INTRODUCTION TO PEACE AND CONFLICT STUDIES

LOIS EDMUND

ROWMAN & LITTLEFIELD

LANHAM • BOULDER • NEW YORK • LONDON

Executive Acquisitions Editor: Mark Kerr
Assistant Editor: Courtney Packard
Sales and Marketing Inquiries: textbooks@rowman.com

Credits and acknowledgments for material borrowed from other sources, and reproduced with permission, appear on the appropriate pages within the text.

Published in cooperation with the Association for Conflict Resolution

Published by Rowman & Littlefield
An imprint of The Rowman & Littlefield Publishing Group, Inc.
4501 Forbes Boulevard, Suite 200, Lanham, Maryland 20706
www.rowman.com

6 Tinworth Street, London SE11 5AL, United Kingdom

British Library Cataloguing in Publication Information Available

Library of Congress Cataloging-in-Publication Data
Names: Edmund, Lois, 1951– author.
Title: Introduction to peace and conflict studies / Lois Edmund.
Description: Lanham : Rowman & Littlefield, 2021. | Includes bibliographical references and index.
Identifiers: LCCN 2020058422 (print) | LCCN 2020058423 (ebook) | ISBN 9781538117620 (cloth)
    | ISBN 9781538117637 (paperback) | ISBN 9781538117644 (epub)
Subjects: LCSH: Conflict management. | Peace-building.
Classification: LCC HM1126 .E36 2021 (print) | LCC HM1126 (ebook) | DDC 303.6/9--dc23
LC record available at https://lccn.loc.gov/2020058422
LC ebook record available at https://lccn.loc.gov/2020058423

♾️™ The paper used in this publication meets the minimum requirements of American National Standard for Information Sciences—Permanence of Paper for Printed Library Materials, ANSI/NISO Z39.48-1992.

To every student who wants to create a more peaceful world.
"Let there be peace on earth, and let it begin with me."

Brief Contents

■ ■ ■

Contents

■ ■ ■

SECTION II GROUPS IN CONFLICT

SECTION III CONFLICT AND VIOLENCE

SECTION IV CONFLICT RESOLUTION

Introduction

Getting Your Study of Peace and Conflict Started

■ ■ ■

This textbook presents a survey of the social science called Peace Studies or CRS: Conflict Resolution Studies. It is intended for people who are curious about human relationships and the dynamics of conflict in the world, but whose background is uneven. Consider this a good-news textbook: conflict can be a constructive force in relationships, in groups, and even in large-scale political and international contexts. Each chapter includes discussions about conflict, but also about pathways to peace. Each chapter will present skills that you can practice and incorporate into your life. This is our plan:

In *Section I, Interpersonal Conflict*, you will begin to explore the following:

- Chapter 1, Individual Factors Related to People in Conflict, delves into the psychological aspects of emotion, personal needs, perception, and personality and the ways they affect your behavior when in conflict.
- Chapter 2, Interpersonal Factors Related to People in Conflict, focuses on several dimensions of interpersonal relating and shows that competent communication supports peaceable relationship while adversarial communication can cause interpersonal trouble.
- Chapter 3, Sources and Drivers of Conflict, and Perception of Problems, helps you identify some of the main problems that trigger conflict, particularly in an interpersonal context.
- Chapter 4, Conflict Development and Process, follows the unfolding process as conflict develops, escalating and deescalating with the sequence of moves and countermoves.

In *Section II, Groups in Conflict*, you will explore a larger circle of groups in conflict.

- Chapter 5, Diversity Studies, Intersectionality, and Conflict, investigates the amazing array of human diversity that results from factors like culture and gender, and some of the ways that multiple identities contribute to peace and conflict.

1

- Chapter 6, Conflict within Families, looks first at the many complex functions provided by the family, then examines some of the reasons for the development of positive and negative conflict among family members.
- Chapter 7, Conflict in the Workplace, explores the unique setting of workplace relationships, and the particular dynamics of conflict among coworkers.

In *Section III, Conflict and Violence,*

- Chapter 8, The Problems of Interpersonal Violence, begins to unpack the many forms of aggression and violence that affect people in relationships, and some of the reasons violence develops and some strategies for ending it and mending the fallout.
- Chapter 9, The Problems of National and International Violence, moves to a wider horizon of costly political and larger-scale violence, discussing its forms, the ways it escalates and deescalates, and begins to examine some ways of peacemaking.

In *Section IV, Conflict Resolution,* the focus is on multiple solutions to conflict in interpersonal, group, and broader levels.

- Chapter 10, Justice Making and Third-Party Resolution, examines social systems that support justice when conflict has harmed relationships.
- Chapter 11, The Goals of Peacebuilding, describes conditions that maintain peaceable interactions, and some of the formal peacebuilding efforts possible.
- Chapter 12, Transformative Conflict Resolution and Social Change, distinguishes among solutions to conflict called conflict resolution, conflict management, and conflict transformation, and the processes of interpersonal and social transformation that can result from dealing deeply with any factor that contributes to the existence of conflict.

In the *Conclusion,* you will survey the many practical options and choices for professional careers in the peace and conflict field.

In this brief introduction, you will prepare with some vocabulary and foundational concepts related to conflict. You will define what conflict is and is not, and the creative potentials for constructive processing. You will learn a method for organizing your thinking about complex conflict called "Quadruple-P" or 4-P, referring to People, Problem, Process, and Potential Solutions. You can see an image of conflict flowing and unfolding, through a simplified visual flowchart of events (illustrated by Figure I.1). You will survey the scholarly field of Peace and Conflict Studies.

This book is a good-news textbook in that it will deepen your understanding of yourself, and help you connect meaningfully with people close to you and with your fellow students. You can help each other as you study by asking questions, exploring your own experiences and concepts and being open to alternative viewpoints.

Figure I.1 4-P Flowchart of conflict analysis

CONFLICT CASE I.1 ■ COMMUNITY TROUBLE IN NORTH VIRGINIA

Maire Dugan (1996) was asked to help resolve a racial confrontation. Two groups of boys from a Northern Virginia high school, one black and one white, became involved in an on-campus fight after some white boys came to school wearing jackets decked out with Confederate flags, viewed by some people as an emblem of white supremacy.* The fight did not lead to any lasting injuries, but it deepened already existing racial wounds in both the combative boys and others attending the school. In addition, news coverage led to widespread community reactions and disturbance.

When the school principal asked Dugan for advice to resolve the conflict, she was faced with a dilemma: although local, the incident had ignited a major and divisive conflict throughout the community. It involved many different levels (personal, relational, group, and community) simultaneously. Dugan observed that the immediate conflict (the boys' fight) was probably nested within a broader social problem of racial inequity.

As she planned her intervention, she considered several possible approaches:

1. Deal with the immediate causes of the fight;
2. Address relationship issues among the antagonists, both before and after the confrontation;

---

*Since dissolution of the "Confederate States of America" (which existed only during the American Civil War, 1861–65), the flag has been an emblem of deep historical, cultural, political, and racial conflict. Some people believe it is a symbol of racial hatred.

3. Focus on trouble in the school that seemed to mirror wider community conflict; and/or
4. Alter the underlying racial inequities that the boys had experienced in the surrounding community.

Dugan decided that intervention within the school (#3, preceding text) would be the most effective, thinking that indirect changes in the relationships (#2) and resolution of the issue (#1) might follow, with potentially positive consequences in the community (#4).

Her actual intervention was based on a *futures intervention*, a concept created by Elise Boulding (Boulding and Boulding 1995). First, each participant lists things they would like to see in the future, based on hope and not on fear; working together next, the participants picture a hopeful future, 30 years from that day; then they imagine possible actions, organizations, and values that could make the hope a reality; finally, working back from the future to that day, they ask one another, "what actions can I/we offer?"

Think About and Discuss with Your Colleagues

1. Do you think the boys who wore the jackets to school intended that their actions would ignite such a deep argument? What was the message in the jackets? What unspoken rules were violated?
2. Who were the antagonists? Was there a foreseeable outcome? How could Dugan predict the probability of success of her conflict-resolution efforts?
3. How did this conflict spread from one, somewhat insignificant, event? In what controversy was it rooted?
4. How did the buildup of racial tension, contrasting views about its causes and legitimacy, and unequal abilities and understandings among the participants contribute to the conflict?
5. This event and its resolution undoubtedly had long-lasting impacts on many people. Can you predict the uncertain outcome of the intervention?

Your beliefs about conflict shape your responses to it. Contrasting views of the same event and the same problems may be the reason behind contradictory approaches to conflict: some people freeze, some flee, some (like the North Virginia high school boys) fight, and some (like the school administrators) engage in a process to resolve it. Associated beliefs about conflict form a **paradigm**, a mental model based on images and assumptions that frame conflicts, affect both perception and response, and determine a course of change that can be either useful or limiting (Coleman, 2004). A paradigm is not objective or factual: it can be connected to central assumptions developed from previous experiences, fears, and beliefs, even geography.

A **negative paradigm of conflict** divides the parties because it is connected to fear, can lead to silence or contrived communication. According to the negative paradigm:

- Good relationships have to be harmonious, with no conflict;
- Conflict is a potentially dangerous sign that something is seriously wrong;

- Disagreements should be discouraged and/or minimized;
- Conflict is best resolved by limiting and suppressing it.

In contrast, a **positive paradigm of conflict** tends to draw parties together in a joint effort to solve the problems and restore harmony. According to this approach:

- Many factors create conflict and harmony;
- Conflict is inevitable; it is present in the ebb and flow of every relationship;
- Differences are signs of an honest, interdependent (mutually dependent) relationship because you matter to one another and are part of the same community;
- Dealing with conflict requires flexibility, hope, and patience;
- Conflict is best explored through interaction from all sides of an issue, even if the conversation is difficult, to gain understanding.

These contrasting views are illustrated in an interesting way that the Chinese language depicts conflict (see Figure I.2). The individual characters do not suggest conflict. The symbol on the left can be interpreted as "dash" or hurry; the one on the right has the connotation of "sudden." Taken together, the symbols depict conflict as a "sudden dash" or a crisis. Conflict is a challenge of both crisis and opportunity.

Figure I.2 Chinese symbols used to represent conflict

Because most people have had unpleasant, regrettable experiences with hurtful conflict, many come to believe that avoiding conflict will prevent its harm. However, avoiding conflict does not prevent it. Instead, avoiding conflict tends to defer problems that remain unresolved. Silencing a conflict may have a negative impact on relationship, with one party remaining oblivious or helpless and the other harboring resentment. When the initial problems remain unsolved, a conflict can grow, becoming more intense and prolonged when it does erupt.

Admittedly, conflict is difficult, but all relationships (even strong pleasurable ones) will undergo disagreements. Conflict in any relationship has negative, destructive possibilities that can seriously hurt people, but also brings with it positive, constructive potential that can result in better understanding of self and the Other, smoother interpersonal functioning, and closer, more harmonious relating.

CONFLICT DEFINED

Conflict is tension or an interactive struggle between two or more seemingly incompatible participants. Conflict is like a dynamic dance: it changes mysteriously, is

Table I.1   Concepts of Conflict, Compared

Conflict is tension or an interactive struggle between at least two seemingly incomplete participants		
Conflict is NOT ...	Conflict IS ...	Conflict CAN BE ...
• Simple • Every struggle • Useless • Sudden • Destructive	• Relational • Purpose & direction • Embedded • Uncomfortable	• A corrective change • Creatively effective

puzzling, and can be difficult to understand. Like a series of dance steps, it is predictable and controllable only under limited conditions. Table I.1 compares some of the defining elements of conflict discussed in the following text.

Conflict Is Not...

It is easiest to understand conflict by starting with what it is *not*.

Conflict Is Not Simple

We cannot just say "conflict happens ... people hurt each other ... don't do it ... end of story"! As the chapter opening example and the examples presented throughout this book show, conflict is complex. Every conflict, no matter what type, is caused by multiple factors, occurs on several levels simultaneously, takes numerous steps related to moves and countermoves, and presents numerous opportunities for processing it.

Conflict resolution is not simple either. As stated by author Charles Hauss (2019), conflict resolution is never easy, and peacebuilding is even harder. Although you can learn and practice a number of helpful skills, there exist no fail-safe techniques or methods for resolving conflict. People will not necessarily follow even wise advice to settle their differences. Uncertainty is inherent in conflict-resolution work. That said, it is important to be as well equipped as possible when facing a serious conflict. This text will explore many different pathways to resolution, as well as the skills required to do this well.

Not Every Struggle Is Conflict

Some negative paradigms are so powerful that people become oversensitized to any perceived tension in a relationship, interpreting every difference as a conflict that must be sidestepped. Unhappiness and differences of opinion are sometimes simply that, and not conflict. Instead, conflict occurs along a continuum (illustrated by Figure I.3), ranging from mild tension to extreme conflict. An important skill in conflict resolution is learning to differentiate conflict from milder situations when processing or resolution is unimportant, or more severe situations that require outsider help.

Conflict Is Not Useless

Many people fear that conflict accomplishes nothing except stalling a relationship with an unwanted and useless digression from normal functioning. In fact, conflict always accomplishes something. It may be related to the issues that started

(Enriching) - ∙ **(Serious)**
differences - - -
       - - - conflict is absent - - -
            - - - dispute - - -
                  - - - coercion - - -
                         - - - abusive harassment - - -
                               - - - fighting - - -
                                     - - - extreme conflict

Figure I.3 Continuum of conflict seriousness

it, the background history of the relationship, or the methods the parties choose to resolve it. When conflict bursts out it can scare everyone so much that it is suppressed and silenced, making it latent again; when this happens, the conflict does indeed become useless for the moment. However, most often it resurfaces. It is best to accept it, discern its purposes, and work to resolve it.

Conflict Is Not Sudden
One mistake many people make when analyzing conflict is focusing solely on the immediate disagreement. This gives the impression that conflict comes "out of the blue." Instead, a **precipitating event** (a spark or trigger to the conflict) is just part of a longer process that both precedes and follows the event. Many factors contribute to a buildup of tension, and precipitating events may be compounded by combative responses.

Conflict Is Not Always Destructive or Violent
Because some conflicts lead to hurt feelings, broken relationships, and (rarely) injuries or death, many people fear it. However, not all conflict leads to violence, and not all violence is rooted in conflict. Aggression such as the fight that broke out in North Virginia over the jackets decorated with Confederate flags may be one outcome, but it is personally and relationally expensive. Yes, conflict can be destructive if engaged in particular ways. Conflict may be a fact of life, but peace-building and violence are not predetermined outcomes (Hauss, 2019). There are many options for processing conflict that can lead to satisfactory outcomes or even to improved relationships.

Conflict Is...
Now that you know what conflict is *not*, let's turn to what it *is*.

Conflict Is an Uncomfortable Challenge
Very few people enjoy conflict because of sensitive feelings, opposition, uncertainty of the direction or ending, and the anticipation of a failed resolution. This text does not present conflict as pleasant or enjoyable but as a challenge to be overcome with skill, patience, and hope.

Conflict Is Relational

Conflict is a neutral fact, a part of every relationship. "Conflict does not happen to people, it happens between people" (Hauss, 2019). Conflict involves at least two identifiable parties, and the conflict occurs in the context of a relationship with a past, a present, and (optimistically) a future.

Conflict Has Purpose and Direction

Although sometimes obscured by the intense interactions, conflict is goal-directed and has purpose. Although at times masked by tension, the goal or goals usually are directed toward solving a problem, satisfying a need, or improving the functioning of a relationship.

Conflict Is Multilayered

Conflict occurs on multiple levels, often simultaneously. A particular incident of conflict is viewed as embedded or nested within a personal and social context. The concept of embedded layers is depicted in Figure I.4, somewhat like an old-fashioned Russian matryoshka doll. **Intrapersonal conflict** occurs within an individual, the "conflicted self." In Maire Dugan's example in North Virginia, individual students and others who initially saw the offensive jackets must have had serious negative feelings and inner debates about what to do about them. **Interpersonal conflict** occurs between at least two people. In North Virginia, aggressive action began between one boy hitting another boy. **Group-level conflict** occurs among several parties who are associated in some significant way, like the white and black friendship circles, all whom belonged to the same high school. *Large-scale conflict* refers to conflict between large groups of people or an entire community. In North Virginia, the conflict spread from the boys' groups to the whole high school to the surrounding community. The layering of conflict brings with it the possibility of multiple solutions, as illustrated in Maire Dugan's work.

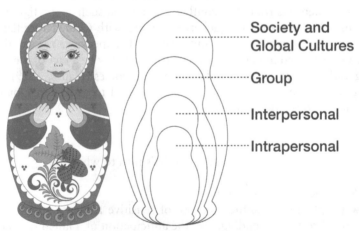

Society and Global Cultures

Group

Interpersonal

Intrapersonal

Figure I.4 Illustration of embedded levels of conflict
Drawing reproduced with the permission of Olga Ozyrina.

Conflict Can...

Now that you know what conflict is *not* and what it *is*, let's turn to what it *can be*.

Conflict Can Bring Needed Change

Important corrective changes may be needed in relationships troubled by factors like competition, imbalanced power, or injustice. Although it is disruptive, conflict can become a catalyst for change. In fact, according to some optimistic scholars, no relationship can survive and mature without conflict; without it, the relationship will stagnate (e.g., Rummel, 1991; Lederach, 2005). As problems are explored, alternatives can be imagined and priorities reexamined and revalued, strengthening the relationship.

Conflict Can Be Creative

Conflict can be effective and sustainable if the parties are satisfied, the problems are solved, the process has been amicable, and the resolution is fair. Creative goodwill between the parties is critical to sustainable relationship. Goodwill lends objectivity to communication, and adds flexibility to potential shifts and changes in relationships.

> *For the optimist, every difficulty is an opportunity; for the pessimist, every opportunity presents some difficulty.*
> —*Bertram Carr, 1919*

4-P: QUADRUPLE-P ANALYSIS: PEOPLE, PROBLEM, PROCESS, AND PRACTICAL SOLUTIONS

Now that you have learned what conflict is *not*, what it *is*, and what it *can be*, how can you go about addressing it? This text uses 4-P: "Quadruple-P" analysis as a guide. The approach sees actual conflict as the outcome of interactions among four main elements: people, problem, process, and potential solutions. The systems approach to conflict emphasizes links among these elements.

People

People are at the heart of all conflict as actors, parties, opponents, or adversaries, who might be individuals, groups, governments, or nations. Conflict tends to uncover people's honest selves; they are less polite and censored than in peaceful times. Conflict can bring selfishness, greed, or cruelty to the surface, but it can also bring out the best in peoples' connections, generosity, and kindness. Interactions become even more complex among people of widely diverse identities. At its best, conflict can be an opportunity to understand more about what really matters to people.

A conflict **party** is someone who has an interest in or cares about the conflict or its outcome. A **primary party** is involved in the dispute. In most instances, this is an arguing dyad whose tactics escalate or deescalate the conflict. For example, in a family conflict, this could be the arguing parents. A **secondary party** is not involved directly, but is affected by the conflict or any solution found. This could be, for example, the children of disputing parents. A **third party** is someone from outside the conflicted relationship system who becomes involved, such as a neighbor or relative. Sometimes third parties can be facilitative and help find a solution; sometimes the presence of third parties, either as audience or in taking sides, can complicate and even stall the resolution process. You will learn more about these personal elements of 4-P analysis in Chapters 1, 3, and 5.

Problem

A **problem** is the stimulus for conflict; it can arise from incompatible needs, principles or values, or goals among the parties. The problem must be resolved if the relationship is to continue functioning. The perceived causes of conflict are usually a complex blend of immediate problems, short-term events and actions that highlight the problem, and long-term history of problematic interactions among the parties. Some deep causes of problems are wrongdoing and injustice, and the misuse of power. Conflict alone rarely solves a problem; real changes must occur to acknowledge party differences to create justice and peace and to amend problems of power. Many problems are never fully resolved, but are solved only partially or temporarily (Mayer, 2009).

An important skill is to consider whether a problem can reasonably be solved, or it if is a **perpetual problem** caused by nonnegotiable issues like personality or lifestyle (Gottman and Gottman, 2008). Some problems, called **dialectic tensions**, are seemingly contradictory elements that challenge the core of every relationship (Baxter and Braithwaite, 2008). For example, dialectic tensions may center in struggles about whether to depend on others or to remain independent, whether to maintain a status quo or risk change, or whether to express the true self or not. These tensions are often revealed in conflict dialogue. Dialectic tensions cannot be dismissed with an "either-or" choice, but are best resolved by accepting "both-and." They are managed by viewing problems from multiple perspectives. You will learn more about the problem aspect of 4-P analysis in Chapters 2, 8, and 9.

Process

Conflict follows discernible sequences as conflicts occur and subside, and ebb and flow. **Process** is the word used to describe how a conflict unfolds. Processes are related to the tactical patterns the people use as they confront a problem and communicate (or don't) in their attempts to find resolution. An essential feature of this aspect of conflict analysis is whether or not a conflict is processed respectfully and assertively, or in a disrespectful way with the goal of defeating the opponent. Proceeding with respectful kindness is a key to healthy, trusting relationships on any level, and to conflict resolution (Lawrence-Lightfoot, 2012). The word *kind* is related to *kin*: if, in conflict, you treat an opponent with the same respectful kindness you would offer a close family member, a positive outcome is much more likely than treating them with animosity as an enemy.

A **conflict curve** is a conceptual tool that represents a simplified view of how conflicts progress over time (for example, see Braithwaite and Lemke, 2011; USAID, 2012; DFID, 2017). This simple model illustrates conflict developing in four phases: discussion, polarization, separation, and destruction (Fisher and Keashly, 1991). Understanding the evolving phases of conflict is an important foundation for imagining and designing methods to resolve it. The conflict curve is usually captured in a graph illustrating the dynamics of escalation and deescalation toward resolution such as the one in Figure I.5. You will learn more about this process aspect of 4-P analysis in Chapter 4.

Potential Solutions: *Praxis*

The availability of *potential solutions* can determine whether a conflict is constructive and satisfying, or destructive and harmful. Conflicts open up numerous

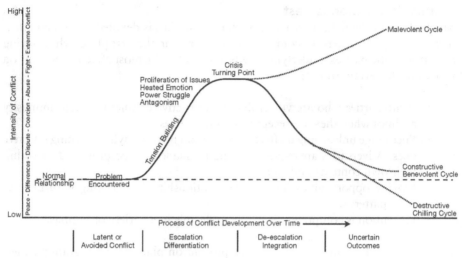

Figure I.5 The conflict curve illustrated

opportunities for understanding and for skill building. A durable solution deals with potentially confusing conflict paradoxes, described by Bernard Mayer (2015):

    a. Competition and cooperation;
    b. Optimism and realism;
    c. Avoidance and engagement;
    d. Principle and compromise;
    e. Emotions and logic;
    f. Neutrality and advocacy; and
    g. Community and autonomy.

Much of this textbook will detail potential pathways toward resolution, but solutions are the particular focus of Chapters 10, 11, and 12.

Think About and Discuss with Your Colleagues

Briefly write out the events of a conflict that recently involved you as an antagonist or a peacemaker.

- Apply the Quadruple-P method to analyze this interchange.

PRAXIS: PUTTING CONFLICT RESOLUTION PRINCIPLES INTO ACTION

Now that you know how conflict is defined and understood, and have learned the basics of Quadruple-P analysis, it is time to focus your thinking on conflict resolution. *Praxis* is an ancient word that describes practical ways of putting knowledge into action.

Conflict Prevention Is Best

Much effort in the field of Peace and Conflict Studies is devoted to finding effective ways to prevent serious conflict from occurring in the first place, while paying attention to the parties' underlying needs and goals. The most effective prevention programs do certain things:

- Invite parties who are vulnerable to destructive conflict to divert animosity at times when they are receptive to alternatives.
- Encourage unlearning ineffective resolution methods while learning effective ones. Adversaries are exposed to and persuaded to accept new ideas within their own contexts and culture.
- Provide opportunities for positive relationships by working with interactions patterns.
- Prevention is comprehensive, and applicable in a variety of settings.

One example of a conflict and violence prevention plan is the program partnership between ACT: Adults and Children Together Against Violence and NAEYC: the National Association for the Education of Young Children. The program, associated with David Hayes and Peggy Hayes, is used to address problems such as youth bullying, homophobic conflict, interracial interactions, and even self-directed violence (Portwood et al., 2011). It has been adapted for use in many settings, including schools, workplaces, and teen dating and family relationships.

Conflict Resolution Is Peacemaking

Peace is the overriding goal of conflict resolution, but is an elusive quality. Harmony is defined in different (sometimes contradictory) ways in relationships, families and groups, society, and global relations. In Peace and Conflict Studies, the goal is to make peace real in real situations. Peacemaking sometimes requires crisis intervention to bring an end to fruitless conflict and violence; this is called **negative peacebuilding. Positive peacebuilding** is a more difficult, long-term route to build peace by setting up sustainable conditions for solving problems and improving relationships. Both negative and positive peacebuilding are essential to creating a peaceable world.

Conflict Resolution Is Justice Making

Justice is key. As long as unjust, unfair conditions affect or limit peoples' life possibilities, peace will not exist. Resolving some conflict therefore often involves justice making through larger systems (Meadows, 2008).

Conflict Resolution Utilizes a Wide Variety of Methods

There is no one right way to solve a conflict. **Equifinality** refers to the existence of many pathways to a desired peaceful end. There are numerous possibilities and choices along the way, and their effectiveness varies according to the specific situation. In fact, problem solving often results in "finding what you are not looking for." Each party must determine what they judge to be a satisfactory resolution. If a resolution is unsatisfying because the problem remains or the relationship is damaged, then the parties will be more willing to continue the disagreement until a satisfactory solution is reached.

Escalate

- Instigate a fight
- Agitate
- Manage conflict

Resolve
1. Forgive
2. Problem Solve
3. Negotiate
4. Coaching
5. Mediation
6. Arbitration ⎤ Third Party
7. Adjudication ⎦

Suppress

- Control people or conflict
- Ignore the conflict
- "Forget"
- Repress

Figure I.6 Range of ways to manage conflict
Based on Laue, 1987.

James Laue (1987) described a continuum of possible ways to manage conflict (see Figure I.6). Some of these methods escalate conflict and might be used as a last resort by people who perceive themselves to be powerless. Other methods suppress conflict by controlling the people or the interactions, and are used by people who enjoy and use greater power. Between these two extremes is an array of methods that result in constructive conflict resolution.

CONFLICT RESOLUTION IS A PROFESSIONAL CAREER

Broadly speaking, careers in conflict resolution include conflict management, conflict resolution, and conflict transformation.

Conflict management is control of the processing of a problem to express the conflict within acceptable or safe limits and to minimize losses for all parties. In addition to solving the problem, the focus is on managing the relationship and the conflict process and dynamics. It is a process that is guided by ground rules for expressing differences and objections fairly. Conflict management is often used in workplace settings, where coworkers must continue to function cooperatively, but deeply harmonious relationships are not necessary. Many court systems also have the goal of managing conflict.

Conflict resolution is less common than conflict management. As the term implies, the parties try to conclusively solve the problem causing the conflict, in hopes of eliminating it entirely. This requires dealing with the deeper causes of conflict rather than simply controlling conflict events. Conflict resolution is effective, for example, in situations involving friends and neighbors.

Conflict transformation is a thorough conflict process that focuses on all elements of a conflict: peoples' needs, intentions, emotions, goals—virtually any

Table I.2   Ten Principles of Peacebuilding

a. Peacemaking works through problems and conflicts by seeking sustainable solutions rather than superficially polite behavior or uneasy and fragile truces.
b. In peacemaking, truth telling and truth seeking are honored, integrity is valued, and trust is given because it is earned.
c. Peacemaking offers an opportunity to explore and discover that which is as yet unimagined.
d. Peacemaking techniques are creative, exploratory, and filled with the risk, fear, and excitement of discovery.
e. Peacemaking is a refuge, a safe haven from incivility and outright nastiness of conflict.
f. The peacemaker is charged with a sacred duty of creating a refuge where people … know they will be heard and understood, where their needs and ideas will be respected, and where they can safely do the difficult work of reconciling their differences.
g. The peacemaker must create a place where people are able to approach, rather than freeze, flee, or fight.
h. Peacemaking seeks to disenfranchise … those who seek unfair advantage.
i. Peacemaking involves risk, not the least of which is failure.
j. Peacemaking requires tremendous courage.

Source: Noll, 2003. Reproduced with permission of Douglas Noll.

factor that plays into the existence of the conflict. This deep, detailed process examines the relationship along with multiple problems and possible solutions, and requires deep investment by the disputants. As the term implies, it has the potential to transform people and relationships. It can be effective in serious situations such as long-term sibling or marriage relationships, or those involving incarcerated criminals.

To reiterate, conflict resolution is never easy, and peacebuilding is even harder (Hauss, 2019). Douglas Noll (2003) outlined ten principles for the aspiring peacebuilder, as shown in the Table I.2.

Think About and Discuss with Your Colleagues

Earlier, you applied the 4-P analysis to a conflict that involved you as an antagonist or a peacemaker.

- What are the differences between conflict management, conflict resolution, and conflict transformation in this situation?
- Which of these methods would be most applicable to that conflict event?

THE SCHOLARLY DISCIPLINE OF PEACE AND CONFLICT STUDIES

Conflict Resolution Studies (CRS) is also called **Peace and Conflict Transformation Studies** in varied settings. It is a social science that explores conflict through the interchange of theory and practice. Attention is given to the personal, interpersonal, group, and international origins, dynamic processes, and outcomes. At the least, the hope is to limit the intensity and severity of conflict when it does occur and to design effective and long-term peaceful functioning. The deeper goals of CRS are to improve the ways conflict is processed, to minimize the harm that often accompanies conflict, and to create more peaceable relationships.

Multidisciplinary studies and data add insight to the body of CRS knowledge. This textbook includes research and ideas from longer established disciplines such as anthropology, communication, diversity studies, economics, geography, political science and justice studies, psychology, sociology, and others. CRS appeals to scholars and researchers, political and community leaders, field practitioners, and even business people who combine their knowledge and experience to assist in this perpetual hunt for healthy, constructive relationships. It is an active science, engaged in real conflicts to guide constructive problem solving.

Problem solving can involve two different types of thinking. *Linear thinking* is the logical examination of the causes and complications of disagreement. It is a method that sequentially examines the separate parts of a conflict. Conflict elements can be clarified with inquiry using question/answer, true/false, and certainty/uncertainty.

However, when analyzing conflict, you discover that the elemental parts like people and problems cannot be completely segregated without overlooking significant information. *Nonlinear thinking* uses many starting points to explore ideas in many directions at once. Conflict can be demanding because of these simultaneous points of attention, but the resulting insight is inventive. Linear thinking uses logic; nonlinear thinking uses accumulated experience and understanding. CRS requires both linear and nonlinear thinking, as illustrated by the Quadruple-P analysis presented here.

Another important starting point for exploring conflict is perspective, or point of view. As you perceive and define concepts like peace and harmony and conflict, your point of view is not singular or static; instead, your point of view intersects with those of others. In conflict, *intersectionality* (your personal and social identities) affects your point of view that, in turn, affects your views of conflict and willingness to engage in it. As you study, be aware of your point of view, but listen to others flexibly to avoid unnecessarily rigid thinking. This influence will be explored in more detail in Chapter 5.

Praxis Skill Builder I.1 ▪ Improving Your Study of Peace and Conflict Studies

Your study of peace and conflict will be stronger and more interesting if you use *multiple sources* of information and knowledge to explore each topic:

- Use this text;
- Actively participate in this course, and others offered within the program;
- Watch and read the news daily with a healthy dose of skepticism. You won't learn something new every day, but over time the correlation between the global stories and your conflict resolution study will become clear.
- Read expert scholarly sources such as books, journals, and articles;
- Explore statistical databases and mapping websites;
- Refer to dictionaries and encyclopedias; and others.

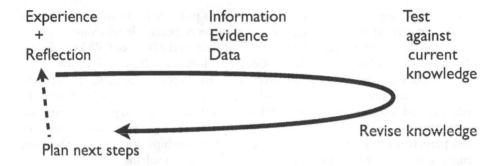

a good attitude: *skepticism*

Figure I.7 Experiential learning and reflective practice cycle

First, and possibly foremost, you can explore your own experiences and connect them to your learnings to make them relevant and applicable. There are, however, several cautions:

- Keep an open mind and be *curious*. This will help you integrate your own interests and concerns with wide social knowledge to provide in-depth understanding of the field. Again, healthy skepticism is in order. Do not believe everything you read, or even everything you think.
- Engage in *transformative learning*. Relinquishing an old interpretation to construct a new view is usually unsettling, but can lead to perspective change.
- Have the *courage* to take risks. Do not expect to be completely comfortable as you study conflict resolution. Your own ideas and convictions will be challenged.
- Engage in *reflective practices*. It is a central habit for any serious student of CRS. As you encounter new ideas and experiences, accept and reflect on the challenges, and experiment with new ways of responding. This approach, called a reflective practice cycle, is illustrated in Figure I.7.

PEACEBUILDING PIONEERS: CHEYENNE PEACE CHIEFS

The Cheyenne are an ancient Indigenous people who live in the Central Great Plains of the United States. The Cheyenne of the 19th century had two contrasting approaches to peace, conflict, and battle that were embedded in two sacred social structures. The "Council of Forty-Four" was made up of 44 *peace chiefs*, called *vehoe*: four male chiefs from each of ten bands, plus four elders with history on the council. The council met annually to share responsibilities for day-to-day community functioning and keeping a peaceful community. They were entrusted to lead the community as models of courage and wisdom, not force. The peace chief had a position of respect and authority based on restrained and careful judgement (Hoig, 1990). The council held community gatherings, *powwow*, and negotiated friendship treaties with outsiders. Their influence declined in the middle 1860s with increased conflict with new settlers, often instigated by mutually misunderstood cultural ways and manners (Harjo, 2014).

The second approach to conflict was led by military societies devoted to following the teachings of an ancestor, Sweet Medicine, who bequeathed four sacred arrows: two for killing bison and two for killing enemies (Moore, 2011). They provided military leadership through the *war chiefs*, called *notxevoe*. They were responsible for maintaining discipline within each community, organizing whole community events like tribal hunting. They were known as fierce battle warriors, including suicide warfare, and had a complex system of war honors (Moore, 2011).

A great conflict divided the community with disagreement about how to relate to settlers. The *vehoe* promoted conciliatory, nonviolent solutions to problems with outsiders, but their courage was exploited by unfair settlers and government aggression. The *notxevoe* advocated retaliation against settler violence. Both peacebuilding and battlement approaches failed, as the Cheyenne eventually became entangled in the tragic cultural genocide that included residential schools, forced relinquishment of traditional customs, as well as executions and community massacre.

Today, the peace council tradition is active, and the Cheyenne continue to maintain the Council of Forty-Four (Smith-Christopher, 2007). The tradition is the basis for an active peacebuilding organization called the Circle Keepers (Pranis, 2014).

CHAPTER SUMMARY AND STUDY GUIDE

- Conflict is interactive tension or a struggle between two or more seemingly incompatible participants. Conflict is not simple, useless, or sudden; not every tension is conflict, and not every conflict has to become destructive or violent. Conflict is relational and multilayered; it has purpose and is an uncomfortable challenge. Conflict solutions can be sustainable if they bring necessary change.
- Conflict is always complex, so a method of analyzing conflict, called 4-P: Quadruple-P, explores the people, problems, process, and potential solutions involved in conflict.
- Conflict prevention avoids the need for conflict resolution. Conflict resolution is peacemaking and justice making, and involves a spectrum of methods.
- Conflict resolution can also be a professional career.

The scholarly field of CRS: Conflict Resolution Studies, also called Peace Studies, is a social science that uses multidisciplinary data to explore the origins, dynamic processes, and outcomes of conflict in the personal, interpersonal, group, and international spheres. It draws from a number of other disciplines, and involves both linear and nonlinear thinking. We sincerely hope that, for you, this will be a book of many possibilities for insight and for praxis.

TERMS IN FOCUS

4-P analysis 9
conflict 5
conflict curve 10
conflict management 13
conflict resolution 13
conflict transformation 13
dialectic tension 10
Equifinality 12
group-level conflict 8
interpersonal conflict 8
intrapersonal conflict 8
negative paradigm of conflict 4

negative peacebuilding 12
paradigm 4
party 9
perpetual problem 10
positive paradigm of conflict 5
positive peacebuilding 12
precipitating event 7
primary party 9
problem 10
process 10
secondary party 9
third party 9

SECTION I
Interpersonal Conflict Resolution

1

Individual Factors Related to People in Conflict

■ ■ ■

As you learned in the introductory chapter, looking closely at four integrated "Quadruple-P" components of conflict (4-P = People + Problem +
Process + Potential Solutions) can help you understand the bigger pictures
of conflict. In many ways, the content of this chapter is *the* beginning of the study
of peace and conflict. People are central to every moment of every conflict. Understanding feelings, needs, actions, and reactions, the choices made as conflict
unfolds, and the interpretation of their efforts are central to conflict resolution.

In this chapter you can begin to analyze and deconstruct conflict by examining the people-related *intra*personal issues that affect a conflict experience: the
inner thoughts, feelings, and conflicts that motivate behavior. Chapter 2 turns
to the *inter*personal issues and communication patterns that affect conflicts. In
Chapter 3, you will explore problem sources, and Chapter 4 helps you focus on
how conflicts develop and unfold.

Intrapersonal conflicts happen within your mind, within the "conflicted
self," related to incompatible feelings, goals, and needs (see Figure 1.1). These
conflicts can be expressed in silent thinking, writing in a private journal, or out
aloud. You usually keep the struggles private until you decide to express them,
but they may sutly show in body language and your actions. Intrapersonal conflicts are often difficult to settle because significant values are involved. This
type of conflict can use up intense inner energy, leading to troubling feelings of
being "mixed up." Until the struggle is resolved, your ongoing inward battles
can cause self-doubt, self-blame, or self-criticism. If incorrectly identified, you
might displace intrapersonal conflict to blame other people who are not responsible for a problem. You have to pay attention to the mixed feelings and issues
to resolve intrapersonal conflict.

A complementary type of conflict, **interpersonal conflict**, occurs between
people. Because of the close link between inward experiences and outward behavior, intrapersonal and interpersonal factors often blur each other. In this chapter,
our focus is on the intrapersonal people issues.

Figure 1.1 The intrapersonal "thinker"

It might help you to consider these observations about people in conflict as you think about your own experiences (after Coltri, 2020):

1. People behave in ways that make sense to them but, possibly, not to other people.
2. Everyone's interpretation of reality is subjective, but largely automatic and subconscious.
3. Everyone is motivated to improve well-being and happiness, and to minimize discomfort, pain, and damage to themselves. People in conflict do not always fulfill their goals.
4. Numerous, often contradictory and hidden, motives are behind behavioral choices during conflict.
5. Hopes about the results of behavior are not always fulfilled because conflict tends to result in self-fulfilling prophecy.
6. Conflict is often based on misperception that, in turn, makes a conflict more persistent.
7. Conflicting parties use the conflict to make assumptions about the motives of their opponents.

INTRAPERSONAL FACTORS IN THE EXPERIENCE OF CONFLICT

Inner Dialogue

In the **Dialogical Self Theory,** Dutch researcher Hubert Hermans (2006) introduced the idea that an inner dialogue quietly voices intrapersonal conflicts between an internal "speaker," a "listener," and an "observer." This inner dialogue might sound something like this:

- Speaker: "Would it really matter if I cheat on my girlfriend?"
- Listener: "Of course it would! That could ruin my relationship completely."
- Observer: "What would my friends think of me?"
- Yourself: "I could feel guilty for a long time."

Hermans used the phrase "moving through three persons yet remaining the same thinker" to express the idea that your whole self can imagine and pay attention to conflicted inner voices as you struggle with dilemma and temptations. One part of your mind might be demanding and responsible while an opposing inner voice might rebel against rules and expectations; one part of your mind might be experimenting with unfamiliar ideas. They are all "you." Herman's conclusions are similar to a therapeutic model called the **Internal Family Systems Model,** which suggests that you learn and repeat habits from experiences with your family to conduct an unconscious inner family dialogue (Schwartz, 2020).

A key to insight is to attend to the multiple "voices" in dialogue to clearly identify the tensions that are causing your intrapersonal conflict. Awareness is an important step toward acceptance, which then opens the way for resolution. As you dare to listen and reflect, analyze, or even argue the contrasting viewpoints, you can clarify key issues, beliefs, and values, sort through what is true or false and right or wrong, and rehearse events you hope or dread will happen. Insightful interpretations of feelings and events emerge (Schwartz, 2013). Hermans also noted that skills for internal dialogue often generate interpersonal dialogue, resulting in more effective listening and communicating.

Praxis Skill Builder 1.1 ■ You Can Benefit from Intrapersonal Dialogue

Understanding your dialogue of inner "voices" is a developed skill. Consider practicing the following steps (Dreher, 2000):

Attend   1. Take time for silence.
Aware   2. Listen to inner dialogue through reflection and meditation.
        3. Open yourself to the whole truth.
Accept   4. Accept fear, accept the darker side of reality and yourself.
        5. Accept that few things are simple; balance many complex factors.

Conflicted Motives

The forces that motivate actions are also mixed. An **approach motive** is the need to satisfy a desired goal such as getting a new job. An **avoid motive** aims to prevent something or avoid doing something distressing or unpleasant such as sitting in bumper-to-bumper traffic after a long day's work. Kurt Lewin (1935) suggested that a comfortable equilibrium normally exists, but he identified three scenarios of conflicted intrapersonal motives. These conflicts can destabilize a person's well-being and result in an urge to figure out the conflict.

- *Approach-approach conflict*—you have two mutually exclusive needs or goals, both of which are desirable. For example, you might have difficulty deciding whether to spend time with your best friend or with a new friend.
- *Approach-avoid conflict*—fulfillment of a single need has both positive and negative consequences, and you cannot decide whether the rewards outweigh the risks. For example, you might be interested in socializing at a dance party, but believe you are a clumsy dancer and want to avoid embarrassment.
- *Avoid-avoid conflict*—you are forced to choose between two unpleasant options, such as being alone on a Friday night versus going on an unwelcome blind date.

Avoid-avoid conflict happened to Bob Vanech, a competitive Scrabble player. He taught his fourteen-year-old son, Tristan, to play competitively and always cheered him on. Bob found himself scheduled to play against Tristan at the US National Scrabble Championship:

> The feeling was "I'm going to play the way I always play—I'm going to beat this kid!" And then I thought "Oh, no, but then he's going to lose ... I can't really want to beat this kid" ... The emotional roller coaster was that no matter what the outcome was, I was going to lose: I would feel horrible if I beat him, or I'd feel horrible if I lost.

Bob strongly wanted to win the tournament, but didn't want to defeat his son. He believed "to let him win is an unfair leg up that I don't think is good" and "to purposefully lose is bad parenting." In the end, Bob didn't hold back and outmatched Tristan by 63 points (Wendy Leung, *Globe and Mail*, October 16, 2010). In addition to illustrating conflicting motives, this story illustrates the multiple emotions that most people experience during conflict.

Dissonance is a contradiction between two ideas. This tension can be a strong motivator to reduce inconsistency and intrapersonal conflict (Festinger, 1957). Dissonance is so unpleasant that it commonly results in **cognitive distortions** including simple denial, self-justifying interpretation, or blaming others. For example, if you lie to your best friend you might tell yourself, "I didn't really lie—it was only an alternative fact" or "she deserved my lie because she was acting like a jerk." Distortion of dissonant beliefs, attitudes, or behavior can decrease inward tension and improve consistency,

> *Those who know that they do not know gain wisdom.*
> *Those who pretend they know remain ignorant.*
> *Those who acknowledge weakness become strong.*
> *Those who flaunt their power will lose it.*
> *Wisdom and power follow truth above all.*
> *For Truth is the way of peace.*
> —*Taoist saying*

but at the cost of accurate thinking. It may seem to others that these distorted ways of thinking are illogical or exaggerated. Cognitive distortions can contribute to the intensity of conflict because others perceive you as defensive and self-serving.

EMOTIONS PROFOUNDLY AFFECT CONFLICT

Surprisingly, there is no single definition of emotion. After a thorough review of current research, Izard (2010) concluded that emotion has "interesting and challenging complexity" and "cannot be defined in any unitary way." For our discussion here, **emotions** are conscious feelings that happen in response to circumstances or events. Conflict and emotions are closely connected, causing and complicating each other: emotions are provoked by conflict and can seriously confound it (Lindner, 2014). Sherod Miller (1988) stated that emotions are "the greatest challenge to relationships." Eran Halpern (2016) asserted that powerful human emotions are central engines for both peacemaking and for aggression.

First Emotional Challenge: What Is the Emotion?
More than four hundred subtle but distinct feelings can be identified (Baron-Cohen, 1997), and emotions related to conflict can be especially strong and mixed. Feelings are useful sources of information about what's happening:

> like a thermometer, emotions tell us about inner events,
> like a barometer, emotions help us understand the environment.

Emotions are often referred to as *affect*, while an enduring affect is called a *mood*. Important skills differentiate one feeling from another when decoding our own and others' affective signals.

    Primary, or **primal emotions** are basic, simple, and somewhat intense. Although debate continues over precisely which emotions are primary and even how many there are, consensus suggests that they include happiness-joy, surprise, sadness, anger-rage, excitement, disgust, fear-terror, and love or admiration. **Secondary emotions** are more subtle and mixed. They elaborate the primary feelings like the infinite variety of colors elaborate the primary colors. For example, fright is a secondary form of fear, and disappointment is a form of sadness. Secondary feelings build on past experiences that, through memory, become emotionally connected to current events. Secondary emotions are influenced by a social context, shaped by culture through socialization that ensures that some feelings in the repertoire are "trained out" or "trained in." A person from North America, for example, may not feel the same deep shame that an Asian person would when they disappoint their family members.

    Varieties of fear, anger, despair, and confusion are common when a conflict is going badly. Simultaneous feelings might even be contradictory, so it may be difficult even to name them, let alone clearly understand or moderate them (Larsen, 2017). Dominant primary emotions can lead to impulsive, poorly planned behavior. Secondary emotions might be subtly hidden by the vividness of primary feelings, but they provide important cues to experiences.

    No emotion, whether simple or complicated, is useful or unhelpful; what *is* important is how the feeling affects your behavior. A **facilitative emotion** clarifies what events mean, providing insight and deliberation. People who are emotionally intelligent use their emotions in a facilitative way to deepen their understanding and regulate their behavior, and this can lead to constructive responses like emotional moderation, focus on relationship, and problem solving. When expressed respectfully, facilitative emotions contribute to open, peaceful relationships. A **debilitative emotion** exaggerates the intensity of the moment, interferes with clear thinking and problem solving, and can hinder effective relationship functioning. Any emotion such as anger might be facilitative or strongly debilitative, depending on how it is interpreted.

Second Emotional Challenge: Should Emotion Be Expressed? If Expressed, How Should Emotion Be Expressed?

There are many reasons to express—or not express—your feelings, particularly when in conflict. Anyone might be afraid to talk about their feelings if they signal vulnerability. You might be afraid of the effect your feelings could have on others; most people do not want intense emotions to become a burden on others or escalate a conflict. *Introspective* people do not readily expose their feelings; rather, they work to resolve them through private reflection. *Extroverted*, outgoing people are more likely to talk through their emotions or their conflicts with others. Social context and cultural background also shape how emotions are displayed and interpreted.

Miriam Greenspan (2003) noted that healthy emotions are experienced in an interplay of "light and dark." Pleasant *light emotions* such as happiness and hope are readily tolerated and expressed because they are viewed as acceptable. Painful *dark emotions* such as anger or despair are unpleasant. Because they are painful, you prefer not to experience them and you learn not to express the dark feelings. The specific approval and avoidance patterns differ in groups, across families, across contrasting cultures and genders, and so on. In Greenspan's view, denying or suppressing feelings does not abolish them, however. Rather, discomfort with certain feelings results in distorted *toxic emotions* of self-pity, shame, anxiety, and painful solitude, tangling and paralyzing the pain. Toxic emotions conceal authentic experiences and alienate you from yourself and other people (Bowen, 1978).

Hidden and denied emotions can cause multiple self-defeating problems. Suppressing emotion requires a great deal of effort that can affect both mental health and physical illness. Suppressed emotion does nothing to help a person feel better or resolve a conflict (DeSteno, 2013; Gross, 1997). Conflict can simmer if you harbor or nurse a secret emotion, gradually building until it erupts. Hidden emotions can also initiate a chilling influence on a relationship. When you are convinced that your efforts will change nothing and resolution is hopeless, you stop expressing your feelings and withdraw your investment from the relationship, which can result in cold indifference. Mending toxic emotion requires uncovering the natural sources, and restoring the interplay of light and dark.

> When emotions are hidden or disguised, a dispute becomes a labyrinth, with layers and layers of thoughts, feelings and behaviors, so concealed that a conflict becomes inevitable and insoluble.
> —*Thomas Scheff*

Dramatically venting emotion is not a good approach either (Bushman, 2002; DeSteno, 2013). Most research shows that after people vent their anger or behave aggressively they feel worse and even more intensely emotional than before. For example, yelling or hitting in frustration will not help and will often derail a conflict. Moderated emotions assist the process of conflict, but most people find this a real challenge.

Suppressing and venting are not the only options. There is a third, facilitative option: careful, constructive expression of the emotion. Well understood and expressed emotions can contribute to your well-being as well as to greater understanding and closeness in a relationship. Emotional experiences and expression can be remarkably facilitative during conflict if they accomplish two goals: 1) they clarify perspectives of what the conflict issues are and why they are important; and 2) they improve mutual knowledge and supportiveness (Halperin, 2016; Heitler, 1997).

Aristotle suggested that emotion should be expressed thoughtfully:

- with the right person,
- to the right extent,
- at the right time,
- with the right motive, and
- in the right way (Aristotle, Ethics)

Aristotle's ancient advice is important, but requires a great deal of personal control (Bartlett, 2011). The term **emotional intelligence** (EI or EQ) is used to describe this complex ability. EI improves your abilities to identify, make sense of, and moderate emotions within yourself, in others, and in groups. EI is recognized both as a natural ability (J. D. Mayer, 1997) and a developing skill (Goleman, 1998).

To develop conflict resolution competence, you must work skillfully with emotions, both yours and those of the other parties. Daniel Goleman described four component abilities of EI:

1. Awareness—the ability to recognize your own emotions and accept their importance.
2. Regulation—the ability to regulate your feelings and reactions and use them to guide sensible decisions.
3. Empathy—the ability to sense, understand, and respond with understanding to others' emotions.
4. Relationship skill—the ability to manage emotions and conflict and use them to influence and build up other people.

All these abilities are helpful when moderating conflict. Practicing reflective thinking and, specifically, mindfulness helps develop emotional intelligence (Segal, 2019).

In conflict resolution, a three-step process helps when dealing with emotions generated by conflict: 1) recognize and process the emotions privately, 2) express them in effective ways, and 3) accurately hear the heated emotions of others. This involves inner work: understanding the triggering conflict and using feelings to recognize the importance of the issue, defining the emotion, teasing out its hidden motives, and moderating it to a manageable intensity.

Praxis Skill Builder 1.2 ■ Conflict Resolution Principles Related to Emotion

As you develop your emotional intelligence, think about the following ideas:

1. Simple feelings require thought before action; complex and mixed feelings require even more careful consideration.
2. Understand your own feelings as useful information.
3. Maximize facilitative feelings to think clearly and solve problems slowly; minimize emotions when they debilitate or compromise your thinking.
4. Feelings, especially intense primary ones, should be a guide but not a prescription for action. Notice that the intensity of emotion varies throughout a conflict and avoid impulsive decisions and actions. Take special care when dealing with your negative feelings. Aim for moderated feelings: be watchful of long brooding moods, and avoid acting on fast changing emotions.

Third Emotional Challenge: Interpersonal Empathy Is Facilitative; Contagion Complicates Conflict

Emotions are a gateway to the deeper dimensions of experience and relationships, even when in conflict. Understanding emotion relies on **empathy**, the ability to accurately sense multiple feelings, paying attention to more than simple facts or words and perceiving the underlying meanings. Empathic understanding relies on respect for self and the other person. It can be the foundation for a cooperative, amicable relationship, and can decrease the animosity and potential aggression of conflict.

Over a century ago, Gustav Le Bon (1895), described a process called **emotional contagion**, which is the transmission of emotion from one person to another; in other words, sometimes you feel emotion that is not genuinely your own. People sense and are influenced by each other's feelings which may "spread" subconsciously from one person to another to form a collective emotion (Hatfield, 2014). Contagion is especially relevant to conflict-related anxiety, fear, and anger; when one is angry, others often react with mirrored anger. When you sense that another person is anxious or fearful, you scan the environment for the cause. In conflict, fear and anger spread very quickly, creating a charged atmosphere that may be difficult to calm. Contagion is probably influential in the development of crowd and mob behavior. However, cooperation and kindness are just as contagious. When you experience kindness you are more likely to be kind to or to cooperate with other people. A kindness wave cascades through an interpersonal network, and one positive action can multiply by three (Christakis, 2010).

Contagion of positive feelings can be facilitative, moving toward problem resolution. Contagion of negative feelings can be debilitative when in conflict (Hatfield, 2009). To prevent this while processing conflict, it is important to first deal with emotion empathically and compassionately, before turning to deal with the substantive issues.

There is no doubt that emotions can contribute positively to a conflict experience; as you have already learned, they can help to identify and prioritize issues and open up communication. However, extremely intense emotions frequently interfere with both intrapersonal and interpersonal conflict resolution.

Fourth Emotional Challenge: Extremes of Emotion

Four emotional clusters complicate conflict when they are particularly intense: 1) fear, anxiety, and worry, 2) hurt, 3) shame and humiliation, and 4) anger and rage. Before exploring them, let's look at degrees of emotional expression.

Reactivity and Apathy

Reactivity refers to a hasty, intensely emotional reaction to events. People who are reactive are likely to experience **emotional flooding** (overwhelming levels of emotion), and feel compelled to respond instantly or in an exaggerated way. They experience their feelings so intensely that thinking shuts down. Goleman (2012) coined the term **emotional hijacking** to describe the way intense emotion can interfere with rational, logical thinking and activate a desperate fight or flight response. Reactive people tend to be dramatically changeable, showing quick temper tantrums, anxiety and panic attacks, and/or sudden tears. They say and do things they regret later. Reactivity can add stress to an already strained relationship and can be damaging if it becomes habitual or severe.

However, when emotional reactivity and flooding become debilitative, some people use excessive control. They might disengage from their feelings and deny that distress even exists. The indifferent, disengaged absence of emotion, concern, or even interest is called **apathy**. The long-term problem with this strategy is that neglecting emotions can result in depression and estrangement from yourself (De France, 2020). Apathy becomes a silent barrier to effective conflict resolution. The futility that results from repetitious, unresolved conflict may permanently damage a relationship. The apathetic pattern also creates subtle power by acting as if an issue or person simply does not matter. It is disempowering and frustrating to sustain dialogue or argue with someone who doesn't care, so apathy often leads either to conflict impasse or escalation.

The goal of a mature conflict resolver is to use emotional intelligence to be **emotionally responsive**, which is neither reactive nor apathetic. People who are emotionally responsive take time to analyze their feelings, sources, and think through potential responses before acting (Hill, 2012).

Vulnerability, Fear, Anxiety, and Worry

Fear, anxiety, and worry all belong to a cluster of feelings related to alarm and vulnerability. Extreme anxiety becomes self-reinforcing: when you are anxious, you are likely to perceive threat in exaggerated terms; then if the conflict intensifies the anxiety seems like a natural response. In a situation of sustained vulnerability, protective defensiveness can silence any useful communication and interfere with effective conflict processing.

Hurt

When you are harmed physically, you instinctively react to protect yourself and stop the one hurting you, even by harming them. This is also true when interpersonal conflict causes emotional pain. When you are hurt you naturally become defensive, but may also become offensive in a retaliatory way. There is a saying, "Hurt people hurt people." Hurt is both the result of conflict, and also escalates it.

Shame and Humiliation

Just as strong self-esteem is a pillar of a resilient identity, shame is central to a negative identity. A person who feels shame believes "I am flawed … I don't measure up … I am worthless." The connection between shame and conflict is that, when humiliated, you may react by treating yourself and others poorly, acting out aggressively. People who suffer shame often overreact to differences, but then violate others' rights to justify or prove themselves. Painful shame can cause a conflict or intensify an ongoing one.

Experiences of humiliation can be so prevalent that they affect an entire culture. In a **shame-based culture**, the primary devices for teaching are shame and embarrassment to penalize people who do not conform, and honor to reward those who live up to social ideals (Morrison, 1998; Wong, 2007). Honor reflects what is considered to be worthwhile and dignified in a culture. The values are evident, for example, in the many rewards for thin women, contrasted to the shame of being "fat" in some cultures. In another example, gangs are shame cultures that use humiliation to enforce strongly defined expectations when members are unable or unwilling to fulfill the rules. The use of prisons to censure criminals also creates a shame culture.

Anger and Rage

When your expectations of yourself or other people are disappointed, you become discouraged and angry. Anger helps you to believe that you are in control, even when that is an illusion. Anger may be an unconscious "cover" for another emotion that is passive or difficult to manage, such as loneliness or helplessness. When any intense emotion is stalled, you might transform it into anger, blame, labeling, and/or judgments of others. These can distract from or disguise anger's true cause.

Anger is often unpleasant, but it can also be healthy when it identifies an important issue that needs attention (Lerner, 2014). When people feel threatened or afraid, anger can be a reasonable response to try to alter the situation or resolve the crisis. Anger is also a healthy response to perceived unfairness or injustice. Not all anger is dangerous or destructive, but it must be carefully understood and regulated.

> *Speak when you are angry and you will make the best speech you will ever regret.*
> —Ambrose Bierce

Intense anger can seem compelling, so it increases the likelihood of conflict and the probability that the conflict will become serious or even violent. Cycles of anger can occur: one person's behavior may cause others to become angry or aggressive, which aggravates the original person's anger, and so on. Think of anger as an accelerator, fueled by unmet expectations, frustration, or injustice (see Figure 1.2). Anger does not have to be a "zero-to-sixty experience" that inevitably results in rage or conflict. Rather, if you pay attention, its escalation can be traced and understood as a growing, developing response that can then be moderated.

Before we move on to explore perception, take note of these conclusions about emotion and conflict:

- Feelings are not "crazy." Emotions are arrational, NOT irrational.
- Accept feelings as no less, and no more, than feelings. They should not be neglected, but they are not a prescription to act.

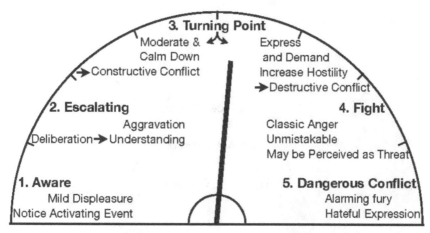

Figure 1.2 Anger development diagram

- When you pay attention to feelings, their information can lead to better choices and enhanced self-control (Lindner, 2014). By paying attention, you can name specific emotional experiences, recognize the many dimensions of feeling, their sources or triggers, your own and others' patterns of reaction, and work toward balanced affect.
- A key to sustainable conflict resolution is reduction of vulnerability (Halperin, 2016), which happens when complicated feelings are both moderated and communicated.

MIXED NEEDS MOTIVATE YOUR BEHAVIOR

Needs are more central than wants; if needs are not satisfied, your well-being and quality of life are compromised. People have personal and social needs, instrumental needs to get things done, and identity needs that confirm or challenge who you are. In the following discussion, notice that all the needs are interwoven even though we segment the personal, social, instrumental, and identity needs for the sake of clarity.

A Needs Hierarchy Suggests That Some Needs Are More Central Than Others

The **Multiple Needs Theory**, extended from Abraham Maslow's original Hierarchy of Needs (1943), suggests that needs and motives are rarely simple. Instead, any behavior is likely motivated by multiple, often competing and fluid, needs. When in conflict, these motives can become both pressing and unstable. According to this theory, personal needs occur in a ranked hierarchy (see Figure 1.3). As the needs are fulfilled your attentions expand outward from self to others to the broader environment.

Deficiency Needs—these are the most basic; when they are threatened or deprived, they will cause somewhat urgent action.

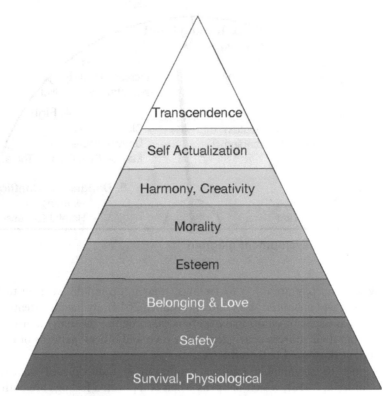

Figure 1.3 Hierarchy of personal needs
Based on Maslow, 1943.

1. The need for physical *survival* is the most foundational and urgent. When survival is threatened, this need overshadows all the rest.
2. Next come the needs for *safety and security*. When you feel insecure, like in a strange environment, seeking safety becomes your main concern.
3. If physical survival and safety are reasonably assured, your need for *belonging* and love are the next priority, and your attention can turn to relationships.
4. Maslow suggested that, when those are fulfilled, *self-esteem* is next in importance in the motivational mix, including both a personal sense of competency and success, and interpersonal recognition.
   Growth Needs—these needs are not essential for survival, but are crucial for thriving.
5. When deficiency needs are mostly satisfied you can pursue behaviors that feed *intellectual-cognitive* challenges like problem solving and the creation of order.
6. Next in priority are the *aesthetic motives* for beauty, harmony, and goodness.
7. *Self-actualization*, which is growth and the fulfilment of your best potential or best self, is crucial to a settled identity and dignity.
8. Maslow later adopted a higher need for *transcendence* that searches for a spiritual dimension in life, from Viktor Frankl (2006).

We can apply this theory to examples of conflict:

1. Physical *survival* is not an issue during most conflicts *unless danger or violence are experienced*; however, many conflicts take on a "do-or-die" tone when you feel you cannot survive intact in a relationship.
2. *Safety and security*—because many conflicts can seem strange and unwelcome, most people feel insecure and apprehensive.
3. Many conflicts threaten love or *belonging* if there is doubt that the relationship can continue.
4. *Self-esteem* is often a casualty of conflict because of self-doubt, interpersonal offenses, or failure to reach resolution.
5. *Intellectual-cognitive* satisfaction is compromised by the confusion and lack of insight that often accompany conflict.
6. *Aesthetic* needs are inherently threatened by the disharmony and disorder of conflict.
7. *Self-actualization* can be stalled when identity and dignity are endangered.
8. The *transcendent* dimension may become involved when disputants process issues of values, meanings, power, or the presence or absence of the divine.

Unmet needs become a recipe for deep conflict. The **Frustration-Aggression Hypothesis** focused a long-presumed link between frustrated needs and conflict. According to this view, when people are unable to satisfy their needs, frustration and an urgency for fulfilment both increase. The more frustrated and urgent the needs, the more likely it is that interpersonal conflict will occur. Redekop and Rioux (2002) also correlated unsatisfied identity needs with the likelihood of violence in conflict.

Needs Are Fulfilled in a Social Context
We are social beings, and most life experiences happen in the context of relationship. The fact that people have social needs for belonging and affection seems almost too obvious to state, but some needs theories overlook this dimension. Social needs include the drive to be in intimate, meaningful relationships with a few primary people, as well as the desire to participate in a broader social environment such as a school or workplace.

Urie Bronfenbrenner's **Ecological Systems Theory** (1979) focused on individual needs and actions within a social environment. You act to fulfill your needs within five unified environments: within yourself, close family and peers, formal institutions, broader society, and culture. He believed that unsatisfied basic need leads to conflict. Bronfenbrenner's work founded the Head Start program in the United States, which is designed to reduce long-term social conflict related to poverty and hunger.

Instrumental Needs to Get Things Done
Individuals are "doing" people and you need settings in which to use your abilities and skills. The need for personal growth in your abilities to get things done through learning and education is driven by intellectual curiosity. Most people thrive when they can significantly contribute to getting meaningful things done,

but they are frustrated when achieving something takes too long or seems impossible. Increasingly, the need for useable information becomes central to your work in society. Instrumental needs extend to the desire for safe work (although "work" does not necessarily imply employment). A sensible activity and leisure balance is also a part of this need.

Identity Needs

Identity refers to your view of your own character, sometimes called the *self-concept*. **Personal** or **core identity** refers to your unique qualities, independent of others. **Social identity**, also called *relational identity*, is expressed when interacting with other people and their expectations. Refinement of a coherent identity involves an integration of core and relational identities. There are four main influences on the formation of identity (Erikson, 1980; Shapiro, 2017; Vignoles, 2006):

- Relationships, especially ones that are crucial to your sense of *belonging*, form the most central core of identity.
- *Competencies*, your strengths and skills as well as your weaknesses and challenges, become integrated into a concept of yourself as capable.
- *Continuity* across time gives you a sense of consistency. The present makes sense because of your past, and the future is flowing sensibly out of your present.
- Values and *ideals* form the part of identity that lends meaning to what you do.

Early in life, identity is assigned by people close to you through interaction, their expectations, and feedback. Eventually, most people challenge an assigned identity, forging something unique through experimentation, conflict, and even rebellion (Erikson, 1980). In adulthood, you choose the identity that provides the most self-respect.

Conflict is inevitable when your established identity is threatened. Called **identity-based conflict**, it develops when a person or group believes that their identity is threatened or denied legitimacy or respect. Identity-based conflict is particularly fierce because it demands defense of your essential values and beliefs.

In contrast to the Frustration-Aggression Hypothesis, the **Identity Needs Theory** recognized that deeply rooted identity needs are a core of serious conflict and of conflict resolution (Burton, 1990; Shapiro, 2017; Stone, 2010). John Burton believed that knowing, understanding, and accommodating everyone's identity needs (*tout le monde*, or "all the world") could eliminate deprivation and frustration as sources of conflict. This viewpoint challenged prevalent conflict resolution practices that directed peacebuilding primarily toward meeting material needs or controlling aggressive behavior.

This theory combines personal and social needs with meaningful *recognition*, *identity*, and a desire for *collaborative relationship*. If satisfaction of these immaterial needs is threatened, some people become offensively competitive, satisfying themselves at others' expense. However, satisfaction of identity needs is limitless, can be shared by everyone, so noncompetitive, cooperative conflict resolution is entirely possible. Burton's work focused on conflict resolution that is based on uncovering unfulfilled identity needs, and creatively exploring ways to promote peaceable satisfaction for everyone (Burton, 1998).

Think About and Discuss with Your Colleagues

1. Record the self-talk related to your self-concept and identities, distinguishing the positive and negative themes. Make note of any self-defeating behavior that results from negative self-talk. Question the "truth" behind negative self-defeating thoughts, and identify possible errors. Reframe a factual, logical alternative way of thinking.
2. Reflect on a recent incident of conflict you experienced within your circle. To what extent was it exacerbated by unmet personal, social, instrumental, and/or identity needs? Understanding that, is there something you might do differently as you approach a similar problem?

The sociological concept of "face" is related to both personal and social identities. **Face** is a personal measure of respectability, asserting an outward impression that you are strong in four ways: 1) you have friends and are worthy of love, 2) you are competent and intelligent, 3) you are consistent, and 4) you are in control (Ho, 1974; Stone, 2010). Face is enhanced through correct behavior, social status, and dutiful conformity, but lost through weakness (Goffman, 1967). In parallel with good face is bad face, when your actions disgrace you in at least one of four opposite ways: 1) you are a loner, rejected by people who matter, 2) you are stupid and not good enough, 3) your actions are contradictory, or 4) others can easily take advantage of or control you. Face threats can be deeply wounding if they are internalized, and humiliating experiences, dissonance, and cognitive distortions often trigger serious identity-based conflict (Stone, 2010). Gaining and losing face and preserving it involve complex maneuvers called *facework* (Domenici, 2006; Goffman, 1967). Although more prominent in eastern cultures, face functions in western relationships as well (Guo, 2011).

Emotions and needs, together, form the basis for human motivation. Perception is a mental process that integrates it all.

PERCEPTION IS CRUCIAL, BUT IT MUST BE ACCURATE

Perception is the process by which you make sense of information and experiences. Every day, you are bombarded by innumerable bits of information that must be sorted and filtered. Perception is obviously influenced by simultaneous sensory, auditory, and visual information, but less obviously by other factors including emotions, relationship history, and context.

Perception is fallible and can deceive you. A commonplace belief is that your own perception is real, true, or "common sense" (Fisher, 2011) and, if others differ from you, then they must be wrong. However, your subjective assumptions, inferences, and explanations usually influence perception more than the objective reality of a situation (Bar-Tal, 1986).

Gary Johns and Alan Saks (2020) divided perception into three components: the perceiver (the People element); the situation in context (the Problem element); and the data received (the Process element).

> *We don't see things as they are.*
> *We see things as we are.*
> —Anaïs Nin

Perception Issues Related to the Perceiver

People do not passively receive incoming information but, rather, actively filter and organize it. In three subconscious operations you filter, choose, and organize, and then interpret what is worth paying attention to. These operations are impacted by many personal qualities such as attention, openness to new experiences, emotions, the intensity of the stimulus, past experiences, and expectations. The timing of a conflict can change a perceiver's reactions—for example, whether you are tired or fired up. Judgments about the "messenger" strongly affect receptiveness to the data—for example, if the information comes from a friendly, respected source, it is likely to be trusted; if the source is threatening, the data may be credible but activate intrusive anxiety. Any past relationship between the disputants (or even with similar characters) can influence the perceiver and move a conflict in unpredictable directions.

Divergent Perspectives Add Relevant Information

Different information is available to disputing parties, so a problem can seem very different to you and other people. For example, the owner of a company, its workers or union members, or its customers do not view a strike in the same way. Especially when a relationship is tense or conflicted, perspective can either broaden or limit the information available to deal with a problem.

There are four potential perspectives:

- *First perspective*—This represents the point of view of a perceiver who is involved in a situation. The focus of the first perspective is primarily your own thoughts, feelings, and needs.
- *Second perspective*—A situation is seen through the eyes of another party who is also involved in the situation. To consider this perspective is to "walk in someone else's shoes." This viewpoint is essential to compassion, and shifting to it may help you see yourself more fully.
- *Third perspective*—This detached, impersonal view observes behavior and its consequences as if from outside the situation, with an objective, unbiased viewpoint. From that perspective, you might notice, for example, when conflict vocabulary escalates already existing tensions.
- *Fourth perspective*—This perspective notices the qualities of a conflicted relationship and how a conflict is unfolding. Observations are "big picture," and using it can often help you grasp the direction of a conversation, conflict and/or the relationship.

Alternative interpretations of a conflict often hinge on the perspective of the perceiver and on contrasts among the four perspectives. In many instances in history, a polarized perspective labels an individual as a "revolutionary terrorist" but, in time, these same individuals may become patriotic governors or even peaceful leaders in their countries—for example, Fidel Castro first rose to prominence as a communist revolutionary, then served as the highest political leader in Cuba from 1959 through 2008.

Remaining "stuck" in a single perspective (usually an **egocentric**, self-centered first viewpoint) severely limits the information available to solve a problem. The skills of empathy and good listening help establish a "learning stance" to explore different perspectives on events, emotions, and identities, adding new information and enriching your perception (Stone, 2010), often leading to new choices and responses. Testing several perspectives is preferable to only one. Thoughtful exploration of all four perspectives will broaden your insight and can restart a stalled argument. This is illustrated by the following quotation: "My vision of myself and the way others see me are frequently very different. If I go through life insisting that others see me the same way I see myself, I am setting myself up for conflict. I need to look at myself through the lens of others' experience of me to understand" (CanMediate International). This is a skill called reframing.

A *frame* refers to a view of the world bounded by assumptions. As you shift perspectives you use new frames, considering other possible views and interpretations. **Reframing** assumes that every action is sensible in some context and tries to discover the frame. Fear can be reframed as caution, anger can be reframed as determination, and underlying causes of conflict such as personal antagonism can be reframed as problems to be solved, a weakness or disadvantage in one context can be a very useful strength in another (B. Mayer, 2012).

Gender Affects Individual Perception

Stereotyped perception can be powerful through cultural expectations associated with gender assigned roles, sometimes called a "culture trap" (Claes, 1999). The expectations were summarized by Theresa Welbourne (2005) as *feminine take care behavior* contrasted with *masculine take charge conduct*. Karima Merchant (2012) described how those feminine and masculine stereotypes are internalized and alter individuals' perception, communication, and talent development. Altered behavior then feeds self-fulfilling prophecies of existing status differences and views of success.

Stereotypic perception can affect the ways women and men see conflict, and shape their focus of attention and effort. Women tend to attend to the relationship and family aspects of conflict, sensitive to issues such as power imbalance, competitive argumentation, keeping a group together in a situation of conflict, and caring for victims of conflict such as family, displaced persons, and refugees. Women and girls emphasize emotional expression, anger, and critique in peacebuilding. Men tend to focus on the task aspects of conflict and conflict resolution, and their past experiences reinforce peacebuilding skills for solving dilemmas and problems (Canary, 1988). In the stereotyped equilibrium, women are encouraged to follow men and men are permitted to claim success.

Such stereotyped perception reinforces some traditional exclusion of females from formal peacemaking efforts, but it is increasingly clear that successful peacemaking addresses both womens' and mens' concerns and input. In Africa, for example, changing perception of women and their roles have become essential to enduring postconflict peacebuilding (Agbalajobi, 2010; Ogunsanya, 2007).

The Relative Power between the Disputants Affects Their Perception and Interaction

Power provides individual choices, opportunities, and resources, but the comparative balance of power in a relationship is very important, especially when in conflict. Issues related to the *structural elements* of power (Galtung, 1969) focus on the ways that dominance and leadership are regulated between the disputants. Power balances and inequalities between the disputants influences their perception of possible choices of action, reactions, tactics, and strategies that, in turn, can determine how the conflict unfolds. For example, the conflict behavior patterns of a parent and a young child, or a parent and an adult son or daughter will be very different; your own conflict patterns will be different when you are arguing with a friend or with your employer. As a dispute escalates, it may convert into a power struggle because of perceived helplessness.

Problems Are Entwined with the Situation in Context

Every conflict situation is associated with evolving, but often mismatched assumptions about what is worth fighting for, what conflict means, appropriate conflict behavior, a preferred method of resolution, and hope or despair of reaching peace. All those perceptions and assumptions are shaped by social learning. When encountering an ambiguous conflict, you actively scan the entire setting for cues from the environment about the seriousness of the problem and potential paths toward solutions (Johns, 2020).

When disagreement is mild, perception is a somewhat accurate reflection of the situation. Disputants tend to trust each other, can acknowledge their similarities, and discussion is respectful. The main focus is on the situation and problem that need resolution. As tensions build, open communication continues, but leans toward more insistent language. Perception is shaped more by personal feelings than by the situation, and assumptions of opposition are likely. Interpretations are dominated by polarized thoughts of "I'm right … you're wrong and need to see it my way." When conflict reaches a tense point of confrontation, distrust is common and respect weakens. Communication narrows to the problem alone. If confrontation does not end the conflict, perception might scarcely resemble the objective realities and the context of crisis can cause disputants to withdraw, giving up on the relationship and on conflict resolution (after Keashly, 1996).

Cultures Differ in Their Approaches

Emotions are experienced within a cultural context (see Chapter 5), in socially prescribed ways, and this might be especially true in conflict situations (Ting-Toomey, 2019).

In *collectivist* cultures (Eastern, rural, and Indigenous), restraint is valued, so emotions are mostly veiled with a public "face" of calm. Collectivist expression tends to be indirect, and the context is relied on for communication. Indistinct communication can be perceived by outsiders as vague, indecisive, or elusive. Meticulous maneuvering is used to prevent confrontation in friendship, family, and employment situations. When differences arise, tactics are chosen to emphasize interpersonal accommodation and collaboration, while argument is severely limited because it is believed to threaten collective harmony. Perceivers' familiarity with the relationship expectations and the context are necessary to make accurate interpretations. Resolution is often created through the fulfilment of expectations and subtle demands within a social network.

In *individualistic* cultures (Western, urban, and multicultural) individual needs and rights are centrally valued. Emotions, even intense varieties, are expressed openly, both nonverbally and verbally. The explicit communication and mannerisms are often seen by collectivists as abrupt, rude, or even aggressive. Conflict is not consistently perceived to be threatening, but may even be seen as a positive opportunity, a "cleansing storm" that clarifies issues. Confrontation is accepted as appropriate if it makes a persuasive point. Resolution is achieved by compromise that integrates divergent interests (Hammer, 2009; Kammhuber 2010; Ting-Toomey, 2019).

An important element of the context is the intercultural familiarity or perceived different-ness of an opponent (Thomas, 2010). Emotions, especially those expressed vividly, are often misunderstood in intercultural discussions. Intercultural conflict can easily be misjudged by over- or underestimating its significance (Kammhuber, 2010), which can lead to perceived over- or underreaction.

Processing the Information Received

Subjective perception may seem to effortlessly integrate information, but it is a highly complex process of making sense of multiple ambiguous stimuli received from the environment. It is understood as a system of processes with *three nearly simultaneous steps*: selecting sensory information for attention, organizing and categorizing it, and interpreting it. The outcome, the perception that you act on, may or may not be an accurate representation of the original stimulus. Especially in situations of intense emotion and intrapersonal or interpersonal conflict, perception can be shaped more by personal factors than by "reality."

First Perceptual Step: Receiving the Information

If you really slow down and pay attention, you are amazed by the bombardment of sensory information you receive in any given five minutes, and all the series of thoughts and reactions to it. Paying attention is not as simple as it seems.

Active attention is the deliberate effort to concentrate on an item such as a task or book. **Passive attention** is not paying attention to any specific item but, rather, letting something capture your notice because it stands out from others: it is louder, moving, bigger, brighter, and so forth. When you are thinking through troublesome or complicated problems and conflicts, most of your focus will be through active attention. **Divided attention** occurs when several relevant items compete for your attention but interfere with one another. This could happen, for example, in a conflict within a group, when there are chaotic conversations all happening at once. **Focused attention** occurs when you consciously select a single stimulus for attention but ignore other, apparently irrelevant stimuli. In a chaotic conflict, you might focus your attention only on one person, for example. **Perceptual defense** is a subconscious censor that affects conflict perception by preventing you from attending to or perceiving obnoxious stimuli such as offensive comments about a loved one.

Receiving accurate and relevant information is vital to working out the important issues when conflict demands your attention. There are many possible intrapersonal sources of error, identified by Leonard Riskin and Rachel Wohl as the "six obstacles to awareness" (Riskin, 2015):

1. Excessive self-centeredness,
2. Strong negative emotion,
3. Automatic, habitual ways of thinking, feeling, and behaving,
4. Too much or too little sensitivity to emotion,
5. Insufficient social skill, and

6. Paying too little attention to important things and new information, or too much attention to trivial information.

Mindfulness is a popular silent meditation that people use to maximize the power of attention. It involves taking deliberate quiet time to focus on present, moment-to-moment thoughts while detaching from the muddle of the past or future. Although it began in ancient Eastern religion, mindfulness is used across the world as a simple daily healthy contemplation. Paying attention to deeper, mostly hidden, thoughts and emotions and meanings beyond obvious, well-known factors can lead to additional insight. This is why Reflective Practice is valuable. See Praxis Skill Builder 1.3 for some tips for developing Reflective Practice through mindfulness.

Praxis Skill Builder 1.3 ■ Mind Full, or Mindful? Reflective Practice and Mindfulness

Guidance from "Mindful," the website of the Foundation for a Mindful Society at mindful.org:

1. Set time aside each day to reflect by yourself.
2. Observe your immediate experiences: your feelings, thoughts, and body sensations.
3. Accept what comes to mind without judgment, and let it simply pass by.
4. Notice when your mind wanders away, but gently keep returning to this present moment.

Mindfulness takes practice! The more you use it, the easier it gets.

One of the originators of the reflective approach to conflict analysis, Donald Schon (1983), distinguished **reflection-in-action** (which is careful thought during a conflict) from **reflection-on-action** (which is retrospective analysis after a conflict has ended). Using this method, a responsible conflict resolver habitually sorts through experiences and both successful and unfortunate actions, continuously learning and reaching insight. Reflective practice is a basic component of your conflict-resolution toolbox. Reflective practice is taught in most conflict resolution education and skills development programs, to sort through "lessons learned." Review the description in the textbook Introduction and Figure I.7 for a more detailed look at reflective practices.

Second Perceptual Step: Collecting, Categorizing, and Organizing the Information
All day, multiple simultaneous stimuli have to be organized to make sense. Your mind is structured to organize information so that comprehension is as quick, simple, and orderly as possible, keeping change and dissonance to a minimum.

When incoming data is ambiguous, you must find ways to "fill in the gaps." Perception is therefore vulnerable to **suggestion**, which is categorizing an experience with something similar from the past. When you hear a loud voice, for example, you might associate it with a remembered loud conflict and "hear" more animosity than is intended. Perception is influenced by expectation—you see what you expect to see. If you expect a lecture to be boring, you will likely think it is; if you are excited about UFOs, you are likely to interpret a strange phenomenon as a UFO. **Perceptual suggestion** might be part of a **perceptual set**, the predisposition to perceive events in an expected way. If, for example, someone says, "Caroline's in a foul mood today," the next time you run into Caroline you are "set" to confirm the suggestion. This is the basis for stereotyping too. Previous conflict with Caroline can shape expectations of her behavior and potential disagreements with her.

During a fast-moving conflict, it is easy to focus on irrelevant details or unhelpfully categorize people because of expectations. Subconscious selection may or may not help: the processes of narrowly focused attention, perceptual defense, and perceptual suggestion may incorrectly or inadequately meet the demand to truly understand a heated conflict. Difficulty arises when an interaction differs from the expectations used. For example, verbalizing absolute judgments by saying things like "you always..." or "you never..." can easily lead to inappropriately fixed perception that traps a conflict into rigid patterns, making resolution less likely.

Third Perceptual Step: Interpreting Meaning

The third step of the perceptual process is interpreting the received and organized information. This is the perceptual stage with the greatest impact on a conflict. Although a few stimuli have clear meanings and are easily placed into context, conflict is usually a complex, ambiguous experience that may have several possible interpretations. Perceptual interpretation is usually determined more by personal factors than by situational factors.

Care must be taken during this process. "Jumping to conclusions" on the basis of incomplete or partially analyzed information can lead to excessively tangled conflict. Blaming one family member as "reckless" or believing that "all teenagers are impossible," for example, can block avenues toward new understanding.

Accurate and Inaccurate Perception

Accurate perception is crucial to successful conflict processing and resolution. If you believe your perceptions are true, you act on them as if they are correct and real. Inaccurate perception can happen in many ways, and is a great source of interpersonal tension and conflict. Negative perceptions can spiral, leading to defensive or aggressive reactions and behavior. This then affects the responses of other parties, and so on. The negativity continues to spiral and it inevitably results in conflict.

Perceptual errors can be experienced from several sources:

- *People* make mistakes by focusing on only one part of an experience or the opponent, assuming that first thoughts are true. Especially in conflict, your perception tends to narrow to singular impressions, and it is easy to neglect possible alternative factors. For example, before giving it thought, most people assume that their perception is correct and right, and that it should be understood by everyone.

- Perception can be complicated by unexamined assumptions about the *problem*. For example, you can generalize and misinterpret conflict behavior to be more aggressive than was intended.
- When *interpreting* conflict, you might experience bias in explaining it. A self-serving bias explains your own behavior in favorable ways that reinforce positive self-esteem; you might also tend to blame others in negative or hostile terms that also reinforce your self-esteem. When an ambiguous incident happens, several different explanations are possible, so you might jump to conclusions and fill in the gaps of what is unknown.

Praxis Skill Builder 1.4 ■ Strategies for Improving the Accuracy of Your Perception

1. Notice the important role that perception plays in everyday events and conflict.
2. Notice people and events with curiosity. Notice subtle details, but don't neglect the context or the bigger picture.
3. Reflect on your own perceptual processes, knowing that your perception of reality may not be the same as everyone's. Ask yourself: Is my information complete? Is my perception accurate?
4. Notice the meanings you assign as you interpret events and people's actions. Aim for the most respectful interpretation.
5. Observe several alternative perspectives or interpretations of a situation. Ask yourself: Could this experience be different from another perspective?
6. Recognize repeating biases that may affect your interpretation.
7. Accept errors in perception without judgment, but find ways to improve your accuracy.
8. Check your perceptions with people who you know will give you honest feedback.

PERSONALITY SHAPES CONFLICT BEHAVIOR

One of the great curiosities in Conflict Resolution Studies is the relationship between personality and conflict behavior. The reasons for a "personality conflict" are somewhat disconnected from events, decisions, or problems, and are more related to personal incompatibilities. Specific reasons are seldom clear and are perplexing as you work toward achieving harmony. **Personality** is the complex mix of traits, thoughts, emotions, and behavioral habits that describe and distinguish one individual from another. Personality assumes that your characteristics are unique, organized, and relatively consistent in a variety of settings over time.

The correlation between personality and conflict behavior is exploratory at best, and the subject of much ongoing research. Here, we summarize one theory that has shown some promise. The **Five Factor Model** (FFM) (see Figure 1.4) identifies five personality domains, expressed as contrasted traits (Digman, 1990; McCrae, 2008; Tupes, 1961; and others). Notice the acronym "**OCEAN**":

1. **Open** means openminded and willing to try new experiences. The contrasting quality is **closed minded**, overly cautious, or somewhat inflexible.

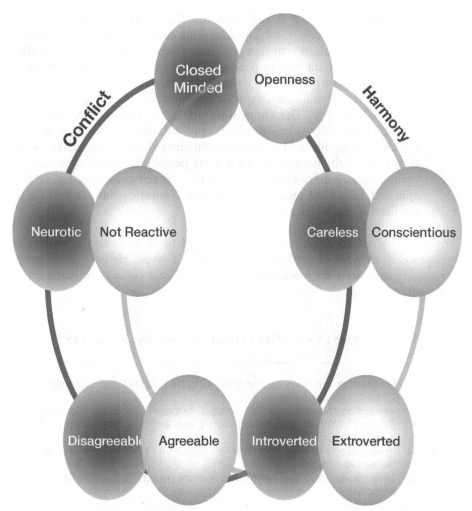

Figure 1.4 Five factor model and conflict behavior
Based on Tupes, 1961.

People who are open, curious, and imaginative are likely to approach conflict in an optimistic way, prepared for insight. They take interest in conflict as a chance to learn something.

2. **Conscientious** is careful, thoughtful, thorough, and diligent. The contrasting feature is **careless** or thoughtless. People who are conscientious engage in conflict in an organized, disciplined, goal-directed, and responsible way.

3. **Extroverted** is enthusiastic sociability, being oriented toward other people, and assertively expressive. Extroverts understand themselves through relationships with other people. The contrasting characteristic is **introverted,** which describes people who take comfort and energy from solitude. Extroverts need to talk as they think through conflict; introverts prefer to be alone to settle issues before they approach a dialogue. When in conflict, introverts may view extroverts as pushy, and extroverts often think of introverts as guarded or resistant.

4. **Agreeable,** tolerant, kind, and forgiving. This requires listening well, taking others' requests seriously, and working cooperatively. The contrasting trait is **disagreeable,** which is unpleasant and oppositional. Even in conflict, agreeable people interact in patient, courteous ways; disagreeable people escalate conflict with repeated debate and argument.

5. **Nonreactivity** to emotions, expressed in qualities like calm, security, and emotional stability. The contrasting quality is **neuroticism,** also called *emotional volatility* or moodiness. People with this characteristic are emotionally changeable, and sometimes dramatize their feelings. Even in conflict, emotionally nonreactive people are persistent, remain confident and optimistic, and do not suffer from anxiety or self-consciousness, so their approach to conflict tends to be objective. Neurotic people contribute unpredictably and illogically to conflict.

Any given individual displays a combination of behaviors that lie somewhere between each extreme of the Five Factor Model. Two people with incompatible personality tendencies are less likely to understand each other or to reach resolution easily.

Praxis Skill Builder 1.5 ■ Conflict Resolution Principles Related to Personality

1. Emphasize curiosity rather than judgment when approaching conflict with someone else.
2. Always be thoughtful about conflict, but don't avoid conflict issues.
3. Be careful to use courteous words and actions, and avoid hurting another person.
4. Invest efforts toward cooperative resolution rather than toward being defensive or silent.
5. Slow down and be optimistic before reacting or taking events personally.

The goal of peaceful relationships as well as effective conflict resolution is to create ways of interacting with others with mutual compassion and fairness. Intrapersonal qualities you have explored in this chapter all become integrated into and expressed in both peaceable and antagonistic behavior. Turn to Chapter 4 to explore issues related to interpersonal relationships.

COMPASSIONATE PEACEBUILDER:
THICH NHAT HAHN (1926–)

"If you want peace, you have to be peace."

Thich Nhat Hanh is a Buddhist monk and peace activist. He was born in Vietnam. He became a monk in 1951 after studying many Buddhist teachings and deep meditation habits. He was convinced by the Vietnam war that Buddhists can and should actively improve lives affected by the turmoil of conflict. Hanh developed

Engaged Buddhism, and wrote and traveled internationally to teach it. This led to the creation of a corps of nonviolent peaceworkers who assist refugees and rebuild communities after war, setting up health care services and schools. After teaching at several universities in the United States in the early 1960s, Hanh was exiled by Vietnam and moved to the south of France. In 1982 he founded a mindfulness peace center called Plum Village, in Dordogne, France.

Hanh believes that the roots of war are within the minds of people and the energies of fear. A peaceful world will begin only when people find an inner peace that is compassionate and free of anger, despair, and hatred. Hanh practices and teaches daily mindfulness as a path toward inner peace and compassionate ethics, which he believes build a collective will for peaceful transformation.

CHAPTER SUMMARY AND STUDY GUIDE

To grasp the complicated ways people behave, whether in peace or conflict, this chapter separates out and discuss several dimensions of *intra*-personal functioning:

- Intrapersonal conflict and interpersonal conflict are different, but are inextricably linked.
- Four possible perspectives or points of view on the same event are possible and can be valuable to understand a conflict.
- Emotions have a deep impact on both peace and conflict, so careful discernment of feelings is helpful to effective conflict resolution. Sometimes emotions facilitate harmony; sometimes they debilitate thinking and problem solving. In peacebuilding, it is useful to identify complex emotions, decide whether and how to express emotion, and recognize their facilitative or debilitative aspects. Not all emotion should be expressed: those that are too intense, unsettled, or debilitating should probably be reserved until they can be moderated.
- Personal, social, instrumental, and identity needs are strong motivators of behavior. Satisfied needs are usually part of a harmonious, constructive relationship. When deprived, unknown, or hidden, needs can cause or exacerbate conflict.
- Three sequential steps that establish perception can be distinguished, and each step presents multiple opportunities for accurate and inaccurate perception.
- Personality can influence the choices that you make while interpreting, processing, and resolving conflict. People whose personalities are open, conscientious, extroverted, agreeable, and nonreactive (OCEAN), and have high emotional intelligence resolve conflict most effectively.
- Explore reflective practices and mindfulness, and how to improve your skill with these abilities.

TERMS IN FOCUS

2

Interpersonal Factors Related to People in Conflict

■ ■ ■

In Focus in This Chapter:

■ identify some principles that govern everyday interpersonal relationships and communication;
■ learn skills to improve your own communicative competence;
■ recognize the influence of diverse identities on communication patterns;
■ understand the potential role of mass communication and social media in the development, maintenance, and resolution of conflict;
■ recognize fighting tactics that tend to escalate conflict; and
■ develop clear, effective communication skills that resolve conflict

CONFLICT CASE 2.1 ■ TYLER AND SOPHIE'S ARGUMENT

Tyler and Sophie had been together for about three years. This conversation took place on an early Friday evening in a busy restaurant, but it was not the first time. Although they seemed relaxed when they first got there, throughout the meal both tensed up. Their voices were raised and everyone around them could clearly hear what they were arguing about. Sophie's arms were crossed over her chest and Tyler played with his water glass and made minimal eye contact. Table 2.1 is a verbatim transcription of their conversation.

Table 2.1 Conversation

	Conversation	Commentary
Sophie	Did you spend that $100 I told you to save?	Trying to control
Tyler	Yep. Did you finish your homework yesterday?	Avoiding the subject
Sophie	Yes. How much money have you saved now?	Continuing intrusion
Tyler	I don't know.	Voice becoming louder
Sophie	How do you not know? I don't believe you saved that $100.	Deteriorating trust
/30 seconds of silence/ Tyler	How would you know? We never spend good time together. You're no fun! I work. It's my money.	Complaining Struggling for control

47

Sophie	Well, I sacrificed to save my share, so it's time for you to do your part. My money is your money and your money is my money. You have no right to spend it. Give me your bankcard, and *do it now.*	Ingenuine disclosure Controlling Coercion
Tyler	I work for my money. *You are not getting my card.*	Regaining control
Sophie	Yes, I am. I will take it when you're sleeping then. You have nothing to show for your supposed work. You owe money to me and everyone else.	Devious Criticism Crossing boundaries
Tyler	*Shut up! Shut up!* You don't care about me and I don't care about you. Go get a new boyfriend then. I'm sure Mark has more money than me.	Aggressive language New conflict
Sophie	What? What a jerk! Mark is just a friend. And, yes, he probably does have more money than you.	Disrespectful comparison
Tyler	You need some serious help. I am just wasting my time with you.	Judgment
Sophie	I love you.	Afraid of loss
Tyler	Yeah, whatever you say. I don't care.	Still upset, rejecting

The waiter came and distracted them, ending the argument without an end.

Think About and Discuss with Your Colleagues

In addition to your own observations and ideas, think about these factors:

- This conflict was fueled by accumulated and unresolved differences and conflict. Although money was definitely important to both Tyler and Sophie, other issues complicated the argument. Identify some of their communication tactics and patterns.
- This seems like a new-old argument, probably repeated over and over. What reasons could you guess for this cycling repetition?
- Sophie and Tyler appeared to be unaware of the escalating tension as the argument developed. More issues were included, more people became involved, emotions heated up, mutual resistance increased. Could they have diverted the energy into more constructive problem solving?
- Can you describe how power differences and struggles might have affected this argument?
- What would you recommend for this couple to improve their communication or problem solving?

In Chapter 1, you studied some intrapersonal factors (personal, inner feelings, needs, perception, and perspectives) related to conflict. Although intrapersonal and interpersonal factors blur and cannot be truly separate, in this chapter you begin to explore some of the (infinite) *inter*personal features of relationship dynamics under ordinary circumstances and under conditions of conflict.

Interpersonal relationships are affiliations between two or more people. The specific nature of an interaction is defined by the context, and shaped by history, setting, culture, and the type and purpose of the relationship. For example, interactions differ greatly in family, friendship, romantic, and professional relationships. Connections are sustained by interaction, communication, cooperation, and, ironically, by positive and negative conflict. Some scholars (e.g., Rummel, 1991) even believe that a relationship will stagnate if there are no challenges or conflict. Constructive conflict results in the elimination of problem sources, but even troubled conflict can lead to better interpersonal understandings and more effective problem solving (Deutsch, 2014). Differences and conflict have the potential to be catalysts for new perspectives, renewed creativity, and expanded choices. Few relationships are static; rather, they shift continuously and they require nurture and skill to maintain.

An important question is "whose problem is it, and who is in conflict"? Processing an intrapersonal conflict does not necessarily involve other parties. In contrast, an interpersonal conflict tends to draw in any parties who share the problem or are affected by the dispute. Many conflicts reverberate beyond the central parties. The people who are directly involved are called *primary parties*, while others who are affected but not involved in the dispute are *secondary parties*. The term *stakeholder* denotes a party on the periphery of the conflict who has something to gain or lose from its outcome. A *third party* is an outsider who becomes involved, usually to help find a solution; sometimes the presence of third parties can be counterproductive or even stall a conflict.

Communication is at the core of all actions and all relationships, even if it is silent. Most relationships are peaceful and interactions are ordinarily enjoyable and productive. For most people, conflict occurs only a small proportion of the time. However, when the differences are deep, ideas are miscommunicated, and perception is inaccurate, the disconnection can lead to conflict. The closer the relationship, the more painful are the differences and conflict. However, troubled communication is not inevitably negative or destructive but can also lead to repair and renewed closeness. Ever deeper communication, using persistence and courage, is essential to resolution. Communicative competence skills facilitate effective connection and, when needed, become the basis for discussing and resolving conflict.

DEFINING THE TERMS

"Everyone knows that communication is important, but nobody knows how to define it" (Greenman, 2008). An internet search for a definition produces a dizzying array of literally millions of references. Even a search limited to scholarly research yields more than 100,000 references. There are many relationship and communication theories (Donahue, 2014; West, 2018), each of which selects a focus on individual and interpersonal factors, the conversational process, or relationship dynamics (Braithwaite, 2015). A definition based on the Oxford English Dictionary states that to communicate is to share, to inform, or to convey or transmit information, thoughts, and feelings to others. This definition, however, is static and hardly captures the centrality or the dynamic.

Think About and Discuss with Your Colleagues

Notice your own communication patterns, and reflect on the following nine questions:

1. Notice why and when you need to communicate.
2. How would you describe effective or good communication? Are there signs that show good, effective communication?
3. What are the greatest challenges to good communication?
4. How important is listening?
5. In your experience, do culture, gender, nationality, or social class affect communication?
6. Notice the role of facial expressions, gestures, and pauses.
7. Has the development of internet and social media affected the ways you communicate?

Discuss your answers with your colleagues, and compare your thoughts with those of Dave Charon, at Voices of Youth (2017): https://www.voicesofyouth.org/blog/9-questions-about-communication.

The frustrating fact is that defining communication depends on many factors. Perhaps its complex elements can be summarized with W6 enquiries: *who* the people are to each other, *what* they intend to communicate and what is transmitted, *how* the message is sent, *why* each person communicates, and *when* and in *what* situation or context communication happens.

1. *Who* refers to the people relating to each other. This usually includes a communicator and a recipient, and there may also be a private or public audience.
2. *What* refers to the meaningful content of the message. Often, the content is mostly deliberate but some elements are unintentional. The message might seem obvious, but it is always accompanied by symbolic meanings. Communicated meanings are inferred and interpreted by the recipient so, very often, the message sent is not the message received. Any element of content might therefore be the impetus for conflict.
3. *How* refers to the process used to communicate. Often, how things are said is more important than what is said. It could be direct or indirect, and always uses multiple channels." The method used becomes the complex *code* for ideas, which then must be decoded by the receiver.
4. *Why* refers to the motives or goals for communicating that could include cultivating a relationship, sharing information, influencing or controlling someone else, and so forth. Each reason is associated with the use of certain tactics.
5. *When* communication happens is, simply, all the time and in every relationship. We cannot not communicate. Even silence can speak volumes.

6. *Where* refers to the situation and context of the interaction, which also links with the "why." For example, interpersonal versus technological contexts, even global systems, influence communication.

Notice all the opportunities for communication going wrong and relationships getting tangled up! These complex elements will be part of your reading in this chapter. As you explore peaceable, difficult, and conflicted **communication**, it is defined as the reciprocating process of conversation using symbols to express and comprehend ideas, thoughts, feelings, and responses.

> *I know that you believe you*
> *understand what you think*
> *I said, but I'm not sure you*
> *realize that what you heard is*
> *not what I meant.*
> —*Robert McCloskey, 1960*

BASIC PRINCIPLES OF EVERYDAY RELATING

The heart of relationships is communication. When you connect, you trustingly disclose yourself to someone, and they reciprocate. Even the process of communication can enhance interpersonal trust. Relationships are complex, and the communication process goes through multiple channels simultaneously, with words and with actions.

The Self Is the Starting Point

The starting point of communication is your Self. Inner dialogue of memories, thoughts, opinions, and debates form and refine your "Who am I?" personal identities and determine how you choose to interact with others. A foundation of authenticity and awareness, developed from listening to yourself, enables you to approach others with an open mind and an attitude of curiosity.

Inconsistencies between an ideal self-perception and actual behavior can cause ongoing intrapersonal conflict; for example, if you think you value diversity then make an angry racist comment to someone at a bus stop, that discrepancy can bother you like a stone in your shoe. Interpersonal conflict can result when your personal sense of self varies from others' views; for example, teen-parent disagreement often results from conflict between a teen's sense of self and parents' more conventional interpretations (Smetana, 1988). Even on a global scale, intractable conflict often results from discrepancies in the views of ourselves; for example, a rebel group might perceive its real identity to be as a needed social corrector while a government in power perceives them as malicious terrorists (Northrup, 1989).

Many scholars including Deborah Tannen (2007) emphasize the importance of *authentic voice*, which involves disclosing deeply personal concerns, beliefs, and values without censorship. The authentic voice is not always simple, as Nicole Ellison and her colleagues (2006) noticed in their research on online voice: the **ideal self** or **enhanced self**, describes an ideal person or the way a person hopes to be; the *ought self* represents what you believe you should be to measure up; and the **actual self** represents the truth in all of its complexities. All the "selves" participate in communication and relationship. As you accept feedback from others and reflect inwardly, you integrate and express the many selves into authentic voice.

Interpersonal Disclosure Is Essential

A genuine relationship depends on open disclosure in the context of trust. Sometimes you reveal only impersonal, easily known facts about yourself. This usually happens when strangers are just getting to know each other, or between people who only minimally trust each other. **Disclosure** occurs when normally private personal information is expressed out loud. Disclosure is risky because it exposes vulnerabilities, so not all disclosure is equally revealing.

> *I meant what I said, and I said what I meant.*
> —*Theodor Seuss Geisel (1940)*

In 1955, Joseph Luft and Harry Ingham created the **Johari Window** (see Figure 2.1) to illustrate the limits of disclosure. We are aware of some things about ourselves, but are blind to others; we let other people know certain aspects of our true selves, but choose not to disclose others. These two defining dimensions result in four types of disclosure:

- *Open Information*—Public information that is readily known to you and to others; it increases with self-disclosure.
- *Hidden Information*, or "The Façade"—Information that is known to you, but not disclosed to others; it limits mutual understanding.
- *Blind Information*, or "Blind Spots" —You only subconsciously communicate, so they are interpreted from your behavior; it decreases by listening to other peoples' feedback.
- *Unknown, Hidden Potential* Area—Neither you nor others are aware of this information; it decreases with self-discovery, and then choices are made about disclosure.

Sherod Miller and his colleagues (1988) described the layers of disclosure in relationship, beginning with impersonal door-openers called Shop Talk and

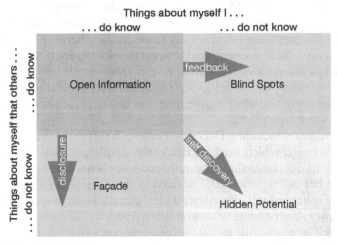

Figure 2.1 Johari window
Based on Luft, 1955.

Small Talk on the surface, Search Talk in the mid-level, and Straight Talk at the deepest and most personal. Although the seemingly trivial interactions of **Shop Talk** and **Small Talk** reveal little personal information, they are important forms of acknowledgment and "civil reciprocity" (Truss, 2005) that build rapport and trust. Conflict is rarely part of the impersonal layer because interchanges are safe and factual. This surface level is enriched by nonverbal components, and may also include playful communication that can be helpful for conflict resolution (Gottman, 2015).

A moderate depth of disclosure includes **Search Talk**, which uses careful inquiry about perception, problems, feelings, and memories. Search Talk can be used to clarify things that are uncertain to reduce anxiety and to improve understanding, so it is a good tool for resolving conflict. Using searching questions, issues are identified and clarified. Search Talk supports trust, defuses struggles for control, and makes authentic communication possible. Parties can then move toward deeper disclosure.

According to Miller, the deepest and riskiest layer of disclosure uses **Straight Talk**, a style of reciprocal dialogue. It is implicitly based on trust, care, and respect. Conflict is rarely a part of this deeply personal interaction because of its elemental honesty and mutuality.

In conflict terms, the layer that is most sensitive is the middle depth. In addition to Search Talk, which can deescalate conflict, this level includes Control Talk, which can escalate it. *Control Talk* is action-oriented with the purpose of guiding, leading, or directing the recipient. If used supportively by mutual consent, Control Talk can be safe and helpful; if used with kindness and respect, it does not cause problems or conflict. For example, employers, teachers, and parents appropriately use Control Talk to teach skills; consenting employees, students, and offspring benefit from the guidance. However, Control Talk can potentially lead to bitter conflict if it is used with criticism or without consent. Then the conflict can easily be transformed into fighting (Fight Talk) or spiteful interchanges (Spite Talk).

Interpersonal Trust and Trust Building

If trust is dependable, disclosure through all the layers can be easy. If trust is only beginning or has been threatened by previous conflict, disclosure will not seem safe, so you maintain interpersonal distance and control. As trust for another person increases, you risk sharing deeper personal thoughts and feelings. The main tools for trust building are integrity and trustworthiness, and dependable empathy. Acts of kindness help others feel safe enough to disclose their thoughts and feelings.

Because of the personal risks inherent in disclosure, when you meet someone you test their trustworthiness within seconds, mostly using nonverbal data. **Trust** is experienced as confidence (but not certainty) of a partner's goodwill, demonstrated in positive actions, reliability when it counts, and predictable concern and responsiveness (Lewicki, 2006). Trust is cultivated by honest disclosure and reciprocal openness, not making promises that cannot be kept, and demonstrated safe behavior. Consistency in actions is particularly crucial in conflicts complicated by a long history of animosity.

Trustworthy people make it acceptable for others to talk about themselves. They listen with warmth and appropriate empathy while communicating support and unconditional respect that transcends disagreement or disapproval (Zimbardo, 2009).

Trust is fragile and easily jeopardized. When trust is slow to develop, is betrayed, or when expectations are disappointed, wariness and conflict result. The intensity of erupting conflict is directly proportional to the initial trust and closeness (Tavris, 1989). Distrust develops when you sense selfishness or hostility, which might then justify retaliatory behavior (Eidelson, 2003). Conflict might fuel defensiveness, further reducing the likelihood of effective resolution (Gibb, 1961). Without trust, the best approach might be skepticism.

Think About and Discuss with Your Colleagues

- Everyday, ordinary relationships are founded on rapport and trust, but they are fragile. Think of a conflict during which you jeopardized someone else's trust. What did that cost you? Did you do anything to actively repair or restore trust? Is there anything you might do now, or do differently?

Repairing broken trust requires commitment and effort from both parties. Commitments to work toward reconciliation depend on such factors as the nature of the original relationship (e.g., whether it was work or personal), the personal resources of the parties (such as wisdom, strength, and courage), or the severity of the conflict events and history. The first step toward repair is the deescalation of a heated interaction. The complex and perilous process of trust repair then requires the restoration of trustworthiness on the part of a betrayer, plus a victim's willingness to put in the effort to reinvest in the relationship. Janis Spring (2004) wrote extensively about the restoration of damaged trust. She identified a set of *trust enhancing behaviors* that involve low-cost and high-cost tactics. Low-cost approaches include being positive, respecting requests as important to the Other (even though they may not be to you), and discussion of new ideas. High-cost efforts, such as sincere apology and sacrificial gestures, provide reasons to restore faith in the relationship. Trust enhancing behaviors begin relationship repair by promoting honest communication, and provides a foundation for new interactions.

Meaning Is Communicated through Many Channels

Messages are communicated with more than words: the *content*, the *nonlinguistic elements*, the communicator's *emotions* and *intentions*, the *context*, and the *process*. Observers have to decipher the whole message and each channel can contribute to conflict or block its resolution. Albert Mehrabian's classic study (1972) on the transmission of complete meanings among North Americans suggested that "actions speak louder than words." He found that only approximately 7% of meaning is taken from the verbal *content* (the words and topics); 38% of the meaning comes from interpreting *nonlinguistic* embellishment (such as vocal pitch and inflection, tone, speed, emphasis, and volume); and the majority of the meaning, 55%, is communicated through *body language* (including facial expression, gesture, body movement, distance between speakers, and so forth). For accurate interpretation to occur, all three elements must be congruent. If they are not consistent, you will trust actions before words.

Content

The content of communication can include impersonal facts, positions, or opinions, but also might involve more risky information such as intentions, interests, or thoughts about a relationship. Disclosure of content could be deliberate or subconscious and unintentional. When in conflict, the content is often displaced from a "true" concern that remains disguised.

Nonlinguistic Elements

Nonlinguistic elements elaborate verbal communication. Content is elaborated nonlinguistically. These aspects are always active and have many functions. However, nonverbal signals are ambiguous and require "reading between the lines" so they are easily misinterpreted.

Emotional Content

Emotions are crucial to accurate interpretation, as discussed in Chapter 1. For example, the simple phrase, "I'm pregnant!" communicates a fact, but full understanding of the statement can only be inferred through hearing the emotional quality of joy, fear, or distress. The impact is not always consistent with the intended message. Inaccurate inference and misunderstanding are frequent triggers for conflict.

Motives for Communicating

There are both obvious and subtle reasons to communicate, and these are particularly important when in conflict. Some obvious motives are to express feelings and intentions, or share simple information, but it could simultaneously satisfy underlying needs for connection, or to dominate another person. A crucial motivational element is the receptivity of the listener (whether they are willing to listen or resistant). If the communicator misreads receptivity, a simple statement can function like aggression and lead to conflict.

Context

Using a cell phone might be completely appropriate in a cafeteria, but deeply disrespectful during a church wedding or Grandma's birthday party. The context in which a conversation takes place communicates meanings beyond the obvious content. Unique contexts such as family, workplace, and friendship develop unique communication codes with distinctive vocabularies and connotations, roles, rules, jokes, and stories. For example, teasing someone about a new hairdo might mean one thing between friends, but an entirely different thing between professor and student. When a message is inappropriate in its context, it can cause considerable harm and conflict.

Process

Process refers to the flow of one topic or focus to another, how the conversation is organized, and the meaning of the unfolding flow. It is the process element that escalates or deescalates during conflict (see Chapter 4). Process is often the primary transmitter of underlying factors such as identity, intention, and relationship, so the flow strongly influences eventual interpretation.

A **linear flow** is cool and clear, as in a meeting. Speaking and listening are rationally organized, shared equitably, and topics are dealt with one at a time. People address current concerns but personal issues tend to remain unspoken. In a **nonlinear flow**, also called *chaotic communication*, conversation meanders and can become tense with many things happening at once. The discussion can therefore become heated or even muddled with emotion, but it is less constrained and dialogue is more genuine. People disclose core issues, risking the unknown. Conflict usually includes a rhythm of linearity and nonlinearity (Mindell, 2014), but most conflicts will calm down from chaotic toward linear process during resolution.

Deborah Tannen (2007) drew attention to the message behind your words. The **metamessage** expresses unspoken qualities like how the parties are connected or the power balance between them. She used a common example of a mother sarcastically asking her teenaged daughter, "You're wearing *that*?," which indirectly implies both disapproval and a directive (Tannen, 2006). Gregory Bateson (1972) identified another process called **metacommunication**, which is communicating about the process. It begins with noticing a metamessage, then commenting on it. Examples are "You're being deliberately provocative," "I'm confused. Could you make your point in another way?," and "I'm pretty nervous about saying this, but I think it's important." Metacommunication is a kind of feedback that can enhance or detract from your message, clarify relationships and the process, or remove obstacles.

Another aspect of process is to determine whether an issue is finished or settled when a conversation ends. If discussion of an issue is left incomplete or if parties do not address the central concerns of a conflict, that leaves the conflict prematurely closed and adds to the need to revisit the problem.

COMPETENT COMMUNICATION SUPPORTS A HEALTHY RELATIONSHIP

Communication is never static or even predictable but, rather, resembles a complex interactive dance. This dance is an everyday pleasure that most people take for granted. There are numerous ways it can go right, and just as many ways it can go wrong.

An important component of the dance is sequential dialogue, which is both simple interaction and a way of relating respectfully (Maise, 2003). **Communication Accommodation Theory** suggests that you adjust your own part of the dance subconsciously to imitate your conversation partners (Giles, 2016). When the responses echo each other, the dance is *convergent*, reinforcing friendship and harmony. When the patterns contrast, the dance is *divergent*, accentuating differences and separation, and often escalating conflict (Gallois, 2015).

Competent communication = active, empathic listening + assertive speaking in dialogue

Developing communicative skill improves the chances that your relationships will be satisfying. A cluster of skills called **communicative competence** is essential (Canary, 2006; Cupach, 2015). Communicative competence has three characteristics:

1. *Appropriate*—Both the speaker and the listener understand the content and process within its relational context;
2. *Flexible and versatile*—It is adapted to the context and to others' expectations and actions. Communication avoids obvious pitfalls and conflict escalation. This requires both planning beforehand and empathy during the interaction;
3. *Effective*—Communication goals are fulfilled, getting the desired result (Maise, 2003; Spitzberg, 2015; Walker, 2018).

John Gottman (2014) noted that key skills are founded on positive strategies like an optimistic attitude, the ability to regulate intense negative feelings during conflict, and a kind approach. Positive tactics go a long way toward soothing rough relationships and solving problems:

- expressing fondness and admiration when not in conflict;
- turning toward (not away from) your opponent;
- establishing reciprocating, balanced sequences;
- using positive, encouraging statements, and reframing negatives respectfully;
- leaving uncrowded space and silence;
- repairing mistakes with apology, connection, or humor.

Cooperative Versus Competitive Patterns

Communication has the power to produce functional, constructive relationship and dysfunctional, harmful conflict. Daniel Maltz and Ruth Borker (1982) described two fundamentally different patterns of communication: cooperative and competitive.

Cooperative communication reinforces or strengthens your relationship. The primary purpose is connection and empathic understanding. Constructive conflict is strongly correlated with cooperative strategies like courtesy, direct assertiveness, mutual decision making, needs validation, and fair solutions (Gibb, 1961; Gottman, 2014; Sillars, 2013). Tactics include disclosure and the tentative exploration of usually private thoughts. Conversation partners tend to interpret cooperative communication as supportive and caring.

Morton Deutsch (2014) described cooperative communication as demonstrating open trust and friendliness, reciprocating empowerment and supportive gestures, and seeking positive common ground; conflict is seen as a joint problem to be solved. These qualities result in dialogue based on assertive skills including self-monitoring, listening, asking useful questions, exchanging feedback, modeling, and dialogue (Walker, 2018). Notice that any these qualities can be offered in a tone of cooperation or antagonism.

Competitive communication is an adversarial interaction with the goal of being right or winning a contest. It reinforces a one-up relationship by tending to focus on demonstrating who is best, wisest, or smartest. Mistrust results in veiled and strategic communication that is designed to dominate the opponent (Maltz, 1982).

Competitive conflict is characterized by disorganized, chaotic dialogue. The sequence typically begins with describing the concerns, followed by limited and

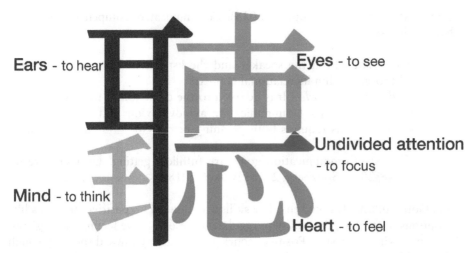

Figure 2.2 Chinese character "to listen"

controlled disclosure. Little reciprocal interaction occurs or, if it does, it is directed toward getting the upper hand. The problem might be solved, but at the cost of greater interpersonal distance.

Most conflicts involve a mix of cooperative and competitive communication. Competent communicators ensure that conversation partners feel safe; only then can trust develop. Communicative competence requires both open disclosure and accurate hearing, so effective listening skills are essential.

Effective Listening Skills

Listening is a fully rounded mental activity that ideally uses input from all the senses. Hearing and listening are not synonymous. One of the Chinese characters for "to listen" illustrates the breadth of skills involved in truly hearing another person (see Figure 2.2).

Careful listening is more important than we typically recognize since it:

- expresses supportive respect;
- encourages the expression of thoughts and feelings to allow exploration of a variety of ideas;
- helps to create a deeper and more honest relationship; and
- leads to cooperation.

Figure 2.3 "I hate listening, I like talking"

Unfortunately, most people have experienced (and been hurt by) disastrously poor listening. There are many errors of listening (Bolton, 1979), and some are exaggerated by confrontation and conflict:

a. *Simple overload*—We are bombarded by messages from multiple sources. It is awkward to pause conflict for solitary silence and thought;
b. *Personal "noise"*—You have private distractions, feelings, and intentions that interfere with hearing another person's concerns;
c. *Mistaken assumptions* or expectations shape what you hear;
d. *Premature evaluations* of the credibility of your opponent may result in selective listening;
e. *Defensiveness* and closedmindedness can severely limit your willingness to listen;
f. *Context*—Placing past events into the framework of current experiences overshadows the immediate reality.

Most people experience relief when you have been fully heard. *Attentive listening*, also called **active listening**, means that the listener is fully *with* the person speaking, taking them seriously as shown in responses like interested concentration, responsive body language, and accurate paraphrasing and summarizing. It goes beyond ordinary hearing to attend to a whole person. This is based on multiple skills that can be learned and refined with practice.

Empathic listening is a related skill. It is listening with the intent to intellectually *and* emotionally understand the meaning from another person's perspective. It uses Miller's (1988) concept of Search Talk. The listener carefully listens and encourages without intruding with his/her own thoughts. The purpose of empathic listening is to understand deeper ideas. Empathic listening is based on **empathy**, the ability to connect with feelings and understand ideas the same way another person perceives them. Empathy is the classic "walk in another person's shoes" skill. Empathy requires the courage to stand by another person as they explore deeply personal experiences and feelings that might be quite different from those of the listener. An empathic connection is the foundation of interpersonal harmony and cooperation.

Several component skills contribute to empathy (Bolton, 1979; Wiseman, 1996):

1. Avoid premature and negative judgments by understanding the *situation* that triggered the other person's reactions;
2. Recognize the *emotions* involved;
3. Use perspective-taking to sensitively and accurately *understand* another person's viewpoint and feelings; and
4. *Communicate* that understanding so the speaker feels understood.

For some people, empathy is a natural talent, but it is also a learned skill that can be refined with practice. See Skill Builders 2.1 and 2.2 for ways to develop your empathic listening skills and engage in assertive dialogue when it's your turn to speak.

Praxis Skill Builder 2.1 ■ Empathic Listening Skills

As you listen, do the following:
1. Focus first on the other person to accurately hear their message. Use the 80/20 Rule: listen 80% and speak 20%. Use encouragers such as door openers and interested silence, interrupting only when absolutely necessary to understand the message.
2. Listen simply, without thinking about how you will reply. Do not correct the speaker or defend yourself. Keep your own mental "noise" to a minimum. Although you may have doubts or arguments or reactions such as anxiety, irritation, or sadness; suspend their expression until you have received complete information.
3. Draw the person out by using open-ended questions one at a time.
4. Develop dual concentration: attend to the Other's thoughts and feelings while simultaneously being aware of (but muting) your reactions.
5. Notice patterns rather than focusing on any isolated cue.
6. Be open to the possibility that what was said was not what was meant. Respond only when you are sure of what the other person really meant.
7. Observe the context and reflect on its impact.
8. Pay attention to nonverbal as well as verbal information. Use your own body language to show sincere curiosity, respect, empathy, and acceptance.

Praxis Skill Builder 2.2 ■ Assertive Dialogue

When it is your turn in a dialogue, use the following skills:
1. Validate the speaker's experiences or feelings, even if you do not share or agree with them.
2. Check the accuracy of your understanding of the facts, feelings, and whole message by *paraphrasing* with two elements: summarize the key point, and briefly rephrase the message.
3. Reframe, relabel, and reinterpret events to reflect positive perspectives.
4. Deal with resistance by minimizing "right and wrong."

Assertive Speaking Skills

Another complex skill that contributes to communicative competence is assertively stating your own thoughts without arousing defensiveness or resistance in the other party. *Assertive* statements involve careful self-disclosure, directly and reasonably stating your needs, thoughts, and opinions in nonthreatening, nondefensive ways. Assertive speaking expresses self-respect and respect for your dialogue partner by subtly conveying a willingness to listen to alternative viewpoints. Assertive behaviors are most likely to result in problem resolution.

In contrast, strictly *passive* responses to conflict solve nothing unless they represent taking time to cool down. Passivity results in conflict avoidance and relationship chilling. Negative, *aggressive* responses risk escalating a disagreement to a fight. Insistent pursuit of an opponent during a conflict can also provoke a reciprocating fight. Aggressive statements can sometimes masquerade as assertiveness, but when used properly, assertiveness tends to free everyone to relate comfortably.

Ethical principles are useful guidelines when planning correct actions and preventing wrong ones. **Personal ethics** guide individual actions in relationships, while **professional ethics** guide professionals' actions toward clients, patients, students, and so forth. Ethical communication shares at least five important qualities:

1. Open, uncensored expression of thoughts, feelings, and opinions;
2. Accurate and honest self-disclosure;
3. Fair disclosure of information;
4. Accepting responsibility for the consequences of communication; and
5. Respect for diverse viewpoints.

Personally ethical and peaceable speech suggests that it is important to convey an attitude of sensitivity, tolerance, and inclusion of anyone relevant to a point being made, and to avoid words that perpetuate stereotyping and marginalization of certain people. As you pay attention to language, you become aware of the subtle ways certain phrases exclude some. See Table 2.2 for suggestions and illustrations.

Table 2.2 Respectful, Inclusive Language Is Important (Age-Fair, Nonsexist, Racially Transparent Language)

It is important to represent in words an attitude of sensitivity and inclusion of anyone relevant to a point being made, and to avoid words that perpetuate stereotyping and marginalization of certain people. Some general rules:

1. Don't single out ethnicity, gender, race, or personal characteristics that have no direct relevance to the point you are making. For example, don't point out gender when it is irrelevant, e.g., "I was grateful to the male nurse who took good care of my mother."
2. Be consistent in describing members of different groups. For example, don't describe White people on the basis of occupation, and Black people on the basis of their geographic residence: "A Caucasian lawyer was confronted by a Black boy from the ghetto."
3. Don't use judgmental terms where they can be neutralized. For example, don't condescend to someone with patronizing language, e.g., "The unfortunate man in the wheelchair."

Practical ways to carry this out are:

- Add words to include those who are usually excluded
- Omit words or phrases that actively exclude selected people
- Use plural instead of singular language
- Alternate between "his" and "her"
- Use inclusive pronouns such as "we" or "our"
- Address the reader with "you"

Examples	Don't say ...	When you mean ...
Age	Good parents guard their children.	Concerned parents attend to their offspring.
	Forefathers	Ancestors, forebears, precursors
	Old	Elderly, experienced, mature, advanced

(continued)

Examples	Don't say ...	When you mean ...
Gender	Brotherhood	Community, fellowship
	Mankind	Humanity, human beings, people
	Man-made	Synthetic, manufactured, artificial
	Chairman	Committee chair
	The average student is worried about his grades.	The average student is worried about grades.
	A careful student consults her dictionary often.	A careful student consults a dictionary often.
	The average man ...	The average voter ...
	Bogeyman	Villain, scoundrel
	Man and wife	Husband and wife, life partners
Race, Ethnicity	Indian	First Nations, Indigenous
	She welshed on a debt.	She refused to pay her debt.
	I think we should Jew him down.	I think we should bargain for this.

Silence and avoidance can also be strategic choices (Wang, 2012). Min-Sun Kim (2002) compiled the reasons people choose *silence* over assertive disclosure:

1. To avoid hurting another person's feelings;
2. To minimize imposition on another person;
3. To block another person's criticism;
4. To avoid compromising a previously clear relationship; and
5. To improve the overall effectiveness of the interaction.

Notice that many silencers rely on questionable assumptions based on a desire to maintain a positive relationship or prevent further relationship deterioration. See Praxis Skill Builder 2.3 for ways to develop assertive speaking skills.

Praxis Skill Builder 2.3 ■ Assertive Speaking Skills

Prior to interaction:
- Do some personal reflection to decide whether something needs to be expressed.
- Be clear about what you want to convey, using "I" messages—I think ... I feel ... I need ... I want ...
- Pay attention to receptiveness—is the other party ready to hear your thoughts?
- Plan a convenient time and place for the interaction.

During the interaction:
- Using Small Talk, offer and invite rapport;
- Always be courteous and respectful;
- Start with an intention statement about your purposes and goals, such as "I'd like to stop fighting with you"; "I think fighting disrupts our relationship and I'd like to ...";

Praxis Skill Builder 2.3 ■ Continued

- Use and encourage progressively deep disclosure: describe events, express thoughts, share feelings, metacommunicate about the relationship;
- Acknowledge the other point of view, especially with body language;
- Speak for yourself alone, stating your viewpoint as simply and authentically as possible. Be specific and concrete (not vague or abstract). A four-part message is often effective: 1) when (specific behavior) happens, 2) I feel (describe the feeling), 3) because (tangible effect), and 4) corrective statement (I would like this to happen). For example: "When you arrive late, I'm frustrated because I can't make last minute plans for the evening. I wish you would let me know if you can't meet me on time.";
- Explain, but don't defend, your feelings and preferences, possibly beginning with a phrase like "the way I see it ..."; and
- If the first attempt to express yourself did not succeed, try again, perhaps with a different approach.

Think About and Discuss with Your Colleagues

- You have learned that competent communication relies on empathic listening, and ethical, assertive speaking. How would you define and describe "incompetent communication"?
- In what ways is competitive communication less competent than cooperative communication?

INFLUENCES OF DIVERSE IDENTITIES ON COMMUNICATION AND CONFLICT

Patterned communication is part of every conversation, but strategies are typically quite different with strangers, family members, friends, and authority figures. All these interactions are shaped by deep personal identities. This section explores some complex gendered and cultural communication patterns and how they affect conflict and conflict resolution. Always remember that identified patterns are only potentials when applied to actual people, conversations, and relationships. Daniel Maltz and Ruth Borker (1982) argued that all communication is fluid. Because it is situational, interactive, and occurs in a particular sociocultural context or community, it is incorrect to apply it to an imaginary homogenous gender, cultural group, or setting.

Genderlect: Gender-Specific Tendencies

In Conflict Resolution Studies, fascination with differences in how females and males engage (or don't engage) in conflict, the patterns of tactics learned and used, and conflict outcomes has resulted in a great deal of published research with mixed results. We live in an era when many social factors result in somewhat transitional concepts of gender identity (Fixmer-Oraiz, 2019). Some caution is appropriate. The supposedly essential differences that distinguish gendered behavior are challenged as we discover the overlap of behaviors among real people. There may be differences, but there are more similarities. A statement like "womens' communication is more personal than mens'" may accurately describe some people, but certainly not all. Substantial variation within each group is found; not all women can be grouped together; not all men can be grouped. Communication is improved by not expecting the Other to respond exactly "in kind" or as you typically do.

In her studies of mixed-gender conversations, Deborah Tannen (1994) found that, on average, women tend to emphasize verbal patterns that she called **rapport speech**, a person-centered strategy that creates connection and cooperation. Disclosing personal information and story are used, and probing questions are asked. Reactions tend to be encouraging and supportive. Sherod Miller (1988) added that females express themselves primarily verbally rather than nonverbally. When discussing difficult issues women tend to interpret tension as lively interchange rather than conflict. Dalton Kehoe's (2013) conclusion was similar: in general, women communicate to create and build connected relationships, so are more likely to use expressive, invitational tactics and "take care" goals.

Tannen (and Ivy, 2016) found that, on average, men tend to use **report speech**, a problem-centered strategy that provides factual information, expresses positions, and explores problems, solutions, and accomplishments. Mens' interactions tend to be less directed toward collaboration than those of women. Miller also found that men use actions to express and demonstrate their feelings, often without verbalizing them, and John Gottman (1999) suggested that mens' factual communication is dependent on habitual masculine subordination of emotions. Kehoe agreed: men tend to use communication to maintain their independence, assert leadership, and accomplish tasks and "take charge" goals, so they are more likely to use personal assertiveness and power language (Merchant, 2012).

Gottman noted that few obvious gender differences are found in peaceable mixed-gender conversations; however, differences in expectations, role, and communication styles can be significant in distressed relationships. His research identified the following trends:

1. Men are more easily emotionally flooded and likely to withdraw.
2. Women view emotional intensity as a way to maintain intimate connection.
3. Men and women pay attention to different grievances.
4. Women are more prone to state their tensions in the relationship.
5. Women are more likely to bring up the past.

These observations portray relationship connections that are important to both men and women, but strategies for establishing and maintaining them tend to differ.

Another topic compares the use of silence. Women tend to assume that resolving issues requires talking them through, and are more comfortable with direct communication than men. For females, silence may cause worry about avoidance, overlooking the problems, or the interpersonal "cold shoulder." Men tend to be more comfortable with silence, and assume that if no one is talking, all is well. Extended verbal conflict and resolution through talking may drive men to be defensive, especially if conflict partners insist on continuing discussion before they are ready.

Think About and Discuss with Your Colleagues

- What is your experience with the differences in communication tendencies used by females and males? Articulate your opinion about any differences you see, starting with, "I see that females and males differ in these ways ... I see that males and females are the same in these ways...." Discuss your views with your classmates.

Cultural Patterns

"Culture is communication.... All communication is cross-cultural" (Tannen, 1984). Communication is the central system that perpetuates every culture. Different cultures reinforce complementary ways of dealing with conflict, but conflict behavior is multidimensional in all cultures (Cai, 2010). Deborah Tannen concluded that culturally learned patterns influence your perception of attentiveness, politeness, and relative status. Perceived rudeness, distractedness, and dominance frequently spark conflict. Her earliest research compared the habits of numerous linguistic groups and found that culture regulates dialogue tactics in many ways such as:

1. What to say; for example, using questions, story, and jokes;
2. Using pauses to pace a conversation;
3. Nonverbal signals of listening;
4. Emphasis on selected portions of a message;
5. Conventional versus creative figures of speech; and
6. Use of hints and assumptions versus directly speaking your mind.
7. When to talk or be silent;

All cross-cultural communication has high potential for misunderstanding. "Language contact means language conflict.... Problems viewed as political, economic, or sociological in nature are often rooted in linguistic conflict.... Language contact and conflict ... occur only between speakers of languages, not between languages per se" (Nelde, 1987).

Edward Hall (1976) was one of the first researchers to compare behavior of individuals from dissimilar cultures. He proposed a polarity that distinguishes two contrasting cultural patterns: high-context and low-context cultures. In Hall's work, **context** referred to any influence that contributes both to individual behavior and to collective practices. Conversations are governed by assumptions, symbols, and codes embedded in the context (Cai, 1997).

In a *high-context culture* (also called an *associative* or *collectivist culture*) like Japan's mainstream culture, the most meaningful clues are expressed implicitly through the context of a conversation, expressed through indirect, mostly unspoken content. A significant listener responsibility is to "hear" and interpret the whole meaning from the interpersonal and physical contexts in which the conversation takes place. People from associative cultures tend to value a positive public image and politeness (face-saving for themselves and others) as an important rule. Because of the relational context, conflict is viewed as personal confrontation, so individuals tend to sidestep disagreement by dealing with it indirectly (Ting-Toomey, 1991). A high-context conflict emphasizes messages communicated nonverbally (Alson, 2003). Deborah Cai (2010) found that people from this cultural context work hard to compromise to satisfy all parties' needs.

In a **low-context culture** (also called an *individualistic culture*) like most of western Europe, messages are communicated prominently with words. The emphasis is on informational content, transmitted verbally and directly with less attention to nonverbal components. Listeners hear the central meaning explicitly and literally. When in conflict, disagreement is addressed openly and impersonally, not necessarily as personal hostility, but often with attempts to dominate the discussion (Ting-Toomey, 1991). People in typically individualistic cultures rate transparency and clarity as the most important goals of both ordinary relationship and conflict interactions. Cai (2010) found that individualists tend toward resolution strategies that focus on problems, but may overlook subtle relationship dynamics. Do notice the parallels between these patterns and more typically masculine strategies.

Tannen (1999) wrote that the United States demonstrates an **argument culture**. By this term she meant that the prevailing social norm is *agonistic debate* or opposition based on an adversarial frame of mind. Truth is treated as dichotomously true *or* false; only one of two alternative viewpoints can be valid. Tannen suggested that productive dialogue requires both disagreement and harmony, speaking and listening, difference and connection, so they should not be suppressed. Her critique of the argument culture was that oppositional dialogue and conflict are overused, leading to extreme viewpoints and fault-finding rather than serious interactions that take diversity into account. "Often, the truth is in the complex middle, not in the oversimplified extremes." Communication from former US president Donald Trump might illustrate the argument culture. The impact of culture on conflict patterns will be explored in greater detail in Chapter 5.

Think About and Discuss with Your Colleagues

- When you have experienced cross-cultural relationships, what was the mix of positive and negative aspects?
- What do you find as effective bridges to people of cultures different from yours?

MASS COMMUNICATION, SOCIAL MEDIA, AND CONFLICT

Journalism

Journalists collect information and distribute it to a consumer audience through media like print, public broadcast, and the vast internet. Although journalists gather information, there are many filter points (and potential conflicts): reporters select what information is gathered, writers decide how this information is worded, and editors and publishers choose what information will be distributed.

Recent shifts in **journalism** have included marked trends:

1. *Reporter credibility issues*—There are concerns about the credibility of information when it has a deliberate agenda. For example, during the Arab Spring uprisings of 2011 (see Conflict Case 2.2), government news reports sharply contradicted citizen reports from individuals experiencing the events on city

streets. While on-the-spot citizen journalist reporting decreases the possibility of strategic manipulation by editors with hidden agenda, their reports may be based on faulty or insufficient information. Peer-gathered information often fails to distinguish fact from opinion, reliable assertions from frank fiction, or misinformation and deliberate disinformation from the truth.

2. *Sensationalism*—Objective factual information is increasingly displaced by material that has sensational consumer appeal. For example, in the 1995 news, the trial of O. J. Simpson took precedence over the Rwandan genocide of nearly one million Tutsi people.

3. *Crisis-centered reporting*—Short-term crisis situations are reported more often than stories that unfold over longer periods. Crisis reports may be distributed prematurely, before complete information is available. For example, reports of the killing and humanitarian crisis in Myanmar in 2017 changed repeatedly as more information became available.

4. *Conflict-centered reporting*—Events characterized by competition and aggression are the focus, with few reports of cooperative and prosocial situations. For example, you often hear news of conflict between police and citizens while rarely hearing about their many cooperative activities.

5. *Questionable accuracy*—Distribution of timely information has accelerated, but this increases the chances for inaccuracy. This is nothing new. A famous case of mistaken reporting occurred in the 1948 US presidential election, which pitted incumbent Democratic president Harry Truman against the Republican governor of New York Thomas Dewey. In an effort to be the first news outlet to declare the winner, the *Chicago Daily Tribune* trumpeted the headline "Dewey Defeats Truman!" Although it was a close race with narrow margins throughout election night, Truman, in fact, defeated Dewey to retain the presidency.

6. *Single viewpoint reporting*—The consolidation of professional sources decreases the number of outlets and results in the proliferation of single-viewpoint reports. Data that explores the background and context of the information or provides alternative viewpoints may or may not be included.

Social Media and Conflict

Social media and conflict intersect in many ways. As most people are aware, social media can ignite serious conflict within friendship circles and community groups. Fewer are aware of its role in forcing the resolution of serious justice and equity conflicts in employment and social settings.

Social media refers to all forms of electronic communication that distribute information, ideas, and commentary. A vast array of forms are readily available, ranging from personal messages between two people to communication that builds networks of like-minded people throughout the world. Many of its uses are constructive, such as bringing together a virtual group that shares rare medical information; some uses can be controversial, such as Alex Jones's use of the extreme media platform "Infowars" to promote fear, prejudice, and hatred. The power of social media was readily apparent in the events of January 2021, when the riot at the US Capitol Hill occurred.

The startling expansion of social media has broadened access to vast amounts of information through internet media that reaches most homes and workplaces in the developed world. Also dramatic is the shift from mere reception of information (such as from a radio) toward media in which much of the content is user-generated, and audience interaction is cultivated.

Positive outcomes of these developments include the immediacy of reporting and timeliness of information disseminated. Widespread event reporting improves global awareness, redefines political concepts like democracy or war, and provides a platform for raising awareness, knowledge, and support for specific ideas.

Shortcomings involve the transfer of information gathering away from trained sources toward informal, less reliable peer sources. Rapid, uncontrolled development of these new resources creates fresh challenges. Both social and mass media are vulnerable to agenda manipulation. There is an old Russian saying: "Paper lets itself be written on." We have few ways to guarantee the accuracy or truth of what is presented on the internet. Misrepresentation in a variety of forms is common, but often difficult to detect.

These inherent shortcomings are easily manipulated in what has been called "the architecture of disinformation" (Ong, 2018). Social media can even be "weaponized" and used as a significant instrument of war, resulting in what some people call Information Warfare. This occurs when inaccurate information contributes to an agenda designed to confuse recipients and citizens, manipulate public debate, and influence political outcomes.

Misinformation is the unintentional spread of incorrect information based on insufficient data available at the time. For example, during the 2017 Rohingya crisis, Burma/Myanmar leader Aung San Suu Kyi attempted to reassure her people that any human rights violations that did occur were scattered, disorganized, and did not represent ethnic cleansing. These statements were found to be mistaken by the 2018 UN Independent International Fact Finding Mission on Myanmar.

Sometimes full information is concealed through omission or evasion because the truth is difficult or shameful and/or the reporter wishes to uphold a positive public impression. This ranges from mild exaggeration or overreporting of facts to deliberate fiction, and has many motives and degrees. **Fake news** is distribution of misleading content, sometimes based on so-called alternative facts. It may result from careless information gathering, misunderstanding the actual data, knowingly slanting real facts, or trying to benefit a specific cause. Recently popularized by US former president Donald Trump, the term "fake news" was named a 2017 "word of the year" by Collins Dictionary.

Disinformation, also called **strategic misrepresentation**, deliberately misstates or distorts information with a purpose to influence people making decisions, such as voters or important opinion leaders. Frequently, this is done to support a public image that might be damaged by true reports. For example, substantial disinformation from leadership regarding a "stolen election" in 2020 was designed to support a positive view of Donald Trump's leadership, but caused enduring confusion and social division in the United States.

Social media plays increasingly active and important roles on the global scene (Bock, 2012), perhaps especially in regions where personal media are the primary means of communication. One example occurred a decade ago in northern Africa when mass protest movements spread from Tunisia to Egypt, Libya, and other regions collectively called the Arab Spring (see Conflict Case 2.2). There were many reasons that this phenomenon galvanized thousands of people of divergent backgrounds to demand social change at that time. Social media became the platform that created a virtual, participatory, collected community.

CONFLICT CASE 2.2 ■ EGYPTIAN ARAB SPRING, 2010–2012

For several generations, politics in northern Africa were dominated by dictators who granted privileges and diverted huge sums of money exclusively to government officials and their friends and allies. So-called elections were orchestrated by corrupt officials who permitted no real opposition. Coupled with economic stagnation, high inflation, and energy shortages, this resulted in dire life conditions for a majority of the Egyptian population by the middle 2000s. Protest was generated by multiple organizations with divergent political views and motives. As the voices of protest became bolder, authorities began to selectively control media outlets to disseminate misinformation.

The youth especially (but not exclusively) experienced alienation from and mistrust of government leadership and information sources. Consequently, people took advantage of the proliferation of social media to access articles written by known nongovernmental writers. Consumers believed that these sources were more reliable and applicable to their real lives. They were inspired as they observed the events of the 2010 "Jasmin Revolution" in Tunis.

Many people had regular access to internet media outlets, mostly Facebook, YouTube, and Twitter, and used them daily. When authorities shut down one channel, the youth simply tried another or created new ways of communicating. Through these alternative media, Egyptians of divergent backgrounds and viewpoints exercised their voices in national affairs for the very first time, making use of this improved ability to interact and debate with others. The intense virtual discussions led to increased in-person conversations, but also heightened conflict between citizens and government.

As a result, people began to understand events as they unfolded in real time, and realized that their individual problems were experienced by others living in similar conditions. Gatherings and protests were initiated by Egyptian activists in the Kefaya Movement of apolitical youth, the April 6 Movement of Youth, the Muslim Brotherhood, and labor rights groups. Nonviolent protests (such as civil disobedience, strikes, and street demonstrations) and violent protests (including rioting and coups targeting government officials) became common and turmoil increased.

Many of the protests were answered violently by ruling authorities and government groups. Counterrevolutionary and military responses quickly dimmed the peoples' hopes for broad social change. Political power struggles ensued in most areas, adding to other complex historical factors. The formidable revolution faded within 18 months after its initial spread. Success was defined in terms of igniting many opportunities for dialogue, uniting the will of the people, and calling global attention to their situation, but the protest movements were hardly successful in stirring lasting improvements to their social conditions. Large-scale conflict and revolutionary war were incited in Syria, Libya, Yemen, and other regions. Some writers refer to these later and largely unsuccessful struggles as the "Arab Winter."

Think About and Discuss with Your Colleagues

- In 2010–2012, were you aware of these Arab Spring events in Northern Africa? Evaluate your own media sources of information. Did they do an adequate job of giving you relevant information at that time?
- In your geographical area, are there any issues that could or should be promoted by social media and result in large-scale demand for change?
- In the United States, recent Black Lives Matter protests opposing unwarranted police violence have been prominent in the news. What is your opinion about these protests and their outcomes? Evaluate your sources of information.

Some Solutions to Media Communication Problems

Some solutions to media challenges include responsible, ethical reporting, media literacy, and peace journalism.

Responsible, Ethical Reporting

Views on responsible reporting are debated and standards vary widely throughout the world. In some locales, the media serve and are controlled by government or power leadership and in others they are fully independent; most frequently, public media are partially independent but influenced by editorial boards with a financial or political agenda. Laws governing freedom of speech, source protection, and prevention of deliberate libel and defamation are by no means uniform or static. These factors raise issues which rise out of diverging values, and they cause repeated public controversy.

The TARES test of ethical persuasion was designed to determine the reliability of journalistic sources (Baker, 2001):

- Is the message Truthful?
- Is the reporter Authentic?
- Does the story Respect multiple viewpoints?
- Does the story address issues of Equity among the parties involved?
- Is the story Socially responsible and directed toward the common good?

Another commonplace attempt to improve the objectivity of reporting is to establish codes of ethics. There are more than 240 codes of conduct for journalists (W. Yang, 2015). Examples include the Independent Press Standards in Britain, Ethics for Journalism in Europe, and the Credo for Ethical Communication in North America. Although such standards exist, they are rarely enforceable because adherence is voluntary.

Media Literacy

A recent focus of many educational programs encourages you to develop **media literacy,** which is the ability to distinguish types of media, and to understand, interpret, and use the information conveyed. Media literacy has become a very important skill for responding to messages from social media. The core skill is *inquiry*, or exploring the background of the message using seven key questions:

1. Source—Who created the message? Credible writers are unbiased, have nothing to gain, and identify their work by signing it.

2. Differentiate the claims—A **fact** includes indisputable information or evidence; an **opinion** communicates a viewpoint or belief that is not necessarily based on fact or knowledge; **rhetoric** and **editorial comments** are intended to persuade or influence the audience.
3. Reliability—Can the information be verified by other reliable sources?
4. Pertinence—Does the message identify centrally relevant issues and facts that have been gathered recently?
5. Attention-getting—Were specific techniques used when constructing the message to attract your attention?
6. Purpose—What was the purpose in sending the message? Possibilities are providing information, persuasion, propaganda, or promoting pop culture.
7. Diversity—Are there lifestyles, values, or viewpoints that are not represented or misrepresented in this message? How would people with different viewpoints understand and interpret this message?

- Take one or two stories from the front page of your local newspaper. Apply the seven inquiry questions to analyze its source(s), purpose(s), and viewpoints.

Peace Journalism

Traditional journalism is effectively **conflict journalism**, according to Johan Galtung (1998; Hawkins, 2011). Mainstream journalism is biased to report violence and war, highlighting sensational violent events without any resolution story. Conflict journalism supports unrealistic views of the potential of violent responses to resolve conflict. It is one significant contributor among many to antisocial behavior and problems (Donnerstein, 2008). **Peace journalism** focuses on the selection and media distribution of nonviolent stories. Its goals are to sensitize the consumer public to the true costs of violence and the real effectiveness of peaceful and constructive conflict solutions (Lynch, 2005). The Oxford International Encyclopedia of Peace estimated that only 17% of world conflicts are resolved through violent strategies (Young, 2010). Peace journalism focuses on the 83% of conflicts that are solved through nonviolent means. For example, "Yes!" magazine presents "solutions journalism" with articles about social justice, environmental issues, health and happiness, economy, democracy. Access it at https://www.yesmagazine.org. Peace journalism has ignited significant debate within the journalistic and peace and conflict disciplines (Kempf, 2007; Lynch, 2008).

DIFFICULT, ADVERSARIAL FIGHTING TACTICS: COMMUNICATION PATTERNS DURING CONFLICT

As you observe people arguing, the first thing you notice is their behavior. A loud voice may be used to emphasize a point or outshout an opponent, standing up could signal impatience or heated emotion, and silence might be used to calm everyone down. These behaviors, called **tactics**, are the moves and countermoves used during a conflict as it unfolds. There are two broad categories of tactic: prosocial and antisocial. *Prosocial tactics* strengthen a relationship and sooth conflict. Personality factors of openmindedness, conscientiousness, extroversion, agreeableness, and nonreactivity to emotions correlate with prosocial tactics. Based on an attitude that acknowledges that all parties' viewpoints are important, prosocial actions benefit everyone.

Antisocial tactics cause or aggravate conflict and hasten the deterioration of a relationship. Challenging characteristics of closedmindedness, carelessness, defensive quiet, disagreeableness, and unpredictable moods commonly contribute to conflict escalation, and usually result in passive, passive-aggressive, and aggressive responses. High-conflict people rely on these tactics. They tend to experience changeable emotions that overshadow logical reasoning and result in two-faced actions (for example, they are charming in public, but confrontational in private) (Antonioni, 1998; Eddy, 2005). High-conflict people have long-term (chronic) relationship problems, but may find it difficult to reflect on their own role in causing them.

Cate Malek and Susana Hayek (2018) presented an example of a conversation that illustrates difficult conversation. An immigrant family included elders who experienced dangerous travel and risked violence to emigrate from their homeland. Their lives had been a difficult climb to prosperity that drew distrust and animosity from local groups in their new homeland, so the elders continued to approach life in fear and isolation. However, the family grew to include young individuals who enjoyed the prosperity and education typical of a free society. They wanted to build up their community by accessing government resources and grants designed to expedite nonimmigrant and immigrant collaboration.

Because both the topic and the people mattered very much to this divided family, strong emotions and convictions were involved. Before the conversation even started, their worry was that threatening, irreconcilable differences would be uncovered. No one really wanted to talk, and the issue was avoided to forestall potential conflict. When it finally began, the dialogue between the elders and young family members became a tense discussion, then developed into an argument laced with fear and warning. Older members forewarned that taking action would expose their family to heightened resistance; younger members were disgusted that the older generation allowed their fear to hinder progress. The conversation ended in stalemate and inaction, becoming a family fiasco.

Douglas Stone and his colleagues (2010) suggested that every difficult conversation is associated with three deeper themes:

- What is happening? In this conflict, there was disagreement about facts, who caused the tension, and what should happen to resolve it.
- How do we feel? There were contrasting strong emotions and worries about the validity of each other's viewpoints.
- Who are we? Family members considered what the issue said about who they were and who they were together.

Working through these tense issues requires a "learning stance" and deep cooperation that prepare you to really listen.

Two adversarial tactics are especially likely to escalate a fight (Miller, 1988). **Fight Talk** is harsh, negative, and judgmental. Because it vents anger or animosity, it often ignites conflict. Common tactics include demands, insults, blame, and threat. Listening is minimal. Similar to Maltz and Borker's concept of competitive communication, you focus on supporting your own opinion, using Fight Talk to control people or the conversation or to force a solution,. Fight Talk conveys that you are right and others are wrong, which creates defensiveness.

Although unpleasant and intimidating, Fight Talk can lead to resolution *if* everyone eventually discloses their actual concerns and becomes willing to listen to each other and to move toward solving the identified problems. If resolution is frustrated by continued unwillingness to listen or solve problems, the interaction is likely to escalate to Spite Talk.

Spite Talk is even harsher than Fight Talk. Using this strategy, you attack your opponents. The primary goal of Spite Talk is to humiliate, hurt, or defeat the opponent. Four spiteful tactics that contribute to all-out emotional war and inevitably damage a relationship are defensiveness, stonewalling, criticism, and contempt (Gottman, 1999). Although common, these tactics are never part of a positive or constructive conflict process. When the conversation deteriorates into spite, the origin of the conflict is overlooked and problems are not solved. Spite Talk can result in real hurt and withdrawal from the relationship.

Deadly Weapons

In addition to the adversarial dynamics of Fight Talk and Spite Talk, other approaches can be associated with drastic consequences. When every "try" and strategy has failed, you become threatened by hopelessness and the relationship has become more distant, you are more likely to use tactics that are potentially lethal to healthy relationship (Omer, 2004) with increasing intensity and force. These include defensiveness, deception, control talk, violent communication, and hate speech.

Defensiveness

Defensiveness reacts to perceived threat or attack. When talking becomes threatening, people move to defend themselves. Signs of defensiveness include intense speech, predictable conflict "scripts" that repeat arguments, emotional reactivity that overrides rational thinking, and increasingly polarized and stereotyped perception of yourself as good and right and the Other as wrong and hungry for power.

Jack Gibb (1978) identified trends in the conversational tone that tend to increase or decrease defensiveness. He found a correlation between competitive communication and hidden ulterior motives, judgmental statements that condescend or criticize, attempts to control or force another person to do something, and blocking new ideas. These tactics increase defensiveness and decrease the possibility of constructive resolution.

Gibb also discovered patterns that rely on honest, open dialogue, an attitude that supports strength, descriptive wording that does not imply criticism, empathy for your opponent's emotions, and focus on a common solvable problem. These redirected tactics are likely to decrease defensiveness and help conflicting parties to trust each other and improve the likelihood of resolution.

Manipulation and Deception

Deception is knowingly misleading another person. Some people are really bad liars whose deception is easy to detect through nonverbal "leakage"; others are successful deceivers who create outright fiction, conceal parts of the truth, or skirt an issue with equivocation (Buller, 1996); most people fall somewhere in between. Deception requires more effort than telling the truth because the deceiver has to find ways to appear to be honest, hide the reasons for deception, provide some kernel of verifiable fact, and sound logically consistent. Deceptiveness can seriously damage a relationship.

Some deception is motivated by selfish wishes to exaggerate one's own character or abilities, or to conceal flaws. Michael Lewis (1993) identified three degrees of deception:

1. Deception despite conscious awareness of the truth;
2. Deception of others that necessitates a degree of self-deception; and
3. Self-deception to maintain one's own illusions.

Everyone tells lies, but most people are honest most of the time. As noted by the **Truth Default Theory** (Levine, 2014), you are influenced by a *truth bias* and assume honesty unless you become convinced to do otherwise. Making the assumption of friendly truthfulness is adaptive and efficient because it is the simplest approach. Even if you become suspicious that what you hear may not be completely true, you default to trust and assume that inaccurate information is an honest mistake or a "white lie." There are no simple methods to recognize manipulative deception. Rather, most lies are detected after the fact because of confession or discovery of new evidence (Levine, 2014). Even lie detector tests are considered untrustworthy in most court situations.

Most deception is used to control others. It may be used to avoid hurting or offending someone (such as telling Grandma you love the ugly sweater she knit), to cover guilt and avoid consequences (such as manipulating events to cover cheating), or to avoid conflict (Buller, 1996). Lewis asserted that all deception is unethical because it exploits trust and risks the health of a relationship when the lies are exposed.

In November 2017, a good news story was circulated in Philadelphia. Kate McClure admitted that she had run out of gas and money on a highway off-ramp. A homeless veteran, Johnny Bobbitt, found her and spent his last $20.00 to buy her some gas. Kate and her boyfriend, Mark D'Amico, were so grateful that they began a GoFundMe campaign to help Johnny. Within several months 14,000 people had contributed more than $400,000.

In the summer of 2018, Bobbitt sued McClure and D'Amico, stating that they were using the fund for their own luxury auto purchases and holidays. Police investigation uncovered a completely fictional story, and charged the trio with deliberate fraud. In 2019, all three pleaded guilty to fraud.

Think About and Discuss with Your Colleagues

- Do you think deception is ever acceptable or even ethical? Under what circumstances is deception acceptable?
- What if deception results in a positive outcome, such as avoiding harm to others?
- What if a lie safeguards a larger truth?

Communication to Gain Power and Control

Power is a factor in almost every relationship. We discuss power dynamics more broadly in Chapter 5, but this section explores the communicative dimensions of interpersonal power. **Personal power** is a fundamental need that gives you the

ability to control yourself and your immediate environment. **Interpersonal power**
is the ability to influence other people's
activities or environment, and ideally is
related to consent (W. Yang, 2015).

> *What upsets me is not that*
> *you lied to me, but that*
> *from now on I can no longer*
> *believe you.*
> —Anonymous, attributed (wrongly)
> to Friedrich Nietzsche

People generally have mixed reactions
to powerful figures. On the one hand, leadership provides a comfortable structure and
direction for followers. People who habitu-
ally use powerful language are typically rated as more credible, and their positions
are more readily adopted by others (Erickson, 1978). Sherod Miller's (1988) **Control
Talk** is acceptable when it is used respectfully and with consent. This power language
is directed toward a listener-learner, empowering them with useful information and
skill. On the other hand, power language can be threatening or even dehumanizing.
The use of powerful speech to dominate people or ignore concerns usually results in
more resistance and less courtesy, and violence becomes more likely.

Power differences are less noticeable in a healthy, trusting relationship but
more significant in a distressed relationship (Ury, 1988). Think, for example,
about a positive employment team in which most employees are unconcerned
with differences between themselves and the boss. In a hostile work environment,
power differences can become an aggravating factor in the escalation of tension.

The speech patterns of powerful leaders (e.g., think of Adolf Hitler or Angela
Merkel) are socially influential, and can quickly set the tone and agenda for
public debate in popular culture. Linguist Jennifer Sclafani (2017) analyzed the
influence of former US president Donald Trump. He was noted for using simple
vocabulary, repeated and catchy phrases like "campaign for change," "culture
war," and "believe me," along with abrupt changes of topic and strong, direct
statements that include repetitious hyperbole. Sclafani noted that this introduced
an everyday, less formal and "brawling" tone to US public dialogue.

Violent Communication

Considerable debate exists about the definition of and criteria for violence. Does
a show of strength always degrade to violence? Is all coercion violent? Does violence solve problems? Does nonviolence solve problems? Violent communication has several distinctive attributes. According to Gerda Siann (1985), violence
occurs under four conditions:

1. There is an intention to harm someone.
2. Violence occurs in the context of already conflicted relationships.
3. The purpose or goal of aggression is to gain advantage over the opponent.
4. Violence, often provoked by conflict, also provokes deeper conflict and
   thereby escalates the conflict. Aggression and conflict are therefore mutually perpetuating.

The National Communication Association defines **violent communication** as any
words or actions that degrade other people and undermine their dignity. Sample
tactics that are directly violent include manipulative shaming that labels someone as inferior, and coercive threats that generate fear and unwilling compliance.

Violent communication can also occur more subtly through using "cold shoulder" gestures, or using supposedly funny "zingers" that are humiliating ridicule. Marshall Rosenberg (2001) noted that violent communication inhibits the interpersonal compassion that is fundamental to every healthy relationship. Violence will be explored in more detail in Chapters 8 and 9.

Offensive Hate Speech: Words That Wound

Hate propagates extremely hostile feelings. More than intense dislike, it expresses malicious wishes for harm to come to the hated person or group. Hate is often rooted in fear. **Hate speech** degrades or attacks, or incites prejudice and violence, by manipulating personal characteristics such as religion, personality, or disability.

The corrosive potential of hate speech is recognized around the world (Waldron, 2012) and attempts to prevent it are central to many educational systems and entrenched in a variety of legal systems. Controversy persists because of two seemingly paradoxical goals: protection of individual rights and preservation of the public good. For the public good, hate speech is prohibited in some countries. Very recently, social media firms such as Facebook and Twitter voluntarily agreed to follow a European Union standard of conduct that obligates them to monitor and remove hate speech postings.

The controversial nature of hate speech is illustrated by the landmark court case, *Snyder v. Phelps*. In 2006, Lance Corporal Matthew Snyder was killed while serving in the US Marines in Iraq. As they had done in similar situations, members of the Westboro Baptist Church of Topeka, Kansas, picketed streets leading toward Snyder's funeral, condemning Matthew's openly gay father, Albert Snyder, and decrying the increasing social tolerance of homosexuality.

Albert Snyder sued church leader Fred W. Phelps Sr. and others from the church, claiming defamation, intrusion into a private family matter, and intentional emotional distress. During the trial, Snyder testified, "They turned this funeral into a media circus and they wanted to hurt my family. They wanted their message heard and they didn't care who they stepped over. My son should have been buried with dignity, not with a bunch of clowns outside." In their defense, members of the church testified that their protest did not violate any local regulations or police instructions. The US Supreme Court ruled against Snyder in 2011, stating that even offensive and outrageous speech that is used publicly (on a sidewalk or street) to address a matter of public concern (the morality of homosexuality) is protected by freedom of speech and could not be considered to be hate speech.

Think About and Discuss with Your Colleagues

- If you had had an opportunity to be on this jury, what information would you want as you consider the criteria for hate speech and form your judgement.
- What is it about "adversarial, fighting tactics" that fuel conflict? In the next few days, notice some tactics that you think are particularly inflammatory, and imagine ways to reframe or divert those into more constructive methods.

COMMUNICATION THAT RESOLVES CONFLICT

Communication creates a reality shared between people, so a revised, amended relationship between conflicted opponents can be generated with modified communication. There is a wide range of options for improving communication and resolving conflict, all based on positive, transparent disclosure. As long as there is a foundation of trust and safety, conflict can be addressed directly through dialogue and negotiation. If trust has been jeopardized, specialized conflict resolution facilitators can assist with building consensus, formal negotiation, and mediation.

> *A gentle answer quiets anger,*
> *but a harsh word stirs it up.*
> —*Proverbs 15: 1, GNT*

Effective conflict resolution relies on shared understanding more than insisting on policies and rules. Transformed behavior is more important than the blunt exchange of information. Robert Kegan and Lisa Lahey (2007) detailed some of the gentle changes in language that can turn a conflict from harsh to satisfactory:

- Starting with internal dialogue, waste little energy complaining; instead, direct your efforts toward an ongoing relationship with your opponent.
- Question assumptions rather than automatically accepting a single version of truth.
- Rather than blaming the other party, take responsibility for your own part in the conflict.
- Don't make weak promises simply to end a conflict; instead, commit to the full harmonization of differences.
- In problem solving, ongoing deep respect replaces calculated praise.

Direct Conflict Communication

Most conflicts are addressed and solved by the parties speaking with each other about shared concerns. When the intensity of these conversations is moderated, they are quite successful: the problem is solved and the relationship is retained or even improved. When the conversation becomes intense and heated, a three-step process of interpersonal clarification is helpful (see Praxis Skill Builder 2.4).

Praxis Skill Builder 2.4 ■ Three-Step Process for Clarifying Concerns

1. Retreat and
   a. Reflect on your contribution to an argument until you are ready to share your insights;
   b. Observe your own and others' behavior until you can clearly describe the concerns; and
   c. Deliberate your most effective method to prevent escalating conflict, contain intense affect, or resolve the current problems (Littlejohn, 2007).

2. During dialogue
   a. Invite your opponent to a corrective conversation;
   b. Set a tone by committing to respectful listening;
   c. Listen, ask good questions, and acknowledge the main points discussed;

(continued)

Praxis Skill Builder 2.4 ■ Continued

    d. If tension increases, don't "rise to the bait"; continue empathic listening;
    e. Apologize when you have wronged or hurt the other person;
    f. Ask what could repair the hurt now; explore options for change or solution;
    g. Assertively describe your perspective without defending it;
    h. State your goals and hopes for the relationship; and
    i. Repeat this process as needed until understandings are reached.

3. With time, open a larger conversation about concerns and issues with a focus on facts, feelings, and needs, working out alternative solutions (Rosenberg, 2001).

Negotiation and Bargaining

Negotiation is part of everyday living as you bargain who will sit in the only remaining seat on a bus, who will buy a friendly coffee, or how much you will pay for a new car. **Negotiation** is a reciprocating give-and-take dialogue and exchange of information, opinion, ideas, and promises, usually between two parties, that results in joint decision making (Wertheim, 1996). Rapport is the starting point for effective negotiation. Most everyday negotiation seems a natural part of functioning with other people and finding a fair division of something: time or activity or work, and so on.

Negotiation techniques mix both competitive and cooperative patterns. Three methods of negotiation are distinguished. **Distributive negotiation** is used when only one person can achieve what they want. It is often used for a one-time competitive dialogue to distribute a limited resource. What one party wins, the other party loses (called the *zero-sum outcome*). The win-lose outcome is successful in the short term, but does not address long-term or repeating problems. If necessary in ongoing relationships, parties can take turns, "You win this one, I win next time."

Another type of negotiation is called **integrative negotiation**. Parties focus on incorporating and balancing everyone's interests and possible benefits. It is usually applied in ongoing, trusting relationships. Because the goal is to find solutions that satisfy everyone without unreasonable compromise of high-priority interests, the dialogue is friendly and direct. It requires more conversation and more time than competitive negotiation does. If confrontation is used, the dialogue will often switch into competitive negotiation.

A third type of negotiation, called **principled negotiation,** is used in formal negotiation, but the principles can also guide informal dialogue by sidestepping enduring tensions. Problems are not the starting points; instead, four principles or ground rules are agreed before negotiation begins:

1. People are not the problem: separate the people and the problem;
2. Ways will be found to focus on interests, not positions;
3. Potential alternative solutions for mutual gain will be brainstormed; and then
4. Objective criteria will determine when closure or "success" are achieved (Fisher, 2011).

When these principles are agreed, the negotiation is usually straightforward.

William Ury (1991) noted that unsuccessful negotiation is usually tainted by fear or anger. He described five common obstacles to successful problem solving: your own emotional reactions to others' actions, others' emotions, sticking to one position without considering other perspectives, dissatisfaction with potential losses, and power that might interfere with collaboration. Ury suggested five strategies that are likely to overcome these obstacles:

1. Control your own emotions by shifting to an objective observer perspective;
2. Do not argue; listen and react to differences with an optimistic assumption;
3. Reframe positions in terms of shared interests;
4. Build bridges with cooperation that addresses needs, identity, and security; and
5. Use your own power to provide information and clarify both parties' interests.

Some of these strategies are discussed in Chapter 3, and Chapter 10 contains a more detailed discussion of distributive, integrative, and principled forms of negotiation.

Alternative Dispute Resolution

Fighting parties occasionally need assistance to resolve their issues. Formally, the techniques are called **Alternative Dispute Resolution** (ADR), referring to conflict resolution outside a court system. A **third party**, respected by all parties, guides a difficult conversation to ensure that the process is respectful and orderly. The varied tools available to the third party include facilitated dialogue, negotiation, and mediation. A *facilitated dialogue* encourages constructive, transparent communication. As you have already learned, **negotiation** attempts to find a reasonable path to a satisfactory agreement. During **mediation,** the third party assists the parties to focus on their needs, rights, and interests and to generate mutual understanding and a satisfactory solution. The third-party role is described in more detail in the Conclusion of this textbook.

CHAPTER SUMMARY AND STUDY GUIDE

- Communication sustains the core of every relationship, but is imprecise. It is risky because, at its best, an interpersonal relationship is built on trust, disclosure of the authentic self, and the process includes a number of different channels that convey meaning, including verbal and nonverbal content, emotion, motives, context, and process.
- Competent, ethical communicators use active empathic listening to encourage others' disclosure, and assertive speaking when in dialogue. Competent communication is constructive and positive, relevant to the situation, and encourages collaboration.
- Communication patterns in commonly occurring interactions include gendered and culturally embedded forms that shift over time and experience. To be effective, all communication must be rooted in respect.

- Mass communication, particularly social media, have recently become even more crucial in causing and processing conflict.
- Fighting tactics, including Fight Talk and Spite Talk as well as defensiveness, deceit, power and control, violence, and hate speech, all escalate conflict and make resolution more complex and difficult.
- Clear, competent communication is essential for fair conflict processing and resolution. This might occur directly between opponents using distributive negotiation, which is competitive and has a zero-sum outcome; integrative negotiation, which is primarily cooperative and has a collaborative outcome; or principled negotiation, which is based on established principles of argument. Resolution might be facilitated by third parties, who engage in ADR activities like facilitated dialogue, formal negotiations, or a mediated conversation.

TERMS IN FOCUS

actual self 51
argument culture 66
communication 51
communicative competence 56
competitive communication 57
context 65
Control Talk 75
cooperative communication 57
deception 73
defensiveness 73
disclosure 52
Disinformation 68
distributive negotiation 78
empathic listening 59
empathy 59
enhanced self 51
ethical principles 61
Fake news 68
Fight Talk 72
Hate speech 76
high-context culture 65
ideal self 51
integrative negotiation 78
Interpersonal power 75
Johari Window 52
journalism 66

linear flow 56
low-context culture 66
media literacy 70
mediation 79
metacommunication 56
metamessage 56
Misinformation 68
negotiation 79
nonlinear flow 56
nonlinguistic communication 55
Peace journalism 71
personal ethics 61
Personal power 74
principled negotiation 78
professional ethics 61
rapport speech 64
report speech 64
Search Talk 53
Shop Talk 53
Small Talk 53
Social media 67
Spite Talk 73
Straight Talk 53
strategic misrepresentation 68
trust 53
violent communication 75

3

Sources and Drivers of Conflict, and Perception of Problems

■ ■ ■

In Focus in This Chapter:

■ Finding the specific problems that cause conflict may not be as straight-forward as you might hope. Many problems are compounded and often elusive. Obvious substantive problems may be distracting covers that obscure deeper issues.

■ Because you come from different contexts, people in conflict have incompatible perceptions and explanations of problems and subsequent events, realistic methods for solving them, and goals for the interaction.

■ Conflict responses depend on the whole situation but actions do lead to future relationship patterns, so problem-solving processes can have many purposes. Simple communication does not always clarify or improve the interactions. Some processes are cooperative, but others are competitive.

■ Problems fall on a continuum, ranging from the easily found and solved to perpetual and intractable problems that may never be solved. Solutions may not be equally satisfying to all the parties.

■ Formal outcomes of problem solving include eliminating the problem, managing it through conflict management, resolving it through conflict resolution, or reformulating it through conflict transformation.

In the last two chapters, you explored conflict issues related to the people engaged in the argument. In this chapter, we deconstruct the many aspects of problem analysis (see Figure 3.1). Conflict is, literally, a daily event for almost everyone, but personal interpretation is subjective. Some people anticipate that even hints of problems will lead to unpleasant, painful, or threatening conflict, so they may be too quick to deny problems when they arise. A few people feel most alive when they are faced with problems, but they may too quickly seize issues to ignite unnecessary conflict. Others can engage in problem solving without anxiety and may be able to use the processes to improve their reactions. Patience with conflict is partially based on confidence in a relationship and in the probability that reaching resolution of the problems is possible. Problem solving involves skills that can be learned. Therefore, analyzing contributing elements to conflict, the people, the problems, and the process can lead to clarity in solving those problems (Wright, 2013).

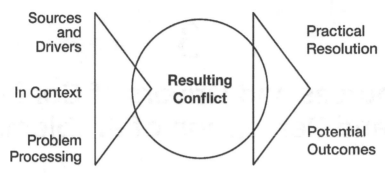

Figure 3.1 Summary of problem elements

CONFLICT CASE 3.1 ■ "WEST-EAST ISLAND"

Lawrence Kohlberg (1927–1987) did research into ethical decision making using fictional moral problems to observe problem solvers' strategies (Garz, 2009). This story is one of his hypothetical dilemma.

There were two islands that were joined by a bridge.

John and Mary met and fell in love on the West Island. After several blissful years, Mary felt the need to better herself through education. There was no university on the West Island, though, so she traveled to the East Island to attend E. I. University.

After about six months, John was lonely and wanted to visit Mary on the East Island. Sadly, when he arrived at the bridge, he found that it had been washed out by a recent storm. He appealed to his friend, Deanna (who owned the only boat close by) to take him across. She said, "Sure, I'll take you—if you spend the night with me." John was miserable and didn't know what to do. He went to his friend, Samantha, to ask her advice. She only shrugged and said, "Follow your heart." John still didn't know what to do and he was still miserably lonely, so in desperation he spent the night with Deanna. The next morning she ferried him across for his reunion with Mary.

When Mary heard what he had done, she flew into a rage and soundly rejected him. Mary, in her own misery, told her friend, Chuck, who then went and beat up John.

Kohlberg's fictional story (1969) is an amusing preview of some of the concepts in this chapter. The story is the depiction of a tangled problem, to which each party contributes and then detracts from the solution. You read that, whatever Mary and John's goals were, they were poorly translated into action. John and Mary ended their relationship in serious conflict and both experienced unintended harm. Much about this story is untold, and much was unspoken between the main characters.

The sources, causes, and drivers of conflict can be seen along a continuum of time: **triggers** are key actions or events that will set off or escalate conflict; **proximate causes** are factors that contribute to a readiness for conflict or for its escalation; and *structural causes* are pervasive tensions that are built into habits or policies, relationship issues, or the fabric of relating that create the preconditions for conflict.

Roxane Lulofs and Dudley Cahn (2000) summarized some starting points for our chapter with *functional beliefs* about the sources of conflict, the unfolding process, and possible outcomes that facilitate managing problems.

Sources:

1. The perception of people in conflict situations shapes their actions.
2. People are responsible for how they feel, what they say, how they respond, and how they act in conflict situations.
3. The context of a conflict gives it meaning and creates expectations.

Process:

4. Communication will not necessarily make things better.
5. People are guided by goals that may be ill-defined prior to enacting a conflict, and the goals may change in the course of the conflict.
6. People are motivated both to cooperate and to compete in conflict situations.
7. Depending on the situation, both confrontation and avoidance are legitimate options.

Outcomes:

8. Any action in a conflict situation affects future choices of action.
9. Not all conflicts are resolvable.

BASIC TERMS AND CONCEPTS

Defining the Problem

A **problem** is any element of a conflict related to an unwelcome or potentially harmful struggle that must be settled in some way. Often, multiple problems contribute simultaneously to the development of a specific conflict. Even with this simple definition, we acknowledge several qualifying issues:

Sometimes, Defining the "Problem" *Is* the Problem

To do effective problem solving, the participants must reach basic agreement on what the problem is. Discussion of this defining dimension can clarify conflicting differences of perception of the problem and is often the first step in a systematic problem-solving process. If one party believes that there is a problem that is solvable if everyone works on it while the other party believes that the opponent *is* the problem, their argument is likely to go in circles. Effective problem solving will begin with consensus by discussing the problem sources and the reasons each party has for the argument before hastily jumping to conclusions or imagined solutions. This is a step that in some ways predetermines the solution: if a problem is formulated too broadly, effort will be wasted in exploring more resources than are helpful; if a problem is defined too narrowly, solutions might only address the obvious warning signs (Volkema, 1997).

Table 3.1   Escalation of Problem Focus

Stage of Conflict Intensity	Focus of "Problem" Addressed
Discussion Stage	Problem content and personal interests
Tension Building	Dynamics of the relationship
Confrontation	Threats to fulfilment of basic needs
Crisis Stage	Survival of the individual or the relationship

Source: Based on Fisher, 1991.

Some Problems and Their Solutions Are Elusive

Conflict escalates along a continuum from effective communication through aggressive attack (Kriesberg, 2020). Problems can shift or multiply with escalation. Roger Fisher and Loraleigh Keashley (1991) noted that as conflict grows in intensity, the problem focus may change in predictable ways. As the emotional dynamics and communication intensify, a stepped shift in focus from impersonal problems to problematic opponents can be observed, a shift that detracts from consensual definitions of the problem and from effective problem solving. This escalation will eventually shape the resolution arrived at (see Table 3.1). Analyzing the problems in context of the duration of the conflict can provide useful clues to problem solving (Folger, 2018).

Some Problems Are Perpetual

One way to consider problems is to assess the likelihood that they can be solved. John Gottman (2015) wrote about two kinds of interpersonal problems. **Solvable problems** are here-and-now, situational, time-limited struggles, such as housecleaning and work responsibilities. Processing solvable problems requires good conversation and, in some cases, considerable skill to negotiate tense issues, but settlement can be reached. However, in a close, interdependent relationship many problems are simply unsolvable; Gottman called these **perpetual problems**. Because perpetual problems are caused by differences in personality, lifestyle, or values, no amount of processing is likely to resolve them. He estimated that less than 30% of perpetual problems can be finally resolved. In a deeply bonded and committed relationship, the primary parties must find ways to manage perpetual differences, to "live and let live." If this equilibrium cannot be reached, **irreconcilable differences** could mean the end of the relationship.

In a broader context of group or international conflict, this type of problem is called **intractable** (e.g., Coleman, 2014) and **wicked** (Conklin, 2006; Rittel, 1973). These are complex, long-lasting problems and conflicts that seem to resist solution. Many factors contribute to intractability (Conklin, 2006):

- The *people* share long-standing relationship in the context of historical grievances and a strong desire for vengeance. Both parties use us-them stereotyping that results in a polarized, hostile perception. Under these circumstances, destructive or violent behavior can supposedly be justified as normal, even necessary.
- *Problems* involve such intangible basics as needs, domination and autonomy, identity, and values and beliefs.

- The conflict *process* is unique, so it has few counterparts from which to learn, no natural stopping rule, and takes place in episodes of calm and storm over a long period.
- *Potential solutions* are elusive because there are no obviously correct answers, and the parties resist attempts to deescalate or manage animosity. Intractable conflicts therefore often have a history of failed peacemaking.

REFINING SOME INTERLOCKING SOURCES AND DRIVERS OF CONFLICT

When examining the interlocking problem sources of a conflict, you will find that some are fairly straightforward and obvious, some are complex. Generally, problems are driven by a tense combination of disagreement plus interdependency: disagreement between parties who are connected in some meaningful way. Disagreement might center in incongruent perspectives on the facts, ideas, or incompatible positions regarding the solutions,

> *If I had an hour to solve a problem, I'd spend 55 minutes thinking about the problem and 5 minutes thinking about solutions.*
> —Attributed to Albert Einstein, but no definitive source is found.

or center in deeper issues of competing but interdependent goals for the relationship or personal values. Together, they can compound a tangled argument where individual disputants are focusing solely on the problem or the relationship. All effective strategies address both problem and relationship dimensions.

Displaced Problems
Problems can become displaced, disguising the central issue with one that is safer, more tangible, or less likely to provoke a confrontation. A *hidden agenda* can result in baffling conflict dynamics that may seem illogical. Some people may be motivated to hide problems and their goals because of vulnerability or hopelessness. For example, instead of confronting difficult issues of closeness in a relationship, parties might engage in endless debate about plans for the future.

Compounded Problems
A specific conflict could be driven by several problems simultaneously. For instance, although the topic in dispute may be obvious, some participants may overlook underlying emotional or identity dynamics. These overlooked factors may serve as catalysts to ignite **latent conflict,** a conflict brewing below the surface of the relationship but not yet overt. For example, in romantic relationships such as that between John and Mary, arguments about seemingly trivial topics often disguise brewing but unspoken tensions about closeness and independence. The ideas of an early political scholar, Immanuel Kant (1724–1804), can be extrapolated to note that conflict can be compounded by at least six sources: unfinished problems, habitual hostility, disputant interference with each other, unwelcome domination, friction with outsiders, and irreconcilable differences of perception, values, and identity.

The Stories You Tell Define the Problem

You tend to perceive a conflict as a coherent event organized around personal themes, not as a disconnected jumble. An important part of coping is making sense of it through personal storytelling that explains the problem and your experiences. Your reaction corresponds with the inner "stories told," called the **narrative frame** (Cobb, 2019). From that frame, archetypes or paradigms for interpreting experiences (Wright, 2013) then become the frameworks for making decisions and acting (Herman, 2019).

Fabled Illustration: Aesop (1919)—The Bundle of Sticks

A farmer had three children who quarreled from dawn to dusk. One day, the farmer fell gravely ill. Wishing to make peace among his children before he died, he called them to his bedside and asked them to bring a bundle of thin sticks.

The father separated three sticks from the bundle and handed one to each of his children. "Can you break the stick?" he asked. Each one did so easily.

Then the father handed the eldest child the bundle of sticks. "Can you break this in two?" he asked.

"Of course!" the eldest answered scornfully. But even with great effort, the bundle of sticks was not broken.

"Those sticks are no thicker than my finger," mocked the middle child.

"I could break those sticks like straw," boasted the third. They all tried with all their might, but could not break the bundle of sticks.

"Let the sticks teach you," said the father, "How easily you can be broken on your own, and how strong you are when you are allied together."

This narrative summarizes a meaning: for the farmer, each stick represented one child and each singular stick signified weakness when divided; the bundled sticks denoted strength in harmony and alliance within the family. Aesop's story about conflict frames a lesson in the reader's mind. The challenge in conflict framing is that participants see and interpret a story with different narrative frames. The actual event, including the perception of the problem that caused it, is uniquely interpreted and those differences are often the base for ongoing conflict. Explanatory narrative that ends hopelessly, such as "She's out to get me and I'll never get away," centers in themes of threat and fear. Stories of hope during conflict, such as "She's a good friend; we'll find a way through this," can inspire efforts to mend troubled relationships.

CONTEXTUAL DRIVERS OF PROBLEMS

Three contextual factors that can fuel the development of a problem or conflict are the parties' history of relationship; positive or negative climate of perception; and beliefs within the social surroundings (Folger, 2018). These factors predispose disputants toward trust or suspicion and toward habitual or innovative methods of problem solving. The factors can therefore have a significant impact on the degree of escalation or deescalation present, and on the resolution process.

History

The past can affect current conflict by aggravating or mitigating the problems and dynamics you encounter. Everyone copes with two streams of history: your personal experiences and those of your related groups.

Your personal experiences with conflict and its resolution influence your perception and guide the plans you make and the tactical styles you select for resolving problems. When you relate closely with specific individuals, like your best friend or the town bully, you accumulate a model interpretation of what sparks tension, how the processing conversations go, and what potential solutions might be realistic. That model sensitizes you in current and future interactions with those individuals and even with people in similar situations. The context of family or friendship or the public is a part of this dynamic too. If you have had a dreadful work experience with a toxic boss, for example, you might forever avoid workplaces in which you could be subject to an authority of any kind.

The social history around you also has an effect. You are brought up within a social environment, primarily a family, that exists within a society that is shaped by its history. This socially shared history might even be somewhat remote from any individual, but it affects the common perception of conflict and expectations and norms for how conflict is best resolved. Even the language used to process problems is deeply enmeshed within these collective experiences. If you live in a region of long-standing conflict and war, for example, traumatic experiences will be part of the milieu of your upbringing; if you were brought up in a society that has experienced decades of peace, that will help shape your outlook on relationships, problems, and conflict. This shared quality is one of the reasons for gaps in perception and understanding between older generations who survived horrifying experiences like the Holocaust and younger generations for whom war is merely an abstract fact.

Climate

Climate refers to generalized energy and attitudes that characterize a whole social group. Although affected by individual behavior, climate is a quality diffused throughout a whole system that continuously changes, as the weather does, influencing the emotional tone of calm or storm of most interactions. In quite specific ways, the climate shared by a group or society shapes the ways its members approach relationships with their problems and projected solutions. Climate creates varied expectations related to trust, respect, and cohesion, and communicates to group members things like whether they can anticipate being valued and supported, and how power will be exercised when dealing with differences. These expectations would inevitably affect the course of problem solving.

Some Conflict Is Fundamentally Friendly; Some Conflict Is Frankly Hostile

Even during difficult and heated conflicts, parties' aims can still be friendly—designed to solve a problem and/or improve an interaction or a relationship. For example, imagine that two people are arguing over one's use of alcohol. One friend is concerned about the effects of excessive alcohol use on the drinker's life. The drinker believes their consumption is acceptable, stating, "I can stop any time I want to." Even though the argument is difficult, the intention of the person raising the issue is a friendly concern about the well-being of the other party. In another example, Mahatma Gandhi wrote to Adolf Hitler, once in 1939 and once in 1940, hoping to persuade the German leader to adopt nonviolent policies.

Despite their diametrically opposed views and politics, Gandhi addressed the Hitler letters to "my friend," and his intention was friendly: prevention of war. Hitler ignored him.

In other instances, the underlying aims may be **hostile** or **malevolent,** not to solve a problem but to deliberately harm or defeat the other party. Malevolent intentions are seldom expressed directly. They are more likely to be hidden behind less hostile topics or content and only implied. For example, malevolent intention to get a work partner fired through criticism might be hidden behind syrupy words like "I'm just trying to help."

Problems in the Context of Diversity: Culture, Gender Role, Power and Status

Although the diverse viewpoints might suggest a fruitful area of interest, no research has made clear if or how diversity influences disputants' perceptions of a problem. Rather, most research reports focus on resulting styles of action when conflict has begun. Findings at the intersection of multiple identities are largely mixed, and clarifying research is needed.

The myriad cultural forms across the world are based in unique perspectives, shaped by a group's history, norms and practices, and values (see Chapter 5). Some conflicts result from perceived incompatibilities in these forms (McGoldrick, 2012; Ting-Toomey, 2010). Cultural studies show that individuals from *collectivist* or *associative societies* tend to deal with problems without confrontation by emphasizing problem solving, compromise, and withdrawal (Holt, 2005). Disputants from *individualistic societies* are quicker to respond when a problem arises, and more likely to emphasize direct resolution by using coercion to force resolution (Holt, 2005; Knutson, 2000).

Gender research does not consistently distinguish between genetic gender and social gender role, leaving some ambiguity when interpreting research results. Response patterns were predictable by the gender of the disputant in only 1% of individual cases, but strategies may be chosen according to the gender of the opponent (Ivy, 2016). *Feminine* individuals tend to interpret conflict within an *affiliative frame* (Donahue, 2011) and therefore emphasize the relational dimension of an interaction. They tend to use rapport, compromise, or avoidance to resolve conflict (Brewer, 2002; Ivy, 2016) and are unlikely to attempt force, especially with their superiors (Holt, 2005) Women report finding agreement more readily than do men (Ivy, 2016). *Masculine* individuals more often rely on facts and information (Ivy, 2016) to interpret conflict from an *instrumental frame* (Donahue, 2011). They tend to use competitive processes and dominating styles (Brewer, 2002; Thomas, 2008). *Androgynous* individuals were more likely to use integrating tactics (Brewer, 2002).

Findings generally do point to a complicated interaction involving gender roles, cultural background, relative power balance, and conflict styles. Leaders were more likely to use assertive tactics to find integrative solutions, while lower-status individuals reported using unassertive avoidance and accommodation (Brewer, 2002; Thomas, 2008). The use of compromise was most likely at the middle levels of power, but decreased at both the highest and lowest levels (Thomas, 2008).

A common power tactic is to use problem control by narrowly limiting the discussion. Issue control can be accomplished in several ways:

- *Suppression* of a problem by creating anxiety about raising it among the concerned parties. For example, "We wouldn't want to upset Dad by contradicting his opinion."
- *Mindguarding* misdirects attention away from a problem by limiting the information available (Janis, 1971). For example, "We don't need to study that issue, it's only a minor detail."
- *Stonewalling* is refusing to answer questions or cooperate, resulting in a stalled dialogue. For example, "We won't talk about that until you see the problem my way."
- *Sequencing* of discussions can direct problem solving toward easy or difficult processing. For example, "Let's see if we can solve the income issue first, then move on to spending it." Sometimes, successful resolution of an easy problem will provide momentum to tackle more difficult ones. By contrast, it may be more useful to solve the difficult problems, and then the easy ones more readily fall into place.

Problem control must be used judiciously because it is not always inappropriate. When it is used to calm heated feelings and give parties time to think about how they want to proceed, it can positively influence the process. However, imposing power might effectively smother debate, leaving problems unsolved and parties feeling silenced, demeaned, and frustrated.

PROBLEM-SOLVING METHODS LEAD TO THE OUTCOME

Underlying dynamics can serve as sources of conflict. Let's turn next to three related dynamics, a destructive problem-solving process, positions versus interests, and unspoken problems.

Uncooperative, Destructive Problem-Solving Process

Morton Deutsch's early work (1969) moved scholars to view process on a continuum of productive and effective interactions, and destructive, competitive processes. Any conflict event can be escalated if the basic process is destructive. Deutsch outlined some criteria for judging that a process is ineffective:

- Opponents lose sight of the original goals for the relationship or for the conflict;
- Hostile behavior becomes the norm, and conflict is a regular part of the interaction;
- The relationship is harmed by the animosity;
- The issues driving the conflict have a tendency to expand and escalate; and
- The outcome is not satisfactory to the opponents.

William Zartman (2008) added that this is particularly true when the opponents believe "there is no way out." Destructive problem solving leads to an outcome of hurting stalemate.

Positions and Interests

When in conflict, a **position** expresses what you say you want, stating a definite viewpoint or demand about a problem and/or its solution. At times, positions may be based on fears or payback for past events or losses. A position might disguise unstated expectations about a relationship. For example, partners might take demanding positions to force decisions and make the partner give in. Positions can also be related to particular responsibilities or roles. For instance, in a family argument, parents will often take a different position from the children about how to define and solve a problem.

Positional conflicts are often futile. When you put effort into defending a position, you spend energy guarding it instead of solving the original problem. Then the conflict becomes argumentative and **positional**. Louis Kriesberg (2020) wrote that a conflict escalates when opponents demand that a position must be implemented. Commitment to positions can be rigid, especially when parties believe that they are not being taken seriously or that they are losing an argument. The trouble may have its source(s) in a goal that the opponent dismisses as illegitimate or unfair. This usually results in an impasse, with no party willing to give in, and the conflict then becomes a contest. Reactive, habitual responses are activated, people stop listening, and the possibilities for resolution are reduced drastically. Compromise could be a solution, but then both parties lose something.

In contrast to a position, an **interest** represents the central goals and underlying needs and hopes. While a position expresses *what* a party wants, an interest reflects *why* you want it. Having an interest makes participation in a conflict appropriate; in other words, my interest makes it "my business." Interests are often unknown or unstated. Some examples of underlying, hidden interests would be to gain approval, be liked, maintain control, or obtain justice.

When interests are stated, parties will often discover common, shared interests that can be satisfied even when initial positions seem incompatible. To broaden the possibilities for discovering common interests, Fisher, Ury, and Patton (2011) recommend a **problem-solving strategy** that separates positions from interests (see Figure 3.2). This shift suggests that conflicting parties should explore more than the incompatible positions or competing interests. Uncovering your common interests requires significant communication and sincere efforts to listen, but can break through an impasse to achieve a solution. Unlike **positional arguments** that can only be resolved through compromise, discussing interests can produce mutual understanding and create a range of possible solutions that satisfy everyone's interests, resulting in a win-win solution.

Hidden Issues Can Derail Problem Solving

One key to finding an effective solution is knowing and working with all relevant factors and influences, and understanding the priorities and resources of each participant. Shadow issues are important but unspoken factors that can undermine a problem-solving process because solutions have to account for both what is admitted and what is hidden (Kolb, 2000). The sources of these issues, hidden from the opponent, might be a reputation or a past history of animosity, for example, or a secret plan, or a stereotype held rigidly. They can result in puzzling statements and decisions during problem solving.

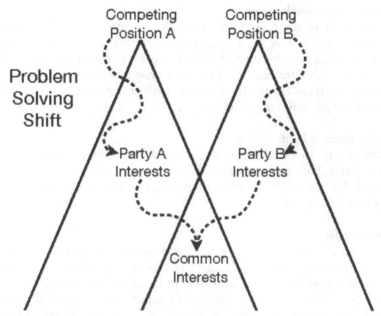

Figure 3.2 Problem-solving shift from position to common interests
Based on Fischer, 2011, public domain.

A precondition for effective discussion is a safe and factual process. Hidden issues must be clarified to reach mutual trust in a climate of positivity, kindness, and respect. Effective processing results from engaged, active listening. Two-way information sharing and disclosure are therefore essential to effective problem solving.

GOALS UNDERLIE CONFLICT DYNAMICS

Every conflict is motivated by a purpose that affects how it begins and unfolds and where it ends. In this sense, conflict is positive and useful, fulfilling its purpose of solving problems and discovering a new equilibrium. If you pay attention, you can discern the aims that each disputing party is working toward.

Contrasting Goals of the Conflict

Most conflicts can be seen to be attempts to reach a future goal in the relationship or to accomplish a purpose, but many factors can cloud the goals:

Variations in Clarity of the Goals

Some goals may be openly acknowledged, but many may remain subconscious, unstated, or hidden. The more obscured or unfocused the goals are, the less likely it is that they will be accomplished. For example, the vague goal of "working on our relationship" is less likely to be fulfilled than action goals of spending more time in conversation and relaxed recreation.

Divergent or Incompatible Goals

When the goals of the parties appear to clash, conflict is likely. For example, many young people look for a "gap year" after high school and before going on to a job or higher education. When their parents push them to decide about a career and further training, conflict often arises. However, there can be ways of harmonizing these apparently divergent goals. For example, the young person could look for job training in Europe.

Different Procedural Points of View

Two parties may share the same goal but have different opinions of how to achieve it. For example, both an employer and an employee share the goal of completing a job well, but the employer might demand greater attention to detail than the employee is willing to invest.

Changes over Time

Goals are rarely static and may evolve as a conflict unfolds. **Prospective goals** are those that start a conflict. **Transactive goals** emerge during the transaction. **Retrospective goals** become evident only in hindsight, after engaging in conflict (Hocker, 2018). For example, a workplace conflict might begin with the prospective goal of settling a scheduling problem, but evolve into a serious transactive power struggle; retrospectively, both parties might recognize that their hope was to get the other person fired.

Unspoken, Implicit Issues Can Also Spark Conflict

Implicit, underlying issues are rarely the subject of open conversation, but it is helpful to identify these influential factors. As you read this section, notice that the issues discussed are not mutually exclusive but, rather, simultaneously affect the conflict.

What Do We Want?

The content of a conflict is expressed in differences of viewpoint, opinion, or priorities. This substance or topic of the dispute, called the **substantive issue,** is what people usually identify when asked about the nature of a conflict. Substantive issues can be about space, time, or money, for example. The substantive issue is the objectively identifiable topic of dispute. The goal of conflict over substantive issues is a straightforward resolution of the identified problem. For example, the substantive issue for members of a family arguing about where to go on vacation might be the ideal destination.

Discomfort about raising substantive issues is common because of anxiety over the possibility of uncovering deeper incompatibilities and causing relationship disruption. However, open processing of substantive issues can lead to clearer thinking, fairer decision making, and more creative solutions that incorporate differing viewpoints.

Why Is This Important?

Another implicit issue is emotional investment. **Emotional** or **affective conflict** occurs when people have significant feelings about a disagreement, and express themselves with emotional heat, animosity, or antagonistic remarks. For example, a family discussion about plans for graduation celebrations might get fairly heated if the parents demand attendance at a Safe Grad celebration and the graduate insists on making his or her own plans. Such conflicts may be generated by strong opinions about how things "ought" or "ought not" to be. Emotional conflict is often triggered by implied or open criticism, punishment, or unpleasant hostility. Intense feelings, such as fear, frustration, and anger, can sometimes become contagious and escalate the conflict by drawing in outsiders who are not directly involved. Resolving affective conflict involves cooling the heated feelings and finding a calm solution.

How Should We Do It?

Another important problem arises from differing opinions about procedure or how to get things done. **Procedural conflict** exists when people disagree about how to solve substantive issues, or how to fulfill goals for a relationship. Parties may disagree about how closely to follow implied or formalized rules of the relationship, or the "right" way to accomplish things. Parties to a procedural conflict must find the most effective way to solve a problem before taking action. For example, two parents might agree on the major goal of raising a child to be a respectful contributor to society, but strongly disagree on the methods used. One parent may use strictly demanding tactics while the other parent uses lenient questioning and quiet instruction. This is a recipe for whole family conflict!

A common procedural conflict relates to the appropriateness of communication patterns: who communicates with whom, or not; how good communication happens; when behaviors such as shouting or leaving are allowed; and so on. Communication is a particularly ambiguous procedural issue when the parties in the relationship have markedly different roles and power, such as parent-child or professor-student.

Another contentious issue can be the procedures for making decisions: by adhering to principles, by consensus, by logical processing, by following "hunches," or by dictator edict? Power struggles are often procedural conflicts.

Interference is yet another problem related to procedure. When one party interferes with another party's activities (or is perceived to do so), underlying needs may be neglected or goals left unfulfilled, resulting in frustration, resentment, and conflict.

What Matters Most About Me?

Convictions about self are a centrally important issue that are often difficult to describe. **Identity** is a term that refers to the core factors that are the foundations of self-respect, personal freedom, gender and cultural integrity, and respectful relationships.

When these core personal needs are threatened, **identity conflict** arises. This experience can become the cause of deep, intense, and sometimes long-lasting discord. The goal of identity conflict is to preserve individual or group identity, roles, or responsibilities, or to restore them when they have been compromised. For example, a family argument about a teenager's choices of friends and activities might reflect deeper identity conflict about the right of the teenager to be independent of the parents' expectations or demands.

Values help determine what is most worthwhile, reflecting individuals' deepest commitments and personal measures of what is good and meaningful. **Personal values** are held by individuals, while **cultural values** are those that are shared with larger groups of people. **Principal values**, are the fundamentals of a personal value system; examples include honesty or loyalty. Because values lead you to judge what behavior is moral or immoral, or to expectations of how good or "normal" people will act, **moral** and **values conflicts** can become some of the most volatile, perpetual conflicts. In identity conflict, disputants believe it is necessary to defend deeply held, precious values.

A useful goal is to try to uphold principles but prevent the interaction from escalating into a life-and-death struggle. In working through this type of conflict it is useful to distinguish between **negotiable** and **nonnegotiable values**. Negotiable values can be discussed and reconsidered; nonnegotiable values usually cannot be resolved with discussion and, therefore, become a conflict demand. If every value in dispute is treated with the same importance, arguments can become extreme and prolonged. One example is the commonly experienced tension between home and work life. For most people, it is important to work in a meaningful, rewarding setting, but it is also important to maintain satisfying family relationships. If both are nonnegotiable, family members will live with unresolved tension and guilt as they try to be perfect in both realms. Most people negotiate inwardly to decide which of these competing values takes priority.

Depending on the centrality of the issue and the power dynamics of the relationship, identity and values conflicts can result in extreme forms of perpetual conflict, uncivil behavior, and sometimes reciprocal violence. You may be surprised how many people are prepared to die rather than compromise their values. For example, many of the combatants in the ongoing Middle Eastern wars are motivated to defend values that have come through many generations and adopted by the individuals. Because of beliefs that these values must not be compromised, the identity struggles are perpetuated, becoming intractable.

Think About the East-West Island Dilemma, and Discuss with Your Colleagues

- What are some of the unspoken issues that might be driving this problem? Identify the types of conflict: substantive, emotional, procedural, identity, and values—how did those types affect the unfolding of the conflict?
- Think about the intentions of each of the five parties as they act in this scenerio. What underlying goals could the conflict be addressing?

Intention

Fully understanding the intentions that motivate actions helps you clarify conflict. **Intention** is defined as the reason(s) behind actions. Understanding intention is not, in fact, a simple matter because intentions are usually *covert* (hidden, possibly even to yourself) rather than *overt* (openly stated).

Intentions are sometimes clear and singular; a simple problem requires a solution, and the intention is to solve it and get on to more pleasant matters. More likely, however, intentions are more complex; they may be mixed or change over time.

A party who genuinely wants to solve a problem might covertly want to express pent-up frustration, avoid a confrontation, or "teach a lesson."

Was the Effect Intended or Unintended?

All actions have consequences. Whenever an action has harmful consequences (even though the intention may have been positive), there is a risk that conflict may erupt. For example, someone communicating criticism may have the genuine intention of helping the other person improve some aspect of a skill, but the recipient of the criticism might feel hurt or insulted by the comments, interpreting the intention as malevolent. Another example is texting while driving: a collision can have brutal consequences that were not the intention of the texter.

Actions are public and evident to all observers, but intentions are rarely communicated openly (see Figure 3.3). Bringing intentions into the open by voicing them is often crucial to conflict resolution. People rarely clarify, "What I meant to happen was ..." or "What I'm hoping for is...." This type of **intention statement** that expresses the intent straightforwardly is helpful to mitigate the impact of words said in conflict. An example might be, "When I said that, I didn't mean to hurt your feelings." Acknowledging that actions have effects that were quite different from what was intended can be part of an effective apology. Even though harm was not intended, a person may need to apologize for a hurtful consequence.

What Is the Difference between Blame and Responsibility?

People often try to explain others' actions by interpreting their intentions. Negative or hostile intention may be assumed, sometimes without sufficient evidence: "You hurt me deliberately!" **Blame** is finding fault, criticizing, or condemning a person for their actions or assumed intentions. Blame often escalates conflict. The blamed person feels compelled to defend their innocence while the hurt person insists their hurt should be heard.

To acknowledge **responsibility** is a no-blame approach; everyone agrees that someone suffered as a result of specific actions, regardless of intentions. For example, in the case of medical accidents, the intention was to cure, but the effect was damage. Accepting responsibility can take many forms, including regret, acknowledgment of harm experienced, apology, and/or compensation. Ideally, people should take responsibility for their own behavior before anyone else has to blame or hold them responsible.

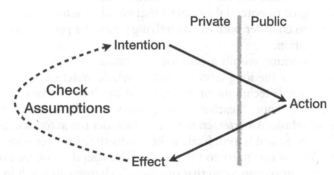

Figure 3.3 Actions are public; intentions and impact are private.

PRACTICAL PROBLEM-SOLVING METHODS AND PROCESSES

Phases of the Problem Cycle

Several problem phases are discernible: first there is a *triggering event*. Reactions to the event result in growing problems, called **differentiation**, during which disputants argue over differences between them more than the over problems they face together. A *turning point* develops when at least one disputant recognizes the futility of the conflict and changes course. The disputants then move on to an **integration** phase, looking for ways to agree on a problem-solving method. This ends in a process that is significantly more orderly than the original (based on Walton, 1987).

Techniques and Strategies for Problem Solving

Problems are rarely considered in isolation from the other elements of the relationship system. The people, the processes, and the problem all contribute to the rhythm of the relationship on a harmony-to-conflict continuum. Appropriate and durable solutions usually result from careful thinking that includes assessment of all sides of a conflict, analysis of possible factors contributing to the current tensions, creating a mental map that will point to possible options for resolution.

A common obstacle in problem solving is uncertainty or disagreement about the scope and seriousness of the problem, and this is aggravated when the data is ambiguous. An example was provided by Michelle Wolfe (2016) who studied the complex issue of climate change. Because both the problems and the solutions to climate change are complex and politicized, many debaters experience "problem uncertainty" compounded by "muddled" prioritizing. Policy makers are left with the tension of knowing there is a problem, but not having a vision of how to move forward. Wolfe noted that uncertainty can motivate debaters to more clearly define the problem, clarify supporting data, and delineate the solutions.

In instances like that, two general strategies are used:

1. **Problem reduction** narrows the scope of a complex problem under consideration. One effective way to do that is to consider only one segment of a problem before moving on to address others.
2. **Problem expansion** broadens the matters for consideration.

Roger Volkema (1997) proposed the Problem-Purpose Expansion (PPE) exercise. Disputants first simplify the problem definition, then expand it by analyzing the purpose or goal of potential solutions that could be attempted. This allows problem solvers to consider both the underlying goals of a problem and of a desirable, effective solution.

When working within a problem or conflict system, one small change can reverberate over the long term to cause a whole system change (Wright, 2013). There is no single technique or strategy that can bring certain success. Rather, as Kriesberg (2020) noted, each solution is likely to address one aspect of a conflict, but not the whole. An *interactive process* includes the active engagement of most or all the parties, and is most likely to be productive. Another option is a *unilateral process* taken by one party to the dispute. The operation of reciprocity processes within a human system mean that one party's change can result in other changes.

To Address a Problem ... or Not Is an Additional Issue

Now that you have learned more about the problem issues, an early step is careful deliberation about whether to take any action at all. The consequences of action or of inaction may be difficult to live with. Taking action can sometimes aggravate or ignite an already strained situation, but inaction might do just as much harm. Reluctance to address an issue may be too easy. Remaining silent and inactive may be more about lack of courage than about lack of skill.

Everyone is a problem solver. Just as people vary in their tolerance for problems and conflict, so there are variations in how you choose to react and the methods you use to solve your problems. Most of the time, personal, informal methods result in good enough, livable solutions. However, that creative process might be shortened by prematurely grasping at solutions before a problem is fully understood (Volkema, 1997). This can cause you to settle on conventional solutions that skip the complexities of the problem. Volkema recommended deferral of judgment by thorough discussion that might end in redefining or reframing the problem. On occasion, a more systematic, orderly problem-solving cycle facilitates consideration of complicated issues.

Orderly Problem Solving

Orderly problem solving uses a combination of **divergent process**, which creates additional choices, and **convergent process**, to choose from among a variety of options. A common procedure is a planned five-step process to recognize and identify the problem(s), dialogue to generate ideas and explore resources, evaluation of possible choices and then taking action, and assessing the progress and evaluating the success (see Praxis Skill Builder 3.1). You might find that you prefer and are better at one stage of this process. The steps can be repeated until satisfactory plans are made.

Win-Lose Problem-Solving Strategy

The **win-lose problem-solving method** is somewhat aggressive, based on the perception of a competitive *zero-sum* solution: whatever I win, you lose, or whatever you win, I must lose. Winning the argument and defeating the opponent becomes the objective rather than resolving the problem. Power is often behind a win-lose strategy: resisting real or implied coercion or domination may push the parties to compete. One party dominates the process to accomplish their goal, while the others compete to satisfy their goals. At least one party insists on a fight-defeat goal, behaves uncooperatively or badly, and/or uses some type of force (Folger, 2018). Win-lose problem solving is most effective when the disputed resources are truly scarce and cannot be shared or when time is short and urgent decisions must be made. For example, in the competition for a workplace promotion, only one candidate will be successful, so the strategy may focus more on discrediting the competitors than on featuring one's own skills and ambitions. However, a win-lose solution is self-centered, and risks weakening a relationship bond.

Lose-Lose Problem-Solving Strategy

A **lose-lose problem solving** shows a lack of faith in the resolution of the problem and in the sustainability of the relationship. Although few conflicts begin with this strategy, many conflicts devolve into a focus on mutual defeat. The argument may be bitter and fierce, but no underlying problems are resolved. There is no one "bad-guy" because each party is working to defeat the other. Neither party leaves the conflict satisfied or with goals achieved. This interaction may originate as **win-lose problem** solving but escalate until both parties lose. For example, in an ongoing workplace dispute, if two employees refuse to work together or end the conflict, both parties might end up unemployed.

Compromise Problem-Solving Strategy

When you engage in a **compromise problem-solving strategy,** you settle the differences by giving up on some goals and yielding to the needs of others. Both parties must sacrifice something, so your goals are only partially satisfied, but neither of you is fully satisfied. Usually, problems are solved incompletely, and may reemerge. In the long run, uneven or unwilling compromise may switch into win-lose or even **lose-lose problem solving.** Compromise rarely results in a truly satisfying, sustainable resolution, but may be effectively used when partial satisfaction is the best outcome for which to hope. For example, many employer-employee negotiations about working conditions or salary involve markedly contrasting initial demands, resolved by compromise on both sides to generate a settlement. In another example, many politicians find themselves caught between the voices of their constituents and the directives or demands of their political party. There is often little harmony or compromise between these divergent demands. Neither side is fully satisfied but parties must be willing to yield to find a compromise to resolve the debate.

Win-Win Problem-Solving Strategy

A **win-win problem-solving** method uses collaboration to solve the problem. The argument addresses both the problem at hand and any underlying issues in the relationship in a collaborative, trusting way, dealing with individual needs, preserving the relationship, and finding a fair outcome. All parties commit to working cooperatively, reject using defeat to end the argument, and avoid compromising or sacrificing satisfaction (Folger, 2018). For example, a workplace dispute might be addressed in a meeting that involves the parties openly naming their concerns, identifying their needs and goals, and coming to a mutual understanding of the whole situation. Then they can find a solution that satisfies all needs, creating a new sense of partnership. Win-win problem solving does take more effort, care, and time than the other approaches, but is most likely to result in problems being solved. Both parties achieve their goals and needs, and the solution is sustainable.

Praxis Skill Builder 3.1 ■ IDEAL Problem-Solving Technique

The following guidelines (after Bransford, 1993) can form the basis for planning effective resolution of problem issues in conflict. Notice the acronym **IDEAL**: identify, dialogue, evaluate, act, and look back.

1. Identify—Carefully analyze problem sources, conflict dynamics, and goals before jumping to premature conclusions or hastily constructed solutions. Improved self-knowledge and mutual understanding are

(continued)

Praxis Skill Builder 3.1 ■ Continued

achievable goals in preparation for a good communication process, but there must be consensus on what the problem is and who is responsible for fixing it.

DIVERGENCE or DIFFERENTIATION

2. **D**ialogue—Explore possible ways to dialogue about the perspectives and problems at a suitable time and place. If one party has a problem, then the relationship has a problem. It is only acceptable to overlook a problem if all parties agree that it is not important enough to deeply process together. A collaborative process, in which all parties have some level of control, is always preferable to a unilateral or coercive process.

a) Supportively listen to one party's needs. When listening, dig more deeply than the obvious, substantive issues to address underlying issues. Invite verbal, assertive expression of thoughts and feelings. These tactics can result in a shared understanding of the problem and lead to a shared goal.

b) Communicate the needs of each party. Use and encourage the use of "I" language. "I want ...," "I need ...," "I think ...," and "I feel ..." are powerful phrases that ground a dialogue.

c) Focus on common interests rather than on positions. Use descriptive, not blaming, vocabulary. Find ways to minimize harmful words. Recognize human tendencies to make mistakes and forgive when actions are forgivable.

d) Reframe the views of those involved, redefining the problem or the entire situation, usually with the input of people outside the dispute.

e) Together, generate and evaluate creative possibilities that will satisfy the needs. There will be no formula.

CONVERGENCE or INTEGRATION

3. **E**valuate—Look for *integrative strategies* that harmonize diverging needs and accommodate differences in core personal identity, morals, and values. Choose a win-win solution that satisfies everyone's needs and goals.

4. **A**ct to Address the Problem—For a time, test the chosen solution. Specifically address who does what, when, and for how long?

5. **L**ook Back—After a time of testing, look at the problem again: Was it solved? Did it result in win-win, as hoped? If so, great! If not, start over.

POTENTIAL OUTCOMES

Like problem elements, the outcomes of conflict are rarely simple. Sometimes issues are resolved and never need to be revisited. More often, problems reemerge and evolve into new ones or are compounded by additional dynamics. In Conflict Resolution Studies, potential solutions are usually categorized as effective or ineffective, rather than good or bad. Laue (1990) noted that an **effective outcome** meets three criteria: 1) solution of the underlying problem,

2) improvement in the parties' relationship, and 3) a fair and inclusive process—in simple words, the conflict fulfills its purpose. An **ineffective outcome** leaves a problem unsolved, or solves the problem at the cost of a damaged or broken relationship. Lacking a workable solution, the problem then returns to trouble the relationship again.

A number of potentially effective outcomes are observed:

The problem was eliminated—Ways can occasionally be found to eliminate the problem and its tension using techniques like *expand the pie* (identifying additional benefits), cutting costs (reducing the costs of the problem), and *logrolling* (taking turns and exchanging compromises). The problem might also be eliminated by one party's exit from the situation, or by decision by an outside authority such as a judge or parent. For example, in many workplaces solutions are worked out that simply limit the contact between contending parties by transferring one to a different department. Sometimes, if the parties simply wait long enough, the problem can become irrelevant or solve itself.

The problem was managed—**Conflict management** focuses on limiting a conflict over the problem to activities that are successful and minimize the possibilities for eruption of ongoing discord or harm. It may not solve problems thoroughly, but a base of successful interactions can build enough goodwill that the parties can then work through the problem. In a workplace example, disputants might reach an equilibrium of "live and let live."

The problem was solved—**Conflict resolution**, also called *dispute settlement*, solves a particular problem and satisfies the conflicted parties' interests, but places little priority on activities that preserve a relationship. For example, in a workplace conflict, options might be created that support the individual parties' needs for independence and pride in their work, without interfering with each other.

The problem was reformulated—Participant insight can result in changes to the disputants' approach or attitude, or the relational roots of a conflict. **Conflict transformation** is used to modify the sources of the problem, which is seen as a signpost to deeper relationship issues that need adjustment. Your perspective and interpretation of problems and conflict, often connected to the context of a conflict and the explanatory stories you use, is a major determinant of the actions you take during conflict. This opens the way for potential reformulations of causes, dynamics, and solutions. For example, in a workplace transformation might involve revision of basic perception of the Other that effectively prevents future conflict by bettering the relationship between working partners.

Think About Mary and John on the "East Island" and Discuss with Your Colleagues

- In what ways are their problem-solving strategies effective or ineffective? What could shift these methods toward a more effective outcome? What is a reasonable outcome of this situation—conflict management, conflict resolution, or conflict transformation?

CHAPTER SUMMARY AND STUDY GUIDE

In this chapter, you have read about many sources and drivers of problems that cause conflict.

- Differing viewpoints related to diverse identities, social background and participant history, and a continuing relational climate affect each participant's interpretation of the problem and of conflict events.
- Participants begin a problem-solving process with differing goals and responses that depend on the whole situation. Cooperative and competitive responses shape conflict that, in turn, shapes the future of the relationship.
- Problem solving usually involves informal conversation. Such communication does not necessarily improve the interaction, and it may overlook potentially creative solutions. On occasion, a methodical process to identify the problem(s), dialogue about them, explore a variety of solutions, take action, and then evaluate the result can order the problem-solving method.
- Not all problems are solved. There are many possible outcomes of problem solving, including eliminating the problem, managing the conflict interactions, resolving the problems, and transforming the relationship.

TERMS IN FOCUS

affective conflict   92
Blame   95
climate   87
compromise problem-solving   98
conflict management   100
conflict resolution   100
conflict transformation   100
convergent process   97
covert intent   94
cultural values   94
differentiation   96
divergent process   97
effective outcome   99
Emotional conflict   92
friendly intent   87
hostile intent   88
Identity   93
identity conflict   93
ineffective outcome   100
integration process   96
intention   94
intention statement   95
interest   90

intractable conflict   84
irreconcilable differences   84
latent conflict   85
lose-lose problem solving   98
malevolent intent   85
moral conflict   94
narrative frame   86
negotiable values   94
nonnegotiable values   94
overt intent   94
perpetual problem   84
personal values   94
position   90
positional argument   90
principal values   94
problem   83
problem expansion   96
problem reduction   96
problem-solving strategy   90
procedural conflict   93
prospective goal   92
proximate cause   82
responsibility   95

4

Conflict Development and Process

■ ■ ■

In Focus in This Chapter:

- ■ Learn to recognize constructive, cooperative conflict, and understand the ways it differs from destructive, competitive processes.
- ■ Identify process factors that shape conflict behavior, including tactics, style, and strategy.
- ■ Distinguish malevolent, benevolent, and chilling process phases and cycles of conflict.
- ■ Use these concepts to learn from a particular conflict episode by conducting conflict assessment and analysis and using these activities to move toward resolution.
- ■ Understand how different conflict process theories add to your broad perspectives on conflict and guide practitioners toward an effective resolution plan.
- ■ Apply effective conflict resolution skills to build cooperative relationships

CONFLICT CASE 4.1 ■ THE LEGENDARY STORY OF THE HATFIELDS AND THE MCCOYS

The dreadful events of this conflict began a century and a half ago, near the Tug Fork River that divides West Virginia and Kentucky. The original parties were "Devil Anse" Hatfield, patriarch of the Hatfield family on the West Virginia river bank, and Randolph "Ran'l" McCoy, leader of the McCoy family on the Kentucky side.

Around 1860, an argument arose between the families over land and rights of access to the river. By 1863, the Hatfield men had formed a militant band that repeatedly raided McCoy properties. The first death from these raids was Ran'l's son, Asa McCoy, but that death was not prosecuted. The conflict was quiet for 13 years. Then in 1876 Ran'l McCoy accused Floyd Hatfield of stealing his razorback hog. When the conflict went to court (with six Hatfields and six McCoys serving on the jury) Floyd was found not guilty. In the ensuing chaos, the Hatfield manager, Bill Staton, was killed. In a later trial Sam McCoy was acquitted of causing Staton's death.

The 20-year-old conflict became even more complicated when Roseanne McCoy and Johnse Hatfield met at a summer election gathering in 1881. They fell in love, and Roseanne went to live in the Hatfield home. Love was too difficult, however, so Roseanne moved back to her family. When Roseanne learned about an ambush planned against Johnse, she rode through the night to warn him. She remained there, and became pregnant. After the baby died in a measles epidemic in 1888, Roseanne returned to live with her own family. That same year Johnse Hatfield married her sister, Nancy McCoy, and Roseanne died grief-stricken.

Ellison Hatfield was fatally wounded in 1882 in a fight with Bud, Pharmer, and Tolbert McCoy. This initiated a brutally violent period between the feuding families, during which the three McCoy brothers were tied up and shot 50 times by Hatfield family members. Four years later, Jeff McCoy was killed by Cap Hatfield. When Ran'l McCoy unsuccessfully tried to extradite Hatfield members to Kentucky for trial, he raided the Hatfield property and kidnapped his daughter, Nancy McCoy Hatfield. In 1888, the Hatfields raided the McCoy cabin, burning it to the ground and killing Alifair and Calvin McCoy.

The governors of Kentucky and West Virginia became embroiled in the feud, as did the National Guard and the courts. Several Hatfields were tried in 1889 for a series of McCoy deaths, resulting in prison sentences for seven Hatfields and the execution of Ellison Mounts for killing Alifair McCoy. The execution seemed to satisfy the antagonists because no further incidents of violence were recorded (Waller, 1988).

In a count of casualties, 5 members of the Hatfield family and 12 McCoys died. Strictly by the numbers, the McCoys surely seemed to be the losers, but in reality everyone lost because the origins of the conflict were completely obscured by the dynamics of hatred and retaliation.

The feud was formally ended with a truce signed in (... wait for it ...) 2003!

Think About and Discuss with Your Colleagues

- What might have been the motives behind the many chapters of this nearly 30 years of violence? What role did the substantive issues involving land and water access play?
- There are only a few instances where isolated individuals may have tried to make peace in this long-standing rivalry. What did some people do to stop what must have seemed like madness?
- Accounts of this conflict portray escalating sequences of violence that appeared to have little purpose or logic other than simple hateful retaliation. Are there signs, though, that there may have been more systematic process between the two warring families?

When confronted with stories or experiences of conflict, most people are mystified by the frustration and futility so often evident. The destructive hallmarks of conflict are familiar: parties use divisive and harmful tactics, problems become personal, confrontation occurs, and relationships are jeopardized. Too often the potential for genuinely constructive process and outcomes are overlooked.

Identifying ways in which conflict can be constructive is a recurring theme in Conflict Resolution Studies.

This chapter explores the conflict **process** that describes the dynamic steps through which a conflict progresses as it advances toward its outcome. Most processes include a combination of positive and negative dynamics. Morton Deutsch (2014) identified seven variables that influence process. Notice the echoes of your 4-P analysis.

1. Characteristics of the individual parties, such as beliefs and values;
2. Tactics and behaviors used during the conflict, such as aggression or avoidance;
3. The previous relationship between the parties, whether generally harmonious or antagonistic;
4. The nature of the problem, and how "close to home" or personal it is;
5. The context in which the conflict begins, such as private or public, home or work;
6. An interested audience or other people affected by a potential resolution;
7. Anticipated consequences of the conflict, such as whether parties expect hope or hopelessness for the relationship.

RECOGNIZING COOPERATIVE, POTENTIALLY CONSTRUCTIVE CONFLICT AND COMPETITIVE, USUALLY DESTRUCTIVE CONFLICT

According to Deutsch (2014), conflict can be useful and benefit a relationship. During **cooperative conflict**, the parties have similar or compatible goals for problem resolution. Dialogue includes a friendly attitude of respect, curiosity, and humility, anticipating agreement; divergence of interests is treated as a joint problem to work out together; you communicate honestly and openly; and you help each other to enhance the chances of resolution. The result is almost always a conflict limited in intensity and scope, with a beneficial resolution.

Competitive conflict tends to expand and escalate because it is approached disagreeably, from a mistrusting, hostile perspective. Although not all competition intensifies to become conflict (Redekop and Rioux, 2012), when conflict takes on competitive characteristics parties' actions tend toward misleading communication; efforts are divided, duplicated, and you aim to obstruct or overpower your opponent to impose resolution. The result is almost always damaging to the relationship and unproductive to resolve the problem.

Even when a relationship is healthy and functional, inevitable differences of goals and values may affect the process. **Latent conflict** results from unexpressed, hidden differences. Because discomfort or irritation does exist but remains hidden, it can lead to competitive functioning and there is potential for the conflict to erupt. **Overt** or **manifest conflict** is open conflict that varies in intensity from cooperatively mild and transitory to destructively unrestrained and violent. Overt conflict can be fundamentally constructive or destructive, or a combination of the two in succession. Although it is overt, **moderated conflict**, also called **regulated conflict**, can be more constructive than either latent or unrestrained conflict because underlying differences are disclosed and can then be harmonized. John Paul Lederach (1992) correlated emotional intensity, conflict intensity, and interpersonal connection with the conflict process:

Table 4.1 Cooperative Versus Competitive Conflict

Cooperative Conflict	*Competitive Conflict*
Effective disclosure of feelings	Obstructed, strategic communication, impersonal information only
Friendly approach, maintain mutual support and connection	Suspicion, negative perception, maintain status and independence
Tentative assertions, coordination of solving efforts	Divided, duplicated efforts
Feeling of understanding and agreement in values and beliefs	Confront differences, disagree, and reject the other's ideas
Willing to share power, compromise where possible	Other's power is a threat, so increase own
Conflicting interests are mutual problem	Believe that coercion will resolve conflict, demand solution or give advice

Source: Based on Deutsch, 2014.

- When conflict is latent or unexpressed, resolution is rare;
- When heated emotions and conflict are unrestrained, resolution is rare; and
- When conflict is moderated and intensity is manageable, improved communication, understanding, and productive conflict resolution can happen.

Moderated conflict and a constructive process are in everyone's long-term interests. Table 4.1 summarizes the differences between cooperative, constructive conflict and destructive, competitive conflict (Deutsch, 2014).

Relationships, conversations, and conflicts unfold in reciprocating sequences, turn-by-turn, move-by-move. This was obvious in the Hatfield and McCoy saga. Relationships can be seen as a sort of "dance," developing as one action provokes another. Because of mutual influence, each move by one party affects the next action of the opponent that, in turn, influences the first person's reaction, and so on. In a healthy relationship, give and take moves and countermoves even out over time to produce a comfortable symmetry. According to **Reciprocity Theory**, most relationships are based on the assumption that people engage with each other in similar ways to create balanced relationships. In a reciprocal relationship, influence is approximately balanced. Giving and receiving are fluid among partners, and there is a reasonably mutual exchange of strength and support. Reciprocity Theory is not associated with any one theorist, but is a common assumption in most cultures.

Reciprocity is obvious during conflict; positive goodwill is reciprocated in friendly conflict, and negative malice is reciprocated in hostile conflict. The underlying assumption is that "you get what you give." Conflict escalation and deescalation result from reciprocal processes. The conflict dance illustrates two broad process patterns. In a **symmetrical process**, you match or exaggerate each others' actions. Even when in conflict, opponents tend to behave in similar ways; for example, both parties are veiled or heated, both reciprocate the other's actions in a "tit-for-tat" manner, or both are kind. Some common symmetrical patterns are Flight-Flight and Fight-Fight. In *Flight-Flight conflict*, avoidance snowballs in counteravoidance and parties eventually refuse to talk. In *Fight-Fight conflict*, one party is hurt, so they hurt back; one party is insulted, so they insult back. Particularly in fight-fight sequences, the responding behavior often increases in intensity: a great

Table 4.2   Summary of Conflict Tactics, Styles, Strategies, and Outcomes

Tactics	Style	Strategy	Likely Outcome
Overlook problems and solutions Evade conflict	Avoid	Two avoiders Two validators Validator + Volatile	Lose-lose Chilled relationship
Passively engage Indirect communication Deny, give up	Accommodate	Volatile + Avoider	Unfair lose-win
Emotional warfare Dominate people and conflict Direct, tactical communication	Force, coerce	Volatile	Escalation Unfair win-lose Mutual harm
Direct, assertive communication Exchange negotiation	Compromise	Validate	Reasonable 50–50 win
Direct, assertive communication Collaborative decision making	Collaborate	Validate	Fair win-win Mutual gain

hurt follows a small hurt, escalating the conflict. In most cases, reciprocal hostility confuses and derails a conflict rather than leading toward settlement. In the extreme, symmetrical hostility results in escalating chains of retaliation or revenge like those experienced over generations by the Hatfields and the McCoys.

In a **complementary conflict**, argument is conducted with contrasting, sometimes opposite behavior. Loud speech is met with quiet; calm approaches are the response to tense movements. A common complementary pattern is *Fight-Flight*, which usually results in a stalemate. For example, when one party uses fight tactics of loud or abusive speech, you might exit the room in a hurry. *Flight-Negotiate-Fight* or *Fight-Freeze-Flight* are more complex complementary patterns. For example, after one party derails the argument by exiting the room, you might pursue, insisting "We have to talk this through." That might then threaten the first party who responds with fighting words. In another example of complementary conflict, one party may begin with quick escalation to fighting tactics that emotionally freeze the other party, resulting in one of the parties ending the confrontation by leaving.

When analyzing conflict events, several components can be distinguished. Conflict **tactics** are specific behaviors and methods employed by opponents pursuing their goals. Conflict **styles** are patterns or clusters of behavior that are used repeatedly in a variety of conflict situations. Styles are habitual ways of relating to others and interacting when in conflict. Conflict **strategy** is a deliberated, planned response to conflict. In a soccer contest, for example, a player would use specific tactics to move the ball toward the goal, using an aggressive or a sporting style, and follow the coach's strategy for outsmarting the opposing players. In an example from war, the battlefield moves are the tactics, the style might utilize crisis diplomacy versus force in the face of opposition, and the strategy is usually to win the war with as few casualties as possible. These three components are summarized in Table 4.2 for your reference as you read; they are explored in detail in the following text.

INDIVIDUAL CONFLICT TACTICS

When individuals respond to conflict, their tactics fall into three main categories: passive, aggressive, and/or assertive. *Passive responses* are used to disengage from a conflict, often resulting in conflict avoidance and relationship deterioration;

withdrawing from the conflict solves nothing unless it represents a "timeout" taken to cool down. *Aggressive tactics* use coercion to overcome an opponent. Aggressive tactics usually escalate a conflict so that it becomes a fight. Assertive tactics are most likely to result in problem resolution. Passive and aggressive tactics can also be combined in a *passive-aggressive response*, which is subtle resistance to others' requests or demands while avoiding direct expression. In passive-aggressive interactions, your words are contradicted by your actions, so you could be labeled manipulative. *Assertive responses* state a person's viewpoint without forcing the point.

John Gottman (2013) identified four specific tactics that are especially conducive to destructive conflict and inevitably damage a relationship:

- Defensiveness—You ward off an anticipated attack by portraying yourself as a victim through tactics such as denying responsibility, defensive countercomplaining, or justifying misbehavior. Defensiveness is a passive tactic, and usually results in one party feeling shut out, unheard, or misunderstood.

  Alternative: Listen carefully to what is being said, take responsibility for your part in creating a problem, agree on what you can while respectfully questioning points with which you disagree.
- Stonewalling—You disconnect from a conflict with icy distance and indifference, refusing to engage or respond. This is a passive aggressive tactic that often results in suffocation of the conflict and, possibly, of the relationship.

  Alternative: A temporary timeout can soothe heated feelings and permit participants to gather their thoughts before engaging in open discussion of the pertinent issues.
- Contempt—You use overt disrespect, communicated through such tactics as insults, scorn, or ridicule. This is a covertly aggressive tactic. It usually results in one person feeling humiliated while the other feels superior.

  Alternative: Contempt is never appropriate. If you truly disrespect the other person, try to adopt an attitude of curiosity at a minimum, or offer appreciation for what you can see as their strengths, then deal with the issues in conflict.
- Criticism—You attack the other person's personality or abilities with disapproval, judgment, or blame. This overtly aggressive tactic usually results in injury for at least one person, and it solves nothing.

  Alternative: Focus on troublesome behavior, not character or blame.

Several dialogue tactics can help arrest escalating fights: focus on the present rather than the past; emphasize similar goals rather than differences; adopt a "conciliatory set": assume the opponent is a friend and be a friend; and look for solutions in small steps rather than in one grand gesture (Price, 2012; Stuart, 2004).

FIVE STYLES OF CONFLICT RESPONSE

Conflict styles describe clusters of similar tactics that are repeated in different contexts. For example, if you repeatedly use tactics of shutting down and refusing to discuss anything or continue a conflict, you could be using an avoidant conflict style. A **conflict style** is a repeated, habitual way of relating to and interacting when in conflict. A combination of factors shape an individual's conflict style:

- temperament or genetics make some people more fiery, others more placid;
- family and social training about the "right" and "wrong" ways to deal with conflict;
- accumulated experiences of success or failure with conflicts; and
- personal choice.

The styles concept can be understood as the intersection of the following three dimensions:

Dimension 1. Degree of focus on the *problem and solution*—People who concentrate on problem issues are likely to assert specific positions or interests, and actively search for solutions to a conflict. People with high problem focus bring high energy to conflict, while people with low problem focus tend to consider the problem of little importance and show little interest in either the conflict or its resolution. This appears on the X axis of Figure 4.1.

Dimension 2. Degree of focus on the *relationship* with the other person—People with high relational focus cooperate to preserve or improve a relationship. People with low relational focus put little effort into maintaining a relationship. This appears on the Y axis of Figure 4.1.

Dimension 3. Degree of willingness to maintain active *engagement* in conflict—People who are engaged stay connected and remain involved until a solution is found. Disengaged people are more likely to passively accept someone else's solution, or detach themselves and walk away. This appears on the Z axis of Figure 4.1.

When combined visually, these three dimensions produce the approach that is strongly supported by scholars: the Five Conflict Styles Model.

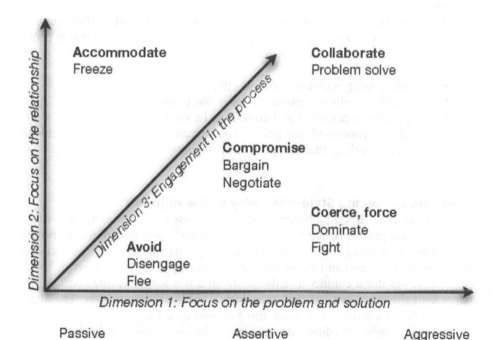

Figure 4.1 Five conflict styles model

Avoidant Style—"I Don't Want to Think about It"

The avoidant style is used to evade conflict. People put little effort into dealing with issues, too often overlooking problems and potential solutions. You also put little priority on a functioning relationship. A conflict in which both parties use avoidance often results in a *lose-lose solution* because neither party accomplishes their goals or has their needs met, and problems remain unsolved. Over time, avoidance tends to increase the tension in a relationship. Frustration with the disengaged relationship and continuing issues or problems is common. However, avoidance can be an effective style when:

- A period of cooling down and reflection will facilitate later conversation;
- Confrontation is too risky and there is too much to lose;
- An issue is not important to either party; it is easier to simply go your own ways; or
- Other people are addressing the issue and do not need support.

Accommodating Style—"Go Along to Get Along"

People who use accommodation rarely assert their needs or directly address problems. You do place a high value on a relationship, however, and often consider a problem that causes relationship tensions not worth tackling. Accommodators care about the opponent, but care less about the problem. Sometimes this style results in a *lose-win solution* because the accommodating person loses the chance to have their needs met, preferring to maintain the relationship and allow the opponent to win. An accommodating person is sometimes misjudged as weak or careless.

Accommodation is generally positive for a relationship because of the emphasis on the tactics of cooperation, giving in, and self-sacrifice, but it leaves problems poorly resolved. Accommodation can be quite useful when:

- The relationship is desirable and worth preserving;
- The problem really is important to only one party;
- The problem is perpetual and unlikely to be solved; or
- You change your mind, recognizing you've made a mistake or you're able to let go of something that was previously important.

Coercion, or Forcing Style—"My Way or the Highway"

The coercive style uses a high degree of assertiveness or, sometimes, aggression. You emphasize problems, assert your opinions or positions, and might use power over others to control the conflict discussion and its outcome. While focusing singly on the problems and solutions, the relationship might be neglected. Using coercion to resolve a conflict usually results in a *win-lose outcome* because one party wins the argument but the other party's needs are passed over. The argument can become stalled or develop into a contest of wills.

A coercive style risks direct, unpleasant escalation. You may begin by expressing frustration over the lack of problem resolution, but gradually become more coercive and demanding, and start using verbal and nonverbal aggression; in extreme cases, the frustration is expressed through physical violence like that reported in the Hatfields and McCoys situation.

Use of the forcing style is likely to incite resistance or counterforce. At best, the relationship can develop a chilling resentment that ultimately threatens its survival. However, force may be effective when:

- The consequences of doing nothing are unacceptable;
- There is a crisis or urgency to solve the problem;
- The issue has dire implications because of unethical or illegal misbehavior; or
- Strong beliefs or values are attached to the problem and its solution, affecting long-term consequences.

An important component of this style is interpersonal power, which is both expressed in and reinforced by coercion. Power or its interpersonal balance is not usually a problem in a functional, amiable relationship. However, in a distressed relationship power can become the prominent aggravating point (Ury, 1993). Parties to a conflict rarely have similar power; often, power is deeply skewed. For example, a partner in a violent domestic relationship may not be able to leave or to negotiate resolution because she and her children are financially dependent on the violent partner. How a conflict unfolds, how it is resolved (or not) is partially shaped by the distribution of power among the parties. When coercion is used to prove power over an opponent, it aggravates inequities and a power struggle can quickly eclipse any effort to solve a problem.

In a common dynamic of divergent conflict styles, a dyad of people who use force plus accommodation are amiable on the surface. The coercive person insists on their position and the accommodating person willingly gives in. Such a pair works hand-in-hand, with one person focused on the problem and its solution, and the other maintaining the cooperative relationship. This is not usually a sustainable balance, however. When the accommodating person stops pleasing and giving in, the forceful tactics begin to escalate, causing the relationship to deteriorate. The accommodating person might also resort to passive-aggression, which results in a similar clash of tactics.

Compromising Style—"Let's Negotiate"
People using a compromising style try to satisfy all parties through bargaining. You negotiate problems and tensions, then settle them by mutual concession. Compromise addresses the problems somewhat assertively, but also requires at least elementary cooperation. It can be viewed as an exchange; both parties relinquish and gain something to resolve the problem, and the relationship is preserved. Effective compromise requires that the bargain is reasonable, mutual, and consensual. It is reasonable to give up something that has little value to you if it is desirable to the opponent. If everyone is satisfied with the sacrifice-benefit equation, compromise can result in a *win-win solution*. However, if not mutual or consensual, a compromising style can result in a *lose-lose resolution*.

Compromise is often a successful style when:

- A relationship is desirable but somewhat impersonal and not deeply meaningful;
- There are mixed goals in the conflict, some negotiable and others nonnegotiable;
- Other creative efforts to resolve the conflict have stalled;
- The parties are locked in an impasse that deepens into hurting stalemate;
- Failure of both the problem resolution and the relationship could result;
- Efficiency is required; little time, energy, or commitment are available for problem processing.

Though common, compromise solutions are not ideal for several reasons. First, although a solution emerges, neither party is fully satisfied and their commitment to carry out the solution may falter half-heartedly. Second, a 50/50 compromise, though amiable on the surface, deals only with 50% of the problem and 50% of the relationship. Third, a compromise solution simply does not exist for many problems and conflicts. Examples include a choice between two cities or the decision to marry.

Collaborative Style—"We Can Work It Out"

Collaboration implies "co-laboring," working jointly and cooperatively to solve a problem. Significant effort is invested in solving a problem because the issue is important, but you remain engaged until a good solution is found and the relationship is supported and preserved. This style requires considerable investment of time and a high level of commitment, but the rewards in sustainable resolution are usually worth it. The nearly 150-year Hatfield-McCoy saga was finally concluded because of collaboration among the descendants in 2003.

Because the collaborative style invests in both the problem resolution and the relationship between the parties, it eventually leads to a *win-win solution*. Both parties are likely to be satisfied because you have been heard, your needs are met, and the problem is solved. The collaborative style is a both/and style: it is *both* cooperative *and* assertive; it *both* solves the problem *and* sustains the relationship; and it satisfies *both* parties' needs *and* their goals. Perhaps a good guideline in selecting a conflict style would be "When in doubt, collaborate." The one downside to collaborative problem solving is that it requires the most effort and time. It cannot be rushed, and the resolution may need to be revisited several times.

Collaboration is therefore effective when:

- It is important that all parties be satisfied.
- There is time to process the conflict.
- Everyone's full support is needed for the success of a solution.

See Praxis Skill Builder 4.1 for practical suggestions.

Each style is effective in some relationships and at some times. Most people use all of the styles, but one style predominates perhaps as much as 50% of the time. A skilled conflict resolver is able use all the conflict styles and knows under which circumstances each is likely to lead to resolution.

Praxis Skill Builder 4.1 ∎ Collaborative Partnering Strategies

Before a conflict begins:
- Affirm interdependency and the value of the relationship.
- Discuss constructive ways to process differences and tensions.
- Use methods that balance everyone's power, and use power cooperatively.
- Identify the risks of the conflict process and address them proactively.

During the conflict:
- Commit yourself to expressing your concerns openly, and to listening nondefensively to the other party's problems. Adopt a conciliatory approach in which you are ready to learn some new things about yourself, your opponent, and conflict.
- Share information in the forms of facts ("I know..."), feelings ("I feel..."), opinions ("I think..."), needs ("I need..."), and wants ("I want ...").
- Find a goal that benefits everyone.
- Emphasize present circumstances and issues rather than the past.
- Take small steps toward a solution.

Concluding the conflict:
- Expand your choices by considering many options.
- Experiment with potential solutions before making final decisions.
- Do not close dialogue prematurely; rather, summarize, acknowledge, and agree to change.

Joseph P. Folger, Marshall Scott Poole, and Randall K. Stuttman. 2020. *Working through Conflict.* 8th ed. Routledge.
Paul E. Wehr. 2019. *Conflict Regulation.* 2nd ed. Westview.

Although research continues, these five styles represent a good consensus among many experts in the field (Blake, 1970; Rahim, 1983; Ruble, 1976; Thomas, 1976; among others). That said, there is still significant debate in Conflict Resolution Studies concerning these ideas:

- Conflict styles are not permanent; they are learned and relearned. Most people use all the styles at some points, but do tend to use one more frequently than the others.
- Although the concept of a conflict style is helpful, it does not explain how specific tactics, style, or strategy are chosen or used.
- Style often depends on the context of a specific conflict. You might be quite aggressive in one relationship, using a coercive style, while in another relationship you use a collaborative or compromising approach.
- The same style and related tactics can have different impacts in different contexts and on different opponents.
- The style and its related tactics may change as a conflict evolves through phases of intensity.
- Generally, style is not consistently confirmed by observing behavior. Instead, self-reflection and self-report are the usual methods, and may reflect biased viewpoints.

Every conflict style is appropriate in some situations. Be aware of the differences and of your own habits before selecting one. Skill and flexibility in the uses of all the tactics and styles is an advantage during conflict. Let's turn next to an exploration of conflict strategies.

CONFLICT STRATEGY

A conflict **strategy** is a deliberated approach that a person uses to think through conflict issues and plan a response. The plan might be responsive, defensive, or offensive but strategy sometimes has the unnecessary connotation of manipulation. Strategies that accentuate negative tactics can nurture antagonism and escalate a conflict. Several considerations can improve the effectiveness of conflict strategy:

1. Anticipate the likely effect of an approach on your opponent or on the conflict. Could using a specific tactic or style provoke an unwanted response?
2. What could be the long-term consequences of choosing specific tactics or style? Recognize that some conflict behaviors have minimal consequences while others have serious ones and could prompt a turning point in a relationship.
3. Consider the potential effectiveness of a tactic or style to achieve a sustainable resolution. What could encourage all parties to remain involved, preserve the relationship, and solve the issue?
4. Evaluate the appropriateness of certain tactical and conflict style choices, and avoid unethical behaviors.

Individual Strategy

Crucial choice points occur during conflict that change the expression of feelings and attempts to influence others. Gottman (1993) identified three personal strategies.

- *Avoider*—Avoiders remain somewhat peripheral to the interactions, not engaging actively or readily expressing emotion. The strategy is to veil feelings, deal with the issues superficially, and not try to change the opponent. You invent multiple ways to minimize conflict, but you might be seen as passive or passive-aggressive. If conflict persists, avoiders tend to detach emotionally and reduce contact (Wang, 2012).
- *Volatiles*—Volatile individuals tend to be strong and passionate, even "in-your-face." The strategy includes feeling all emotions intensely and expressing them quickly and dramatically. You believe in change, so you exert and permit interpersonal influence. For volatiles, conflict is intense and features strong argumentation using forceful words or actions, so you might seem to others to be aggressive.
- *Validator*—Validators are relationally connected, communicating and acting out of a sense of "we." When in conflict, the strategy is to listen carefully before expressing your feelings or opinions. When validators do express themselves, it is usually respectful and assertive, but not insistent.

Five factors seem to influence the choice of an individual strategy (Kriesberg, 2020; Park, 2007): the parties' personal *characteristics*, the relationship *history* of the opponents, the immediate *responses* of each opponent, their *goals* for the conflict, and the *context* of the conflict. When a strategy has been selected, tactics then follow. For example, persuasion may be used to influence the opponent; rewards may be offered when something unfamiliar is requested; or threats and coercion could be used to stop an undesirable action.

Interactive Strategies

Some individual strategies can be used interpersonally to create effective combinations; other combinations increase friction during a conflict. There are two conflict-positive, deescalating combinations, and four conflict-negative, escalating combinations (Gottman, 1993).

Conflict deescalating combinations diminish the intensity of a conflict or minimize developing harm:

- *Two Validators*—This pair places a high value on relationship, and take the strategy of listening and accurately expressing your own needs and views. Conflict is not threatening, so differences are noticed, expressed, possibly even enjoyed.
- *Two Avoiders*—These parties are content with the state of the relationship, although outsiders might observe little depth or satisfaction. Both parties veil their emotions while affirming the relationship. Your strategy is to skip over conflict issues.

Conflict-escalation strategies broaden and intensify conflict interactions, which may increase the likelihood of harmful actions. Here are conflict-escalation combinations:

- *Two Volatiles*—This relationship is unusually intensely conflicted, and may not last through fiery encounters and fights. If the relationship endures, the interactions may take on a bickering form that other people find tedious.
- *Validator plus Avoider*—The validator pursues the partner, then feels shut out emotionally by the avoider. The avoider feels crowded and starts emotional flooding when conflict begins. This strategic combination rarely results in constructive dialogue.
- *Validator plus Volatile*—A validator feels overwhelmed by the volatile's expressiveness, as if on constant "combat duty." A volatile may perceive the validator as cold, disengaged, and distant. As they grow tired of trying to connect, the strategy of both leads to minimize communication.
- *Avoider plus Volatile*—The avoider fears that the volatile is inexplicably out of control, so their conflict strategy is to keep the opponent at a distance. The volatile feels underappreciated, unloved, and rejected even while pursuing resolution. This strategy also leads to diminished communication between the parties.

As the intensity of a conflict increases, actual conflict strategy is likely to change (Keashly, 1996), as illustrated in Table 4.3. When conflict is a latent mild

Table 4.3 Predictable Changes to Strategy as Conflict Escalates

Conflict Stage	Conflict Dynamic	Strategies Used
Stage I	Prelude	Shared problem solving, decision making, balanced gain
Stage II	Tension builds	Dialogue and compromise are the primary methods
Stage III	Confrontation	Win-lose, defensive tactics, competitive conflict
Stage IV	Conflict crisis	Lose-lose warfare, mutual destruction

Source: Based on Keashly, 1996.

disagreement, the conversation centers in balancing the gains through collaboration, shared decision making, and problem solving. As the tension builds, you focus the dialogue on problems, attempting to find acceptable compromises. When confrontation and more intense actions are added, you become defensive and possibly competitive, and the interaction tends to go in the direction of a win-lose outcome. The most intense conflict feels like a crisis to the participants, igniting aggressive tactics that are often hurtful and destructive, and might resemble lose-lose emotional warfare.

Collaborative Strategy

Collaborative strategies can be quite constructive in soothing rough relationships, solving problems, and making conflict processing productive. A **collaborative strategy** is, above all, adaptable. There are three reasons for this. First, because a single style or tactic does not succeed every time, using a broad repertoire of useful styles and tactics is advantageous. Second, communication adapts to behavioral strengths and skills, the roles of the participants, and the purposes of the conflict. Third, flexible responses adapt more realistically to dialogue than rigid ones.

It is important to choose among responses rather than using them automatically or thoughtlessly. When style and strategy match a specific conflict or opponent, the process is more likely to be constructive. Gottman (1993) noted that key resolution skills are focused on positive principles, which include underlying kindness, a generally optimistic attitude, and the ability to moderate heated feelings during conflict.

Processing conflict is energy consuming and it takes real commitment. You may judge that some issues and relationships do not merit the investment. In such cases, many people choose to simply walk away and drop the issue. The relationship might have been important at one time, but if previous attempts to deal with the problems have resulted in making matters worse, you are likely to gradually withdraw.

Decision Theory, a branch of philosophy related to Game Theory, is focused on the decisions people make and what factors they take into account as they do it. According to this theory, four factors play into conflict decisions: other people who have input or are impacted by the decision, the complexity of the problem, the timing and phase of a conflict, and projected outcomes with potential benefits or risks of failure (Steele, 2016).

Using Decision Theory, Paul Wehr (2019) outlined four central questions to ask when choosing conflict strategy. Those questions can be used to construct a decision tree, as seen in Skill Builder 4.2 and Figure 4.2.

Praxis Skill Builder 4.2 ▪ Questions to Help Develop a Strategy Decision Tree

After Paul E. Wehr (2019). *Conflict Regulation*. 2nd ed. Westview.

People
1. How important is the relationship to you? To the other party?
2. How important is the issue to you? To the other party?
3. Is the degree of trust critical to the outcome?

Problem
4. How complex is the problem? If highly complex, can it be reduced to manageable proportions?

Process
5. What is the degree of urgency? Is there time or other pressure?

Potential Outcomes
6. What are the possible risks and benefits of different decisions and choices?

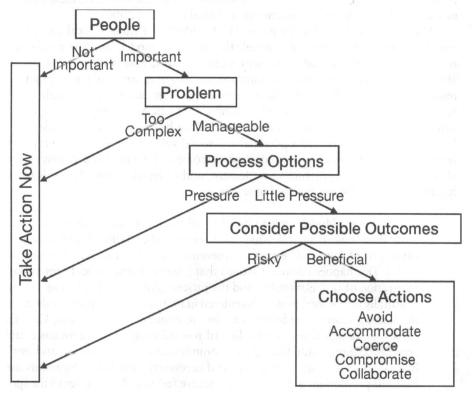

Figure 4.2 Questions to develop a strategy decision
Based on Paul E. Wehr, 2019.

The Influence of Diverse Identities on Conflict Tactics and Strategy

Knowing the significance of personal identities on behavior (also see Chapter 5), you could rightly expect that the choices people make while processing conflict are strongly influenced by factors like cultural background and gender standpoint. Some trends are being explored by many authors, with most findings focusing on behavioral styles more than on conflict process.

The Influence of Culture

Stella Ting-Toomey's early work (1985, 1991) analyzed the conflict styles of people in five countries along the associative-individualistic culture continuum. She found that people from traditionally *associative* cultures tended to be motivated to preserve relationship and positive face for their opponents (more than their own image), so they chose avoidance, accommodation, and collaboration more often than other styles (Gabrielldis, 1997). These results were later confirmed by Holt (2005), who also found problem solving in the associative repertoire.

People from *individualistic* cultures seemed more concerned to maintain their own positive image and interests, so tended to use confrontation, domination, and coercion (Brett, 2014).

These results were shown to be somewhat more complex in Brew's (2004) *intercultural* study. In that context, conflict styles were correlated more with relative status and crosscultural factors than with cultural background per se, and comparative power of the opponents determined their use of direct, higher-status or indirect, lower-status approaches (also found by Tyler, 2000).

Michel Kozan's productive paper (1997) identified three typical models of conflict process: the regulatory model, the harmony model, and the confrontational model. These **models** represent shared norms, assumptions, and beliefs about conflict that are used to interpret experiences and to guide practical responses. The models are in the background as disputants sift through issues to establish those that are essential and those that can be set aside as peripheral. Models tend to prescribe tactics and styles on the basis of what is considered to be appropriate (they represent personal and social values) and what is expected to be successful (they work toward a desired outcome). The models affect perception of what is a fair and constructive settlement, and of equal benefit. Kozan's work has been the base for much ongoing research.

- The *Harmony Model* tends to influence disputants from associative cultures more than those from individualistic backgrounds. Conflict is anticipated to cause loss of face and respect, so prevention is a central goal (Gabrielldis, 1997). This happens through actions that preserve harmony and prevent disintegration of the relationship and the process (Anedo, 2013; Leung, 2010). Culturally established protocols centered in mutual obligation and respect for the status hierarchy are believed to lead to constructive resolution. Conflict tactics are designed to smooth discord toward cooperation: avoidance and accommodation, with little direct communication of concerns, and with mutual needs reaching a compromise if necessary. Associative disputants use little self-promotion or disclosure of negative feelings. Parties defer to the spoken needs of the Other, or defer to a community elder or leader. Resolution is judged to be successful if relationships are sustainable in the long term.

- The *Confrontational Model* tends to be favored by disputants from individualistic cultures, and is mostly used in the West. This model corresponds with the Latin origins of the word "conflict," which is *conflictus* or a collision, fight, or contest (Oxford Latin Dictionary). Frustrated needs are seen as the primary cause of conflict, so processing is needs-based. The method emphasizes promoting relationship through problem solving, so conflict is viewed as an opportunity to "clear the air." Using this model, people forcefully pursue their own goals and interests and express the feelings associated with them. Tactics include directly expressing discontent and tension, engaging in actions that tend toward argumentation and confrontation, like assertiveness edging into aggression. Third-party intervention, if used, facilitates the parties coming to a reasonable compromise to meet their competing needs. Success tends to be measured in terms of shorter-term wins rather than long-term relationship.
- The *Regulatory Model* is a somewhat "legalistic" approach based on relationships ordered by stated rules and principles. Personal aspects such as emotions are viewed as less than legitimate determinants of agreement, so they are downplayed or ignored. Perception of the problem focuses on discordant priorities and rights. Conflict processing is grievance-based, emphasizing formal, "proper" methods used to minimize and avoid overt or escalating conflict. Disputants might begin with avoidant or competitive tactics, but then appeal to an authoritative third party who has the power to enforce agreed rules. Outcomes are judged to be successful if they adhere to the original principles and regulations (Haines, 2003) because rules are assumed to support long-term peace. A long-term relationship is a lesser goal.

The Influence of Gender

Holt (2005) used meta-analysis to summarize 36 research studies of diversity influences on conflict style by culture, gender, and organizational status. Although her results were somewhat complex, she reported that *females* are more likely than males to use compromise, regardless of culture; individualistic *males* are more likely than females to use coercion. These results are consistent with other research studies.

Research of this genre presents a number of interpretational difficulties. The described identities are unlikely to exist in any pure form, so their practical usefulness to any individual or conflict is questioned. Many scholars and others protest individaul freedom to be different from generalizations. Conflict is a fact that implies differences, even disagreement but, because perspectives differ, actual and perceived differences may not be identical. Conflict processing assumes an interactive process and is, therefore, dynamic and not likely to be predictable.

Some common denominators of process can be acknowledged. First, regardless of personal identities, people try to move toward secure connection and inclusion in others' lives. You tend to approach this need from an interdependent versus independent stance, placing emphasis on "our" versus "my" concerns, and this affects specific goals for the relationship and for conflict behavior. Second, people tend to imitate behavior in ambiguous or risky situations that result during conflict.

This means that you tend to match the actions of your opponent, and imitate actions you see in broader society. Third, most people desire an orderly resolution to their conflicts. All these factors are addressed by each of the models in different proportion.

Meanings and actions are related, so these common denominators are reflected in your efforts to promote peaceful resolution process and prevent escalation. That said, there are few constants or uniform patterns. Differences in conflict strategy result from variables within the situation and specific episode of conflict, influenced by individual choice. This frequently results in the perceptions or judgments of "inconsistent" conflict processing to people from alternative backgrounds.

The question for the field is how to understand differences in a practically useful way. As asserted by Kevin Avruch (1998) and others, conflict-resolution practices must find methods to deal with the intersection of diversity and difference.

In summary, in the context conflict-resolution processes, diversity factors do affect choices and events. A complex mix of personal and social influences interact to determine individual choices and process:

Personal Identity Influences

1. Gender;
2. Cultural background; and
3. Age.

Contextual Factors

4. Nature of the relationship between disputants—in particular, orientations toward interdependence or independence, and the power relationship and relative status;
5. Role in the relationship;
6. Social expectations and perception; and
7. Local, situational factors.

An obvious observation is that the conflict process is anything but static; rather, conflict is constantly, fluidly changing and follows identifiable process cycles that will be explored next.

PROCESS CYCLES

The dynamic steps through which a conflict progresses as it advances toward its outcome are called **process**. There are three basic conflict process forms: escalation, avoidance, and deescalation. None of these is exclusively destructive or constructive. All change dynamically according to the approaches of the parties or the point in the development of the conflict. A conflict becomes destructive when it is predominantly negative, when harmful tactics are not moderated, and when parties fail to reach satisfying resolution.

Escalation and the Malevolent Cycle

Escalation refers to an increase in the severity of the dynamics of a conflict. A conflict might escalate as a natural part of the conflict or it may be provoked by a *malignant catalyst* such as jealousy or a need for control (Maiese, 2003). For example, during a conflict, you might deliberately increase the use of provocative language because you fear you are losing the argument.

Malevolence is hostile ill will expressed through nastiness or spite. An *escalation cycle*, also called a *malevolent cycle*, occurs when you choose greater hostility and conflict intensity increases, issues proliferate, the number of involved parties multiplies—sometimes called "kitchen sink fighting" (e.g., Heaphy, 1999; Reiger, 1987) because everything except the kitchen sink is thrown in. This is the type of cycle that was recorded on the Hatfield-McCoy war ground. The tactics that fuel conflict escalation are patterned and predictable:

- Incompatibilities and differences are exaggerated and compounded.
- Negative communication is used with increasing frequency, breadth, and sharpness, while more positive feelings are diverted and veiled.
- Tactics with hurtful consequences are used with increasing frequency and less discrimination.

The cycle is both intrapersonal, involving a souring of attitude and amiability, and interpersonal, involving malevolent actions. The intrapersonal dimension is characterized by a **negative frame,** in which pessimistic perception and negative interpretation steadily add to the dispute. You anxiously inflate contrasts and emphasize negatives: ambiguous or neutral behaviors are reacted to as if they were negative, differences are emphasized and interpreted as resistance, and troublesome experiences are exaggerated in scope and consequences.

The negative frame fuels an interpersonal spiral of abrasive behaviors that initiate and justify defensiveness (such as poorly expressed emotion), and rude, hostile behavior or fight tactics (such as argumentativeness, contempt, threat). Reciprocating interpersonal attack-withdraw, pursue-flee, and domination-subordination result. The malevolent cycle is created by negative reciprocity. Some harmful tactics lead to others in an action-reaction cycle—spiteful words and Fight Talk and a coercive conflict style are reciprocated and intensified with retaliation. When aggression occurs, you increase defensiveness and indirect confrontation.

An escalating conflict is often difficult to regulate or solve, and sometimes spins out of control toward outright violence. When negative tactics are used by both parties, responsibility for harm is shared. Malicious behavior and hurtful communication erode the relationship and wear down your willingness to work toward resolving the problem, so sometimes people choose to go outside the conflicted relationship to seek allies.

The malevolent cycle cannot resolve conflict constructively for several reasons:

1. You become weary of great effort, experienced harm, and a lack of progress.
2. Problems and arguments remain unresolved, become amplified, and inevitably repeat.
3. The process creates artificial polarization and defensive coalitions.

Avoidance and the Damaging Chilling Cycle

Sometimes conflict adversaries are unable to tolerate escalating tensions. You escape, avoiding the discord, and protect yourself from arguments with detachment. This self-perpetuating *avoidant cycle*, also called the *chilling cycle*, progressively distances and cools a relationship. Obvious outcomes of an avoidant cycle are an ineffective relationship, unsolved problems and repeating arguments, and, often, a broken relationship.

There are many legitimate reasons, and many poor ones, that people avoid conflict or break off a relationship:

- You become convinced that your opponent cannot work through the conflict;
- You feel unskilled, especially compared with the opponent;
- You fear or have already experienced loss or harm; or
- You experience only the frustrating, unproductive possibilities of conflict, and none of the clarifying possibilities that could result.

The chilling cycle often results in the demise of the relationship because the underlying aim is to *not* deal with the issues. By the time a conflict reaches the point of chill, the intrapersonal dimensions are usually the central drivers of response strategies. At least one of the parties experiences diminishing warmth, feels hopeless, and believes that continued processing of differences is futile. You might decrease your attachment and commitment as you begin to think that better alternatives exist outside the relationship. You might experience significant anxiety about the other party's reactions, fearing loss or harm, and decrease engagement in the conflict or the relationship even further.

This underlying protective stance then plays out in conflict behavior. Communication decreases or uses more diversion and deception, thereby causing a reciprocating cycle of concealment (Afifi, 2010). The conditions for cooperative interaction are compromised, and self-centered behavior increases in place of relationship-centered, interdependent behavior.

Deescalation and the Constructive Benevolent Cycle

Deescalation is a decrease in severity that occurs when calming words and actions are used to limit the factors in active dispute. Deescalation can end up silencing the issues if the parties are frightened by intensity, but could also lead toward resolution by introducing more reasonable communication. Deescalating tactics are as follows (Deutsch, 1994):

- You take time and effort to reflectively analyze the conflict problems and process;
- You remain constructively engaged in the process;
- Conflict tactics are conciliatory, respectful, and inclusive;
- Negotiation is the primary method of conflict resolution;
- Communication is open and allows mutual listening;
- The tension of conflict is accepted as an opportunity to explore change; and
- Conflict dynamics are only moderately intense.

A *deescalation cycle* occurs when at least one party offers conciliation or friend-liness. A *benevolent cycle* is initiated by moves that soften tension and hostility, calm the interaction, and restore respectful behavior and true dialogue. Although deescalation does not eliminate the conflict or solve a problem, it does result in more manageable processing. Deescalation is causally linked to collaborative actions that can help you to be more cooperative and clearer as you communicate your con-cerns. The presence of onlookers may become a turning point toward deescalation because you are less likely to use hurtful tactics when witnesses are present.

If strategic deescalation occurs to calm a disagreement, the defusing process is quite different from avoidance or flight. Deescalation decreases the number of peo-ple involved in the conflict, fewer contentious issues are in active play, and an over-all lowering of the intensity of conflict happens. In those ways, this cycle can serve as a catalyst for improved interpersonal relationships as problems begin to be solved.

A deescalation cycle, even if used by a single party, can become a reciprocat-ing benevolent cycle through self-understanding; knowledge of each other's needs, wants, and interpretations, and achieving solutions to the precipitating problems. The attitude underlying a benevolent cycle is goodwill and respect, a **positive frame** that helps you to perceive and interpret both your opponent and the conflict in friendly terms. A respectful party can acknowledge and give attention to others' con-cerns and consider multiple viewpoints and interests. Prompted by a positive frame, benevolent actions assertively face and articulate problems until they are clear, per-sist in communication until everyone is heard, try to find common ground for agree-ment, and use conciliatory tactics. In addition to conflict resolution, this cycle can enhance learning and skills that can be applied to future relationships and conflicts.

Process Cycles Are Sequential
The work of Richard Walton (1969) suggests that, within limits, the escalation and deescalation cycles are both necessary and helpful in the process of conflict devel-opment and movement toward resolution. The cycles may occur out of sequence and may be repeated several times, but are still recognizable (see Figure 4.3).

According to Walton, escalation initiates a *differentiation phase*, during which differences become magnified. Differentiation can be unstable and disorganized as

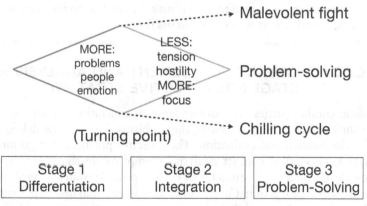

Figure 4.3 Process cycles in sequence
Based on Walton, 1969, public domain.

issues proliferate, new people become involved, emotions become heated and intensified, and peripheral factors become complicated. Although differentiation may seem poorly controlled, this phase has constructive purposes. Issues are clarified, and their importance is expressed. The increasingly intense engagement reinforces everyone's involvement and interdependence, solidifying your commitment to resolution.

The conflict typically reaches a crisis point of tension when it appears that no one is ready to give in. If this impasse is not resolved, it leads to a malevolent cycle of unrestrained conflict, or to an avoidant cycle. Walton notes that a *turning point* is reached when at least one party becomes aware of experiencing more harm than good, and recognizes that concessions are necessary to break the impasse. This party may also recognize the legitimacy of the opponent's argument. The turning point initiates more cooperation, which moves the conflict toward the next process phase. The greatest risk at this point is anxiety, which could cause withdrawal.

Walton calls deescalation the integration phase. During this stabilizing phase, emotions cool, issues are prioritized, and peripheral issues are set aside to concentrate on the central issue. Parties voluntarily calm their own tensions, moderate the heated feelings associated with differentiation, and become motivated to collaborate. When differences are fully aired and honored, problems can be managed (if not resolved), and the potential for a normalized relationship is restored. The actual issues of contention are then processed through conciliatory dialogue. The temptation during this third phase is to concede too quickly to preserve the relationship.

Rudolph Rummel (1991) observed that no relationships can remain static without stagnating; instead, conflict and peace phases repeat and cycle like a spiraling helix of relationship growth. He used the terms *conflict phase* to depict differentiating escalation, and *peace phase* to depict integration and deescalation. In Rummel's optimistic view, the conflict and peace cycles create opportunities for mutual understanding, learning new skill, and adjustment of tactics and strategies.

Think About and Discuss with Your Colleagues

- Although somewhat unpredictable, conflict does follow recognizable process cycles. Many factors contribute to the process, and cycles often occur in sequences that can facilitate problem solution. Use an illustration from your own experience to notice and discuss this.

PRACTICAL CONFLICT ASSESSMENT AND ANALYSIS SET THE STAGE FOR EFFECTIVE STRATEGY

Too often, conflict parties prematurely jump to conclusions or attempt trial-and-error solutions before fully reviewing the problems. You can use deliberate reflection for clarification and evaluation. The reflective practices that go into **conflict assessment**, also called **conflict analysis**, attempt to clearly define the problem, describe the dynamics of a conflict, and explore possible routes to resolution before taking any significant action. Careful analysis is an essential first step toward resolution that enhances the possibility of reaching a constructive, sustainable solution. In addition, it can serve as the prelude to effective consensus building (Susskind, 2009).

Assessment begins with observation, usually through simple active listening, or it may be conducted with more systematic interviewing. Observations are written or visually drawn to make the factors tangible. The gathered data is then synthesized carefully and used to design a strategy for processing the conflict. Conflict practitioners have developed a number of different methods for this reflective inquiry.

Conflict analysis can be organized with your familiar quadruple-P: identifying problems, people, process, and potential solutions. See Praxis Skill Builder 4.3 for some questions that guide your reflective assessment.

Praxis Skill Builder 4.3 ■ 4-P Conflict Assessment and Analysis Guide

Assessment and analysis skills and practices can give you a "big picture" of a conflict, and set the stage for planning an effective resolution strategy. The following questions can be a guide to that process.

People Factors
- Is this conflict primarily intrapersonal, interpersonal, or broader?
- Who are the parties involved, and what is their role? Are the parties primary, secondary, interested, or neutral?
- Are the disputants conscious of their interdependence?
- What tactics and styles have contributed to this conflict?
- What are the power relationships among the parties?

Problem Factors
- What facts are known? What facts are suggested, but unconfirmed?
- What needs are unsatisfied?
- What goals motivate this conflict?
- What positions and interests are expressed by the parties?
- What values do the parties support and defend?
- Are there hidden problem sources outside the immediate context?

Process Factors
- What were the triggering events? Within what context and relationship history did they occur?
- How did the problems emerge, develop, and proliferate?
- How far has the conflict progressed?
- How did the parties become polarized?
- What type of negative and positive cycles are evident as the conflict unfolds?

Potential Solutions
- What alternative possibilities exist for solving the problems?
- What internal or external factors could limit the conflict or inhibit its solution?
- Could intervention improve the dynamic or deteriorate and increase risk?
- What would conflict management be like? What would conflict resolution be like? What could conflict transformation be like?

For an example of detailed guidelines, see:
Department for International Development. 2002. Conducting Conflict Assessment: Guidance Notes. UK DFID.
http://www.conflictrecovery.org/bin/dfid-conflictassessmentguidance.pdf.

Think About and Discuss with Your Colleagues

- Even though the Hatfield-McCoy conflict was complicated, try to apply the 4-P conflict assessment guide to it. What more would you need to know to design a resolution process that would take less than 150 years?

PROCESS THEORIES USED IN ASSESSMENT AND ANALYSIS

A **theory** is a unified concept formed to explain observed facts and known principles. Theoretical ideas form the beginning of direction as you try to sort out a set of facts. Several process theories highlight specific aspects of the conflict process for attention, resulting in somewhat different analyses.

Systems Theory

Systems Theory provides one approach to the complexity of most conflict. There is no one theorist responsible for this approach; instead, it has many applications.

A **system** is a multilevel network of interacting elements that relate to one another. The elements can be parties, relationships, roles, events, process sequences, or even ideas. Conflict emerges within a whole system, shifting over time intricately and quickly, to produce chains of actions and reactions. **Systems analysis** acknowledges the role of individual decisions and actions in the development of conflict, but also plots the sequences of events, showing how one action results in reactions from others and identifying the impact of these events on the relationship network or system of conflict. It explicitly describes behavioral chains. Systems theory and systems analysis capture the relationships within the social network to represent how the system interacts as a whole. The central goal of the systems approach is discerning influences among the conflict elements to lead to conflict prevention, resolution, and shaping conflict development toward positively constructive outcomes (Gallo, 2012).

Social Field Theory

Kurt Lewin (1951) coined the term **Social Field Theory** to highlight the concept of a continuous dynamic in the relationship field that is similar to weather patterns: sometimes calm and sometimes turbulent. Interactions among intrapersonal and interpersonal factors create forces that influence the development of a *relationship climate*. The relationship climate (think of weather patterns like stormy and dark, or calm and bright) can influence the frame and direction of conflict events. Communication and interaction processes shift the climate of a conflict from friendly to hostile, or from placid to stormy, for example. Climate sets the background for positive or negative *critical incidents* that serve as catalysts for development of positive or negative frames. Examples of critically positive incidents could be kindness or apology offered; examples of critically negative incidents could be telling a lie or refusing to fulfill a promise. Together, communication, interactions, and critical incidents can become *helping forces* that facilitate conflict resolution, or *hindering forces* that block it.

Game Theory

Game Theory centers on the idea that rules govern relationships, just as rules shape the way games are played. Rules can subtly determine whether a conflict remains latent or emerges into the open. Axelrod (2006) noted that conflicts that are most beneficial are shaped by a strategy of reciprocal cooperation, guided by the following action rules:

1. Parties are reliably engaged, and do not shut down prematurely.
2. Parties use decision strategies rather than blind trust or suspicion.
3. A forgiving approach defaults toward cooperation.
4. Parties do not try to selfishly gain more than the opponent.

One goal of Game Theory is to discover the rules or ground rules that are shaping particular events and how they affect fighting behavior. Ground rules can be inferred from the "plays" or strategic moves made during conflict, especially as they progress toward cooperative or competitive conflict. **Explicit rules** are definite, specific, and agreed on by the parties to a conflict. "We don't swear at each other, no matter how bad we feel" might be an example of an explicit rule. **Implicit rules** are unspoken, but compliance is assumed. "If you expect to win an argument with your professor you don't point out her faults," for example. We are scarcely aware of implicit rules, but they have powerful effects on the nature of relating. Unfortunately, the primary way to discover implicit rules is to make mistakes and suffer the consequences, so they easily escalate a conflict.

People who perceive others' concerns as legitimate and within the rules are more likely to express their own concerns openly and cooperate in a conflict resolution process (Klein, 1996). According to Louis Kriesberg (2020), orderly adherence to rules is more likely when the following conditions are met:

1. The rules are explicit;
2. The rules are unambiguous and consistent;
3. The rules are fair to both opponents;
4. The rules are agreed by all parties;
5. There is significant social approval for compliance and criticism for violations;
6. Violations are evident to outsiders;
7. Following the rules in the past has helped in conflict situations; and
8. Parties anticipate utilizing the rules in the future.

When the ground rules are clear, fair, and consistently used, conflict is usually moderate. Conflict intensifies when parties are, in fact, "playing by different rules." A common dynamic occurs when one disputant's tactics are based on decent and respectful principles while the other party uses an "anything-goes" approach. This ensures that conflict will be difficult to moderate.

When the parties play by ambiguous or contrasting rules, the conflict will be chaotic, absurd, and maybe even dangerous. Consider a sports illustration: if one team is playing by the rules of American football and the opposing team plays by the rules of European soccer, the ridiculous game will make no sense to either team. The players are likely to run into each other and may even sustain injury. In her novel, *A Certain Justice*, P. D. James wrote of the relationship between Octavia Aldridge and Gary Asch. The problem was that Octavia and Gary were operating under different rules. Gary was secretly paid to initiate the relationship as an act of revenge for someone else, so he played a "tolerate-and-use-her" game. Octavia was playing the "bonding" game, and behaved in supportive, kind, and loving ways. Gary's appalling behavior only made sense when you understand that they were playing the relationship game by different rules.

Conflict rules are usually informal, subtly negotiated, and learned during a lifetime of conflict. They are also grounded in culture. People using typically Western rules are more likely to be open and assertive about their needs, opinions, and rights; in contrast, people using typically Eastern rules are more likely to suppress or yield their desires to those of the opponent or the group, expressing themselves only indirectly. Some situations operate by formal and explicitly agreed rules. For example, teachers, counselors, conflict mediators, and other professionals behave according to the rules described and limited by Codes of Conduct.

Military *rules of engagement* prescribe reasonable military force, identifying when, under what circumstances, against whom, and with what goals force may be used legitimately. Maneuvers considered acceptable in one situation may be unacceptable in another. In a shocking example, international military forces that attempted to intervene in Bosnia-Herzegovina in 1994 encountered the deadly consequences of dissonant rules. The North Atlantic Treaty Organization (NATO) rules applied to situations in which violence is not imminent; the UN peacekeeping rules applied to already violent situations. Many soldiers in the field, operating under both organizations and rules simultaneously, were confused by the contrasting NATO and UN rules of engagement. They were not always able to determine which set of rules applied, making them tragically unable to fulfill their responsibilities to protect civilians from harm. A high proportion of peacekeeping soldiers suffered from posttraumatic stress disorder following that conflict.

Another concept of Game Theory is the **game changer,** a single tactic or event that completely upsets an established system of relationship rules or assumptions, similar to Lewin's idea of critical incident. For better or for worse, relationships are never the same after such an upset. For example, cheating affairs can upset the balance of most committed relationships, and the parties are often unable to recover.

Although Game Theory cannot predict how or when conflicts will erupt, it has generated much data that is used to describe cooperative behavior, the spread of information and resources within relationship networks, and conflict moves and countermoves.

CONSTRUCTIVE, COLLABORATIVE PROCESS LEADS TO SUSTAINABLE CONFLICT RESOLUTION

Conflict solutions are sustainable when they have three qualities:

1. The problem has been addressed in ways that are reasonably satisfactory to all parties.
2. The relationship is preserved or, even better, may be stronger with improved communication and trust.
3. No one has withdrawn from the relationship.

Although a constructive process can begin with one party's conciliatory actions, it requires the eventual cooperation of all parties. You have to be committed, or recommitted, to the relationship and to the task of resolving the problems. Parties in constructive conflict operate with six crucial practical skills (Deutsch, 2014):

- You can describe your own viewpoint, and know that others may differ.
- You are able to acknowledge that you need each other, and feel equally valuable.
- The conflict is expressed through respectful dialogue.
- Substantive issues are reframed to be workable and solvable rather than confrontational or perpetual.
- Conflict tactics are flexible, exploring a variety of ways to express yourself.
- You are willing to work toward resolution, even though it may not be the easiest way.

When parties engage with these skills, communication is more likely to be mutual, accuracy increases, interactions are more amicable, multiple interpretations can be considered, dynamics are explained in generous ways, and an optimistic attitude toward the conflict is maintained.

CHAPTER SUMMARY AND STUDY GUIDE

- Cooperative conflict is friendly conflict between parties who share the same goals for resolution. Competitive conflict is hostile conflict in which parties aim toward forcing a solution and defeating each other.
- Tactics are the specific actions used during conflict that logically move a conflict process in the direction of cooperation or fighting.
- The Five Styles Model describes five clusters of responses to conflict: avoidance, accommodation, coercion, compromise, and collaboration. These five conflict styles are mainly distinguished by their emphasis on solving the problem or on preserving and improving the relationship itself.
- Both individual and reciprocating strategies are influential in the unfolding of a conflict process and in its disposition and outcome.
- Most conflicts occur in recurring process cycles: the escalation or malevolent cycle clarifies multiple issues in contention, but with increasing intensity; the avoidant or chilling cycle is characterized by withdrawal from the conflict or even the relationship; during the deescalation cycle the conflict becomes more moderate and reasonable, which helps parties to create a workable solution. These cycles occur somewhat sequentially.
- Quadruple-P conflict assessment is a systematic method for analysis of the Problem, People, and Process factors. The main goal of conflict analysis is to facilitate a process for envisioning effective Potential Solutions.
- Process Theories such as Systems Theory, Social Field Theory, and Game Theory help explain the complex processes that conflicts seem to follow.

- Skills for building collaboration are essential to finding sustainable resolution that keeps parties relating with each other, satisfactorily addresses the problem, and preserves or improves the relationship.

TERMS IN FOCUS

SECTION II
Groups in Conflict

5

Diversity Studies, Intersectionality, and Conflict

■ ■ ■

In Focus in This Chapter:

- ■ You encounter a diversity of identities like race, gender, socioeconomic status (SES), religion, and culture every day, in every situation. Diversity can be the source of positive connections and creativity, or can be the base for deep injustice and conflict when diversity is associated with unfair conduct.
- ■ Intersectionality explores personal and social identity factors and their intersections. This forms a complex body of inquiry that helps decode complex intrapersonal, interpersonal, social, and even global systems and conflicts.
- ■ Culture affects your life inescapably, but nearly invisibly. There are three primary layers to cultural identities: visible actions, invisible ways that relationships are operated, and invisible beliefs and values.
- ■ Race seems personally and socially important, but many of our concepts of race and many interracial interactions are influenced by assumptions not based in fact.
- ■ Gender is a factor of deep interest to most people and to conflict studies, but much remains unclear. Misleading beliefs about gender profoundly affect your relationships and conflicts.
- ■ Religion includes traditional practices, rules and expectations, and deep beliefs about the spiritual life. Although it can be a binding influence, it is also the impetus for some of the most intractable conflicts.
- ■ Socioeconomic status is usually not chosen, but has immense implications for quality of life.
- ■ Conflict, conciliation, and harmonious relationships demand diversity-sensitive tolerance that promotes equality, equity, and inclusion of all, regardless of intersected identities.

CONFLICT CASE 5.1 ■ DR. KENNETH HARDY AND THE POLICE

When Kenneth Hardy was 29 years old, he had a PhD in family therapy and was working as a therapist and the deputy director of the American Association of Marriage and Family Therapy. He was a middle-class black man with a polished manner, and economically privileged with a thriving professional career.

While riding his motorcycle on his way to watch a basketball game, he was stopped by a police officer for a traffic violation. When the officer looked at Hardy's license, he scolded, "Says here you're supposed to be wearing glasses."

Hardy replied, "I'm wearing contacts, sir."

"Okay, you're gonna have to show me—pop one out."

Hardy objected, "That would be difficult. My hands are filthy and I wouldn't be able to put it back in."

With a low, tight voice, the officer demanded, "Take the *!* contact out." Hoping to avoid antagonizing him, Hardy removed the contact.

"Where's your owner's card?" the officer snapped.

Hardy admitted, "I was in a hurry and forgot to take it out of my car."

"That's a good one. Nice try, boy." The officer spoke on his radio. Within minutes a tow truck pulled up. "Put that bike on the truck, boy. We'll see who owns that cycle. Do you hear me, boy? I said put the *!* bike on the truck!"

Frightened, but trying to salvage his dignity, Hardy responded, "You know my name, sir, it's on my driver's license. Until you call me by my name, I'm not answering any more."

The officer laughed. "That a fact, boy?" He jabbed Hardy in the nose with a series of hard punches, causing a nosebleed, then used his radio again. Suddenly, tires screeched, lights flashed, and five more officers jumped out of patrol cars. "Now you're gonna behave, boy" smirked the officer.

A crowd gathered. An elderly woman shook her head and asked no one in particular, "Why do these police have to be so nasty? " Something snapped in Hardy and he said, loudly and clearly, "I understand why, ma'am. You see, they find these fragile men, give them a badge and a gun and, suddenly, they become supermen overnight."

Silence ... staring. The officer said with a crooked smile, "I get it. You're one of those smart-assed niggers." Grabbing Hardy by the neck, he threw him on the patrol car hood and handcuffed his hands behind his back. With nightsticks, he and another officer beat Hardy on his neck, back, and thighs while the other officers laughed. Bloody and unconscious, Hardy was shoved into the patrol car, arrested for disorderly conduct, disturbing the peace, and making terrorist threats against a police officer, fingerprinted, and jailed overnight. He felt utterly degraded and powerless, invisible, voiceless. His father advised him, "You're naive if you think you'll get a fair trial, son. Keep yourself safe and alive. Admit to something, plea bargain and get your sentence reduced to probation." Hardy pled not guilty.

For 18 months, he waited with anxiety and dread. At trial he was found not guilty of all charges. In the meantime, he began to explore the ways society had robbed him of his voice and benefited from his silence, how stunted and warped he had become, and what he could do to recover his voice and sense of Self. He discovered a growing desire to work with larger social forces of racism, sexism, homophobia, and poverty that silence and dehumanize many people. He committed himself to help transform not only individual pain but also to make visible the larger conditions of separateness, misunderstanding, and hate that aggravate hurt and voicelessness (Hardy, 2001).

This is a horrifying story of clashing identities that, sadly, is not uncommon. Dr. Hardy and the police officers approached their lives from worldviews with incompatible assumptions and expectations. The resulting conflict turned into an awful interracial struggle that diminished every person. This chapter explores **diversity** describing the qualities that define fundamental differences among people. Those differences are enjoyable, expansive, and creative in many situations but, when understanding breaks down, navigating a path through diversity can be tricky (LeBaron, 2003a). Ideally, conflict need not happen but, bluntly put, it does. In this chapter, you are challenged to explore worldview identities and find the heart of tolerance.

As you read, think about these questions:

- How is diversity defined, analyzed, and understood?
- What are potential sources of diversity?
- How can diversity be a source both of creativity and conflict?
- What do social and cultural systems contribute to identity conflict?
- What can be done to improve appropriate ways of managing diversity?

Kimberle Williams Crenshaw is an American civil rights lawyer and law professor specializing in gender and race issues. She introduced and is still developing the **Theory of Intersectionality** (1994), which explores individual and social identities, and social and political systems as they relate to domination, subordination, and discrimination.

Dr. Crenshaw's insight is that personal and social identities develop from multiple sources, woven together like a fabric. Crenshaw's work advocates for equal recognition of identities, racial justice, and fair law enforcement. She believes that any threat to opportunity should be met actively with just correctives that improve social justice. When sources of disadvantage (for example, vulnerability to violent assault and poor health) are addressed separately, the resulting conclusions and policies unjustly overlook the complex experiences of actual people who experience compounded discrimination (for example, an immigrant woman who is poor because of underemployment). "Antidiscrimination law looks at [identities] separately. The consequence of that is when African American women or any other women of color experience compound discrimination, the law initially is not there to come to their defence" (London School of Economics lecture, April 26, 2014).

The central concern of diversity and intersectional studies is justice for everyone, sustained by circumstances that are right, fair, and reasonable. Fair justice making supports equity, equality, and inclusion, regardless of identity. This is a field of popular interest in the globalizing world. It is also of great interest to conflict scholars because diversity studies inform many other fields such as social services, history, human rights, international relations, and global affairs.

DIVERSITY STUDIES, CONCEPTS, AND TERMS

The concept of **diversity** condenses the many qualities that define personal differences. Diversity has multiple sources that are mostly invisible. It is always present, but frames every action, relationship, and belief. Individual identities are diversified to include a mix of ethnic and family background, age, gender, status

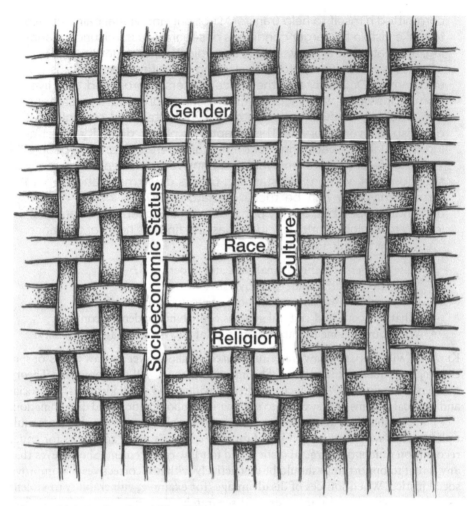

Figure 5.1 Intersectional identities
Jan Redekop, used with permission.

in society, and so on. A diverse group is one that incorporates an assortment of many qualities. This can be enriching when the mix adds new perspectives, creativity, and practical options. However, diversity can also consume time and effort due to discomfort with unfamiliar viewpoints and tangled communication patterns, so collaboration can be awkward.

Intersectionality highlights the fact that no person is entirely defined by one personal quality, as illustrated by Figure 5.1. No one is solely "black" or "disabled" or "rich," so singular descriptors become useless when trying to understand someone. Rather, each individual's background forms an intersection of interlocking qualities that shape complex identity at one point in time such as "gay white student," "Filipino female peace officer," "homeless male army veteran," and so forth (McCall, 2005). That intersection forms a unique combination of identities, privilege, and disadvantage in different contexts, so people experience shifting status and power: they are honored and "somebody" in one context and belittled as "nobody" in another. This shapes accumulated experiences of justice and injustice.

Concepts of intersectionality are by no means universally accepted (Nash, 2008). There is considerable scholarly debate concerning intersectional studies, the scope and value of the concept as it affects real life, and decision making based on intersectional principles (Cho, 2013; Collins, 2016).

Diversity Studies explores social diversity and its influence on relationships and culture. Diversity analysis attempts to improve ways of using identities to enrich our self-understandings, knowledge, and work. Interests in this field include any source of diversity associated with inequality like differences of gender and sexuality, age, race, religion, ethnicity, culture, beliefs and values, and national origin. It is a challenging study because biased ideas, long assumed to be fact, and subconscious discrimination are confronted. It is particularly important because if diversity is not respected then most efforts to resolve identity-based conflict will falter.

The complex experiences at the intersection determine your **standpoint**, which is your unique perspective for viewing the world and gathering knowledge. Aspects of standpoint are partially shared with other members of a similar group (for example, among females or people of color) but because standpoint is multifaceted each one is unique.

A **worldview** is a mental model of the world based in a particular standpoint. It is a starting point that you use to explain experiences, assume causation, anticipate the future, and determine a course of action (Aerts, 1994). Worldview affects what you hear and understand, what experiences you consider relevant, and what conclusions you think are persuasive and true or false (LeBaron, 2003). Core worldview beliefs are often deeply rooted and are best understood through crisis. Like Ken Hardy, when confronted with an experience that does not comfortably fit into your existing worldview, your choice is to overlook the experience or to alter your worldview to incorporate the odd experience.

Michelle LeBaron (2003) linked worldview with conflict:

- Though susceptible to deep conflict, worldviews can also be the starting point from which shared new meanings and values emerge.
- Communication that overlooks differences of worldview and values will fumble.
- If conflict opponents' worldviews are fundamentally different, incongruent deep values can fuel division and conflict.
- Subconscious worldviews may be imposed by strong disputants or conflict "winners," destroying some peoples' foundations of living.
- Sustainable conflict resolution demands some attention to worldview diversity.

Social identity is an assembled mosaic of characteristics—gender and sexuality, age, race, culture, religion, SES, dis/ability, for example—that denote group affiliation. Identity is socialized, which means it is learned within a social context. This concept suggests that if you want the approval of your social group, so you learn proper behavior that will ensure approval, and that includes adopting beliefs about diverse identities. The expectations transmitted during upbringing are powerful influences on your behavior and beliefs, and they direct people toward social positions.

Socialization, also called **social learning**, is lifelong learning of the norms and standards for behavior, relationships, and attitudes necessary to act appropriately in society. For example, conflict behavior is learned through direct teaching, imitating respected models, selective approval or disapproval, as well as ongoing experimentation and practice. A **social norm** is a standard behavior expectation that defines and controls actions viewed as "normal." Nonconforming patterns are disapproved and regarded as inappropriate. Norms tend to be subconscious and unspoken, but powerfully demanding. *Descriptive norms* refer to ideas about what people should do to fulfill expectations. *Prescriptive norms* refer to what you believe people must do if you want to remain a member of a group. *Proscriptive norms* are beliefs about what people must not do; otherwise, they are labelled as "abnormal."

Bobbie Harro's (2018) analysis resulted in her description of the **Cycle of Socialization** [of Injustice], shown in Figure 5.2. The *first* socializing force is the

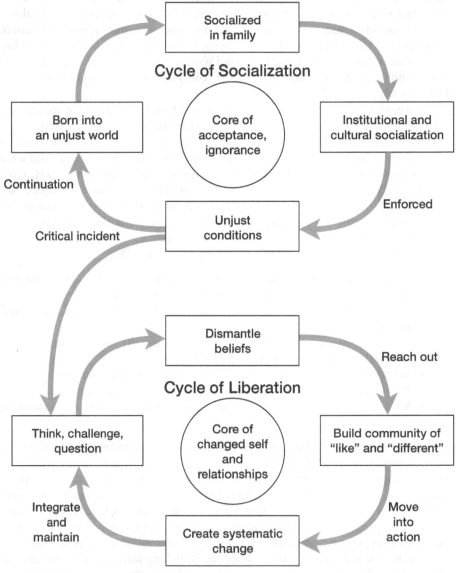

Figure 5.2 Cycles of socialization
Based on Harro, 2018, public domain.

world of your birth, set in history, habits, and biases. *Second*, the family teaches you to accept defined roles and obey conventional rules that sketch your self-concept, perception of Others, and values. *Third*, within a broader community environment you experience and observe innumerable lessons about privilege and limits, and who holds what power (Crenshaw, 1994). *Next*, conformity, testing, and defiance are selectively rewarded and corrected with mainstream rules. These steps lead toward an *outcome* that reinforces structures of privilege and power, sustaining groups in leadership with control while disadvantaging others (Butler, 2016; Crenshaw, 1994; Farmer, 2003).

Socialization occurs on all sides in your environment; it is consistently patterned, is predictable, and perpetuates the rules. If you accept an unjust outcome, the cycle continues. Hope of changing the cycle lies in questioning and challenging the existing system, but this brings with it both serious resistance and immeasurable justice. This tension is illustrated by Ken Hardy's break from his compliant heritage to become an active peacebuilder.

Notes about Intersectional Terms, Definitions, and Concepts

When asked to define "time" in 400 CE, Augustine said, "What, then, is time? If no one asks me, I know; if I try to explain it to someone who asks, I do not know." This depiction shows parallels in deeply meaningful concepts like race, gender, and culture. Definitions of most concepts addressed by Diversity Studies are familiar if no one asks, but are ambiguous and debated.

When exploring intersectionality and conflict, there are many obstacles to clear thinking:

- This is an area that is personally challenging. Untangling the layers of actual knowledge alongside natural blindness and learned bias can be unsettling, even resulting in shame.
- Memories and perception are shaped by your own multiple identities. Having always lived in and experienced society from your specific standpoint, you have a subjective worldview. Accumulated identity-related experiences inevitably influence expectations of yourself and of others.
- Scientific evidence is often at odds with popular assumptions. For example, most people would say that behaviors are distinct for the genders or social classes. When in conflict, their comfort varies, feelings differ, behavioral tactics contrast, you anticipate different degrees of success or failure in resolving conflicts, and so on. However, scientific evidence does not confirm these common personal conclusions. It might surprise you to learn that actual individual differences in conflict behavior are, in fact, almost random.
- Scientific evidence is mixed and inconsistent. Intersectional research tends to be theoretical, and there is little consistent correlation with practical conflict resolution. Theories and studies are emerging, but findings are at best complementary and at times contradictory. Even metastudies report mixed and contradictory results.
- Another dimension of complexity results from the tendency to polarize intersectional issues. You would be hard-pressed to find a person who has no opinion on the issues, and most beliefs are tested and strong. Most peoples' opinions, including many scholars, are linked to predetermined conclusions.

- An important factor when exploring diversity and conflict is that inequities and injustices have been and are experienced every day. Many disappointments are encountered despite the best efforts of justice makers. For example, the 20th-century civil rights turmoil in the United States may seem to have made little actual progress in the plight of marginal people.

DIVERSITY, POWER, AND PRIVILEGE

Power is found in the freedom to accomplish a particular goal by choice or by directing other peoples' actions. Power inequities of dissimilar social groups (for example, management vs. employees) create differences in personal power that represent a microcosm of larger systems of rank and privilege (for example, the "mainstream" vs. the "margins" of society).

Systems of power intersect in what Patricia Hill Collins (2016) variously called the **matrix of privilege**, the *matrix of domination*, and the *matrix of oppression*. **Privilege** is an unearned right or advantage that is granted to a particular person or group. The matrix of privilege refers to a web of "big seven" sources of privilege and power in Western society: gender (male) and sexual orientation (heterosexual), race (white), culture (mainstream), religion (Christian), and SES (wealth and education). This is complex: although many people enjoy multiple forms of privilege, not all are powerful; although many people cope with multiple forms of marginalization, not all are left powerless.

Privilege and power are neutral facts. The matrix of privilege causes trouble because of **normativity** assumptions that specific qualities are a valid baseline for comparing everyone. When norms are assumed as if they are facts, behavior and relationships are affected. For example, the normative assumption behind the English use of the patriarchal term "man" to refer to humanity, both male and female, was that masculinity was the peak of normal and femininity was a lesser, weaker form. Therefore, it became the duty and privilege of more powerful males to dominate and protect members of the "weaker sex."

According to Evelyn Young (2011), there are four degrees of conscious action:

- some people are conscious of their privilege and power and use it to improve equity;
- some understand the concept of power, but are blind to the personal benefits of privilege;
- some people consciously deny power and privilege and therefore unintentionally put others down; and
- some people intentionally take advantage of their power and privilege.

Entitlement is the attitude that "I am, or we are, better than other people, and therefore deserve special treatment." Such assumptions result in voicelessness for the powerless, called **muted voice** by Shirley Ardener and Edwin Ardener (2005; Wood, 2017). Recall Ken Hardy's experience of being silenced and invisible. The voice and the expectations of a dominant group (for example, men) mute the needs and voices of a marginalized group (for example, women).

Cultural issues are relevant here, too. In associative cultures (where group cohesion is more valued than individual ambition), privilege and power tend to be inherited from or granted by the holders of power. Relationships are viewed within a hierarchy that is exerted indirectly. In individualistic cultures (where individual identity is valued), power and authority may be earned by anyone, everyone's opinion matters, and power is more directly expressed (Ting-Toomey, 2011).

The key to effective power is using it with consent and with respect. Power and privilege are abused when they are used nonconsensually or disrespectfully, to benefit someone exclusively, or to intimidate someone. Conflict arises from privilege when it unfairly stratifies people, imposing social levels (strata) that enforce domination-submission pecking orders. The reality is that many people experience intimidation and injustice every day. Power used in abusive ways can be expected to result in resistant protest at best, and violent conflict at worst.

It might be obvious that conflict involving intersectional identities takes generations of development and reinforcement; working through and managing such identity conflicts may take an equally long time. Entrenchment of these problems occurs at the individual level, among groups, and as part of whole societies.

THE ROOTS OF IDENTITY CONFLICT

Diversity studies acknowledges that some differences of behavioral style are desirable and beneficial, and should be cultivated in a thriving society. Conflict results when unfair use is made of differences, or when diversity is suppressed. Now that we have defined some central concepts, let's look at how they translate into deep identity conflict.

Think About and Discuss with Your Colleagues

- Investigate a recent example of serious identity conflict such as the ongoing plight of the Rohingya people of Myanmar (Council on Foreign Relations, 2021), or the conflict in Sri Lanka in 2020 (Anandakugan, 2020). What was the actual basis for the conflict? What factors would you distinguish as the root causes? Can you think of better policies or practices that might have prevented a conflict of that nature?

---

1. Miscommunication
   Ambiguous perception and incorrect interpretation are very common as people communicate intersectionally. This is particularly true when communication is deeper than task related, and in undertones of tension or emotion.

2. Nonconformity to Dominant Norms
   Norms are behavior patterns, like "scripts," used as you function in relationships. Conflict often arises when you behave in ways that do not conform to your visible group membership. Social norms constantly (but slowly) evolve, often in response to conflict, so there is a global trend toward more equitable attitudes. One example of this is the roles expected of military personnel. Fifty years ago, soldiers were expected to be impervious to pain and emotion; today, soldiers are taught multiple skills and roles that require emotional intelligence, including negotiation, diplomacy, and peacekeeping.

3. Construction of "the Other"

The Other is a term that refers to another person who is obviously different from yourself. Otherness is subjective, and is perceived in contrast to what is familiar, expected, and socially common. **Othering,** or the **construction of the Other,** describes the process of defining and reducing another person's identity to labels. This process is inherently dehumanizing because personal and interpersonal sameness and difference are manipulated (Dervin, 2012) to form an inferior label that reinforces the view that the Other does not properly fit. The process essentially constructs an us–them *enemy.*

The escalating dynamics of Othering are deeply embedded in relationships as follows.

Categorization of Identities Leads to Stereotyping
You tend to perceive identities in similar/different dichotomies, with one quality in contrast to another (Bauman, 1996). "I am like X," "I am different from Y," "I would not want to be like Z." A primary line of division is **foreignness,** which is a subjective sense of resemblance versus strange or alien. You tend to presume that those who resemble you are safe because they think the same way you do, while those who are foreign are threats. These categories are subconscious and subjectively based on inexact criteria, but they create a false "us–them" contrast. This is the foundation of **xenophobia,** which is fear and distrust of the Other. For example, many people do not want to think about the unknown homeless in society, and respond with disdain and fear.

You categorize for several reasons:

- Categories are simple. They provide ready information (only partially accurate) that reduces the need to discern and decide how to behave with someone else.
- Categories provide shortcut explanations that help you make sense of confusing or ambiguous behavior. Categorization classifies unfamiliar people, helping interpret their behavior and reduce ambiguity.
- Categories become a source of bonding and boundary keeping within a social context—"us" against "them." By sharing labels with other members of a group, and these labels are taught to inexperienced members.

However, as with most generalizations, some people fit a category some of the time, but many do not. For example, many stories can be found of compassion and generosity within homeless communities. You also tend to be affected by a confirmation bias, which means that you pay attention to factors in the Other that confirm your existing category assumptions while overlooking observations that challenge them. A **stereotype** is a simplistic perception of the Other that labels someone merely as a member of a class while obscuring personality and dignity; for example, associating dog ownership with good character, or athleticism with low intelligence. Stereotypes affect both group functioning and individual belief systems (Tajfel, 1981). Stereotypes lead to the amplification of the goodness and worth of people similar to you, and exaggeration of the perceived faults of those foreign to you.

Recall, for instance, the police officers apparent perception of Ken Hardy. When judgment inflates foreignness, individuality is obscured. Though common, stereotypes are starkly incomplete and inaccurate, and they become a "culture trap" (Claes, 1999). Stereotypes can lead to stratification and are used to justify actions that oppress or exclude.

> *If something is perceived as real, it becomes real in its consequences.*
> —W. I. Thomas, 1928

Stratification Arbitrarily Assigns Worth

Stratification describes the organization of individuals into hierarchical social divisions (strata) of society. These can strongly shape the status and opportunities of individuals within those strata. Historical prestige assigns "higher/superior" power and status or "lesser/inferior" value to particular categories. Only some groups have prestige, creating a distribution of privilege and power that benefits some and harms others. The strata are observable across the globe, but are even more starkly evident during times of conflict and war.

Stratification means that most apparent differences are related to assigned status, creating a limiting, harmful system of privilege and power. Stratification is based on disrespectfully normative **ethnocentrism**, which compares the Other against the standards and customs of your own group. For example, Aboriginal peoples across the world were labeled for generations as "savages" because their cultures were different from the colonizers, and they were judged to be inferior. Stratification is linked both to ignorance and to condescending entitlement (Adams, 2018; Harro, 2018). Stratification is the pretext that leads to deeper prejudice. It can be the base of escalating hostile attitudes such as "they're taking our jobs" and "they're all terrorists."

Prejudice Leads to Dislike

Prejudice means, literally, prejudged. You judge the Other unfavorably. based on unfounded assumptions about a group rather than on actual experience. Several components contribute to the content of prejudice (Allport, 1979):

- assumptions learned from an affiliation group, plus
- inaccurate or incomplete information, plus
- negative and hostile feelings, and
- beliefs that have no factual foundation.

Prejudice provides a "reason" to dislike the Other, going beyond ignorance to maintain blindness by resisting factual information (Allport, 1979). In addition, Harro (2018) noted that this unfair attitude affects social institutions of education, the economy, health care, and so forth (also, Farmer, 2003). Prejudice leads to discrimination and a vicious cycle of marginalization.

Discriminatory Actions Intensify Disadvantage

Discrimination expresses prejudicial attitudes in action, creating unjust exclusion and exploitation of the Other. Discrimination expresses structural violence and systemic cultural violence, described by Johan Galtung (1969, see Chapter 8).

Inequality becomes embedded and is supported by unjust and inaccurate belief systems that invalidate some groups.

Gordon Allport (1979) described the acceleration of discriminatory actions. The mildest expression is *verbal*, indirectly through "joking ridicule" or directly through name-calling and devaluing insults. The construction of the Other then leads to literal *avoidance and separation*. As discrimination spreads, it is sanctioned through formal *regulations and legislation*. This then opens the way for *violence* against people and their property. A dreadful example of this occurred with the policies of apartheid in South Africa that restricted "colored people" (blacks and Indians) from opportunities for employment and housing, and their rights to vote, engage in business contracts, bring lawsuits, and intermarry. The most severe discrimination involves systematic attempts to destroy a group through various forms of *genocide*.

Discrimination formalizes in the law results in multiple marginality and injustice for groups judged to be inferior. Members of the group may be displaced and ghettoized to specific territories, like "the other sides of the tracks." They are economically marginalized through educational disparities, and restricted to low-skill, entry-level jobs, and inadequate living wages. Socially costly discrimination results in precarious family and community structures. Political marginalization limits equal access to power and decision making.

When privilege is restricted to some groups, suffering is experienced by disenfranchised groups. The implications of discrimination are enormous, and whole communities absorb the misfortune. The lives of both the excluded margins and the privileged are negatively affected.

Extremist Attitudes Aggravate Otherness

Extremism is defined inconsistently (Berger, 2018), often contrasted to mainstream norms and used simply to label and divide. To an insider an extremist may be a "freedom fighter"; to an outsider an extremist might be a "terrorist." Even among scholars, the meanings are inconsistent. Simply, **extremism** is fanaticism, holding extreme beliefs. Examples in political discussion today include *jihadism* (a struggle against the enemies of Islam) and white nationalism (support for an independent white nation that excludes other skin colors). Simply defined, "extremists are extreme," so the term inadequately unifies a vast spectrum of ideas and practices that range from mild curiosity through a lifestyle molded by fanatical views (George, 1992). Religious scripture and language might be used to justify negative attitudes, but actions that are forbidden to some extremists are moral obligations for others (for example, honor killing). Extremists often (but not always) advocate militant action to broadcast their views, and a few resort to violence. Processes that converge to produce extreme activism are called **radicalization**. Radicalization seems to occur in three phases, beginning with 1) *sensitivity* activated by personal experiences of injustice and loss that are 2) heightened by group *affiliation*, then 3) consolidated into taking *action* (Doosje, 2016).

Enemy Making: Hatred and Alienation

Hate is a complex, multidimensional experience that has very personal meanings. **Hatred** is psychological and relational antipathy that develops in response to perceived offenses. It aims to shame, humiliate, and disempower the Other, but has unexpectedly corrosive implications for the hating person and an alienated relationship. The natural result of hatred is aggravated animosity and conflict.

A continuum of hatred ranges from mild aversion that motivates you to simply avoid the Other, through extreme irrational loathing for a whole group, with brutal actions directed toward random individuals. Much literature is concerned with hate-motivated behaviors such as hate crimes and genocide.

Fair consensus is found in the literature that the development of hatred is progressive (Sternberg, 2003). *Individually*, hatred is often a reaction to humiliation. The experience is internalized as indignity and personal violence, painfully nursed and resented, becoming passionate fear and rage. Distance from the Other grows, symbolically or literally, through dehumanization (Yang, 2015). A relationship can then be consumed by bitterness, thoughts that reinforce foreignness, and hateful actions. In a *group*, hate develops in a similar way. Groups use direct transmission of hatred through modeling and teaching, maintained and transmitted through retold stories that portray the enemy as threatening or evil. Hatred may be used to consolidate group identity by disparaging the Other.

Personal and group hatred can become catalysts for endless interpersonal and social conflict, and hateful violence may be the final outgrowth. Hateful actions are motivated by hate, but hate does not invariably translate into hateful action. Hatred is sustained by violence that is reciprocated between the adversaries.

4. Use of Exclusion, Domination, and Force

The use of force in any interaction eventually results in defensiveness and counterforce reactions which incite or aggravate conflict. Identities can also be the hot spot in conflict when group membership is used to restrict individuals from accomplishing desired opportunities. When identities are mistreated through force or discrimination, identity injury happens. The result, according to Kenneth Hardy (2001), is the "assaulted sense of Self," invisibility, and muted voice. This can be the foundation for deeply significant conflict such as the Black Lives Matter protests in 2020.

CULTURE

Culture is made up of collected society, gathered in all we know, accept, trust, and value as meaningful. Culture responds dynamically to global social changes, constantly changing to meet the needs of its members (Avruch, 2008). An early study by Alfred Kroeber and Clyde Kluckhohn (1952) identified more than 160 definitions of culture at that time; surely, there are more now. Though mostly intangible, culture establishes ways of living that shape behavior, guiding toward the "right" way to do things and the way things "should be," governing and regulating lifeways. It shapes perception, organizes relationships, and forms meaningful values.

Enculturation is the process by which you absorb the rules of a group's culture. Culture is so deeply absorbed that it anchors what makes sense and is usually taken for granted. This may not be the case to observers: other people might easily identify—"That person is an Orthodox Jew" from his clothing, or "That person is from the Guatemalan culture" from her speech, or "That person is a pacifist" from his belief system. Every person belongs to several groups at once and, therefore, your own perspective integrates transcultural worldviews. Even within one

Morphological (Visible)	Gentleness, supportiveness Cooperation (the leaves)
Structural (Invisible)	Kindness, civility Peaceable language Amiable relationships (the trunk)
Worldview Meaning	Constructive traditions Norms of tolerance Respectful values, beliefs (water)

Conflict most likely

Figure 5.3 Three levels of cultural identity
Based on Das, 2007, public domain.

group, members never completely agree on ways of living. Instead, variations of practices and belief are found within every group. Cultural diversity and variation are universal (Avruch, 1998, 2015). Let's try now to explore the universal features of culture.

Elements of Culture

Kalpana Das (2007) described three levels of cultural identity using the metaphor of a growing tree. See Figure 5.3 to illustrate this analysis while you read the following text.

At the *first* level of culture, the most visible and expressive **morphological level,** are distinctive customs, manners, and etiquette, as well as material artifacts such as art, music, costume, food, and home style. The history of a group, its geography and climate (for example, hot–cold, North–South, plains–mountains) are also embedded in cultural morphology. The practices establish *savoir faire,* knowing how to do things. This visible layer of culture expresses deeper but often unspoken beliefs about what behavior is "right" and polite or "wrong" and rude. As you imitate and repeat customary actions, you subtly adopt the corresponding values. In the Das metaphor, these elements are the "showy" leaves, fruit, and flowers.

This level of culture presents you with delightful experiments, and you probably enjoy **recreational diversity** by sampling the morphological aspects of alternative cultures like enjoying Ethiopian food or wearing Latinx embroidered clothing. Distinctive customs are frequently the content of crosscultural training for international workers, according to Roger Axtell, who was called the "international Emily Post." Certain behaviors and etiquette become signs of prestige and success. Conflict originating in this level is uncommon, but conflict results when behavior patterns or language are either severely imposed or forbidden, as happened during the colonization period.

The *second* level of cultural identity, called the **structural level,** is less tangible and must be inferred from observing how people organize their relationships.

These aspects of culture describe appropriate interactions between elders and children, for example, between the genders, and between people of differing levels of authority. Structures mark family belonging and community identity and, often, national identities of who belongs here or does not. The structures largely determine control of material resources, status, and power (Avruch, 1998). Even political and social welfare systems (for example, health, legal, and education) reflect the prevailing cultural structures.

The standards for structural relationships are rarely explained to people verbally, so learning them is through observing others, often with mistakes corrected by social disapproval. Traditional structures preserve stability; changes to structures often cause turmoil (A. Thomas, 2010). Das noted that this level guides you how to live well with Others, *savoir vivre*. In her metaphor, structures are represented by the roots, trunk, and branches of a tree.

The ways a culture organizes its members can be a source of conflict when the associated power distribution is not consensual or equitable. Many ongoing regional conflicts have their roots in the discontent of powerless groups. For example, bitter conflict can erupt when immigrants are excluded from social benefits, or when women are excluded from political office, or when a country is ruled for generations by exploitive officials.

Das's *third*, deepest and least tangible level of cultural identity is associated with worldview, values, and meaning. Values are subconscious and must be inferred. This layer of culture goes beyond outward symbols to encompass your reason for being in the world. This foundation tells you how to be, *savoir etre*, and it shapes your assumptions, perception, values, and goals. Jayne Docherty (2004) suggested that a useful way to explore worldview is to answer the following five questions:

1. What is real in this culture (things, people, institutions, traditions, ideas, etc.)?
2. How do I/we know what is real?
3. How is real organized?
4. What is valuable about real things?
5. How should I/we act, or not act?

For Das, the deepest layer of cultural identity is likened to the water that enters a tree, traveling to the visible parts and keeping the whole tree alive.

Worldview is influenced by traditional, deeply held values that combine to form a social consensus that does encompass a certain degree of diversity (Avruch, 2008). Just as your personality is a mix of characteristics, specific countries or cultural groups demonstrate a mix of worldviews. The cultures of the United States and Israel, for example, are generally more violent than those of Canada and the Scandinavian countries, but wide diversity exists within each of those societies. An interesting assessment of values and global changes is found in the **World Values Survey** (2019), available on their website.

An unusual example of cultural consensus is found in the Gross National Happiness of Bhutan, coined in 1979 when King Jigme Singye Wangchuck stated, "Gross National Happiness is more important than the Gross National Product." This philosophy now guides government officials when deciding policies to consider the happiness and well-being of the population rather than productivity. The culture of happiness has inspired many other principles.

Although diversity at this level can be intriguing in relationships, it can also be the most challenging and the most likely to cause conflict. Dialogue about values frequently leads to what is deeply profound, and differences may uncover non-negotiable, ultimate values and identity conflict. Conflict is sensitive and intense and may suffocate dialogue and change the nature of a relationship. Positively, Michelle LeBaron (2003) stated that worldview is the "seedbed" of culture that might also be a resource for understanding deeply divisive conflict.

Cultural Studies is an interdisciplinary area of scholarship that analyzes contemporary culture, concentrating on its history, distinctive traits, influences on everyday living and relationships, political dynamics between cultural groups, and conflict and peacemaking.

Two Models of Culture Are Useful: Associative and Individualistic

Categorization of culture and worldview generally settles on two major forms: associative and individualistic cultures (LeBaron, 2003a; Triandis, 1994). The "associative" and "individualistic" models are understood as a continuum, with hypothetical forms on the poles and mixes of actual practices and values found in the center. Associative values tends to be found in older societies such as in Asia and the Middle East; in Western regions, rural and Aboriginal groups tend to be more associative than are urban cosmopolitan groups (Hall, 1989). Historically, individualism grew from a mix of cultures and tends to be newer, less traditional, and more transitional because of social mobility (Thomson, 2018).

Associative Culture

The **associative** (also called *collectivist*) form of culture rests on group identification: personal connections, relationships, and family, all regarded as interdependent. The collective identity is more important than the individual: you have to forego self-centered concerns when it ensures the well-being of all (Nisbett, 2001). Associative relationships are formalized, governed by tradition, rules, and detailed protocols. In associative cultures, values are transmitted in implicit, unspoken ways, and you understand the values from the context. Uniqueness is seen as rebellious, and deference produces harmony. When rules, roles, and traditional manners are known, degrees of security and comfort are found in knowing what is expected and how to behave. Power is inherited or granted, and authority operates and controls from the top.

Stella Ting-Toomey (1982, 1991) found that the face or honor of the group bears a higher priority than any individual in collectivist cultures, especially when in conflict. Harmony, or at least the appearance of harmony, is highly valued. A notable sample of this philosophy is in the custom of arranged marriage, which joins two families more so than two individuals. Individuals are expected to defer to the arrangements planned by the family, and expressing resistance or will is seen as defiance of the family wisdom and honor, and risks permanent family rejection.

Conflict, even open differences of opinion, are avoided in associative cultures as if they threaten the integrity and face of the family or group. Conflict reflects badly on a relationship and is a source of shame, so it should never be expressed directly in confrontation. You are expected to divert conflict by skirting around controversial differences, topics, and actions. If conflict does erupt, you are expected to suppress your own interests and feelings and conform to the collective will to maintain smooth group functioning with avoidance or accommodation (Ting-Toomey, 1991). Third-party intervention is authoritative, and mingles group input that reveals conflict issues, priorities, and potential solutions. Because community and group elements are so important in the perception of and resolution of conflict, surrounding members of a group are actively involved to provide calming witness and constructive suggestions (Ury, 2000).

Individualistic Culture

The systemic contrast is called *individualism* (Triandis, 1994). In this culture, rules and expectations are less formal and more flexible. The stories and legends of individualist cultures favor lone heroes who go against the status quo (often violently) to create justice. Autonomy is valued, and personal choice, goals, and achievement are encouraged. Authority is earned, power is shared, and roles shift. Individual identities are primary, and group membership is somewhat incidental.

Conflict in individualistic cultures is accepted as normal and useful. Conflict occurs when differences of opinion come to the surface, or when personal expectations are disappointed. Differences of standpoint, worldview, and goals are expressed directly and explicitly, and are processed with dialogue and even confrontive argument. Reasoning and factual truth are central to harmony, establishing which party is right and correct. Truth is seen as fairly absolute: something is either true or false, with little consideration for finer paradoxes. Conflict is as an opportunity to debate truth with a focus on impersonal facts. Domination or collaboration effectively address a problem (Ting-Toomey, 1982). Third-party intervention facilitates dialogue, confrontation, and debate using orderly rules and guidance to find the best solution.

Culture as we have presented it, might seem static to you, as if established mainstream views are constant. This misconception overlooks the fact that culture shows unending progress (Avruch, 2008). Check the latest World Values Survey (2020) website for an interesting illustration of this dynamic fact. Constantly changing language—words invented, added, appropriated, and dropped—illustrates this progress. Subcultural forces such as dissatisfaction with existing values interweave with influences from other worldviews to produce cultural identities that persistently, though slowly, transform and evolve. Think about North American culture of the 1960s, for example, when many now aged people were teenagers. Think about the never static music or art culture. Within an associative culture, subcultural members may find it necessary to withdrawal from the mainstream as they refine their worldviews. In an individualistic society, demonstration of alternative views is tolerated and, in fact, nonconforming individuality is viewed as courageous.

As cultural changes verge closer to the heart of a group, however, tenacity increases, sometimes causing resistance to change, and conflict. When language is threatened, for instance, whole societies can be galvanized to protect symbolic language rights of the "mother tongue." Preservation of tradition becomes especially passionate when issues echo family habits related to gift giving, sexuality, or life transitions (birth rituals, emergence from childhood into adulthood, marriage, and death). At such times, cultural incompatibilities are sensitive, and group members become defensive of the rightness of specific traditions.

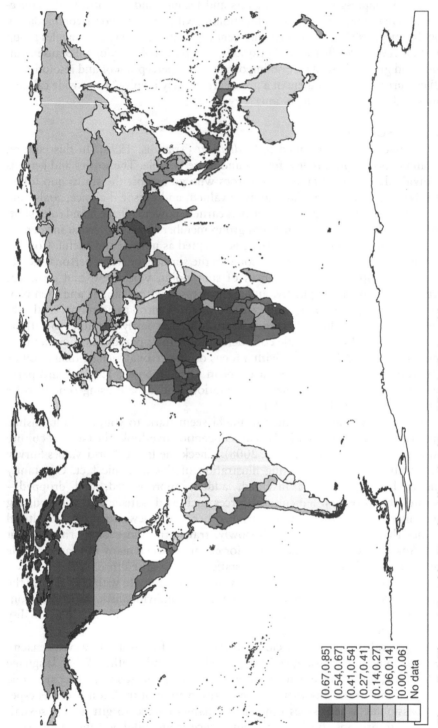

Figure 5.4 The most and least culturally mixed countries in the world

Based on Morin, 2013, Pew Research, public domain.

[0.67,0.85]
[0.54,0.67]
[0.41,0.54]
[0.27,0.41]
[0.14,0.27]
[0.06,0.14]
[0.00,0.06]
No data

Globalization and the crosspollination of resources, ideas, and viewpoints bring faster-paced cultural change. It results from expanded international networks of communication, trade, travel, and migration that ensure vigorous exposure among many cultural identities. Our globalizing environment encourages **cultural diffusion**, which is the spread of one society's cultural distinctives to another. Some analysts view this as a positive force for social development while others dread the passing of lost traditions (Paczynska, 2008). "McDonaldization" was coined by George Ritzer (2009) to describe a diffused culture that is driven by large corporations and dominated by homogeneity and uniformity, especially in popular practice (Pieterse, 2020). **Cultural pluralism** or **multiculturalism** is the respectful coexistence of different forms, each retaining some of the original distinctives. For a graphic illustration of global cultures, see Figure 5.4.

There is a subtle difference between multiculturalism and diversity, though. Multiculturalism is the parallel existence and tolerance of multiple forms; within that variety, invisible hierarchies of preference might present advantages to some forms and not to others. For example, to gain entry to a specialized multicultural arts high school, candidates had to pass an examination and present a portfolio, essay, or experiment. Presumably, students from white, Asian, black, Latinx, and some European traditions were at similar levels of ability. However, among students, a distinct social hierarchy developed: male athletes were the most honored, followed by white students of both genders, followed by brown students (females over males), then black students, with mixed-race students at the bottom. This hierarchy was reinforced by actions of the administration too, for example when a black student was expelled for vaping in the washroom while three white students selling cigarettes behind the school were only required to write an essay on the dangers of smoking.

In fact, diversity ensures that every individual has multicultural identities. Diversity goes beyond coexistence to seek out and appreciate alternative perspectives, understanding the value and even necessity of multiple viewpoints to represent a full view of reality. Many countries deliberately adopt diversity policies of multilingualism and multiculturalism. In 2001, the United Nations declared in the Universal Declaration on Cultural Diversity that culture is one of four pillars of human sustainability, and diversity is the "common heritage of humanity" (Stenou, 2002).

Think About and Discuss with Your Colleagues

- In the West people tend to think of ourselves as more socially advanced than in less developed countries. Yet, the cultures of Eastern origin are much older than ours—ancient, in fact. What does this say about our assumptions, or theirs?

Culture and Conflict

Culture and conflict are deeply and inextricably linked. Douglas Noll (2003) said "culture affects conflict behavior, and conflict can also be understood as cultural behavior." He outlined these deep links:

- culture explains what people value;
- culture defines what issues people find worth fighting about;
- culture defines appropriate ways to behave when in conflict; and

- culture creates the methods of communicating needs and the processes and institutions by which conflicts are handled.

In many ways, every intercultural encounter is a "complex improvisational experience" (Avruch, 2009). When we encounter people with a different cultural base, we tentatively improvise our way through the interaction, often making mistakes. Particularly when in cross-cultural conflict, many disputants find they cannot rely on previous habits, and feel off balance as they try to settle issues. Intercultural conflict can rarely be separated from tribal or ethnic history, religious differences, political ambitions, or economic realities. Ting-Toomey (2001) identified seven sources of intercultural conflict, all of which were evident in the Kenneth Hardy case:

- frustrations and mismatched expectations, interpreted as disrespect;
- divergent communication, conflict styles, and methods;
- biased intergroup perception and explanations of the conflict episode;
- divergent face needs to be treated with respect or honor;
- incompatible conflict goals;
- situational factors such as the context of the conflict and the roles played out; and
- thinking restricted to limited factors rather than larger systems.

Beyond those, serious intercultural conflict is ignited by cultural violence of any sort. **Cultural imperialism** is the term used for cultural conquest, when members of one culture aggressively impose their own worldview on others, supposedly to reform or civilize the Other. The extreme form is **cultural genocide**, which attempts to obliterate the cultural heritage of a group completely. Originally called *ethnocide* (Lemkin, 1944), cultural genocide forbids the practices, language, values, and religion of a group judged to be inferior, while mandating the adoption of worldviews of the conquering group. This was the centuries-old policy of most Western nations during the colonial era, for example, and the policy continues to actively drive many regional conflicts such as those in the Middle East today.

Though culture is the "seedbed" of identity (Le Baron, 2003), many other factors such as race, gender status, religion, and SES contribute to the intersection of social identities.

RACE

John Howard Griffin, a white journalist, underwent a series of medical treatments that made him look like an African American, to investigate the American black experience of the middle 20th century. For six weeks in 1959, he traveled as himself in the segregated southern United States, with the exception of his false skin color. At that time, the Jim Crow Laws, based on the Black Codes, were used to maintain white supremacy and strict racial segregation. The civil rights movement had begun to dismantle segregation, but people of all races were struggling to understand social responsibility. The report of Griffin's experience, called *Black Like Me* (Griffin, 1961 [2010]), was made into a dramatic film in 1964.

Griffin reported, under the original title "Journey into Shame," that his experiment uncovered shocking racism, demonstrated in constant exclusion from such ordinary resources as food and shelter, ticket sales, and public drinking fountains.

Black and white communities occupied different parts of town, had distinct codes of behavior and manners, had discrepant opportunities, and had contradictory standards of safety. Although he found that some whites were friendly and helpful, Griffin reported on his frequent encounters with white suspicion, prejudice, threat, and hatred. He later wrote, "All the courtesies in the world do not cover up the one vital and massive discourtesy—that the Negro is treated not even as a second-class citizen, but as a tenth-class one."

When he returned to his home in Texas, the publication of the story resulted in hostility and threats against him and his family, as well as public protests defending white rights. In 1975, he was severely beaten by the Ku Klux Klan. He continued to write and to lecture on race relations and social justice making, and he received many awards.

Race is a concept that refers to classification of human groups based on inherited visible characteristics like skin color, hair color and texture, and eye color. Race is blurred by many historic and cultural factors. In fact, there are no "pure" races, and racial classification is often erroneous. Global racial distribution can only be estimated. In one attempt to map the global racial distribution (Mason, 2018) 8 main categories and 69 subcategories were used, but several include multiple ancestry groups that further complicate the wide diversity.

Almost no one can claim a singular or even dual racial identity; rather, your so-called racial identity is made up of a mix of racial and ethnic backgrounds. *Biracial identity* results from the mix of two main heritages; *multiracial* or *mixed-race identity* is made up of scattered sources of genetic inheritance.

Ethnic Studies is an academic specialty within Diversity Studies. It is motivated by the goals of understanding and moderating racial and ethnic tensions and conflict globally. It is an interdisciplinary study of ancestral origins, racial differences, diverse forms of ethnicity, and national identity. Another focus is the intersection of social, political, and cultural power with ethnicity and marginalization.

Genetics and Race

In 1839 and 1849, Samuel Morton used the measurement of skull shapes and structures to correlate five "races" with behavior, character traits, and abilities. Morton believed that the races resulted from five separate acts of divine creation, and that the Creator established a human hierarchy based on racial character. Superiority was attributed to the white (Caucasian) race, judged by Morton to be the most beautiful, intelligent, courageous, civilized, and industrious; East Asians (Mongolians) were described as resourceful, but teachable; Southeast Asians (Malay), American (Aboriginal), and black (Ethiopian) were reverse ranked as the so-called inferior races that Morton believed would ultimately become extinct.

By reporting these conclusions, Morton became the "father of scientific racism" because assumed superiority of white men (*sic*) and their right to rule over the inferior races was legitimized. His theories were accepted by teachers, journalists, politicians, and many religious leaders, and can be seen as part of the fabric of racial prejudice even today. Morton's conclusions were accepted as factual: that humans can be separately categorized by biological race, that variation within a race is minimal while variation between the races is significant, and that race is the basis for observable appearance, character, and abilities, notably intelligence. These myths dominated racial beliefs and prejudice for generations and, in fact, they continue to do so. Perhaps the deepest impact of these misconceptions is their pervasive effect on racial self-identity.

Most contemporary research on racial genetics happened in the 1990s and was finalized in the early 21st century with the completion of the human genetic map at the Human Genome Project. There is a genetic basis for visible racial differences (the **phenotype**); these differences are, however, "only skin deep." The **genotype**, which is the whole genetic inheritance, is 99% homogenous for all races (Rosenberg, 2002). The Human Genome Project found: all humans are closely related, human origins were in Africa, and racial variation is blurred. Racial genetics are therefore far more alike than different, and variation that does exist tends to be determined by geographic and community location (Jorde, 2004). Current scientific consensus concludes that "The concept of race has no genetic or scientific basis" (Venter, 2001).

Culture and Race

Race terminology is often the source of misunderstanding and, sometimes, of conflict. In common language, "race" is a hazy term that can connote biological race, ancestry or descent, social ethnicity, and kinship, depending on context and without clear definition. David Williams's (1997) survey of scientific dictionaries and journals concluded that the term is often used in thoughtless ways as a substitute for unmeasured biological, socioeconomic, and/or sociocultural characteristics. Here, **race** refers to a group of people unified by inherited characteristics, geographic boundaries, and/or lifestyle. Race is based not singly in genetics but also in shared cultural heritage. An **ethnic group** is one whose members identify with each other because of common culture, history, and language, such as the Han Chinese. Another blurry term is **kinship**, which refers to a group of people who develop attachment and mutual loyalty through historical origins, such as Jewish people. **Nationality** names the political state in which a person is a citizen. **Nationalism** is the belief that societies or nations should be "pure." Nationalism is usually based in racial stereotypes, and advocates the establishment of separately pure nations.

Critical Race Theory

Critical Race Theory began with the early stages of intersectional studies to examine the crossroads of race, national origin, power, and law. Some of the themes of Critical Race Theory (Delgado, 2017) are:

- Power, race, and racism are inextricably linked.
- All races and ethnic groups have unique historical, experiential sources of knowledge that are passed on orally.
- The racial beliefs of mainstream societies show self-serving bias.
- Even in societies where social justice is valued, unconscious bias is betrayed in countless experiences of **microaggression** and **microassault**, which are subtle indignities that are elusive and usually subconscious. Examples are calling Dr. Hardy "boy," or moving when an Asian person sits beside you on a bus. These derogatory or prejudicial insults highlight marginalization.
- The search for equality among the races, and equitable power and emancipation under the law are central justice making activities.

This interdisciplinary study is typically offered in schools of law. Prominent writers are joined by postcolonial specialists and thinkers from the global south.

Conclusions about Race

The study of race is complex and difficult. At this point in time, several conclusions can be extrapolated:

1. Two randomly chosen people from the same perceived racial group are no more genetically similar than two randomly chosen people from apparently different races. Variation in genetic inheritance exists, but the concept of race does not capture it (Williams, 1997).
2. Visible racial differences are partially determined by genetic inheritance and by familial associations, but cultural influences are far more dominant than the biological (Black, 2008).
3. Visible racial differences interact with other factors such as employment, transience and migration, and socioeconomic status to produce marked inequities of prestige, tangible benefits, and resulting wellbeing (McCall, 2005).
4. Seven anthropological theories are currently under debate regarding racial differences. Of those theories, none are focused on genetic identity; all are concentrated on cultural and social sources and functions of diversity (Wimmer, 2013).

Racism and Conflict

Racism is any belief or attitude, action or practice that is founded on a racialized worldview. Racist beliefs are that humans can be divided into genetic classes called "races," that common descent is a link to personality, intelligence, morality, and other characteristics. In this worldview, differential treatment of people distinguishable by race is justified. **Racial profiling** (which is treatment based on visible characteristics that suggest race, religion, or national origin) appears to be based on that worldview, so the practice is offensive to many people. Because racism is associated with unequal treatment, it always leads to identity conflict.

Foreignness divisions are deeply rooted in most social and cultural systems and racism is inescapably embedded to some degree in everyone's belief and value systems. Called structural violence (see Chapter 8) and popularly called **systemic racism**, social power structures originating in privilege and supremacy perpetuate the exclusion of members of visible racial groups like Aboriginals, blacks, and Latinx (Feagin, 2006). Unjust systems generate profound invisible wounds like racial antagonism and learned voicelessness (Hardy, 2001), and those systems continuously deprive people of rights and positions to which they are entitled as humans. Growing national and international protests against police violence toward people of color, such as the Black Lives Matter movement, are attempts to right this source of conflict.

Think About and Discuss with Your Colleagues

- What does the suffix "-ism" mean to you? What was your first encounter with racism? How are racism, conflict, and violence related? In your own words, define racism.

GENDER

Gender is the category used to describe multifaceted male and female identities. "Sex" and "gender" are often used interchangeably and they are linked but not identical concepts. Whereas **sex** refers to biological, genetic nature at birth, **gender** refers to cultural expectations for different behavior. Sex is popularly assumed to correspond with gender, but neither sex nor gender are as absolute as many people believe. The real frequency of diverse, nondichotomous gender identities (collectively called LGBT2QSI+: lesbian, gay, bisexual, transgender, 2-spirit, queer, questioning, intersex, and so on) is unknown. The value of any estimates is limited because of rapidly shifting social approval or disapproval that favor open versus hidden disclosure. In previous generations, alternative identities were not unknown, but usually hidden. Younger people today are more likely than in the past to acknowledge alternative gender identities openly.

Gender Studies is a scholarly discipline devoted to the exploration of gender effects on behavior, social relationships and functioning, and values and attitudes. *Gender analysis* compares experiences in society from the differing standpoints. *Gender literacy* is awareness of gender diversity, associated expectations, and the consequences of those expectations.

Conflict Resolution Studies points to the ways that gender is a factor in conflict and violence and, more importantly, in conflict resolution and peacemaking. Gender can be viewed in many ways, raising many (often unanswered) questions, even for researchers. For some scholars, outstanding questions and data relate to *behavioral similarities and differences*:

- Are there consistent differences in the ways females and males engage in conflict?
- If so, how do those differences affect the dynamics of conflict or conflict resolution?
- If there are differences, what explains them?

Some scholars are more concerned with the *social dimensions of gender*:

- Does gender affect participation in society?
- Why are a majority of leadership roles held by males?
- How do gender and power interact? Why do males typically have more power, or at least different forms of power, than do females in most societies?
- What is the role of the media in portraying females and males in conflict?

Many scholars associate gender with *positive and negative attitudes*.

- The same behavior can be judged positively or negatively, depending on whether it is carried out by a male or female individual.
- Are females or males differently valued and treated? If so, how does this affect them and society?
- Stereotypic expectations affect judgments about conflict and its outcomes.
- Negative attitudes toward one or both genders are often at the core of hateful attitudes and offensive discrimination that fuels conflict (Shields, 2008).

Genetics and Gender

Sex is genetically determined by the natural "X" and "Y" genes inherited at conception. This might imply that sex is **binary**, having one of two distinct and "opposite" forms, female and male, corresponding with the pink or blue bonnets babies are sometimes given at birth. Indeed this is the most common concept of sex. Gender is much more complex than that.

Intersex individuals are born with ambiguous chromosomes, genitalia, or hormonal functioning. The true incidence of intersex is unknown because detection and record keeping are neglected and flawed, but 1.7% of births are estimated to be affected by intersex identities (IHRA, 2013). The main suffering for intersex individuals and their families results from misconceptions, secrecy, and associated stigma.

Ongoing controversy surrounds a South African athlete named Caster Semenya, a much-decorated runner. After her performance showed dramatic improvement in 2009, she was suspected of hormone use and subjected to sex verification testing. Although cleared several times to compete in womens' events, this suspicion has followed her career. For Semenya, such testing creates personal anxiety, depression, and social isolation, as well as identity and social crisis, public humiliation, and political uproar. Many people believe that her human rights were violated by this repeated testing and that it was motivated by racism, but there is significant history of this verification testing in single-sex athletic competitions.

Gender identity is psychological identification with a particular gender, established early and firmly. Gender identity is not the same as *gender expression*, which is how a person chooses to communicate gender identity. Gender identity can also be complicated by alternate *sexual orientation*, which expresses sexual attraction toward others. Gender identity is not biological. Genetic heritage and identity may not be in harmony, so there are many variations.

Scientific consensus is that the genetics of sex and gender are not as simplistically binary as many people think. Although most individuals have a distinctively male or female genetic mix, this is not always the case and the phrase "opposite sex" is distracting.

Culture and Gender Roles

Social conversation on sexuality and gender is adapting rapidly, but this results in significant controversy. Culture defines the patterns that are considered appropriately feminine or masculine behavior, called **gender roles** or **sex roles** (Fixmer-Oraiz, 2019). Typically, gender roles and behaviors fall on a continuum with characteristically masculine "macho-man" behavior at one pole, and contrasting feminine "fair lady" behavior at the other pole. For example, females have been described as taking a more "take care" relationship approach compared to the males "take charge" approach (Merchant, 2012). Specific expectations depend greatly on surrounding culture that is affected, in turn, by multiple factors such as history, ethnicity, and SES.

The genetic base is not correlated with masculine or feminine sex roles. No one portrays a singularly masculine or feminine role; rather, enactment of each gender role becomes a unique expression of many qualities. **Androgyny** (literally "andro-" man + "-gyne" woman) is neither feminine nor masculine but, rather, is a mix of gender role features.

Social anthropologist Margaret Mead (1935) studied personality and behavior seen as culturally proper (normal) to the genders. Mead concluded that some transcultural regularities do exist:

- Most cultures invest authority in males more than in females;
- Most societies are *patriarchal* and organized around unconcealed male power; and
- Males tend toward dominance, and engage in observably aggressive conflict; females tend toward emotional responsiveness, cooperation, and strategic conflict.

Mead's conclusion was that masculine and feminine roles are primarily determined by culture and socialization rather than by biogenetic factors. Her conclusions formed part of the foundation of feminist studies.

Scientific consensus in Gender Studies is that gender role traits are taken on gradually and refined through a wide array of socializing forces. Lifelong frameworks of female and male perception, strengths, and response patterns are founded on unique standpoints constructed from birth onward.

Sexism and Conflict

There are many conjunctions between gender and conflict. According to the United Nations (Goetz, 2006):

- Conflict has multiple causes, but simple gender is rarely at the root. Any gender inequality can be the catalyst for conflict, and gender injustice is often the manifestation of conflict;
- Gender hierarchies intersect with other social causes of conflict such as race, class, age, and geography; and
- In conflict, males are perceived primarily as aggressors, females are perceived primarily as victims. Both of these ideas obscure the many roles and consequences of violence.

Even though standpoints and experiences may differ, women and men share common vulnerabilities. Both females and males are subject to violence but the intensity of force is often of a different order. Women tend to bear the major burden of care for survivors of conflict and violence. Violent conflict displaces whole families, often subsequently led by women as they search for safety.

Inequitable beliefs and practical injustices mean that conflict and gender can disadvantage most people except powerful men. Nearly a century ago, Mead observed that the masculine-feminine binary is used to enforce gender based segregation and repression. Differential treatment results in disadvantage for women all across the world, causing varying degrees of limitation. Women are at increased risk of underemployment and poverty, and are vulnerable to serious illness, including mental illness. The basic needs and health of relatively marginal women and children are often neglected, both in times of peace and of war (WHO, 2012). Too often, violence is closely linked to the collision of the genders, such as in dating and family situations, and in war.

Social Exclusion, Dominance, and Violence

A conflicted, uncertain environment correlates with family tension and increased violence in homes, schools, and workplaces, as was observed during the recent coronavirus pandemic. Increased risk of sexual and **gender-based violence** (GBV) often accompanies the escalation of conflict. The actual frequency of GBV is probably like a pyramid, with only a small proportion visible and acknowledged.

Some GBV has its roots in specific cultural beliefs. **Harmful traditional practices** place females at higher risk of sexual abuse and rape, marital rape, and domestic violence. Ritual genital mutilation and forced early marriage are still used in some societies, supposedly to preserve the girls' purity and the honor of the family. These forms of cultural violence are serious and surprisingly widespread, especially in Africa, Asia, and the Middle East (Boyden, 2012; Wadesango, 2011; Watson, 2020).

Although violence places everyone at risk of harm, vulnerable females of all ages are targeted and at high risk during serious conflict. Females are targeted for sexual exploitation and trafficking. Girls and women are targeted for **instrumental violence** as part of a wartime strategy (Zenn, 2014). Armed groups commonly use rape and female disfigurement to demonstrate their power and defeat an enemy. A still unresolved tragedy was the kidnapping of 276 girls from the Nigerian Chibok school by the terrorist group, Boko Haram, in 2014.

Sexism is prejudice or discrimination based on sex, gender, or gender roles. Misperception and stereotyping are important factors. *Misogyny* is the perception that women are threats, resulting in distrust or even hatred of females. Girls' and womens' needs and positive contributions to our world are overlooked. *Misandry* is a complementary perception that men are treacherous, with accompanying distrust or hatred of males, or disregard for mens' and boys' needs and full contributions. Both attitudes aggravate ongoing conflicts all over the world. Based on belief in the superior or sole legitimacy of heterosexuality, *heterosexism* is a prejudicial attitude or active discrimination against alternative sexual expressions.

Systemic violence operates throughout a group of people, often so subtly that it is invisible even to those affected by it. We are most familiar with the dynamics of relationship violence in abusive relationships, but there is another level of violence. You don't have to personally abuse the vulnerable—society does it for you. Misogynistic or misandronistic models experienced in everyday events like jokes, public interactions, news articles, or authority invested exclusively in one gender ensure ongoing social tension regarding gender. Gender gaps in opportunity, success, and attitudes are substantial, and they also form the backdrop for childrens' opportunities. The practical implications of the gap are poorer health and health care, economic struggle, lower educational achievement, and lesser political and social participation (Leopold, 2017).

These factors can become so normalized as to be nearly undetectable. They reinforce and subtly legitimize gender exclusive actions. Gender parity is fundamental to a thriving society (Leopold, 2017); without parity, societies are unable to benefit from the resources of excluded groups, mostly women. Although many societies have advanced toward gender parity and representative leadership, there is a long way to go. Some recent movements like MeToo and Time's Up are gaining attention, but some notice they are also creating a backlash of resistance.

RELIGION

Religion is a source of vast human diversity, reflected in estimates that 75% to 84% of the world's population claim spiritual belief. **Religion** refers to a sacred belief in the transcendent or supernatural dimension of life, shared with other devotees through a set of faith practices, a study of doctrine, and a system of beliefs. Religion implies community affiliation with some degree of organization, whereas **faith** and **spirituality** are personal systems of belief and practice. Faith has widely different meanings to individual adherents and to collective groups. The definition of religion in Religious Studies is controversial, with much disagreement about what qualifies as a *bona fide* religion or a small, loosely affiliated sect.

A poll conducted in 2015 by the Pew Research Center found that the five major world religions attract 84% of religious believers (Hackett, 2017). Christianity is the dominant religion with a numerical majority in 157 countries and 30% of worldwide adherents; second is Islam, which has a numerical majority in 27 countries and is claimed by 23% of global adherents; 16% of respondents claimed atheism, agnosticism, or no formalized affiliation, but report continuing to believe in God or a higher power; 15% of adherents are Hindu; 7% are Buddhist; and 5% of adherents follow traditional indigenous and folk religions. Current estimates of the number of religions vary from more than 4,000 to more than 10,000, but religions can form and disband elusively. Although most countries have a majority religion plus many others, 25% of countries place restrictions on religious practices, or even encourage government harassment of adherents.

Controversy also exists in scholarly circles about the origins of and explanations for this pervasive influence, with theories including an individual psychological need for belonging, and an "exotic," group need to establish and maintain boundaries as a method of self-definition, and a social need for civic order and control through religious expectations and ethics (Strausberg, 2009). Other ideas emphasize the mythology of religion, or the conviction that religion is the product of actual superhuman intervention in the universe.

Religion, Peace, and Conflict

Even though religious conflict is often mysterious, some facts about it can be extrapolated (Cavanaugh, 2009; Fitzpatrick, 2014; Goldberg, 2011; Smith-Christopher, 2007):

- Many of the deepest and most intractable conflicts have religious dimensions.
- When doctrine is used to foster animosity or promote violence, religion might be viewed as the problem.
- Religious conflict often centers in seemingly nonnegotiable values disputes.
- Religious war is caused or justified by religious differences. Religious doctrine is often prescriptive, which jeopardizes the autonomy and neutrality of any intervenor in an active conflict.
- Religious differences can aggravate a war that is fought for other reasons.
- The legitimacy of religion as a political influence is controversial, often causing conflict.

- Controversy also continues about the specific role of religion in conflict: whether it is a trigger or a tool.

Historically, many or most religions develop as a result of significant internal and external conflict. Many religious groups initially form under the leadership of one charismatic person such as Moses or Muhammad or Mary Baker Eddy. New movement groups might be regarded by the religious mainstream as illegitimate, causing resistance and conflict until they are more fully developed and established. Most religious groups undergo recurrent differentiation and branching as a result of changes in leadership, doctrinal debates, and advancing faith practices.

Many religions attempt to construct a common set of conservative "fundamentals" (such as the five Christian fundamentals, the five pillars of Islam, and the Tripitaka and *vinaya* of Buddhism), but consensus is not uniform even around those. Fundamentalist beliefs often stimulate resentment and rebellion among subgroups of adherents. There is no exclusively "true Christianity," "correct Islam," "uniform Buddhism," and so forth; instead, every religion shows internal diversity of interpretation and practice, especially about how the faithful should live and what religious duties are. Contemporary Western debate among evangelical (actively preaching), conservative (traditional or orthodox), and liberal (tolerant of progress) devotees draws on the deepening divides of North American and European societies. In the name of religion, much good is done, and much evil is done (Smith-Christopher, 2007).

Many currently valued social services such as health care and education grew out of needs for service and charity during conflict, and much of this benevolence continues. Most religions support acts of donation that express followers' spiritual gratitude. Religious leaders are often called to be peacemakers and reconcilers in times and regions of conflict and war (Horowitz, 2001). Interfaith dialogue and cooperative work is often able to unite divided communities. The first formal interfaith conference occurred at the 1893 Chicago World's Fair, where the universality of spiritual values and diversities of practice were affirmed.

Most religions have Scriptures and traditions of both nonviolence and violence, so they can be used to justify adherents' responses to conflict (Cavanaugh, 2009; Gentry, 2016; McClymond, 2006; Smith-Christopher, 2007). Sometimes religions claim special status as the exclusive domain of truth and morality. Therefore, religious teachings are sometimes mobilized as offensive and defensive weapons.

Religious Extremism

Religious extremism is at the crossroads of political views and religious doctrine. It often emerges to defend religious identity, violently if necessary. Extremism identifies secular law and political forms as the sources of evil, and faithfulness to the doctrines as the solution. Many scholars argue that religious terrorism is probably rooted in social, ethnic, and national grievances and tied to revolutionary politics, and religion should be viewed as only an incidental factor rather than as the primary motivator. The religious ideology is justification that disguises the political motivation.

The assumed association of extremism with mainstream religion or the majority of religious adherents (primarily with Islam) is a stereotype that overlooks the reactive roots of extremism in intolerance and exclusion (Cavanaugh, 2009; Iannaccone, 2006; Stueland, 2013). A Pew Research Center 2017 survey of 12 countries found virtually no difference between Muslim adherents and the general public: 82% of American Muslims, 83% of the American public, and 79% of European Muslims said they were concerned about global extremism committed in the name of Islam (Poushter, 2017).

SOCIOECONOMIC STATUS

The terms **socioeconomic class** (SEC) and **socioeconomic status** (SES) refer to the stratified social rank of a group of people with similar levels of wealth and power. Class differentiation is reflected in the relative unity of a society; a differentiated society, such as in parts of India, has organized and separated standards for the classes that determine individual autonomy, family structures and resources, and inclusion in decision making within a community (Higley, 2000). **Class Studies** and **Working Class Studies** are specialties within Diversity Studies that explore social strata and class, working-class culture, status-based inequity, and social policy.

There is no one definition of class, and criteria used to describe SES vary from region to region and discipline to discipline. Formally, status is measured by **social capital**, a recently identified concept with three primary components: education, income, and occupational prestige, all which raise status. Relationship networks and political power are also indicators, although they are not usually included in formal measures. SES determines the lifestyle factors that create a safe and secure home: knowledge and culture to pass on, a living income, relationship networks, and meaningful work. The upper SES strata are reinforced by hereditary resources, opportunities, privileges, and political control (Galtung, 1969). Class is also marked by place: a homeless person should not enter certain places but, by the same "rules," a rich person should not enter a homeless village.

Three categories were historically used in the developed world: *upper class*, who control the generation and distribution of wealth; the *employed middle class* of professionals and managers ("white collar"); and the *manual working class* ("blue collar"), for whom low-paying jobs and poverty are typical. As societies develop, new classes emerge and status adjusts, as typified by the recent refinement of seven British categories (Savage, 2015):

- 6% Elite, upper class—This group is the most privileged with highest status, having high levels of all three types of capital. This group controls the majority of wealth and power, so paid employment is optional. Resources and privileges tend to be inherited within a family, generation to generation.
- 25% Established middle class—This is the largest single group. They have moderately high levels of education, income, and status, and are socially connected and culturally engaged.
- 15% Emerging service workers—This group tends to be young and urban. They have high social capital and high cultural engagement. Because they are young, economic capital is low but increasing.
- 14% Newly affluent workers—This is a newly emerging class that has autonomy, has moderate to high economic capital through earned wealth, and is developing cultural and social capital.

- 6% Technical middle class—This is a group whose employment depends on high-demand specialized technical skill, so they have high economic capital. However, they tend not to be culturally or socially engaged.
- 19% Traditional working class—The second-largest group is made up of older workers. Although they are not poor, their social capital is low in all three areas.
- 15% Precarious poverty level—This group is the most deprived with precarious living due to low employment and income, poor education, and low status.

The **Human Development Index** (HDI) is compiled from statistically comparable education, per capita income, and life expectancy, and is used by the UN Development Program to rank national well-being. The overall trend is toward improvement in national HDI since its invention in 1975, but marked discrepancies are consistently found. As globalization spreads, inequality between nations decreases, but inequality within nations increases, meaning that the gap between the "haves" and "have-nots" is increasing in most nations (Milanovic, 2016). The **Inequality-Adjusted Human Development Index** (IHDI) compares national achievements with potential contributions lost because of socioeconomic inequality, so it is in some ways a measure of the costs of inequity. This index suggests dramatic discrepancies within and between countries. A corresponding statistic is the **Multidimensional Poverty Index** (MPI), which records acute gaps in standards of family living. The 2018 MPI report estimated that 1,334 million people (almost 18%) live in acute poverty worldwide, most in Sub-Saharan Africa and South Asia, and the majority of them are children.

Classism and Conflict

Classism includes any situation that assigns different value to people based on social status. Problems occur when those in the more powerful strata feel entitled to exclude Others from their privileges (I. Young, 2008). **Disenfranchisement** occurs when identifiable groups are deprived of rights, privileges, or opportunities. The most rigid form of classism occurs in countries that have a caste system. Castes are hereditary boundaries of culture, status, power, and occupation that still prevail in discriminatory restrictions in some areas of Asia (for example, India, Pakistan, Sri Lanka, Japan). UNICEF estimates that 250 million people are currently disadvantaged by caste discrimination.

Intersectional studies of socioeconomic conditions show that status functions to benefit a few, at the expense of many. In most societies the highest percentage of wealth and property are concentrated in the upper class (Black, 2008). According to 2016–18 *Forbes Magazine* data, the fortunes of the three wealthiest American men were greater than the combined assets of the lower 50% of Americans. The *New York Times* (2014) reported that the richest 1% of Americans own more wealth than the poorest 90%. These discrepancies are even more marked when race and gender are considered into the calculations.

Classism affects individual and family choices, prejudice, and belief systems, and is equally active in social institutions when peoples' needs are substantially unmet. Tangible inequities that result from socioeconomic conditions are obvious causes of conflict. However, the immediate sources of conflict can be linked only indirectly to status, and are often obscured by compounded marginalization (Crenshaw, 1994). **Class conflict** or **class struggle** occurs when social tension and conflict result from competing interests and intergroup interference. Class struggle aims to reform local and global systems that perpetuate class and status gaps. It is demonstrated in social upheaval, political unrest, and sometimes in violent conflict. Dramatic movements such as the 2010 Arab Spring (see Conflict Case 2.2) and the Black Lives Matter campaign illustrate widespread projects intended to promote social and economic justice. Consensus is that such movements are important for raising awareness, but were largely unsuccessful in bringing about sustained cultural change.

Culture, race, gender, religion, and SES—all are at the intersection of social identities; all offer opportunities for generating artificial boundaries and enemies; and all offer priceless resources for compassion, conflict resolution, peacemaking, and reconciliation (Armstrong, 2010; Shapiro, 2017).

CONFLICT RESOLUTION AND JUSTICE: DIVERSITY, EQUALITY, EQUITY, INCLUSION

> *There is no such thing as a single issue struggle because we do not live single issue lives.*
> —*Audre Lorde*

When division is caused by stereotyping and prejudice, establishing friendship will challenge every level of a system and every skill available. This is difficult work that includes uncovering deep assumptions and biases, making you aware of them, overcoming long-standing resistance, and using creativity to imagine tolerant ways of being together. Kenneth Cloke (2007), Laurie Coltri (2009), and many others, call this work risky, even "dangerous," for several reasons:

1. No one escapes the influence of their own invisible culture, values, and perspectives;
2. Existing social structures support a prevailing status quo;
3. Support is hard to generate; instead, sustained resistance is likely;
4. The acute stress of working with these deep problems tempts you to deflect to less critical tasks, or to accept simpler paths of less resistance;
5. It is very easy to try short-sighted, misplaced conflict resolution methods;
6. It takes great skill and experience to competently apply the most useful tools; and
7. It is not always possible to find amicable solutions that truly respect identities.

Seven Principles of Diversity Sensitive Conflict Resolution

Conflict related to intersectional factors is often referred to as "struggle" because it is so subtle, far reaching, and all consuming. No simple answers are adequate. The search for clear-cut understanding, resolution, and peacebuilding seems, at times, desperate. Personal search, partisan division, institutional reform, and international politics are all involved. Social alienation will intensify unless there is commitment to civil relations and to social justice.

Some principles guide the process.

1. Intersectional conflict resolution is a lifelong, generations-long process.
2. The roots of identity conflict are subtle, and detection is the first challenge. It can be perplexing to accurately perceive your own identity as privileged or disadvantaged. Intersectional conflict resolution involves complex processes that address deep roots of conflict to alleviate the consequences.
3. Potential solutions need to move beyond immediate conflict partners to recruit influential leaders and groups and obtain their support.
4. Sustainable reconciliation must address all forms of inequity, subordination, and oppression, notably marginalization, powerlessness, exploitation, cultural imperialism, and violence (I. Young, 2012).
5. Intersectional culture change is systems change. In an **open system**, the norms are flexible, so individuals can make changes relatively easily, and there is tolerance of diverse forms. In a **closed system**, there are more rigid definitions of proper and desirable behavior, so that individuals making changes often encounter resistance and disapproval. North Americans and many Europeans experience a contradictory environment. Overtly open systems encourage people to pursue their dreams regardless of gender, race, and so forth; however, social change is covertly closed. It results in a sheltered *glass ceiling* discovered by many competent but marginalized minorities who want to rise in leadership.
6. Hope of changing the socialization cycle lies in questioning and challenging systems personally and socially, and this brings with it both serious resistance and immeasurable justice. Bobbie Harro (2018) revised her Cycle of Socialization [of Injustice] to become the Cycle of Liberation. Refer to Figure 5.2 as you read the following text. *First*, do not sidestep critical incidents that challenge your assumptions, upbringing, habits, or biases. Respect yourself enough to trust that you will find balance without guilt. *Second*, challenge social rules that enforce an estrangement of identities. Experiment with alternative identities, yours and others. Reach out to Others, both trusted familiar people and strangers. Appreciate your privileges, share them with others, and exercise power constructively. *Third*, connect with the broader community. Explore what you hear in the social environment about power and its limits, privileges, and justice. Engage with other people who are challenging assumptions or working to change the situation. *Next*, be prepared for strong reactions from others. Some will passionately support you; some will oppose you with efforts to reeducate you, ridicule, or possibly even reject you. *Fifth*, take action personally and in your environment. Make every effort to live consistently with respectful and inclusive values. Loan your efforts to projects that confront injustice.
7. The goals of conflict resolution are an appreciative approach to establish equality, equity, and inclusion, and just reconciliation between alienated groups (see Figure 5.5).

Figure 5.5 "Equality, Equity, Liberation, Reality"
A collaboration between Center for Story-Based Strategy & Interactive Institute for Social Change. Created by Angus Maguire.

Preventing Overt Conflict and Violence Cessation Are Crucial

Preventing or ending open, violent conflict is crucial. Clearly, this does not mean suppression or silencing the conflict. Instead, active methods that support real encounter and dialogue are effective. Joseph Bock (2001) described four types of peacebuilding that occur in sequence as tensions escalate and conflict becomes overt (see Figure 5.6).

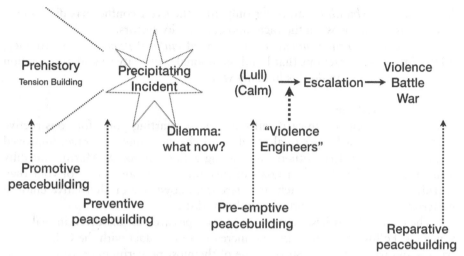

Figure 5.6 Escalation and proactive peacebuilding
Based on Horowitz, 2001, public domain.

- *Promotive peacebuilding* intervenes when open conflict is minimal to promote collaboration and relationship building across intersectional divides. Activities include things like international sports or conferences;
- *Preventive peacebuilding* assertively addresses intersectional divides using education, activity projects, and informed debate to cultivate goodwill and foster positive interpretations of the Other;
- *Preemptive peacebuilding* occurs during a looming crisis, focusing actions that deescalate tension by encouraging public calm, calling for help from peaceable people, and peace dialogue; and
- *Reparative peacebuilding* applies after violence and damage have happened, to repair relationships and improve root problems; this is usually the most expensive intervention.

A recent illustration was the trial of police officer George Zimmerman, who was charged with second-degree murder after he fatally shot Trayvon Martin in Sanford, Florida, in 2013. Zimmerman is white, and Martin was young and black. The case ignited grim tension in the already seriously divided community between law enforcement and the community, the black and white factions, and conservative and liberal politicians. Zimmerman was injured during the encounter so used self-defense to explain his actions, and was found not guilty by the jury. In 2019, Zimmerman sued the Martin family for US$100 million. *Promotive peacebuilding* would have happened years earlier by promoting constructive activities between racial groups and identifiable sectors of Florida society. *Preventive peacebuilding* would gather mixed groups of people for joint projects like community beautification, informative evening classes, or public debates. After the trial, when many predicted and prepared for vengeful violent clashes, *preemptive peacebuilding* did happen as prominent Americans called for calm. President Barack Obama said, "We are a nation of laws, and a jury has spoken. I now ask every American to respect the call for calm reflection from two parents who lost their young son."

Reparative peacebuilding can occur only after the overt conflict has died down, to repair relations between the races and community sectors.

Practicing *cultural competence*, also called *cultural fluency* (Ting-Toomey, 2019), includes interactions that build intentional sensitivity to and appreciation of divergence. You can do this in many ways.

Inner, Intrapersonal Work

Many writers focus on inward reflection as the starting point for constructive reconciliation. Clearly, personal insight and change require courage, improved awareness, support from others, and taking action. Mercedes Martin and Billy Vaughn (2014) identified four goals of this inner work: awareness of your own worldview, a positive approach to difference, knowledge of alternative cultural patterns and worldviews, and cross-cultural skills.

The **contact hypothesis** states that stereotypes are best dissolved in real relationships. Follow your curiosity and increase your contact with the Other. Make friends and work together. Story is one of the most powerful expressions of personal identity; be brave as you actively listen to others' experiences of cultural exclusion; be brave to tell your own hurtful stories. Study personal accounts of both injustice and of hope.

- It takes courage—As you begin this exploration, question the objectivity of your anxieties and perceived threats. Do expect to feel safe as you explore, but do not expect to feel comfortable. Be patient with tension and discomfort. Adopt an open, learning stance and commit yourself to the long process. Think positively about how you want to approach people, or have them approach you. What values are deeply important to you and how would you express them when you meet a stranger? Be ready to notice unconscious bias as it affects your everyday behavior.
- Awareness is the reward—You will never fully know yourself. Develop awareness of your own tangled identities and privilege. You do not create the privilege, but do benefit from it. Develop awareness of the ways that you unintentionally treat some people disrespectfully.
- Don't do this work alone—Find support and opportunities to work with like-minded people.
- Action is necessary—Consolidate new insights with actions.
- Use and support social media that present alternative identities positively.
- Try to influence others' beliefs and actions. Make tolerance the norm, and Othering unacceptable. Challenge bias and stereotypes, even seemingly "innocent jokes" that are not funny. In doing this, you can expect discomfort and resistance. If you push too hard, people shut down; if you do not push hard enough, people will not see the need for change.

Interpersonal Conciliation Work Requires Dialogue

Conciliation is friendship making. Working in diversity-sensitive ways requires repeated dialogue. Your personal horizons widen as you refine trust in yourself and the Other. Anticipate that change provokes anxiety in most people. The process begins with unsettling experiences that initiate a pause to question familiar biases and assumptions. This can lead you to insight that can then be shared in dialogue with others. People are more alike than different, and discovery of shared values and commitments can lead to new dimensions of relationship.

Here are some starting points for interpersonal diversity work;

- Speak out loud for justice, speaking against both obvious and subtle injustice.
- Facilitate friendship in your own community, between individuals and groups.
- Help create a supportive and safe space for frank dialogue and problem solving. Loan your support to an already active campaign that uses its resources to organize, coordinate and multiply efforts, plan strategically and professionally.

Society's Work Is Part of Diversity

The most complicated and difficult part of improving equity, equality, and inclusion is facilitating the culture change necessary to dismantle unjust systems and establish new ways. The central aims of social justice making are repairing past injustice, remediating ongoing suffering, and building new systems around respect. These activities occur in individual, cultural, and universal contexts that usually require deep changes of legal processes and legislation, such as the real desegregation of public services and the establishment of uniform human rights. Given the power of community narrative, social reconciliation is aided by corrective story that means rewriting history accounts composed exclusively from the standpoints of power. Accomplishing these changes is often a tricky process, but sustaining the changes created is even more difficult. Strong leaders and decision makers must be identified and engaged. These parties need to have vision and power to make relevant decisions.

In the long run, concern with enduring peacemaking is more useful than short-term agenda. As shown by numerous historical transformations, the results of changing social institutions and policies are far-reaching.

There are three potential strategies to cause social change (Keashley, 2000):

1. Gradual reform, usually initiated by decision makers within, through policy change, programming, or affirmative action projects, for example;
2. Nonviolent confrontational activity that challenges the status quo, sometimes in significantly organized movements such as the civil rights movement led by Martin Luther King; and
3. Violent confrontation, for example using violent protest, insurrection, or coup d'etat.

CHAPTER SUMMARY AND STUDY GUIDE

- Personal identities are created at the intersection of diverse factors like race, gender, SES, religion, and culture. Intersectionality explores the personal and social identity factors and systems that shape most human interactions. Diversity Studies is specialized scholarship that explores the potential for positive connections and creativity result-ing from diverse identities, and the roots of deep injustice and conflict when unfair practices are used.

- Cultural identity affects everyone behaviorally, relationally, and at the level of deep beliefs and values. Our own cultures are largely taken for granted, whereas other cultures are more easily evident. Culture can be intriguing, or can become the base for fear.
- Gender identity is interwoven with dimensions of genetic inheritance, self-identification, and cultural and role expectations. There is much that remains to be understood.
- Race is an influential factor in the development and resolution of many conflicts. Nonetheless, racial differences are more closely linked with social factors than with biological features.
- Religious identity, or beliefs about the spiritual dimension of existence, is formed through association with like-minded people, through per-sonal study and choice. Religion is a weak influence in some societies, and a powerful force in others. Religion can be used both for social integration or also to support deep, enduring conflict.
- SES is largely a matter of heritage, despite Western popular beliefs in individual power to determine one's own status. Socioeconomic resources are highly correlated with quality-of-life outcomes such as health, life expectancy and expectations, independence, and self-determination. Gaps in relative status are inevitable sources of lasting social conflict.
- Reconciliation of conflict, and sustainably peaceable relationships and society, cannot happen without diversity sensitive functioning that produces equality, equity, and inclusion of all, regardless of intersec-tional identities.

TERMS IN FOCUS

6

Conflict within Families

■ ■ ■

In Focus in This Chapter:

- There are many variations of family and family functioning. Definitions of the family evolve over time and culture, with no static agreement.
- Families provide four foundations for individual members: offer and nurture secure belonging, shape competency strengths and resilience, provide continuity through time, and socialize deep values and beliefs.
- Families are structured with power, roles, and rules to accomplish the adaptive tasks of socializing the young, adapting to change, and solving problems.
- Conflict in effective, functional families becomes a creative force for bonding and prosocial learning; in dysfunctional families, high conflict perpetuates corrosive effects on everyone.
- Families deal with multiple problems simultaneously. Problems cluster around frequent, common sources of argument, including universal dialectic tensions that arise in every relationship and those linked to maturation through the family life cycle. To move beyond conflict, the family must find consensus that a problem exists that is worth working on, and they must remain engaged until the problems are settled.
- All families cope persistently with change, some natural and some forced. Any change can be a source of growth and maturation, but also of tension and conflict.
- As complex as the family is, so too is conflict resolution. Prevention of family division is the best option. However, families do experience ordinary conflict every day, resolving it with dialogue. Serious, intense, or prolonged family conflicts require outside intervention. There are four models for this: legal justice, settlement mediation, therapeutic mediation, and problem-solving conciliation.

The family is a unique organization, so conflict in a family takes on unique characteristics. The family exists in two worlds: it is a group of individuals affiliated for life and also a group that must fulfill legal responsibilities and obligations. In this chapter you will explore these unique features by discussing individual membership within the family, look at the essential functions of family in the lives of its members, explore family conflict, and sketch some possibilities for resolving serious conflict.

DEFINING THE FAMILY

Common Western definitions of family focus on the **nuclear family**: "a married woman and man, with at least one child." However, actual families include many alternative forms, some originating in non-Western cultures. Alan Mirabelli, of the Vanier Institute of the Family, noted that "the family unit is varied and ever changing, and the definition has a long history of expanding and contracting." Lynn Turner and Richard West (2015) stated that defining the family is an "incomparable challenge."

In contrast to the nuclear concept, here are a few realities of contemporary Western families:

1. Approximately 70% of children live in nuclear families; 19% of children live with one single parent; and 9% live in a stepfamily. These statistics vary according to economic and geographic circumstances and alter as a family ages (Statistics Canada, 2018).
2. More than one-third of contemporary marriages begin with an online introduction. For homosexual couples, the internet provides the most common way to meet dating partners; for heterosexual couples, it is the second most common (Ortega, 2018). Divorce rates are slightly lower for those who meet online than for other couples.
3. A sexual relationship is not the central defining factor of a family. Rather, factors like economics (opportunities to earn a wage), relationship dynamics (domestic partnership and extended family), and reproduction shape perceptions of family. Emotional, economic, and legal dimensions of family are often at the core of family conflict.
4. Nonheterosexual families (LGBTQ2+) are not uncommon. Families with LGBTQ2+ heads of household could include about 10% of families in North America and Europe (Statistics Canada, 2015); LGBTQ2+ families are less common in other cultures. Conclusive figures are difficult to establish because statistics are gathered for different purposes among diverse populations. Alternative configurations may occur more frequently than census data suggests because acceptance of LGBTQ2+ relationships is not universal. Legal rights and privileges granted to heterosexual families are not uniformly granted to alternative families.
5. Families have a certain stability but also constantly change. The instability of members entering and leaving through birth, marriage, divorce, the addition of foster and adoptive children, and death can be a source of serious conflict.
6. Family breakup is usually associated with conflict and alters many long-standing constellations. Current estimates are that 40% of committed adult relationships eventually dissolve (Kazdin, 2002). Rates vary widely across professions, ethnic groups and cultures, and religious affiliations. Many conflicts require professional assistance to handle the legal challenges of the dissolving family.
7. The previously mentioned statistics refer mostly to contemporary Western patterns. Non-Western and tribal cultures' family groups are more often united by ancestry, kinship networks, cultures, and lifestyles (Red Horse, 1980; Vidyarthi, 1976).

The "normal family" is a matter of considerable curiosity. In fact, there simply is no normal family—there are average family statistics; there are imperfect families who are not "abnormal"; and there are families who appear drastically different on the surface and in private. The very definition of normal is shaped by dominant cultural values that surround the family (Walsh, 2012). Your personal concept of family is shaped by your experiences and cultural roots, although we tend to assume that our own family patterns are "normal." A more useful concept is a **functional family**. This includes diverse forms of operational family (Walsh, 2012; and others). A **dysfunctional family** is an unsafe or neglectful one that does not adequately support the members' needs for any number of reasons. This can result in silenced members, negative or chaotic interactions, asocial or abusive behavior, and endless conflict.

It is useful to distinguish between a **household**, which is a group of people occupying a home, and **family**, which is a group of people bonded in time and space by a variety of factors such as ancestry, common fate, and economic dependency. Mirabelli stated, "If you feel like a family, you probably are."

PERSONAL IDENTITY IS SHAPED IN THE FAMILY IN THE CONTEXT OF SURROUNDING CULTURE

Family is the origin and foundation of identity, self-esteem, and respectful relationships. You are given identity early—no one chooses gender or siblings or your surname, for example. During adolescence, most people experiment with alternative identities and the accompanying behavior patterns. In young adulthood, healthy identity results from deliberate investment in the sort of adult character you personally value.

Four Family Foundations of Identity

The family is a nucleus that provides for the needs of individual members in four essential ways: attachment and belonging, teaching skills for competent functioning, continuity through time, and values and beliefs. Some family conflicts begin when members believe the family has failed in these functions.

The Family Is the Seat of Attachment, Security, and Interdependence

A vital human need is to belong, to give and experience love. When connection needs are met, people feel well. Healthy families provide the secure base from which members venture into the world. The family is a source of belonging that can become a template or a working model against which later relationships are experienced (Bowlby, 1988). Attachment relationships make each family constellation unique with shifting variations of closeness in subsystems of parents and siblings, nuclear and extended family, and established members and new.

Specific family attachment patterns occur within their cultural surroundings (McGoldrick and Shibusawa, 2012). In collective societies, attachments tend to be close and more whole-family; in individualistic cultures, spousal and sibling dyadic relationships tend to be central.

Shared experiences bring people together, so attachment is a theme of encounters every day. Even conflict, if resolved amicably, can strengthen bonds. A *bid for connection* is any action that communicates, "I want to feel close." The bid can seem trivial, like a quick touch, eye contact, a quiet question; it could be a receptive response to another person's bid for connection.

Research by John Bowlby was pivotal to our understandings of attachment. Contradicting Maslow's theory (see Chapter 1), Bowlby demonstrated that emotional security is more important to human well-being than physical safety. His findings form the core of **Attachment Theory** (Ainsworth, 2015; Bowlby, 1969), a body of work that highlights the lifelong benefits of attachment as well as the potentially harmful consequences of poorly or excessively attached relationships. Secure and reciprocal **attachment** creates an incomparable safe haven from which the individual operates. Individual benefits of healthy attachment include a strong Self with positive self-esteem and a prosocial attitude of concern for others.

CONFLICT CASE 6.1 ■ LOST ORYSSIA

Oryssia was 7 years old in 1942 Russia when nearby war combat caused her family and entire community to flee their homes to go to Germany. They took with them only precious articles. As their flight became more and more desperate, articles and animals were discarded along the road. Oryssia clung to her family, fearing that she would be so slow that they would discard her too.

Tragically, Oryssia and her 8-year-old friend, Anna, did become separated from their group. After wandering for several days, they were taken in by a farmer family, who then took them to a Red Cross orphanage. Oryssia and Anna stayed at the orphanage for 8 months, believing that their people had abandoned them. When they were eventually located by their despairing families, they were so traumatically wounded that neither girl was ever able to accept or believe that they were secure. Oryssia is now 85 years old and still does not believe she is good enough to belong. She has never had a friend or romantic relationships that lasted more than a few months.

Oryssia's family safely immigrated to North America, where she was educated as a nurse. She spent the next 65 years nearly homeless, moving from city to city, 37 in all. In her work, she was often fired for conflict with coworkers.

Mary Ainsworth et al. (2015) described the qualities of secure and insecure attachment. The large majority of people experience **secure attachment**, with little or no anxiety about belonging or abandonment. The attachment figure, usually a parent, becomes a base for exploring the world because of confidence that the Other's help will be sensitively protective, responsive, and supportive. **Insecure attachment** may take one of three conflicted forms, even in adulthood. *Fearful-avoidant attachment* motivates people to turn away from each other because of distrust. In relationship, these individuals oscillate between intense attachment and avoidance. In *anxious ambivalent attachment*, separation anxiety is prominent because a person does not feel confident that the Other is reliable. *Disorganized detached* is a state where true attachment is absent.

A **Reactive Attachment Disorder** (RAD) is the term used to describe a seriously disturbed attachment-affection bond such as experienced by Oryssia. Interrupted natural attachment prevents security from developing. This can occur when love is stressful and unreliable or abusive, when a child becomes separated from the family, or when there is an early death of an attachment figure. The insecurity leads to feelings of unworthiness, distress, and disengagement, and interpersonal difficulties with anger, insensitivity, and domination. Oryssia's adult relationships demonstrated insecure identity and RAD. The incidence of RAD is unknown, but rare. It is estimated that, even among neglected and abused children, about 10% develop RAD (Zeanah, 2010). Attachment is a central issue and often a serious challenge for adoptive families. Close attachments confront everyone with a fundamental dialectic dilemma of balancing independence—*my* wishes and goals, *my* values—with unselfish altruism—*our* goals and expectations, *our* needs for cooperation (Baxter, 1990). This natural tension can become the source of considerable interpersonal conflict when:

- individual needs for attachment or for independence are unfulfilled;
- two related individuals experience mismatched needs; or
- family affection is jeopardized by trauma.

As for Oryssia, attachment habits influence conflict behavior later in adulthood. Positive connections make room for a positive frame during conflict, which helps prevent the escalation of arguments. People who avoid close attachments are more likely to engage in hostile conflicts with their partners (Steuber, 2005). Not surprisingly, insecure people also report significantly less satisfaction in adult romantic relationships.

Romantic Attachment

Robert Sternberg (1986) wrote the **Triangular Theory of Love,** illustrated in Figure 6.1. Three connected factors contribute to the existence of romantic love:

- *passionate* emotional and erotic connection;
- *friendship* based on intimacy, communication, and shared living; and
- *commitment* through a conscious decision to be indefinitely faithful.

> *In contrast to how a child belongs in the world, adult belonging is never as natural, innocent, or playful. Adult belonging has to be chosen, received, and renewed. It is a lifetime's work.*
> —John O'Donohue

Ideally, mutually affectionate intimacy develops slowly and gradually. The first year of a romance is the most formative because it provides opportunities to learn to operate jointly, and establishes habits that can continue for the duration of the relationship. As two adults encounter each other in different circumstances and discover shared goals, the components of love develop in varying pace. John and Julie Gottman (2017) noted that love tends to develop in sequence: the passionate connection of falling in love is usually first, building a trusting friendship comes from that infatuation, and loyalty and commitment take time. According to

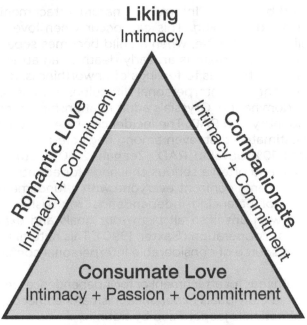

Figure 6.1 Triangular theory of love

Based on Sternberg, 1986, public domain.

Sternberg, when the three elements are in relative *balance*, an equitable, maturing attachment exists that is usually satisfying. When the relationship is *imbalanced* and dominated by one element while the others are neglected, the relationship can be unsatisfying and cause conflict. Sternberg's (2005) **Triangular Theory of Hate** described the keen animosity that can sometimes develop when a loving relationship is damaged by conflict.

Cheating and Infidelity Break Romantic Attachment Healthy romantic relationships depend on a core of mutual trust, understanding, reciprocal loyalty and support, and harmonious rules and boundaries. If partners have drastically different expectations, confusion will be the pressing result. Serious conflict can develop. Infidelity involves the violation of core assumptions: truth is obscured, trust is broken, and loyalty is weakened. Some research suggests that infidelity is common: approximately 12% of men and 7% of women admit to extramarital affairs, although this varies with individual age and social era (Wang, 2018). Most affairs develop from a nucleus of unexpressed or unresolved anger (Spring, 1997).

> *Love is the hot water for Relationship Soup. There's nothing nourishing unless you add trust, compatibility, great sex, common interests, understanding, selflessness, fun, and support you can count on.*
> —Maureen Scurfield

Disclosure of infidelity creates "an avalanche of feelings and a labyrinth of choices." Janis Abrams Spring (1997) noted that a quick forgive-and-forget reaction is common, but very unlikely to resolve the affair and its resulting harm. Conflict-resolution professionals are often engaged to help couples work through the pain of cheating, particularly when the parties' intend to remain together and rebuild the relationship. Many decision points must be navigated. Spring mapped out a process for healing that involves separate paths for the cheater and the injured party, and much authentic communication that was not typical in the past.

The Family Nurtures Competence and Resilience

Personal competence is the ability to successfully apply knowledge and skill to master life's challenges. The development of competence begins at birth and, of course, is never complete. The role of the family in encouraging and monitoring competence cannot be underestimated because it touches every aspect of personal functioning. Fundamental skills include emotion management, social-interpersonal sensitivity, mastering stressful problems and conflict, working rationally, and acquiring specialized abilities.

Family competence is the ability of the family whole to organize and manage itself to productively accomplish its tasks. One essential family task is to instill in young members an accurate perception of their personal competence: healthy individuals must be able to acknowledge their strengths without conceit while also relying on others in times of weakness without embarrassment or shame. This perspective comes from a family that can accept both strength and weakness.

An important correlate of family competence is **resilience**, the ability to adapt to sudden misfortune or to ongoing difficulties and stress. A functional family is a resilient family (Rolland, 2004). Not only so-called normal families are resilient, and normal families are not necessarily resilient. *Psychological resilience* is an individual's ability to remain calm and successfully cope with crisis without enduring negative consequences. Harmonious relationships facilitate development of psychological resilience skills. *Family resilience* is the ability of the whole system to withstand and adapt to changes within the family and in the environment, and recover a workable equilibrium. The family may need to make temporary adjustments to cope with passing crises such as temporary unemployment, or might need to absorb more permanent losses such as divorce or death to shape a new way of operating. Families marked by mutual support, shared responsibility, flexible structure and boundaries, and teamwork tend to be more resilient (VanBreda, 2001).

Community resilience is even more complex, affecting everyone within a community (Chandra, 2011). **Community resilience** is the ability of a social system to protect against, prepare for, and respond to a variety of emergencies that affect many people at once. Resilient responses might demand coordinated *short-term responses* that care for the vulnerable during crisis, *longer-term crisis recovery*, and long-term *community building* or rebuilding when the crisis has ended. Essential functions of a healthy community system are fostering individual and family resilience.

The Family Ensures Continuity and the Presence of the Past

Family continuity conveys security through reliable, predictable consistency. Tradition, cultural identity, and heritage create a sense of continuous progress. Connections to the past generate confidence in the durability of the family unit into the future. Continuity suggests an uninterrupted quality that is, in fact, an unrealistic expectation in a family, and yet it is a necessity for individual and group identity. On an individual level, continuity expresses itself as the family of origin becomes a sort of template for other relationships.

Among other factors, family habit patterns shape continuity. **Habits** are routine actions and interactions that are acquired through repetition, usually without thinking or choosing. Habits are cocreated and shared, which means that without realizing it family members instruct each other to constantly learn and unlearn habits. Cues about what is acceptable or offensive are received, exchanged, responded to, or ignored, becoming part of reciprocating behavioral cues that add to the overall dynamic of the family. Some habits can be simple, such as the fact that Mom parks the car just like Grandpa did, or they can relate to style issues such as tidiness or how you all treat pets, or they can profoundly influence how you live out your values or operate arguments. Day-to-day family functioning is often entrenched in automatic patterns, and habits can be very hard to change. Some members may feel confined and unable to grow.

Systems do not remain static, however, because families constantly change in membership and functioning. A dialectic tension between stable continuity and pervasive change confronts everyone (Baxter, 1990). The individual members' constantly evolving and maturing needs and growth challenge a family to flexibly adapt. Influence exists between the family system and its cultural and global environment, and a family must adjust to changes surrounding it too.

Discontinuity occurs when consistency and predictability break down, resulting in uncertainty and insecurity. There are myriad sources of discontinuity and transition. A parent's change of employment, a child moving out of the parental home, a period of illness, or adding a pet to the family are some examples of ordinary stressors that necessitate transition and adjustment. Every family must also cope with serious, sometimes shocking sources of discontinuity. The continuity of peaceful family living was never recovered by Oryssia or her family, for example.

Family Discontinuity Due to Adoption

Adoption is a well-known source of discontinuity. Although practices vary, approximately 30% of people globally report adoption within an extended family (UNDESA, 2009).

The adoption process is usually difficult and stressful at best. In North America, the average child waits for a suitable adoptive family for 3 years; more than 10% of children wait more than 5 years; prospective adoptive parents wait between 9 months and 7 years (Adoption Network, 2018). Eighty percent of placements become finalized with legal adoption, but many legal hurdles must be addressed along the way, such as birth relatives' and the child's rights, government jurisdiction, ancestry and inheritance issues, medical factors, and international law in the case of transnational adoption. Most aspiring adoptive parents feel great pressure to present their motives and abilities as "perfect" to gain approval.

Aside from the legal issues, adoption discontinuity refers to an equally difficult emotional process of forming new family attachments, which has great potential for intrapersonal and interpersonal conflict. The deep hopes and demanding adoption process often set up unrealistic expectations and ideals that may prove impossible to fulfill. Bonding is never instant but, rather, is slow, uneven, and awkward, necessitating a preparation phase called *adoption courtship*. Some families and cultures do not accept adoption as legitimate, so some adoptive families must cope with the stigma of not being regarded as "normal" or "real." There may be visible dissimilarities that inadvertently broadcast the history of adoption. Sometimes there are medical implications of not being related by ancestry or birth. All these issues can slow the process and affect the success of new attachment and the long-term identity of a "forever family."

Several recent trends assist adoptive families to cope with or overcome discontinuity. Although legal adoption is usually permanent, open adoption now permits ongoing contact between birth parents and children. Birth records, traditionally held secret, can be opened upon consent of the child and the biological parent, and this can lead to reunion. Another trend has been to preserve the original culture and religion in a child's upbringing rather than to obliterate it. Safe Haven Laws have decriminalized the anonymous relinquishment of a healthy child, which makes unwanted parenting less likely. New legislation is enacted in some areas to protect international adoptions.

When a child's life or the family constellation is disrupted by serial foster placements or unsuccessful adoption, everyone must cope with the emotional contradictions of transient attachment and traumatic separation. The majority of adoptions are successful, but 10% of families still deal with compounded disappointment or dissolution (Adoption Network, 2018). The probability of breakdown increases with the age of the child at placement, with the number of previous placements and ongoing disability as factors. The child may cope with Cumulative Adoption Trauma.

The Family Establishes Values and Beliefs

Values are relatively permanent principles that are considered important and worthwhile guiding principles behind character development and behavior choices. Examples of values are "honesty," "serve the common good," and fairness. **Beliefs** are standards that guide true, right, moral actions. Examples of beliefs are "adventure is good" and "cheating is wrong." One feature that contributes to family uniqueness is their management of values and beliefs. Some families hold them rigidly and resist variation; some families have a flexible approach. For some families, beliefs are open for explicit questions and conversation; some families maintain covert silence and expect members to figure them out and comply.

Personal identity is strongly influenced by family cultural roots, and tradition (McGoldrick and Shibusawa, 2012). **Culture** is made up of complex systems of behavior, values, and beliefs learned from and shared by members of a group. With a degree of choice, culture creates a "blueprint" for correct behavior, thoughts, emotions, and judgments through which you interpret your experiences. In this far-reaching way, culture influences most of what you do. *Family culture* is the assembled objects, habits, beliefs, and ideals that make up shared family identity. This heritage contributes to the consolidation of individual identity, as you accept, reject, modify, and choose identity. Ernest Burgess (1931) coined the term with these words: "Whatever its biological inheritance from its parents and other ancestors, the child receives also from them a heritage of attitudes, sentiments, and ideals which may be termed the family tradition or the family culture." One family responsibility is to transmit cultural identity to young generations and new entrees into the family.

Beliefs about what is considered to be appropriate and proper behavior are rooted in culture, circumstances, and family history. Values and behavioral rules intersect. *Core family values* are fundamental, and rules connected to them rarely change; *peripheral family values* apply to more pragmatic concerns, and rules are negotiable and can change with maturity and under new circumstances. Five unhealthy beliefs are likely to create an anxious, antagonistic family identity that leads to conflict (Eidelson and Eidelson, 2003).

1. *Entitlement*—I am, or we are, better than other people, and therefore deserve special treatment;
2. *Mistrust*—Other people are intentionally hostile toward me or us, and will take advantage of or hurt me/us, so it would be unwise to collaborate with anyone else;
3. *Vulnerability*—I, or we, live in a world where harm cannot be controlled, and fear about the future means I/we should defend ourselves;
4. *Injustice*—When I, or we together, are mistreated, retaliation is a necessary response; and
5. *Helplessness*—Even carefully planned actions will fail and I, or we, are powerless to fulfill desirable goals, so I/we needn't bother trying.

Mixed-Cultures Family It is a challenge even in the best of circumstances for a new member with unfamiliar behavior, values, and beliefs to assimilate into the family culture. It is particularly acute when new family members have identities with diverse origins in race, culture, country of origin or birth, or religion. Mixed cultures highlight alternative standards and values although, in fact, every family is intercultural. Figures vary, but in Western countries the number of mixed culture families is increasing, becoming one of the fastest-growing distinct population groups (Parker, 2001, 2004). These unions tend to occur among younger members who live in major city centers (Statistics Canada, 2011; US Census Bureau, 2018).

Though common, this joining of cultures challenges family and societal acceptance in ways that affect later lifestyle and family style decisions. Judith Martin and Thomas Nakayama (1999) outlined four possible ways of blending dissimilar cultures:

1. *Submission*—One partner relinquishes a source culture and accepts the other;
2. *Compromise*—Each partner gives up some and takes on some elements of the others' culture;
3. *Consensus*—Some elements are adopted from a "best of both worlds"; or
4. *Obliteration*—Both partners relinquish their own cultures and create a "third culture."

Family culture can become a source of conflict in many ways. An individual's divergence from the family rules and expectations might shape friendship, romantic, and work relationships in ways that differ from their parents' or extended family plans. In some families, this is regarded as defiance. Newfangled values and beliefs, especially religious ones, can ignite intense family judgment and conflict.

A FAMILY IS A COMPLEX WHOLE

A family is an excellent example of a complex adaptive system, continuously evolving to meet changing circumstances. You are interdependent, bonded by love and history and conflict and forgiveness. Whole family functioning is organized by factors like power, rules, roles, and coalitions. Information is processed by your family as it operates within larger community and national contexts. Family systems are goal directed and have purpose (Meadows, 2008). Family is the primary context in which individual identity and group boundaries form and reform throughout life.

The analogy of a ceiling mobile is aptly applied to a family system (Miller, 1992, see Figure 6.2). A mobile is a single piece of art with many connected pieces. Like your family, the parts are organized, and dance around each other in patterned and somewhat predictable ways. They move within a limited perimeter but do not escape it.

The "Smith family" may be a group of 27 people, each with their own characteristics, needs, skills, and so forth, but the Smith family is greater than the simple collection of individuals named Smith. It is like an amazing sociological piece of art. The whole has properties and functioning that are different from the functioning of any individual member. It is perceived as a connected whole, but the boundaries and psychological distances shift. Although there is constant change within, many things remain the same.

Figure 6.2 A complex family system is illustrated by a ceiling mobile

A Family Is Organized and Structured

A family is organized by power relationships, defined roles, and rules of behavior. Structures include and influence (but transcend) every member. Organization is a source of dependable comfort, but can also cause frustration if it unnecessarily limits personal freedom and development.

Power Relationships

Every member has a place in the family structure, like one piece hanging in a mobile. Most families are only partially democratic, and members' use of power and influence is an important dimension of structural organization. Power models tend to resemble one of two forms on a continuum. Leadership and power might be *symmetrical*, where influence is an outgrowth of the connection between people. Power is shared and exchanged, fluctuating collaboratively according to individual strengths to cope with specific situations. This **relational paradigm of power** results in consensus decisions made after full communication that considers diverging feelings and needs (Young, 1973). Alternatively, the members may function in **complementary** ways, so that one member takes the leader role while others function as followers. Each member has a limited domain of power with little sharing or overlap of control, such as "mens' work" or "kids' chores." In this model, one decision maker makes decisions, usually benevolently. Sometimes called a **dominator paradigm of power and control**, this pattern creates an unequal, dominant-deferential relationship. The leader who exercises power is viewed as stronger or even superior and the followers defer, usually consensually. However, this can lead to power struggles when individual needs, strengths, and competencies mature. When the singular decision maker uses power defensively rather than benevolently, conflict is ignited. Negotiating family power habits often becomes the source of serious conflict (Peterson, 2013):

- To the degree that power is not recognized, it is probably not fully consensual.
- Inequitable distribution of power and responsibility usually creates uneven dynamics such as codependency, or asymmetrical helpfulness and helplessness, with resentment.
- Sudden, unexpected changes in power relationships usually cause resistance.
- The unfair use of power by "lording it over" others with threat, punishment, or harmful exploitation will always lead to turmoil.

Roles Are Imposed and Enacted

Structured **roles** are recurring behavior molds you are expected to fulfill as part of the whole system. Roles are shaped by positive and troubled interactions and both subtle and overt communication. Roles establish an interacting network of responsibilities that interlock for family operations to succeed. They facilitate a division of labor so that not every member of the family has to accomplish every task, like housekeeping, money earning and spending, care of children, and so forth. *Task roles* depend on specific abilities and contribute to efficient family and home operations; for example, bill payer or message taker. *Positional roles* are behavior patterns expected of family members linked with position in the constellation, such as "big brother" or "the baby," but

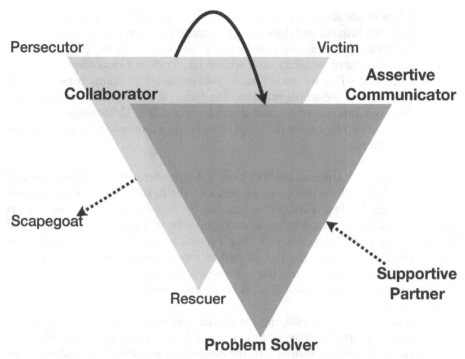

Figure 6.3 Tragic drama triangle, reframed
Based on Karpman, 2007, public domain.

people might feel uncomfortably locked into these roles. *Process roles* contribute to smooth relationships among family members; for example, emotional caretaker or problem member.

Roles support stability and predictability, but can also be confining, so they must be flexible enough to accommodate ordinary development and growth as well as unforeseen events and challenges. Other members expect recurrent patterns; for example, the role of "wife," "grandparent," or "sibling" has specific expectations. Expectations can cause repeated conflict if the demanded responsibilities are ambiguous or compulsory or do not suit the individual's desires, talents, or development.

Stephen Karpman's (2007) **Tragic Drama Theory** describes four stereotypical roles that seem to emerge during conflict (see Figure 6.3).

- *Persecutor* (aka Villain)—When in this negative role, you engage in conflict with unreasonable demands and coercive actions. You blame and attack others, and accept no responsibility for the conflict.
- *Victim*—This term does not refer to an actual victim, but to a Victim perception. When in this powerless role, you feel and act defenseless and incapable, are frozen and mostly unable to contribute to resolution. Feeling victimized by others, you take no personal responsibility. You are often treated by other members as Victim too.
- *Rescuer* (aka Hero)—This person "saves the day" or the Victim, whether or not it is necessary. Rescuing establishes a power role as a "good guy."

When in the Rescuer role, you step in hastily, and your actions may reinforce the helpless and dependent feelings of the Victim, and be resented by the Persecutor. Rescuing enables everyone to overlook the underlying feelings or roots of a conflict, so it seldom facilitates true resolution.

- *Scapegoat*—This somewhat minor role in the tragic drama is perceived as the source of the whole problem. The focus on Scapegoat serves to distract the disputants from the actual dynamics of conflict. The Scapegoat function may be filled by one of the three primary actors, or might by someone else in the family.

According to Karpman, conflict usually begins between the Persecutor and the Victim, but both recruit other players into the drama. The Rescuer is often the first to get hooked. Family conflicts can be very confusing because players repeatedly switch tactics, strategies, and roles during a conflict. Any individual in the family might play any role. The Persecutor can quickly switch to play the Victim, for instance. The drama seldom moves toward problem solving or resolution because it plays out like a theater script, and individuals feel unable to deviate from the prescribed lines. A repeating, sometimes malevolent, conflict cycle traps the actors.

Karpman stated that escaping the drama begins with discomfort in it. Key skills must be learned to recognize the roles and switch patterns while reframing the source(s) of conflict. Insight into the motivation and beliefs behind each role is useful. Other writers (Emerald, 2015) have focused their work on exploring the positive aspects of each role, so that:

- a Persecutor, instead of demanding and attacking, can learn to collaborate;
- a Victim can end the passive acceptance of misery, and become a pragmatic communicator, assertively contributing their thoughts and opinions;
- a Rescuer can learn the restraint of objective and factual problem solving; and
- a Scapegoat can be responsibly supportive instead of the target of blame.

The Karpman theory has proven useful in family therapy and mediation, but has received only limited scholarly support.

Work and Family Role Conflict

Many people find that having dual work and family responsibilities benefits their performance in both because of personal enrichment, skills growth, and broadened relationship supports. However, the pressures of the competing roles of healthy family member and valued employee can be incompatible and difficult to limit. In times of stress, the demands of work can interfere with important life priorities and/or family tensions interfere with performance of work responsibilities (Byron, 2005). This intrapersonal conflict is especially common for people who are socialized to be the "breadwinner" for a whole family. The work-family role conflict can cause significant discontent, shown in unreliable physical and mental health, relationship conflicts in both realms, and unsatisfactory effort, absenteeism, and turnover at work.

Think About and Discuss with Your Colleagues

- Do you remember either of your parents experiencing the family-work role conflict? How did this show in their behavior at home?
- When and how did you start paid or volunteer work outside your home? Did you experience conflict between the dual roles? Do you think the work-life role conflict might affect you in the future? Are there characteristics in your personality that might make this more or less likely?
- In 5 years, as you build your career and your home, which of these phrases do you think will be your attitude (and why): "Family comes first ..." or "If you love your work, you always put success first ...."
- If or when you experience this family-work conflict, how will you figure out a solution?

Solutions to this ubiquitous conflict are hard to find. Clearly agreed work and home expectations, roles, and balanced responsibilities will help. Open communication both at home and at work is critical and does not signal weakness or failure.

A Family Is Governed by Rules

Rules are guidelines actions in specific situations. Family rules crystallize what what is desirable and allowable or forbidden (Shannon and Sutton, 2018). Family rules are mostly *implicit* and unspoken, but can be inferred from repeated habit patterns (Ford, 1983). Some rules associated with security and self-confidence *facilitate* positive emotional connection and closeness by encouraging honest communication; some rules *constrain* and limit family functioning by communicating negative messages such as blame or be silent (Carlson, 2017; Crane, 2013). Healthy rule systems share a number of characteristics: they are *explicit* and discussed; they promote openness, equal application, and dignity; they benefit every family member; compliance is attainable; and degrees of diversity and difference are permitted. Significant sources of conflict are hidden rules that are unknowingly violated.

For most people, rules are ranked subjectively into personal priority systems. *First-level rules* guide behavior and daily actions, such as the implicit rules we have for time management and emotional expressiveness. *Middle-level rules* deal with family-as-a-group relationships, including divisions of labor, decision making, interpersonal coalitions, and ways of using power. A *family paradigm* consists of core values and commitments that guide management of dialectic issues such as togetherness and independence, responsibility and blame. The paradigm also sets the methods used to correct error: reward, punishment, guilt and shame, and acceptance and rejection. *Metarules* are agreements about how strictly rules are enforced or changed. Notice the resemblance to Kalpana Das's analysis of cultures in Chapter 5.

A Family Has Many Tasks that Must Be Accomplished

Family Is the Primary Agent of Socialization

An essential task of the family, while sheltering members from the storms of life, is to teach principles that will enable maturing children to become independent (Walsh, 1994). Parents are the central agents of **socialization**, which is the process of learning behaviors, relationship patterns, and attitudes necessary to act effectively in family and in society. Socialization occurs in positive ways that encourage desirable behavior and negative ways that are designed to reduce undesirable actions.

Parenting and Child Raising Child raising is a profound challenge that most people voluntarily take on. Approximately 85% of adults do have children, although this has decreased in Western regions in recent decades (Blackstone, 2012). Parenting raises cycling tensions of demand and tolerance, protection and control, correction, discipline, and punishment, all very likely to cause conflict.

Robert Epstein (2010) studied the effectiveness of practices recommended by experts and used by parents. He found ten parenting skillsets that are correlated with childrens' secure attachment, overall happiness, social competence, academic confidence, and infrequent problem behaviors. In order of importance, these trainable parenting skills are:

1. First and foremost, expressing love and physical affection through attention, acceptance, and support;
2. Stress management and reduction, and positive interpretation of events;
3. Strong spousal relationship and healthy modeling for children;
4. Respect for a child's autonomy that encourages self-reliance;
5. Learning promoted through example;
6. Providing a stable and predictable family environment;
7. Behavior correction that emphasizes positive reinforcement, punishment is rare;
8. Modeling healthy lifestyle habits;
9. Providing religious education and spiritual community; and
10. Providing a protective, safe environment.

These skills facilitate what Donald Winnicott (1973) called **good enough parenting**, which is imperfect parenting based on a core of positive practices and stable family.

Parenting style, a pattern of parent behaviors toward children, is defined by the cluster of strategies a parent uses, as they fall on two intersecting dimensions (see Figure 6.4): *responsiveness* (the degree of sensitivity to and acceptance of a child's emotional and developmental status), and *demandingness* or control (referring to parental control vs. child responsibility) (Darling, 1999).

Diana Baumrind (1967, 2012) described four typical parenting styles based on decades of family observation.

- *Indulgent* or *permissive* ("too soft") *parents* exercise little control or direction, letting the child's impulses and demands be the guide. Permissive parents tend to overlook a child's need for correction. Conflict communication is somewhat covert and ambiguous.
- *Authoritarian* ("too hard") *parents* restrict and control misbehavior through coercive power, punishment, and fear. An already established status quo is maintained, and change is difficult. Parents tend to be domineering and concerned with efficient obedience rather than with understanding the child's needs or behavior. Authoritarian parents often rely on corporal punishment. Conflict is limited, but repetitive.

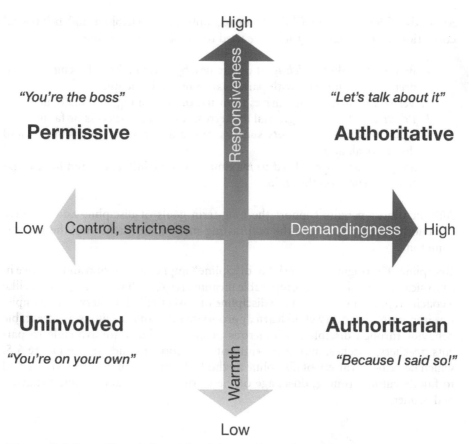

Figure 6.4 Parenting styles at the intersection of two dimensions
Reprinted with the permission of Graeme Stuart, Sustaining Community.

- *Uninvolved* ("not enough") *parents* use a laissez-faire indifferent approach, providing less attention, nurture, discipline, and guidance than the child needs. These families tend to avoid conflict because of weaker connections and a lack of effective stress management.
- *Authoritative* ("just right") *parents* balance consistent rules and limits with warm emotional responsiveness and respect for the child's autonomy. They use open communication and positive affirmation of the child's character, independence, and success. They model reasoning, focus on positive results, and negotiate behavioral consequences. Arguments are taken in stride with a strong repertoire of potential solutions. Authoritative parenting is repeatedly found to promote positive self-esteem and prosocial behavior in children.

> *Parents can only give good advice or put children on the right path, but the final forming of a person's character lies in their own hands.*
> —Anne Frank

Methods of Socialization Children unarguably need discipline and behavioral correction. Five primary methods are used to shape social learning:

1. By imitating the *modeling* of others nearby and in a broader culture, children learn to identify with particular noteworthy people;
2. Verbal *instruction* emphasizes information, reasoning, and dialogue;
3. *Practicing skills* through trial and error, resulting in success or failure;
4. Behavioral *reinforcements* such as praise and reward, punishment, and disapproval; and
5. *Selective exposure* is used to maximize positive influences and limit negative influences on the child.

Although most parents support the long-term goals of discipline and adaptive behavior, controversy about the contrasting methods for achieving the goals is common.

Discipline The origin of the verb "to **discipline**" implies instruction and practice in a physical or mental skill. A comparable meaning is to coach with skill practice, like a coach prepares an athlete in the discipline of basketball or archery, for example. It is important that every child learn appropriate rules and the limits of acceptable behavior through discipline. Numerous positive methods are available to parents, teachers, coaches, and other authorities to correct children. See Figure 6.5, which describes a variety of discipline methods. Variations in the methods are tied to family culture, timing, dose, age of the learner, type of undesirable behavior, and gender.

Unhealthy - Abuse	Distraction	Unhealthy - Neglect
Threats	Reminders	Safety ignored
Shaming	Supervision	Basic needs unmet
Spanking	Monitoring	Emotionally deprived
Rigidity	Encouragement	Not noticing child
Physical Abuse	Rewards	
	Incentives	
	Choices	
	Time-in	
	Time-out	
	Teaching	
	I messages	
	Negotiable Rules	
	Problem Solving	
	Consequences	
	Non-negotiable Rules	

Figure 6.5 Alternative discipline methods
Reprinted with the permission of Deborah MacDonald, The Center for Parenting Education.

Discipline strategies are most effective when:

- they are rooted in a positive relationship;
- discipline is part of a long-term instruction process;
- discipline is consistent, with a degree of flexibility;
- desirable behavior is taught, encouraged, and reinforced;
- undesirable behavior has predictable, consistent consequences; and
- discipline is sensitive and responsive to a learner's development and personality.

Punishment Punishment imposes an unpleasant penalty such as a time of isolation or corporal punishment with the goal of reducing improper or wrong behavior. A reasonable critique is that punishment might eliminate undesirable behavior, but does not present positive alternatives.

Think About and Discuss with Your Colleagues

- Would you or should you spank your own children? Under what circumstances could you imagine spanking your children?
- Imagine that someone in authority is displeased with you—perhaps your employer or a professor. Under what conditions might this authority be justified to hit you? (You probably answered "None"!)
- … can a parent hitting a child be justified?
- … a majority of parents approve of some use of spanking or corporal punishment.

Corporal punishment, or *spanking*, causes pain with slapping or hitting. Spanking is often intended to ensure a child's attention to the seriousness of their misdeeds. Boys experience more spanking than do girls, and fathers are more likely than mothers to use it (McKee, 2007). Although most people detest child abuse, few parents regard spanking to be abusive. ABCNews reported that, in a 2012 random sample of more than 1,000 American adults, 66% approve of parents spanking children. Significant variation relates to parents' own experiences, gender, culture, education, and geographic region. Few parents approve of spanking in schools.

Although some controversy persists (Larzelere, 2005), parents are discouraged by experts and by legislation from using corporal punishment. The majority of child psychologists and development specialists are opposed to spanking under any circumstances, and this is supported by the American Academy of Pediatrics (AAP), the American Psychological Association (APA), and other expert organizations. In 2006, the UN Committee on the Rights of the Child released an advisory report that starkly equated physical punishment with violence. This report was endorsed by 192 countries, with only Somalia and the United States failing to ratify it. Corporal punishment of any type is legally banned in more than 50 countries (Grogan-Kayler, 2018). In the United States and Canada, corporal punishment is legally permitted but is limited to "reasonable punishment," not assault. The distinction is fairly subjective.

The results are very clear. Corporal punishment is successful to bring about momentary behavior change, mostly because children are afraid of and avoid pain. However, corporal punishment simply does not work in the long run. To the contrary, many negative consequences are found:

- Within the *family*, strained relationships result, and an intergenerational echo of a malevolent violence cycle is risked (McCoy, 2014).
- For a *parent*, corporal punishment can initiate habits that are part of a family violence continuum that can slide into abuse and child injury (Grogan-Kayler, 2018).
- In a *child*, spanking is strongly correlated with contradictory outcomes such as antisocial behavior, aggression, and problems with anxiety and depression (AAP, 1998; Afifi, 2012; Grogan-Kayler, 2018).

A Family Is Challenged to Continually Adapt to Change

Every family system is an emerging, developing organization of "these people, at this particular time" whose arrangements change continuously. Change is not a discrete event but, rather, is part of an ongoing flow of change. Slow change is accepted as stability; rapid, sweeping change is perceived as chaotic stress and can be an inevitable source of ambivalent feelings and conflict. Most families are also forced to confront unplanned changes. The collective challenge everyone has to navigate is how to conserve enough stability from the familiar (even though it may no longer be comfortable) versus how to make the necessary changes (which demands the relinquishment of the familiar to venture into the unknown). Adjustments to change are easier when they are planned and gradual and accomplished with everyone's participation.

Some Change Is Motivated by Individual Discontent One way family changes begin is with dawning discontent and agenda building of one individual. It may result from a time of intrapersonal conflict that clarifies the source(s) of discontent. With that awareness, the individual can think about alternatives and decide whether or not to demand change from other family members. Voicing or acting out the discontent can result in argumentation that can potentially cause hurt and turmoil for others.

Family changes rarely happen smoothly but, rather, with many missteps along the way. There may be foot dragging and resistance from some members, so changes rarely happen with synchronicity. The family must negotiate decisions. The action phase is often the most challenging: enduring change happens because of actual changes in behavior that must occur and be sustained, or the family will quickly revert to old, familiar habits.

Dialectics in the Family Dialectic tensions are a set of seemingly contradictory forces that are present in all connected relationships, and they are active most intensely within an intimate group. They can be difficult to manage and balance because they cannot be resolved with finality (Baxter, 1990). Within a family unit, dialectic tensions revolve around *cohesion and bonding*. Individual members and dyads must find a workable balance between contradictory factors of a) connection versus independence and distance regulation, b) predictable stability versus change and growth, and c) transparency versus safer privacy. As the family interacts outside itself, the tensions revolve around *adaptation to the world*. The family as a whole negotiates d) inclusion versus exclusion of outsiders as part of the family unit, e) conventional forms of relationship versus unique arrangements, and f) family boundaries that disclose versus conceal private information in public. To deal effectively with these tensions and problems, the family must find some degree of consensus and cooperative functioning.

Natural Change through the Family Life Cycle Families are anything but static. Some natural developmental changes can be predicted and mapped with the Family Life Cycle (McGoldrick and Shibusawa, 2012). There is general agreement that:

- Families develop repeating interaction habits over time.
- Stages in the family life cycle can be distinguished, but vary and are reversible.
- Norms from other social groups such as the extended family and the surrounding culture affect the timing and sequencing of development.
- Past adjustments influence current functioning. Causes and effects can be cyclic; either can become the other.

Pulling several scholars' work together, the **Family Life Cycle Theory** (see Figure 6.6) observes that healthy family evolution occurs in seven predictable transitions with no beginning or end (McGoldrick, 1989; P. Murphy, 1979; Rodgers, 2009).

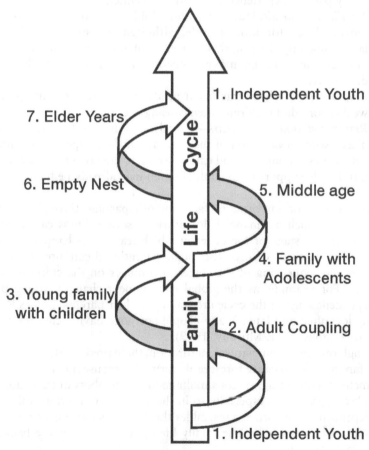

Figure 6.6 Family Life Cycle: Simultaneous family development stages
Based on McGoldrick, 1989; P. Murphy, 1979; Rodgers, 2009.

1. *Single independent youth*—With a focus on the future, youth at this time invest in peer attachments and influence, consolidating personal competencies, and experimenting with identities, values, and religion. Their independent explorations can be the source of considerable parent-child conflict.

2. *Young adults coupling*—Before children, there is an inward focus on the couple attachment, establishing a joint home, and applying competencies to work. When conflict happens, it is usually focused on perpetual, lifestyle differences, moving toward a more comfortable equilibrium.

3. *Family with young children*—Most time is spent at home with highly dependent children. Conflict between young parents is common because competencies as a parent and partner are tested, and differences of values are exposed.
   a) Family with *preschool children*, birth to 5 years old;
   b) Family with *school-aged children*, 6 to 12 years.

4. *Family with adolescents* 13 to 18 years old—Both the children and the family are expanding commitments outside the home. Parent-child conflict can result from parents losing their influence over kids' experimentation. Many parents experience work-family conflict.

5. *Middle-aged adult*, launching adult children—This is a time of welcome independence for most people, although the social trend is toward later launching. During this phase, whole-family conflict is likely when independent children make decisions of which one or both parents disapprove.

6. *Empty nest family*—Attachment needs are strong for many parents, but weaker for adult children, often causing friction.

7. *Retirement and elder years*—Usually and hopefully this is a peaceful phase, with reevaluation of the past, and little interpersonal conflict. Parents' needs for support and care increase at the same time as demands for intrafamily support from adult children may already be high.

Families are not uniform; in fact, smooth passage through the stages is unusual. Events such as financial downturn or severe illness can affect how a family navigates a stage or the order in which transitions happen. Events such as unexpected death or divorce and single parenthood can alter the cycle. The expression and sequencing of the stages also hinges on the cultural context of the family. For example, as the global environment changes, young people in the independent stage of the cycle are staying in their parents' homes longer and marrying less often and later. Many people postpone having children until their careers are established (P. Murphy, 1979).

Though resulting from natural maturation, these predictable changes destabilize the family and can cause foreseeable turmoil. Because members are at different, sometimes competing, stages simultaneously, members in transition interact in complex ways. This is especially so in the areas of connection, values testing, and independence. The process resembles the relentless movement forward of an old-fashioned barber's pole. The family life cycle therefore is the backdrop for frequent family conflict.

Conflicts arise throughout the family life cycle when people's needs and competencies become incongruent. What was functional at an earlier age becomes confining if members feel obstructed. Deborah Tannen (2012) described a common conflict that stems from the "love-control continuum" between parents and their offspring. What a parent communicates with intentions of being lovingly helpful (for example, "I'm worried about your studies"), can be perceived as controlling and interfering with childrens' independence (it sounds like "You're slacking off again"). It is a difficult challenge for a parent to recognize how and when to give up control. Tannen recommended setting aside the control and power issue, and emphasizing the connected dimension of the relationship.

Changes Due to Relationship Dissolution, Separation, and Divorce Common sources of discontinuity are separation, divorce, and family resettlement. Although separation usually occurs within a primary parental relationship, seriously stressful loss and transitions ripple to every individual. Rates of separation vary widely, influenced by surrounding historical and cultural factors linked to the acceptability of divorce. In North America and in Europe, divorce rates for first marriages currently average around 45% (OECD, 2018). The highest rates are found in eastern Europe, and the lowest are found in Chile and Ireland.

There are statistical peaks for separation when a relationship has lasted 3 years (due to emotional disengagement), 7 years (due to high conflict), and 20 years (due to an erosion of connection) (Gottman, 2015; Regina, 2011). If the relationship outlasts those high stress points, it is more likely to endure, so divorce rates decrease with the length of a relationship. A **risk factor** is something that increases the likelihood of developing serious relationship difficulty. Known risk factors for conflict and relationship dissolution are:

- early marriage between ages 15 and 19;
- high school education or less;
- the presence of children at the start of the relationship;
- short courtship;
- cohabitation to test the relationship;
- conflicted, never married, or divorced parents;
- religious and/or cultural conflict;
- family or friends' disapproval; and
- unstable employment and financial stress.

Knowledge of these risks could be discouraging but knowing the possibilities can open the way for exploration and deliberate choices. For example, having unhappily married parents might darken your perspective on long-term commitment, but could also open the way to solidify your own hopes and beliefs.

Realistic expectations can sidestep these risk factors more than simply "hope for the best." Taking a period to slowly get to know each other and develop mutual commitment can provide a genuine picture of lifestyle habits, values and character, and life goals. Authentic communication, ideally facilitated by premarital counseling and workshops, is facilitative. Gaining the support of both families is an advantage. Concerns about temper, substance abuse, or violence should be taken seriously.

Think About and Discuss with Your Colleagues

Leo Tolstoy (1877) wrote: "All happy families are alike; each unhappy family is unhappy in its own way."
Vladimir Nabokov (1969) wrote: "All happy families are ... dissimilar; all unhappy ones are more or less alike."

- In your experience, which of these statements sounds more realistic or familiar?
- Which of these statements might describe your own perspective on families?
- What have you seen as the major sources of happiness, and the major causes of unhappiness?

The Separation Process The process of emotional detachment is prolonged for several years for most people. Usually, one hopeless partner thinks, "Why bother? It's no use." Rarely is there **synchronicity** when the partners come to a decision simultaneously, so overt conflict often increases as one partner stays invested while the other has silently left (Kaslow, 1996). The end of commitment destabilizes individuals, the relationship, and the family, with chaotic painful mourning, anger, disorientation, longing for reconciliation, and quiet adjustment to the reality.

A decision to separate unleashes a complicated series of events, each with its potential for compounded conflict. Separated living arrangements must be made, child well-being and custody considerations discussed, and property divided and financial concerns addressed. When extended family and friends are informed, they may become polarized, believing that they must support one "victim" against a "bad guy." Legal matters come into play, and processes are begun that can take many months or, in some cases, years to resolve. Legal separation and divorce are discrete events. As time goes by, most separating adults do resolve their substantive issues and develop conflict patterns that are more effective than when they lived together.

Adult Resettlement As the disruptions of family separation and child issues stabilize, a newly single person will usually experience a period of intrapersonal turmoil that is unsettling but not necessarily unpleasant. It is a time of exploring and renewing identity that can lead to new relationship directions. The healthy need for this time of inner debate makes it inadvisable to begin a new relationship prematurely.

Legal divorce permits remarriage, and about three years after divorce that is likely: approximately 75% of men and 66% of women remarry (Walsh, 2012). This provides no guarantee of peace, though, and the divorce rate for second marriages is 60%, and 75% for third.

Resettlement of Children For children, there is no standard outcome: for some, it is the end of a period of family uproar, for some it is a devastating loss. Generally, the more continuity in the child's life, the easier the transition. Some crucial factors (Kelly, 2012; Kressel, 1977) that ease childrens' reactions are:

- *precursors*—reduced intensity of parental conflict;
- *during separation*—preservation of central sibling and extended family attachments, reactions of significant other people, and overall continuity of lifestyle; and
- *after separation*—reliability of care and positivity in parent-child relationship, supports from people in the child's environment, the parents' ongoing conflict and abilities to cooperate, and parents' choices regarding new romantic attachments.

In the first year after separation, family financial resources are often drastically reduced because of new expenditures. After five years, while womens' income recovers to 94% of predivorce income, mens' income is substantially higher at 110% (Amato, 2014). Eighty-two percent of single-parent households are headed by a woman, and only 30% of noncustodial parents make regular child-support payments or follow visitation agreements. Of course, these factors are contributors to ongoing stress and conflict, particularly regarding the child.

Converging Information 6.1 ∎ Parent Alienation Syndrome

Parent Alienation Syndrome (PAS) is a distorted relationship between a child and a noncustodial parent after separation. PAS was identified by Richard Gardner (1985) to summarize one potential outcome of severe dispute over child custody.

PAS results from one parent deliberately communicating scorn and even hatred toward the other. Conflict tactics can include:

1. *Use authorities such as child protection agencies and the court* to block access and parent-child contact, making unreasonable applications for court intervention or making unfounded abuse allegations.
2. *Undermine the parent-child relationship* by portraying the opponent parent as selfish, unavailable, unreliable, and unsafe;
3. *Demand divided loyalty*, coaching a child's animosity and distrust, or using the child to gather damaging information. This demand for loyalty may also extend to friends or extended family (Baker, 2011).

The child is the central victim of this syndrome. Because false perceptions and exaggerated behaviors are cultivated, the child's alienation follows. Emotionally, the child shows unreasonable, extreme feelings of fear and distrust, hurt, and anger. Their hostility rejects one "all-bad" parent while outwardly colluding with the other "all-good" parent. PAS is relational "poison" to the child and to the whole family. When it occurs, it is emotionally harmful and unjustified. The child may become completely estranged from one parent.

In the field of conflict resolution, PAS has been controversial. On the one hand, signs are readily recognized by legal and mental health professionals in a small minority of cases. Michael Walsh and Michael Bone (1997) found that some degree of PAS was detectable in the majority of high conflict divorces. On the other hand, the concept is severely criticized for three main reasons: first, it is not universally accepted by court-appointed decision makers; second, it may be nearly impossible to identify subtly devastating cases and scientific reliability and validity are mostly unproven; and, third, because parental vigilance on behalf of the child is fully a parent's responsibility, criticism is justified when maltreatment or abuse is suspected but unjustified as a tactical weapon in a custody war.

Blended Family Settlement Resettlement is usually a prolonged mix of both positive elements such as relief and greater harmony, and also stress, disequilibrium, and conflict. The frequency of remarriage after divorce means that whole families must adjust to a **blended family**, which creates a household that includes members from at least two backgrounds. This is neither a magical happily-ever-after situation nor one resembling the wicked stepparent fairytales. Rather, it takes considerable time, careful effort, and attachment by degrees, often under resistance from some members (Braithwaite, 2013). When two families blend, internal restructuring happens, with many corrections as the family cultures are mixed. Froma Walsh (2012) drew parallels between remarriage and the enculturation necessary after immigration to a foreign country. Individual members and subgroups adjust at differing rates, and mistakes are common (Baker, 2011).

Patricia Papernow (2015) described a 2–8 year emotional blending process. When the blended family is first established, differences are amplified by divergent lifestyle habits, skills, and balance, so instability and conflict are common. Dissatisfaction with the turbulence can lead at least one member to mobilize the others to begin resolving the troubling differences. Successful actions lead to calmer family functioning that is accepted as different from both original families. Secure step-attachments and loyalty can then take root.

Family Migration and Traumatic Change Migration from a homeland to another home disrupts the continuity of the "old," commonly resulting in distress and whole family disequilibrium and conflict. Migration requires adjustment to a new culture that involves **acculturation**, the painful relinquishment of the familiar, along with **assimilation**, the process of adopting the ways and values of the new culture. Parents, raised in the old culture, may be tied to treasured patterns of language, relationship, and belief and therefore less willing to make the adjustments. Younger family members, especially if born and raised in the new culture, may be drawn away from the original culture through interests, friendships, and involvement outside the family. The generational disconnect usually requires modification of whole family patterns and habits, which often generates conflict.

When the migration is forced by environmental disaster, hardship, or violence, as happened to Oryssia and her community, the adjustments can be compounded by prolonged crisis and trauma recovery. In those instances, restoration of both the reality and feeling of safety are crucial. Crisis management is slowly paced, painful work that deals with the trauma experienced, so a base of family strength is necessary.

Family Problem Solving

As the material so far suggests, the causes of conflict are complex, involving multiple sources and influences at any moment. The family, more than any other human group, is characteristically conflictual.

To effectively overcome problems, the family has to recognize and agree that *a problem exists*. This might not be as simple as it seems. Problems exist on a continuum of intensity, from ordinary predicaments (like conflicting schedules) to seriously corrosive elements (such as lying or aggression) that threaten a relationship. Family members often do not agree on what sort of problem it is. Parents, for example, might think that a teenager's use of social media is a problem with extensively negative effects, while the teenager views the media as a lifeline and the problem is the parents' interference. Consensus must also be found about whether the issue is a *perpetual problem* or a *solvable problem* (Gottman, 2015). Effectively, though, if one person has a problem then the relationship has a problem. The family is processing a **metaproblem** when there is disagreement about whether a problem exists or not, or whether a problem is important or not.

Sources of Conflict The family has to recognize *complex root sources*. Some families fight primarily about content; some families disagree on the process of resolution; and some fights are about both content and process, simultaneously or sequentially. Arthur Bodin (1996) analyzed family conflict and described **content clusters** are related and linked problems. Bodin discovered the following clusters, in order of frequency:

1. Activities,
2. Change,
3. Personal character,
4. Communication,
5. Lifestyle, habits, rules and conformity,
6. Taste preferences,
7. Relationships within and outside the family,
8. Fulfillment of responsibilities, and
9. Values.

The collective interpretation of the problems shapes the resolution. A simplistic view of tension is that there is one single cause in a person or an event. This view is likely to lead to scapegoating one member for blame. That will not go far toward a sustainable solution but, rather, leads to cycling conflict. A more realistic and useful view is that problems and solutions are shared, each member contributing both positively and negatively to the tensions. Families also have to cope with problems resulting from interactions with and pressures from the environment. The family power hierarchy can influence recognition of a problem; a whole family can be controlled by one person's stonewalling ("This. Is. Not. A. Problem!").

The family must work patiently to continue communicating and jointly *testing possible ways* of resolving the issue. Even when there is consensus that a problem exists that is worth working on, other factors can affect the resolution. If one party is working on simply getting along while another is demanding complete agreement, there will be a mismatch of goals. Disputants might resort to habitual interpersonal alliances and subsystems without thoroughly considering the issue. Antisocial or aggressive behavior can escalate conflict and inhibit peace. If habits of processing conflict become ritualized and resistant to change, the family can become stalled by patterns of ineffective communication, closeness, or power inequity (Goldman-Wetzler, 2020).

CONFLICT IN THE FAMILY

John Gottman's (2001) research findings identify some crucial relationship factors of both intact and broken families. The degree of satisfaction or unhappiness and the frequency of conflict are *not* conspicuous causes of relationship breakdown. Gottman discovered that, particularly in times of conflict, it is the seemingly mundane and trivial communication, actions, and reactions that most powerfully set the tone and quality of a relationship. His findings and insights can be helpful to understand most intimate relationships.

Functional Family Conflict

There is no ideally harmonious family. The fact is that all families argue, most even fight at times. However, some ways to resolve conflicts are more and less effective, while some are inherently destructive. We have discussed the contrast between constructive and destructive conflict elsewhere (see Chapters 3 and 4), but some principles apply specifically to family.

Constructive and functional individual tactics use what Melissa Hawkins (2002; Gottman, 2015) called **positive sentiment override**, a positive perspective that is based on core habits that turn disputants toward each other. A positive past builds a reservoir that helps keep conflict friendly. If conflict begins with enough positive feeling "in the bank," that perspective will override pressing negative feelings so that everyone can remain safely engaged until the conflict is paused or resolved. Tactics concentrate on contact and affection, calmed emotions, soft speech, and listening, leading toward collaborative solutions that avoid impasse, and repair when someone is hurt. Gottman (2002) called this foundation in family friendship a **sound marital house**.

The functional family's central goal is to meet every member's needs. Functional families clarify the issues: they are able to discuss feelings and opinions, and needs and wants, and members hear each other accurately. Problems and fair processing are the focus, with steady movement toward solution. Members recognize that every conflict has more than one source or cause, so simplistic solutions are questioned.

Constructive strategy is marked by the use of tactful ways to bring up a problem, quiet body language, moderation of heated emotion, hearing and cooperating with the other's wishes. A *repair attempt* is an action offered to deescalate or cool a conflict by fixing an error. Examples of repair attempts are self-directed humor, apology, or giving in. Effective repair is easier to accomplish when there are already strong bonds of mutual support.

Dysfunctional Family Conflict

High-Conflict Individuals

Undoubtedly, every participant has a role in conflict, but **high-conflict individuals** share qualities that reinforce frequent arguments. Gottman (2015) called these harsh individuals **masters of disaster**. Poor underlying emotional coping is the key because logical thinking can be overruled by emotion during conflict. Masters of disaster experience emotional duality: on the one hand, they are sensitive and reactive to others' emotion; on the other hand, they are only vaguely aware of their own emotions and needs, so that feelings build quietly in intensity in the background until they erupt. Emotional flooding happens, and anger and fighting show a build-and-explode pattern. Although aware of tension with other people, they cannot respond constructively, so they find fault with others' and do not reflect on their own roles. Sometimes they have a dual face, publicly polite to outsiders but privately confrontive or surly (Eddy, 2005).

Several rare forms of mental illness can cause significant distress and conflict with other family members. **Oppositional Defiant Disorder** (ODD) is an illness that affects approximately 3%–5% of families. ODD begins in late childhood but continues into adulthood. Signs of ODD are frequent angry mood, irritable argumentativeness in most relationships, weak respect for authority and persistent defiance of rules, and spiteful pleasure from irritating others. Professional treatment is challenging for the whole family, usually involving child psychotherapy and social skills training, behavior management, and family or parental counseling.

A similar illness is **Conduct Disorder**, a long-lasting behavioral disorder of childhood and teen years that affects the life of a whole family with disruptive conflict. Seven to twelve percent of North American children are diagnosed with Conduct Disorder, boys more often than girls. There are four signal behaviors: interpersonal mistrust and deceit; impulsive violation of age-appropriate expectations; extreme expression of anger in disruptive fighting and antisocial aggression; and destruction of property. Long-term professional treatment usually includes child psychotherapy and skills training, family therapy to strengthen communication and parenting skills, and environmental supports at school and in the community.

An **Intermittent Explosive Disorder** (IED) affects up to 7% of families. It begins in childhood but is usually not diagnosed until adulthood. Repeated episodes of instantaneous, explosive rage occur that are disproportionate to any provocation. IED does not involve premeditated aggression but, rather, violence results from a sort of daze when thinking shuts down and rage takes over. Many who suffer are also anxious and depressed, especially just prior to an outburst. After the episode is over, people with IED do experience remorse and guilt, and many try to prevent the episodes with substance abuse. Professional treatment usually involves education and psychotherapy, habit modification, and, often, medication.

High-Conflict Relationships in a Family

High-conflict families spend too much energy on chronic fighting. Typical interactions could begin with only one provocative high-conflict individual, could be limited to two high-conflict individuals, or draw in other family members. Common characteristics at the base of severe conflict are insecure attachment, poor management of intense feelings, ineffective communication and unsuccessful problem solving, and unequal or abused power. High-conflict families are at the extreme end of a conflict continuum (Maccoby, 1992):

- *Minimal or mild conflict* (about 15% of family arguments) is characterized by quarrelling with anger, but hurtful interactions are quickly brought under control. Arguments usually end with cooperative actions that validate the needs of each individual.
- *Moderated conflict* (approximately 65%) might become verbally loud and attacking, but with no history or fear of violence. Attempts are made to overpower the other party by forming alliances or manipulating threats.
- *Substantial conflict* (15%) is more severe in intensity. Some emotions are expressed physically with slamming or throwing objects. Threats to use

children against the Other are used. Threats of violence are frequent and adults might endanger each other. Children are not at risk of physical harm, but do experience emotional distress and fear.

- *Intense conflict* (5%) endangers every family member with out-of-control emotional, verbal, physical, or sexual violence. Heated emotional outbursts, character attacks, blame, and caustic conflict are common. Children are openly used as weapons in the fight. Mental illness and/or substance abuse may be factors. Typically, outside social agencies such as child protection and police become involved (Maccoby, 1992; Stewart, 2001).

High-conflict families use tactics that are likely to aggravate problems, escalate conflict intensity, and damage relationships. Factors that predict destructive, dysfunctional conflict seem to correspond with qualities of what Florence Kaslow (1996) called a **corrosive adversarial relationship**. Other family members may eventually accept and accommodate to the discord.

Converging Information 6.2 ■ Violent Relationships in Dating and in the Family

With the exception of the military and the police, there is no more violent social group ... than the family. A person is more likely to be hit or killed in his/her own home by a family member than anywhere else, or by anyone else.—Straus and Gelles, 1980

Violent Relationships Defined

Intimate violence is controlling behavior or violence that occurs between any individuals in a trusting, close relationship. Mistreatment exploits someone's weakness through that trust. The usual goal is control—making another person do or stop doing something against their will. The violence can be *emotional* like intimidation, stalking, or threatening violence; *physical* like hitting or assault with a weapon; *sexual* like forcing sexual activity on someone who does not consent; and *spiritual* like imposing religious practices on someone or forbidding them. Intimate violence is simply that—violence. It is *not* conflict, although it sometimes occurs in the context of conflict. It involves people known and related to each other, of all genders, ages, cultures, and social circumstances: parents and children, siblings, dating relationships, friendships. It damages direct victims, those who witness the violence, some who try to intervene, even bystanders.

Family violence, also called **domestic violence**, endangers wellbeing, security, or survival in an ongoing family relationship or home. It can cause physical injury, psychological trauma, social isolation and fear, economic disadvantage, sexual risk, and spiritual lifelessness. The effects are long-lasting, even for several generations.

Intimate and Family Violence Are "A Hidden Epidemic"

The accurate incidence of intimate violence is unknown because it is a hidden problem. Nearly four million cases of child abuse are reported every year, but childrens' "cries for help" are often disguised, and often are understood only after 20 tries. Thirty-six percent of adult females and 17% of males report relationship violence. Statistics show a pyramid of actions ranging from friendship violence and invisible injuries (incalculable victims), corporal

punishment and other parental violence (experienced in a minority of fami-
lies), intentional and unintentional injury (uncommon), to homicide (rare). In
North America:
- Between 6 and 10 children die from neglect and abuse every day.
- Fifteen percent of all violent crimes occur in intimate relationships.
- Nineteen percent of intimate partner violence involves a weapon.
- One in 4 women experience severe violence at the hands of a "loved
  one"; 1 in 7 sustain physical injury; 1 in 9 men experience severe vio-
  lence; 1 in 25 sustain injury.
- Only 34% of people injured by a family member receive medical care.
- Twenty percent of homicides are committed by a family member or
  friend of the victim.
- One in 5 women and 1 in 59 men is raped during her/his lifetime.
- Access to a firearm by an abuser increases the risk of partner femi-
  cide by 400%.

Intimate Violence Patterns, supported by numerous research studies, are
as follows:

Victims
- Boys experience higher levels of aggression as children.
- Girls and women victims are most likely to be injured.
- Victims often accept self-imposed or social blame, and are encour-
  aged to "forgive."
- Adults who report are in a no-win situation; if they leave the rela-
  tionship they are at higher risk of violence and also at risk of social
  isolation and poverty.
- Victims often leave the relationship but then return ostensibly to
  mend the relationship.

Offenders
- Offenders are most likely male.
- Offenders may be reacting to a specific situation, or using a general
  habit of power and control.
- Boys and men are more likely to use escalating violence against oth-
  ers in adulthood.

The Dynamics
- The core issue is power and control—violence reinforces an abuser's
  distorted power.
- Violent episodes are not isolated; rather, cycles of escalating threat
  and harm occur.
- BEHAVIORAL
- violent pattern
- violent assault incident

Verbal
- verbal assault
- verbal threat
- intimidation, stalking

Passive
- neglect
- Violent episodes are perceived and explained differently by victims,
  offenders, family members, and society.
- North American society generally considers a dating and family relationship to be a "private matter," and impotently overlooks violence.

Information Box 6.2 ■ Continued

Authorities
- Law enforcement personnel often do not know how to deal with intimate violence.
- Twelve percent of events that trigger police calls result in charges of assault.
- Consequences and convictions are inconsistent.
- There are few successful prosecutions, partly because victims at risk may decline to testify.

Effects
- Violence can become reciprocal, especially after a prolongued history.
- About 80% of young adults who lived in violent homes are diagnosed with a psychological disorder.
- People who experience childhood violence are more likely to engage in violent relationships in adulthood; they are 30% more likely to commit a violent crime; 36% of women and 14% of men in prison were abused as children.
- Violence is correlated with marital separation and dissolution, but leaving or police charges rarely stop the violence.

The challenges for professionals
- Healing of relationship violence requires both "ending" and "mending."
- *Ending* means to build negative peace with early detection, protecting the vulnerable, and containing the violence or minimizing its damage.
- *Mending* means to build positive peace among all who are affected: victims, offenders, family witnesses, and society. This requires drastic changes to education, power dynamics, and creating positive relational conditions in which violence is no longer thinkable. Intimate violence can rarely be mediated successfully.

For additional information, explore University of Wisconsin website "Campus for awareness and relationship education."

Chronic, recycling conflict relates to several factors:

a) *Emotional connection is faulty*—If an emotional connection does not deepen, unmatched attachment and subjective loneliness result. When bids for connection that invite or reinforce bonding are ignored or rejected, discouragement can lead to withdrawal and ultimately to a chilled bond.

b) *Problem solving is endless*—69% of everyday tensions, most having to do with personality differences, lifestyle, and values are virtually never settled. Problems remain generalized and abstract, effectively blocking solution. Gottman (1999) called these **perpetual problems**. If you persist in demanding solutions, frustration will result in gridlock and conflict at ever higher intensity; if a family can agree to disagree but stop fighting, a foundation of positivity can be rebuilt.

c) *Harsh tactics and argumentation are used*—When you become emotionally overheated, you are more likely to perceive the opponent as an enemy, and justify use of the four "poisons" of defensiveness, criticism, disdain, and stonewalling. Blaming the opponent, judging and character attacks, or labeling each other with terms like "crazy" or "hateful" are examples. If there is a mismatch in styles of conflict, both parties may conclude that communication is useless. This results in distancing and avoidance, or mounting confrontation.

d) *Poorly balanced negativity*—Hawkins (2002) identified a **negative sentiment override**, which means that negative, harsh behaviors and comments far outweigh shared positive history. The balance of positive (e.g., compliments, thanks, appreciative comments) versus negative (e.g., criticism or antagonism) is revealing. In amicable relationships, positivity is offered on an average ratio of 20 positive to 1 negative; in conflicted relationships, the ratio is five or fewer positive to one negative, which feels like constant criticism. The lesson is that if you must criticize your family member, do it against a background of many positive interactions.

e) *Ineffective methods are used to finish a conflict and repair the past*—Ending a conflict with accusation or insult or with an exit will make peace unlikely if not impossible. Deescalating repairs might involve conceding a point, apology, self-directed humor, or affection, for example.

Predictable, repetitive patterns emerge, dramatized like a choreographed dance sometimes called a **conflict ritual**. Rather than to focus on solving problems, members tend to learn conflict avoidance. Family members use repeated win-lose argumentation and coercive power tactics. Under these conditions, conflict frequently ends with a chilled standoff, a disengaged exit, or the hostility spirals out of control.

Effects of Conflict on Children
All families experience conflict, and all children witness and engage in it. This can be a positive force if children observe constructive endings of tension peaks. Nonetheless, prolonged intense conflict can have negative effects on children, especially if they become entangled or blamed.

Children demonstrate the sometimes hidden effects in multiple ways. Physically, most experience sleep disturbances with daytime concentration problems, as well as unexplained physical symptoms and aches. Emotional distress, anxiety, and depression are common. Mistrust and insecurity, as well as aggression and conflict with peers and siblings, are recurrent.

There is a broad range of child adjustment. Some children show resilience while others are overtly stressed. Boys tend to act out their feelings in overt behavior, while girls tend to experience the effects in covert emotion. Disturbances tend to settle over time, so that older kids tend to show better adjustment than do very young children. Overall, children living with ongoing dispute show poorer adaptability than children from amicable families.

CONFLICT CASE 6.2 ■ THE "SARGENT" FAMILY

The Sargent family consisted of "Christine" and "Victor," married for 6 years, and Victor's 28-year-old son, "Kevin." It was Victor's second marriage and Christine's first. Father and son had lived together until his marriage to Christine, and they remained close. Christine and Victor jointly owned an electronics business, and Kevin worked there as the sales manager.

Christine was an outwardly charismatic woman, lively, and magnetic. Beneath the surface, however, fiery emotions flooded her thinking. She controlled most details of Victor's life, and was resentful and jealous of any time Victor and Kevin spent together. Her temper was quick and explosive, and she was in frequent conflict, especially with Kevin but also with employees and some people in her social circle. She insisted that other people were at fault, and was unable to think constructively about her own actions in those relationships. The relationship between Kevin and Christine was marked by mutual aggravated hostility, with nearly every interaction degrading into a skirmish. Victor had been a peacemaker many times, but was tired and had given up.

One outstanding event made everyone realize that "something had to be done." Victor and Christine were opening a new business location. During the grand opening, on the sales floor in front of many customers, Christine and Kevin got into a loud argument over who was boss. During the fight, Christine insulted Kevin's mother and slapped him, so he slapped her back. Later, Christine confronted Victor, "You have to choose—it's him or me."

Kevin was charged with assaulting Christine. During the trial, Christine became angry with the judge and loudly accused him of bias. The trial was adjourned and they were referred for family mediation.

The mediation was challenged from the beginning. The mediator, "Melanie," planned to see each of the three individuals alone as a first step, then propose joint sessions to establish some groundrules that might calm the battles and, hopefully, work toward more constructive problem solving. Both Kevin and Victor were open to discussing resolution; Christine refused to meet alone with Melanie. She saw the situation in black and white terms and could not back down: she had done nothing wrong, Kevin was a fault, and Victor was weak because he did not control his son. She demanded apology from both Kevin and Victor, and demanded that Kevin participate in treatment for his anger. When Melanie proposed dealing with anger issues separately and suggested there might be several solutions, Christine was insulted and accused Melanie of taking Kevin's side. She became very angry, left the room, and refused to meet again.

When the case went back to court, the judge dismissed the charges against Kevin.

On the surface, you might notice:

- It was difficult to discover whether the fights were over Christine's power, Victor's loyalty or love, or something unknown.
- Christine seemed to be in contentious conflict with many people. Within the family, Kevin easily took her bait.
- In some ways, Kevin and Christine were arguing "apples and oranges": Kevin resented Christine's interference in his relationship with his father, Christine defined the problem as Kevin's insubordination.
- A repeating destructive loop resulted. If Victor was to have any peace, he had to play the peacemaker in this cycle.

- During the frequent conflicts, Kevin, Victor, and Christine each habitually took positions and roles that in many ways programmed an unsuccessful outcome
- All the relationships were tangled by family, marital, stepfamily, and work roles. One source of conflict that surfaced at the store opening was the contrasting interests, goals, and roles of family and employer/employee.
- It was difficult to find a path toward resolution because Christine needed control and insisted that Kevin was to blame and had to change.

POTENTIAL SOLUTIONS TO CONFLICT

The fact that family conflict is so complex also means that the possibilities for constructive resolution are many. The best option is conflict prevention with strong and functional relationships. Most conflicts are "ordinary," everyday disagreements that are solved with conversation and negotiation. Third-party assistance is also available through professional family mediators.

Prevention Is Always Best: Build Strong Relationships

Elise Boulding believed that global peace could be imagined through the vital foundations of the family and, especially, through nurturing relationships. She believed that children are innately generous and peaceable, connecting naturally with others, so they inspire affection, compassion, and peace. She pointed to children as the microcosm and practice ground for producing "global civic culture" (Boulding, 1988). To create lasting peace, she proposed that every person can participate in collective peacemaking by being a peace learner, teacher, and problem solver within the family.

Rudolph Rummel (1991) explained how collective learning takes place. As you experience interactions that are rewarded with peace, you learn to repeat those exchanges; as you experience tension that escalates toward conflict and warns of violence, you learn to prevent the escalation. Rummel's optimistic view was that every experience of conflict therefore becomes a potential learning that can guide the future and, over time, your relationships become smoother and more cooperative and peaceable. The sequences of these conflict-peace interactions form a spiral of learning that has the potential to lead to benevolent nonviolent conflict resolution skills and conflict prevention.

Tensions and complaints will always arise. When you "pick your battles," the relationship is likely to be more amicable. Gridlocked arguments are avoided by exploring the underlying reasons for conflict and finding ways to meet everyone's needs. Learning to stop arguing about perpetual problems effectively blocks futile argument (Gottman, 2015).

Ordinary Conflict: Conflict Resolution in Conversation and by Negotiation

Peacebuilding is an ordinary, everyday goal accomplished with daily peaceful habits. Managing tension with regular, respectful dialogue means that the majority of conflicts are resolved using conversation and negotiation.

The base skill is calm negotiation that minimizes argument by discussing each parties' interests. Robert Selman (1984) described the maturation of family negotiating strategies. Early in life, the focus is to accomplish self-centered aims without considering any other person. The next phase has a focus on "what can you give me?" As maturation continues, people develop reciprocity and can offer more cooperation and collaborative dialogue. In a mature relationship, balanced interpersonal openness exists with truly give and take conflict resolution. As you review Skill Builder 6.1, imagine how these principles could apply to the Sargent scenario.

Professional Intervention with Serious Family Conflict

A few family conflicts become so intense and entrenched that intervention from an outside third party is enlisted—like Melanie and the judge dealing with the Sargent family.

The Professional

Family conflict professionals simultaneously work with many fields of knowledge, so several human science disciplines (like psychology, social work, counseling, justice, and the law) are used in training:

Praxis Skill Builder 6.1 ■ Ordinary Family Conflict Resolution with "Clean Fighting"

DO	DON'T
• be realistic, not idealistic	• emphasize negative insult or criticism
• move toward each other, not away, and respond to bids for connection	• reject a bid for connection or withdraw from discussion abruptly
• stay in the here-and-now	• demand change
• speak for yourself, and no one else—"I think ... I feel ... I want ... I need ..."	• never use poison: criticism, defensiveness, stonewalling, contempt
• take responsibility for your own part first	• do use: tactful complaint, accept responsibility, self-soothing culture of appreciation
• actively listen, use "Search Talk," accept the Other's perspective with empathy	• engage in gridlock, an Escalation Cycle, or the Chilling Cycle
• tolerate emotions and keep them cool; take a break if they become too heated	
• slow down reactivity and assumptions to communicate calmly and tactfully	
• embed critique into positive statements at a rate of 20 to 1	
• reserve battles for the truly important matters	
• recognize when the discussion reaches an impasse, take a break	
• offer a compromise or call a truce: agree to disagree, but stop fighting	
• quickly reach out and make repairs with humor, apology, forgiveness	

- individual development and childrens' needs and best interests;
- family dynamics, including resilience, life-cycle milestones, functional communication, parenting patterns, and cultural influences;
- mental health and illness;
- effective and dysfunctional conflict, crisis, distress, and domestic violence; and
- collaborative problem solving, and mediation theory and intervention models.

Work with highly distressed people can be personally challenging and stressful. Professionals use reflective practice to ensure ongoing learning through self-correcting review and insight. They must manage their own thoughts and feelings to ensure a safe environment and process. One important skill is critical thinking about one's own family experiences, assumptions and biases, as well as cultural values. Professionals are sensitive to their own impact on the momentary interactions.

Ethical decision making is another critical component of family conflict practice that protects vulnerable people. Ethical dilemmas are particularly common when working with conflicting parents and/or family members. Family conflict workers are guided by the Model Standards of Practice for Family and Divorce Mediation in the United States, and the Code of Professional Conduct of the ADR Institute in Canada. See the Conclusion to this textbook for fuller descriptions of professional career preparation.

Three Stages of Intervention

Stage One of professional intervention is assessment of the family strengths and difficulties. Management of crisis elements if they are present is also essential. Stage Two is consideration of multiple options available, to decide on and plan the intervention. When sufficient information has been gathered and discussed, Stage Three intervention can go forward. With the Sargent family, the mediation that Melanie attempted never went past Stage One because of Christine's adamant need to control the process.

Stage One of Intervention: Gathering Family Information with 4-P Inquiry The professional begins with inquiry into significant 4-P factors: the people, problems, the process to date, and potential solution. All affect both the origins of the conflict and, probably, the future. Before proceeding further, an evaluation of the degree of distress is also relevant. If family distress is too low, motivation for change might be minimal; if the intensity of crisis and distress are severe, the family might be paralyzed and unable to deal with substantive issues. In that case, simple crisis intervention is used to restabilize the family before dealing with dynamic issues later.

Some 4-P detailed assessment questions follow:

a) Assessment of the People

- Who are the primary disputing parties? Who contributes to the ongoing nature of the conflict; who contributes to calming and forward motion of solution?
- What are the individual and collective resources that family members bring? What strengths hold the family together? What potential skills are present?

- How attached and committed are members, to the family and to resolving the conflict? Has anyone already silently left the relationship?
- Are individuals ready to make relationship changes or do they resist?
- Are there cultural issues that can influence the intervention?

b) Assessment of the Problems

- Trauma Informed Care always explores traumatic experiences which the family may be revisiting in the current conflict or crisis.
- What substantive content divides the family? What are the solvable problems?
- Do individual conflict styles aggravate friction?
- Is the family struggling with natural dialectic tensions and life-cycle transitions?
- Are there unusual stress factors the family has to cope with?
- Who is vulnerable? Are family members safe or is there risk of greater danger?

c) Assessment of Relevant Processes

- How weary or despairing are family members?
- What elements of the current conflict are healthy and functional?
- What are the dysfunctional aspects of the conflict?

d) 4-P summary of the people, the problems, the processes, and potential solutions.

- Should the process be diverted toward immediate crisis intervention and the reestablishment of safety?
- In balance, are the positives and strengths greater than the challenges?
- Can the family as a whole manage the chaos and anxiety that change brings?

Stage Two of Intervention: Analysis, Feedback Conversation, and Plan
A professional first does the analysis privately then a feedback conversation is held that includes all relevant parties. When family mediation is used, it leaves the primary control and decision making with the disputants rather than an authority dictating resolution. As planning goes forward, decisions are made about who should be and is willing to be involved in any combination of individuals, a dyad, or the whole family. The general principle is to involve any member who is part of the family problem, and anyone who is part of the solution.

Is the relationship trouble primarily an individual problem, a personal problem affected by a relationship, a disturbed dyadic relationship, or a whole-family problem?

- Is there consensus or denial that there is a problem that warrants necessary work?
- Is there an informal intervenor such as a clergyperson who could help? Is a professional facilitator required?
- Could outside intervention make matters worse or endanger some members? A decision is made about whether to suppress and quiet the conflict, or to expose the topics for open processing. If conflict is shut down, family members need to decide if they can live with conditions as they are; if conflict is facilitated, members need to decide their degree of involvement. If conditions include substance abuse, mental illness, or domestic violence, family mediation is rarely used, and success is risky.

- Together, a plan is made for next steps. If a professional is uncertain of a useful course of action, their responsibility is to refer the family to another expert.

Stage Three of Intervention: Consider Multiple Options

So many intervention methods can be used to address the problems that this stage is often the most challenging (Mosten, 2015; J. Murphy, 2015). Establishing clear goals, shared by all participants, will help with the selection of method. Dozens of third-party procedures are currently in use, and new methods of intervention are under development.* There are four basic models of intervention, illustrated in Figure 6.7:

a. *Legal, procedural justice* uses a professionally controlled process that suppresses conflict;

b. *Settlement mediation*, primarily controlled by disputants, is designed to suppress conflict and reach simple agreements;

c. *Therapeutic mediation* is professionally directed with the aim of discovering and dealing with root causes of a conflict; and

d. *Problem-solving mediation* or *conciliation* is primarily directed by disputants with the goal of solving the problems uncovered.

a) Legal, Procedural Justice

This method of settling family disputes goes through family court systems to address the legal and contractual dimensions of marriage, child custody, adoption, and inheritance. A court official, usually a judge, balances the best interests of family members. The goals are to find resolution that is safe and fair. Solutions are shaped by applicable laws and are to some extent predictable but they are not debatable

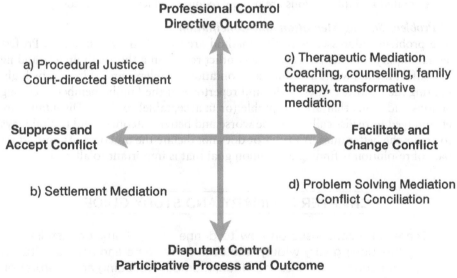

Figure 6.7 Four models of professional family conflict intervention

*For a wide ranging catalogue of the variety of family conflict resolution, see Gurman (2015).

after judgments are made. Advantages of this method are that blatant power differences between disputing parties are minimized, and previous conflict tactics are largely irrelevant. Disadvantages are that issues are often logistically complex and always emotionally troubled. Intervention occurs in family systems that are already in disequilibrium and distress, and final decisions may be difficult for disputants to accept. This was the ultimate procedure used with the Sargents because Christine could not voluntarily relinquish control to the judge or the mediator.

b) Settlement Mediation
Settlement mediation is a procedure that is mostly directed by the disputing parties with the guidance of a professional mediator. It is designed to manage the outstanding issues of conflict in an organized way with low emotion and little overt conflict. Because the goal is to reach a settlement that all parties can find agreeable, it moves forward in the present without dealing with the underlying problems or the history of the conflict. Advantages are that it is a brief and relatively simple focus on solutions. An example of this method is Jay Haley's Directive Family Therapy (2007). Agreements may not be durable if the problems are not really settled.

c) Therapeutic Mediation
This process is directed by a professional like a psychologist or a family therapist. The goal is insight into the underlying causes of a conflict. As previously hidden causes are brought to the surface, disputants can begin to brainstorm solutions. Transformative forgiveness may be a part of this facilitated process, unblocking past resentments by providing ways to make mistakes right. The process typically alters relationship dynamics toward improved communication, more reciprocal support and positive reinforcement, greater harmony and compassion, if not restoration of the relationship. An example of this procedure is Transformative Mediation, associated with Robert Bush and Joseph Folger (2002; see Chapter 12). Advantages are that the procedures are systematically applied to uncover new insights. Disadvantages are that multiple sessions are usually required, which are often costly.

d) Problem-Solving Mediation and Conciliation
The problems addressed with this method are identified by disputants. Professional inquiry into the reasons for a conflict results in a thorough understanding of conflict themes while avoiding confrontation. Problems are addressed by highlighting the conflict tactics, style, and repertoire of the family members, refining actions and limits that are acceptable (or unacceptable) to them. Disputants are encouraged to realistically describe worse and better outcomes, and to find ways to create the better ones. A mediator does not dictate the outcome. An important part of resolution is finding a common goal that is important to all parties.

CHAPTER SUMMARY AND STUDY GUIDE

- There is no consensus on how to define family. Family constellations and functioning vary widely, and evolve over time and across cultures.
- Four functions critical to individual member wellbeing and maturation are provided uniquely by the family: secure belonging and attachment, individual and collective competency and resilience, continuity through time, and the socialization of values and beliefs.

- Change is a persistent challenge for every family; some changes are natural and some are forced. They can be the source of tension and conflict, but also of growth and maturation.
- Multiple problems confront families simultaneously. Natural dialectic tensions arise from maturation through the family life cycle, and clusters of common problems become sources of conflict for most. The family must reach consensus that a problem exists that is worth working on, and must stay committed until a solution or settlement is found.
- Conflict can provide creative learning opportunities in effective, functional families; high conflict impacts every individual negatively in dysfunctional families.
- Many pathways exist for resolving family conflict, starting with prevention. Everyone copes with ordinary family disagreement that can be resolved with dialogue. A minority of family conflicts require third-party intervention, and there are four models for this: legal justice, settlement mediation, therapeutic mediation, and problem-solving mediation and conciliation.

TERMS IN FOCUS

acculturation 198
assimilation 198
attachment 176
Attachment Theory 176
belief 181
bid for connection 175
blended family 198
community resilience 179
complementary 184
conciliation 211
continuity 179
corrosive adversarial
   relationship 202
culture 181
dialectic tensions 192
discipline 190
discontinuity 180
dysfunctional family 175
family 174
family competence 179
family culture 181
functional family 175

habits 180
legal, procedural justice 211
mixed-cultures family 182
metaproblem 199
negative sentiment override 205
parenting style 188
personal competence 179
positive sentiment override 200
problem-solving mediation 211
punishment 191
resilience 179
role 184
rule 187
settlement mediation 211
socialization 187
symmetrical 184
task role 184
therapeutic mediation 211
Tragic Drama Theory 185
Triangular Theory of Love 177
values 181

7

Conflict in the Workplace

■ ■ ■

In Focus in This Chapter:

- ■ The workplace is a unique system with special characteristics.
- ■ There are many personal contributors to conflict in the workplace such as personality, emotions, interdependence, roles, and territories.
- ■ A functional, positive workplace climate includes constructive conflict; dysfunctional conflict is destructive.
- ■ Conflict analysis is crucial to effective conflict management and resolution, and it includes distinguishing many contributing elements such as agents and stage.
- ■ The measurable and immeasurable costs of workplace conflict can be very high.
- ■ Many methods are available to deal with workplace conflict.

CONFLICT CASE 7.1 ■ CAPSTONE'S IN TROUBLE

A small Canadian film producer, "Capstone," developed a strong team of seven staff, supervised by the owner of the company, Greg. Each employee was uniquely skilled, but they worked collaboratively and amicably. For three years the company was a creative leader in documentary production. They produced an informative documentary about Fetal Alcohol Spectrum Disorder (FASD) and its treatment.

One fall, the regional arts council invited nominations for their annual award called the Blizzard award. Without consulting Greg or the rest of the team, one member, Sean, nominated the FASD film. In March of the following year, Sean was informed that the film had won the highest Blizzard. He bought a tuxedo and invited his wife and parents to the ceremony. He did not notify the other team members, so the team only learned of the award the day after the ceremony, when the newspaper ran a front-page story with Sean's picture, elated as he accepted the award.

A fierce conflict ensued, with the other six employees protesting, condemning, and attacking, while Sean stoutly defended his actions. Greg attempted to moderate the conflict. The team argued furiously for several hours until Greg finally asked them all to go home and return the next day to process the problem. When they resumed the next day, everyone was calmer, but no one had changed their perspective: team members were boiling, Sean was

215

defensive, and Greg alone was looking for ways to work through the conflict. After much argument, the team came to the solution that Capstone would sponsor a large Blizzard "thank-you" advertisement in the newspaper with all their names listed.

Although this action partially soothed the hurt and angry feelings of team members, the working dynamic was never the same. An atmosphere of distrust persisted. Within 6 months the team had disintegrated as most of the team members found other employment, and the remaining few were drained. It took several years before Capstone recovered its former level of creativity.

This is one example of thousands of conflicts that occur every year in workplace systems. Although an unusually dramatic story, it highlights key issues in workplace conflict, including the following:

- Conflicts in a workplace demonstrate specific dynamics unique to the setting.
- The actions and conflicts of a minority can infect a whole group.
- There are many types of conflict, sometimes layered and simultaneous, involving personal issues, task priorities and procedural differences, emotions, and ideas conflict.
- Workplace conflict is risky, so many people try to bury it or overlook it, with the hope that resolution will happen spontaneously. When they do attempt to address conflict directly, many people do so privately, but feel unprepared and unskilled.
- Workplace conflict is costly, literally financially, but even more emotionally.
- Many workplaces invest considerable resources in efforts to prevent conflict or to resolve it effectively.

The Capstone episode was unusually dramatic, but workplace conflicts are more often of the "ordinary," everyday variety. Many studies report that people in all occupations find the most stressful aspects of their jobs come from the conflicts they experience on a daily basis. As you have discovered in other contexts, such stresses affect several levels simultaneously: 1) conflict within, 2) conflict among people, 3) conflict across divides, especially of culture and gender, and 4) conflict across the world (following Axelrod, 2005). Sometimes workplace conflicts are confined to events with a few individuals involved, but they often expand, drawing in teams of people or even a whole system. The Public Service Commission of Newfoundland and Labrador estimated that more than 65% of work performance problems result from strained relationships rather than from deficits in motivation or skill (Government of Newfoundland and Labrador, 2020). Supervising managers commonly spend between 25% and 40% of their time handling workplace conflict (Ilgaz, 2014). In this chapter, you will explore aspects of conflict uniquely found in the workplace.

THE WORKPLACE REPRESENTS A UNIQUE SETTING

The workplace represents a unique setting with multiple dynamic factors that predictably promote conflict. Loraleigh Keashly and her colleagues have devoted most of their careers studying workplace dynamics. She stated, "The workplace is the most profound social context we have.... Work is a place of connections and relationships ... that affect the quality of our work, the meaning and identity we derive from it, and the overall climate and culture of the workplace." Here are a few distinctive features.

Mismatched Priorities

Individuals with little in common are gathered in workplaces and assigned to work units, rarely with choice. People present differing commitments: for some, it is "just a job" and their life goals are fulfilled through activities outside of work; for some, identity is invested in vocation and career, and activities and accomplishments become central to their self-concept. For most, survival depends on the livelihood gained from employment, and this depends on job security. Dramatic mismatches of needs, personality, and styles of work often happen.

These factors combine to create a dialectic tension between the working "I" and the team "we." Individual needs differ from group needs, and employees participate with different priorities. A common source of workplace conflict is the *hidden agenda*, which happens when an individual's concealed goals drive their working behavior (Barnlund, 2012). Although a person may appear to be acting cooperatively, their work is fulfilling personal goals that may compete with collective goals. This often causes frustration and lurking conflict.

Individual and Collective Stress

Stress is a universal experience. Employees and larger systems struggle to manage stressors and pressures in effective ways, and poor stress management can be costly to employee health and wellbeing, efficient functioning, and organizational productivity. A personal stressor commonly reported by committed workers is feeling caught by conflicting loyalties to work and home. In addition, many employees feel insecure in their positions. Nearly half of jobs are in transition toward automated and artificial intelligence methods (Frey, 2013), and many employees are vulnerable to corporate downsizing. In many workplaces, significant resources are directed toward stress management to support job performance, creativity, and smooth functioning.

Organized Hierarchy

Workplaces are necessarily structured, organized into functional divisions and usually into hierarchies of power with leaders and followers. Structures are designed to plan direction for the organization, improve efficient operations, delegate responsibility, and assign specialized roles. The inevitable divide within the structure plays out in dissimilar or even competing perception, interests, and priorities, for example, between management with formal authority and employees who follow orders.

Legitimate power is authority and power derived from a position within the hierarchy, such as supervisor or manager. It determines the areas where you may legitimately exert power and order others' actions (Raven, 1958). Legitimate power may or may not be accepted within the social structure of the organization, so there are elements of consent and respect. It is associated with trust, a shared task, and voluntary cooperation (Hofmann, 2017). The power goes with the position so, when you no longer fill that role, your authority disappears.

The contrast is *coercive power*, which authorities exercise through monitoring, threats, and consequences to force someone else to follow expectations (Raven, 1958). It might be directly used with threats of punishment, for example, or subtly or indirectly used with manipulation or deception. Coercive power is correlated with enforced compliance, and an antagonistic climate (Hofmann, 2017), because others are stalled with few options. If coercive power is used to impose the solution to a problem or conflict, it may lead to counterproductive low motivation and cause a backlash against the solution (Northrup, 1989). The costs of coercive power are amusingly illustrated by Logan's drawing, "The Queen" in Figure 7.1. Notice the facial expressions of each person, and the presence or lack of hands.

Although these two sources of power are distinct in definition, they are not completely separate. For example, former US president Donald Trump possessed almost immeasurable legitimate power within the position he held, but he had a reputation for the coercive use of threats of public humiliation of all opponents with his ill-mannered insults.

Studying the power patterns of leaders, Bertram Raven and John French in their classic study (1959), identified six bases of power:

1. *Legitimate power* or *positional power* is asserted from a position or role of dominance within an accepted hierarchy. Often called *authority*, this is the power held by teachers, elected officials, and people with occupationational titles such as Esquire or Captain, for example.
2. *Information power* or *expert power* is influence that results from having knowledge or know-how that is needed and respected by others. For example, this is the power held by a professional conflict mediator.
3. *Reward power* or *coercive power* is the ability to force others' actions through reward (or promises of reward) or punishment (or threats of punishment). This power is held by anyone with control of evaluation measures such as salary or grades, for example.
4. *Referent power* is based on identification and connections with socially powerful people. This is why prominent musicians and celebrities attract "groupies."

THE QUEEN   LOGAN

Figure 7.1 Logan's drawing illustrating coercive power

5. *Charisma* is a natural ability to charm or inspire followers through personality, modeling, and/or compelling speech. Storied hero figures had charisma because of their apparent invincibility. Historical figures with strong charisma include Napoleon Bonaparte and Barack Obama.

6. *Ethical power* or *moral power* is the ability to inspire others with authority through beliefs, values, and actions that seem inherently right. Some of Mahatma Gandhi's power derived from the fact that his viewpoint seemed so right to so many Indian people.

Notice that these formal categories do not take into account the everyday power of interpersonal connections and influences of friendship that inspire loyalty. Power is inherent in a relationship, not a quantity or ability that someone has or does not have. Everyone utilizes several types of power. Combinations form a style of leadership and followership that determines workplace climate and functioning. French and Raven's classifications were elaborated by many others.

Power relationships and struggles within the hierarchy are often at the center of workplace conflict, and differing expectations regarding power and its uses can aggravate otherwise trivial conflicts. Power cannot be indefinitely sustained without respect for the leader and the consent of the followers. Both of these are the outgrowth of two pivotal factors: the repertoire of influence tactics used, and the balance of power experienced.

Influence tactics express power in actual behavior, with varying degrees of effectiveness (Yukl, 2012). They can be divided into positive, *soft (pull) tactics* that do little harm, and negative, *hard (authoritarian push) tactics* that resemble military command that must be followed but strain relationships, damage reputations, and are likely to harm other people (Yukl, 1992). Soft tactics are more likely used during initial attempts, to be modified if more influence seems necessary. Different sets of influence tactics are used when dealing with bosses, peers, and subordinates. Specific choices of tactic are determined by subjectively judged factors: *effectiveness* for a particular goal (accomplishing a task or changing people), cultural *acceptability*, matching both the personal *power* and the organizational position, anticipated *resistance*, and *cost* in time, effort, loss of resources, or interpersonal alienation (Shewchuk, 2010; Yukl, 1992). Workplace influence is best exercised in such a way as to promote cooperation and empowerment (Hallet, 2014).

Another pivotal factor in the use of power is the effective management of relative balance or inequity. Although the contemporary trend is toward more *flat structures*—employee *empowerment* with more balanced sharing of power—most work settings still have *hierarchial structures* where it is clear who has the power and how it is wielded. Employee power can be allocated by degree: in some situations, no discretion is permitted; in some, power is participatory and shared; and some employees are given virtual autonomy and self-management (Ford, 1995).

A new tension arises out of our information era: the visibility of structural inequity within a power structure; for example, inequities of salary or different rules and privileges that are based on status and not on performance or merit. It is easily discovered that the highest paid executives earn nearly 200 times the average worker's salary, and will have received the equivalent of an average yearly salary by 10:30 in the morning on January 2nd (Mackenzie, 2016). These known inequities can cause pointed resentment and conflict. The **gender wage gap** is the difference of earnings between female and male workers. The Canadian Centre for Policy Alternatives reported in January 2019 that the average North American full-time female worker earns 77% of the average male, especially if there are children in the family. These statistics are even more divergent in less developed countries. UN commissions have published numerous documents to express concern that the marked long-term consequences of these gaps extend to entire families and into old age.

In-Group Membership and Communication Develop a Bonded Identity

Workplaces develop unique communication patterns that distinguish in-group members, and simultaneously (if unintentionally) exclude outsiders. Insiders know and understand local jargon and humor through the context and situation. They understand and go along with the quirks, and can sense and respond to the feelings of the whole group. Words used may not convey what common meanings would suggest; rather, private meanings are understood indirectly through subtleties, in-jokes, acronyms, and nonverbal signals, but that feels like cliquish exclusion to those who do not get the meanings.

To move from the periphery of a workplace group toward a sense of belonging, people are expected to learn in-group speech. Outsiders and newcomers are often embarrassed by their awkward, bewildering mistakes. Everyone knows that someone is not part of the in-group if they have trouble understanding the roundabout communication pathways. They lose face, but can earn respect by learning the in-group language.

In many ways, workplace cultures resemble the characteristics of a bounded **high-context culture**, first described by Edward Hall (1976). Conflict in high-context groups results mostly from unspoken, misunderstood, and violated expectations, especially about cooperative activity. Direct confrontation is discouraged for fear of fracturing the group. When conflict does arise, it focuses on feelings you might be reluctant to articulate. High-context conflict can seem disjointed and confusing to people unfamiliar with it. These are some of the reasons that conflict in workplaces is often latent, hidden, and difficult to address appropriately. It is worth noting that abrupt changes to the working context due to the recent coronavirus pandemic will have lasting but as yet unknown impact.

Global Marketplace

Workplaces function within fast-paced multidimensional economies, sometimes operating across the entire globe. Change is a fact as workplace systems respond continuously and even urgently to the environment. Preserving sufficient stability while, at the same time, responding creatively and successfully to changing demands can be challenging and stressful. Employee needs for stability and goal fulfillment can conflict with the urgent needs present in changing workplaces. Many corporations are confronted with new versions of old dilemma such as child labor and intense competition. It becomes necessary to repeatedly recalibrate individual and system equilibriums to adapt to changing demands.

INDIVIDUAL FACTORS AND WORKPLACE CONFLICT

Personality

Understanding personality within a team can make the team's functioning more effective because it helps improve task assignment and appropriate specialization of labor, and enables teammates to predict and prevent conflict. Workplace problems, often called "personality clashes," originate in style friction between individuals and can result in deeply personal relationship conflict. A large majority of dismissals can be attributed to personality conflict.

Much research explores personality and style differences in the workplace, its effects on group interactions and success, and ways of promoting interpersonal harmony. The findings of several studies show that personality conflict results from a combination of incompatibilities in individual traits and preferences, variations of workstyle within a team, and overall team equilibrium. Some insurmountable incompatibilities can arise from differences in openness to novel ideas and change, and from using constructive or avoidant approaches to conflict. Recall and review the discussion in Chapter 1 of the Five Factor Model that identifies the OCEAN personality as the most amiable (Moberg, 2001). Personality cannot be changed, but behavior can.

Emotions in the Workplace

Employees usually try to behave in professional ways that might obscure their true feelings. Realistically, though, events activate emotions that, whether expressed or silenced, can contribute to conflict. In a multinational survey, 65% of respondents noted that emotions and personal pride affected the solutions reached to tense situations (Stewart, 2008). Anxiety and anger are especially relevant in the workplace.

Insecurity, Anxiety, and Fear

Anxiety and conflict are mutually causative: anxiety and fear cause conflict, and conflict causes anxiety. Because anxiety can interfere with effective thinking and problem solving, both anxiety and conflict can undermine job performance and personal satisfaction (e.g., Coy, 2011). Some insecurity and anxiety results from ordinary problems such as deadlines or frustrations about success and advancement. In mild forms this type of anxiety can be a motivator for hard work (Mathews, 1990). However, intense anxiety can quite literally interfere with good, logical thinking. Long-term, chronic anxiety can reach levels that compromise individual and team effectiveness. Anxiety and fear tend to be contagious and, therefore, when they persist, they can create a seriously negative influence in the social milieu.

As individuals and groups develop better strategies for conflict management, people respond with less anxiety and the whole team can benefit. Open communication patterns that strengthen relationships, diffuse potential tensions, and deal directly with problems all help to reduce workplace anxiety.

Anger

Anger rests on a fine balance. When it becomes a motivator of positive actions, anger can improve relationships, work functioning, and success. When anger is silenced but nursed, it causes resentment that can continue to simmer until it boils over (Lerner, 1997). Fury, in the extreme, may manifest in hostile harassment, vandalism, and other forms of violence.

Anger can be constructive in the workplace when it:

- is straightforwardly accepted as a signal of discomfort,
- is taken seriously,
- can be expressed respectfully,
- is driven by the wish for smooth relationship functioning, and
- has the goals of restoring a positive relationship when an offense has occurred.

Anger was the primary emotion that ignited the firestorm at the Capstone film group. Resentment of Sean's selfishly taking credit for the film became mixed up with incredulous embarrassment of other staff members. Sean responded with his own anger, and the conflict raged for hours. The meaning of anger for each side was not addressed. Even months later, the entire working group was compromised by unresolved anger.

Deciding if or how to communicate anger is often a dilemma. Expressing anger can make a situation even more tense and conflictual. It is important to take some time to sort through the feelings. Radio host Bernard Meltzer developed a guideline for deciding whether or not to confront someone about their actions (notice the acronym THINK). Effective confrontation includes statements that are:

- True
- Helpful
- Inspiring
- Necessary
- Kind

Until you can communicate anger clearly in this manner, it is best to continue an inward reflection process.

Workers Are Interdependent

A degree of interdependence is necessary for productive teamwork, but individual needs vary. Some people are most comfortable working independently; some people desire collaboration and interdependence; some workers may be overly dependent on others. When these needs are mismatched, employees become frustrated and might blame each other for their dissatisfaction. At one extreme of independence is a person who is self-serving and does not willingly contribute to the group. This person may force their own way with subtle behaviors such as lazy footdragging or procrastination, or openly with deception, backstabbing, or sabotaging others' efforts to make themselves look competent. Any of these conditions can cause conflict.

Morton Deutsch was one of the early founders of Conflict Resolution Studies. He noted that *promotive interdependence* is based on the belief that any one person's success promotes the entire group. Therefore, group members who believe this will cooperatively assist each other toward fulfilling their joint goals. *Contrient interdependence* is competitive because it is guided by the belief that one group member's success competes with that of another member, therefore leading to negative, group hindering tactics and sabotage (Deutsch, 1973).

It seems obvious that peoples' actions and reactions can cause, soften, or escalate conflict, and can affect the way conflict is processed and resolved. Conflict can be friendly and constructive if it is expressed with courtesy, in ways that are intended to maintain trust and acknowledge interdependence. Disrespectful or selfish tactics like insensitivity, impatience, or rudeness will almost always escalate conflict and block its resolution. Group irritations such as gossip or open antagonism are sure to cause divisive conflict. Negative tactics have serious individual consequences like significant worry and decreased productivity, or even consideration of quitting. The negativity can also quickly become contagious, lowering morale, and compromising the cohesion of a whole system.

Varied Roles Influence Behavior

Roles are important influences on both perception and actions in a workplace. A **role** defines behavior a person is expected to fulfill as part of the whole. A role is played by a specific worker, but transcends the person. Within an organization, roles establish an interacting system or network of positions and responsibilities that interlock to get the job done. Most employees have a formal role specified by a job description and a title that outlines performance measures and related rewards such as salary. Roles must be somewhat flexible to accommodate unforeseen events and challenges.

Kenneth Benne and Paul Sheats (1948) described three central roles displayed in work settings:

Task Roles relate to completing the work. Task roles include directed action like information seeking and sharing, maintaining focus, and coordinating activities that help a whole system solve problems. When members of a system disagree about facts, information relevance, or procedures for task accomplishment, or if responsibilities are blurred or misunderstood, a **task** or **procedural conflict** occurs (also called *substantive conflict*), focused on ideas and problems. Conflict might also arise if a coworker is perceived to be excessively task focused at the cost of relationship.

Group Maintenance Roles describe activities that support the functioning of the relationships by regulating and strengthening the group's cohesion. This type of role emphasizes communication, encouragement and praise, and harmonizing differences. When individuals behave in ways that disrupt relationships, an **affective conflict** occurs, the fuel for which comes from emotional differences and interpersonal resistance. Sometimes, group relationship builders are perceived as nosy or bossy, and this might backfire when in conflict.

Individualistic Roles are shaped by self-interested needs or goals more than by the collective good. People who fill this role would tend to use help- or recognition-seeking, dominate others, or attack coworkers insensitively when they need to win. They can become the source of conflict because they do not operate as "team players."

Most people cope with multiple roles that may be selectively valued. Many workers experience role strain when competing, contradictory, or impossible demands have to be balanced. For example, work demands often intrude into responsibilities outside of work, and vice versa. The increasing use of technology, while facilitating communication, also leaves people feeling "permanently wired" to their jobs. Thus, overloaded roles can be the source of significant distress. Employees may be assigned roles for which they do not feel qualified, and demands that are beyond individual abilities can cause significant self-doubt. Inconsistent expectations must be sorted, and many people feel unable to fulfill all expectations without disappointing someone. Interpersonal conflict can happen when individuals have differing or unspoken perceptions of a role, such having unrealistic expectations of a leader or supervisor. Organizational strain is also common when individuals are not able to perform to standards or expectations, and crucial tasks remain unfinished.

A **conflict of interests** is a specific type of role conflict that arises from potentially incompatible interests. It occurs when someone has multiple roles that lead to competing interests, one of which could unfairly influence the other. It contains the old idea that we cannot "serve two masters." This often happens, for example, when family members work together. The boss might also be the mother, or the employee may also be a nephew. The roles and resulting incompatible interests can interfere with objective work related decision making. Conflicts of interest are the subject of significant ethical debate and are often prohibited in Codes of Conduct. They are often the cause of conflict in family-based industries.

Territoriality

Humans seem to function most comfortably when engaged with familiar people, spaces, and tasks. A common stress reduction strategy is to maintain familiar conditions that minimize change. This is why people prefer to use the same seat on the bus or the same parking spot every day, minimizing decisions of where to sit or park.

The essential rights of territory are ownership, use, and control (Brown, 2005). Territory or resources are "yours" because you own them, you use them, or you control how they are used by others. There are three zones: **primary territory**, such as a specific work space, is under individual or small group control; **secondary territory**, like a building or cafeteria, is used regularly by many people, but only if they comply with agreed-upon norms, such as nonsmoking rules; and *tertiary* or *public territory*, a sidewalk or public transportation for example, is available to anyone who needs it (Altman, 1984).

"Invasions" such as going through someone's desk or using "their" coffee mug cause feelings of threat, anxiety, and resentment that may escalate into defensive conflict. Julia Wood (2018) described three typical responses to the discomfort of perceived territorial invasion:

a. Give way, welcome the invader and share the space. Wood described this as a typically feminine response.
b. Stand your ground, claim your space defensively or even aggressively. Wood described this as a typically masculine pattern.

c. When forced to fit into close spaces such as a crowded elevator, people avoid direct contact or eye contact to signal that they are not intentionally invading the other's space.

Territorial conflict occurs because people have different interpretations of the zones, and expectations about shared spaces, possessions, responsibilities, and rewards. Problems arise when people become territorial or attached to something they believe is theirs, while others want to share. The territory is defended, and people try to claim exclusive ownership or jurisdiction where it may not exist.

THE INFLUENCE OF DIVERSE IDENTITIES IN THE WORKPLACE

In the context of the workplace, **diversity** refers to the degree of heterogeneous mixing versus homogeneous similarities among workers. All workplaces are diverse; the mix is a mosaic of gender, cultural background, family history and circumstances, degree of disability or coping with chronic illness, education, and other personal factors. There are three primary ways that identities affect workers: in the language used to operate with tasks and conflict, in the cultural context of the interaction, and most prominently in the thinking patterns of the workers (Oetzel, 2003). *Surface-level diversity* refers to visible qualities such as age and ethnicity; *deep-level diversity* results from differences of thoughts, attitudes, and values (Ilgen, 2005). While surface-level diversity sparks conflict in the early phases of a group's functioning, it is the deep-level diversity that becomes more prominent over time. Diversity differences appear to impact work process and performance initially, but less over time (Watson, 2017).

Homogeneity of background appears to correspond with relational trust, and similar patterns of thinking and problem solving, and norms and social values, so workers more readily understand each other and have more efficient work processes, with stronger effectiveness (W. Watson, 2017). Both men and women report higher levels of happiness, morale, and cooperativeness in homogenous offices. However, due to assumptions made, homogeneous groups tend to be less rigorous in their decision making and make more mistakes than diverse groups (Apfelbaum, 2012), and show lower productivity as measured by company income (Ellison, 2014).

Heterogeneous groups contain a wider variety of experience, skills, and priorities, which results in more robust and innovative problem solving and task completion but, at the same time, higher frequency of conflict (Bersin, 2015; Lorenzo, 2018; Watson, 2017). Consensus suggests that workplaces need a diverse portfolio of ideas, skills, and interests to best complete its tasks. Heterogeneous diversity is preferred by most workers and in the majority of workplaces (Glassdoor, 2014). Diversity in one dimension is likely correlated with diversity in other dimensions like ideas, skills, and interests (Ellison, 2014).

Identity Factors

As an averaged group, *females* invest in relationships and tend toward the use of rapport speech, signaling qualities like interpersonal connections and solidarity, offering and receiving support (Kehoe, 2013; Tannen, 2007). *Males* seem to value accomplishment and solving problems, so as a group they tend to use report speech, emphasizing problem solving with impersonal information, facts, and unemotional processing. The influx of women into the workforce during and after World War II resulted in more competitive conflict (Ellison, 2014).

Many women in the workforce work out of economic necessity, but have competing responsibilities for child and home care. Men experience less work-home struggle, and may tend toward attitudes of entitlement at work. These factors challenge employers to provide family-friendly policies and practices, and to develop diverse opportunities for professional and management training.

Workers from *associative* cultures value trust and personal relationship. They tend to prefer indirect, nonconfrontational patterns of communicating their needs and opinions, and use indirect forms of influence. Work processes seem to be more intuitive than objective. Tactics tending toward conflict avoidance and facilitating the formation of integrative coalitions were preferred by associative managers. Information tends to flow upward toward leadership (Fu, 2000; Oetzel, 2003). Workers from *individualistic* backgrounds tend to prefer direct statements and dominating processing that emphasize facts (Fu, 1998; Ting-Toomey, 2001; Triandis, 2018). Communication of information is spontaneously shared. Individualistic managers prefer rational persuasion and fair exchange (Fu, 2000).

Generational strata are identifiable groups loosely defined by demographics and key life events (Tolbize, 2008; Urick, 2017). These groups are at different stages of their career so they bring different knowledge and skill sets and sense of responsibility. Priorities change as workers age (compare this idea with the Cycle of Family Life in Chapter 6). The presence of several generations sharing workspace is usually a positive factor for the transfer of knowledge needed for adaptative learning (Bennett, 2012), but the generations have different views and ideas, values and aspirations that are not readily compatible. Common consensus is that there are five generations working side by side today:

- *Traditionalists* (born before about 1945) grew up expecting to work hard, save money, and delay gratification, so they value stability and tend to resist change;
- *Baby boomers* (born between 1944 and 1964) value tangible signs of a peaceful and prosperous life, so place importance on salary, leisure opportunities, and economic independence, and are willing to work longer to sustain the lifestyle;
- *Generation X* (1965–1980), experience the highest levels of education, but grew up in an era of social turmoil and doubt about peace because of ongoing war. Work is not the priority it was for earlier generations, so they tend to be contented in job satisfaction and advancement;
- *Generation Y* (1985–1996) are technologically competent and connected to world events. They tend to be skeptical of the integrity of authority. They often must compete with job outsourcing and the reluctance of older generations to retire, so look for opportunities to be creative within a positive work environment; and
- *Generation Z* (1995–2015) are usually immersed in training and planning their career, so tend to delay relationships and family, and plan life to include more than work. They value tolerance and inclusion and meaningful work.

Many intergenerational workplaces include a large number of healthy, relatively educated and experienced employees who are on the verge of retirement. Many employers are limited in their capacity to hire younger, typically lower-paid workers (Shewchuk, 2009). Younger generations are also more challenged by competing demands of their work and personal lives, and training or relocation are less negotiable.

Mixed-Identity Workplaces

In some ways, research that divides people and amalgamates their responses provides only fractured data. Generalizations do make somewhat useful distinctions, but they also obscure real differences. They can deepen stereotyped perception, devaluing others and disregarding differences, and segregation, reinforcing common ideas that people live in "different worlds." In actuality, no average adequately describes either real behavior or variation within a group. The interaction dynamic is key, and appears to have a stronger influence than any single identity factor (Stainback, 2012; Triandis, 1994).

Some studies indicate that in mixed-identity groups lower power individuals tend to adopt the communication style and work habits that are more typical of higher power individuals (Giles, 2016). For example, two individuals of different genders are communicating, report talk is a more typical pattern than rapport talk (Michel, 1994).

When mixed-identity groups are located in the same workspace, less task and interpersonal conflict is reported than for groups working in separated locale (Hinds, 2005). Spontaneous communication (as contrasted with planned, formal communication) is associated with stronger interpersonal identification and sense of shared context, and also with lower levels of conflict (Hinds, 2005).

Organizational Approaches to Improve Diversity, Equity, and Inclusion

Contemporary trends across the globe are increasing diversity in workplaces. The fact is that both visible and invisible diversity are part of every workplace, whether or not it is recognized. Addressing Diversity, Equity, and Inclusion (DEI) is supported by research and by legislation. In this environment, a range of options are observed (Shewchuk, 2009):

- Differences and the impact of diversity can be *denied*, so nothing need be done.
- Differences can be acknowledged, but group problems avoided by expecting *acculturation*.
- Differences can be acknowledged by taking only basic, *legally mandated* action;
- Differences can be acknowledged and any troublesome impact minimized by promoting *understanding and acceptance*. This usually involves training in local organizational culture, including efforts to address stereotypes, biases, and prejudice.
- Diversity influences can be assertively *managed* by recognizing differences, enhancing potential benefits of heterogeneity. Leadership transparently

challenges programs that present barriers to specific groups and to diversification of the workforce. For example, this can mean proactively recruiting employees who present a variety of diversity characteristics.

This latter option is the most effective in terms of employee wellbeing, work processing, and success, but it also requires significant attention and investment.

PROBLEM FACTORS THAT RESULT IN WORKPLACE CONFLICT

Significant research is conducted every year to advance problem prevention and resolution, using informal and formal approaches. These goals are advanced by reasonably consistent findings that describe sources and causes, the frequency, the effects on individuals and groups, and organizational problem-solving effectiveness. New problems also emerge in response to the developing environment. For example, new work is being done now to combat cyberbullying and discover potential roles of conflict bystanders.

Dysfunctional Dynamics Can Ignite Conflict

Of course, not all workplace conflict is damaging. In fact, the creativity of a workplace is directly related to vigorous discussion of everyday perspective differences (Chen, 2006). Many researchers distinguish between beneficial, meaningful conflict, called *functional conflict* (usually constructive and creative), and harmful conflict, called *dysfunctional conflict* (usually destructive conflict). Both types of conflict are illustrated in the Capstone functioning before and after Sean's misstep with the Blizzard award. The main factor that distinguishes functional from dysfunctional conflict is the way the conflict is processed, as compiled in Table 7.1.

Table 7.1 Functional and Dysfunctional Conflict Compared

Dysfunctional, Destructive Conflict	*Functional, Creative Conflict*
Polarization: needs fulfillment is competitive	Integration: everyone's needs are legitimate and considered
Opposition: other parties are seen as competitors and opponents	Cooperation: work together to satisfy everyone
Disconfirming: defend yourself and attack people to deal with problems	Affirming: conflict parties support and validate each other
Coercion: power and dominance are used to win or succeed	Consensual agreement: group members emphasize agreement rather than dispute
Escalation: problems are compounded	Deescalation: problems are solved
Drifting: irrelevant problems are brought into the disagreement	Focus: one issue or problem is dealt with systematically
Shortsighted: long-term relationships and goals are lost in the immediate argument	Foresightful: arguments are handled with care for the future of the relationship
Negative results for relationship: problems remain unsolved, relationships are damaged	Results positive: relationships are strengthened through understanding, problems are solved

In functional conflict, people are able to support and validate each other, preserving the relationship for the future. Problems are dealt with systematically, one at a time. Everyone's needs are considered to be legitimate as the teams work to satisfy everyone. Final decisions are made by consensus. In the end, relationships remain strong. In dysfunctional conflict, people distrust each other, viewing others as competitors or opponents, so their tactics switch into rivalry and opposition (Adler, 2012).

Conflict in a workplace always has the potential to jeopardize constructive, creative functioning, as you saw with the Capstone fiasco. When the group or organization denies or fails to deal successfully with conflict, it is likely to continue brewing. This usually points to a fault within the system structure or the attitude and values base.

Group Climate

Group or corporate **climate** refers to the prevailing interactions, energy, and attitudes within a group. Group climate is critical to team functioning, pervasively influencing individuals and the collective. It is partially created by individual behaviors that fall on a hypothetical spectrum of respect and disrespect, but corrosive patterns can disseminate within the group. Group climate is a quality of a whole system culture, constantly streaming to influence the emotional tone of most interactions. It is created reciprocally as members of the group affect each other, then is diffused throughout the group,. Climate is as tangible as the weather. Individuals have differing sensitivity to it, but perception of climate is shared by all (Folger, 2018). It becomes part of the enduring stability and predictability of a work system.

Kurt Lewin (1943) identified four sources of climate which are part of almost all working interactions. These represent particularly sensitive interactions, and how they are handled influences the climate. A positive climate is sustained by:

a. Dominance and authority appropriately fitted to the situation;
b. Interactions that are perceived as supportive;
c. Personal identification with the workplace and its goals, reinforcing group cohesion; and
d. Satisfactory levels of interdependence.

Climate can be affected by the ways that conflict is processed within an organization. The **explicit conflict system** is what the organization says it does with conflict; their **implicit conflict system** is what members do in practice. Most conflicts are handled according to implicit norms. When the explicit and implicit systems are inconsistent, conflict resolution efforts may be futile, and a negative, hopeless climate can result.

Positive, supportive climate can be fragile; conversely, a negative climate can persist long after the precipitating problems are resolved, as was the case at Capstone. Negativity seems to survive even when employees leave and new ones are hired. Workers in an unhealthy climate feel confused and devalued. They report high levels of frustration and agitation, and tend to be less productive than workers in healthier environments.

A **toxic workplace** is an organization with a negative, mistrusting, or threatening climate. Destructive actions such as dramatic displays of opinion, manipulation, infighting among colleagues, and behavior that harms perceived rivals can be observed. In extreme forms, a toxic workplace sets the stage for poor productivity, serious disloyalty, rampant conflict, and even emotional violence (Keashly, 2012). Many governments are enacting respectful workplace legislation to prevent and address these developments. Although the Capstone film company had been an exemplar of creative teamwork, Sean's actions at the Blizzard award ceremony jeopardized the team, causing toxicity that lasted for many months and was really resolved only by the disintegration of the team.

Think About and Discuss with Your Colleagues

- If you have worked in several environments, what were the differences and similarities between them in the interpersonal relationship patterns? In working climate?
- Can you outline what factors contributed to those differences and similarities?

Some Potential Problems of Power

Power is loosely viewed as the ability of one person to exert influence or control over another. Although this is a necessary and good dynamic in every workplace with more than one employee, power is tricky to manage and is a frequent source of conflict. For many workers, there is a basic incompatibility between power structures and personal needs for autonomy. Also, some employees are more comfortable with power relationships than others are, and some managers use power in healthier ways than others do. Some people misuse their power simply because they are unaware that they have it; some people try to use power that they do not have; and some people use power to achieve results, but in rough ways. When an authority steps outside the bounds of accepted or consensual power, it usually rouses opposition (although it might be covert).

Disparities of power are often an important key, especially when in conflict (Ury, 1993). In amicable workplaces, authority is accepted as a normal condition of the setting, and does not cause tension. The power relationship is one of trust and consent, influence is mutual, and no one has to accept inordinate domination. Power is used to facilitate the success of the group by showing empathy, respect, and kindness when providing direction. However, in an already distressed setting, power can become a sore focus and can cause deeply harmful conflicts. Then other work priorities risk neglect, and important tasks remain unfulfilled. There are many common forms of power abuse.

Interference with Work can happen directly or indirectly, through tactics like providing misleading information, overloading a person with unrealistic expectations, or interfering with skill development opportunities. *Work and reputational sabotage* can undermine an employee's momentum or value by, for example, damaging equipment, plagiarizing work, or spreading distorted information about a person.

Favoritism, or differential treatment and privilege granted by someone in a powerful position, is a common cause of conflict. In such cases, less favored people experience interference with reaching their goals, and struggles for favor or power can disrupt an entire system. Jealousy and jurisdictional disagreements among individuals, departments, or unions and management can absorb impressive amounts of effort.

Heavy-Handed Leadership is another source of conflict. This is the common mistake of equating leadership with coercion. Sometimes called *command and control leadership*, this style can easily become oppressive. Centralized entitlement, authority, responsibility, and directive decision making are emphasized. Less powerful members are expected to comply with orders without input. Many people are uncomfortable with the unequal distribution of command and control power. Then, if the expectations for obedience are not met, conflict can escalate to patterns of reciprocating resistance, threat, and coercion, or even misconduct.

When a leader's use of power violates established policies or becomes intense enough to be unacceptable, it is called **professional misconduct**. Addressing and stopping this escalating type of behavior might eventually require the intervention of an outside third party such as someone trained in human resources. Graduated correctives of power abuse were recommended by Gerald Hickson (2007):

1. If abuse occurs as a *single incident*, approach the offender for an informal conversation about the incident and a desirable resolution.
2. If several incidents suggest a *pattern* of abuse, the abuser may benefit from awareness and skills training about relevant policies and acceptable leadership tactics, directed by a third party (someone other than the victim).
3. When *persistent patterns* can be identified, authoritative direction is needed to develop alternative behaviors and ways of dealing with the problems.
4. If *no correction* occurs, formal disciplinary measures should be taken by authorities with more power than the offender has.

Ultimately, it is in everyone's best interests to deal quickly and thoroughly with conflict and misconduct to restore a positive climate of collaboration. Conflict escalates when people think all creative options for constructive change are exhausted.

Disrespectful "Bad" Individual Behavior

Any particular interaction can be seen to fall on a hypothetical spectrum of respect that encompasses healthy interactions as well as unhealthy and abusive patterns. Some difficulties are encountered because what is perceived as "bad," disrespectful behavior to one person may be considered rather normal to another or in another situation (Moule, 2017). Subjective interpretations can vary drastically among the person acting, the recipient, and the surrounding people.

Objectively, **disrespect** is expressed in behavior that you reasonably expect would cause harm or humiliation. It affects work because actions are offensive and hostile, repeated over a considerable length of months, and result in inferior positioning (Einarsen, 2003). It can be described to include five defining categories: *disruptive*, inappropriate actions that block others' abilities to accomplish their goals; *passive-aggressive* patterns that fail to cooperate with or passively resist others' requests and needs; *dismissive treatment* of others that implies that they are of lesser value; humiliating, *demeaning treatment* of others; and *systemic disrespect* such as chronic lateness to meetings (adapted from Leape, 2012a). Disrespectful behavior does not refer to something that you simply don't like or find objectionable, like that disgusting Stinking Bishop's cheese sandwich in the lunchroom; it does not refer to a disagreement that is isolated or occurs between disputants of approximately equal power or status.

There are two subtly disrespectful actions. **Microaggression** is an insensitive act that violates common social norms and is perceived as an indignity or insult. Examples include the common assumption that all LGBTQ people are or would like to be friends, or that passionate women are "hysterical." **Uncivil behavior** is low-intensity discourtesy or rudeness with ambiguous intent to harm. For example, you find a colleague's name difficult to pronounce, so you impose a nickname on them.

In the workplace, disrespect, microaggression, and incivility can be ambiguous and veiled, and often rise out of ignorance (Bartlett, 2009). They become an aggravation, like the incessant dripping of a tap. Because they are hard to prove they are associated with *unseen injustice* (Rayner, 2005). Disrespectful actions help support workplace disparities based on history, ability, gender, and race (Cortina, 2008). Several scholars report that although overt disrespect has diminished and workplace climates appear to be improving, in reality such behavior may have gone more "underground" and is underreported (Bendersky, 1998).

Harassment and Discrimination

Harassment refers to the hostile, aggressive behavior that could appear in many types and intensities such as ridicule and criticism, offensive jokes or pictures, verbal abuse, sexual harassment, and outright violence. *Bullying* is merely another word for repeated aggression. It is never welcome or deserved, but has the same harmful effects as any aggression: fear, intimidation, humiliation, anger, and depression. **Discrimination** is an action or decision that treats someone unfavorably because of a presumed (but incorrect) correlation between ability and a personal characteristic such as age, religion, gender, or gender identity.

Harassment and discrimination contribute to fierce conflict when power is used aggressively (Rayner, 2005). Gary Namie (2003) devised a ten-point scale for measuring potential compromised safety and organizational disruption associated with harassment:

1–3 Rude discourtesy, causes irritation but little measurable harm;
4–9 Task interference, escalating abuse causes increasing harm;
10 Assault, battery, and homicide cause complete work shutdown. This type of abuse occurs on an escalating pyramid:

- 2% of workers admit that they have personally hit someone (#10);
- 10% work in an area where physical violence has occurred in the past (#10);
- 14% were tempted to strike a coworker in the past year, but didn't (#8); and
- 18% reported threat or verbal intimidation within the past year (#4) (Statistics, 2017).

These problems affect the working lives of many people. Almost one-third of the approximately 90,000 complaints received in one year by the US Equal Employment Opportunity Commission involve allegations of workplace harassment (Feldblum, 2015). Statistics that describe workplace discrimination are somewhat difficult to find because of the varied forms that originate in intersectional gender, physical appearance, age, and other factors.

Official acknowledgment of the importance and harmful consequences of workplace harassment has gained credibility in recent years, in part due to protest movements like "Me Too" and its global variants. Dealing with harassment can take three directions, ideally all of them in concert: *social response* to develop healthy workplace legislation, *organizational response* for prevention and intervention, and *individual methods* of responding to it. See Praxis Skill Builder 7.1 for a review of possible options for dealing with workplace harassment.

Praxis Skill Builder 7.1 ■ Dealing with Workplace Harassment

Harassment is improper, unwelcome, undeserved badgering or treatment based on identities like age or gender or personal likes and dislikes, not based on ability or performance. Resulting feelings of discomfort, humiliation, or, even worse, unsafety can negatively impact your health and job, career, and an entire workforce. Some types are prohibited by human rights and workplace legislation, and are criminal. Although there are many possible responses, none are guaranteed to successfully eliminate it. Prevention is probably the best approach whenever possible. Effective approaches usually begin at the organizational level, but individuals are not powerless.

1. Organizational Measures
   An organization has a responsibility to establish a respectful workplace that protects all employees from harassment. Actions of organizational authorities communicate and reinforce a respectful workplace, so leaders must be fully committed to supporting this culture.

   Every setting should have a formal protection policy that defines and prohibits all forms of harassment, specifying the consequences if it is found. It helps if the organization outlines a complaint procedure that can and should be followed to report harassing events, including reports made to civil authorities when needed. There should also be protection for "whistleblowers" so that people are not afraid to report what they know. Policies and procedures are somewhat toothless, however, if employees are unaware of them, so repeated information and training about respectful practices is essential.

   Organizations can actualize their protective responsibility by providing aftercare. Reports of harmful events have to be objectively investigated to establish and document what happened. If harassment is found, it must be ended decisively. This usually involves direct confrontation of the harasser that spells out escalating consequences if the behavior continues (Raynr, 2005). The organization should also prepare to provide trauma-informed restoration of respect to both the target and the harasser, either through in-house support or through referral to expert outside resources. Organizational control may be required if punitive measures become necessary to ensure accountability.

(continued)

Praxis Skill Builder 7.1 ■Continued

Individual Alternatives

A target of harassment should write down and carefully analyze the whole situation before taking any clear action. You may need to access support and information as you do this and make a plan.

Direct action could include:

- Quit your job—although not a fair option, many people weigh the risks and benefits of continuing in the position and conclude that looking for a better work opportunity is the best option.
- Accept the harassment—it is a valid alternative to focus on your task and avoid getting sidetracked. In the long run the costs might include deteriorating self-esteem and satisfaction in your job.
- Retaliate with counterharassment—revenge is not uncommon, but is not recommended because escalating intensity is more usual than ending it.
- Decide to deal directly with the harasser. You might cultivate a relationship with a safe colleague with whom you can rehearse the events and your plan, while you imagine both positive and negative conversations. Arrange a conversation with the harasser and possibly with a witness in a work setting, and describe 1) what happened, 2) the explicit consequences you have experienced, and 3) what you expect to happen now. Documenting later events and interactions is part of this step.

Indirect action would mean reporting the incidents to a work authority such as a human resources manager. There are also governmental agencies mandated to protect individual rights and prevent criminal abuse. With your cooperation, the person in authority would take responsibility for carrying the grievance forward.

Bystander Role

An important role in the harassment scenerio is played by bystanders to the abuse. If you have the courage to speak up as a witness to a disrespectful or harassing interaction, that can often stop escalation toward increasing violence.

When a colleague asks you for support as they deal with harassment, first listen with an emphasis on the facts of the story. It is probably important that you reassure your colleague with 1) "That was wrong" and 2) "It was not your fault." Suggesting "You should have done something else..." amounts to blaming the victim. The victim may want to rehearse possible conversations with you. Later, check in privately with the victim so that you are aware of ongoing events. If the victim decides to deal directly with it, it might be helpful to provide them with later debriefing.

"Romantic" Sexual Relationships create an especially murky area because multiple, complex issues are involved. On the one hand, employees tend to believe that voluntary relationships are sweet, and a right. On the other hand, romantic relationships open the possibility of "influence peddling" and conflicts of interest. Behavior is sexually harassing if it is unwelcome, intimidating, or coercive in any way; it is offensive or humiliating; and you cannot reasonably consent, refuse, or control it.

Broken romances often complicate office dynamics unbearably. Some people fear that their job benefits are contingent on compliance with sexual advances. When a benefit such as a favorable work schedule is offered in exchange for a sexual relationship, it is called *quid pro quo harassment*.

Sexual harassment often begins in mild, passive forms such an inordinate focus on appearance, gender, or sexual orientation. It might then escalate to spreading gossip or rumors of a sexual nature within the company network. Direct intimidation and harassment involve overtly sexual comments, invitations, or actions. Women are more frequent targets than are men. A 2014 survey reported that approximately 80% of women and 40% of men have experienced sexual harassment at some time (Kearl, 2014). Harassment might also manifest in gender inequality and discrimination, which is less personal but more widespread.

Women and men may experience sexual harassment differently, differing in their thresholds for judging offensiveness, and in their perception of the power-sex correlation. Men tend to view sexual advances from peers as misunderstandings, while the same behaviors from managers are perceived as harassing power moves. Women are more attuned to those behaviors within a male-dominated society, and tend to view any fellow employee with power as a potential harasser (Dougherty, 2007).

Employers are legally responsible to create respectful environments, and may become vulnerable to accusations of hostile environments based on negative sexual and gender dynamics. Considering the potential costs, most employers are cautious, and many Codes of Conduct discourage or prohibit romantic relationships between coworkers.

Emotional and Verbal Aggression might take place subtly through exclusion or freezing a person out of critical opportunities, or openly with insults. The emotional significance of these actions is often intensely personal, and may not be understood by observers or investigators. The harm is caused by broken trust. Nearly half of employees report that yelling and other verbal abuse is common in their work setting, and about one-third admit to yelling at other coworkers because of workplace stress (Statistics, 2017).

Physical Intimidation, Threat, and Violence are rare but, when they occur, detection is clear and is often treated as criminal. Approximately 15% of all employees report witnessing some level of violent behavior at work (Global Human Capital Report, 2008). The US Bureau of Labor Statistics reported that, in 2015, workplace homicides accounted for approximately 9% of fatal occupational injuries (Statistics, 2015).

Workplace violence is often reactive. When chronic stress or frustration result in poor coping, violence may be an outcome. Threats or intimidation may also be the consequence of reciprocating and escalating conflict among colleagues. Many aggressors have been the past target of others' aggression. Feelings of victimization fuel an observable and predictable escalation of frustration and potential for violence that is often overlooked or "forgiven" in the interests of peace at any cost. In these ways, aggression may be a manifestation of a destructive, toxic work environment and negative culture.

PROCESS FACTORS WHEN A WORKPLACE IS IN CONFLICT

Minor conflict occurs in every place where people work together, simply because of diversity of perception, needs, opinion, and interests. Conflict episodes can often be patiently overlooked, or solved with direct communication. Some conflicts develop because of the presence of an intentional troublemaker. Some conflicts develop mutually, with both or all parties contributing to the animosity. Conflicts involving heated and escalating emotions usually require outsider intervention to prevent them from becoming serious and widespread. Personal and identity conflicts result from perceptions of disrespect or threat to core qualities essential to a party's wellbeing. It is important, before attempting conflict resolution, to clearly understand the nature of the conflict affecting the group.

Who Are the Agents of This Conflict?

Sometimes people become involved who have little real interest in a problem or in its solution. **Primary parties** are those directly and immediately in conflict. **Secondary parties** are allies or people whose work may be affected by the conflict or by its resolution. **Change agents** are those people who influence the conflict process positively as *peacemakers*, or negatively as *troublemakers*. **Third parties** are those who are not directly involved in the conflict, but whose focus is on potential solutions. The question of who should rightly be involved in conflict processing is represented in the phrase, "Anyone who is part of the problem, and anyone who is part of a solution should be involved."

At What Stage Is This Group Functioning?

A significant body of scholarly work describes the normal developmental stages through which most groups evolve over time. Conflict can be distinct within these lifespan milestones, with their cycles of task, learning, and conflict. Each phase seems to incorporate times of inertia, "punctuated equilibrium," and revolution (Gersick, 2017).

Bruce Tuckman's (1965) early theory provides the framework.

1. *Forming*—Group members learn about each other and develop a common purpose. They begin to test ways to interact interdependently at the same time as they become oriented to the tasks. Conflict is usually tangible but latent, and discomfort tends to revolve around feelings, confusion, and mismatched commitment to the group, but they have not yet developed skills to effectively cope with open conflict.
2. *Norming*—The group establishes cohesion by testing and settling what is implicit and explicit: ground rules, expectations, roles, the exchange of collaborative skills, and differences of opinion. Friction is articulated but of low intensity, and usually results from ineffective communication. Uncovering conflict at this stage usually has long-term benefits of improved cooperation and problem solving.
3. *Storming*—This is the phase of actively tackling the group task with brainstorming. It is most vulnerable to conflict and some group members may be uncomfortable with the sense of crisis. Group members can show emotional volatility as they contest relationships, roles, and values, and blame for struggles. Conflict tactics and styles are tested, and some discarded.

4. *Performing*—The group is at its most creative and functional phase, having developed a base of consensus and deescalated the storm. Work processes are established and the group performs within those limits, so solutions begin to smoothly emerge.
5. *Adjourning* and *mourning*—Not every group reaches this phase because some are ongoing (based on Tuckman, 1965, 1977).

Judith Kolb noted from her literature review (2013) that by building on the accumulated insight of each phase, workplace conflict can be functional. Conflict should not be denied or overlooked, but should be part of every group's early skills repertoire. Ground rules established during early phases can be made explicit, then used to productively discuss disagreement. The group benefits from open discussion of substantive, task-related conflict, but rarely learns from open discussion of specific interpersonal conflict unless a solution is directly related to the task and skill sets.

WORKPLACE CONFLICT IS COSTLY

Conflict in the workplace is costly in many ways: it is expensive to manage, and the costs of unresolved conflict can rise dramatically. Conflict within, among people, and across groups results in decreased wellbeing, and employee quality of life, satisfaction, and productivity. The enormous impact of workplace conflict cannot be fully measured because of significant underreporting and because of varying tolerance.

Costs are estimated using associated losses in time and money. An international study was conducted with five thousand workers in nine countries. The Global Human Capital Report (2008) found that 85% of all employees reported some degree of conflict, with 29% reporting conflict frequently or daily. Many workers spent several paid hours per week dealing with conflict (for example, 2.1 hours in the United States, 3.3 hours in Germany and Ireland). In 2005, the *Washington Business Journal* reported that a typical manager spends between 25% and 40% of worktime dealing with conflict. That time spent was estimated to cost approximately US$359 billion in 2008.

The impact of conflict can be described at several systemic levels. For both victims and witnesses, conflict compromises health and mental health, with many people reporting headache, anxiety and depression, and distressed emotions. Disrupted sleep is common, with accompanying fatigue and difficulty sustaining concentration. Significant sickness and absenteeism is attributed to dealing with (or avoiding) conflict. Many people seek the treatment of mental health or medical professionals. Some people resort to the use of prescription medications or alcohol and other drugs. Thinking back to the Capstone film group, the conflict ultimately cost the entire staff individually and threatened the company.

Conflicted work systems also show decreased employee morale and commitment, as well as pervasive feelings of betrayal and mistrust. These individual feelings generate a divided workforce, which translates into decreased collaboration and mutual assistance. Employees tend toward defensive tactics like silent noncooperation and passive aggression.

Beyond the individual level, many systemic and organizational costs can also be observed. The Global Human Capital Report (2008) reported that conflict most frequently affects inexperienced new workers at the frontline levels, but it exists throughout all levels of an organization. It can be financially expensive to the system because of task sabotage and purposeful waste. High turnover means increased resources are devoted to orienting new employees. Time and resources are wasted throughout the system when dealing with increased complaints and grievances, when time and energy are diverted from productive tasks and goals, and team productivity shows decreased quantity and quality of output. Creativity is jeopardized and disrupted by decision deadlock.

However, the costs of conflict are not limited to the work system only. Outsiders such as customers and partner organizations become aware of workplace trouble, and satisfaction with and the reputation of a stressed workplace suffers in consequence.

POTENTIAL SOLUTIONS AND METHODS FOR CONFLICT PROCESSING

Most workers behave professionally most of the time. Most people, when encountering a conflict, are sincere in their efforts to quickly resolve it and return to positive functioning. Hickson (2007) found that when dealing with work conflict, one of the most influential factors is employees' experience with and role modeling of a trainer or supervisor.

Prevention Is the Best Way

Benjamin Franklin is often quoted to have said in 1736, "An ounce of prevention is worth a pound of cure." The emotional and productivity costs of conflict can be substantially reduced if efforts are made to prevent its development or escalation. In North America, employers have a legal responsibility to protect and preserve employees' dignity and wellbeing. In most workplaces, this means active efforts to create and maintain a fair, safe, and respectful environment (Leape, 2012b).

Process Design, Systems Design

Because conflict is costly and results in many systemic losses, many organizations invest in process design to implement better ways to prevent and deal with conflict. A neutral designer is professionally trained and skilled in conflict resolution. This person is designated to explore the explicit and implicit processes for processing conflict within an organization, and to recommend improvements. The designer is a "big-picture" thinker looking at the whole organization. They do not work on an urgent conflict but, rather, the designer considers a series of conflicts within the whole work system with observation, interview, and process analysis to assess such factors as:

- short- and long-term communication patterns,
- problem-solving patterns,
- repeating causes of friction and conflict,
- stressful times and environmental factors that increase the risk of disruptive conflict,
- typical employee responses to conflicts when they do arise,
- the effectiveness of resolution attempts within the organization, and/or
- potential future conflicts to be imagined and explored.

The hope behind process design is that the impacts of conflict can be diminished through advanced systems analysis and process design (Ury, 1993). The designer uses historical data to organize methods for dealing with future conflict, beginning with the simplest and most direct, and advancing toward more formal, complex, or power-based forms.

Process design is particularly important when:

- parties in the system expect or desire a continuing partnership,
- disputing parties are not typically included in existing conflict-resolution processes,
- there are repeating patterns and/or irritating complaints behind conflict,
- dispute resolution takes too much time away from productive work, or
- resolution efforts are ineffective because parties remain dissatisfied even when they "win" an argument.

Think About and Discuss with Your Colleagues

- If you were the boss of a work unit, supervising 10 to 15 workers, what early designs could facilitate harmonious working relationships and minimize conflict?

Respectful Workplace Codes of Conduct

Most organizations encourage or require employees to use respectful, courteous behavior, specifically to prevent the development of conflict causing dynamics. Tactics that express trust and respect can minimize conflict; insensitivity, rudeness, or antagonism can create and escalate conflict. Most workplaces adopt codes that systematize the mission and values of the organization and lay out rules for behavior. Respectful workplace policies vary widely because every organization's mandate and situation is unique and the services provided may be more or less risky.

A **Code of Ethics** usually refers to the principles and values of the company; a **Code of Conduct** describes behaviors expected of individual employees; a **Code of Practice** represents professional standards for using specialized knowledge and information. Most companies require that employees and associates support and comply with the policies as a condition of continuing employment. See the Conclusion of this textbook for a more detailed discussion of Codes of Ethics.

Codes cannot address every potential problem. They are structured to include descriptions of both desirable and prohibited behavior. Typical codes address issues like:

- expected attendance rates and reasonable absences,
- job responsibilities, including decision making and task completion,
- honesty, integrity, and fairness when dealing with coworkers and customers,
- attitude toward authority, and
- prohibitions against harassment, discrimination, intimidation, and aggression.

One weakness of a code of conduct is that it may be good in principle, but may be very difficult to effectively enforce in everyday situations. People may outwardly agree with a code because their employment depends on it, while inwardly opposing it. The code may have little to do with choices made when actual conflict arises. Research by Boris Kabanoff and his colleagues (2017) found that the implicit values of many organizations determines their expectations of employees, but different codes seem to apply to a) elite individuals, b) leadership positions, c) merit and accomplishment, or d) collegial, cooperative functioning.

Face-to-Face Negotiation

Approaching a supervisor about conflict can be risky, so most people are tempted to simply suppress their emotions, refuse to pay attention to a conflict, or avoid the people involved. These strategies might succeed in the short term, but everyday friction, unusual stress, and new disagreement can easily rejuvenate a latent conflict. It is best to deal with tension assertively before it escalates into open conflict.

The worker should start with careful self-assessment, thinking through

- What is the problem?
- What are my interests related to this problem?
- How did this conflict develop?
- Whose problem is it?
- Who can help find a solution?
- What is important to me?

Praxis Skill Builder 4.2 might also help you develop a decision tree before you proceed.

Answers to this thinking could help shape a viable plan for negotiating a conflict informally. The most constructive goal is harmony or, if that is not feasible, then agreement on the issues of conflict and maintaining a reasonably smooth working relationship is usually possible.

The core negotiation skill is active listening. This might be the first thing compromised "in the heat of the battle," if you insist on your own way, focus on the past, or assign blame. The techniques for active, respectful communication are to:

- avoid defensiveness;
- minimize argumentation;
- address the problem jointly;
- ensure clear communication by using paraphrasing to check understandings; and
- focus on the future; talk about what can be done.

Briefly, four principles of effective negotiation (Fisher, 2011) are:

1. Separate the people from the problem—Value the relationship and commit yourself to improving it. Focus on a solvable problem, not on complaints about a person.
2. Focus on interests, not on positions—It is important to agree early on the focus of the discussion. All relevant needs must be considered, both

tangible and intangible. Negotiators must remain openminded as they explore perspectives. It is also helpful to identify common interests and goals.

3. Explore opportunities for mutual gain—Together, generate multiple possibilities that satisfy both sides, and test them against the goals of the discussion.

4. Set goals based on objective criteria—These criteria will help set problems to rest by objectively measuring successful resolution.

Third-Party Facilitation and Intervention

Third-party facilitation occurs when someone who is not involved in a conflict works with the parties to assist them to stop the conflict and to address the source problems. The third person takes an intermediary role between the disputants. This type of intervention requires specific training and should not be initiated by peers.

Supervisors and human resources personnel often must take the third-party role. In the Capstone film case, Greg attempted to facilitate, but without training or expertise. Although his actions were generally appropriate, he was unable to help the group to find resolution and get back to productive functioning. Skilled conflict resolvers use systematic steps that lead the participants to identify what is important, creating openness and willingness to dialogue and explore possible solutions.

There are five basic methods, starting with the simplest:

Skills-Based Methods use education and training to improve the parties' Emotional Intelligence. This is based on the assumption that inadequate skills for respectful processing cause people to conceal their distress or to use wornout tactics that result in the prolongation or escalation of a conflict. Some of the skills needed are these:

a. Stress management—Sometimes, conflict is the outcome of fatigued and stressed workers' limited energy and imagination. Stress moderation skills can improve overall wellbeing so that workers can invest more energy in a positive working environment or relationships. One common focus of this training may also be ineffective habits that develop when chronic conflict is experienced. Ongoing peer supports are a positive outgrowth of this type of training.

b. Communication—Because many conflicts begin or are perpetuated by poor communication patterns, improving workplace communication can be effective.

c. Conflict-resolution skills—Specific training in conflict-resolution methods can be helpful to improve insight and the effectiveness of tactics used when processing conflict.

d. Management training and coaching—Developing skilled leadership and management practices can contribute dynamically to improve work satisfaction and conflict prevention. Coaching is a new type of intervention. A trained coach and a manager work together to develop and practice specific techniques for staff management, conflict analysis, and resolution. Coaches support individuals whose own role is to deal directly with conflict.

Interests-Based Facilitation
—A trained mediator helps the parties to specify their own interests, acknowledge common interests, and then negotiate satisfactory solutions.

Rights-Based Facilitation
—Here, the focus is on individual rights, exploring the reasons for competing or incompatible rights, and then granting appropriate rights in ways that do not undermine each other. This method usually follows a prescribed procedure for filing a **grievance**, which is a complaint about a perceived injustice. This, then, proceeds through formal mediation or an arbitration process toward resolution.

Advocacy
—An **ombudsperson** is someone officially appointed to communicate between disputing parties, a neutral advocate for each to clarify the limits of reasonable conflict in a workplace, interpret positions, and suggest potential resolution.

Power-Based Methods
—A third party has authority over the employees to impose a solution. Little negotiation occurs; rather, this method resembles legal adjudication. The disputing parties have little choice other than to comply with the solution prescribed. This may take the form of workplace discipline spelling out corrective actions that must be taken. There might be a short-term or permanent change of role and responsibility. In cases in which workplace discipline is used, dismissal from a position could be the extreme consequence for noncompliance with the resolution imposed.

Another form of power-based resolution might be to require counseling. This is appropriate in instances where anger problems, mental illness, or substance use is a factor contributing to the conflict. This might be quite effective, for example, when severe anxiety compromises work efficiency, substance use interferes with work performance, or when poor anger management jeopardizes team relationships. A drastic power-based option, rarely used, is litigation through the conventional civil court system.

The success of power-based resolution depends greatly on the wisdom and perspective of the person in authority. Such methods are, in fact, used often, because they are efficient. Nonetheless, power-based methods should be used sparingly and as a last resort (Lytle, 2007). Because of the power element, outward compliance might be gained, but not always be accompanied by inward change. Also, many people feel disempowered by the process, so the power balance of an entire workplace can shift. Power-based methods are usually necessary in serious cases of employee misconduct, ethical violations, or violent behavior.

SUMMARY OF QUADRUPLE-P FACTORS IN WORKPLACE CONFLICT

- Think of the most serious workplace conflict that you experienced, and describe how it unfolded. What underlying problems were part of that conflict? How could those problems have been addressed to prevent or minimize the conflict that occurred? If you were the boss or supervisor, what would you do if you noticed problems like those beginning again?

People
- Because people have different personalities, needs, interests, and workstyle, disagreeable discord or frank conflict are inevitable in workplaces.
- People experience friction arising from hidden or minimized emotions, especially anxiety or anger.
- Morton Deutsch drew attention to promotive (cooperative) or contrient (competitive) interdependence within the working unit as a determinant of the extent to which working partners assist or hinder each other.

Problem Factors
- Role expectations can be harmonious, or the source of conflict. Individualistic roles are particularly disruptive to group functioning, while task roles focus on the work, and relationship building roles attend to the interpersonal dynamics of workplace interactions.
- Inappropriate territoriality can become offensive in the workplace.

Process Factors
- Kurt Lewin's work on group climate noted four important influences on workplace functioning: dominance and authority, supportiveness, identification and cohesion, and satisfaction with interdependence.
- The developmental stage of the working group and of the conflict can drastically affect how a group processes conflict and how individual members will function to escalate or deescalate it.
- Workplace conflicts are enormously expensive for individuals, groups, and entire organizations, consuming many paid hours per week.
- Tactics that express trust and respect do minimize conflict, while negative insensitivity, rudeness, or antagonism can create and escalate it. Many organizations use Codes of Ethics, Codes of Conduct, and/or Codes of Practice to guide employees toward positive tactics.

Potential Conflict Resolution
- Many options are available for resolving conflicts when they arise, but prevention and process design plans effectively minimize the risks. Most resolution attempts occur through individual conversation and negotiation. Third-party intervention, usually through human resources departments, makes use of skills-based methods, active intervention, and power-based methods.

TERMS IN FOCUS

SECTION III
Conflict and Violence

8

The Problems of
Interpersonal Violence

■ ■ ■

In Focus in This Chapter:

- ■ Interpersonal violence is a complex phenomenon related to, but distinct from, conflict. Even defining the terms and concepts is complicated.
- ■ People are at the center of violence. Individual perpetrators resort to violence, individual victims and witnesses are harmed; all are personally affected and bear the consequences.
- ■ There are no single problems or simple causes of violence. Johan Galtung's "Vicious Violence Triangle" helps begin untangling some of the sources. Interpersonal power is a central dynamic.
- ■ Interpersonal violence develops over time in dyadic cycles that involve both perpetrators and victims, with traumatic consequences for individuals and for society.
- ■ If interpersonal violence is complex so, too, are the potential practical solutions. They begin with prevention, then deal with violent events with violence ending intervention and postvention mending. Society also has work to do to decrease violence.

CONFLICT CASE 8.1 ■ GABRIEL AND THE LOS BRAVOS GANG

Gabriel* was a 12-year-old boy living in the inner city of York Park, Maryland.* Although Gabriel was born in the United States, his parents had (legally) emigrated from their home in Nicaragua just before his birth. His parents worked in three impermanent, low-paying jobs. Gabriel's family lived in isolation and poverty, and was perpetually exhausted.

Gabriel was born with no left hand. As a teen, he often spoke disparagingly about himself at home, and rarely spoke at school. He was in constant trouble: at home, he was disobedient or absent; academically, his grades were low, and he was frequently truant; socially, he had no friends, and was bullied by some classmates and occasionally tried to fight back. He felt unsafe and rejected. By the time he was 12, Gabriel had entered the fringes of a local gang, Los Bravos, occasionally working for them as a courier. The gang used threats and violence to intimidate rivals, and crimes to finance their operations. In Gabriel's world, the group appeared to be wealthy, independent, disciplined, and supportive (like a pseudofamily). However, respect, for Los Bravos, meant intimidation: you showed "respect" with submission to their power and coercion.

Gabriel's mother, Marie,* approached the guidance counselor at his school, asking for help to manage the challenges. Realizing that the gang's appeal to him had to be overcome, it was decided that he needed to be turned back toward his family and a connected community. Unknown to Gabriel, a plan was made to coordinate family, school, and community efforts.

He was invited by one of the student leaders to participate in a biweekly social skills development peer group that included topics like study skills, decision making, respectful relationships, and internet safety and cyberbullying. A teacher-mentor was recruited to check in with him regularly. He was allowed to take charge of some small jobs in the school gym. His parents were enrolled in the Community Parent Education Program (CoPE) to discuss with other parents issues like home expectations and chores, positive rewards, transitional warnings, when/thens, and sibling conflict management.

Within 4 months, Marie and Gabriel's father, Daniel,* reported real changes for him. He was less self-conscious and less critical. He had made two friends and was participating more often in classes at school, and was accepting some responsibilities there. A developing sense of humor was making friends for him.

Violence is a highly complex human phenomenon that the World Health Organization (WHO) calls "a universal challenge" (Krug, 2002). Violence is shockingly common and occurs in many forms and contexts. It is perpetrated for complex reasons by very different types of actors; there are multiple contributing factors, causes, and aggravators; it impacts millions of people around the world, changing their lives at tragic cost to individuals, families, and communities (Morris, 2007).

Jennifer Langhinrichsen-Rohling (2005) summarized research findings regarding interpersonal violence:

- Violent acts are most often perpetrated within relationship rather than between strangers.
- Interpersonal violence typically evolves from relationship dissatisfaction.
- Both men and women use violence and are affected by it.
- There are several subtypes of interpersonally violent perpetrators, but most are men.
- The saying, "hurt people hurt people," confirms the generational transmission of violence.
- We need to consider all dimensions of violence, including what is beyond the physical.
- Substances, including alcohol, are important in the origins of interpersonal violence.

*Names and circumstances have been altered to protect the anonymity of the individuals.

DEFINITIONS AND CONCEPTS RELATED TO INTERPERSONAL VIOLENCE

Aggression and Violence

Here are some Webster dictionary definitions:

> **Aggression:** Violent behavior with the intent to dominate or master another party.
>
> **Violence:** An act of aggression that has the intent to harm another party.

Notice how closely linked these everyday definitions are. Aggression and violence are often (and appropriately) used interchangeably. As you survey terms and concepts related to violence, you can begin to untangle the varied forms and describe some of the consequences of violence for individuals and small groups. Even the WHO noted that defining violence is not precise; rather, it is a matter of varied perspective (Krug, 2002). Sometimes the image of a prism is used when discussing violence. A prism is transparent glass through which something can be viewed, but it confines the light so that it becomes distorted and dispersed. As we define violence, you will see that it partly confines, partly clarifies the discussion.

Conflict is not necessarily violent, but aggression and violence are both associated with conflict. Conflict and aggression can be mutually perpetuating. According to Gerda Siann (1994), they occur under four conditions:

1. There is an intention to harm.
2. Violence occurs in the context of an already conflicted relationship.
3. The purpose or goal of aggression is to gain advantage over an opponent.
4. Although often provoked by conflict, violence escalates animosity and, in turn, provokes deeper conflict.

Whether an action is considered aggressive or violent may depend on point of view and knowledge of a specific relationship or situation. For example, *self-defense* from a perpetrator's perspective might be *criminal* from that of the victim. Violence is antisocial behavior that contrasts with prosocial actions.

According to the WHO, **violence** is the intentional use of physical force or power, threatened or actual, against oneself, another person, or a group or community, that either results in or has a high likelihood of resulting in injury, death, psychological harm, maldevelopment, or deprivation (Krug, 2002). This inclusive definition addresses both physical and psychological violence. In fact, they often occur at the same time and both cause harm. The definition introduces three potential sites of violence: self-directed, interpersonal, and collective violence. In the case example of Gabriel and Los Bravos, self-directed violence occurred as he disparaged and emotionally harassed himself; interpersonal violence resulted from peer bullying; and he experienced collective violence from a society that devalues immigrants and the handicapped, and fails to provide a living wage. The WHO publishes a helpful chart that systematizes the many forms of violence (see Figure 8.1).

Think About and Discuss with Your Colleagues

- In the WHO typology of violence (Figure 8.1), notice that there are only two categories that are not sexual in nature. How has your life been touched by events that are described by WHO? Does the widespread nature of interpersonal violence surprise you?

Human violence is a highly complex phenomenon, with many definitions, dimensions, and determinants. For your reference, we define **interpersonal violence** as intentionally antisocial actions, relationship patterns, or attitudes that result from multiple source problems, develop and escalate over time, harm countless people, and suggest many potential solutions. We begin this chapter with detailed exploration of personal and group violence such as that experienced by Gabriel. In Chapter 9 we will explore terms and concepts related to large-scale international violence and war.

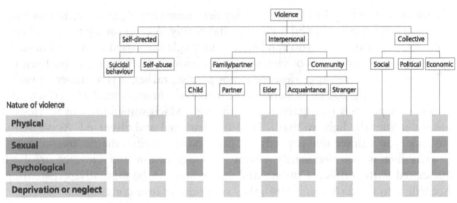

Figure 8.1 World Health Organization typology of violence
Based on Krug, 2002, public domain.

Prosocial Actions

Prosocial tactics lead toward positive, harmonious relationships. Based on acknowledgment that all parties' viewpoints are important, prosocial actions benefit everyone. The personality factors of openmindedness, conscientiousness, extroversion, agreeableness, and nonreactivity to emotions correlate with prosocial tactics (Roccas, 2002).

Prosocial tactics support relationship and peaceful interactions and conflict processing even during the heat of conflict. A prosocial person courteously expresses their needs and wishes, but also listens to the opponent's perspective. *Assertive responses* are honest and respectful. You express your discontent and ask for what you need in a way that does not override or insult the opponent. This response is sometimes called "the third way": it is neither passive nor aggressive. Everyone expresses their opinions about a problem and works together toward a solution. Because these tactics likely result in satisfaction for all parties, they lead to *win-win outcomes*. Although anyone can use prosocial tactics, females' predominant prosocial responses tend toward expressiveness and caring, whereas males' most salient prosocial responses are more interactive and instrumental (Larieu, 2010).

Antisocial Actions

In stark contrast, **antisocial tactics** cause or aggravate conflict and hasten the deterioration of a relationship. High-conflict individuals tend to experience changeable emotions that stall logical reasoning and result in two-faced behavior (for example, they are charming in public, but confrontational in private), and find it difficult to reflect on their own role in a conflict (Antonioni, 1998; Eddy, 2005). Characteristics like closedmindedness, carelessness, introversion, disagreeability, and unstable moods add fuel to conflict escalation and result in passive, aggressive, and passive-aggressive responses.

When someone lets a conflict unfold with little input, they submit to the other parties, not disclosing their needs, ideas, or goals. Examples of such *passive responses* include people-pleasing, changing the subject, or simple silence. Because the person is willing to relinquish personal satisfaction, passive responses usually lead to *lose-win outcomes*.

The aim of an *aggressive response* is to gain or express power. When used to excel or to thrive, aggressive responses can be useful, but there is a very fine line between self-promotion and provoking conflict. Control or intimidation used in a hostile manner allows aggressive people to succeed in forcing their position, dominating others, and coercing others to accept solutions unwillingly. The outcome of this tactic is usually an unsatisfying, one-sided relationship. Negative experiences with aggression often result in habits of conflict avoidance. Because these tactics all result in the defeat of one party, they are called *win-lose outcomes*. Aggressive responses may take varied forms, like concealed *covert aggression*, hostile overt aggression, and frustrating *passive-aggression*.

PEOPLE ARE ALWAYS AFFECTED

Interpersonal violence occurs between two individuals. The systems perspective suggests that any level of society can implicated, though, so when conflict escalates, it can quickly spread to involve other individuals in groups like families and neighborhoods, and beyond.

The contextual environment is relevant and should not be overlooked. The environment holds both protective and risk factors. **Protective factors** act as buffers, either decreasing the likelihood of experiencing violence or moderating the harm (Howell, 2010). Key protective factors (among other factors) for individuals and families are interpersonal connections with prosocial groups, and an emotionally and economically healthy environment. **Risk factors** are life events, conditions, and experiences linked with problems, antisocial behavior, and violence (Howell, 2010), such as having lived in a violent neighborhood, learning disabilities during childhood, and being victimized. They potentially make life less healthy and more dangerous (Byrne, 2012). These seem to mount up so that the more factors are present, the more likely violence will occur. Once again, the quality of personal relationships with peers and family is crucial, along with a stressful or violent family or community environment (CDC, 2020).

Individual Perpetrators of Violence

A **perpetrator** of aggression is a person who carries out an illegal, immoral, or intentionally harmful act (from the OED). Perpetrators of violence are dissimilar, showing few comparable patterns. Individually, they are probably not what they seem to be because they seem "normal" or unremarkable to almost everyone who knows them. They are not purely evil; they are not usually mentally ill. Rather, they are fallible human beings whose actions are a mixture of bad and good and fall along the fine line between good and evil (Zimbardo, 2007). Hannah Arendt (1963) is famous for identifying "the banality of evil," meaning that violence can seem unremarkably ordinary.

Although most violent perpetrators appear on the surface to be strong, confident, even liked by others, this sometimes differs dramatically from their intrapersonal reality. Studies consistently conclude that people who abuse others display lower self-esteem and are subtly depressed. They have not learned the skills for positive identity, so they perceive themselves as vulnerable. They compensate for insecurity and inadequacy by using violent power to fortify themselves. It is also clear that most perpetrators of violence were previous targets of violence. Thus, they become a part of a repeating cycle of violent coping.

According to Leonard Berkowitz (1993), most individual violent behavior is motivated by one of three discernible goals:

1. *Defensive* or *reactive violence* attempts to preserve survival in the face of a perceived threat or attack. For example, a majority of states in the United States have adopted "Stand Your Ground" laws, which legitimize even lethal defensive aggression if family members, possessions, or safety are believed to be threatened.
2. *Instrumental violence* is used in a strategy to accomplish a goal in the relationship or resolve a contentious issue. It has an aim, is planned, and is usually fairly controlled in intensity. Instrumental violence usually occurs only after repeated nonviolent attempts to accomplish the goal are unsuccessful.
3. *Hostile* or *retaliatory aggression* is impulsive dominance or revenge. It is often unplanned, and is linked to the presence of a very hot emotion such as rage.

Twin studies conducted by Philippe Rushton (2004) estimated that prosocial actions are associated more than 60% with environmental influences, and about 40% with genetic determinants (also the conclusion of Pepler, 2018), with likely parallels for antisocial patterns.

Influences from the Social Environment

Social attitudes, especially the endorsement and tolerance of certain types of violence, create a climate that bypasses its outcomes. Common themes such as "boys will be boys" or "it's a private matter" discourage a closer look. Victims frequently blame themselves, so they may be reluctant to disclose the violence publicly. Witnesses may hesitate to intervene for fear of becoming the target of retaliation.

Some social environments enforce the paradigm of power and control. For example, aggression may be commonly seen as an acceptable (or the only) way to resolve conflict in a relationship, and passionate behavior viewed as compelling and uncontrollable. This social tolerance makes it too easy to focus on the victim's behavior, and to overlook and normalize aggressive actions.

Think again of case of Gabriel and his family. Their risk was endemic: they were immigrants with less than perfect English skills, few extended family supports, and chronic financial stress; Gabriel was disadvantaged by his handicapped hand and had few meaningful links with the school community. These factors resulted in Gabriel's acceptance of outsider status within his environment, and his being drawn to the tightly structured Los Bravos pseudofamily despite its ethic of domination and violence.

Genetic Influences: The "Nature-Nurture" Debate

The search for individual causes of violence still reverts to an age-old controversy, the **nature-nurture debate,** which was revisited in the late 20th century as the genetic components of human behavior were decoded. On one side of this debate are *nature theorists* who believe that aggression is instinctive or in some way caused biologically. There is some evidence and much current research investigating the hypotheses that aggression is linked to specific brain structures, hormones (especially sexual hormones), abnormal DNA coding, and other biological factors. On the other side of the debate are *nurture scholars* who look at the learning environment, believing that humans are taught to be violent (or peaceable) through modeling, overt instruction, selective rewards and punishments, and successful practice.

Although the controversy continues, the results are not ambiguous. Scientific consensus is clear: the primary determinant of individual violence is social learning. In 1986, the UN Educational, Scientific, and Cultural Organization (UNESCO), convened an international conference at Seville, Spain, to discuss the evidence for biological correlates of world violence. This conference resulted in repudiation of the nature theory.

Core ideas of the Seville Statement on Violence (1986):
It is *incorrect* to say that

1. ... We have inherited a tendency to make war from our animal ancestors.
2. ... War or any other violent behavior is genetically programmed into human nature.
3. ... The course of human evolution has shown selection for aggressive behavior more than for other kinds of behavior.
4. ... Humans have a "violent brain."
5. ... War is caused by "instinct" or any single motivation.

The statement was signed by many international scientists and officially adopted by UNESCO, it continues somewhat controversial. Nurture theorists believe that most perpetrators of violence are unaware of methods or skills for coping with conflict appropriately and responsibly. Violence is caused by learning within a social environment: violent patterns are learned, and perpetrators fail to learn alternative prosocial responses.

Consequences for Perpetrators

Mostly, violence is perpetrated for several situational reasons. First, it works. It results in the victim stopping whatever the perpetrator found objectionable. Second, most perpetrators "get away with" most violent incidents. They have typically experienced the high probability of **impunity,** or not having to face negative consequences or punishment. Third, they know their actions can successfully overpower a relatively powerless victim, such as a woman or a child. Interpersonal perpetrators are rarely indiscriminately violent, and do not engage in violence against more powerful adversaries (DCP, 2013).

Violent perpetrators may use numerous methods to hide the violence, possibly appearing in public as amiable and helpful. They also hide (and might not even be aware of) the intrapersonal consequences of their behavior. Nonetheless, violence is traumatic even to the perpetrator. **Perpetration Induced Trauma Stress** (PITS) is a syndrome similar to Post-Traumatic Stress Disorder (PTSD, which affects victims and witnesses). It results from active participation in violent actions, especially prolonged or repeated, such as gang and military force action or even animal slaughterhouse workers. PITS is not a formally recognized diagnosis at present, but sufferers experience chronic stress symptoms: mentally intrusive memories, flashbacks, and nightmares, emotional numbness alternating with anger, shame, and guilt, interpersonal detachment, alienation, and disintegrating relationships (MacNair, 2012). Many sufferers self-medicate with substance abuse or cycles of dangerous behavior.

Individual Victims of Violence

A **victim** of aggression is a person who has experienced or witnessed the harm of a significantly violent event. Although the term is in everyday use, its meaning is ambiguous. So many victims are hidden.

The word "victim" can be a controversial stereotype, even in formal scholarship. To many, it incorrectly implies conditions that confine the sufferer to perpetual suffering because victims are naively reactive and not proactive, have no ability to better her/his situation (Lamb, 1996, 1999), and "help" is too arbitrary. There are very few potentially neutral synonyms.

There is no singular "type" of victim. Vulnerability is a human constant within degrees, but becomes evident differently in individuals (Fineman, 2008, 2017). Actual vulnerability to violence is multidimensional and intersectional, involving many simultaneous factors such as age, family status, economic dependency, cultural-ethnic group, and so forth. Research finds a dynamic interplay between some factors that can be improved (for example, economic or immigrant status or substance abuse), and some factors that are static and cannot be changed (for example, age or ethnicity). A few common factors that increase vulnerability are denial of the risks and a lack of intuitive fear, mental illness diagnosis, and social isolation (Museilak, 2018))

Think About and Discuss with Your Colleagues

- How do you define a "victim" of violence?
- What signs would you look for to identify such a person?
- Is she/he a victim if they do not see themselves that way?
- Is she/he a victim if the violence is self-directed?
- Is she/he a victim if they are simultaneously a perpetrator?

Victims Coping with Violence: Post-Traumatic Stress Disorder

A very high proportion of victims experience enduring trauma and grief reactions. **Post-Traumatic Stress Disorder** (PTSD) is a psychological condition caused by experiencing or witnessing a seriously stressful or traumatic event. PTSD is not a mental illness but is a normal response to an abnormal event. It is heightened by a number of factors: the intensity of the originating event, repeated or ongoing trauma, unexpectedness or unpredictability of the trauma, and self-blame (Herman, 1997). Each person has a unique reaction pattern, but primary warning signs include repetitious recall and reexperience of the event, avoidance of similar situations, and excessively vigilant attention to the environment. Secondary signs include expression of extreme forms of emotion during conflict, and substance abuse in an attempt to alleviate tension.

In Western populations not directly affected by war, approximately 5% of males and 10% of females experience PTSD because of experienced threats and life trauma. Virtually 100% of victims of violence demonstrate some degree of PTSD. In military populations deployed to a war zone, 15–30% experience PTSD; of those, approximately 30% manifest a chronic form (NIH, 2014). Many PTSD sufferers encounter the added stigma of public misunderstanding, shaming, and disrespect because of the disabling effects of the condition. Canadian General Romeo Dallaire, who announced publicly that he suffers with PTSD as a result of the horror of the Rwandan genocide in 1994, has become an outspoken advocate for accurate diagnosis and treatment.

Although incurable, PTSD is controllable with appropriate treatment. Therapeutic programs for the treatment of trauma are increasingly accessible. Keys to effective management include 1) ending the violence and trauma; 2) early trauma debriefing; 3) accurate information about the condition and its management; and 4) emotional processing of the trauma and its meaning. Clearly, the longer it remains secret, the more difficult is the healing.

Victims Coping with Violence: The Victim Identity

Victims of interpersonal violence develop some coping patterns that compromise their ability to cope. Aphrodite Matsakis (1996) identified three components of a *victim identity*, which develops in response to severe or prolonged violence:

1. Belief in the goodness of the world is shattered. The environment seems disorderly, and the victim feels vulnerable and incapable.
2. Victim identity is internalized; the trauma becomes the one, central defining fact of identity. The victim may relive the violence, fearing and acting as if it is still happening, or even suffer with a repetition compulsion.
3. New wounding is caused by others' reactions that deny or minimize the violence, or shame and stigmatize the victim through neglect and blame.

Victims are not doomed to this identity, however. With appropriate, enduring support and treatment, those identity factors transform the victim to *survivor*, then to *thriver* (Hansen, 1991). The *victim* has not been able to grow beyond the traumatic situation, and is dominated by guilt, shame, and fear. The *survivor* is determined to resume life and growth, and is able to access the help and support they need to mourn the violence and take new control of life. The *thriver* experiences the wellbeing of life satisfaction and resilience despite the trauma, and may be able to use new insights to assist others in their healing.

SOURCES OF PROBLEMS CAUSING VIOLENCE

The causes or sources of violence are present at every level of the human system in "a web of violence": individual and group contributors, social, and cultural features (Byrne, 2012). Violent conflict occurs at all levels, often spreading from one segment to another. A systems analysis proposes that:

- Peace and violence are both complex phenomena.
- People and their social environments are interactive, with continuous "bottom-up" and "top-down" influences toward peace or violence.
- Peace and violence have no simple causes and do not develop straightforwardly.
- The causes of violent or peaceable behavior exist within a complete social system. Violence is the complex result of four entwined influences: individual, relationship, community, and society (Byrne, 2012; Cashman, 2013; Garcia-Moreno, 2012).
- Discussions of violence is entangled within our understandings of ownership and entitlement, the acceptability of superior, dominating hierarchy, and the social legitimacy of violence (Byrne, 2012).

Johan Galtung's Analysis of Forms of Violence

Johan Galtung (1971) was, and is, a major contributor to understanding *the vicious violence triangle*. He noted that we too often focus exclusively on overt, visibly aggressive behavior and its causes. Obvious, dramatically aggressive behavior can be difficult to overlook or keep in perspective, but there is only illusory comfort in paying attention to overt violence: if it happens to someone else, then it is not happening to you. If affected individuals or families can be identified, then prevention and control might be possible.

Galtung suggests looking deeper to recognize that not all violence is clearly visible. Some sources of harm comprise what he calls invisible and indirect violence. For example, people living in certain areas may be at higher risk of violent events than others, so the actual extent of violence could be linked to economic geography. Men are more likely to use or be the target of direct physical aggression; women are more likely to use and experience covert, subtle forms of violence. Also, cultures vary widely in their tolerance of violent behaviors and in their attempts to provide members with effective alternatives.

According to Galtung, three categories of violence are interwoven; cause and effect are mutually reinforcing (Figure 8.2).

Behavioral, Direct Violence   refers to violent actions with identifiable victim(s), and identifiable perpetrator(s): "So-and-so hurt so-and-so." This type of violence is usually somewhat impulsive, and is not associated with any group or cause. It is a significant source of suffering all over the world. The Small Arms Survey (Mc Evoy, 2017) estimated that, in 2016, 385,000 people died as a result of intentional homicide, a type of direct violence. Albert Bandura's experiments (1973) demonstrated that behavioral violence is highly influenced by observing and *modeling* others, especially high-status individuals. Other

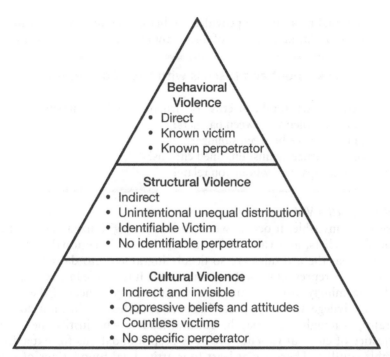

Figure 8.2 Johan Galtung's vicious violence triangle

contributors to this type of violence include intense emotion (especially fear and anger), frustration with goal achievement, a need for power or status, or revenge for previously experienced violence.

Structural Violence or Institutionalized Violence occurs when a society is organized or stratified in such a way that significant groups of people are disadvantaged by the unequal distribution of resources or power. Unjust access to collective resources results in restricted past and future opportunities, diminished quality of life, and even shorter life spans. It is colloquially called *systemic violence*. Daniel Christie (2001) and his colleagues identified three primary mechanisms for structural violence: social dominance, political oppression, and economic exploitation. Structural violence is insidious: it is indirect and unintentional, with identifiable victims but no identifiable perpetrators.

The **Theory of Multiple Marginality** (Vigil, 2016) was developed from research into gang relationships and violence in society. **Marginality** is the unchosen and probably undeserved situation of an individual or group being relegated to the margins of mainstream systems and institutions. It crucially compromises individuals' abilities to access resources such as health care, employment, and education. Therefore, marginality ensures that crucial survival and identity needs are inadequately met, and results in pervasive status as an outsider. According to this view, then, violence is correlated with institutional, political, and social influences such as economic disadvantage, racism, voter suppression, and exclusion. Those forces undermine community bonds and family supports, and compel an individual to find support elsewhere, among alternative peers. Irrespective of values, marginal peer culture provides the belonging and social learning that are absent from traditional sources of disadvantaged families and communities.

Think About and Discuss with Your Colleagues

- How could "structural concerns" or structural violence affect:
  - o domestic violence between partners?
  - o family violence between siblings?
  - o police violence against unarmed citizens?
  - o other groups with whom you relate?

Cultural or Collective Violence
is indirect and invisible. It occurs when violence is legitimized and justified by the attitudes, beliefs, and values of a society. It is unintentional and invisible in the sense that the attitudes are so deeply ingrained into daily life that you assume that they represent something that is true. It is visible in its consequences every day: seemingly insignificant but devastating experiences of the injustices of unequal privilege and prejudice. There are countless victims but no specific perpetrator, although there may be cultural leaders who justify the attitudes. The injustice of cultural violence provides deep foundations for extended and intractable conflict. There are at least four attitudinal foundations of cultural violence:

First, the *normalization* of violence and cultivation of a violence-desensitized environment happen gradually through frequent exposure to violence. Some neighborhoods are more dangerous than others, exposing their residents more frequently to violent events. Frequent graphic media reports of dramatic events help to normalize them, but leave out relevant information regarding causation and resolution.

Think About and Discuss with Your Colleagues

- In your experience and opinion, how influential are media portrayals of violent and nonviolent behavior? Do you think they "desensitize" viewers? Consider multiple media: news, TV, video games, advertising, and so forth.

Second, misunderstandings and *stereotypes* lead people to devalue and demean anyone who appears to be different. Unfamiliar experiences are discounted when compared with the understood "normal," forming the base for an us–them distinction. It can be difficult to acknowledge stereotype because it separates the distance between "us" and "those other brutes." For example, it is inaccurate, but convenient, to scapegoat men or ethnic groups or youth for violent events. At the same time, victims of violence are misunderstood by those whose reality does not include vulnerability or powerlessness.

A third assumption and attitude that enables violence is called the *Just World*: you get what you deserve. This implies that those who enjoy peaceful privileges and benefits deserve them; by the same token, those who experience violence

Table 8.1   Honor Code of Violence

1. The Principle of Defense
   Never use unprovoked or undeserved violence. Therefore, "someone else started it."
2. The Principle of Retaliation
   Retaliation is not a choice; it is required. Therefore, reciprocation of violence is necessary.
3. The Principle of Ownership
   If you own it, you can hurt it—but no one else can, so…. If you own it, you must defend it. Therefore, violence is merely protective.
4. The Principle of Pain
   Giving pain should not be outwardly enjoyed. Therefore, "someone's got to do it." Enter the battle with manly "courage."
5. The Principle of Better Behavior
   Excessive behavior is excusable as long as a rationale is upheld; for example, real men are active, not passive. Therefore, for real men excessive aggression is better than passivity.
6. The Principle of Strength
   A chain of command is fundamental to strength, which is the exact opposite of weakness and chaos. A chain of command is to be followed simply, not to be questioned. Therefore, the highest nobility is to follow orders, even if they are violent.

Source: Based on Joseph A. Kuypers.1992. Man's Will to Hurt. Fernwood.

deserve it. This leads to suspecting, discrediting, or blaming the victim: "He always did make up stories." "She was exaggerating and lying." "What did he do to provoke that?" And so forth.

Fourth, members of society define social roles and *power* in ways that justify domination as a legitimate (or only) source of personal power. Sometimes called the privilege of power, this attitude leads to the use of an escalating continuum of influence and coercive control that includes thought manipulation and isolation from social supports (Singer, 1995). For example, many cultures confine "act like a man" to being sexually relentless, tough and in control, and, therefore, successful. Joseph Kuypers (1992) studied these attitudes in an "Honor Code" (see Table 8.1) that is used to justify violence as moral and right.

Interpersonal Power and Violence

A core dynamic of violent relationships is interpersonal power: gaining it, losing it, challenging it, and fighting for it. No one is completely powerless, but power inequities do exist and can strongly affect every interaction. It is part of relational balance and consent, but power is contextual and may be useless in a given situation. Power can be used to enable or to disable others.

Violence is, ultimately, an expression of or a demand for power. Aggressors have a sense of entitlement to lead or control others and, therefore, view all interactions through the lens of compliance or disobedience, or power challenge. Violence grows gradually and often subtly, as a way to maintain relative control; if it is abusive, it is to ensure others' deference to the leader.

In real relationships, power is an unavoidable factor that shifts with circumstances and situations. The actual source is less important than the ways in which power and power imbalances are handled. When power is used with consent and respect to support and empower everyone's wellbeing, it can be the basis for important social change. For example, the support of celebrities advertising intolerance for drunk driving helped make driving under the influence shameful. Power is abused when it is used nonconsensually and/or disrespectfully, or to exploit, humiliate, or coerce someone. Power used in abusive ways can be expected to result in resistant protest at best, and violent conflict at worst.

Rollo May (1998) identified a continuum of ways of using personal power that range from prosocial through destructive, antisocial uses (see Figure 8.3): healthy, prosocial power is *nurturing*, power used "for" others, to provide supportive caring to others; **integrative power** is used "with" others, to unite, advocate, collaborate, and promote cooperation; either healthy or destructive, **manipulative power** is used "over" others to control through persuasion and management; **competitive power** is used "against" other people for personal gain at someone else's expense; and the least healthy, most destructive and abusive power is **exploitive**, taking power "from" others to fuel one's own private ends, without concern for other peoples' needs. This personal power could use influence methods like direct exploitation, deliberate deception, and physical coercion (Singer, 1994).

Because it is a factor in every relationship, power plays a role in escalating or deescalating most conflicts. Certain conditions contribute to violent conflict (Kraybill, 1992):

a. Ambiguity occurs when power is granted within a structure or hierarchy but rules are unspoken or limits are poorly defined. This can contribute to power struggles.

b. A reactive power struggle is ignited when legitimate power is used without consent, is imposed coercively or oppressively, or interferes with others' fulfillment of their goals.

c. When power and privilege are used to stratify relationships with an unsupported superior-inferior judgment, resistance is created.

d. Unstable power can become an issue when the powerful feel compelled to protect it or use it to improve their status.

Figure 8.3 Continuum of power uses
Based on May, 1998, public domain.

The power used by perpetrators of violence is malevolent and unhealthy, and is associated with destructive consequences for everyone. It uses threat that may be implicit or explicit. The most "effective" violence is arbitrary and unpredictable, ruthless, and absolute. The horrifying obedience experiments of Stanley Milgram (1963) are well known for their conclusions:

1. Authority is very powerful, and most people allow authority to overrule their own judgment and morals.
2. Depersonalizing and dehumanizing a victim justifies bad behavior.
3. Power, expectations, and dehumanization need not be explicit.
4. Few people have the courage for noncompliance with power.

PROCESS AND CONSEQUENCES OF VIOLENCE

The Development of Violent Relationships

Violent relationships occur most often in close, intimate relationships such as family, but can occur in any setting and all socioeconomic, religious, and cultural groups. A study conducted by the US Centers for Disease Control (Black, 2010) found that 33% of American women and 25% of American men have experienced some degree of violence in a close relationship. Females are more likely to experience violence by people known and close to them; males are more likely to experience violence by an acquaintance or stranger.

Maryam Monsef, Canada's parliamentary minister for Women and Gender Equality, called the problem of female-targeted violence a "four-alarm fire." Violence against females happens everywhere, but certain places (like campuses, the military, and RCMP) have especially high rates. Certain groups like women with disabilities and Indigenous women and girls face higher rates of violence. The effects of the damage caused by most violent relationships ripple outward, impacting many people beyond the aggressor and the victim.

Dyadic Cycles of Violence

Some incidents of violence are situational and episodic. Isolated actions, when they occur, are shocking to both the perpetrator and the victim, and can result in a sudden reevaluation of conflict strategies. However, even though assault may occur only once, or rarely, the threat of future violence allows a perpetrator to exercise control in a victim's life. The development of habit patterns suggests that "one hit leads to another."

More usually, incidents of violence are part of a repeating cycle of days or months, first identified by Lenore Walker (2017). It is perpetuated by a continuing contradiction between hope that all will be well and denial that all is not well. This cycle eventually forms the foundation for a regular habit of using violence in response to conflict. The cycle has three phases (see Figure 8.4, which illustrates these interlocking dynamics).

Phase 1: *Tension Building*—Tensions, possibly arguments, begin to dominate everyday interactions, threatening the perpetrator's equilibrium of control. Typically, a perpetrator of violence blames the victim for the arguments, justifying increasing control by the victim's behavior. A victim, sensing the signs of escalating control, typically experiences dread and anxiety, and possibly also accepts the blame for increasing tension. The victim responds by trying to deal with the conflict issues with nonviolent discussion and resolution, but this is likely to increase the tensions further. Phase 2: *Critical Incident*—A harmful episode of violence erupts and harm is done, but the tension is relieved. Some victims fight back with reciprocal violence.

Phase 3: *"Peace"*—The critical incident shocks both parties into establishing an illusion of **pseudopeace**. The victim reacts with withdrawal, rejecting the perpetrator to seek support from outside the relationship. The perpetrator feels shame and expresses remorse, often blaming external factors such as alcohol or stress, and promising the violence will never happen again. Because the relationship is valued by both parties, the relationship usually continues, but enters a phase of pseudopeace that is a form of denial. The perpetrator pursues the victim with attention and promises of a better future. The relieved victim responds to the perpetrator's remorse and promises by using pleasing actions and maintaining the fragile peace at all costs.

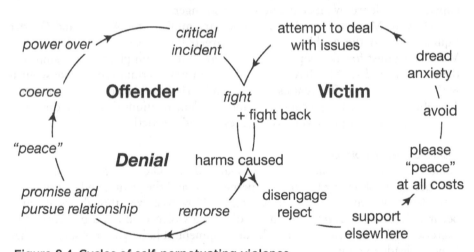

Figure 8.4 Cycles of self-perpetuating violence

This cycle represents events that are most common in individualistic Western societies (Straus, 2012). Because of differences of family structure, economic status, and community response, less is known about the frequency or dynamics of similar violence in associative cultures (Garcia-Moreno, 2006). However, associative cultures place more emphasis and value on family bonds and internal loyalty. Family honor is maintained by observance of traditional patriarchal roles and structures, which relegate dominant decision making power to males, and modest obedience to female family members (Khan, 2018). Risk of relationship violence in these settings appears to be tied to actual decision-making equity and economic resources (Xu, 2011).

Traumatic Consequences

The effects of violence are inevitably and pervasively traumatic. **Trauma** is an intense threat to wellbeing and the damage that results from a disturbing or distressing event. It may result from a one-time incident (*Type 1 trauma*), a repeated event (*Type II trauma*), or violence so numerous and pervasive that the experiences mingle together (*Type III trauma*).

Trauma Studies is a social science that investigates healthy and maladaptive responses to traumatic events like conflict. Some conclusions seem obvious:

1. A traumatic event cannot be solved; it must be endured;
2. The event overloads normal coping and problem solving abilities;
3. Trauma and reactions to it disrupt existing life meaning and goals;
4. The long-term individual impact of trauma waxes and wanes, shifting from disorganized crisis to stabilization and back to crisis; and
5. The reactions often compound earlier unresolved issues (McCann, 2015).

Costs to Society

Violence is incalculably costly. In 2019, it was estimated that the global impact of violence totaled US$14 trillion, or more than 10% of global economic activity, and $1,853 per person (IEP, 2019). The actual cost varies greatly from region to region. Direct costs include emergency and ongoing medical care for victims and witnesses of violence, operating shelters for victims fleeing violence (sometimes for years), trauma and mental health care, military forces and security operations expenditures, and dealing with crime and justice. Indirect costs include lost wages due to undermined personal functioning and reduced community productivity. Repeating violent cycles also result in inevitable, but long-term, costs.

PRAXIS: POTENTIAL PRACTICAL SOLUTIONS

Conflict and violence are fundamentally different (though related) processes. Conflict does not necessarily include violence, but aggression and violence grow out of unchecked escalation. It is as if conflict takes a tangential pathway as violence develops. When considering practical solutions to violence, traditional conflict resolution techniques are not sufficient. Dealing with conflict issues during a violent episode or in an ongoing violent relationship is virtually impossible. Going beyond conflict resolution, you could use the convenient catchphrase:

Ending and Mending

Only after the violence has ended can a mending process begin and the initial conflict issues be discussed. Strategies for peacekeeping in diverse situations include many challenging tasks:

- *Prevention*—significant effort is invested to understand the dynamics of escalating conflict and detect the risk factors and early warnings before violence occurs;
- *Intervention*—this is work done during and shortly after (usually about 3 weeks) a violent crisis to improve the immediate crisis or lower the harm caused by it;

- *Postvention*—dealing with the aftermath of violence is critical to future prevention (usually several years);
- *Society's Work*—reforming the base of norms and values that tolerate violent responses and provide few workable alternatives (an unending task).

The process of dealing with interpersonal violence are sequential: first, protect everyone, but especially the vulnerable, by ending existing violence; second, devise systemwide, comprehensive approaches to dealing with the sources and the effects of violence and; third, prevent new development of violence. To be effective, practical solutions must deal with each level of violence envisioned by Galtung (1969).

Trauma-Informed Practice

Many conflict practitioners work with victims traumatized by violence in a variety of situations like family, communities, refugees, and military members and their relatives. Often, the trauma history is ongoing or hidden. Trauma-Informed Practice deals with conflict issues with sensitivity to past trauma, consequences, and coping mechanisms. Understanding that victims' "symptoms" are primarily expressions of the trauma reaction can alter a conflict settlement plan entirely, and the same might be found for perpetrators of violence. Specific training in Trauma-Informed Practice is essential for competent conflict professionals.

Nonviolent Communication

Marshall Rosenberg (1983, 2015) developed a process called nonviolent communication (NVC), and founded the Center for Nonviolent Communication to train practical peacekeeping skills. NVC supports communication in connected relationships, conflict prevention planning, and peaceful living.

The base of the process is deep compassion toward the people whose harmful experiences lead to violent feelings and strategies. NVC is used intrapersonally, interpersonally, and within groups and social systems. Core skills use authentic communication, empathic connections between people, and collaboration, with the goal of free, harmonious relating. The model integrates the awareness that is found in many other peaceful strategies: careful observation followed by the clarifying disclosure of feelings, needs, and values, and an assertive request for what is wanted.

Ongoing training is conducted by the Center. NVC has many global applications, from children's books to racial desegregation to international peacekeeping.

Prevention Strategies Are Always Best

Prevention programs are positive approaches that improve community living conditions generally, and so reduce the frequency of violent events. The human and economic benefits of prevention are vast. There are four conventional strategies:

Relationship Building and Community Development

Active personal connections and involvement in a safe, protective community environment are powerful ways to prevent individuals from developing violent patterns. This can mean, for example, providing constructive community activities for youth and other vulnerable groups. Many communities create multisectoral partnerships among families, schools, police, and political administrations to provide comprehensive approaches to community building. For example, "Project Safe Neighborhoods" is an American national program that forms teams that include partners from community leadership, law enforcement, and several levels of government. These teams confront the most pressing problems of crime and violence that a neighborhood is dealing with, and brainstorm effective solutions to address them.

Enhance Protective Factors

Risk factors make it more likely that violent events will occur; protective factors lower the probability of violence, improve stress resilience, or mitigate the harm inherent in violent events (Howell, 2010). Protective influences include such factors as strong family structure, positive school experiences, and support and supervision from the community. This type of influence prevents violence through community partnerships that promote healthy social development for all community members. It can include encouragement of strong, close, prosocial friendships; support for local business; and open community discussions of social challenges such as racism and poverty. For example, the Seattle Social Development Project was designed to reduce aggressive children's behavior by strengthening family and school attachments, commitments, and attitudes toward education. It worked with teachers, parents, and children (Hawkins, 2007).

Reduce Risk Factors

Violent patterns are clearly related to specific experiences and life events that place vulnerable individuals at risk of entering cycles of antisocial and violent behavior. Many of these factors are related to unmet needs for personal stability, protection, and social advancement (Howell, 2019) in a troubled milieu. Risk factors are locally identified and evaluated, then prevention programs designed to alleviate potential areas of personal and family frustration. Effective programs usually include the participation of local community members and legal and sometimes mental health professionals (Monahan, 2016). For example, the field of environmental design uses architecture and landscape planning to reduce community danger and fear (Crowe, 2000).

Education and Training

Because much violence occurs because individuals and groups are not prepared with prosocial skills to resolve problems, prevention that results from skills enhancement can be effective. Generally, access to high-quality, well-rounded education programs is part of this strategy. Specific lifeskills such as respectful communication, conflict-resolution processes, and maintaining employment can improve the milieu. With respect to aggression and violence, prevention requires proactive work and the participation of a substantial number of community members. Training focuses on recognizing risks and escalating behavior patterns, proactive safe preparedness and nonviolent crisis intervention for situational crises, specific deescalation techniques, and responsible communication, debriefing, and reporting procedures.

For example, Adults and Children Together (ACT) against Violence is an 8-week training program designed to prevent child maltreatment by teaching positive parenting. The program addresses both child behavior and parent's and caregiver's emotional management. After training, measures showed increased use of mutual nurturing and effective discipline, and decreased harsh verbal and physical punishment. Positive community connections and support were unexpected benefits (Portwood, 2011).

A number of challenges are present when prevention programs are designed. The context is important. Because of a plethora of historic, cultural, resource, and economic differences, parallel communities with equivalent populations or types of violence do not exist, so success in one community cannot necessarily predict success in another. Ongoing research tends to yield only weak evidence and diverse conclusions.

Effective prevention programs share a number of characteristics (Nation, 2003). First and foremost, they are based on personal relationships among the participants. Growing from that, effective programs integrate and coordinate the input from a comprehensive collection of community members, including family, police, street workers, and school personnel. Programs are proactively long term, to be activated at appropriate times. They are locally designed and culturally relevant, based on accurate data on identifiable patterns and trends. They are part of a continuum approach to prevention and early intervention.

Violence Ending Intervention Strategies

Violence intervention is initially focused on crisis response and support services during and promptly following a violent crisis. Immediate security of the vulnerable may be in jeopardy at this time, so risks must be dealt with. This often means involving law enforcement and protection, and investigation services. For safety and therapeutic reasons, most perpetrators need to be temporarily distanced and disengaged from the community in which the violence occurred. Although the longer-term goal of this strategy is reintegration with the community, many perpetrators are unable to tolerate the separation and many return to former relationships prematurely.

The primary need for victims is for crisis recovery and intervention to relieve the harm left by traumatic violence. Debriefing of the incident as soon as possible after the incident is a crucial step for the victim's recovery. It is a guided retelling of the incident and thoughts and feelings remaining. When the victim and perpetrator are prematurely reunited (which often happens), this can short circuit the later mending processes for both parties.

Postvention Strategies for Mending the Wounds of Violence

Postvention refers to actions taken after violence has occurred and the crisis has stabilized. This is the "mending" phase referred to earlier, which can take several years' time. The process is very different for perpetrators and for victims and witnesses.

Perpetrators need comprehensive treatment to prevent future problem behavior, but are often the most resistant to treatment. It is essential that everyone recognize the basic principle of responsibility: the perpetrator alone is responsible for violent actions, the perpetrator alone is responsible to make a decision and commit to relinquishing violent behavior. No one else can coerce or guarantee the transformation needed. A perpetrator must experience a transformation that fundamentally alters their worldview, with implications for behavior patterns, relationship assumptions, and attitudes and values. This is not a quick insight and promise. Until it is complete, perpetrators are no safer than before, and are likely to eventually return to coercive and violent habits. Programs will include relationship nurture to address interpersonal isolation and alienation, empowerment to address underlying feelings of inadequacy, substance abuse rehabilitation if that is a factor, and training in leadership skills, study, and job preparation. The international work done by the British charity, The Forgiveness Project, is an example of this treatment. Work with both victims and convicted criminals to help them face the story of the crime, to forgive themselves and, when possible, to reconcile (Noor and Cantacuzino, 2018).

Victims and *witnesses* of violence are relatively easy to engage in treatment programs, although the treatment is complex. The actual plan depends on the context and severity of the incident(s) and traumatic impact. It usually involves development of a trusting therapeutic relationship. Victims have to integrate the real losses that resulted from the traumatic incident or relationship. A quick "forgive and forget" approach will usually result in ongoing trauma effects that continue to impact future relationships. The first step is to (re-)establish both the reality and feeling of safety. It may take a victim some time to overcome the anxiety of threat before confidence develops in renewed safety. A victim then begins a process of healing that includes remembering, grieving, and rebuilding lifestyle and meaningful connections (Herman, 2015).

In addition to providing prevention, intervention, and postvention resources, society also has its work, suggested by Galtung's layer of cultural violence.

Society's Work to Transform Attitudes

Lasting peace can only be created by changing the social norms and values that support and normalize violence (Galtung, 1971). Social changers can work negatively to eliminate the drivers of violence, and positively to cultivate constructive, peaceable environments. Probably the most effective methods use coordinated, comprehensive approaches that aim toward the eventual transformation of any aspect of a social context that perpetuates violence. A positively *constructive plan* encourages strength development within an identity community by a) modeling behavioral alternatives to violence, b) functioning with just, equitable social order, and c) cultivating respectful attitudes that value diversity. With that, existing behavioral expectations and relationship structures can be altered to create a nonviolent culture (see Chapter 12 on Conflict Transformation).

Stopping violence from happening through such concepts as *safe schools*, for example, that use effective campus monitoring and surveillance and prohibition of any gang affiliation markers on campus. *Safe communities* benefit from such activities as graffiti removal, constructive activities for youth, and positive partnerships among community, law enforcement, even business agencies. One example of a positive and negative prevention program is the "Safe Streets Campaign" in Tacoma, Washington, providing neighborhood dispute intervention, workshop seminars, encouragement to complete education programs, and employment preparation.

Authority Methods
People in authority and leadership have an important role in helping end violence and build community. They must provide strong voices to consistently condemn violent power, and model respectful relationship. The power and authority of school or police might be needed to separate the perpetrator from the victim, which is an unfortunate but usually necessary step. Schools, for example, can expel students found in possession of weapons or using aggression to address their conflicts, and can provide students with (among other things) skills to manage friendship and resolve conflicts.

Authorities must model respectful nonviolent relationships and conflict management, first of all. All authority figures need clear knowledge of the sources, dynamics, and prevention of violence, and effective intervention methods. Decision-making leaders can ensure access to intervention programs for victims, willing perpetrators, family, and community members.

Many agencies, including the WHO, urge authorities to implement and enforce existing policies and laws that prohibit violence. Many societies and cultures (and also religions) have existing principles and values based on interpersonal responsibility and nonviolent relationships. Those laws and principles need to be actualized.

In this chapter, you explored interpersonal violence in detail. In Chapter 9 you will encounter terms and concepts related to large-scale, international violence and war.

CHAPTER SUMMARY AND STUDY GUIDE

- Clarifying terms and concepts related to interpersonal violence reveals complex phenomena. We defined **interpersonal violence** as intentionally antisocial actions, relationship patterns, or attitudes that result from multiple source problems, develop and escalate over time, harm countless people, and suggest many potentially practical solutions.
- People are intricately involved and affected by violence, as perpetrators and as victims and witnesses, and develop several distinct coping mechanisms.
- According to Johan Galtung, violence occurs in three simultaneous and interwoven forms: behavioral violence refers to violent actions; structural violence encompasses the ways that relationships and institutions are organized to selectively privilege some people and disadvantage others; and cultural violence is the attitudes, beliefs, and values that are used to justify violence in all its forms. Power is always a factor.
- Interpersonal violence develops slowly to become a habitual dyadic cycle for both perpetrator and victim. The presence of violence in any relationship has costly consequences for the people and for society.

- Practical solutions to violence go beyond traditional conflict-resolution procedures. Resolving interpersonal violence requires a comprehensive approach that is both negative (ending violence) and positive (mending the effects and preventing new violence). Prevention, violence ending intervention, postvention mending strategies, and society's transformation are all parts of this work.

TERMS IN FOCUS

aggression 248
antisocial actions 250
behavioral violence 256
collective violence 258
competitive power 260
cultural violence 258
exploitive power 260
hostile aggression 252
impunity 253
instrumental violence 252
integrative power 260
interpersonal violence 249
manipulative power 260
marginality 257
nature-nurture debate 253
nurturing power 260
perpetrator 251
Perpetration Induced Trauma Stress (PITS) 254
Post-Traumatic Stress Disorder

(PTSD) 254
postvention 264
prevention 263
prosocial actions 250
protective factors 251
pseudopeace 262
risk factor 251
structural violence 257
trauma 263
Trauma-Informed Practice 264
Trauma Studies 263
Type I trauma 263
Type II trauma 263
Type III trauma 263
victim 254
victim identity 255
violence 249
violence (World Health Organization) 249

9

The Problems of National and International Violence

■ ■ ■

In Focus in This Chapter:

■ Defining large-scale violence has proven surprisingly tricky. In this chapter, we refer to **large-scale violence** as hostile actions, relationships, and attitudes that increase risks and experiences of danger for an identifiable group of people in a community, nation, or international setting.

■ Large-scale violence is the outcome of a longer process of grievance, attempted solution, and desperate frustration. Although phases of the developmental process can be identified, a particular conflict rarely unfolds in an orderly way.

■ Johan Galtung described the "Vicious Violence Triangle" to identify visible behavioral violence, but also to look beyond it to invisible structural violence, and endemic cultural violence.

■ The problems at the source of violent international conflict are complex, and shifting dissatisfaction with political division, unjust resource distribution, and power transitions are three such forces.

■ All large-scale violence has large-scale costs and consequences for people, families, societies, and the environment. Some costs are measured, some are immeasurable.

■ Just as large-scale conflict results from many simultaneous sources, peace results from many practices and resolution methods, some peaceably self-directed, some using interactive dialogue and negotiation, some aggressively and violently coercive. Prevention of violence is fundamental to peace.

CONFLICT CASE 9.1 ■ SOUTH AFRICAN APARTHEID AND F. W. DE KLERK

The 15th through the 18th centuries are called the **Age of Discovery** because relatively developed nations roamed the then-unknown globe to "discover" new territories. The explorers were guided by the **Doctrine of Discovery**, which assumed that land belonged to whomever claimed it. The resulting territorial occupations led to the disenfranchisement of innumerable Aboriginal groups and subsequent policies of "Christianization."

South Africa was colonized by the Dutch, beginning in 1650. Its primary trade resource was human slaves, and racial slavery became its social, economic, and legal centerpiece. Racism existed paralegally from the onset of Dutch colonization and was socially enforced in South Africa as *apartheid*, or the segregation of races, prior to the 1940s. It was legalized after the election of the National Party and Prime Minister Daniel Francois (D. F.) Malan in 1948. Political authority was based on *baasskap*, a policy based on white supremacy and domination, with white South Africans as the beneficiaries and non-whites as its victims. Supposedly, "colored" people (black, Asian, and Indian) were not considered inferior, but were of "lesser development." On this foundation, South African apartheid was formally legalized by numerous acts of parliament. Although it entrenched widespread violations of human rights, apartheid's architects declared that their design would provide "justice to every South African."

The races were categorized and segregated as white, black, colored, and Indian, according to appearance, known ancestry, socioeconomic status, and culture. Everyone was issued an identity pass that prescribed their residence, trade, and political affiliation, but fixed and limited their freedoms. Approximately 3.5 million coloreds were evicted from their homes and farms to arbitrary "tribal homelands" to enforce segregation. Public facilities and services were segregated, free speech became illegal, and interracial marriage was prohibited because it was considered "immoral." Colored people could be imprisoned and tortured without trial, and have their citizenship revoked.

Years of internal resistance followed. Apartheid continued from 1948 to 1990 despite denunciation by international organizations and other governments. The military was deployed to oppose any signs of "rebellion." Penalties included detention without trial and even the death penalty. It is estimated that more than 14,000 colored people were killed during the 44 years of apartheid rule.

F. W. de Klerk, a white politician born in white-dominated South Africa, was only 12 years old when apartheid was legally enacted with the support of his father, Johannes. His powerful Afrikaner family, his education, and South African society all supported the status quo, and he became a known advocate for white privilege, discrimination, and segregation policies. In late 1972, de Klerk became involved in South African politics.

Over time a number of forces helped challenge his beliefs:

- His elder brother, Willem, openly challenged the family's conservative opinions.
- In 1973 the United Nations declared the systemic oppression and domination of colored people to be an "inhumane crime."
- The fall of the Berlin wall in 1989 affected de Klerk's perception of divided societies.

Gradually, de Klerk came to the private conviction that apartheid was morally wrong. After being elected president of South Africa in 1989, he began a personal campaign of opposition to the 350-year legacy of oppression. He took enormous political risks that surprised many of his parliamentary supporters. Between 1990 and 1992 he approved the release of many political prisoners, including Nelson Mandela. When he proposed a mixed-race government and an end to apartheid, some of his supporters walked out of parliament and called him a traitor. Nonetheless, he persisted and succeeded in dismantling apartheid.

In 1993, de Klerk shared the Nobel Peace Prize with Nelson Mandela for their liberation work to establish South African democracy and civil rights.

Think About and Discuss with Your Colleagues

- What influences and factors seemed to push de Klerk to the gradual, but drastic, changes to his beliefs and policies?
- How might he have overcome the fierce resistance to his campaign of reform?
- How do you think his cooperation with Nelson Mandela affected public readiness and acceptance of the end of apartheid?
- How would you judge the success of this drastic change in South Africa's history today?

Conflict Resolution Studies has the urgent task of analyzing the complexes of peace and violent conflict so that peaceable relations can be extended and violence can be diminished or abolished. In Chapter 8, you studied some of the dynamics interpersonal and community violence, defining **interpersonal violence** as intentionally antisocial actions, relationship patterns, or attitudes that result from multiple source problems, develop and escalate over time, harm countless people, and suggest many potential solutions. In this chapter, your focus will be large group national and international violence. In ths chapter, we explore large-scale violence.

DEFINITIONS AND CONCEPTS RELATED TO LARGE-SCALE CONFLICT AND VIOLENCE

Large-Scale Conflict

Although there are some overlaps between conflict on interpersonal and larger scales, there are significant differences between them that make this level of peace and conflict even more complex. You can summarize those distinctives using the familiar 4-P analysis: people, problem, process, and practical solutions.

People

Although people continue to be the actual players, large-scale conflicts involve many connected parties. Tactics, relative powers, and allegiances may shift quickly. When organizations or governments are involved, their input is often through representatives who have no real peacemaking authority. Interested audiences in affected communities become engaged, and their presence on the sidelines complicates peace processes. Negotiations are often overshadowed by a past history of mistrust and conflict, so negotiators provide as little information directly as is feasible. A mixture of national self-interested, competitive, and cooperative intentions can drive the conflicts.

Problems

In large-scale conflicts, especially those with long history, there are multiple root sources that must be addressed to sustain peace. *Conflicts of interest* and *resource tensions* are usually the most obvious, but they are driven by *conflicts of ideology*, particularly about differing political systems and viewpoints. Jay Rothman (1997, 2013) noted the central significance of *conflicted community identities* in perpetuating conflicts.

Process

Conflicts change and progress dynamically. Not all large-scale conflict becomes violent, but all violence relates to unresolved grievances and inadequately contained conflict. Conflicts frequently go through protracted phases of escalation and deescalation that could be several decades or even generations long (Dudouet, 2006). Power imbalances between parties fluctuate with internal and global circumstances, so corresponding domination and control maneuvers are also likely. Retention and displays of power determines conflict tactics of withdrawal and escalating aggression.

An *intrastate conflict* (also known as a *civil wa*r and *domestic conflict*) is a conflict between a state government and a group within distinct boundaries. Most contemporary civil conflicts have racial, ethnic, and class conflict origins. *Interstate conflict* (also called *international conflict)* occurs between two or more sovereign parties, such as Iraq and the United States. Domestic conflict can become international if the violence spreads beyond national borders or if one party is supported by an allied government. One example is the 2020 conflict in Venezuela over poverty and starvation conditions, where the United Nations and United States were on the brink of international intervention. *Extrastate conflict* involves one state and an armed group from outside its borders, such as the Kurdish conflict in eastern Turkey.

Praxis: Peace Process

Peace results from any number of resolution methods, some peaceable, some interactive, some aggressively coercive. There can be no "one-size-fits-all" approach but, rather, resolution must be found that is specific and congruent locally (Wilson, 2019). There are few effective organizations that can provide third-party intervention to end violence, enforce agreements, or transform animosity. Because peace is as highly complex as is conflict, prevention is fundamental.

Peace

The primary dictionary meaning of **large-scale peace** is negative peace: the absence of social conflict, violence, and war (Webster, Cambridge, OED). Most conflict scholars add the necessary qualities of positive peace: concord and a state of justice (Rummel, 1981).

According to Lund (2001), peaceable relations vascillate widely and sometimes end abruptly. *Durable and sustainable peace* demonstrates cooperative, orderly negotiation between opponents, and is marked by justice. During *stable peace*, sometimes called *cold peace*, the risk of open conflict is so small that it is not considered significant. *Unstable peace*, sometimes called *cold war*, involves intermittent periods of order and conflict, but with crisis looming. *Violent crisis* results from escalation of hostility and tense confrontation, and efforts are made to forestall an outbreak of violence. *War* or *hot war* is a condition of chaotic turmoil and violence among multiple organized parties.

Large-Scale Violence

Large-scale violence refers to hostile actions, relationships, and attitudes that increase risks and experiences of danger for an identifiable group of people in a community, nation, or international setting (Byrne, 2012). It is usually motivated to defeat an opponent group. It may take shifting forms such as social protest, contrived humanitarian crisis, or armed conflict. Violence grows out of incompleted problem solving and grievance resolution, but uses aggressive tactics to force a particular point of view. Violence has consequences that involve numerous parties who have little control in a conflict. Traumatic consequences include needs deprivation, maldevelopment, psychological harm, destruction of property and economic loss, injury, and death (Krug, 2002).

Conflict, violence, and war are not equivalents. Not all conflict becomes violent, but all violence is the product of unsatisfied, escalating conflict that could deteriorate into warring conditions. Large-scale conflict demonstrates the following characteristics (Levy, 2010):

- Large-scale conflict happens between organized parties, but has implications for many individuals;
- Violence becomes reciprocal as an outgrowth of conflict interactions;
- Violence is expressed in episodes of fluid magnitude and impact;
- War is a coercive instrument that sidesteps other types of political influence; and
- War is sustained through time and space.

This level of violence is both complex and controversial. There are no simple insights about its causes, functions, or solutions. Most violence is fleeting and peace can be elusive: each exists for short episodes and then ends. There is much contested terminology, profoundly shaped by standpoint, culture, politics, and legal elements.

The **United Nations** agreed that **war** is waged through five intentional actions (1948):

1. Life conditions that are likely to damage or destroy people are inflicted;
2. Measures designed to prevent birth are imposed;
3. Children are forcibly transferred from one group to another;
4. Serious bodily or mental harm are caused to members of a group; and/or
5. Members of a group are killed.

Of the past 3,400 years of recorded history, humans have been entirely at peace for 268 years, or just 8% (New York Times). In 2017, 40 wars were reported across the globe. Figure 9.1 shows the comparative costs of war, but also illustrates the distribution of violent conflict in various global areas.

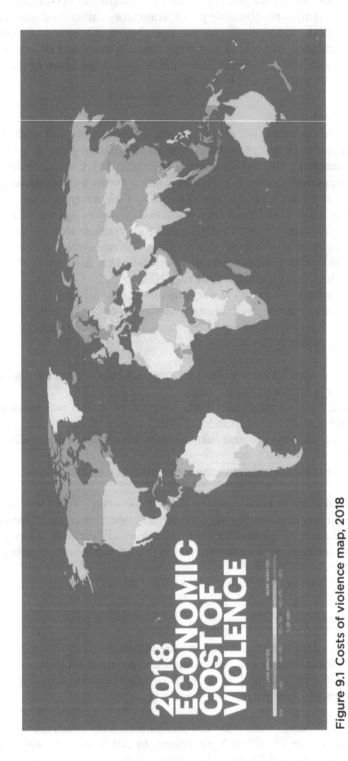

Figure 9.1 Costs of violence map, 2018

Institute for Economics & Peace. Global Peace Index 2019: Measuring Peace in a Complex World, Sydney, June 2019. Available from: http://visionofhumanity.org/reports (accessed 2019 December 9).

Political violence is hostile aggression led by a government or groups of people, with the goal of achieving a political aim. Political violence is the broad term that takes in many different forms, and the methods, objectives, perceived enemy, and tactics may shift suddenly. Table 9.1 summarizes some definitions and concepts of political violence.

Table 9.1   Terms and Concepts Related to Political Violence

Violence is the intentional use of physical force or power, threatened or actual, against oneself, another person, a group or community, which results in or has a high likelihood of resulting in injury, death, psychological harm, maldevelopment, or deprivation (World Health Organization)

Concept of Violence	Scope and Purpose	Example
Asymmetric violence	Guerilla warfare to gain national independence from colonizers	1954–1975 Viet Cong fighting in support of North Viet Nam against South Viet Nam and the United States
Civil war	Intrastate war fought for control of territory or economic or political power	1948–1958 "La Violencia" in Colombia
Conventional war	Two states are engaged in trained and equipped military combat. The goal is to fulfill national priorities using escalating confrontation. "Enemies" are clearly defined and rules of engagement are roughly honored	World Wars I and II
Cultural violence	Violent attitudes, beliefs, and values that are used to legitimize direct and structural violence; invisible and must be inferred	Racism, sexism
Direct violence	Violent behavior with identifiable perpetrator(s) and victim(s)	Verbal attack, assault, homicide, femicide
Family, domestic, and intimate violence	Perpetrators and victims are in relationship of trust	Child neglect and abuse
Genocide	Deliberate, systematic destruction of a people, especially targeted because of religion, ethnicity or race, or nationality	1994 Rwanda
Guerilla warfare	War against conventional military and police forces, waged with limited action by paramilitary force fighting for a political or protest strategy	Current: al-Qaeda and ISIS in Iraq
Insurgency	Violent uprising or revolt against recognized government authority, often multipolar	1998–2006 Somali Civil War

(continued)

Concept of Violence	Scope and Purpose	Example
Just War	The belief that the use of military force is acceptable if it is defensive and meets six criteria: right authority, just cause, right intention, last resort, proportional means, and reasonable prospects of success	2020 Preemptive US bombing of Baghdad, Iran, that killed General Qasem Suleimani
Political violence	Hostile aggression led by a government or groups of people, with the goal of achieving a political aim	Many different forms
Revolution	Organized political violence, dissident campaign	1968–1998 Northern Ireland Troubles
Structural violence	Violent injustice or selective exploitation built into organizational social inequalities; indirect and must be inferred	Patriarchy, abuse of power
Targeted violence	Planned violence against a specific group or location	School and industrial shootings
Terrorism	Violence or threat of violence toward random victims in pursuit of a cause, intended to intimidate the public and coerce politicians with a widespread climate of fear	September 11, 2000 USA, Attacks on houses of faith
Unconventional war	War between asymmetric opponents: one powerful, one smaller or less well organized. The aim is not to defeat, but to exploit enemy vulnerabilities and persuade	US Navy SEALs operations
Unrightable wrong	Atrocious violence used to quell conflict or eliminate a people	1932–1933 Ukranian Holodomor

Conventional and Unconventional Warfare

In **conventional warfare**, two equipped and trained states engage in military combat. The enemy is clearly defined and agreed-on rules of engagement are roughly honored. Tactics of conventional war aim to weaken or destroy the opponent. The strategy is to advance national priorities using escalating confrontation. These battles are usually conducted in ways that do not involve civilian populations, and primarily engage enemy combatants.

Contemporary warfare trends are toward **unconventional warfare** between asymmetric opponents: one powerful, one smaller and less well organized. The aim is usually not to defeat the enemy, but to increase enemy vulnerability and persuade the opponent that negotiation and compromise are necessary to create peace. Tactics tend toward a covert, "anything goes" approach that may use new technological methods such as drone delivery of armaments. Unconventional warfare is likely to involve terrorists and resistance fighters, such as the French resistance during World War II. Although military combatants are engaged, civilian populations are often caught in the crossfire.

DEVELOPMENTAL PROCESS FROM DISPUTE TO WAR

The Wave or Curve of Violence Model

Both conflict and violence are dynamic, and tension continually fluctuates in international relations. When problems are overlooked, issues ignored, or solutions sidelined, conflict may be avoided temporarily, but tension continues to build. The wave model, also referred to as a conflict curve or conflict life cycle (see Figure I.5 in the Introduction), is one way to visualize the fluctuating escalation and deescalation cycles and phases. The phases describe significant changes to the nature of the interaction over time.

Although there are different versions, a curve usually sketches dynamics that shift from a beginning, and escalate through a middle period to a positive, indifferent, or destructive end, in ways that resemble interpersonal conflict. Periods of latency are punctuated with crisis and intermittent progress toward resolution. There is much debate about the **escalation threshold**, or the point at which conflict becomes war because that determination often betrays a particular political agenda.

Roger Fisher and Loraleigh Keashly (1991) labeled four phases: discussion, polarization, segregation, and destruction. Louis Kriesberg (2005), a prominent scholar, expanded those phases, and they can be blended with the "conflict barometer" of seriousness used by the Heidelberg Institute for International Conflict Research (HIIK, 2019).

Nonviolent Stage:

1. *Latent dispute* (intensity 1) occurs when different values and interests exist, but there is no open dispute. Issues and demands are discussed by the parties and perceived in roughly equivalent ways. Episodic *eruption* of conflict may involve previously unresolved grievances or threats. There may be opportunities to explore peacemaking during interruptions.
2. *Manifest conflict* (intensity 2) is ignited by provocative behavior such as distributing propaganda. Polarization of the parties is evident. The dispute is overt, and implicit or explicit threats may be used to emphasize positions, but there is no overt violence. An *escalating onset* of conflict is marked by increasing segregation, antagonism, and destructive moves and countermoves that can aggravate grievances, creating crisis.
3. *Peacemaking efforts* by internal leaders or outsiders risk failure when the parties expect rejection, or when audiences become mobilized.

Violent Stage:

4. During a *violent crisis* (intensity 3), tension is expressed in sporadic violence and destruction by at least one party. Self-perpetuating crisis and deadlock diminish the possibilities for settlement.
5. In a *severe crisis* or *limited war* (intensity 4) violent force is organized and used detructively by at least one party;

6. A *war* (intensity 5) utilizes violence in organized, systematic, reciprocated, and extensive ways, resulting in massive and long-lasting destruction. Most large-scale violence has an element of retribution.
7. Gradual or negotiated *deescalation* of conflict intensity and scope, leads to agreement, conflict resolution, or transformation.
8. *Termination* and recovery might be brief if there are persistent grievances.

Serious conflict is more complex than these roughly sequential stages, and does not proceed in a linear or orderly way. Smooth progress from one phase to another is rare, and phases may be repeated. Because the stages are experienced subjectively, contradictory perceptions can aggravate grievances.

Unresolved conflict may become **intractable conflict**, which is self-perpetuating and self-reinforcing antagonism (Brecher, 2016). Kriesberg identified three characteristics of intractable conflicts: they are not well managed, they are persistently destructive, and most efforts to end them fail for a variety of reasons. Atrocious violence is in a category by itself.

Orchestrated Violence

Some conditions and group dynamics heighten the risk of violent outbreaks.

First, because humans are essentially social and relational beings, empathy is a cornerstone of all interactions. This means that underlying realities are likely to be communicated both consciously and subconsciously. **Emotional contagion** refers to the tendency for feelings to spread empathically through a group to become a shared feeling, attitude, or animosity. Because emotional contagion is especially powerful with feelings of anxiety and anger, an excited crowd can quickly erupt into angry violence, as occurred at Capitol Hill in Washington, D.C. in January 2021.

Second, specific people are motivated to create violence to make a dramatic point or to further a cause. Donald Horowitz (2001) called these parties **violence engineers**, who benefit from generalized social dissatisfaction and divided opinion. Horowitz saw their activity as crucial to the development of violent group behavior. When violence engineers work to agitate a group, encouraging a violent response to the issue, violence becomes likely. If religious and political leaders call for calm thought and strategy, violence becomes less likely.

Another group are called **peace spoilers**. They are individuals and groups who adopt violent strategies to undermine peace processes and agreements (Stedman, 1997). They may have one of several incentives: some are greedy for power or profit and take violent advantage of the settlement terms; some believe they were overlooked in the negotiation process or the terms of the agreement and protest with violence; some are motivated by ideology, believing that the settlement betrays key values and use violence to resist on principle (Newman, 2006). "Spoilers" is a controversial term because some scholars focus more on violent strategy than on the spoiler label (Subedi, 2013; Zahar, 2015).

Atrocious Violence

In a very few societies, conflict is taken to almost inconceivable extremes of atrocious violence. This happened in Ukranian Soviet Union in 1932–1933, for example, where a famine resulted in millions of deaths, becoming known as the "Holodomor" (literally, "killing by a starvation plague"). Responsibility for the deaths is still debated, but many believe that Joseph Stalin planned the Holodomor or, at very least, organized and exploited an artificial famine as a way of eliminating Ukranian nationalist opponents. This type of brutal atrocity, used to quell conflict or eliminate a people leads to **unrightable wrong** in a society.

Franklin Dukes (2008) laid out some criteria defining such profound wrongs. Injustice is intentionally or systematically inflicted on an identity group, often motivated by prejudice, and is usually discriminatory. The wrong has emotional, economic, social, political, and spiritual consequences that are continuous: historic, present, and future. And the causes involve complex sets of issues and people, which makes any resolution seem daunting or even impossible.

Unrightable wrongs cause enormous suffering and social unrest. Under conditions that have such devastating consequences, hate and revenge are likely to develop. However, as happened in the Rwandan genocide of 1994, the victims and perpetrators of such atrocities often have to remain in the same community as neighbors and coworkers. Sometimes the worst enemies are even family members. Martin Luther King poetically said, "Returning hate for hate multiplies hate, adding deeper darkness to a night already devoid of stars. Darkness cannot drive out darkness; only light can do that. Hate cannot drive out hate; only love can do that." For the survival of a torn society, pathways toward harmony must be created, but it involves reconstruction, transformation, and endless peacebuilding.

Atrocious wrongs such as those perpetrated in the Ukraine and Rwanda leave a cascade of harm, extending from direct victims to impotent witnesses to shattered families and relationships that remain. The devastated society must reassemble and create new life with new meanings that incorporate vicious cruelties and remember the victims. Even years later, the traumatic consequences must be transformed into a new, resilient social order, with mended structures. The past must be integrated, possibly forgiven; present traumatic consequences must be mended and people reconciled; the future must be fabricated as a legacy to the innocent. Some of these peacebuilding tasks are described in Chapters 11 and 12.

Experiences of great violence such as the war in Syria can have permanent effects on the formation of a whole society. A society is particularly vulnerable to this alteration when protracted violence and trauma are shared by every member of a community, there is mixed violence among parties and no single identifiable perpetrator, and there is simultaneous, compounded trauma from violence, family death, and widespread loss of home (McAdams, 2013; Volkan, 1990). Under these conditions, common patterns include widespread individual PTSD, intergenerational transmission of fear, and disturbed social and political processes.

When the losses are overpoweringly profound, a whole society can develop a victim identity that expresses the collective trauma. Cultural stories are told and retold to shape a collective memory by renewing the past, either destructively or constructively. Vamik Volkan and his colleagues (1990) defined two types of cultural retelling: **chosen trauma** is the repetition of stories of violence, victimization, and humiliation (such as the retelling of war stories); and **chosen glory** is the repetition of stories of heroism and triumph (such as soldiers' repeatedly recounting a battle win). Volkan's analysis suggests that you choose the cultural stories that shape your own identity. For this reason, many trauma survivors avoid the stories, that former combatants sometimes call "war porn."

Volkan warned that interminable chosen trauma causes *cultural degeneration* into social helplessness that lacks trust in basic order, stalling peoples' mourning and making it difficult to overcome a helpless and humiliated identity. A contemporary example might be the many Indigenous communities devasted by centuries of cultural genocide. Chosen trauma stories can appear to justify or demand retaliation, and may unleash ongoing retaliatory animosity that ensures that peace is unstable at best. However, chosen glory leads to *cultural regeneration* after trauma, restoring basic trust and stability, and lamentation that is necessary to make way for possible forgiveness. A contemporary example of this is Rwandan society as it recovers from the 1994 genocide.

Just War

The **Just War Doctrine** has been developed and debated over centuries in an attempt to limit out of control violence. The theory asserts that force may legitimately be used to correct a wrong—in other words, for a just purpose (Cordeira-Rodrigues and Singh, 2020). The most recent public debate took place in the United States. In response, the US Roman Catholic bishops released a widely circulated pastoral letter detailing the seven criteria of a just and proper war (NCCB, 1983):

1. There must be a *just cause*. To defend against a real and certain danger or to protect innocent people is a just cause; war waged for economic gain is not just.
2. A competent, legitimate *leader* with authority for public order must initiate the war. An attack initiated by a rebel or a dictator is not just.
3. Comparative *injustice exists*. The suffering of one group is much greater than that of another group. Just war is waged on behalf of the weak who are unable to defend themselves.
4. A just war is based on *correct intentions* to restore good, and restrain evil or limit harm. War is the *last resort*. All other, peaceful alternatives have failed to end the injustice.
5. A reasonable *probability of success* (or victory) exists. A war that is ineffectual or futile is not just.
6. The actions taken must be *proportional* to the injustices committed, so that potentially positive results outweigh the destruction necessitated by the action.

Daniel Smith-Christopher (2007) noted that the just war criteria are much clearer in theory than in actuality. Critically, the determination that an attack is just requires accessible, reliable, accurate information; however, under most circumstances, the necessities of secrecy outweigh the availability of clear information. In the absence of full information, the Just War Doctrine reverts to simply trusting the leaders who provide the information. This became terribly clear in the aftermath of "Operation Free Iraq, 2003" when US President George W. Bush was forced to admit that invasion decisions were based on flawed intelligence.

According to political philosopher Hannah Arendt (1970): "Violence can be justifiable, but it never will be legitimate.... Its justification loses in plausibility the farther its intended end recedes into the future. No one questions the use of violence in self-defence, because the danger is not only clear but also present, and the immediate end justifies the means."

Think About and Discuss with Your Colleagues

James Schellenberg (1996) wrote, "We must accept force and coercion as among the ways that conflicts are resolved. At least, a resort to force may provide an end to a conflict's most intense period.... We take seriously the idea that force and coercion may provide one form of conflict resolution."

- Do you accept this?
- What are your thoughts about Arendt's statement?
- When is force the method of choice?

Influences of Diverse Viewpoints

As you noticed in other sections of this textbook, diversity of viewpoints and worldviews can profoundly influence peace and conflict, positively or negatively. Diversity improves the creativity within a group and intergroup interactions. However, diverse viewpoints can also be a direct source of polarizing conflict and can alter individual perceptions of an interaction, some calling it a debate, some calling it a battle.

There are many relevant sources of diversity in the globalizing national and international arena. Every group and society has unique identities shaped by history, custom and conventions, religion, and ideology. Feminism has had enormous influence on the views and interpretations of peace and violence. Some cultural groups like those of Indigenous heritage have traditional definitions of peace, justice, and conflict. Their views of peacemaking are likely to include a central body of treaty law, which differs from and often contradicts mainstream Western social contract concepts. In addition, even scholarship shows great diversity of fundamental beliefs and values, giving scholars a range of concepts for debate and exploration. These diversity factors only add ambiguity to the complexity of understanding both interpersonal and large-scale violence.

JOHAN GALTUNG'S ANALYSIS OF VIOLENCE

Johan Galtung (1971), a major contributor to understanding violence, described the *Vicious Violence Triangle* as part of cycling, interlocking system of violence that encompasses individuals, organizations, and culture. Specific violent incidents or actions are the complex product of all three systemic influences. The consequences of the violence are born by people, but those consequences in turn reinforce violent structures and beliefs.

Direct Behavioral Violence

Galtung stated that too often the focus is on dramatic, visible aggressive behavior and violence, and their causes. **Behavioral violence** describes intermittent, intentionally violent actions against identifiable victim(s) by identifiable perpetrator(s).

But not all violence is clearly identifiable, so Galtung suggested looking deeper. Exclusive focus on visible violence causes you to overlook other types and dynamics that he described as indirect and invisible violence, discernible only in the devastating consequences.

Overall, the statistical trend is toward less overt conflict, violence, and death (Dupuy, 2017; Pettersson, 2020). Integrating fragmented insights and pieces of information is challenging and generalization is risky, but some trends can be extrapolated (UCDP, 2019):

- The number of serious conflicts decreased since 2000, with a corresponding decline of global casualty rates.
- Casualties have shifted from large groups targeted in an organized manner toward individuals or smaller groups targeted deliberately or randomly through terrorist activity.
- Serious conflicts are likely to represent internal rebellion, with specific groups resisting the authority of the leader or government, most often in urban settings.
- Regions with significantly complex history, culture, politics, and current conditions are at higher risk of violence and war.
- High levels of violence are reported in areas of the world affected by long-term struggles for independence.
- Seriously violent areas are mostly concentrated in the southern hemisphere; exceptions include Russia and the United States, where violence is high, and Australia, where violence is low.
- The highest risks are recorded in Syria, the Central African Republic, Iraq, South Sudan, Afghanistan, and several other African countries. The highest levels of complex violence are experienced in Colombia; continuing increases in Afghanistan amount to 40% of global violence fatalities despite ongoing peace negotiations, and increased violence in Africa as organized transnational terror groups relocate their efforts.
- Long-term ethnic conflict is perpetual in the Middle East, Afghanistan, and Asia.
- Canada, middle Europe, and the area around the Mediterranean experience the lowest levels of violence.

Structural Violence

According to Galtung, **structural violence** is unjust suffering that is part of society's organization into hierarchies of power. Some power structures are benevolent, benefiting a majority of the people; some structures are exploitive and incompatible with basic human needs fulfilment. Structural violence is rooted in the power of certain groups that operate to preserve social order and existing concentrations of power while limiting other groups. It is inherently unjust when certain people live with privilege and power while others experience exclusion and relative powerlessness. Achievement of some peoples' full potential is chronically frustrated, so violent conflict becomes more likely. For example, powerful alliances between men, political parties, or states that disenfranchise women eventually cause conflict and possibly even violence.

Structural violence is built into political and economic hierarchial systems. No perpetrator is identifiable, but there are many victims. It is continuous and inescapable, part of an indirect "chain of harm." The distribution of social resources is unequal and unjust, and freedom is restricted (Christie, 2001), so some members of a society suffer. The resulting unmet needs, diminished quality of life, and shortened life spans are the fuel of discontented conflict (Farmer, 2003) that often leads to behavioral violence by the powerless against the powerful. Leaders who benefit from exploitive policies emphasize crisis management and short-term problem solutions that maintain existing social strata.

Cultural and Collective Violence

Cultural violence was defined by Galtung as any belief that is used to legitimize violence in its behavioral or structural forms. Invisible and unspoken beliefs, such as the entitlement to privilege of some people at the expense and hindrance of others, seemingly justify hierarchies of power that are demonstrated in structural injustice. The WHO noted that collective violence has political, economic, and social purposes and results.

Stories from the history of South Africa's *baasskap* white supremacy illustrate the multiple violences that apartheid perpetrated. Black and coloreds were the frequent targets of white officials' violence; the entire society was structured around the separation of the races; the racism and prejudicial attitudes of white supremacy and colored inferiority were deeply ingrained and believed to represent a necessary order of nature and of society. In another example, negative attitudes toward homeless persons such as the Romani peoples in Europe are used to legitimize repeated forced relocation. These beliefs lead toward limiting opportunities for people of a "lesser" group, a situation Galtung labels as structural violence that is likely to incite behavioral violence.

Cultures of War and of Peace

The perspectives of a particular society converge in a collective **culture of conflict**, which refers to culturally developed practices, institutions, norms, and values specifically associated with conflict (Avruch, 1998; Ross, 1993). These norms are expressed generally in the selection of methods for dealing with conflict, tendencies toward constructiveness or destructiveness within that society and with outsiders, and using more or less violent methods to resolve conflict. Societies also designate police and military forces or peacebuilding organizations that reflect the cultural values within. See Figure 9.2, illustrating two contrasting cultures of conflict.

A **culture of war** is marked by common perception of insecurity and threat, with a related belief system and practices that support defensive violence. When fear is shared among many people and reinforced by dreadful events such as looting or terrorist attacks, the collective result is vigilance and defensiveness. Dichotomous distinctions divide friend and enemy, female and male, government and citizen, and human from nature, and one must dominate the other. In this culture, there is confidence that authority, power, and domination provide security and order. Because displays of strength are believed to cultivate confidence and prosperity, investments are made in armaments and military strength. This belief system can be the basis for international policy and is likely to foster conflict (United Nations, 1999).

Figure 9.2 UN cultures of violence and peace

A culture of violence and war is strongly correlated with a culture of fear. Barry Glassner (2009) distinguished two varieties of fear: legitimate fear and suspicion. **Legitimate fear** results from a factual threat to survival. It is adaptive when a threat is imminent because it inspires caution and protection. **Suspicion** is fear that is disproportionate to threat and does not reflect actual risk. This type of fear was dominant in the widespread disinformation about the 2020 US presidential election. Glassner suggested that suspicion is easily manipulated by groups called **fear mongers** who are motivated by a specific interest or cause to stir up troublesome fear. Hot war is expensive in innumberable ways. A far easier option is propoganda and disinformation that damages social confidence is established social order. Glassner also noted that the unique information provided by journalists and the media can either promote or alleviate fear (Sheafer, 2010).

The contrast to the culture of fear is a *culture of peace and nonviolence*, a system of attitudes that are likely to promote peaceful coexistence and the nonviolent resolution of conflicts as they arise. A peaceable society is one in which the people experience secure, stable living without fear (among other qualities). Contrasting views of the sources of that security, vulnerability, and threat are embodied in the debate over national security versus human security (Jolly, 2007) and in contrasting assumptions behind police practices.

Elise Boulding (1988) elaborated the daily practices of such a culture. A **low-conflict society** values connections and equalities among peoples and nations. Individual and community interests are seen as interlinked, so harmonious relationships are actively pursued. This society reduces severely violent conflict by supporting education, promoting long-term sustainable development, and validating diversity and human rights. The attitudes of a peaceful culture are maintained by vigorous dialogue. A variety of viewpoints coexist, including outsider voices, to facilitate cooperative problem solving. Dialogue strategies such as shifts from general grievances to specific goals, clarification of interests and identification of common interests are used to reduce the probability of conflict (Ross, 1993).

National security has a focus on the state, both as the object and the provider of security: if national interests are secure, then life is secure. Perception of threat focuses on challenges like foreign economic domination, crime and international crime, terrorism, and border intimidation (Lama, 2018). Security and protection of the nation-state are provided by law enforcement agencies, government, and military protection, symbolized in the catchphrase "law and order."

This concept is contrasted by *human security*, first identified as a priority in the UN Human Development Report (UNDP, 1994), which identified two conceptual goals of security: freedom from want and freedom from fear. In this view, humanity is the central concern, and citizen stability and wellbeing are the main sources of security. Vulnerability is perceived in critical human threats such as food insecurity, poverty and inadequate shelter, and environmental degradation (Lama, 2018).

In terms of violence, both national insecurity and human insecurity are connected to protracted violent conflict. Some scholars argue that the two securities should not be contrasted, as if they compete. Rather, national and human security priorities should be coordinated by a cooperative strategy that links foreign policy with positive approaches to citizen wellbeing (e.g., Burke-White, 2004).

In another contemporary illustration, Sue Rahr and Steven Rice (2015) identified contrasting police cultures: police as warriors and police as guardians. *Police as warriors* is the concept that the primary function of police is to search for and catch law breakers and threatening criminals. This is evident in the increasing militarization of police tactics and equipment. As was the case in the 2020 events related to the Black Lives Matters movement, the debate is whether police militarization has been a cause of increased social protest and violence, or whether it is a necessary prevention of violent events.

Police as guardians is expressed in "R2P"—responsibility to protect. This idea expects police success from "community policing" that emphasizes service and interpersonal connections. In the security and violence debate, some believe that this policy is insufficiently authoritarian to control negative social influences. Some argue that both images and cultures are important to a unified, effective approach to law enforcement (McLean, 2019).

Problems That Incite Intercultural Conflict and Violence

Intercultural Antagonism

In our globalizing world, we are confronted continuously by a variety of cultural forms, with distinctive practices, relationships, and belief systems (review Chapter 5). Cultural conflicts are very common, ranging from individual experiences of "culture shock" to major conflicts between nations with antagonistic cultural or religious overtones. **Ethnopolitical conflict** is large-scale conflict in which ethnic or religious differences and political disputes compound one another.

There are many sources of intercultural conflict (Taras, 2016):

- Simple *misunderstandings* or misinterpretations of cultural forms. Misinterpretation of traditional dress or appearance can cause conflict, as occurred when Aboriginal officers of the Royal Canadian Mounted Police applied to retain their traditional hair braids.
- *Stereotypes*. Members of an unfamiliar culture are characterized by stereotypes, which polarize members of different cultures, obscuring avenues for peaceful cooperative action.
- *Incompatibility* of deeply rooted values, beliefs, and attitudes. For example, the place of females in many Eastern societies is very different from their role in Western societies because of beliefs about the proper role of women rooted in centuries old practices, often endorsed by religious belief. Thus, Western females often have difficulties integrating in meaningful ways into Eastern societies, and vice versa.

Long-standing distrust, fear and vulnerability, and animosity are seriously aggravated by past experiences of division or violence. Intercultural conflicts are deeply rooted and cannot be separated from other factors such as historical relationships between the cultures, religious differences, political ambitions, or economic realities. This makes intercultural conflict difficult to analyze and often protracted and intractable. Current examples are ongoing in Ireland and in Palestine-Israel.

Cultural Conquest

A **holy war** and **cultural imperialism** are waged to establish dominance and control through religion or culture (religion and culture can hardly be separated). Current conflicts in the Middle East (e.g., Israel-Palestine, Syria, and Afghanistan and Iraq) are holy wars that center in religious control issues. Cultural conquest also may have secular goals such as social, economic, or political dominance that are justified by cultural-religious doctrines. This occurred in Afghanistan when the Taliban took power in 1996.

One strategy of cultural imperialism was the attempted obliteration of Indigenous cultures by imposing foreign culture on a dependent or defeated group. The worldview of the powerful becomes the overbearing cultural norm. When countless regions of the world were colonized during the Age of Discovery, the occupying countries asserted sovereignty over the Indigenous peoples. In what is now regarded as **cultural genocide**, the destruction of the culture that gives a group its identity, the occupying nations imposed their own models of government, education, religion, and health care, eventually overcoming the initial resistance of the defeated people. According to Andrew Woolford (in Hinton, 2014), "genocide should be understood as the destruction of group life rather than lives within a group, what makes them a group, what defines their cultural cohesion." In the 20th century, colonial sovereignty was challenged by Indigenous groups' declarations of self-government, embodied in group names such as First Nations. Many of these groups have regained sovereignty and official recognition and are reenacting full expression of their source cultures.

PROBLEMS AT THE SOURCE OF LARGE-SCALE CONFLICT AND VIOLENCE

Discerning and distinguishing the complex problem sources is a crucial first step toward finding solutions to large-scale conflict. Several linked themes contribute to the risk of serious conflict: political divide among the people, unjust distribution of public resources, national instability and power transitions, territorial and resource rivalry.

Politically Divided Beliefs

Representative government was initially divided into "estates" who debated issues and advised the monarch, Louis XVI of France: 300 members of the clergy, 300 aristocratic rulers and landowners, and 300 peasant commoners. Later, the "fourth estate" press was suggested by Edmund Burke. The clergy and the press were expected to only peripherally and indirectly influence political process. One of the earliest democratic parliaments, in France in the early 19th century, was deliberately built with aristocracy on the right side and peasants on the left. The oppositional debate and negotiation inspired were meant to provide corrective balances on decision making. This right-left axis is still used to explain politics today. The phrase *the loyal opposition* implies that the healthy function of a social minority is to dispute proposals made by the majority without showing disloyalty. Interestingly, the physical space between the right and left sides in British and Canadian parliaments is still the length of two swords plus one meter, so ensure that no injury would result from representative "dueling."

Right-wing politics summarizes a conservative principle that supports national policy making by leaders to conserve existing norms for family, prosperity, law and order, established institutions and borders, and a singular culture. Central beliefs emphasize individualistic freedom, accomplishment, and responsibility with a minimum of government oversight. This strain of thought supports peace through authoritative measures such as the military and international alliances.

Left-wing politics summarizes progressive principles that emphasize egalitarian sharing of power and resources, with particular attention to reformation of conditions that cause social inequality. Core beliefs include collective responsibility through actions that preserve access to community benefits like health care, education, and environmental protection. Leftists tend to favor cultural diversity and open national and international policies. Peace is maintained by democratic and collective security, and free and equal participation in decision making.

In a thriving peaceable society, diversity of opinion is valued and fluid (Horowitz, 1993). Individual citizens, political parties, and governments rarely adhere solidly to one firm point of view. Instead, they support a fluid mix of policies that adjust to local and global events. In today's sophisticated scene, the simple left-right picture is considered passé, and political convictions are viewed on a *political spectrum* based on two or more intersecting axes. One dimension is the traditional right-left; the additional dimension is defined inconsistently, but usually contrasts communal interests decided by individuals representing their own interests, or by benevolent authorities (e.g., Haywood, 2017). It is important to remember that the spectrum contributes to vigorous public debate, like the ancient Chinese whole of "yin" plus "yang." Ideally, they should not behave as adversaries (Haidt, 2013).

However, when there is political scandal, controversy, or conflict, opponents tend to consolidate their own identity over against the perceived adversary. This *us–them polarity* overlooks shared needs and goals, and common values, and virtually blocks understanding and collaboration. When political beliefs and attitudes become enmeshed with fear and intense disagreement, Others are constructed, and society can become fragmented. Fear of injustice, violence, or the potential for violence prevents a society from effectively bridging division to create peaceful debate (Du Toit, 1989; Guelke, 2012). Entrenched polarization results in a *divided society* with recurrent, deeply rooted fault lines or open conflict (Guelke, 2012). The actual divisions may settle in political viewpoint, but often become entangled with such factors as race and financial stability.

These divided political dynamics can be manipulated by political far-right (exclusivist antidemocracy) and far-left (anticapitalist socialist and communist) extremists (March 2012; Mudd, 2019). Views present in mainstream and moderate society can be exaggerated to fuel social suspicion, erode public confidence, and gain the power of unsubstantiated opinion.

Think About and Discuss with Your Colleagues

Even though it is a peaceable society, the United States has increasingly been called a divided society, fragmented by (among other things) social class, race and ethnicity, historical animosity, and political viewpoint. This is echoed in other regions like Europe.

- Describe signs of a political divide in your own environment.
- How would you describe your own experience of the "us–them polarity"? Do fear and Othering aggravate these divisions?
- What efforts to bridge social division do you observe around you?

Imbalanced, Unjust Distribution and Access to Resources

When resources are fairly shared, human misery is generally averted. However, severe imbalance in resources, power, and/or knowledge results in prolonged injustice and struggle such as that experienced in South Africa for decades. Higher powers work to conserve their status and privilege; lower powers strive to overcome the indignity of lesser status, scarce resources, and perceived discrimination. Widespread poverty can perpetuate political instability and cycles of violence and retaliation (Lindner, 2006). Today, large sectors of the global population remain in poverty and debt because of the policies of corrupt regional leadership, reinforced by Western governments' financial practices.

When a markedly unjust distribution of resources exists, many of the dispossessed hopelessly tolerate the situation for many generations. Others protest and demand fairness. If the imbalance persists despite nonviolent attempts to equalize it, violent conflict or class warfare can occur. In response, the greater power can increase defense of the status quo or voluntarily or under negotiated agreement transfer resources through taxation, services, humanitarian aid, and other forms of redistribution.

Political Power Transitions, Failed States, and Violence

Political power provides the ability to ensure that a party's own interests prevail. Through political leadership, individuals can control others' behavior, shape collective consensus, and affect the social environment (Lynch, 2008), but also shape the future by enabling or limiting possibilities. The power of governments is the focus of **political studies**. A balance of power is important to the ways in which groups operate.

There two basic models of political power: an elitist view, and a pluralistic view. In the *elitist view*, society forms a pyramid, with power unified and concentrated in the leaders who control the rest. In the *pluralistic view*, power is dispersed among the many (for example, who might be voters, organizations, or special interest groups). The many exert their influence on leaders and decision makers, so there is a continuously shifting equilibrium of power. Much research and debate continues over what constitutes the legitimate use of political power. The unjust use of power is increasingly regarded as a cause of serious conflict (Sheng, 2009).

National power refers to a state's ability to make independent decisions, combined with an ability to influence other governments. A nation's **tangible power** is power potential beyond its declared borders, backed by resources such as population, economic strength, technology, and military capacity. For example, a *small power* such as Mongolia or Uruguay has smaller population and land size, and limited economic and military capacity. Small powers usually depend on diplomatic coalitions with more powerful nations (Thorhallsson, 2017). The power of a *superpower* or internationally dominant state, such as the United States or the United Kingdom, is based on high population, established culture, and extensive economic and military capacity. It is widely believed that China is attempting to surpass the United States as a global 21st-century superpower. Australia and Canada are self-defined *middle powers*, functioning independently but using extensive diplomacy with other nations to promote their interests (Holmes, 2020).

Kenneth Boulding (1990) observed that political power can be used benevolently to create harmonious society. Power is based on mutually respectful *persuasion* between government and citizens. Most often, political power is self-interested rather than entirely benevolent. When in conflict, a powerful nation is often reluctant to accept anything less than dominance and outright victory (Rupasinghe, 1998). Power can also be based on loyalty *exchanged* between a government and its citizens, balancing the provision of services and citizen compliance with social demands. Strategic political powers try to arrange an exchange balance that promotes powerful groups and a majority of citizens.

Alternatively, political power is maintained defensively or malevolently through *threat* and coercion, resulting in governmental intimidation (Boulding 1990). This is one function of a strong military force in the absence of overt conflict. Although this is not the situation in most Western nations, it is not uncommon in developing nations.

Joseph Nye (1990) drew a distinction between hard and soft political power. *Hard power* uses coercive economic and military methods. These include inducements (offers of humanitarian aid or political alliance), threats, sanctions (restrictions on trade, banking and investment), punitive policies (tariffs on imported material), and the use of military force (Boulding, 1990). The use of hard power is often a prelude to war. *Soft power* is the use of diplomatic appeals and demonstrations of superior national resources to persuade other nations to cooperate. Methods include cultural exchange, strategic communication, formal diplomacy, and appealing to international law. So-called *smart power* is the effective use of combined hard and soft strategies to produce the desired effect. Theodore Roosevelt said, "speak softly and carry a big stick, you will go far." He was describing a strategy of smart power: using soft power for peaceful negotiation, backed by hard power resources. For example, in dealing with Iraq in the early 21st century, the United States tried to achieve the elimination of weapons of mass destruction (WMD) through negotiation, but failure resulted in the Iraq War.

Intangible power is the fluid dynamic of relative power among nations. It has its origins in factors that influence the success of diplomatic and international negotiation, like good-faith decision making, and a minimum of coercion and exploitation. Those factors include charismatic leadership, national reputation, global support, and the use of persuasive soft power. In a **symmetrical power relationship**, national powers are somewhat balanced by independent military, political, and diplomatic resources. The groups are of equal standing in the global political scene. International coalitions ensure the resilience of the global power equilibrium. International coalitions such as the Group of Seven (G7) and the Group of Twenty (G20) sponsor international policy discussions, ostensibly to improve global stability and security. Because the powers are balanced, there is little threat, and conflict is uncommon. In an **asymmetrical power relationship**, one side has more power and higher international legitimacy and status. An example of such a pairing is the United States and Afghanistan.

Political stability refers to a state of minimal social change, upheaval, or violence. It is related to three components: an orderly society in which little change is needed or imminent, fundamental government policies do not waver until changes are perceived as legitimate, and few citizens demand change, and those who do are nonviolent (Margolis, 2010). Political stability is influenced by complex simultaneous forces: international power balances, global economic conditions, employment, education, and standards of living. Steady movement toward sustainable, just governance is desirable.

Political instability occurs during times of political, economic, or financial crisis (Kaufmann, 2011). Instability can range from low-intensity transitory social commotion to long-term chaos and violence affecting an entire population and beyond. Insecurity results in citizen protest and social upheaval. It also becomes an opportunity for aggressive adversaries to take advantage of others' weaknesses. Large-scale social conflict attracts internal parties and external audiences, and incites adversarial tactics, so political restabilization can be a decades-long process.

Governmental stability is remarkably fragile, as seen in many countries with rapidly changing leadership. National power centers rise and fall with some regularity in response to population shifts, economic growth or change, natural forces and disasters, or military conquest. Leadership transition and power redistribution are inevitable. Unstable, fragmenting governments will always be vulnerable to power rivals, and factional, diffused power patterns may be part of the transition process. If no centralized body or group takes responsibility for peace negotiation or conflict resolution, ongoing protracted contests for power may occur for a significant period of time. This dynamic has been evident in Africa over the last three decades as local regions have gained independence from colonizing nations.

Transitional justice (TJ) is an important peacebuilding instrument following periods of violent national transition. TJ governs legal and political decisions in a newly stabilizing region by addressing existing balances of power and providing reparation for victims of large-scale violence. Its goal is to create new models for justice and community healing that are specific and locally designed (Wilson, 2019).

Territory, Boundary, and Resource Rivalry

Territory, an area of bounded space, can be marked or claimed by occupation or establishing boundaries like fences and border patrols. The essential privileges of territory are possession, use, and control, another way of quantifying political power. Under most governments, this extends to immigration matters, trade, and trade barriers. Territorial conflict is particularly common where rival states are in close proximity and their peoples share history but have polarized views of each other, such as the conflict between North Korea and South Korea.

When a state claims and occupies a territory, exerts sovereign title, and controls immigration and/or emigration, the territory is treated as if absorbed into the nation, as has happened in the Crimea since 2014. Political sovereignty is the authority of a government over land, sea, airspace, and a body of people, as well as independence from outside interference. Sovereignty is the basic principle that underlies the current leading model of nation-states.

Territorial and resource conflicts occur for many reasons:

1. Disagreements about the *boundaries* of the territories. Conflict is likely if a nation claims land space that other nations desire, such as the ongoing rivalry among the eight Arctic nations.
2. Disagreements about the *uses* of the territory. A nation claiming territorial waters for military training exercises may be perceived by a tense neighbor as aggressive, as happened recently as the United States conducted military exercises in the South China Sea.
3. Linkage of territory with *valued resources*. Rivalry for scarce resources such as agricultural product, water, oil, and gas reserves is likely. This is the main reason for ongoing rivalry for Artic dominance.
4. Uninvited *intrusion* within the borders is likely to be interpreted as an aggressive attack, and likely to be answered with resistance or with counter-aggression. When Russia controversially annexed the Ukrainian Crimea in 2014, it ignited an international protest. The original power then has the choice to accept the intrusion, or protect and defend the space.

An interesting, though somewhat puzzling, example of territorial conflict occured between Argentina and the United Kingdom. More than seven hundred Falkland Islands in the south Atlantic Ocean, 250 nautical miles east of the Argentinian coastline, have been in dispute since 1690 when Britain seized control. Since then, Argentina has made many efforts to claim sovereignty, but the United Kingdom continues to maintain a disputed presence there through military occupation and trade. In 1982, Argentina claimed sovereignty through military occupation, which Britain interpreted as an act of invasion. This incited the seven-day Falkland War, which necessitated UN Security Council intervention. Argentina eventually withdrew, leaving in its wake a chilly diplomatic relationship, with both parties in an uneasy "agree to disagree" stance. In 1990, full diplomatic relationships were restored. In 2010, the British company Desire Petroleum PLC company began exploration of sea beds around the Falklands, which contain an estimated 60 billion barrels of gas and oil. This triggered diplomatic protest and sea maneuvers by the Argentine government, which were mostly ignored by UK ships.

COSTS AND CONSEQUENCES OF VIOLENT CONFLICT

Viewed individually or globally, violence has direct and indirect victims and tangible and hidden costs. Simply and starkly stated, the costs of aggression and violence to the human race and to our planet are calamitous. The real costs

> *The most expensive peace is still cheaper than the cheapest war.*
> —Alexander Pope

of serious conflict are impossible to estimate for many reasons. Serious conflict is ever-present and repetitious, but measurement is impaired by data and information inconsistencies and gaps. Some costs and consequences are related to slow onset events, which are difficult to predict or measure. There is disagreement about which costs should be considered, such as the care of displaced families. Emergency funding is rarely well counted because of the crisis nature of the activities. Many costs are counted only afterward, in casualty and veterans' health and disability care, and postwar rebuilding.

Economic Losses

The World Economic Forum provides a comprehensive appraisal of the **costs of conflict**, counting activities related to containing, preventing, and dealing with the consequences of violence. It was estimated that in 2018 the economic costs of global conflict and violence amounted to US$14.3 trillion, which is the equivalent of $1,915 per person, or $5.25 per person per day (IEP, 2019; OCHA, 2017).

Measurable Costs

Some of the costs of violence are measurable. Between 1999 and 2002, the World Health Organization (WHO) sponsored a multinational review of the worldwide costs of violence. Obvious costs include lost property, damage to the immediate environment, injuries and deaths, or lost human potential because of permanent disabilities.

Economic costs include regular funding of law enforcement, armed forces and essential materials, containment of violence when it does occur, and postconflict peacekeeping and reconstruction of property and infrastructure.

Injuries and disabilities include people who are wounded or partially incapacitated by violence. Costs include direct consequences such as hospital visits and overnight stays, and health care costs, but are not fully comparable because of divergent reporting systems and underreporting. In Canada in 2010, intentional injuries cost CA$1,140 million. In the United States in 2013, intentional injuries cost US$76 billion. The WHO also speculates on life-years lost due to death in violent conflict.

Immeasurable Costs and Consequences

Many (possibly most) costs of violence are indirect, hidden, and largely incalculable. The WHO attempts to quantify broad social losses attributable to violence across the world. Such factors as health status, injurious cultural practices, crime data, and costs of health care are compiled in an annual, continuously refined report (WHO, 2016). The humanitarian consequences and costs and the invisible harms and disabilities that radically alter peoples' living conditions and wellbeing are the most pervasively devastating.

Consequences include psychological harm, deprivation, and distorted child development (WHO, 2016), all of which cause interminable suffering. Collateral economic costs relate to increased use of health care, higher needs for policing, lost productivity, and the toll of displacement and migration. Assisting victims of violence, and providing safe and educated therapeutic methods and settings are emotionally costly. The costs of mental stress and illness may be quantifiable to some extent, but the emotional costs in wellbeing and quality of life cannot be counted. Incarceration and rehabilitation of perpetrators of violence also cost society. Education and learning are disrupted by violence, often during critical periods of childrens' readiness that can never be revisited. It is possible to imagine, but impossible to quantify, the devastating costs of invisible human suffering that rob the world of human potential and productivity. It is sobering to realize that unresolved conflict only leads to deepening dysfunction.

Full Costs of Violence

An integrated approach to the question of full costs was inaugurated by Michael Cranna's 1994 book *The True Cost of Conflict*, commissioned by Saferworld, an independent international organization working to prevent violent conflict and build safer lives. Cranna examined seven conflicts, analyzing measurable economic, casualty, and death measures, and assessing more covert social, relational, environmental, and community development costs.

Cranna's approach has now become an ambitious multidisciplinary study series called **True Costs of Conflict**, coordinated by the Strategic Foresight Group in Mumbai, India. This group publishes an annual report of the comprehensive costs of conflict, focusing on salient conflicts active during that year. The purpose of this project is to encourage public discussion of violent conflict and its consequences, and to broaden public awareness of the global implications of conflict events and decisions.

Consequences for People and Families: Involuntary Displacement and Forced Migration

Migration is a fact of global history. The world was populated by migrations originating in Africa, and a nomadic, migratory way of life was widespread in countless Indigenous groups for centuries. Barriers to migration include seas and mountains, legal hindrances, and so on. Humans have also constructed artificial barriers to resist migration, starting with the Great Wall of China, including the Berlin Wall that was constructed during the Cold War and removed in the late 20th century, and continuing to the barrier that separates Israel and the West Bank today. A point of social controversy in the United States was former president Donald Trump's insistence on building a barrier to migration on the US-Mexico border.

Think About and Discuss with Your Colleagues

- In your experience, do artificial barriers facilitate or hinder migration? Do barriers have anything to do with peace and conflict resolution? Explain your answer.
- From your observation, do artificial barriers improve safety and security? Why or why not?
- The desperate flight of thousands and millions of people has created a whole class of human smugglers, the so-called *coyotes*, who illegally exploit migrants. In your view, who should be responsible for dealing with coyotes?

Involuntary displacement and *forced migration* describe the unplanned movement of a person or family away from their original homeland. Compelled by persecution, conflict, violence, or war, they cannot return home safely. Involuntarily displaced persons (IDP) are legally protected by the UN High Commissioner for Refugees (UNHCR), but represent a devastating global challenge. The following annual statistics likely underestimate the magnitude of the problem (UNHCR, 2018):

> Over 40 million people are displaced within their home nation
> 25.4 million are refugees (50% children)
> 10 million are stateless
> 3.1 million are asylum seekers

People relocate for many reasons, including safety and refuge, forcible population transfer, and deportation.

a. *Safety and Refuge.* According to the UN Universal Declaration of Human Rights (1948): "Everyone has the right to seek and to enjoy in other countries asylum from persecution." A *refugee* is someone who has fled their homeland because of war related violence. If they return, they face degrading treatment (such as female circumcision or forced marriage), violence, or death. An *asylum seeker* is a refugee who has legally been granted that status by the United Nations or a cooperating state.

   The term *sanctuary* refers to the provision of shelter, protection, physical and health support, and legal advice, sometimes in civil disobedience to local law. The *sanctuary movement* was a campaign by religious and political groups that began in the early 1980s to facilitate the safe migration of asylum seekers into the United States, especially those from Central America. In the middle 1980s some sanctuary providers were tried in the notorious "sanctuary trials." Although eight defendants were convicted of smuggling aliens, most received suspended sentences or short periods of house arrest. In 2018, more than 800 groups were members of this controversial movement.

b. *Forcible Population Transfer.* Sometimes an entire group is forced to migrate because a weaker subgroup is considered undesirable by the powerful. This occurred across the world in the 19th and 20th centuries when Indigenous groups were forced into "reserves" by foreign occupiers. It is still going on today, for example, in Kurdistan where approximately 2.75 million Kurds have been forced away from their traditional territories (Project, 2015).

c. *Deportation.* Also called extradition, **deportation** is the expulsion of a person or group by a government, usually as a punishment. In 1755–1764, approximately 11,000 Acadians were deported by the British government from what is now maritime Canada, and forced to relocate to the United States and other areas. These people were the origin of the term "cajun" in the southern United States.

The UNHCR goals for involuntarily displaced migrants are, first in priority, voluntary return and safe repatriation to their own country; if that is not possible, integration into their new location is explored; or the least desirable option is resettlement in a third country. Regardless of these goals and ideals, the fate of displaced people is often very poor. As many as 10% experience starvation, violence, and death as they flee. Most begin their new existence under "acute and temporary protection and services," which are rudimentary refugee camps or basic urban settings administered by nongovernmental organizations such as the Red Crescent or Red Cross societies. In 2018, the UNHCR estimated that there were about 700 refugee camps operating across the world. Although designed as short-term placements, 66% of refugees have been displaced for more than 3 years, and 50% have been displaced for more than 10 years because of inability to return home or rejection by other nations (UNHCR, 2018).

A more enduring solution is elusive: refugees are usually granted temporary entry visas at best and must sort out governmental bureaucracy and regulations, often without language skills or the demanded documentation. Even those who can return to their original homeland may continue to experience rootless impermanence, and become embroiled in property disputes resulting from their years of absence. After conflict has ceased, insufficient housing and employment for a returning population are common.*

Fatal Consequences

Fatal casualties are deaths that result from intentional violence. At least 108 million people were killed in war in the 20th century (New York Times). The WHO estimated that, worldwide, more than 1.6 million people were killed in violent confrontations in 2016, more than one person every three minutes. In the past decade, more than 2 million children have died as a result of war (UN Special Envoy for Children and Armed Conflict, Jimmie Briggs).

In 2016, there were more than 87,000 battle-related deaths, most in the Middle East. Seventy percent of conflict-related deaths were civilian and, in higher population areas, this increased to 92% (OCHA, 2017). In 2017 in the United States, more than 19,500 people were murdered, and 47,000 people died from

---

*June 20 was designated by the United Nations in 2000 as World Refugee Day.

violent suicide (NVDRS, 2017). In 2015, the highest international concentrations of fatalities resulted from conflict occurring in Lesotho, Honduras (five times the number in Iraq), Venezuela, Iraq, and the Philippines (WHO, 2016).

The Uppsala Conflict Data Program (UCDP, 2018) measures conflict severity by deaths per year.

1. A *serious dispute* involves threat of violence or a show of force, but no death.
2. A conflict is viewed as *low intensity* when there is sporadic but not intense violence.
3. *Minor armed conflict* engages two armed forces, at least one of which is a state. There are fewer than 25 military and civilian casualties each year.
4. *Intermediate conflict* occurs when at least 25 deaths happen in one year's time, and up to 1,000 deaths over the course of the conflict. A war is considered *active* if it has reached this intensity.
5. *War*, or a *major armed conflict,* results in more than 1,000 deaths per year. *Low-intensity wars,* involving between 1 and 10,000 casualties per year, are often ended through diplomatic negotiation, requiring negotiation with the perpetrators of very serious violence. The resulting peace can be quite easily jeopardized. A *high-intensity war* involves between 10,000 and 100,000 annual casualties. *Total war* represents unrestrained conflict escalation and out-of-control violence that results in more than 100,000 casualties per year.

PRAXIS: PRACTICAL APPROACHES TO VIOLENCE AND PEACE

Ending and Mending Large-Scale Violence

Yaacov Bar-Siman-Tov (2004) traced the peacebuilding steps of a society as it struggles with the aftermath of devastating conflict. Many so-called toolbox methods are available and are developing for practical conflict resolution and peacebuilding: some are peaceable, self-directed; some are interactive, some are aggressively coercive.

Conflict Assessment and Analysis

Conflict assessment gathers information and analyzes the elements of a specific conflict and the reasons for violence. To maximize effectiveness, practical approaches must be appropriate to a particular location and time (Midgley, 2015; Wilson, 2019). A detailed assessment usually considers the 4-P elements: the people, stakeholders, and diversities of personal identities; the multiple short- and long-term problems that converged in the present turmoil, including current security and risks of violence; the process of conflict and violence development; and a range of potential solutions to move the group from conflict toward peace. Peacebuilding agencies such as Saferworld, the Department for International Development in the United Kingdom, and the US Agency for International Development provide detailed guidance on how to conduct these assessments prior to planning any action.

Planning for Practical Action

According to Bar-Siman-Tov (2004) the first action step is short-term *conflict cessation* to end hostility. Negative peace is the absence of conflict and violence; **negative peacebuilding,** then, means ending ongoing violence and hindering future conflicts from igniting in group and national spheres. This creates a temporary, brief pause of violence that ushers in an *unstable peace.* Establishing stable, *sustainable peace* necessitates resolution of long-term wrongs. Positive peace is the presence of life conditions, structures and institutions, and attitudes that create and sustain a peaceable society; **positive peacebuilding** is activity that addresses existing sources of structural and cultural violence (IEP, 2019), as well as reestablishes and develops social infrastructure. *Reconciliation,* the restoration of friendship and harmony between former enemies, involves work at the local, neighborhood levels. See Chapter 11 for more detailed discussion.

Preventing Conflict and Violence

"Conflict begins and escalates for a reason, and to arrest its course requires a deliberate effort" (Zartman, 2015). **Prevention** is any action that inhibits disputes from arising between parties, prevents existing disputes from escalating into [violent] conflict, and limits the spread of the violent conflicts when they do occur (Boutros-Ghali, 1992). Figure 9.3, based on the UN peace and security activity planning, illustrates the complexity of the tasks. *Conflict prevention* is most effectively used when unstable, cold peace is present, but no open violence has happened. Political and community leaders are crucially influential, but military intervention may be perceived as provocative.

Figure 9.3 Spectrum of peacebuilding activities

Negative Peacemaking: Ending Violence

Numerous political, community, and military actors and agents of change may be constructively involved in ending violence, but it is most effective when carefully coordinated and linked to the stage of a conflict. Hot peace is the desired goal, when political parties are functioning collaboratively for the benefit of the majority of the people, and the surrounding population has resumed their normal lives.

- *Peace enforcement* and *peacemaking* activities are most effective under cold peace conditions when intermittent violence has begun, but is not yet severe. Political process and military intervention may be necessary to deter more serious violence and protect civilians, and community leaders are not especially effective;
- *Peacekeeping* is the best (possibly the only) option when hot conflict and crisis are ongoing. Military and political intervention are primary, and community leaders and members are beginning to forge their roles.
- Postconflict *peacebuilding* is the best hope of preventing relapse into conflict when a conflict has reasonably ended. Military personnel are helpful for technical expertise and assistance, political leadership is important for conceptual rebuilding, and community members are most active and effective because of their grass roots connections to those affected by the conflict.

Conflict and violence management is the typical outcome of resolution processes that are directed through a wide variety of political activities that could include diplomatic negotiation, international sanctions, and aggressive violence. Violence cessation is achieved, but may only be a "stop fighting" agreement that does not address the underlying tensions and problems. In that sense, violence is restrained to great benefit, but the conflict remains and is likely to be revived by parties with persistent concerns about the original grievances that drove the conflict.

Conflict and violence settlement and dispute resolution might also occur through an adversarial, legalized arbitration or prosecution conducted by an international cooperative body. International parties with legal disputes submit their quarrel for settlement directed by the International Court of Justice (ICJ) for advisory opinion and adjudication of international legal conflicts such as border and sovereignty disputes, the International Chamber of Commerce for arbitration of crossborder trade disputes, or the International Criminal Court (ICC) for prosecution of international criminals. Ideally, these legally settled rulings do end and prevent violent conflict outbreaks, but that is often not so. Because only nations can participate in the processes, nongovernmental groups are often unsatisfied with the resolution reached. Enforcement of the rulings is unreliable.

In setting with long-standing conflict such as South Africa, efforts were and are made to end the violence through negative peace, and to build a healthy society through positive peace. The underlying conflict remains, but violent events are better contained, with fewer casualties.

Positive Peacemaking: Peacebuilding and Social Transformation

Peace and violence are not merely inverse concepts (Diehl, 2016). Positive peacebuilding goes beneath immediate violence to address the long-term sources of the originating conflict. The Institute for Economics and Peace (IEP), in a major work assessing positive peace indicators globally (IEP, 2019), stated that eight qualities are measurable in regions where degrees of positive peace are present. These form the intermediate goals of long-term positive peacebuilding:

- promotion of human rights,
- a strong economic environment,
- equitable resource and power distributions,

- high levels of human skills, knowledge, and expertise,
- well-functioning government,
- free flow of information,
- low levels of institutional corruption, and
- positive neighbor relationships.

Stephen Ryan (2013) noted that conflict, even if it is violent, is both the target and the means of transformative change. The deep and wide changes that bring sustainable peace can be achieved even in the presence of violence. The people must be empowered with groundbreaking thinking and dialogue, sensitivity to area cultures, and work on all levels of society (also Miall, 2013). Such social transformation means that deep changes are promoted that alter long-standing worldviews and unite historical adversaries into actions that maintain peace.

Think About and Discuss with Your Colleagues

The website for the IEP provides the "Global Peace Index for 2019." Explore this report, especially the key findings on page 4.
  http://visionofhumanity.org/app/uploads/2019/06/GPI-2019-web003.pdf

- Does your experience of your country, or your community, generally confirm or contradict these IEP findings?
- On a scale of 0–100, how would you measure the peaceableness of your own surroundings, according to the previously mentioned qualities?
- What sort of improvements would you like to see locally or globally?

Transformation is a long-term, possibly endless, task (Zartman, 1983). David Barash and Charles Webel (2018) suggested that reductions to violence at all levels of society and on a global scale could require five enormous tasks:

1. Establish respect for human rights reliably and universally;
2. Create long-term, balanced economic alternatives to current models of political control;
3. Secure fair and adequate distribution of available resources;
4. Respect the earth's natural cycles and create ecological wellbeing; and
5. Establish reliable nonviolent conflict resolution methods.

Conflict and violence transformation is an outcome of comprehensive peacemaking activities that potentially address direct, structural, and attitudinal sources of violence (Dudouet, 2006; see Chapter 12). Without a doubt, those tasks necessitate comprehensive negotiation on a global scale, with visionary leadership and committed citizens.

Peacebuilding in South Africa was initiated even before *apartheid* was enacted more than 70 years ago, and it continues today. The obvious sources of violence have diminished, governmental reformation and legislation have improved the legal landscape, and many organizations are working to transform the cultural and attitudinal bases of society. The conflicts do continue, and the transformative work will likely extend long into the future.

CONTROVERSIAL PEACEBUILDER:
NELSON MANDELA (1918-2013)

"It is in our hands to make of our world a better one for all."

Nelson Mandela was the black leader who, with F. W. de Klerk, oversaw the genesis of social transformation in South Africa in the late 20th century. His goals were to dismantle apartheid and, most importantly, foster racial reconciliation. His story showed several drastic changes of strategy, as if his life were divided into "chapters."

Chapter 1: Origins

Nelson Mandela was born into a prominent black family in a racially segregated eastern province of South Africa. He was 30 years old when the National Party of South Africa began to formalize apartheid laws and white supremacist policies.

Chapter 2: Political Action

Mandela adopted increasingly anticolonial and antisegregation views. In 1944, he joined the African National Congress (ANC), a black liberation group, beginning as leader of its Youth League. He continued antiapartheid defiance and nonviolent activism in several ANC leadership positions. He studied law at the University of Witwatersrand, and began practice as a lawyer specializing in cases related to apartheid.

Chapter 3: Radical, Violent Rebel

Mandela's activism with the ANC gave him visibility, which added credibility to his arguments but also made him the target of government harassment. When his activities were severely restricted, he went underground. He was acquitted of treason charges in 1961. That same year, police confronted nonviolent, unarmed blacks demonstrating against apartheid at Sharpeville, wounding or killing about 250. After that, Mandela gave up on nonviolent defiance, began to advocate active sabotage, and was trained in guerilla warfare. He cofounded the militant and sometimes violent subgroup of the ANC called Umkhonto weSizwe (Spear of the Nation).

Mandela was tried twice for treason, and sentenced to life in prison. His speech at the 1963 Rivona Trial, called "I Am Prepared to Die," attracted international attention. Imprisonment was often brutal and debilitating, but he refused several government offers of conditional freedom. During his 27 years in prison, he retained visibility and support among South African blacks and the international community. Although refusing to publicly renounce violence, he began to speak about his commitment to personal courage, forgiveness, and interracial peacebuilding. He participated in nonviolent talks to create interracial understanding and reconciliation.

Chapter 4: Politician

From about 1983, as South Africa's social conflict steadily escalated, Mandela was engaged in six years of negotiation with the National Party government. In 1989 F. W. de Klerk was elected president. De Klerk had come to believe that apartheid was wrong and unsustainable, and began a series of reforms to repeal apartheid and end segregation. Along with many other political prisoners, Mandela was released from prison in 1990.

Following his release from prison, Mandela resumed leadership of the ANC. The first multiracial, fully representative elections were held in 1994, and Mandela was elected the first black President of South Africa, with F. W. de Klerk serving as Deputy President. During his 5 years in office, they oversaw the rocky, but peaceful, transition from white rule to multiracial democracy under the new democratic constitution.

Chapter 5: Mandela's Legacy—"The Father of the Nation"
As stated by Chip Haas (2011), no agreement could overcome the tragic legacy of four centuries of white rule and 40 years of official apartheid. However, Mandela is widely regarded as a powerful symbol of democratic social change and social justice. In 1993, he and de Klerk shared the Nobel Peace Prize for their efforts to peacefully terminate official apartheid and found a newly democratic South Africa.

Mandela's leadership was instrumental in formation of the South African Truth and Reconciliation Commission (TRC) in 1995, which investigated human rights violations under apartheid. That TRC, lead by Bishop Desmond Tutu, became a model for similar reparative commissions around the world.

After leaving office in 1999, Mandela continued to advocate for social justice, peace, and reconciliation internationally. In 2007, he was a founding member of "The Elders," an international group dedicated to global problem solving and conflict resolution. He died at his home in Johannesburg in 2013. The Nelson Mandela Foundation continues his work.

CHAPTER SUMMARY AND STUDY GUIDE

- Violence has many (controversial) definitions and dimensions. Large-scale violence refers to hostile actions, relationships, and attitudes intersecting to increase risks and experiences of danger for an identifiable group of people in a community, nation, or international setting.
- Serious violence does not occur suddenly; it develops slowly and and escalates through control, coercion, threat, and harm.
- Many sources of violence are in the organizational structures of society if they privilege some people at the expense of disadvantage for others.
- Cultural violence is invisible in many ways except in its consequences.
- Efforts to quantify simple sources of national and international conflict and violence are probably futile because the root causes are widespread and complex. However, political and social division, political power transitions, and unjust distribution of common resources are central causes.
- Crisis and violence are costly. The main challenges are containment, reduction of violence, and alleviation of suffering.

- Ending and mending violence, and creating both negative and positive peace, are enormous tasks that require the commitment and cooperation of political leaders, community members, with national and international policy makers.

TERMS IN FOCUS

asymmetrical power
  relationship 292
atrocious violence 280
behavioral violence 283
chosen glory 281
chosen trauma 281
conventional warfare 278
cultural genocide 288
cultural imperialism 288
cultural violence 285
culture of war 285
deportation 297
durable peace 274
escalation threshold 279
ethnopolitical conflict 287
extrastate conflict 274
fear monger 286
forced migration 296
hard power 291
holy war 288
human security 287
intangible power 292
interstate conflict 274
intractable conflict 280
intrastate conflict 274
involuntary displacement 296
Just War 282
large-scale violence 271
left-wing politics 289

legitimate fear 286
national security 287
negative peacebuilding 299
orchestrated violence 280
peace spoiler 280
political power 291
political violence 277
positive peacebuilding 299
prevention 299
refugee 296
right-wing politics 289
soft power 291
sovereignty 293
spoiler 280
stable peace 274
structural violence 284
suspicion 286
sustainable peace 274
symmetrical power
  relationship 292
tangible power 291
transitional justice (TJ) 293
unconventional warfare 278
unrightable wrong 281
unstable peace 275
violence (WHO) 277
violence engineer 280
war 275

SECTION IV
Conflict Resolution

10

Justice Making and Third-Party Resolution

■ ■ ■

In Focus in This Chapter:

■ Justice is, above all, fair: it is orderly, respectful, and equitable. Injustice is unfair: it disregards the law, is disrespectful, and is imbalanced. To be successful, peacemaking and justice making must correct injustices.

■ Injustice is at the core of most conflicts, and conflict resolution methods are designed to create or restore justice and peaceful relationships. Many options exist to do this, linked with different concepts or paradigms of justice.

■ Order restoring justice methods include procedural justice, which uses strictly fair procedures to process conflict, and retributive justice, which imposes a penalty on the person responsible for the injustice.

■ Equity-restoring justice includes distributive justice, which redistributes privileges and resources to produce a fairer balance, and restorative justice, which addresses losses and harm caused to people impacted by injustice.

■ There are numerous informal and formal methods of making justice and peace. Single-party conflict resolution deals with a problem privately, emphasizing problem solving or, possibly, coaching. Two-party resolution relies on dialogue and negotiation or, occasionally, force, between the primary parties. Third-party resolution introduces an impartial outsider to help disputants settle a conflict.

■ Formal adversarial methods are governed by the judicial system through orderly adjudication in the courts or arbitration by a trained expert.

■ Formalized nonadversarial conflict processing restores equity with negotiation and mediation with trained facilitators.

■ Although Western thinking focuses on these formal principles of making justice and resolving conflict, non-Western, tribal methods rely on traditional processes that include an entire community.

CONFLICT CASE 10.1 ■ "CONFLICT GONE CRAZY"
—*PEARSON V. CHUNG*, 2007

This outrageous conflict began when an unsatisfied customer complained to the owners of a family business.

In May 2005, Roy Pearson was appointed as a judge in Washington, D.C. He brought several suits to Custom Cleaners for dry cleaning and alteration. When he returned two days later, one pair of pants was missing. Judge Pearson asked the cleaners, Jin Nam Chung, Ki Chung, and Soo Chung, to pay US$1,450 for a new suit. When the pants were found one week later, Judge Pearson claimed the pants were not his, but the Chung family refused his compensation request. Judge Pearson sued the cleaners for fraud (the front window of their store had signs saying, "Satisfaction Guaranteed" and "Same-Day Service") and for damages. Although the Chung family made three compensation offers of $3,000, $4,600, and $12,000, Judge Pearson remained unsatisfied and continued his court action.

The case went to trial in June 2007, with Judge Pearson asking that the signs be removed from the window and for compensation of US$65 million: $1,450 for a new suit, $15,000 to rent a car every weekend for 10 years so that he could take his dry cleaning to another city, almost $500,000 costs to represent himself in court, $2 million for "distress, inconvenience, and discomfort," plus $51.5 million punitive damages to be used to assist other dissatisfied Washington customers. At the conclusion of the trial, Judge Judith Bartnoff ruled in favor of Custom Cleaners, and awarded them court costs.

Still not satisfied, Judge Pearson appealed the ruling in 2007, 2008, and 2009. When his last appeal was rejected, he decided not to take his case to his last resort, the US Supreme Court. Although further difficulties did follow for both Judge Pearson and the Chung family, the conflict between them was considered to be legally resolved.

This type of frivolous court case is rare, and was highlighted as outrageous in popular media reports. In addition to your own impressions, you might notice some aspects of this story:

- Judge Pearson was asking the court system to settle his conflict with Custom Cleaners;
- in many ways, outsiders could criticize these disorderly events as unfair;
- both parties spent a great deal of money in the adjudication process;
- in the end, Judge Pearson received no satisfaction, the Chungs were traumatized by the process, the relationship remained antagonistic, and no satisfactory outcome was realized.

Think About and Discuss with Your Colleagues

- In what specific ways do you think this conflict was fair, or not, and to whom?
- Can you imagine other ways Judge Pearson could have acted? Could the Chung family have acted differently?
- If you were a friend of Judge Pearson, how would you have advised him?
- If you were a friend of the Chung family, how would you have advised them?
- What do you think of Judge Judith Bartnoff's 2007 judgment?
- Do you think Judge Pearson should have taken his complaint to the US Supreme Court, which was his right?

Many serious conflicts result from wrong actions or injustice. Justice is always complex and sometimes elusive, but it is a key concept in Peace and Conflict Studies. Because wrongdoing and injustice are the basis of so many conflicts, then righting the wrongs in just ways should be the basis of most resolution and peacebuilding. Although this is a key principle, it does not suggest specific ways of creating justice. Positive, healthy relationships are an important part of peace. Conflict Resolution Studies emphasizes links between "conflict resolution," "justice making," and "peacemaking." In the context of injustice, conflict can function to correct something wrong, protest against a wrong, or resist unfair treatment. Few conflicts are resolved until a just, fair understanding or agreement has been reached between the opponents. In this chapter we will explore many concepts and ideas related to justice, conflict, and justice making.

> *True peace is not merely the absence of tension; it is the presence of justice.*
> —Martin Luther King *(This was written in 1955 in response to an accusation that his actions to end racism were "disturbing the peace.")*

DEFINING JUSTICE AND INJUSTICE

Many scholars acknowledge that finding a single definition of justice is a failing task (Longres, 2001; Novak, 2000; Sen, 2009). Justice is as multidimensional as a complex mosaic. Unfocused definitions are used casually, as if anyone should recognize it. Who you are and what you care about biases your perception, needs, and goals (Carens, 2000), so your perspective defines justice, as was clear for the Chungs and Judge Pearson (Sitka, 2009).

Think About and Discuss with Your Colleagues

Amartya Sen (2009) offered an illustration of clashing principles in "Who gets the flute?"

> Suppose three children, Anna, Bob, and Carla, are quarrelling over a flute. Anna says she is the only one who can play the flute, so obviously we should give it to her. But then Bob says that he is the only child who has no toys at all, so surely he ought at least to have a flute to play with. Suddenly the question does not look so easy. And finally Carla points out that she spent months actually making the flute. So who should get it?

Abstract theoretical arguments, subjective experiences, and justice systems are not congruent. Generally, there are two approaches to defining justice. Some scholars address the objective question, "what qualities describe a just society?" (Rawls, 1999); alternative discussion centers on the practical question of "how can justice, now, be improved?" Sen (2009). Neither approach helps us understand what people subjectively sense to be just, or what the right remedies are for injustice.

Justice is experienced when conditions are right, fair, and reasonable. Above all, justice connotes fairness. Its strongest purpose is to support conflict resolution through peaceful interactions. There are three common elements of meaning in justice:

1. *Law and order*—Social expectations and the rules of a society are designed to establish security and order. Citizens are expected to obey the law. This element of justice establishes *justice systems*, institutions and procedures that set laws, enforce them, impartially judge peoples' conformity, and apply penalties for illegal actions. However, it is important to recognize that formal justice is limited by those whose power sets the rules, such as supervisors, lawmakers, and judges, and those systems preserve existing power structures (Butler, 2016). Laws are founded on prevailing cultural norms, and unfair laws target people who are less powerful because of race, lack of social support, poor education, and other disadvantages.

2. *Respectful relationships*—Respect implies a positive, appreciative attitude toward another person and their differences. Respect is earned in reciprocal, agreeable relationships. It is also given to a person based on exceptional abilities or achievements, or to a person in authority. One of the functions of a just society is to establish norms that ensure genuinely respectful relationships. Codes of rights, duties, and responsibilities are created as basic standards for respectful actions.

3. *Fairness and equity*—Justice is cooperative, evenhandedly working to support the good of all. A just group or society is one in which the people receive a fair share of resources, applied equally and evenly to everyone. The interconnected qualities of *social justice* refer to conditions of a) equal access to common resources like water and education, b) equal treatment without prejudice that is based on personal traits, c) practical human rights, and d) participation and voice to leadership, for example, by voting (van Tuijl, 1999). Despite virtually universal agreement that equity is just and right, there is vigorous debate in society and in Peace and Conflict Studies about how equity is applied among diverse people, as you saw in Sen's story of the flute (see Chapter 5).

Injustice and wrongdoing cause social chaos. **Injustice** is unfair, but the experience of injustice may focus on particular actions that are abusive or malicious, on a situation marked by imbalance or inequity, or even on the failure of a social system to maintain fair justice. The foundation of a sense of injustice is the harm caused by wrongdoing. Again, perspective matters: underlying this concept are varying interpretations of wrongdoing. If you believe that injustice results from mistakes or failure, then justice making explores repair; if you believe that injustice results from bad character, then the best justice comes through retaliation or punishment; if injustice results from prejudiced policies, then society must change.

Think About and Discuss with Your Colleagues

- What has your real-life experience with "justice" been? Is justice a distant concept in the news media, for example, or have you or your family encountered justice system(s) directly? Given your experiences, discuss and write your own definition of justice.

Three sometimes clashing interpretations of injustice were articulated by Howard Zehr (2014):

1. *Disobedience to the law* defines injustice. This emphasizes that the law must be obeyed to maintain social order, so agencies and authorities such as police and judges are empowered to apply the law to particular situations. They are expected to fairly weigh the injustice or justice of a situation, determine wrong or right, and regulate reparation if it is indicated.
2. *Disrespectful, harmful relationships* are unjust. Mistakes, failures, and wrongdoing inevitably occur in many forms and in all relationships. Trust and respect are fragile and are upheld by trustworthy, responsible actions. When trust is disappointed, people experience injustice. Ways to reduce or repair harm and to restore respectful relationships are guided by community standards and processes.
3. *Inequity is unjust.* An unequal share of common resources and privilege are given to some people, creating injustice. *Social injustice* is defined by any systemic condition that causes inequity or exclusion of an individual or group from opportunities. Systemic inequity often leads to social unrest and disorder such as the Black Lives Matter protests.

A vital component of resolving conflict is the restoration of peace after a relationship has been damaged by wrongdoing and injustice. **Justice making** is both the process and outcome of restoring justice and fairness to all parties to a conflict. People (both victims and offenders) need to be released from the "trouble" of wrongdoing and to be restored to mutual respect but there is no uniform procedure to accomplish this weighty task. Justice making is an interactive process involving many people and many levels of activity. The most effective justice making is holistic and thorough.

- justice making is *relational*: parties needs are satisfied so that trusting, respectful interactions are possible;
- justice making is *reparative*: wrongs have been righted and harm has been repaired; and
- justice making is *social*: the surrounding family or community is functioning in orderly and equitable ways.

PARADIGMS: FOUR JUSTICE-MAKING MODELS

One of the reasons for the evolving development of multiple forms of justice is that societies keep trying to invent successful justice and peacemaking systems that correct previous flaws. Since ancient times, countless ways have been explored that ensure justice and repair when wrongdoing happens. Many traditional concepts survive today.

A wide repertoire of tools, techniques, and possible roles are available and can be put to use. Resolution of conflict does not have to happen through oppositional fighting, called **adversarial conflict resolution**. In **nonadversarial conflict resolution**, peace and justice are created through cooperative discussion, on the principle that satisfaction is desirable and possible for everyone.

A **paradigm** is a pattern used to describe the characteristics of a typical example of something. Paradigms rise out of different interests and purposes, so they shape perception, actions, associated assumptions, beliefs, and values. In Peace and Conflict Studies, there are four distinct paradigms of justice: procedural, retributive, distributive, and restorative. Constructive conflict processing leads to an enduring solution for three main reasons: the relationship between the parties has improved, the process for dealing with the conflict was participatory and satisfactory, and the resolution meets the needs and addresses the problems or issues from which the conflict originated. The ultimate goal of all justice-making paradigms and processes is sustainable peace that fulfills several criteria:

- the conflict was accurately expressed;
- each party understood that their own perspective and the Other's may not be identical, and it might be that neither is fully accurate;
- parties were willing to invest in processing a conflict because they acknowledge interdependence and commitment to each other; and
- respect and power were equalized.

Order-Restoring Justice

Some justice-making methods correct the disorderly nature of injustice, replacing it with order.

a. The central focus of **procedural justice** is the fairness of an orderly process that addresses disputes or injustice. For example, most employment groups such as schools and businesses have prescribed grievance procedures that must be used to ensure that conflicts are properly addressed. The process can be determined either by agreement among those affected or, more often, by an unbiased outside authority or mediator.

b. **Retributive justice** evens the field by punishing injustice with payment or compensation. For example, the police impose speeding tickets which escalate in penalty as the speed over the legal limit increases, and those funds are used to support law enforcement. To provide *restitution* is to return something that was taken by the wrongdoer's actions, or to give a comparable equivalent. Punishment of the Chung's actions, and equivalent compensation, were the intent of Judge Pearson's actions in suing the family. Related concepts are punishment, revenge, and retaliation.

Equity-Restoring Justice

Some methods of reestablishing justice focus on an imbalance caused between the disputing parties.

c. **Distributive justice** attends primarily to the principle of equal resources. Justice making therefore means correcting inequity by redistributing the resource or, even better, dismantling unjust ways of accessing resources. For example, when discriminatory hiring has created a "glass ceiling" for females, some businesses correct the injustice with preferential female hiring or promotion.

d. **Restorative justice** assumes that wrongdoing has caused widespread alienation and harm to everyone: the hurt victim, the shamed wrongdoer, their damaged relationship, and their community. Justice making works out ways to restore relationships, repair the harm, and reconcile the community. For example, offenders may be required to serve community service as an alternative to incarceration, and this gives them job experience, this helps the community, and many victims are satisfied that the penalty is meaningful.

Table 10.1   Comparison of Justice-Making Paradigms

	Order Restoring		Equity Restoring	
	Procedural Justice	Retributive Justice	Distributive Justice	Restorative Justice
Concept of wrongdoing and injustice	Violation of standards and laws	Violation of law creates guilt and debt to society	Inequity creates a responsibility, obligation	Violation of person and relationship
Justice making through	Factual inquiry, strictly fair procedures	Punishment, compensation for loss	Fair resource distribution	Community reconciliation
People involved	Magistrates, judges, tribunals	Adversaries for state and accused	Community dialogue, government	Offender, victim, community
Process	Contest of interpretation of facts	Determination of guilt or innocence	Resource negotiation	Identify needs, dialogue, circle process
Result	One view of the facts is judged correct	Punishment imposed and satisfied	Equitable access to common resources	All communicate, take responsibility
Goals	Maintain safety and order	Maintain safety and order, compensate for harm	Equitable resources	Repair harm, relationships encouraged

Paradigms are often compared side-by-side to help explain the patterns (see Table 10.1). Each paradigm will be explained in detail in the following text.

Order-Restoring Justice

When a society is orderly, successful functioning of that society results in safety, civility, and courtesy. When relationships are disorderly, energy is wasted on basic functioning and the people cannot operate effectively or productively. Order is promoted by laws that regulate individual actions, relationships (for example, in contracts and marriage), prescribe community functioning (for example, campaign and election laws), and guide relationships between nations (through treaties and diplomacy). Procedural and retributive justice attempt to restore order when injustice has occurred.

Procedural Justice Paradigm

The Concept The central focus of **procedural justice** is the fairness of the process that addresses disputes or injustice. Zehr (1995) explained this: "Justice is defined by the process more than the outcome.... Have the right rules and processes been followed? If so, justice was done." Procedural justice relies on established rules that outline fairness and keep order. Practically, the methods usually involve authority figures such as magistrates or judges in a role similar to that of a referee: to guide the conflict through fair procedures that are consistent with the rules. Order might be restored by appealing for protection through judicial peace bonds and restraining orders, or by submitting conflicts to authorities for decision. This was the method used to settle the dispute between the Chung family and Judge Roy Pearson.

Numerous studies have established that when a disputant believes that the process of reaching resolution was fair, they are more likely to accept the outcome; if a disputant believes that unfair procedures were used, they are more likely to continue the dispute. Several key concepts determine the fairness of procedures (Blader, 2003):

- rules are established, interpreted, and applied consistently;
- conflict parties are treated fairly and equally;
- formal discussion of the conflict occurs without secrecy;
- one version of the "truth" is reached through balanced (though adversarial) inquiry into the facts;
- one party is judged to be primarily responsible for the conflict and injustice; and
- a penalty or punishment is imposed on the person responsible, and that dissolves their guilt.

Procedural Justice in Everyday Life Procedural justice making applies formalized methods, monitored and guided by authority figures who represent society and the rules, in many settings such as schools and workplaces. Two social systems deal in this way with claims of injustice: the civil justice system and the criminal court system.

Procedural Justice and the Civil Court System Returning to our earlier case, *Pearson v. Chung*, 2007, procedural justice making was carried out in this way:

- rules of fair business were determined, and Pearson's accusation against the Chungs was compared with those standards;
- balanced investigation resulted in findings of the facts of the interactions between the Chung family and Judge Pearson;
- discussions occurred in open court where both parties presented opposing viewpoints;
- the viewpoint of the Chung family was found to be correct, and the views of Judge Pearson were judged incorrect; and
- Judge Pearson was found primarily responsible and, as a consequence, had to pay court costs and received no compensation.

A weakness of this procedure is that "fair" and "just" are decided by an appointed, powerful authority. The conclusion may or may not match the experiences or satisfaction of the actual people. In the case of the Chungs and Pearson, neither party experienced resolution.

Retributive Justice Paradigm

The Concept The central belief of the Retributive Justice paradigm is "You get what you deserve." If you treat others with kindness, you deserve kindness in return; if you do wrong or are unjust, justice is served when you have wrong done to you.

The emphases of retributive justice are the accused individual and appropriate consequences for proven wrongdoing. **Retribution** is punishment, and retributive justice communicates society's disapproval of harmful actions through the imposition of negative, punishing consequences. The idea is that punishment demonstrates the painful consequences of injustice, so that the offender will become sorry or penitent (notice the obvious connection with the term "penitentiary"). According to the retributive justice paradigm, injustice is righted through accountability and proportional punishment, and this prevents future wrongdoing. Schools, some families, courts, and the military are examples of settings in which the retributive justice paradigm is prevalent.

Five principles determine retributive justice:

- *Rule by the Law*—Everyone should be protected by the law, which prevents bias or imbalanced or abused power and sets the standards by which specific actions are judged.
- *Impartiality*—Similar actions should have the same consequences. This is the principle behind guidelines for minimum and maximum punishment when guilt has been determined. Penalties should be imposed consistently, with consideration of the wrongdoer's specific circumstances.
- The *Rule of Proportionality*—Fair punishment should balance the injustice, the harms or losses experienced, and the moral implications of the wrong. "Let the punishment fit the crime." The severity of punishment should reasonably match the severity of the wrongdoing, but there is much debate over what "fair punishment" is. Over history, reasonable limits on the severity and violence inherent in punishment have been refined. In *Pearson v. Chung*, Judge Bartnoff ruled that Judge Pearson's demands for compensation (US$65 million) were not proportional to his losses (one ruined suit).
- The *Rule of Correction*—Retributive justice results in five correctives intended to prevent future conflict:
  1. Educate to promote social responsibility—Societies maintain behavior standards and, through the imposition of a penalty, denounce wrong behavior as unacceptable. The theory is that, with correction, wrongdoers will learn conformity to social standards.
  2. Accountability and punishment—The root of the concept of punishment is "pain." The intent of punishment is to impose pain on someone who has caused harm to others. The theory is that this will convince the wrongdoer of the harmful impact of their behavior, create some empathy for the victim(s), and encourage future responsibility.
  3. Benefit society by protecting the vulnerable—Punishment should reduce the danger to other potential victims.
  4. Prevent wrongdoing by imposing a deterrent—A painful consequence deters wrongdoers and other observers in society. When the threat of punishment for inappropriate behavior exists, people are theoretically dissuaded from it and persuaded to behave in socially responsible ways. This is one reason for the public transparency of trials and their outcomes.
  5. Rehabilitation—Many offenses are perpetrated by individuals who have developed maladaptive coping patterns like using violation as a

first strategy. The theory is that these patterns can be corrected through relearning and therapy.

- The *Rule of Closure*—when the penalty for wrongdoing is fulfilled, the wrong and guilt are dissolved.

Some issues that challenge retributive justice making are unsolved debates over the causes of criminal behavior, the rationale for incarceration, the criteria used to establish proportional punishment, the methods used for behavioral correction, and the effectiveness of current practices.

Retributive Justice in Everyday Life There is significant ongoing debate and criticism in politics, scholarship, and workplaces about the effectiveness of retribution:

- Retributive justice procedures uphold the rights of an accused person, but do very little to address the needs of victims or communities affected by injustice.
- Retribution is nothing better than retaliatory revenge, shaming the punished wrongdoer without considering the life circumstances that might have contributed to the failings.
- Punishment for wrongs is not corrective because the focus is on *incorrect* rather than on appropriate behavior.
- Although retribution is associated with significant popular approval, punishment seldom results in real change.
- The punitive consequences of offenses (borne by the wrongdoer) have little to do with the natural consequences (borne by the victim and community).

If the Retributive Justice paradigm had been applied to *Pearson v. Chung*, this is how it would have played out (and do notice some parallels with procedural justice):

- A formal accusation would be made against the Chung family, charging them with breaking the laws of fair business.
- A trial would allow both Judge Pearson and the Chungs to present evidence that could be tested, resulting in an impartial weighing of factual guilt or innocence.
- If found liable, a punishment would be imposed on the Chungs, probably in the form of a fine or service in the community, or (unlikely) a term of incarceration.
- If found not guilty, the Chung family would return to their homes and work.

The Problems of Crime and Conflict Crime is always related to some level of conflict: to a deep intrapersonal conflict, family or other interpersonal conflict, social conflict, and so forth. Conflict could be the cause or the outcome of crime. Narrowly, crime is the violation of a law that results in objective guilt. Technically, the wrongdoing and conflict are between society and the accused wrongdoer, so only law enforcement officials can charge offenders with contravening the law.

Quantifying criminal events is difficult and causes many problems and much controversy. Generally, two types of records are tracked for information research. First, statistics are kept by virtually all law enforcement agencies, but these refer only to events that are reported. In the United States approximately 80 crimes per 1,000 people are reported annually, while in Canada approximately 75 crimes per 1,000 people are reported. In Europe and other areas, crime rates vary widely because some areas are experiencing violence related to war. Another way to quantify and compare criminal events is to compile victim-related statistics. For example, the United Nations sponsors an annual record called the UN Survey on Crime Trends and the Operations of Criminal Justice Systems. The former European Crime and Safety Survey recently became the International Crime Victims Survey (ICVS), which is produced by the European Union.

Crimes involving property (such as vandalism or forgery) have serious personal implications for the victims, but are considered to be minor and less serious than *crimes against persons* (such as assault or homicide). *Violent and sexual crimes* are considered to be the most serious violations, causing the greatest degree of individual harm. Some crimes (such as *war crimes* and *genocide*) are directed toward an entire group of people. There are also *victimless crimes* (such as jaywalking or gambling, which involve risk but lack any personal, identifiable victim) but not all jurisdictions recognize this as a valid category. The criminal injustice of some actions (such as political protest and some types of medical research) is debated.

Worldwide, crime imposes enormous costs on people and societies, but precision about the real costs is impossible to discover. There are many reasons:

- The vast majority of crimes are not reported to authorities and are not tracked by official statistics.
- Actions covered by the criminal justice system are technically directed against society, and are considered a breach of society's peace, effectively overlooking the many people who are seriously affected by every crime.
- Crimes are recorded inconsistently.
- Crimes are not isolated actions, but usually occur with intention, planning, attempt, and completion, and they may occur in the context of a criminal lifestyle.
- Crime rates and the safety index of a society vary indirectly: the higher the crime rate, the lower the safety index. However, there is almost no uniformity in these measures.

Justice and the Criminal Court System Retributive justice is the paradigm behind nearly all official responses to crime. The **criminal justice system** refers to the entire network of laws and enforcement through many branches of police work, indictment of infractions, and imposition of penalties on the guilty. Although rules and laws are intended to prevent wrongdoing and crime, the work of the criminal justice system deals with misdeeds. In this system, conflicts are technically between an accused individual and a state, and conflict is resolved by specially trained and empowered authorities such as judges, juries, or tribunals. Carefully detailed fair procedures are obligatory at every step.

Formal charges or accusations are made and the conflict is submitted to the adversarial court system. The state and the defendant each argue for a particular interpretation of the facts, presenting witness testimony to support their position. Inquiry results in a judgment that supports one interpretation and disproves the other. If guilty of the accusation, the wrongdoer bears the penalty dictated by the law, and justice is deemed to have been established.

Incarceration and Imprisonment The ubiquitous influence of crime in our neighborhoods is a concern to most people and to all governments. The need for an effective approach is clear. **Incarceration** is the restriction of an individual's human rights in proportion with the harm or injustice their crime caused (Mauer, 2017). North American prisons were established and are maintained by governments or their designates. Prisons are set up with varying degrees of security and inmate freedom, linked to the seriousness of the crime, the terms of the sentence, and the present risk of violence. Prisons house and work separately with youth under 18 years old, and both male adult and female adult populations. Provisions are sometimes made for female inmates to continue to parent their children while in prison.

Worldwide, approximately 14 million people (144 per 100,000) are detained in pretrial detention or postconviction sentence at any one time, but rates vary greatly across regions. The United States has the highest incarceration rate in the world (655 per 100,000 in 2018), incarcerating more people annually than 35 European countries combined (162 per 100,000). Canada's rate is substantially lower (107 per 100,000). The lowest rate (12 per 100,000) is found in Denmark's Faeroe Islands (Walmsley, 2018).

Recent trends are toward substantially higher rates of incarceration and higher minimum punishments, as well as decreased use of alternatives such as parole and conditional release. During the 1990s, incarceration rates grew by approximately 20% in almost all countries, and that trend continues in the 21st century. In the United States, incarceration rates increased by 300% after 1990 (Walmsley, 2018).

Multiple, complex reasons are behind these apparent trends (Walmsley, 2003):

- increased, more immediate access to media reports of dramatic criminal events;
- higher rates of crime, which may or may not be uniformly categorized;
- lengthening mandatory minimum sentences for conviction;
- probably most important are the changing attitudes of the general public and particularly among key groups such as legislators, prosecutors and judges, and the media, including
  o widespread fear of crime,
  o increased popular support for retributive justice,
  o loss of confidence in justice alternatives,
  o disappointment with the effectiveness of treatment and rehabilitation, and
  o belief that incarceration is preferable to other alternatives (Kuhn, 2001).

These trends lead to secondary problems with overcrowded and understaffed institutions, yielding poor and unsafe living conditions and quality of life for detainees. Increased conflict, as well as potential and actual violence within prisons, are commonly reported. Programs that are likely to support successful transition back into the community following release are imperfect (Walmsley, 2018).

Scholars disagree. Some argue that increases of incarceration rates suggest more effective policing and trial procedures; some argue that our societies are increasingly punitive and restrictive. Many take the view that providing wrongdoers with reformative or transformative experiences is preferable to punishment. For example, in 2010 the American Psychological Association adopted a strong motion urging national governments, agencies, and professionals to develop and support research, education, and services that would more adequately satisfy the psychosocial needs of court defendants, incarcerated offenders, and their families (Western, 2010).

Some certainties of prison systems form the objections to their overuse:

Prisons are expensive.

- Financially: Throughout North America, costs of housing each federal inmate are estimated between US$35,000 and $115,000 annually, with variation according to inmate gender, location, and level of security (Hyle, 2018).
- In long-term impact: Although incarceration is for a limited period, fallout effects are extensive. For example, prior to incarceration, about 66% of inmates were employed and 50% were the primary source of family income. After release, less than 50% are reemployed in the first year and employed convicts experience significant reductions in hourly wages and duration of employment, resulting in a 40% reduction in annual earnings (Decker, 2014).
- In collateral effects: Although punishment through incarceration is directed toward the individual wrongdoer, many other people's lives are affected and the unmeasured costs ripple throughout the interpersonal network. In the United States, 2.7 million children have at least one parent who is incarcerated. Twenty-three percent of these children were suspended or expelled from school annually, compared with 4% of children who had no incarcerated parent (Western, 2010).

Prisons aren't fair.

One of the primary principles of justice is that people are treated equally, without regard for identities of race, gender, or age. However, in the real criminal justice system, there is no way to make identity invisible or irrelevant (Butler, 2016). Even judges who have the intention of impartiality come to different conclusions based on the same evidence, and this forms the basis of the appeals system.

Race and ethnicity are probably the most blatant illustration of these effects. Although less than 1% of white North Americans are incarcerated, people of visible ethnic origin are overrepresented in prison populations: nearly 3% are Hispanics, more than 8% are North Americans of African descent, and something close to 20% are Indigenous peoples (Canada, 2018). The population of North American women inmates is approximately 20% that of men. Youth under 18 years of age represent more than 20% of all charges and convictions (Canada, 2018).

Prisons don't work.

People facing the retributive justice system deal with impersonal judges, not with their victims, and community members participate only as observers or as witnesses to a factual recitation of events. Offenders therefore remain largely isolated from the real human costs and consequences of their actions. One recent development in some jurisdictions is the introduction of Victim Impact Statements after conviction and before sentencing, when the court and the offender can hear the losses experienced by a victim and the community.

Recidivism is a concept derived from the Latin word for "fall"; it means a fall back into criminal behavior and the criminal justice system despite experiencing its punitive consequences. Approximately 15% of all paroled inmates return to jail, varying by the type of crime and later correction methods. Repeated recidivism can result in habitual criminal patterns, or a criminal lifestyle.

In effect, prisons may be part of a retributory cycle: crime occurs in reaction to social injustice, but also causes further injustice; injustice punished retributively furthers the cycle (Redekop, 2008). Corrective learning that results from incarceration is questionable. Michel Foucault (1977) strongly criticized the intended reformation and relearning goals of punishment as ineffective, stating that punishment is merely a controlling force that uses power to threaten, coerce, and suppress people.

Prisons don't provide justice for victims.

Much research on the victims of crime suggests that they are routinely excluded from the justice-making process, and experience only difficult recovery. Victims benefit little from retribution. Rather, to experience justice, victims need:

1. Answers to personally urgent questions—why me? was I to blame? could I have done something to prevent the events?
2. Protection and separation from the offender to reestablish security—this need is a two-edged sword: separation may be necessary for security and safety, but also crystallizes alienating isolation for both offender and victim.
3. Acknowledgment of the wrong and the resulting personal loss—community members can be very helpful with this, communicating "we care, we recognize this wrong, and will work to prevent future problems."
4. Reparation—restoration of safety, trust in the world, and personal control (Newmark, 2006; Zehr, 2014).

Think About and Discuss with Your Colleagues

- People have different ideas about the sentences which should be given to offenders. Take for instance the case of a man 21 years old who is found guilty of a burglary for the second time. This time he stole a color TV. Discuss which of the following penalties you consider the most appropriate: fine, prison, community service, suspended sentence or any other sentence? If you opted for imprisonment, specify the length (after A. Kuhn).

Alternatives to Incarceration within the Retributive Justice System Many unintended but serious complications are related to systems of imprisonment, so scholars and practitioners are continuously exploring alternatives to more effectively accomplish the worthy goals set out. A few examples of currently used alternatives include:

- Court Diversion—accused wrongdoers are referred, or diverted, to community agencies that have expertise in skill building and working through conflicted relationships.
- Sentencing Circle—after an offender has been convicted of a crime, dialogue among members of the community is used to determine the penalty. The circle usually includes the offender, the victim, community support people, and a judge. Discussion of the problems and circumstances occurs, moving toward consensus about an appropriate sentence for the offender, and commitments are made by each participant to keep the peace and cultivate positive relationships. A common outcome is that the offender will agree to make specific amends for the crime.
- Community Service—a guilty person compensates for their wrongdoing with hours of unpaid service to the community.

Experiments with a large variety of alternatives to incarceration are ongoing, including conditional release, conditional sentencing or probation, intermittent sentencing, fines, and therapeutic imprisonment. These options are intended to support reintegration of offenders into the community.

Think About and Discuss with Your Colleagues

- How do you understand "Order Restoring Justice"? In what ways are procedural justice and retributive justice similar and different? Do you think order is restored using these methods for justice making?

Equity-Restoring Justice

One concept of injustice focuses on unequal access to privileges, responsibilities, or roles that betrays a fundamental disrespect for some persons and disregard for their rights. This is also called structural violence (Galtung, 1969). If injustice is caused by inequity, justice making promotes equity and balanced rights and responsibilities so that just relationships are possible and conflict is prevented. Two forms of justice making within this paradigm are Distributive Justice and Restorative Justice.

Distributive Justice Paradigm

The Concept Distributive justice is based on a principle of equality as an undeniable baseline in a just society. Members are equally free, have equal responsibility, and fairly share social benefits. Distributive justice is cooperative and participatory: all members of a just group have the opportunity to contribute to common life. Specific questions addressed are:

- What resources, benefits, and opportunities exist?
- What responsibilities are reasonably demanded?
- What principles of fair decision making are used?
- Are the benefits distributed fairly?

In this paradigm, unfair distribution is wrong. Basic benefits, opportunities, and/or power are available only to some people, and inequality and injustice are experienced as humiliating subordination and dependency, and unmet needs (Butler, 2016). If people think they receive an unfair share of something, they will try to gain their entitlement. This will likely cause social unrest and conflict. Correction of this type of injustice was the driving force behind the Occupy Movement, started in 2011 in the United States.

A graphic illustration of distributive justice and injustice is found in the **Gini Coefficient,** which is a comparative measure of global economic justice. Similarity of family incomes within a nation results in a lower Gini index, or 0% when all resources are distributed identically; income inequity indicates a disparity between the rich ("the haves") and the poor ("the have-nots"), and results in a higher Gini index, or 100% in the extreme. In the latest estimates, highest Gini indexes were found in Lesotho (63.2) and South Africa (62.5) while the lowest ranks were found in Jersey (0.3) and Denmark's Faroe Islands (22.7). Canada's index was 32.1, and the United States was 45.0 (CIA, 2019). This index is maintained by the US Central Intelligence Agency, and extrapolated for use as a predictor of national discontent and divisive conflict.

Distributive Justice in Everyday Life Some practical ways that distributive justice is promoted are through taxation and international aid. Injustice is righted by redistribution of resources held disproportionally by some people or groups. In many societies, distributive justice is achieved through the regular sharing of benefit programs like a minimum living wage, social assistance, and health care access programs.

Several issues and controversies frustrate the principles of distributive justice.

- Some say that there are certain fundamental requirements such as adequate nutrition and health care that are nonnegotiable when considering equity issues;
- Some debate the criteria for "fair distribution" (Konow, 2001). Possibilities are:
  o need—each person's share is based on a minimum human requirement;
  o accountability—a person's share is determined by variables that can be personally controlled (for example, willingness to work) rather than by variables that cannot be controlled (for example, a personal handicap); and
  o efficiency—each person's share represents a reasonable proportion of the total resources available.

- Those with the power to determine the criteria defining "fair" may also have a personal interest in the outcome (such as a government agriculture official who is also a farmer). They may be motivated to analyze and determine justice in ways that benefit and preserve their own group.

In *Pearson v. Chung*, distributive injustice could be identified in two ways: the Chung family may not have lived up to their responsibilities ("Satisfaction Guaranteed"), and/or Judge Pearson may have used the privileges of his powerful position to overwhelm the Chungs with his demands. Distributive justice making in their case could involve inquiring into the factual existence of injustice, followed by negotiating the responsibilities for the problem to determine an equitable balance between the parties, thus settling the conflict.

Restorative Justice Paradigm

The Concept Restorative justice in North America was developed in contrast to the retributive justice paradigm. It is a traditional paradigm, much older than most current models. Most cultures throughout history developed similar community based justice making, so much of our contemporary growth of the restorative justice paradigm is based on the recovery of previously neglected traditional principles and methods.

A main critique of the procedural justice and retributive justice paradigms is their emphasis on abstractions—the wrongdoer's actions, the relevant rules, established procedures, and prescribed consequences for antisocial actions. Restorative justice represents a fundamental shift in how offenses and injustice are interpreted. In the **Restorative Justice** paradigm (often abbreviated RJ), wrongdoing is seen as a sign of a wounded person or damaged relationship. Any wrongdoing that jeopardizes safety and trust is unjust and results in hurt and loss for a victim, the community, and the offender. Restorative justice making occurs in the context of a whole community. Restorative justice asks,

1. Who has been hurt, including the victim, the offender, and members of the community?
2. What are their needs, and how do we ensure those needs are met?
3. How can things be made right, and whose obligations are these? (Zehr, 2014).

There is strong rationale for RJ. The paradigm assumes that the underlying causes of wrongdoing are important, and attempts to correct these. Addictions, weak employment skill, and inadequate family moral base are some potential risk factors for antisocial behavior. Most people on the "wrong" side of society have already experienced too many broken relationships, and their wrongdoing is the outcome of community breakdown. Justice making should provide opportunities to correct wrong actions and form new ways of belonging in their own communities. It is the community that deals with wrongdoing, conflict, and longer-term consequences. Conflict can break or build community cohesion and skill. Restorative practices include everyone affected by injustice, attempting to fulfill their needs. In this way, the original conflict can be used to construct healthier relationships.

RJ provides community members with constructive guidance. Human and financial resources can be redirected away from punishment toward repair.

Restorative Justice in Everyday Life Injustice harms people, sometimes dreadfully, and wrongdoing exposes the need for mending to restore peace. The central focus of restorative justice making is repair, so RJ is sometimes called *reparative justice*.

The restorative justice paradigm developed simultaneously in many settings, beginning in the latter 20th century, and spread rapidly around the world. Exploration continues in countless situations of injustice. Family circle mediation is often used in instances of severe family conflict, for example. Many school systems use RJ to promote positive community building, and as an alternative to the more common punishment system. RJ is used in criminal justice systems to divert people from criminal court procedures. Victim-offender mediation is used to address the human costs of criminal conflict. Indigenous and many other traditional communities are reviving lost customs that are founded on RJ principles.

Each relevant person could be included in the resolution process, so restorative justice making is complex. Practically, it requires careful discernment and does not succeed if a formulaic procedure is followed. Methods used for justice making are called **restorative practices**, founded on four distinct principles (Van Ness, 2010).

1. *Inclusion* and encounter—People affected by injustice as wrongdoer or as victim have an opportunity to work together, with community support, to create solutions.
2. Collaborative, *participatory* resolution—RJ brings together a range of skills to explore, promote, and maintain peace through the collaboration of primary parties and community members.
3. Positive *change*—Restoration of peaceful relationships is the goal. This means, on the one hand, denouncing harmful actions and, on the other hand, exploring reconciliation of everyone affected by the wrongdoing.
4. *Restoration* of what was damaged—Using restorative practices, people causing trouble are offered ways to take responsibility, repair the damages, ease the healing of those injured by their actions, and be restored to healthy participation in their communities.

Restorative practices usually occur in a **circle process**, which is an intense sequential dialogue guided by a facilitator, literally in a circle. The goal of the circle process is for wrongdoers to take responsibility for their actions and the harmful consequences and, in return, to be offered ways of making amends. Intense vulnerability and demanding honesty are required of every participant. First, there is an encounter among the victim and supporters, the offender and supporters, and witnesses and community members. The encounter usually happens face-to-face and in a circle so everyone sees and hears everyone else. Second, participants take turns describing the events and the ongoing aftermath. Third, discussion focuses on the needs of each participant, and actions that could help heal their distress. Fourth, pathways toward reintegrating the wrongdoer into the community are discussed to signal renewed dignity and acceptance (Zehr, 2014).

The results of circle processes have been scrutinized in numerous research studies. Participants report less later conflict, both specifically in troubled relationships and also generally in the community. Circle process, when used as a diversion from court, reduces financial and judicial costs (although RJ practices can be emotionally costly). Victims of wrongdoing experience higher levels of satisfaction, both with the participatory process and also with the outcomes. Offenders accept responsibility for their actions, and recidivism rates are reduced (Public Safety Canada, 2003; Sherman, 2007).

Restorative practices cannot be used in every case of conflict or crime, and not all circle processes are completed successfully. Zehr (2014) described a continuum of outcomes in a range from fully restorative, mostly restorative, potentially restorative, to not restorative. Sometimes vulnerability is so immediate that participants are unable to provide the honest disclosure that is necessary. RJ procedures should never be used if a wrongdoer is unable to accept responsibility because of compromised mental health or development. Sometimes people participate for reasons other than to create justice or peace, and circle process cannot be successful for those who have insincere or selfish motives. More harm than good can result from intense encounters with wrongdoers who deny responsibility for their actions or show little remorse or commitment to safe relationships. Victimless crimes (such as drug possession) also do not lend themselves to the RJ process.

Restorative Justice applied to *Pearson v. Chung*, would probably take the form of facilitated mediation between members of the Chung family and Judge Pearson.

- This would involve a trained facilitator who would initially interview all participants to ensure that their motives and goals were suited to the RJ process.
- If appropriate, then, a face-to-face encounter would be arranged. Each party would detail their perception and interpretation of the unfolding conflict and describe the personal impact. Both sides would be encouraged to take responsibility for any actions that contributed to the trouble.
- Judge Pearson and the Chungs would discuss possible reparation of losses that resulted, and begin the process of reconciliation, if feasible.
- The ideal outcome of such a mediation would be that Judge Pearson and the Chung family would live respectfully and peaceably in the same community, as they presumably did before the conflict began.

Think About and Discuss with Your Colleagues

- How do you understand "Equity Restoring Justice"? In what ways are distributive justice and restorative justice similar and different? What is restored with restorative practices? Do you think equity is restored using these types of justice making?

PRAXIS: PRACTICAL METHODS OF RESOLVING CONFLICT WITH JUSTICE

A factor important to conflict, conflict resolution, and justice making is the involvement of the relevant parties. Simplified, this reasonably involves a few people:

- Include someone who has something to do with the problem, and
- include someone who has something to do with the solution.

Single-Party Justice Making

Some conflicts (likely many) are settled or solved by one single party. Someone can legitimately decide that an issue is not worth fighting over or processing directly, and simply ignore the conflict and choose to overlook it. If the sense of injustice remains unsettled and the party is unable to figure out what to do, they could seek conflict **coaching**, which is expert advice offered to a disputant to coach more effective alternative skills and techniques. Another solo option is the difficult process of forgiving the Other for offenses and hurts, rebuilding trust, and possibly reconciling the relationship. Ideally, this is an interpersonal process, but forgiveness can be found by one party alone. Forgiveness will be explored in more detail in Chapter 12.

Two-Party, Direct Conflict Resolution

Problem Solving

The majority of daily conflicts are resolved by the primary parties using conversation and problem solving to deal with tensions and find reasonable and just solutions. In fact, the many times conflicts are solved directly, agreeably, and peaceably are a testament to everyday skill and values. **Problem solving** is a method of conflict resolution that focuses on the problem causing conflict. Differences of perspective do not necessarily escalate to a conflict because they can be solved by one person or two working together.

Two-party problem solving is known to be a complex human skill, involving component skills of introspection, information processing, and willingness to communicate and cooperate. In its best expression, problem solving challenges relationship skills because good process is based on trust, communication, and supportive collaboration. These skills are used both to address particular issues, but then also to develop competence to solve new problems when they come up. Problem solving can easily become stalled if parties cannot agree on what the problem is, or when they prematurely jump to solutions without adequately considering alternatives. See Chapter 3 for a more complete exploration of problem solving.

Negotiation

Negotiation is a reciprocating dialogue and exchange of information, ideas, and promises, usually between two parties who exchange proposals and counterproposals, and tentative plans. Participants give and gain information about the scope of a problem and their own and others' needs and priorities, in most instances against the backdrop of continuing relationships and events. Most negotiations involve elements of both competitive and cooperative communication. The majority of negotiations are successful and solve contentious issues.

Negotiated justice simultaneously addresses rational, interpersonal, and psychological concerns (Wertheim, 1996). The *rational level* systematically addresses the substantive issues of the conflict. *Interpersonal* rapport and trust are starting points for decisions about participation, expectations of the process and/or the outcome. How much the parties like or dislike each other, how important it is to avoid conflict, and how important it is to win the argument (and not look foolish) influence the negotiations. The *psychological factors* are more complex, and are especially affected by the parties' comfort with and attitude about the problem, the conflict, and each other. They also include assumptions and perception (or misperceptions) of the other party, self, and the problem, which can covertly but powerfully influence the process and outcomes.

a. *Distributive Negotiation*

Distributive negotiation, also called **positional bargaining** and **hard bargaining,** occurs when resources are limited and only one person can achieve what they want (like who will get that last sports ticket or how money will be spent). The parties then assume that their interests are in competition: what one party wins, the other party loses, called the *zero sum* or *fixed pie assumption.* The aim of the dialogue is personal gain using any possible advantage over the opponent, so the negotiation is competitive and the oppositional tone can jeopardize an ongoing relationship. A distributive negotiation strategy emphasizes, first, protecting or defending ones' own interests and, second, confrontive power tactics such as argumentation, self-promotion, threats to fire you or to withdraw an offer, and even lying to control the outcome. Because continuing the relationship is not a central goal, *brinksmanship* often pushes the conversation to the verge of breaking. Deliberately introducing an extreme or unrealistic demand to trick or mislead the opponent is not unusual.

A sample of these tactics is illustrated in the *British Diplomat Service Manual.* "Nothing may be said which is not true, but it is as unnecessary as it is sometimes undesirable to say everything relevant which is true. The facts given may be arranged in any convenient order. The perfect reply to an embarrassing question is one that is brief, appears to answer the question completely (if challenged it can be proved to be accurate in every word), gives no opening for awkward follow-up questions, and discloses really nothing." Strategies such as concealing information or intentions, and flatly resisting the other person's ideas or suggestions form an adversarial dialogue, with an unresponsive, veiled tone. Many people consider such tactics to be unethical.

Emmy Wertheim (1996) articulated a set of questions that underly distributive negotiation, consciously or subconsciously as a negotiation is conducted. **Mini-Max** questions help discover the strongest and weakest points and balance risk with potential gains:
- What is the minimum gain I can accept that will solve the problem?
- What is the maximum I can demand without appearing outrageous?
- What is the minimum I can offer without appearing outrageous?
- What is the maximum I can give away or concede?

"It's not enough that we succeed. Cats must also fail."

Figure 10.1 "It's not enough that we succeed. Cats must also fail."
www.CartoonCollections.com.

The Mini-Max Approach also involves trying to guess the other party's answers to these questions.

Although the outcome is not fully predictable, a distributive negotiation usually has a win-lose result (illustrated in Figure 10.1), with maximum gain for one party and maximum loss for the other. The dialogue risks increasing rather than decreasing the tension between opponents. Negotiators often worry about being overpowered, so defensiveness and dissatisfaction with the outcome are common, meaning that the conflict is likely to be revisited.

Cooperation may not be an option if one party refuses to cooperate, or if the disputed resources are truly scarce. Distributive negotiation is often a one-time dialogue that is successful in the short term but does not address long term problems or solutions.

b. *Integrative Negotiation*

An alternative pattern of negotiation is called **integrative negotiation, collaborative negotiation,** and **soft bargaining.** This pattern occurs in interdependent relationships, allowing negotiators to maximize joint benefits and common interests. As Mary Parker Follett (2013) stated, "[W]hen two desires are integrated, that means a solution has been found in which both desires have found a place, and neither side has had to sacrifice anything." You can address everyone's needs without overriding any. The goal of integrative negotiation is a solution that satisfies all parties without unreasonable compromise.

Integrative negotiation contrasts sharply with distributive negotiation by including such trust-based tactics as information sharing, disclosure of real interests and exploration of differences, reciprocal give-and-take, and noncoercive power sharing. *Expand the pie* tactics can be used to add additional resources to the discussion; *cutting costs* can make limited resources less critical; and *logrolling* occurs when the parties give up something that does not cost very much because it is valued by the opponent.

Because ongoing relationship is valued, integrative negotiators are rarely confrontational. Communication is open and direct; they "mean what they say and say what they mean." It requires a level of risky trust and more time and creativity than distributive negotiation. Negotiators consider multiple positions without overlooking any, and try to find common goals and interests rather than singular ones such as winning. Decisions are reached by consensus. The goal is mutually agreeable maximum gain and minimal loss for both parties. If both sides can see that they are further ahead than when they started, the ongoing relationship is comparatively stable.

Integrative negotiation is best used when an ongoing relationship is desirable or necessary. This process can safeguard the interests of a community beyond the individual bargainers. This type of negotiation is fair to individuals, and generally takes into account other parties affected by the resolution.

c. *Principled or Problem-Solving Negotiation*
In 1979, Harvard University created the Harvard Negotiation Project under the direction of William Ury and Roger Fisher. The project developed a third process for negotiation, called **principled negotiation** and **problem-solving negotiation** (Fisher, 2011). The starting point for negotiation is not problems, but agreement to follow four process principles:
1. Separate the people from the problem;
2. Find ways to focus on interests, not positions;
3. Brainstorm and generate alternatives for mutual gain, creating an extensive list of practical solutions; then
4. Use objective criteria to define "success."

If agreement is reached to use these principles, the negotiation is usually fairly straightforward. Negotiators analyze their own interests, potentially satisfying and just solutions, and possible consequences of accepting each solution. Negotiators realistically consider the **alternatives to a negotiated agreement,** asking themselves, "if we are unable to negotiate a just agreement, what are our alternatives?" Imagining the *best alternative to a negotiated agreement* (BATNA) and the *worst alternative to a negotiated* *agreement* (WATNA) give negotiators a picture of the limits to and urgency of the negotiation. These factors are then openly discussed to create and agree on a testable solution to the shared problem.

Distributive, integrative, and principled negotiation are well researched. They are rarely used singly. Many negotiators begin with distributive tactics; when that is less than successful, they move on to integrative methods; in the best instances, the final negotiations use principled tactics to reach a satisfying agreement.

Nonnegotiation Using Dominance, Force, and Violence

An unfortunate strategy used to deal with a problem or injustice is to bypass negotiation and overwhelm the opponent, using force to end the conflict or compel a supposed solution. It can only succeed when one party has significantly more power than the other.

Clearly, this strategy might silence a problem or injustice, but it does not make justice. Force is experienced by most recipients as illegitimate and unjust, so it usually causes resistance and the use of counterforce. The strategy risks direct escalation of the conflict from confrontation to aggression to violence. At best, the supposed resolution will be unjust, and generate chilling resentment or directly compromise the relationship.

Some people believe that this strategy is legitimately used to address wrong actions and injustice when the consequences of doing nothing are no longer acceptable, an injustice causes a crisis or urgency to solve the problem, or the injustice has important ethical or legal implications.

Think About and Discuss with Your Colleagues

Undoubtedly, you use negotiation techniques for nonadversarial conflict resolution every day.

- Does your style tend to be distributive (competitive) or integrative (cooperative)?
- Do you think the principles of problem-solving negotiation would help? How?
- Under what circumstances do you think it is legitimate to use force?

Third-Party Resolution

Sometimes, the primary parties become so entangled in an unpleasant or perpetuating conflict that they appeal for help. A helper-facilitator, called the **third party**, works with the parties. Sometimes an informal, untrained helper such as a relative or friend steps in as third party; sometimes the appeal is to a trained, professional helper such as a counselor or trained mediator. Third parties might be invited for several reasons: the parties feel stuck and inadequate to solve the problems themselves and the third party is a person trusted by everyone to objectively apply wisdom or justice to influence the process constructively.

Third parties take a variety of roles and they must be ready to switch roles during the process. Expectations of a third party are subtly serious. You generally do not invite help from someone who is biased, so you look for someone who is perceived to be *disinterested* or *neutral,* unbiased and having nothing to gain personally from the conflict or its outcome. A third party who wants one or the other party to win, or tries to direct the outcome toward a specific conclusion, is considered to have a *conflict of interest*. Therefore, they are not likely to be an effective help.

There are many advantages to asking an outside person to facilitate a conflict. Because long-term conflict is emotionally draining, and adversarial processes can be financially costly, third parties can often shorten the periods of conflict and diminish potential costs. A disinterested third party can highlight blind spots or difficulties that could lead to a compounded argument, and also point to common ground for the parties.

The strengths of third-party intervention are criticized by some people because they can artificially suppress conflict. Outside intervention does not always permit the full expression of emotions and concerns and, therefore, may not bring lasting changes in perception or viewpoint. Because the focus is on resolving problem issues, fundamental relationship injustice such as power inequality sometimes remain unsolved. The presence of a third party means that the conflict is no longer completely personal and private.

Adjudication

Adjudication is a form of adversarial conflict resolution in which a dispute is submitted for judgment to a fair, authoritative third party who has the power to issue a binding decision. Typically, judicial justice making happens in several steps. Decisions at each step could settle a conflict, or it might continue to the next step. One party realizes that a conflict exists and efforts to resolve it have failed. The complainant, called the *plaintiff*, lodges a formal grievance, and the other party, called the *respondent*, must answer the complaint. Advocates, usually lawyers, often become involved to indirectly negotiate the complaint or argue the conflict before the third party. The authority considers and recommends alternatives, and the conflict is settled by decision or judgment.

Note several key features of this process:

- A just outcome demands that the authority is independent, unbiased, and not influenced by personal interests.
- Parties become involved who are not affected by the dispute or its resolution.
- The role of the authority is to safeguard the debate process, ensuring fair procedures and conformity to relevant regulations and laws.
- Resolution of the conflict is based on the authority and power of the third party, which functions to equalize disputants' power and limit their tactics. Adjudication therefore takes place within a system of controlled pyramidal power, which has many safeguards, checks, and balances.
- Adjudication is not consensual, and does force participants to comply with the decision of the authority. As happened to both Judge Pearson and the Chung family, this often results in disputant dissatisfaction with the process and/or the outcome. This sometimes results in noncompliance with the authority's decision and then leads to a new complaint and response sequence.

In the United States, several judicial systems exist in parallel: the federal and the state systems, and courts of military appeals, courts of claims, and courts of international trade. Each is governed by a unique system of regulations and personnel. Judges are elected democratically, or appointed by a state governor in the case of a vacancy. The Supreme Court is the court of appeal for all the streams. In Canada, the judicial system of military, provincial, and federal courts is unified. Judges are appointed by the government. The Supreme Court of Canada handles appealed judgments.

Most participants in adjudication complain that the process is expensive: financially, in time, and in stress. Therefore, the legal community has made heroic efforts in recent decades to invent alternatives that divert this adversarial process to resolve conflicts in less costly ways. Formally, this is called **alternative dispute resolution** (ADR), which is a field flourishing within the conflict community. The following are a few examples of ADR:

- In civil disputes, a judge might offer Judicially Assisted Dispute Resolution (JADR). This confidential, nonbinding negotiation is guided by a judge who evaluates the case and tries to advise resolution.
- In family or divorce court, a *case management judge* might divert marital or parent-child conflict to a service such as family conciliation for mediation.
- Neighborhood disputes are frequently referred for community mediation prior to a hearing.

Arbitration

An **arbitration** is controlled and decided by an expert third party called an *arbiter* or *arbitrator*. For a particularly contentious conflict, there may be a panel or tribunal of more than one arbitrator. Professional arbitrators are trained in formal legal procedures, based on the principles of procedural justice, but arbitration is not judicial. Arbitrators have significant influence on decisions about the resolution of a conflict, but do not have the authority to enforce resolution the way a judge might.

A trained, unbiased arbitrator is chosen and trusted by the parties to hear evidence from both sides of a dispute. There are two possible starting assumptions: in *binding arbitration*, the parties agree in advance that they will comply with the arbitrator's decision; in *nonbinding arbitration*, the parties wait to hear the recommended resolution before deciding whether or not to follow it. Presentation of the case is an adversarial process during which each party argues the validity and worth of their position. The arbitrator hears all the arguments and suggests a settlement, but the parties determine actions they are willing to take to solve the problems.

Deliberate escalation of tension may be used at times to force an arbitration, and this may be perceived as unfair. Some disputants object to the outcomes, feeling disempowered by the process, but generally the disputing parties have significant input into the settlement terms.

Arbitration is likely to be successful when it is voluntary and consensual. It is used to assist resolution of many types of conflict, commonly including labor, neighborhood, contract, and financial disputes. Because of its focus on the content of a conflict rather than on a relationship, arbitration is not applied to personal disputes such as family or marital conflicts.

Mediation

Mediation is a nonadversarial negotiation designed to help disputing parties to fully identify and discuss the problems and explore mutually acceptable solutions (Zutter, 2007). The disputing parties participate voluntarily. The mediator typically is a professional person, trained to facilitate discussions without imposing a solution. Their work practices are consistent with the *Model Standards for Mediators* (2005). *Facilitator* and *mediator* are customary names describing this third-party role.

Although specific roles vary according to the situation, mediators use common procedures and skills (Beer, 2012).

1. *Advanced preparation* ensures that parties have consented and are committed to resolution, and are ready for disclosure. This usually involves interviews with the conflicted parties and their support people.
2. After entry into the mediation, the third party assists the disputants to establish **groundrules,** which are guidelines for behavior that participants agree to, that set the tone for the interactions.
3. A face-to-face *mediation* usually involves several sessions, and has some common steps:
   - disputants discuss the problem and find agreement on its meaning;
   - each party details their perspective on the background to the conflict and the issues of contention, and acknowledge each others' viewpoint;
   - the parties develop consensus on the central issues that need resolution;
   - both parties generate and negotiate possible options and solutions; and
   - the parties reach a decision to take a shared course of action.
4. Ideally, the parties *test* out the solution for several weeks or months, and meet again to *review* the relationship and, if needed, revise the plan for continuing or altering the solution.

Mediation is appropriate and effective under specific conditions. Successful resolution is likely when contentious issues are clear and not muddled, disputing parties value a continuing relationship and are willing to work for it, and participants' power is roughly balanced. The process is likely to end in stalemate and is not recommended if used coercively or in violent situations, if it substitutes for proper authority, or when counseling or psychotherapy are needed.

NON-WESTERN JUSTICE MAKING

It is important to know that most of the information in this chapter aligns with Western, Judeo-Christian concepts of justice, which primarily use confrontational transactions to address conflict (Brett, 2010). Those methods are by no means universally applicable (Walker, 2004). Other societies have memorialized traditional methods of creating justice and resolving conflict that have a much longer history than that of the West. Probably a majority of the world's population continues to operate with non-Western, traditional concepts. These traditions are described as community processes for transforming a conflict from a desire for revenge (in our terms, retributive justice) to a willingness to forgive (transformative justice) (Ajayi, 2014; Pely, 2011).

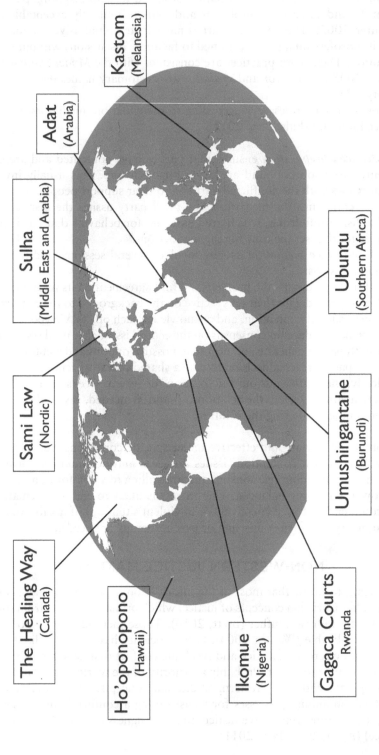

Figure 10.2 Traditional, non-Western justice making and conflict-resolution methods

Alternative traditions are typified by the ancient African term, *ubuntu*. A rough translation is "I am human because of who we all are," and the term connotes "what separates us is not very great" (Tutu, 2012). Even in places where Western justice was previously imposed by colonizers, a global movement is reviving diverse traditional tribal methods of conflict resolution and justice making. See Figure 10.2, which illustrates the locations of a few of these traditional, non-Western methods.

Specific methods of resolving conflict in traditional communities and cultures are highly diverse. However, the methods have some common characteristics:

- They are *community* initiated, often organized by community elders, and the community accepts some responsibility for instigating and resolving the problem.
- They are based on *local definitions* of justice, often closely linked with spiritual practices.
- They are *ceremonial*, and very different from Western justice-making procedures.
- *Goals* of these traditional processes (after Fortune, 2001) are:
  1. truth telling by and for everyone;
  2. naming the injustice and validating the suffering uncovered;
  3. compassion for all, but especially for victims and their healing;
  4. protecting vulnerable people;
  5. wrongdoer accountability, making insight and understanding possible;
  6. repair and restore broken community relationships.
- *Practices* include elder oversight, direct confrontation among conflict parties without self-defense other than the presence of community witnesses, community consent for reparative agreements that aim to incorporate the interests of all parties, and symbolic ceremonial endings (Pely, 2011).

CHAPTER SUMMARY AND STUDY GUIDE

- Most conflicts are ignited by injustice, which in some way disregards the law, is disrespectful, and/or creates imbalanced relationship. Few conflicts can be truly resolved without justice making, which is both the process and outcome of restoring justice and fairness to all parties to a conflict. Justice making is peacemaking.
- The core of peaceable relationships and justice in conflict is fairness. Component meanings of justice are order, respect, and equity. Injustice occurs during conflict, and it creates an unfair situation. Successful resolution of conflict must address the primary nature of the injustice and create or restore justice.
- Procedural justice restores order by using strictly fair procedures to process conflict and make justice, usually involving an authoritative outsider. Retributive justice restores order by demanding a penalty from the person responsible when injustice happens.
- Distributive justice restores equity when privileges or resources have been distributed unfairly. Restorative justice addresses the losses and harm caused to every person affected by injustice.

- There are numerous informal and formal methods and practices for making justice and peace. Single-party, two-party, and third-party processes are legitimate forms.
- Professional adjudication in the courts is a formal adversarial method of addressing and settling conflict; in arbitration a trained expert uses similar procedures to outline a resolution.
- Nonadversarial conflict processing may occur using several types of negotiation; mediation involves the intervention of a trained conflict facilitator.
- There is a recent global movement to revive non-Western, traditional methods of settling conflict that rely on ceremonial community processes.

TERMS IN FOCUS

11

The Goals of Peacebuilding

■ ■ ■

In Focus in This Chapter:

■ Everyone experiences peace, but it is a multipart phenomenon and experience. Negative peace is the absence of conflict and violence, positive peace is harmony created by justice and needs fulfilment. A society's base culture can be depicted with a continuum of conflict to peace.

■ A peaceable society is made up of individuals who operate as global citizens. Good government is peaceable and helps maintain a civil society.

■ Sustained positive peace and harmonious relationships are founded on actions that are just, support human rights, value diversity, provide freedoms for everyone, and ensure a secure society.

■ There are multiple pathways to peace, categorized as negative peacebuilding and positive peacebuilding. Prevention of serious conflict is the first strategy.

POSITIVE PEACEBUILDER:
ASHOKA, EMPEROR OF INDIA, 273–232 BCE

Ashoka was born in 304 BCE, a prince with several older brothers who were in line for the throne of the Mauryan empire in India. As a boy, Ashoka was popular with his peers and excelled in academics and leadership. His eldest brother, Susima, was jealous of his skills and knowledge, so persuaded their father to send Ashoka on a risky military mission. When he was injured, he was treated by Buddhist monks and introduced to their teachings. Ashoka's crusades were repeatedly successful. This occurred at a time in India's history that had a tradition of "sacred warfare," which meant conquering the enemy by killing them. In the later competition to rule Maurya, Ashoka killed several brothers cruelly and ruthlessly.

In 273 BCE, he became the emperor of India, and expanded the empire through war. He won the gruesome Kalinga War in 265 BCE, during which countless people were killed and the region was completely plundered.

This became an unexpected turning point, however, as Ashoka was sickened by scenes of his own brutality. His shock and self-challenge—"What have I done?"—resulted in spiritual and political reformation. Ashoka vowed to model a new civility in India and never to perpetrate such violence again. He became a visionary for social welfare who was respectfully studied for many generations,

337

Figure 11.1 Drawing of Ashoka Chakra

including by Mohandas Gandhi (Schlichtmann, 2016). Sacred warfare became sacred reconciliation. His monarchy became benevolent and his rule was one of the most prosperous in India's history (see Figure 11.1). Ashoka adopted a new symbol for his empire by turning a chariot wheel into a peace wheel: the *Ashoka Chakra* (Violatti, 2018).

The core and ultimate goal of Peace and Conflict Studies is peace, in relationships, families and groups, society, and global relations. The first step toward peace is to deal with conflict in pacific ways that end fruitless struggle and violence. This is called negative peacebuilding. A more difficult step toward peace is to build the conditions that sustain peaceable processes by solving problems and reinforcing human interconnections. This is called positive peacebuilding. Together, negative and positive peacebuilding proactively help create a peaceable world.

When a society is at peace, features of global citizenship, good governance, and civil society exist. Sustained peace

> *We have the choice to live together on the earth like brothers and sisters, or to perish together like fools.*
> —*Martin Luther King*

is founded on vital justice, access to human rights, tolerance of diversity, freedom for all society members, and security from fear. Peace is threatened when any of those qualities are compromised.

The United Nations, in 1999, recognized distinctive cultures of fear and war and of peace and nonviolence. Much dialogue and research has occurred since then to identify and describe specific determinants of those cultures. As complex as peace is, there are numerous methods for establishing and maintaining it.

DEFINING THE TERMS AND CONCEPTS OF PEACE

"Peace" would mean entirely different things to

- a 13-year-old Congolese AIDS orphan trying to raise her three younger siblings;
- a soldier in the armed forces, serving in Afghanistan; and
- a politician in the embattled and divided US Senate.

Peace has been called a "fuzzy concept." Although it is deeply and personally meaningful, a definition is not fixed or precise. Many people use the term, believing that they are communicating an obvious meaning, but in actuality the concept has unique meanings for each person using it, and the implications vary according to context. Definitions of peace are subjective, even among scientists and scholars (Royce, 2004). Wolfgang Dietrich (2012) wrote about "many peaces."

The origins of the concept of peace are ancient, with references found in most societies and languages. The English word "peace" has its origin in Latin *pax* or *paix*, which has two associated meanings: freedom from disturbance, hostility, and quarrelling and, more emphatically, a tranquil relationship of harmony and goodwill.

Negative and Positive Peace

The concept of peace is refined by the distinction between negative peace and positive peace, most often associated with the work of Johan Galtung. **Negative peace** is the absence of tension, threat, open conflict, or violence. This is a typically Western understanding of the concept. Most political bodies focus on the settlement of active conflict, but focus little attention on its roots in adversarial relationships, troubled social conditions, or injustice. In a contrasting view of negative peacebuilding, some people believe that it is the duty of responsible citizens to "make trouble" for an unjust government.

Critique of negative peace is that it merely preserves the status quo of existing relationships but does nothing to relieve the roots of trouble. Leo Sandy and Ray Perkins (2002) proposed that this status quo *cold war* is characterized by mutual hostility but no direct battle; the war consists of indirect tactics such as propaganda and tangible preparations for aggression. In *cold peace*, hostility continues in a frozen sort of way, with no aggressive action, but also no efforts to build trust or collaboration. Peace can be *pseudopeace*, which is a false or sham peace. This occurs when protest and conflict are merely suppressed and silenced, as was attempted in the ongoing government response to thousands of Hong Kong youth protesting mainland Chinese rule. Martin Luther King wrote, "negative peace is the absence of tension; positive peace is the presence of justice" (1963).

Positive peace is multidimensional because it actively prevents conflict and limits violence by addressing the originating problems. Positive peace is inward peace, calm, and honest integrity; it is outward peace in relationships and between nations.

Sandy (2002) proposed the term, *hot peace* for this condition. It involves active bridge building and cooperation between opponents. The foundation of positive peace is justice, so it is sometimes called *JustPeace*. "There can be no justice without peace and there can be no peace without justice" (King, 1967). The peaceful relationship in this sense is founded on justice, mercy, truth, and compassion (Yoder, 2017). Positive peace requires collaborative action to resolve the underlying causes of conflict. The work of Jane Addams, one of the earliest peace activists, correlated poverty and disenfranchisement with serious conflict. She shared the 1931 Nobel Peace Prize for her charitable work to improve the dreadful living conditions of Chicago's poor, and her efforts to find a peaceable end to war.

Peace Perceptions Poll

The international online survey called the **Peace Perceptions Poll** was set up to ascertain global trends in peoples' perception and prospects for peace. In 2018, some surprising results were reported (International Alert, 2018). Most notably, people living in more peaceful countries like the United Kingdom were more pessimistic about future peace and security than people living in countries currently experiencing conflict like Syria and Nigeria. This overall result masked significant variation within between urban and rural regions, however. Check the website for detailed results of the poll.

Insight on Peace and Conflict from the World's Wisdom Traditions

Harmonious and conflicted relationships have been a perpetual social mystery, so the world's innumerable wisdom traditions make valuable contributions to this discussion. While Eastern and Southern thought tends to be heterogenous, Western thinking is overshadowed by Judeo-Christian concepts that underlie Western culture (Johnson, 1987). A contrast can be observed between an Eastern (over-) emphasis on inner, intrapersonal peace, and Western (over-)emphasis on outer-, relational-social peace (Groff, 1996). In this section, you will read about the five most common spiritual traditions; however, these are only the most popular among thousands of religions that form and disband elusively (see Figure 11.2).

There is more variation than uniformity. Within every religion and faith, subdivisions branch and sometimes break from the mainstream (usually because of conflict), producing variations of belief. There are few singularly authoritative wisdom sources. Many formulations are written from limited points of view: conservative and moderate and progressive, believers and secular researchers, mainstream and dissenters, politically aligned thinkers, and so on.

No one peacebuilding approach is sufficient (Bouta, 2005; Frost, 2004). Exclusive focus on a single viewpoint usually leads to misguided projects. Activities are most successful when they are designed to be gender, ethnic, and faith collaborations (Grieves, 2009; Nasir, 2020; L. Smith, 1999), to include both religious and secular peacebuilders (Bouta, 2005; Rouner, 1990; Tanabe, 2019). Several scholars (for example, Johnson, 1987; Mac Ginty, 2008) distinguish customary peace concepts from "liberal peace," which typically sponsors internationally directed, democratic intervention. Liberal peace is criticized for promoting a regimented, top-down Western peacebuilding that often contradicts

Figure 11.2 The golden rule, from the world's wisdom traditions
Reproduced with the permission of Paul McKenna.

long-tested, bottom-up traditional approaches, but the most effective methods may be hybrid (Firchow, 2018; Mac Ginty, 2010; McCandless, 2020).

Judaism, Christianity, and the Bible

The prehistoric origins of *Judaism* were in the culture and beliefs of ancient Mesopotamia, approximately 4,000 years ago. The founder was Abram, also called Abraham. The primary sacred text is the Torah (the first five books of the Bible), but the Talmud, a later commentary and teaching, is also authoritative. These writings contain rich information about conflict, justice, and peace. The ancient Hebrew word, *shalom*, roughly translated to mean "peace be with you," is often used today as a friends' greeting or parting phrase, as are similar linguistic expressions like *salaam*, *schlama*, and *shalom aleichem*. At its root, it has profound historical meanings (Dietrich, 2012), weaving together related qualities of safety, healthy wellbeing, shared prosperity and order, and completion (Freedman, 2016; Yoder, 2017). Conflict is manifest in the chaos of sickness, social discord, and war.

Christianity grew out of Judaic roots during the Roman era, about 2,000 years later, marking the beginning of our current dating system, that divides BCE

(Before the Common Era) from CE (of the Common Era). Together, the Judeo-Christian worldview dominates most Western viewpoints (Bainton, 1960).

Within a wide range of meaning, biblical peace is believed to be established by God as an ideal for human life, a rightness and order to which individuals must commit themselves in daily living. Positive peace is therefore both outward good-will in relationships and between nations, and also inward harmony. Four "dance partners" preserve right living: truth, justice, mercy, and peace (Lederach, 1998).

In Judeo-Christian peacebuilding, the belief that humans must defend God's peace, even to death (Barash, 2017; Green, 2005), is strong. It was carried out, for example, in the five brutal Crusades from about 1,100 to 1,300 CE. Those battles were fought to claim the holy sites that both Christians and Muslims believe are sacred, and some of those tensions exist today. In stark contrast, some believe that if God is the founder of peace in the Kingdom of God, believers must commit themselves to a peaceful end of all hostility and killing (Koontz, 2009). This is lived, for example, in the pacifism of the historic Christian peace churches such as the Church of the Brethren, the Religious Society of Friends, and the Mennonites.

Islam and the Quran

The Quran is the central text of *Islam*, revealed to and recorded by the prophet Muhammad. Muslims believe in life principles of unity, coexistence, and tolerance in one human community. All that is was created together, and all life is believed to be sacred. Therefore, antagonism among the elements of creation is wrong. Belief and practice are not separate: there is an explicit connection between inner and outer peace.

There are two distinct "paths" for living prescribed in the sacred teachings of the Quran and the *Sunnah*. Conflict illustrates the wrong path, causing disregard for the virtues of making positive assumptions, patience, cooperation, and community (Cader, 2017). Peace is created by submitting to the right path of Allah with an all-committed struggle, or *jihad* (Asfaruddin, 2013). Pacifism is the practical framework within which conflict can unfold nonviolently and creatively through truth, justice, mercy, and security to bring positive change. Nonviolence is an everyday habit. Practical peacebuilding is part of a believer's obligation to faith, although there is no standard pacifism in Islam (Johnson, 2002). There is agreement among interpreters that using Muslim belief to justify violence is simply wrong, disguising political aggression with false religious cover.

In formalized conflict practice, Islamic groups often appoint a council, called a *shura*, and a mediator, called a *muslih*. They help disputants fulfill their religious obligations to peace by verifying events and providing advice (Cader, 2017). There are three main goals: halt and prevent conflict, facilitate reconciliation between enemies, and promote social reform and justice making where needed. There seems to be little global coordination, but many individual actors and Muslim organizations are doing significant peacebuilding through interpersonal, community, and humanitarian work (Bouta, 2005).

Hinduism

In the ancient philosophy of *Hinduism*, peace, or *shanti*, implies inner tranquility, happiness, and eternal rest (Pandia, 2017), but it is created by overcoming isolation and creating harmonies and togetherness with the universe (Sinha, 1982; Soni, 2010). All life is one, so peace equalizes and balances all of life's elements.

Wisdom is gained through action. A detached mind and a peaceful Self are linked, so most learning is through repetitive practice and habit. Chanting meditation creates a sacred opening for new learning and peace. The *shanti path* is a meditative prayer for release and detachment from dissatisfaction. Some sacred teachings and guidance are found in the *Upanishads*, and in the epic literature of the *Mahabharata* and the *Bhagavad Gita* (Sinha, 1982).

The spiritual and practical dimensions of Hindu life are inseparable. *Karma* is the result of action: good karma is created by beneficial actions, bad karma is created by the harmful effects of intentional actions. A central principle, then, is to avoid harming humans or animals through a nonviolent lifestyle called *ahimsa*. Conflict results in bad karma, creating a cycle of birth and rebirth until a believer is free of the body, negative thoughts, words, and actions. Bad karma can also be unwoven through living a pure and simple life, performing good deeds for others, worshiping God, and taking pilgrimage to sacred places.

Buddhism

Buddhism, among the oldest wisdom traditions, began in eastern India, approximately 6,000 years ago. Its teachings evolved as it spread through Asia and beyond. Although Buddhism is older than Hinduism, they grew in parallel and have some common beliefs with some distinctive differences. Today, there are several major Buddhistic traditions (Mahayana, Theravada, and Vijrayana) and other minor forms. The authoritative writings of Buddhism are mostly of anonymous source (Lopez, 2004; Winston, 2005), collected as the teachings of the Buddha, named Siddhartha Gautama or Gautama Buddha (Epstein, 1988; Kraft, 1992).

In this tradition, all life forms are connected within spiritual nature (Tanabe, 2016). Living beings exist constantly in relationship to other beings reflected in the changing nature of existence. Even apparently trivial and private emotions, thoughts, and actions have some effect on others (Yeh, 2006). In that way, every small personal action drives the world toward peace or conflict.

Ignorance is blindness to the reality of interdependency; enlightenment is awakening to connection (Hahn, 2008). All suffering comes from an ignorant, superficial illusion that the Self is separate from the world. Self-centered living leads to selfish action based on desire, greed, and pride. When selfish desires are unfulfilled, fear, anger, and hatred cause conflict and violence, and create an endless revenge cycle that can never be solved.

Karma derives from all mental, verbal, and physical activities in the cycle of life. Good deeds result in the fortunate continuation of life; dishonorable actions lead to misfortune. Individual karma determines the conditions of your birth (whether in human or animal life form), your family, state of health, and so on. Shared karma is part of the universe of relationships with people, other living beings, and the environment. The sum of the relational universe leads to community peace or to war.

Karma does not inevitably limit your life, however. Each person decides to be directed by mindless habits or by responsible, mindful choices. Peace is a choice at every moment: a compassionate peaceful mind leads to peaceful speech and actions; selfishness leads to conflict. The root of violence lies in the mind, like the three angry "fires" of greed, hatred, and ignorance, under a "boiling pot of soup" that is conflict. Peace can only be found in the choice to relinquish anger and pursue contentment (Brantmeier, 2007).

Peaceful actions are performed one at a time. Peacebuilding, then, is choosing a lifestyle of nonviolent thoughts, no suffering, no desire, no Self (Soeung, 2017). Harmonious, daily peace conforms to the "Five Precepts" that avoid causing suffering to others (Kraft, 2006; Yeh, 2006).

Although devout Buddhists have traditionally retreated from the concerns of the world, the contemporary "Engaged Buddhism" of Thich Nhat Hahn is a daily discipline within active life (see his biography in Chapter 1). Hahn (2008) advocated four peacebuilding steps:

1. Reduce the flame of selfish fear, and the cause of conflict is reduced;
2. Mindfully choose to avoid stoking the fire with angry thoughts; carry out peace with high standards of truth and self-control of the mind, words, and actions;
3. Thought purification helps you become a source of compassionate peace rather than conflict in the world around you;
4. Connecting thoughts to speech and actions generates compassion in those close to you, and then extends to compassionate communities, countries, and the entire world.

Customary Indigenous Concepts

Indigenous philosophy can scarcely be generalized, as literally thousands of cultures developed globally over centuries of experience.

These concepts of peace and conflict rest on a worldview foundation of flowing connection among all the elements of the universe (Grieves, 2007). No distinction is drawn between the sacred and the worldly, the immaterial and material (W. Edwards, 2002). Peaceful human existence depends on the natural realities of the earth, like the rhythms of the seasons and the endless chains of existence, often depicted as a circle of life. Individual actions reverberate from the past into the future, so present decisions are made with the "7th generation" in view: seven generations of descendants. The resources of the earth and community are given to benefit everyone and ownership has no validity. "This land does not belong to me; I belong to the land" (Neidjie, 2002).

> *Humankind has not woven the web of life; we are but one thread within it. What we do to the web, we do to ourselves. All things are bound together; all things connect.*
> —*Chief Seattle, approximately 1854*[1]

Few Indigenous sources are documented except through artistic depiction and mythology. Authority derives from tradition: knowledge is transmitted orally through community elders, sometimes called the "keepers of the circle." Elders are the bearers of knowledge, medicine, language, and culture (Hoffman, 2013; Wilson, 2004). When outsiders are admitted to the circle, for example through treaty, inclusion is regarded to begin an unbreakable friendship like a family relationship.

Peacebuilding is based on experiential knowledge. Conflict threatens the group; conflict resolution ensures that the tribe will survive, so it is mandatory (W. Edwards, 2002). The circle of life concept is incorporated in a process in which the related community participates, expressed in the phrase "nothing about us without us." Indigenous elders are key authorities who emphasize connection: people with people, and people with nature. Ceremonial procedures and local customary forms provide guidance. Story, analogies to nature, the sacred, and ceremony guide the process (Nasir, 2020). Truth-seeking is used to repair, reconcile, and recreate harmony.

Conflict has been a constant fact in Indigenous communities, particularly since encounters with outside settler peoples who engaged in serious cultural imperialism. Today, many groups are facing continuing systemic issues centered in racist discrimination, political marginalization, and conflict over land, territory, and natural resources. Incorporation of traditional knowledge, environmental protection and human rights are central cultural goals. To assist and provide a mediating influence, the United Nations established the Permanent Forum on Indigenous Issues in 2000, and sanctioned the Declaration on the Rights of Indigenous Peoples in 2007. These institutions provide the right, if not the reality, of entitlements to Indigenous land and to independence and self-governance.

Elements in Common among Diverse Wisdom Forms

Although very different in their specific beliefs, ancient wisdom traditions present themes that are echoed in peacebuilding principles across the world today (Dyck, 1996). Peace is understood, longed for, and worked for by a wide variety of actors across human history. Your actions have implications far beyond the immediate situation. Conflict results when you lose your sense of connection with others, the world, and the environment (Armstrong, 2006). Intrapersonal peacefulness or struggle are expressed in interpersonal actions. Dissatisfaction leads to selfishness, which leads to conflict; contentment leads to harmony and outer peace. Violent responses to conflict spin into a cycle of revenge; compassionate responses generate harmony (Armstrong, 2013). Peacebuilding is an idea, an ideal, and a lifestyle.

Measuring Peace

Because peace, aggression, and violent conflict are complex, integrating the highly varied data is a challenge. However, discernible causes and their impact on human lifestyle can be identified. For example, peace appears to be correlated with higher levels of education; violence appears to be correlated with higher levels of poverty (IEP, 2020). Whether such factors cause peace or violence, or whether they are caused by peace or violence is debatable. Relatively peaceful countries share specific characteristics such as cohesive populations, low levels of internal conflict, efficient and accountable government, strong economy, and functional international relationships. More turbulent and violent regions share fewer characteristics, not resembling each other for complicated reasons (IEP, 2020).

The **Global Peace Index** (GPI) is produced annually by the Institute for Economics and Peace. It ranks nations by analyzing both social turbulence and citizen wellbeing to produce measures of negative and positive peace. The 23 factors are both internal to the country (such as the number of incarcerated individuals or the national military capacity) and external (such as relations with neighboring regions or the displacement of citizens into unfamiliar areas for safety). Some of the findings of the 2020 report are as follows (see the map in Figure 11.3):

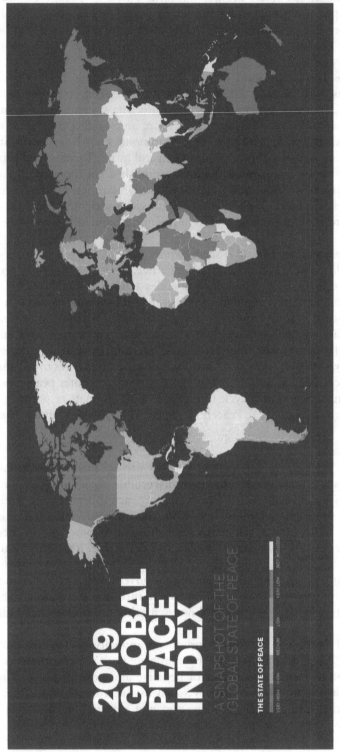

Figure 11.3 Global peace index, 2019

Reproduced with the permission of Janine Lynch, Institute for Economics and Peace.

a. Europe was the most peaceful region; Austria, Denmark, Iceland, New Zealand, and Portugal were the most peaceful countries;

b. The Middle East and North Africa were the least peaceful regions; Afghanistan, Iraq, Somalia, South Sudan, and Syria were the least peaceful countries;

c. Global peace deteriorated in 2019, especially in the Caribbean, Central and South America;

d. Peace in 80 countries deteriorated in 2019 while 81 countries showed improvement;

e. The gap between the most and least peaceful countries continued to grow;

f. There was a sharp increase in global civil unrest, with protests, general strikes, and riots, especially in Europe; 65% of unrest events in Europe were nonviolent;

g. Military expenditures compared with gross domestic product increased in 2019; and

h. Economic losses due to violence amounted to US$1,909 per person globally.

Support for the GPI is mixed because it is a big picture, top-down measure conducted by expert researchers from outside the countries (Mac Ginty, 2016).

An alternative measure is called **Everyday Peace Indicators** (EPI). For this measure, Pamina Firchow and her colleagues (2018) conducted local dialogue with war-affected people where violence had been moderated or ended to measure tangible, bottom-up peace experiences and regional peacebuilding. Firchow claims that the bottom-up and the top-down approaches are complementary and, together, they provide a fuller measure of peace than either measure alone.

POSITIVE PEACEBUILDER:
ASHOKA THE GREAT (REVISITED)

After Ashoka's shocking confrontation with his own brutality after the Kalinga War, his personal turning point introduced new civil policies that inaugurated a unified and peaceful period across much of southwestern Asia, sometimes called the *golden age of India*. His ideas formed the seeds for positive peacemaking for many generations. Ashoka's policies were based on six principles:

1. Natural *interdependency* guided his rule over the people, his territory, and his foreign relationships. He advocated mutual compassion and care. Having experienced the destructiveness of war, he adopted a nonviolent approach that later became known as *ahimsa*, no-injury. This extended to ending the killing of animals, and led to vegetarianism.

2. Development of and access to *social services* such as universities and hospitals was established throughout the reign. He unified the economy and currency systems.

3. *Pluralistic and diverse existence* was practiced politically with ambassador exchanges and alliances and economically with trade and commerce far beyond the borders. Asoka's religious tolerance became the earliest foundations of the nonviolent religions of Hinduism, Buddhism, and Jainism,

4. He created a *loyal opposition government* by treating political opponents with respect, as if they were allies.

5. He established an early form of *distributive justice*, which allocates collective resources fairly. He renovated the road system; he built water systems and encouraged agricultural irrigation; he built thousands of guesthouses for travelers, a tradition that continues today; and he returned land that had been seized from criminals.

6. He created a system for *legal justice*, with a new mercy practiced toward prisoners.

FUNDAMENTAL FEATURES OF PEACEABLE SOCIAL SYSTEMS: GLOBAL CITIZENSHIP, GOOD GOVERNANCE, CIVIL SOCIETY

Global citizenship, good governance, and civil society are practices that provide bridges between people to prevent conflict. The theoretical characteristics of a peaceable society are as follows:

1. Conscious awareness of individual and collective *interdependency* that includes thorough self-awareness and realistic understanding. Connections result in a commitment to tolerance of diversity beyond a restricted community or region, and pursues political pluralism and sociocultural diversity.

2. *Participation* in the community highlights the value of a diversity of opinion and ideology. Members have the freedom to voice their values, and to advocate for reform of a social system where there is injustice. Participatory voting is a crucial responsibility that offers voice.

3. Balanced rights and *responsibility* are closely associated and result in decision making based on the awareness that local decisions affect all parts of an interconnected system. The wellbeing of individuals is protected through balanced human and collective rights in a peaceful, ordered society. Individuals have some responsibility for society's fair, ethical decisions. Valclav Havel said, "The salvation of this human world lies nowhere else than in the human heart, in the human power to reflect, in human modesty, and in human responsibility" (1997). Decisions taken and upheld by a group must responsibly contribute to the collective good. This approach is illustrated, for example, in reluctance to buy goods produced in sweatshops or by child workers.

4. The goal is to positively influence the *wellbeing of all* citizens by creating a community that is governed fairly and justly.

Global Citizenship
A key insight of a peaceable society is that the proper context for peacebuilding is human rather than national. You are a **global citizen** when you think about needs beyond your local community and the narrow "I" or "us," to include concerns of the whole. A global citizen actively pursues benefits for many. Conflict is therefore prevented through the satisfaction of most needs (Burton, 1990).

Good Governance
Governance is the system by which political authority is exercised: how decisions are discussed and made, plans are formed and implemented, and public resources

are managed. Generally, the phrase refers to the actions of a national government, but it can also describe related community activities at other levels of organization. There is no single marker, and it is not a dichotomous quality: any government at a particular time may be observed to operate along a "good-to-faulty" continuum.

A significant factor in a culture is the peoples' perception of whether governors are motivated benevolently or malevolently. *Good governance* ensures responsible decision making. Just decisions are made that benefit everyone, but particularly the most vulnerable. With good governance, people affected by decisions are able to voice their viewpoints. Leaders are accountable and responsive to the people, and decisions are transparently and consensually made. Leaders are subject to established rules and law, and actions do solve problems with the efficient use of collective resources.

In contrast, *poor governance* generally looks out for the wellbeing of a selected few, but not most people. It is increasingly regarded as a root cause of serious conflict (Sheng, 2009). It is characterized by arbitrary, unpredictable, often secret decision making by a few who are unresponsive to the needs of most. Corrupt or abusive use of political power, weak accountability, and legal systems that are unjust or not enforced equitably characterize poor governance.

The World Bank reports regularly on more than 200 countries' governance status through the complex **Worldwide Governance Indicators** Project (WGI) (Kaufmann, 2011, 2018). Recent results suggested that the most effective good governments are found in Sweden, Finland, and New Zealand, while the least effective governments are found in Somalia, the Democratic Republic of Congo, and Sudan.

Civil Society
Civil society is an ideal community that focuses on wholistic wellbeing, to permit all its citizens to prosper (Peterson, 2004). The leaders of such a society are very important models, so that civility spreads throughout to include active partner organizations and grass roots citizens (Paffenholz, 2009). The concept is used to describe an integrated society with engaged citizens, ethical government with a balance of powers, and government active in global networks (Kaldor, 2003). In theory, civil society is related to peacebuilding, functioning through socially cohesive citizen protection, advocating for and facilitating and monitoring social progress, education (Paffenholz, 2009). After his reformative experience, Ashoka's policies made possible the creation of a civil society in India. There are controversial debates and numerous culturally determined definitions of civil society, but it is seen as both an outcome and an agent of globally linked human connection (Kaldor, 2003; Spurk, 2010).

ESSENTIAL PEACE FOUNDATIONS: JUSTICE, HUMAN RIGHTS, DIVERSITY, FREEDOM, AND SECURITY

Justice is complex, with the component ideas include equity and fair dealing, correctness, goodness, and conformity to the law (Oxford English Dictionary). In a peaceful society, justice is linked in the legal and judicial systems, social development, and pluralistic government. Justice-making systems were explored in Chapter 10.

Human rights are fundamental freedoms and privileges that belong to every human. The rights describe how you intuitively expect to be treated as a human being. International human rights law reinforces the obligation of a good government to promote and protect human rights. Human rights are regarded in the Western context as *universal* (they cannot be earned because they are guaranteed without limit or exception), *inalienable* (they cannot be compromised), *interdependent* (one cannot be selected and others ignored), and *indivisible* (you cannot have part if a right). Specific human rights are set out in the Universal Declaration of Human Rights (also known as UDHR). It was adopted in 1948 by the UN General Assembly, and is the foundation for many policies. In international practice and in scholarship there is significant cultural and political debate about specific human rights and how they relate to nonwestern cultures.

Think About and Discuss with Your Colleagues

As central as human rights are, they do not exist without dialectic tensions. Discuss with your classmates some of the controversial issues:

- Take a look at the UDHR. In your view, are there central and peripheral human rights, given the fact that different rights are prioritized by different cultures and political regimes? How do central rights relate to responsibilities and duties?
- Are there natural rights, and are they distinct from legal rights?
- Are there negative rights (freedom from ...) that are distinct from positive rights (that permit or require an action).
- When they contradict each other, should individual rights trump collective rights, or vice versa?
- When rights contradict, how would you decide what takes precedence?

Diversity of viewpoints and ideals is another component that enriches a peaceful society. Contributions to diversity come from different cultural, political, or ethnic and religious backgrounds. Varied training, life experiences, and interpretations add perspective to the mix of thinking and critical dialogue within a community, ideally creating a sense of collective wisdom. Tensions result from diversity because individuals may have difficulty finding like-minded people or a "home" with which to identify. This might force a false consensus (Myers, 2015). For example, although the US culture is frequently identified as a "Christian nation," in fact it includes a highly diverse range of belief and faith.

Freedom of, and access to, acccurate information opens up good thinking and civic participation. A variety of information sources provide content for thought, and challenge both global citizens and leadership to take responsible actions.

Freedom of speech refers to the right to speak both mainstream and dissenting opinions, based on independent thought. Dissent includes the rights to hold unpopular beliefs, criticize decisions and actions, and protest actions of which you disapprove. Dissent is not inherently violent. Dissent is disagreeable and nonconformist, and it causes discomfort in most settings. However, dissent can also enliven civil society by challenging long-accepted assumptions.

Freedom of belief, values, and worship contributes to the spiritual diversity of a society. Tolerance implies appreciating and offering respect to people who differ (Fisher, 2011; Peterson, 2003). One point of debate is the extent to which philosophical or religious beliefs should be the basis for political decisions and actions. For instance, should a Muslim or Christian elected official make decisions based on their own religious convictions? Interfaith dialogue can easily slip into religious debate and even hostility, and many people struggle to reconcile the differences of belief. Unfriendly dialogue frequently centers in the ways that religious language can be used to exclude and invalidate others whose beliefs differ.

Traditionally, **security** has meant freedom from fear and oppression. Every nation tries to create peace and security among its citizens and territories. For governments, this happens, in part, through the formation of international alliances and treaties, increased national spending on military technology and weaponry, and improving military skill.

In the peacebuilding context, the security equation appears to be that fear and defense are associated with increased risk of antagonism and violence, while connection and human security are associated with developing relationships and peace. The emergence of unconventional security threats and new conflict patterns across the globe have prompted extension of society's security beyond defense to adopt priorities involving human rights, humanitarian intervention, democracy, prosperity, and positive peacebuilding (Christie, 2008). When these qualities are jeopardized, conflict is likely and peace is not sustainable. Security is a charged issue. There is much debate about the effective sources of security, and this is a highly politicized issue because it usually touches on national security policies.

POTENTIAL CONFLICT RESOLUTION

In peacebuilding, there are multiple avenues for proactive, committed work in most circles of everyday life and in international settings. Galtung said in 1980, "There are tasks for everybody." Peacebuilding is multidimensional and multilevel, with many entwined methods and varied success. Strategic peacebuilding can be facilitated at several points (Christie, 2008; Lederach, 2010) that have unpredictable effectiveness:

- before conflict breaks out, growing tension can be addressed by revising relationships to improve justice;
- as violence begins to erupt, violence containment and hostility deescalation (called peace enforcement by others) can be used;
- structural and institutional change (called peacemaking by others) can be promoted; and
- after violence has dissipated, postconflict peacebuilding can promote justice and healing.

Defining Peacebuilding
Peacebuilding is a comprehensive concept that refers to all efforts to decrease violence, increase security, and create more peaceable relationships. The key lies in the qualities of the relationships among adversaries (Lederach, 1998) and the activities are wide-ranging. The most effective methods are cooperative, coordinated attempts that address multiple concerns (Woodhouse, 2011; Zelizer, 2013).

Although peacebuilding efforts have been abundant for generations, scholarly interest became focused after the end of the Cold War in the early 1990s. Ongoing efforts deal with many unresolved issues of debate (PBI, 2013). UN Secretary-General Boutros Boutros-Ghali (1992) introduced four consecutive but entwined categories of action for working toward peace in places of conflict. His outline has become an accepted framework for peacemaking design. Table 11.1 compares categories of peacemaking:

- *peace enforcement* through 1) military defense and 2) international law. This is used when violence is intermittent to protect civilians and deter more serious conflict from escalating, usually by separating the opponents.
- *peacekeeping* through 3) disarmament and 4) peacekeeping forces. This is used when a violent crisis is ongoing to reduce violence with its costs and casualties.
- *peacemaking* through 5) diplomacy and 6) civilian-military cooperation. This concept is a somewhat general term that entails cooperative dialogue among the parties.
- *peacebuilding* through 7) postconflict reconstruction. These activities are used after conflict has ended and are aimed to prevent relapse into violence.

The conflict-resolution field of study continues to urgently work to address immense ongoing challenges and gaps in our knowledge (Woodhouse, 2000).

Table 11.1   Comparison of Peacebuilding Concepts

Concept	Primary Personnel	Definition	Examples and Activities
Peace enforcement	Military leaders, combatants	Late-stage, urgent, coercive interposition of third-party military forces or trained civilians, to control or end destructive conflict crisis	1. Military defense 2. International law
Peacekeeping	Immediate adversaries: political leaders military leaders	Used when a crisis is developing, and designed to manage intense hostility that is on the verge of becoming violent	3. Disarmament, demobilization, and reintegration 4. Peacekeeping forces
Peacemaking	Representative citizens, and spoilers	Activities during cold peace that bring hostile parties to negotiate settlement of their grievances to win long-term peace through structural change	5. Diplomacy 6. CIMIC
Peacebuilding	Citizens impacted by violence	Adversaries plan to avoid relapse into conflict, agenda to rebuild peace with justice and healing in a society damaged by violence	7. Long-term post-conflict stabilization, reconstruction, and transformation

Sources: Boutros-Ghali, 1992; Lederach, 1997; Lund, 2001

A vast array of activities are ongoing (Lederach, 1998). You may notice that, although the methods are distinct in definition, in practice the roles are imprecise and less definite (Cottey, 2013).

Some common principles guide peacebuilding work (Peacebuilding Initiatives, 2013):

- peacebuilding is a broad project that should not be limited to postconflict work;
- there is a wide array of activities and processes;
- peacebuilding aims toward lasting prevention of conflict and violence; and
- the impact of peacebuilding is both tangible (measurable) and intangible (affecting peoples' quality of life).

Prevention Is Best

Hot war is expensive, in military costs, civilian casualties, and damage to infrastructure; revention is by far preferable. The first and by far the most effective principle of international conflict resolution is *prevention of disputes*. This is done through promoting positive relationships, and minimizing the spread of open conflict and violence when it has begun (Boutros-Ghali, 1992). Conflict scholars, practitioners, and national leaders have long known that preventing violence is much easier than stopping it. The goals of national and international resolution efforts are always to maintain or improve reliable justice and security. Yet not enough is known about how to do that and, even when necessary steps are clear, it is rare that sufficient resources are allocated to fully accomplish preventive steps (Burgess, 2018). Interstate relationships are in constant flux, like a multiparty dance that depends on political leadership and policies within prevailing global factors. Peacemaking is most effective if it is motivated and designed from within the conflicted society (Firchow, 2019).

Think About and Discuss with Your Colleagues

- As you listen to, view, and read the daily news, can you distinguish international efforts toward conflict prevention, peace enforcement (defense and international law), peacekeeping (DDR and peacekeeping forces), peacemaking (diplomacy and CIMIC), and peacebuilding (postconflict reconstruction)?

PRAXIS: PEACEBUILDING ACTION

Negative Peacebuilding: Ending Violence

Negative peacebuilding reacts to crisis and emphasizes crisis management and violence containment or reduction. Galtung (1980) called this a "dissociative approach" because it often involves at least a temporary separation of adversaries. These actions are very important options that, when effective, save many lives from violent conflict. There are two strategies:

Negative Peacebuilding with Peace Enforcement

Peace enforcement is the interposition of third-party military forces or trained civilians (usually unarmed) between violent adversaries. It occurs when a situation has already grown to a significant, often intense, violent crisis and the move is intended to diminish the violence and casualties. Peace enforcement can deploy military groups designated by a government or the United Nations, or possibly civilian groups like the Nonviolent Peace Force. It is a late-stage urgent move designed to coerce a temporary suspension of the intensity and scope of hot, direct violence or (even better) an actual end of the violence. The enforcers call attention to the real costs of violence and challenge adversaries to cease fire, maintain calm, and work toward peace talks. Joseph Bock (2001) called this *preemptive peacebuilding*, occurring when there is a conflict crisis and general panic.

Although few issues are immediately resolved, peace enforcement clears the way for other peacemaking activities. Actions are directed toward military leaders and combatants with the intention of establishing an urgent end of ongoing violence through a truce or ceasefire. A subsequent goal is to compel enemy leaders to accept and implement a peace agreement. Ultimately, this method creates a safer environment for negotiation of problems and peace agreements by stopping cycles of violence and reducing direct casualties and property destruction.

Peace enforcement was notably used in 1956 when Canadian Prime Minister Lester B. Pearson organized the UN Emergency Force to stop hostility and resolve the Suez Crisis. Pearson was awarded the 1957 Nobel Peace Prize for the concept. Since those operations, the demand for peace forces, especially through the United Nations, has rapidly accelerated. The complexity of peace enforcement and ambiguity of such missions makes their work very difficult and often hazardous (Burgess, 2018).

There are two common methods used to enforce peace: military defense and international law.

1. *Peace Enforcement Using Defense*

    Most governments have, as a high priority, protection of the nation against any chronic threats to citizens' survival, rights, or ways of life. Defense is supposedly used after an attack that necessitates protection of sovereignty. Defenses are developed through early warning systems, technological advances, and political deterrents like economic sanctions and penalizing enemy citizens within the country. A widespread practice in North America during World War II confined citizens of Japanese origin to internment camps to prevent internal unrest and potential attacks. In actuality, the goal is not always clear. Although defensive in design, these interactions are often offensive in both strategy and tactics.

    When there is hostile disagreement, especially with a powerful adversary, fear that something valuable might be lost thrives. The **security dilemma** (Herz, 1951, 2003) refers to a climate of national uncertainty or mistrust that grows in concert with another state's power or perceived threat. It can correspond with a change in the policies or status of a foreign state, which might destabilize an existing political equilibrium. The dilemma is how to avert violence when an adversary has the actual power to harm. A common strategy is to increase and show off national power and defense stocks to stay ahead of the opponent and motivate them to reconsider aggression and reestablish the former equilibrium. However, this strategy can be interpreted as hostile and provoke a mirror reaction, creating an escalating spiral of defense and increasing the potential for violence.

In 1955, Lester B. Pearson said, "A 'balance of terror' has succeeded a 'balance of power.'" Development of the defense spiral sensitizes a government to danger, but rarely leads to international cooperation (Edwards, 1986). Aggression resulting from this dynamic is an artifact of the uncertainty and apparent threat that can occur even if neither state wants conflict.

Maintenance of Military Forces Most governments establish an active military force. Before the 21st century, most forces were used to protect or extend political territories. In recent years, military activities have expanded to include peacekeeping, providing humanitarian aid in response to disaster, and community development rather like diplomacy, sometimes called *peaceful warriorship* (Faure-Brac, 2012; Woodhouse, 2005). Although commanded by the government in power, professional military forces have traditionally been politically neutral. However, recent trends are notable: military candidates are sometimes endorsed during election campaigns, and military leaders occasionally step into elected office and appointed cabinet positions.

While most military forces are under the authority of an established government, some nongovernmental forces, such as a rebel citizen army, have significant capacity to initiate and sustain large-scale conflict. Many of these forces are organized around a cause rather than a political system.

2. *Peace Enforcement Using International Law*

International law refers to a collection of rules that govern the relationships between sovereign nations, particularly when in serious conflict or war. The principle is that war should be as humane as possible, so the regulations attempt to limit the most destructive and gruesome consequences of war. The *Geneva Conventions* resulted in a series of treaties that define humanitarian treatment of soldiers and civilians, and prohibit the use of certain weapons for international conflict. Most of these rules were negotiated under a UN mandate, but they are nationally adopted. The customary term "international law" is probably not accurate because consistent enforcement of the law is ineffective, and conformity depends on voluntary implementation.

Two agencies of international law have gained prominence in the last decade:

The International Court of Justice

The International Court of Justice (ICJ) was commissioned in 1945 by the United Nations to settle legal disputes between nations and to give advisory opinions about contentious issues. Since 1947, the ICJ has dealt with an average of two or three cases per year. Examples of cases currently under consideration are to determine the correct borders between India and Pakistan, the control of assets seized by the United States from the Islamic Republic of Iran, and the 2017 relocation of the US embassy from Tel Aviv to Jerusalem, which crystallized a long political controversy about the capital of Israel. ICJ advisory opinions are not enforceable (ICJ, 2018).

The International Criminal Court

The International Criminal Court (ICC) is an intergovernmental court that investigates and prosecutes accusations of war crime, crimes against humanity, and genocide. Established by a multinational treaty in 2002, the ICC cooperates with national police and legal agencies and occasionally operates independently. Despite early disputes about jurisdiction and usefulness, the ICC is becoming more effective in holding international criminals accountable (ICC, 2020).

Wartime actions are considered to be legitimate when they are part of combat and they conform to the principles of *distinction* and *proportionality* protected by international law. When legal, combatants are immune from detention, arrest, and criminal prosecution for their actions. For example, if a soldier kills an adversary during a battle, they cannot be prosecuted for homicide.

Actions that violate core human rights are never regarded as legal by international law. A **war crime** is an action that seriously violates international rights codes, such as rape, intentionally killing a civilian, and mistreating a prisoner of war. Individuals can be held accountable for war crimes regardless of their military or official status, even when a person is ordered to do something by a higher-ranking superior. When the ICC agrees to process a case, an international arrest warrant is issued that may be carried out by Interpol or by any signatory nation. Every case considered since 2000 has involved one of the African nations in turmoil. In 2020, there were approximately 20 active arrest warrants and 28 people were at various stages of trial. Almost no efforts have been effective to deter or prevent war crimes. Rather, they are dealt with, usually with punishment, after the war has ended.

Several principles of immunity limit individual legal accountability. **Sovereign immunity** or **state immunity** claims that a sovereign head of a government cannot commit an illegal act and is, therefore, immune from prosecution for all official actions. **Personal immunity** applies to state officers acting within the mandate of their office. An example of this is *diplomatic immunity*, granted to official representatives working in an embassy in a foreign country. **Functional immunity** protects actions or functions carried out by professionals on behalf of a state. For example, police officers representing the state are responsible to appropriately protect property and people, so actual police violence is judged according to a standard of *reasonable force* versus *brutality*, which is force that is excessive or unnecessary to protect community safety.

At times, accused criminals are tried together by the ICC. When there are many allegations by innumerable individuals, the ICC might establish a temporary International Criminal Tribunal to investigate events in that region and prosecute accused perpetrators.

Negative Peacebuilding through Peacekeeping

Peacekeeping is used to forestall developing confrontational crisis. This second type of negative peacebuilding is designed to moderate intense hostility that is on the verge of becoming violent. Its goal is to find ways to calm conflict and prevent violence. Actions are directed toward separating political and military opponents, attempting to coerce adversaries to deescalate tension, and ultimately to begin a peace process of deliberate dialogue (Boutros-Ghali, 1992). Bock (2001) called this *preventive peacemaking*.

Peacekeeping includes two common methods: disarmament and peacekeeping forces.

3. *Peacekeeping with Disarmament, Demobilization, and Reintegration*
   Disarmament, demobilization, and reintegration (DDR) are the first phases that deal with combatants during a community's transition from war to peace. **Disarmament** entails the surrender, removal, or destruction of combat arms: "peace without weapons." For individual combatants, this often requires a government sponsored amnesty or a trade of arms for vocational implements such as sewing machines or bicycles. For armed groups, this is called stockpile reduction. Disarmament is rarely rapid but is, rather, a gradual process. **Demobilization** is the term used for disbanding armed groups. DDR is disorienting because it directly contradicts common military training that belonging and loyalty are essential to survival.

   The convoluted process of **reintegrating** combatants into civilian social and economic life necessitates a drastic worldview shift from "war" to "peace," and a new fit into a world and social milieu that are drastically altered by the former violence. It can be bewildering to individual combatants and their families because of the drastic change in identity. Consistent observation shows that those who expect a smooth transition to "normalcy" will likely be unsuccessful, which then leads to continuing violence (Burgess, 2018).

   DDR is transitional at best. It does not bring a permanent end of violence, but it is crucial in the shift from war to peace. The goals of DDR are both short term and long term, and successful completion of each is foundational to the next. In the short term, the hope is to avert lethal violence and, thus, to make room for political stability, citizen security, and peaceful community building. In the long term, DDR contributes to the renewal of postconflict society.

   Disarmament on a larger political scale is called **arms control** or **nonproliferation**. It restricts national arms production, inventory, and use (Boutros-Ghali, 1995). The theory asserts that arms control limits the damages possible during conflict and, thereby, improves national security and stability and diverts funds to more peaceable activities. Nonproliferation treaties are usually negotiated between states, or might be voluntarily and unilaterally declared. Examples of disarmament on this scale are the Outer Space Treaty of 1967, ratified by more than 125 countries, and the START Treaty of 2011 between Russia and the United States.

4. *Peacekeeping with Peacekeeping Forces*
   Peacekeeping activity begins to address the causes of conflict by creating a safer environment in which peace negotiations can be completed and implemented. The goal, after a truce is secured, is to reduce the potential for persistent conflict. Usually, peacekeeping involves a national military or police force, or civilian organization, designated by the UN. They function as neutral third-party forces, deployed at the site of previous violence,

to maintain an existing armistice, support the implementation of signed peace commitments, and monitor and observe the transition from violent conflict to peace. When deployed by the United Nations, soldiers wear blue berets or helmets for identification.

Peacekeeping forces have complicated roles to protect vulnerable civilians (especially women and children), promote the rule of law, and safeguard human rights. Peacekeepers are often in difficult, ambiguous roles, unsure of the prevailing mandate. This sometimes means that they are unable to prevent serious violence, as occurred to the soldiers collaborating under the United Nations and the North Atlantic Treaty Organization (NATO) in Bosnia-Herzegovina in the 1990s.

Positive Peacebuilding: Mending and Building

Positive peacebuilding takes place when adversaries have accomplished an end to conflict and plan to rebuild their damaged societies. Many serious conflicts are rooted in social and structural inequities of resources and power and in injustice, so positive peacebuilding is intended to address the deeper causes of conflict and violence by generating movement toward equity (IEP, 2019). Galtung (1976) called this the *associative approach* because it usually cannot be accomplished by isolated adversaries.

David Barash and Charles Webel (2018) suggested five grand-scale conditions for enduring peace:

1. Protected and promoted human rights;
2. Ethical promotion of environmental and ecological wellbeing;
3. Economic wellbeing and the elimination of poverty;
4. Nonviolent resolution of conflict; and
5. Personal and national reconciliation of previous enmity.

Peacemaking involves activities that bring hostile parties to settle their grievances, with the objective of winning an enduring peace treaty. The most common method uses diplomacy between rival nations, sometimes facilitated or brokered by a neutral nation. National and community leaders are the focus of these actions. Peacemaking activities are effective when tensions are present but not intense, or at an early stage of conflict development. Making peace involves at least two activities: stabilizing the safety of the people, and beginning to correct the issues that ignited conflict. There are two common categories of peacemaking activity: diplomacy and civilian-military cooperation.

5. *Making Peace through Diplomacy*

Diplomacy involves formal discussions that manage international relationships and conflicts through designated diplomats who represent the interests and policies of their sending nation. Drazen Pehar notably called it "words that prevent us from reaching for our swords." Diplomacy is a constant pursuit of most governments. It occurs when tension exists, but there is minimal risk of war. This peacemaking focuses on forms of negotiation that peacefully settle the differences. The central purpose of diplomacy is to persuade other nations of the sending government's viewpoint or position. It often takes a competitive, hard bargaining form that overlooks possibilities for cooperation. Diplomats use a wide variety of procedures—basically whatever accomplishes the goal—such as diplomatic inquiry, alliance formation, negotiation, offering concessions to avoid confrontation, third-party arbitration and mediation, and conferences and congresses. Diplomats draft agreements and treaties that will later be considered for consent by their governments. Training in diplomatic technique is offered by most governments.

Traditionally, diplomacy took place exclusively through professional diplomats like appointed ambassadors, and this practice does continue as *Track I diplomacy*. In recent decades new "levels of engagement" have been invented, so diplomacy is now conducted through at least nine (and expanding) tracks of communication (Burgess, 2018). Louise Diamond and John McDonald (1996) coined the term *multitrack diplomacy* to refer to these simultaneous and interconnected negotiations conducted through separate representative groups. The tracks are used to augment and improve Track I official engagement; at times the alternate tracks can be used to bypass ongoing negotiations. McDonald (2003) described the multiple tracks and their guiding mandates.

Diplomacy might also include activities like fact-finding missions, early warning discussion, and intermediary communications (GPF, 2002)

6. *Making Peace with Civil-Military Cooperation*
Partly in response to the failures of World War II, military strategists began to realize that their task was "winning the peace, " rather than "winning the war" (Burgess, 2018). Military mission options widened beyond traditional security and combat to include humanitarian relief, conflict-resolution training, social development, and social reconstruction. Cooperative partnerships between civilian and military groups have been organized since then, with formal communication lines and designated roles. Building mutual trust and maintaining local independence are essential, but challengingly paradoxical (Bruneau, 2013; Franke, 2006).

In some conflict regions, significant civilian or military groups are opposed to peacemaking efforts. These parties, called **peace spoilers,** may sabotage or undermine peace negotiations and attempt to reignite the war (Newman, 2006; Nilsson, 2011). To facilitate civil-military cooperation (CIMIC) partnerships, governments must create politically pluralistic alliances with other nations, tolerate and encourage sociocultural diversity, and treat opponents with respect, acknowledging common goals (as Ashoka did).

Peacebuilding refers to actions that identify and support local structures that will help to strengthen and solidify peaceful functioning. The primary aim is to prevent a relapse into conflict, although it is increasingly viewed as reparative. It takes place when adversaries have ended conflict and want to rebuild societies that have been damaged by violence. The targets of these activities are the citizens of a society impacted by the hostility and violent conflict. Sometimes called *postconflict rebuilding*, activities focus on repair of damaged properties and the more challenging reparation for damaged people and relationships. To avoid a relapse into conflict, the sources of the conflict must be addressed and resolved.

7. *Building Peace through Postconflict Reconstruction and Transformation*
Active conflict resolution cannot stop with an end of violence without risking a relapse into conflict. Transforming a culture of fear and war into a culture of peace is long-term (possibly endless) work, requiring that a broad range of behaviors, relationships, and structures, and attitudes and values must be addressed (Woodhouse, 2005). These are long-term activities that strengthen people and societies weakened by conflict. Restoration after serious explosive war, such as in many parts of postcolonial Africa rocked by generations of conflict, usually involves a profound rethinking and relearning of relationships and society. Bock (2001) called these transformative activities *promotive peacebuilding* and *reparative peacebuilding*. Positive peacebuilding occurs after violent conflict has slowed down or (rarely) halted, and follows peacemaking and peacekeeping. Examples of settings in which this has successfully begun are the 1998 Truth and Reconciliation Commission of South Africa, the formation of the 2007 Ministry of Peace and Reconstruction in Nepal, and the 2015 Truth and Reconciliation Commission of Canada.

Juan Gutierrez (2009) described the weighty "three Rs" that begin to overcome the destruction of political violence:

Reconstruction involves actual infrastructure repair. Destruction during conflict, though catastrophically costly, can become an opportunity to reimagine and reorient (not simply replace) social infrastructure, social roles, and power and authority, and create a new peacetime economy and society. One challenge of reconstruction is that international humanitarian aid, called liberal peace, is usually indispensable, but granting nations must refrain from imposing foreign assumptions and join a true partnership with a newly empowered local community (Smith, 1998).

Resolution involves changes to and transformation of values and attitudes in ways that address the original injustices. Douglas Fry (2007) described four ways that warring nations can establish nonviolent peace systems. Each requires that past relationships be restructured. *First*, values, beliefs, and attitudes are primary. The renewing society must explore the concepts of violence and war with a truly "never again" approach to war. Common origins of the enemies must be accepted and explored. *Second*, practical mechanisms for just, nonviolent dispute resolution must be established. *Third*, economic interdependence will create the will to develop nonviolent, nondestructive negotiation of disagreements. *Fourth*, personal and community relational links must be encouraged and sustained with deliberate effort.

Reconciliation involves cultural renewal (Lederach, 1998). Elise Boulding's numerous recommendations (2000) warned that this type of work must be based on a growing commitment of a whole society to transform a core culture, newly defined by:

- dealing creatively with individual differences;
- cultivating a stance of listening and learning from an opponent;
- teaching and practicing conflict analysis, dialogue, and negotiation skills;
- learning from womens' experience with peacebuilding;
- removing the game dynamic of winners and losers from diplomacy;
- counteracting the belief in the inevitability and uncontrollability of war;
- making nonviolent alternatives to aggression and war accessible; and
- replacing military and battle honor with civic honor and responsibility.

National and international reconciliation after conflict is a topic of intense research and also disagreement. No uniform methods exist because actual conflicts are ideosyncratic, and success depends on many contextual factors such as the range of reasons for working toward reconciliation, the presence or absence of mechanisms for dealing with past suffering, the willingness of citizens to be patient with real suffering, and the specific role of political leaders. The reconciliation process is undeniably tangled, often both hindered and enhanced by contributions from religious and sociocultural identity groups, individual psychological status, economic factors, and political and judicial processes.

NONVIOLENT PEACEBUILDER: MOHANDAS K. (MAHATMA) GANDHI (1869–1948)

Mohandas Gandhi is widely known as an Indian teacher whose life provided a vivid example of nonviolent social action as a means of bringing about drastic change. Gandhi's historical legacy included the *age of violence* with brutal invasions from central Asia as well as the legends of peaceful Ashoka (Schlichtmann, 2016).

During the *age of discovery* (15th through 20th centuries CE), India was colonized by the Netherlands, Portugal, and, most notably, Britain, with an initial strategy of establishing rich trading partnerships. However, British rule over India resulted from a century of British Government of India Acts, 1833–1935, which granted all trading rights to the British East India Company. By 1855, Britain had seized political, economic, and cultural dominance.

Local resistance to foreign interference culminated in the 1857 Sepoy Mutiny. It was a scene of ferocious reciprocating massacre that included women and children, but failed to secure Indian independence. For the following 60 years British rule became ever more oppressive and brutal. Anti-British rioting led to the 1919 Amritsar Massacre, during which the British-Indian army "restored order" by killing approximately 370 peaceful protestors, and injuring 1,200 Indians trapped in the Amritsar public garden (Britannica, 2019). This critical event influenced the civil rights movement in India from 1916 to 1948, led by Mohandas Gandhi and other teachers.

Family Roots in India, 1869–1893

Mohandas Gandhi was born at Porbandar, India, in 1869, a fourth child. He was married to Kasturbai when both were 13 years old in 1882. They did not enjoy a particularly peaceable relationship and quarrelled often. Together, they eventually had four sons.

After completing legal training in London in 1891, Gandhi tried to elevate his status by imitating foreign culture and denying his heritage. He rejoined his family in Porbandar to practice law (photo in Figure 11.4). His elder brother, Laxmidas, asked Gandhi to mediate a conflict with the British Political Agent. At that time, British colonial rule was entrenched and Indian citizens were regarded as unimportant and inferior. The agent insisted that they must use "the proper channels" (which everyone knew would be futile) to address the complaint, and the agent had Gandhi physically thrown out of the office. Gandhi later related that the shock of the violence and his own failure became one of the defining moments of his life.

Civil Rights Movement in South Africa, 1893–1914, Gandhi Began to Hone His Skills

In 1893, Gandhi was sent to South Africa to represent an Indian shipping firm. He experienced several more incidents of violence there. Although apartheid had not yet become national policy in South Africa, segregation of white people from "coloreds"

Figure 11.4 Gandhi in his time serving as a lawyer

(blacks and Indians) was a widespread custom enforced in facilities like public trans-portation. Gandhi had purchased a first-class ticket for the night train to Pretoria, South Africa. Two white railway officials ordered him, because of his colored skin, to move to the baggage car that was even lower than a third-class car. His valid ticket and his protests were ineffectual. The officials and a white police officer physically threw him onto the station platform, and the station officials impounded his luggage and coat. He refused to move from the station waiting room, and spent a very cold night there.

These events and others exposed a stark reality of the injustice of the custom-ary segregation around Gandhi, and he became involved in the South African civil rights movement and a passionate advocate of nonviolent social change. Living in South Africa for 21 years, he concentrated on politics and ethics. He began to test some activist techniques that later became central to his peacebuilding philosophy and work. He developed his ideas and nonviolent strategies to demand social change, and gained a reputation as an effective thinker and organizer.

Gandhi's experiences and analysis led to core observations about the causes of violence. He identified *seven social sins that cause violence*. All of them rose from entitlement and social irresponsibility and, today, we might call them injustices:

1. Politics without principle;
2. Commerce without morality;
3. Wealth without work;
4. Education without character;
5. Science without humanity;
6. Pleasure without conscience; and
7. Worship without sacrifice.

By 1914, he was somewhat well known for Indian nationalist views. He returned to India with his family, convinced that significant social struggle was timely in his ancestral homeland, to correct the injustices of British rule, racial discrimina-tion, the customary Indian caste system, and religious hatred between the Hin-dus and Moslems. During five dramatic campaigns, Gandhi united the common Indian people to form one of the largest protest movements in history.

India, 1916-1948
Gandhi became active as a leader of the struggle for Indian justice (photo in Figure 11.5). He studied historical peacebuilders, including Ashoka. He initiated many projects that highlighted the brutality and injustice of British rule, and aimed toward independence for the Indian people.

- 1915 Returned to India and became politically active
- 1919 First campaign, against the Government of India Acts
- 1919 Founded the *ashram* at Kheda, Gujarat (his demonstration project for the program to build a just community)
- 1920 Leader of the Indian National Congress
- 1919 Government of India Act revisions, Gandhi proposed civil disobedi-ence and noncooperation
- 1922 First arrest

Figure 11.5 Gandhi as protest leader

Sculpture by Ram Vanji Sutar (2004); photo reproduced with the permission of David Grant Klassen.

- 1924 Twenty-day public fast to plead for Hindu-Moslem amity
- 1930 Second campaign the "Salt March," to protest a proposed British tax on salt, imprisoned
- 1931–1932 Imperial Round Table negotiations in London
- 1932 Third campaign using civil disobedience to protest British rule
- 1939 Fourth campaign, fasting to coerce government reform through public opinion
- 1942 "Quit India" resolution demanding the end of British rule over India
- 1945 Fifth campaign, a fast to end chaotic violence
- 1945–1947 Conferences at end of World War II

Gandhi's campaigns were successful when India gained independence from British rule in 1948. Gandhi experienced significant support and resistance to his ideas and demands, becoming a controversial figure around the world. He was assassinated at New Delhi, India, in 1948.

His cotton spinning wheel symbolized his belief in local industry and self-reliance. Ashoka's peace wheel was modified to be a spinning wheel, and became the centerpiece of the Indian flag when India gained its independence (illustrated by Figure 11.6). Gandhi's name of respect was "Mahatma," which translates to "great soul." In 1981, the United Nations established his birthdate, October 2nd, as the International Day of Peace, and World Peace Day.

The *values* that Gandhi preached were foundational to his peacebuilding work (Nagler, 2019). That they resemble Ashoka's reformed policies is not coincidental.

First, Gandhi's overarching life principle was *ahimsa*, which means no-harm. This was an invitation, adopted voluntarily by his followers. For Gandhi, *ahimsa* was both a principle and an organized movement of nonviolence.

Second, he believed in the interdependent humanity united under one God; human nature was marked by moral goodness.

Third, dignified humans should be self-determining and fairly care for each other, called *swaraj*. For Gandhi, this meant advocating for decentralized social services based on local industry and economy.

Another central belief focused on law and the legal system. Gandhi knew that laws can be unjust and, if they are, believed that citizens are under no obligation to obey them. In fact, he advocated the principle of passive resistance to unjust laws, called *satyagraha*, which means truth force, or acting out the truth. *Satyagraha* included refusal to cooperate with laws that violate fundamental truth, refusal to

Figure 11.6 Flag of India

cooperate with officials who violate truth, or, even more proactively, civil disobedience and contravention of unjust laws.

Gandhi also taught personal practices for peacebuilders that he believed would ensure the success of protests and protest movements:

1. Harbor no anger;
2. Do not submit to orders given in anger;
3. Refrain from insult;
4. Pprotect opponents from insult;
5. Do not resist arrest;
6. Do not resist the expropriation of property;
7. If taken prisoner, behave in honorable fashion; and
8. Obey peaceful leaders.

Think About and Discuss with Your Colleagues

View the 1982 popular film, "Gandhi," starring Ben Kingsley.

- What do you notice about Gandhi's lifestyle(s)?
- What do you pick up from his story about both negative and positive peacebuilding?

CHAPTER SUMMARY AND STUDY GUIDE

- Peace is a highly complex phenomenon that occurs on a continuum of peace-to-conflict. Negative peace is the absence of conflict and violence, positive peace is harmony created by justice and needs satisfaction.
- Definitions of peace and conflict vary widely, both individually and culturally. The world's wisdom traditions provide common principles upon which most peacebuilding is based.
- A peaceable society is made up of individuals who perceive themselves to be global citizens. Good government that is peaceable establishes a civil society.
- Sustained peace and harmonious relationships are founded on positive, proactive actions that support justice and equity, apply human rights, value diversity, provide freedoms for everyone, and ensure a secure society.
- There are many pathways to peace, categorized as negative peacebuilding and positive peacebuilding.
- Negative peacebuilding contains and ends violence. This can occur through **peace enforcement** strategies like military defense and international law organizations, and through **peacekeeping** activities like disarmament, demobilization, and reintegration, and designated peacekeeping forces.

- Positive peacebuilding works to alleviate the causes of the conflict by solving grievances. This occurs through **peacemaking** strategies such as diplomacy and cooperative civil-military activity, and postconflict **peacebuilding**.
- Mohandas Gandhi's life and work became an early model for peace-building and nonviolent social change.

TERMS IN FOCUS

arms control 357
CIMIC 359
civil society 349
cold peace 339
cold war 339
demobilization 357
diplomacy 358
disarmament 357
functional immunity 356
global citizen 348
good governance 349
governance 348
hot peace 340
hot war 353
immunity 356
JustPeace 340

multitrack diplomacy 359
negative peace 339
negative peacebuilding 353
nonproliferation 357
peacebuilding 359
peace enforcement 353
peacekeeping 356
peacemaking 358
peace spoiler 359
poor governance 349
positive peace 339
positive peacebuilding 358
security dilemma 354
sovereign immunity 356
war crime 356

12

Transformative Conflict Resolution and Social Change

■ ■ ■

In Focus in This Chapter:

- ■ Conflict transformation is a long-term, comprehensive process that attempts to resolve deeply rooted problems by revising the perception and beliefs, creating the new constructive dynamic of a sustainably peaceable relationship.
- ■ Conflict occurs on four embedded levels: intrapersonal, interpersonal, group, and large scale. Just so, conflict transformation addresses conflict on all levels, sometimes all at once.
- ■ Harm, injustice, and conflict can be addressed passively, violently, or nonviolently.
- ■ Intrapersonal transformation aims to create an inwardly peaceable spirit that reverberates in interpersonal relationships.
- ■ Interpersonal transformation attempts to repair the harm caused by conflict with apology, forgiveness, and, if appropriate, reconciliation.
- ■ Social turmoil and conflict are usually the result of unjust conditions among the people. The purpose of conflict transformation on this level is to revise social conditions to create a better, more equitable, society.
- ■ Conflict transformation theory welcomes conflict as an opening for insight and amiable relationship.

CONFLICT CASE 12.1 ■ ELVIA ALVARADO IN HONDURAS

Honduran society is characterized by disparities between classes and genders that originated during the colonial period. Hierarchical, unequal application of human rights is systemic: international people are the most privileged, the wealthy have significant advantages, machismo men rule the homes, and women and children have the fewest benefits and bear the greatest burden. Very few agricultural workers own the land on which they work; rather, most peasant workers are employed by international corporations. Most workers (*campesinos*) labor for long hours under conditions that permit beating and severe punishment. Yet more than 60% of the population live in perpetual poverty. Common living conditions include poor sanitation, malnutrition, and related health problems; rates of violent crime are among the highest in the world and police and military forces are ineffective or corrupt; people are vulnerable to natural disaster with few resources for recovery; and education is often nonexistent. Many *campesinos* migrate to shifting sites of work. Many abandon their homes, migrating northward to apply for asylum in the United States. A few remain in place to drive change. Such widespread suffering can only be relieved with social change of Honduran society.

Elvia Alvarado is a *campesina*, a "nobody" in her society, a poor woman supporting her family alone. She is also a human rights activist who progressed beyond her personal challenges. Alvarado thoughtfully analyzed Honduran social conditions and organized the *campesinos* to respond. As a public critic of sexism, she worked to improve womens' and childrens' situations through education and the direct distribution of resources. She promoted sustainable working conditions and land reform through the National Union of Rural Workers (Confederación Nacional de Trabajadores del Campo), at times using protest, strikes, and strategic land occupation. She opposed all forms of violence. She urged social stabilization through the enforcement of existing Honduran law that limits public corruption and force, and interference by international groups (Alvarado, 1987).

Alvarado's story underlines some important ideas that will be explored in this chapter on transformative change:

- Social change of unjust conditions is inevitable, and it is accomplished by both individual and collective action. Those changes can accompany social progress, or can be expedited by violent or nonviolent methods.
- Both violent and nonviolent methods do facilitate social change, but nonviolent methods are preferable to violent methods because they create more lasting peaceful results.
- Systemic social change provides a way to effectively resolve conflict and create peace by altering unjust practices, relationships, and cultures.

> *Never doubt that a small group of thoughtful, committed citizens can change the world. It's the only thing that ever has.*
> —Margaret Mead

DEFINING TERMS AND CONCEPTS FROM CONFLICT TRANSFORMATION VIEWPOINT

Transformative Conflict Resolution

You have explored *conflict resolution*, which works toward satisfactory solutions to problems. The scope of activity is current, and the emphasis is on immediate, urgent issues that ignited a conflict. In Honduras, this might mean, for example, setting up meal programs for poor families or maintaining safer refugee camps for those who have fled their homes.

Conflict management aims to contain conflict within reasonable limits, to settle but not necessarily to eliminate the problems (Wehr, 2019). It might be used when conflict has become embedded, and subduing and containing the conflict is

Table 12.1   Comparison of Conflict Resolution and Conflict Transformation Perspectives

	Conflict Resolution	*Conflict Transformation*
The key question	How do we end an undesirable conflict?	How do we end a destructive conflict and build a desirable relationship?
The focus	Conflict content centered	Relationship centered
The purpose	Achieve agreement and solve the presenting problem that created the crisis	Promote constructive changes, inclusive of (but not limited to) immediate solutions
Development of the conflict	Embedded in and built around the immediate relationship where symptoms of disruption appear	The presenting problem is an opportunity to respond to symptoms, and to engage systems within which relationships are embedded
Time frame	Crisis-driven short-term relief of pain, anxiety, and difficulty	Mid- to long-term changes that are crisis responsive
View of conflict	Conflict processes must be deescalated	Conflict is a relational dynamic with ebb (deescalation to pursue constructive change) and flow (escalation to pursue constructive change)

Source: Adapted from Lederach, 2009. Reprinted from *The Little Book of Conflict Transformation* by John Lederach by permission of Good Books, an imprint of Skyhorse Publishing, Inc.

the most attainable outcome. In Honduras, this could mean establishing problem-solving committees to discuss and address protest and conflict dynamics, decreasing incidents of outright conflict. See Table 12.1 to compare the resolution and transformation perspectives.

John Paul Lederach (2007) wrote that sustainable peace in society is embedded in respectful relationships, fair social structures, and justice (similar to *shalom*, described in Chapter 11). Conflict transformation promotes deep change that creates enduring peace in situations of enduring conflict. **Conflict transformation** is a process by which participants' interests and problems, interactions, and conflict strategies are addressed in integrated ways, reconciling destructive, intractable conflict (Bar-Siman-Tov, 2004). "The goal of transformation ... is not only being better off, but *being better*" (Bush, 2005; emphasis mine).

Useful starting points concentrate on fundamental inequities and injustice, by addressing the immediate context of the conflict, a retrospective view of problems that added to troubled relationships, and a prospective vision that links the past with present with future. The pathway to peace cannot be controlled or prescribed. This long-term, open-ended work usually involves multiple interventions at once. This is the type of work attempted by Alvarado: pursuing equal rights and opportunities for all Hondurans, finding peaceable ways to transfer land-ownership back to the original occupants and legal methods of applying existing law to citizens and to international corporations.

4-P Analysis of Transformative Conflict Resolution

- *Problems* are a natural and normal part of all evolving relationships. No conflict is an isolated event. Rather, each conflict is part of the cadence of calm and tension and is a catalyst for progress and growth. New ways of interpreting problems lead to new, more sustainable solutions. Transformative conflict resolution therefore explores both obvious problems and broader patterns of interaction.

- *Parties* are willing to end hostility and put effort into constructing something new.
- The conflicted *process* can be transformed from antagonistic escalation to constructive relationship by addressing all levels of personal, relational, structural, and cultural conflict. Though complex, constructive change can be devised with the energy generated by a conflict.
- *Practical solutions* go beyond conventional negotiation and problem solving that could be useless or even counterproductive in complex conflicts. Peace is not a static end-state but is, rather, a respectfully engaged relationship. The aims are to reduce violence and suffering by rebuilding justice.

Alvarado's advice to people who want to drive social transformation is this:

- social change calls for personal sacrifice;
- common people must organize to counteract prevailing social institution(s);
- four practical methods to bring change are: educate the people, divide the tasks, form small groups, and make allies; and
- change is long in coming and requires persistence; we work for our grandchildren.

In Chapter 10, we dealt with legal justice making as a method of resolving conflict. In Chapter 11, peacemaking was used to resolve broader social conflicts. In this chapter, we explore conflict transformation. The chapter will be structured almost like three minichapters dealing with three levels of transformation: the intrapersonal, the interpersonal, and the social.

INNER, INTRAPERSONAL PEACEMAKING AND TRANSFORMATION

People Are the Agents of Change

The term, **agency,** refers to the freedom and power to accomplish things. **Change agents** are individuals who are motivated to contribute their efforts to transformation and have the skills and accept responsibility to inspire change. They are sensitive to social problems and broader social-political conditions (Kan, 2004). They might take a role internal or external to the situation, for example as information gatherer, trainer, or consultant (Lunenburg, 2010). A change agent could be an individual or a group within a group (Bartunek, 2013).

For change to be successful, leaders must emerge who can catalyze a collective vision and direction. Peter Senge (2015) predicted that the most successful leaders are those who can view the whole system, positive and negative, who foster generative conversations about assumptions, and shift the focus from problem solving to creating a desired future. Change leaders operate on a continuum of motivation (Mindell, 2014; Moyer, 2002). *Visionaries* (5%) and *reformers* (15%) accept the fundamental goodness of a relationship system, but imagine constructive improvements (an international example is Malala Yousafzai). On the contrasting end of the continuum are *revolutionary leaders* (15%) and *fighters* (5%) who believe the foundations of a system are irreparably flawed and must be coercively, even destructively, replaced (for example, Karl Marx or Fidel Castro).

The middle approximately 60% are followers, or *onlookers* with varying degrees of concern and incentive to participate, a mix of people who are likely to accept change and those who resist. They must be convinced before they will support change. Everett Rogers (2003) described five fluid categories of readiness for change. *Innovators* (something near 2.5% of onlookers) are individuals who can be convinced of the problem, are willing to try new patterns and make lifestyle adjustments necessary to incorporate a change. *Early adopters* of change (approximately 13%) alter their personal habits discreetly and may become opinion leaders for others. *Adopter majorities, early* and *late* (68%) are skeptical of new ideas, slow to be persuaded, and they adjust to new patterns over a longer time period. Changes made are expedient and only behavioral, and their viewpoint is not changed. This level of change might become significant, but people easily reverse direction and resume old patterns of behavior. *Laggards* (16%) are individuals who deny a problem, are generally change-averse, and therefore are slow to accept change (and sometimes never do accept it). Concessions occur but are inwardly resisted, so they are shallow and happen only in a specific context. Long-lasting transformation is unlikely for laggards.

Contemporary adjustments in attitudes toward nontraditional marriage provide an example of this dynamic: some people do become convinced of the validity of alternative relationship forms and change their attitudes to accommodate greater diversity; the opinions of the majority do not change, but they make changes to conform to the tide of society; and some individuals give in to social demand, but continue to resist alternative perceptions and viewpoints.

Intrapersonal Problems
Any close, valued relationship can be damaged by wrongdoing or conflict, but the type and degree of hurt will depend on the behavior and events. The intensity of the response may be, in some ways, a measure of the importance of the problem or the relationship. Some offenses and their damage are *accidental*, no one's fault unless carelessness caused them. The trouble can usually be discussed or privately forgiven. When offenses are, or appear to be, *intentionally* motivated, they can result in serious disruption. Security, trust, and confidence in yourself, others, or the world are shaken. The resulting wariness and distrust are very difficult to neutralize. These injuries are often ignored and overlooked with "forgive and forget," but then the mistrust can mount up. The peaceable response to wrongdoing is to communicate it interpersonally, although this can be very tricky. Some people choose to hurt back with a vengeful response.

Intrapersonal Transformation Process
In Eastern cultures, the emphasis of transformation is on inner peace and psychological peacemaking on the principle that peaceful thoughts and emotions are correlated with peaceable relationships. A Western emphasis is on outwardly peaceful relationships. Both intrapersonal and interpersonal transformation are important to create lasting peace.

For individuals, transformation takes place in five phases.

1. It begins with a *disorienting predicament* that does not fit your worldview. You find that your existing perspective and coping methods are simply inadequate to resolve the predicament. For example, the onset of the AIDS crisis disrupted prevalent sexual trends and caused many people to question their lifestyles.
2. Often, an anxious crisis follows, in which you might feel that "the world has tilted." Though uncomfortable, this fuels a *choice*, usually subconscious, to ignore the predicament and hold to your existing worldview, or to search for a new way of finding sense in the issue.
3. Next, *critical consideration* of assumptions and beliefs generates a readiness to consider potentially useful alternatives. With the threat of AIDS, for example, many people had to examine both their actions and their beliefs about relationship, sexuality, love, and commitment. Other peoples' input during this phase provides the context and support to explore alternative ideas, experiences, opinions, and solutions.
4. A *revised worldview* and organizing principles that accommodate the predicament are constructed from individual and social turmoil.
5. Last, you will experiment with *new action patterns* that integrate significant insights into your lifestyle. Some resistance to change always occurs because relinquishing a worldview represents stepping from certainty into painful (though ultimately rewarding) insecurity.

Jessie Sutherland (2005) identified **worldview skills** that challenge existing worldviews and inspire rethinking. See Praxis Skill Builder 12.1 for some suggestions for cultivating worldview skills.

Both Mohandas Gandhi and Martin Luther King were skeptical about the expected success of any social transformation in the presence of selfish resentment, bitterness, or hatred. Both were determined that social action should not cause suffering or recreate violence in any form. Martin Luther King said, "Nonviolence means avoiding not only external, physical violence, but also an internal violence of spirit. You not only refuse to shoot ... but you also refuse to hate."

Praxis Skill Builder 12.1 ■ Principles for Worldview Skills Building

- Don't wait—Actively pursue understanding and emotional awareness through reflection.
- Practice deep gratitude.
- Be patient with uncertainty, imperfection, and incompletion.
- Invest in connection—Start with "ME" and extend to "WE."
- Live with values of *love* and collective attachment; *honest* transparency; personal *balance*; the *power* to choose; *integrity* of purpose, regardless of emotion or doubt; serving with *charity*; the *wisdom* of humility, personal discipline, flexibility, and diligence.
- Optimistically believe in goals, and take risks to achieve them. "We become what we hope" (Florence Nightingale).

Jessie Sutherland (2005). *Worldview Skills: Transforming Conflict from the inside Out.* New Delhi: Worldview Strategies.

Individuals have to be ready and open to transformation. Conflict transformation is both theoretical and practical. Knowledge is not enough; the insights gained will change your actions. Intrapersonal transformation therefore requires a combination of personal commitment, development, and advanced skill. John Paul Lederach (2009) described some developed insights that prepare a person:

> Insight 1: Interpret the energy of conflict as a dilemma, not a problem;
> Insight 2: Look at presenting issues as a window, not a door;
> Insight 3: Expand time frames beyond the immediate situation;
> Insight 4: Make complexity a friend, not a foe; and
> Insight 5: Hear and engage identities and relationship.

INTERPERSONAL PEACEMAKING AND TRANSFORMATION

Individual Responses to Injustice

When something is offensive—wrong-doing or injustice—individual and community reactions too often pursue the dichotomous options of choosing to escape with passive avoidance, or to fight with violent aggression. Lynne Woehrle and Susan French (1992) challenged this false dichotomy with a violence-nonviolence-violence continuum. Both passivity and violent force are based in fear; both are reactive, not proactive; both perpetuate the belief that power solves problems; both inevitably set up destructive, asymmetric conflict and cycling violence; and both cause harm to someone. The crucial third option is proactive action used nonviolently to oppose what is wrong and achieve change.

> *Watch your thoughts, for they become words.*
> *Watch your words, for they become actions.*
> *Watch your actions, for they become habits.*
> *Watch your habits, for they become character.*
> *Watch your character, for it becomes your destiny.*
> —*Attributed to Laozi in* Tao Te Ching

A few scholars note that a lack of personal awareness is a serious impediment to transformed, peaceful relationships. **Moral blindness** is insensitivity to or denial of the deep implications of injustice and violence, and the alternatives (Bauman, 2013; Drumwright, 2004). It is an outcome, essentially, of self-centered bias that permits much blind, overlooked injustice such as racism. The contrasting ability is the **moral imagination,** which uses empathy to imagine a full range of possibilities that can produce ethical and effective problem solutions. This was prominent in Martin Luther King's "I Have A Dream" speech, given in Washington, D.C., in 1963. In practice, the moral imagination is the capacity to imagine and generate constructive conflict processes that transcend habitual destructive and violent patterns. Using the moral imagination in conflict situations will inevitably lead to diminished violence and constructive social interactions (Lederach, 2005).

Passive-Avoidant Responses Are Defensive, and Bring No Change

Like many of the *campesinos* of Honduras, some victims despair their powerlessness and conclude that nothing can be done. They are defeated or cynical about the risks in taking action (Solnit, 2016). Some accept violence and continue to suffer; others flee their violent settings to find safe sanctuary, protecting the most vulnerable among them: their children, elders, and the "nobodies." The consequences of either strategy are usually dire: suffering is deep, and society loses the benefit of their input. People might be safer, but no social transformation occurs.

Violence Produces Change, but at a Cost

Violence grows in a context of desperation and confrontation using coercive force to impose change. Violence seems faster than slow social evolution, so people become frustrated with the perceived failures of alternative peaceful means. After repeatedly unsuccessful attempts to overcome offense or injustice, some change agents give up on gradual change and adopt tactics that they believe will compel a new order.

The threat of violence or the occasional outbreak of actual violence can demonstrate a will for change and a capacity for action, forcing decision makers to take the demands for change seriously. Limited violence is sometimes perceived to be legitimate. For example, self-defense or the violent potential of police forces are seen by most people as legitimate and necessary for social order. Violence perpetrated by individuals or by groups on the fringe of society is regarded as illegitimate and criminal.

People working toward social transformation also consider reasons to avert violence. Because it erupts unpredictably or often with several simultaneous origins, violence can be disorganized, with stumbling aims and methods. Almost always, it results in costly property damage. Unintended victims are exposed to harm emotionally at minimum, and injuries and even death are also possible. Violence cannot be sustained because of the toll it takes on consciences and on society.

The Third Option: Nonviolent Social Transformation Is Active and Constructive

Alvarado chooses another option. **Nonviolence** is a far-reaching concept that goes beyond both passive acceptance and violent aggression to solve problems. Nonviolent action is not passive but, instead, rejects violence and injustice of any type *and* finds alternatives to achieve a goal. Just as violence occurs on every level of social life, so nonviolent responses are possible on every level. This was illustrated by Erica Chenoweth and Maria Stephan (2011) who found that in the last century violence was a surprisingly ineffective strategy (25% successful, fully or partially); rather, nonviolent methods created more durable peace more often (75% successful, and increasing). The trend is that violence does transform injustice but is used less and less often.

Two complementary forms of nonviolence can be differentiated. *Pragmatic* or *strategic nonviolence* uses nonviolence because it works (Ackerman, 1994). Many activists adopt the strategies of inspirational predecessors such as Mohandas Gandhi, Martin Luther King, and Nelson Mandela, all of whom were successful in generating dramatic social change. *Principled* or *compassionate nonviolence* assumes a responsibility to promote deeply respectful interactions in every relationship. For example, Gandhi's concept of *satygraha* (the force of truth) stated that any violence, whether physical or psychological, causes damage and can be overcome only with compassion and nonviolent action. Although often supported by religious belief, nonviolence is a principle and a practice that spans many centuries and many faiths (Sharp, 1973; Smith-Christopher, 2007).

Martin Luther King was famous and is remembered for leading the refinement of nonviolent thinking and practices. His Six Principles of Nonviolence (1958) emphasized the lifestyle and lifetime aspects of nonviolent peacemaking.

1. Nonviolence is a way of life for courageous people. It is mentally, emotionally, and spiritually aggressive to actively resist evil.
2. Nonviolence seeks to win understanding, friendship, and community reconciliation.
3. Nonviolence seeks to resist and defeat injustice, not people.
4. Nonviolence holds that suffering can educate and transform, so accepts suffering without retaliation.
5. Nonviolence chooses unselfish, creative love instead of hate to resist violence.
6. Nonviolence believes that the universe is on the side of justice, so that justice will eventually win.

Nonviolence is a strategy chosen for many reasons. It grows from confidence that final powers remain with each choice. Nonviolence avoids the property and personal casualties that are inevitable when violence ignites, so nonviolence is more likely to gather public approval and participation.

An unlimited repertoire of nonviolent action has been used throughout history, tailored by the inventiveness of the parties, the issue, and the context. Johan Galtung (1965) stated that transformation includes negative actions that interfere with violence, and positive actions that encourage friendship and cooperation. Gene Sharp (1973) compiled and categorized nearly 200 transformative nonviolent strategies used in history.

Nonviolence has been, and is, controversial, with a range of opinion in every society. Martin Luther King cautioned, "By no means does nonviolence always result in change. Nonviolence is, in fact, often met with violence." Nonviolent strategy does not always remain nonviolent; some people do turn to violence and sometimes nonviolence is deliberately used to provoke violent counteraction.

INTRAPERSONAL AND INTERPERSONAL TRANSFORMATION TOGETHER

Intrapersonal transformation is an inward process that cultivates peaceable character over time. Interpersonal transformation occurs between at least two people who have experienced a damaged relationship. Next, we will explore the complex links among the transformative elements of apology, forgiveness, and reconciliation.

When the qualities of a peaceable relationship are interrupted by wrongdoing and injustice, there is always a protective response such as shock or anger or fear. Most people find it impossible to return to the desired "normal" until some work of repair has mended the rupture. The offended person has choices:

1. Avoid and deny with willful blindness, which results in greater personal damage or a loss of the relationship in the long run;
2. Take revenge, resorting to a "tit-for-tat" version of justice, which results in compounded harm;

3. Process forgiveness that acknowledges the seriousness of the offense but provides release from guilt and harm; and
4. Reconciliation, a renewed relationship built on justice, truth, integrity, and mutuality.

Actions that restore an amiable relationship are twofold: the offender offers apology, restitution, and/or is punished, and the offended person extends pardon. Ideally these responsibilities are shared by both parties. Most often, though, the offended person and the offender have divergent interpretations, needs, and timetables, and the two processes occur asymmetrically. Repair is possible but there are few formulae, and parties may need support and facilitation to deal with a painful injury, and they might have to accept what is possible rather than what is ideal.

Apology

An important facilitator of transformative resolution is an apology by the wrongdoer. Just as offense results in harm, heartfelt apology results in repair (Govier, 2002). Although some people are overly quick to say "sorry ... sorry," an effective apology has to be made carefully. If not offered wisely, apologies can do more harm than good, backfiring into an additional injury. When the words of an apology are too little too late, or the victim senses that the wrongdoer is insincere, has been forced, or is merely trying to avoid responsibility, it is difficult to view an apology as a signal of real healing. Done well, an apology can result in improved communication and lead to less intense or lengthy conflict.

Douglas Noll (2003) described two parts of a *core interpersonal apology sequence*, that Roy Lewicki (2016) augmented with *six components*:

1. The offender offers an apology:
   a. name the mistake and take full responsibility for the harm it caused;
   b. express emotions of sorrow and regret;
   c. express willingness to make at least symbolic amends;
   d. show humility by explaining the facts of what went wrong;
   e. explain a commitment to change and what will prevent a repeated situation; and
   f. request (not demand) forgiveness.
2. The victim begins the lengthy process of forgiving: this might be *unilateral* (a solitary process not communicated with the offender) or *mutual* (based on interactions between the victim and the offender).

Some apology components are more important than others. Taking responsibility is the most persuasive, and asking for forgiveness is the least effective. A sincere apology constitutes a **moral amend** by

> *There is never a great way to apologize, but there are plenty of terrible ways.*
> —*Anonymous*

addressing the victim with dignity, separate from **practical amends** that restore to the victim any material losses caused by the wrongdoing (Govier, 2002).

Apology Acts Legislated

In the past decade, some legal jurisdictions have established Apology Acts to facilitate apology between a professional and someone who believes their professional actions caused a detrimental outcome, such as ongoing losses resulting from inaccurate accounting. This form of apology is usually mediated between the accused and the offended parties, but is not an admission of legal guilt or incompetence. Not all states or provinces have provisions for this process.

Apology and forgiveness are "two sides of the same coin" (Hauss, 2003). Both provide constructive ways to transform suffering caused by wrongdoing.

Forgiveness

Everyone does wrong at some point and disappoints or hurts people. We all need forgiveness, and everyone has experienced and offered some forms of forgiveness. This is what makes forgiveness an **empty universal**: a universal experience that is objectively blank because each person completes its meaning with their own subjective meanings. For this discussion, to **forgive** is to pardon an offense. Forgiveness is a deeply felt, in many ways costly and mysterious, phenomenon. Forgiveness is a gift granted (a noun) and also an action (a verb).

In Peace and Conflict Studies, forgiveness is regarded as a critical harmonizing factor (for example, Enright and North, 1998; Exline, 2003; McCullough, 2000; Shriver, 1995). However, many ambiguities are debated: how to define it, what responsibilities the victim and the wrongdoer have, what is the role of remorse, whether or not forgiveness should be promoted, what process leads to forgiveness, and so on. Some practitioners believe it is too easily misused and it places too much burden on a victim. Forgiveness does not always help heal or transform a broken relationship. Rather, too often it results in repetition of the offense, and the relationship becomes tangled in a cycle of offense and pseudoforgiveness. Table 12.2 illustrates what forgiveness is and, just as importantly, is not.

Forgiveness Paradox #1: Forgiveness is both intrapersonal and interpersonal.

> *Forgiveness is intrapersonal.*

Forgiveness by the person harmed is primarily an inward process of mending that lets go of resentment and the right to retaliate. At points, this seems like an

Table 12.2   Forgiveness Is ... and Is Not ...

Forgiveness is ... difficult	*Forgiveness is NOT ... "cheap" pseudoforgiveness*
A lengthy, individual process	Completed instantly
Naming and facing the hurt	Suppressing the hurt and resentment
Acknowledging bad behavior and its consequences	Excusing or justifying bad behavior
Remembering	Overlooking and forgetting injustice
Working to repair the harm, and rebuild trustworthiness	Kissing and make up
Facing the consequences	Legal pardon or "letting them off the hook"

impossible task because victims essentially give up the anger to which they are entitled and give the offender an undeserved gift (Enright, 2015). Intrapersonal forgiveness rarely manifests itself whole; rather, it advances in discernible degrees (Flanigan, 1992).

1. A reduction of negative emotions leads to ...
2. Neutral feelings toward the wrongdoer, which starts a readiness for ...
3. Risky reengagement with selective disclosure; if it is safe, this can lead to ...
4. Full reconciliation of the relationship with uncensored disclosure and growth.

Ideally, forgiveness is interactive and interpersonal.

The majority of the existing forgiveness scholarship is focused on the injured person's process and tasks, possibly because offenders are difficult to engage. In fact, some wrongdoers may never be capable of what is necessary to help the process. However, wrongdoing is the responsibility of the offender; so, too, transformative mending is primarily the offender's responsibility (Worthington, 2009).

When Sally Kohn became an adult, she gained some insight about herself as a teen bully. She hired a private investigator to find a girl she had bullied and set up an apology meeting with "Vicky Rarsch," the pseudonym Kohn used when she told the story. Rarsch told her, "I accept your apology. Messages such as this cannot absolve you of your past actions. The only way to do that is to improve the world, prevent others from behaving in similar ways, and foster compassion" (Kohn, 2016).

Typically, a wrongdoer's transformation is long and twisted because the hardest work of all is forgiving yourself. Offenders must persistently resist the temptation to accept (or demand) cheap forgiveness (Wenzel, 2012). The process usually begins with denial that downplays the offense or its impact, and sometimes that denial does not fully end. When a wrongdoer does understand the gravity of the wrongful actions, they can be flooded with shame and guilt that they try to appease with confession and remorse. Expressing this remorse often convinces the victim to offer forgiveness prematurely. Properly, though, this is when the difficult transformation and reformation work begins. The wrongdoer must be strongly motivated to persist in the process of change.

To establish a safe basis for a relationship, much is required of an offender:

1. Acknowledge the wrong—One of the greatest impediments to forgiveness is the wrongdoer's unwillingness to fully face the truth of the offense and its impact. Rather, actions are minimized or justified, or excuses are made.
2. Empathy for those harmed—Offenders must be able to take the perspective of the person hurt. Understanding the full consequences of wrongful actions can be overwhelming and seem impossible to remedy.
3. Take responsibility—Wrongdoers must blame no one but themselves for their actions. This is a two-edged sword: the offender must acknowledge their guilt but the admission can be crippling, so nondefensive and humble ways to manage their self-esteem, shame, and guilt must be found.
4. Take specific steps to prevent recurrence of the wrongdoing.

5. Be willing to offer reparation for the harms caused.
6. Then, and only then, the wrongdoer is ready to offer apology and ask for forgiveness (Jenkins, 2009).

Forgiveness Paradox #2: Forgiveness is neither so lenient that it cancels natural consequences nor so harsh that it can never happen.

Forgiveness is not lenient pseudoforgiveness.

Pseudoforgiveness is a victim's pretense masquerading as forgiveness. Many victims are tempted to be too lenient, to "forgive and forget," thinking that this is generous or merciful and a way to resolve their own hurt. It is an ineffective way to hurry the healing, and results only in suppressed issues and hurt. Superficial pseudoforgiveness does nothing to move a conflict toward transformative resolution.

Forgiveness should not be too severe.

However, some victims are tempted to make forgiveness impossible by demanding excessive accountability, reparation, or punishment. True forgiveness is found somewhere in the middle between lenient and demanding, involving an active combination of victim mercy and offender accountability (see Figure 12.1).

Forgiveness Paradox #3: For the offended person, transformative forgiveness is both a decision and a process.

Forgiveness is a choice.

True forgiveness cannot be forced or rushed. Until victims have resolved some bitterness and pain, many actively resist forgiving (Enright, 2015). Eventually, most commit themselves to forgiving for their own peace. Scholarly consensus is that a decision point is part of forgiveness.

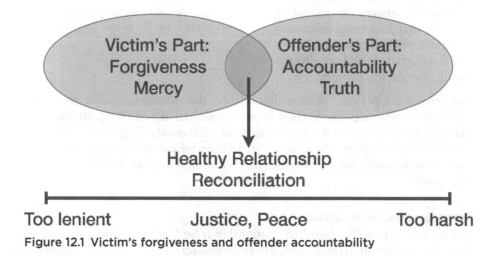

Figure 12.1 Victim's forgiveness and offender accountability

This decisive aspect was vividly demonstrated in 2006, when the children of the West Nickel Mines Amish school in Pennsylvania were attacked by Charles Roberts. The boys were forced to leave; the girls were bound, lined up, and shot, injuring five and killing five; then Roberts shot himself. When the news of this attack began filtering out, community members reached out to Roberts's widow, parents, and parents-in-law to verbally offer forgiveness. One member was quoted to say, "We will not think evil of this man." Later, members stated that this remarkable process was initiated in each case by a decision to forgive Roberts, regardless of the incredible severity of his crimes. Donald Kraybill (2007) described this as *upsidedown forgiveness*.

The community's forgiveness and compassion were the beginning, but certainly not the end, of the process. Many families continue to live with the repercussions of the attack, mourning the deaths and coping with girls permanently disabled by brain injury.

Forgiveness initiates a healing process.

Forgiveness is a choice, but also grows out of a difficult process. As for the Nickel Mines families, it may take a considerable length of time usually correlated with the intensity of the wrongdoing. Victim process cannot be prescribed, but the elements are described (Enright, 2015; Wade, 2005):

- explore what forgiveness does and does not mean personally;
- confront the damage, and reorient fragile feelings;
- discover openness to and possible empathy for the wrongdoer's perspective;
- forgive your own weakness and mistakes;
- choose to forgive; and
- overcome resistance to forgiveness.

Unfortunately, many victims also deal with others who either blame the victim for the offense or demand that the victim forgive. Both of these approaches amount to secondary injustice that sometimes reinforces a victim's own self-blame and unrealistic expectations and can divert a healthy forgiveness process.

> *The stupid neither forgive nor forget;*
> *The naive forgive and forget;*
> *The wise forgive but do not forget.*
> —*Thomas Szasz, The Second Sin (1973)*
> *"Personal Conduct"*

Forgiveness is a personal process that restores the victim; reconciliation restores a broken relationship. Forgiveness is not reconciliation and reconciliation is not essential to forgiveness. A victim might simultaneously forgive and decide to release the relationship. The essential foundation for reconciliation is transformation of the offender, who establishes trustworthiness so that the offense will not be repeated.

Interpersonal Reconciliation

A meaningful, possibly cherished relationship is broken by conflict, offense, and hurt. Painful alienation results and, if the relationship is to survive, a transformative

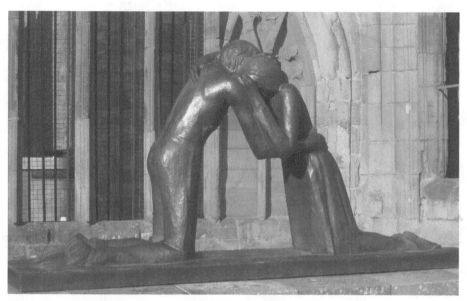

Figure 12.2 "Reconciliation"—Statue at Bradford University
Statue by Josefina de Vasconcellos (1977), Bradford University School of Peace Studies.

peace process of reconciliation must occur. Reconciliation means refriending, reestablishing a broken relationship. The process is usually long; in some situations it may even involve successive generations.

Reconciliation (see Figure 12.2) necessitates that animosity and distrust are overcome to create a new attachment. It is a victim's part to willingly consider this as a possibility, and the offender's responsibility to transform character by (re)building trustworthiness. However, contrition, forgiveness, and reconciliation are autonomous: a victim cannot be held hostage by a wrongdoer's refusal to do the work, and a wrongdoer cannot be held hostage by a victim's refusal to forgive (Enright, 1998).

Paradox #4: Reconciliation is both a process and an outcome (Bar-Tal, 2004).

Reconciliation is a process.

When a formerly open relationship is damaged, revenge and retaliation are common reactions that may take on the rhythm of a continuing cycle depicted in Figure 12.3. The resulting escalation of hostility and cruelty, in their turn, causes a recurring cycle of harm. A *revenge cycle* emphasizes interpersonal alienation and rejection. That attitude seems to justify retaliatory violence toward the Other, but this then perpetuates the cycle of harm (Tutu, 2014).

A more risky but courageous option is to choose healing, with the possibility of new relationship between the offender and the offended person. The *reconciliation cycle* (Kraybill, 2000) validates the hurt and vulnerability, but allows for empathy that accepts human weakness. This leads to a willingness to dialogue, possibly to reconcile. It can lead either to release of the painful relationship, or to restoration of the openly trusting, safe relationship. Reconciliation occurs in the convergence of four dynamic processes that meet like square dancing partners,

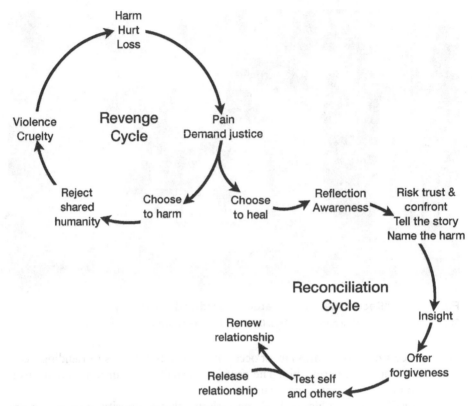

Figure 12.3 Revenge and reconciliation cycles
Adapted from Tutu (2014) and Kraybill (2000).

each taking a turn to function at center stage, and then ceding to another partner (Lederach, 1999).

- *truth* breaks the silence of alienation;
- *mercy* longs for a renewed relationship;
- *justice* is unwilling to accept easy peace; and
- *peace* works to create harmony.

Reconciliation is also an outcome.

Most offenses occur within a meaningful group such as a family, a workplace, or a friendship circle. Most people, when offended, do not want to end the relationship but, rather, they want to rebuild it. The hope and ultimate qualities of reconciliation are that all parties feel valued and loved, feel safe from unreasonable future harm, know their needs will be equitably met, have a healthy sense of boundary and self-responsibility, and enjoy restored friendship or partnership.

Facilitated Intrapersonal and Interpersonal Transformation
Although much personal transformation takes place naturally, some creative influences smooth its progress and speed the pace (Partridge, 2021). Some forms

(such as meditation) are practiced alone, others (such as music) are expressive-receptive, occasionally with an audience; some (such as storytelling) are participatory. The intrapersonal and interpersonal processes are entwined, and rarely completely separate. We will explore four forms, but other varieties are limited only by creativity (Lederach, 2005).

Visual Art Is a Transformative Medium

Visual art symbolizes the creator's deeply personal feelings and ideas. Visual art pieces such as sculpture, painting and posters, photographs, and comic books place color, shape, words, and insights side by side, to express specific ideas about peace and conflict. The visual symbols are linked in a subliminal way with deep feelings, beliefs, and memories associated with conflict, so they become a profound catalyst for viewers to think about conflict while sorting through difficult and discordant images.

The factional Spanish Civil War was fought from 1936–1939. In April 1937, at the request of nationalist Francisco Franco Bahamonde, Nazi Germany relentlesly bombed the Spanish town of Guernica. The town was nearly obliterated as homes and bomb shelters, waterworks, transportation routes and bridges, animals, and citizens were bombed, shot, and burned. From his horror about this event, Pablo Picasso created a painting, "Guernica," to depict the grotesque suffering of all the living creatures there. The controversial painting was unveiled at the Spanish pavilion at the 1937 Paris International Exhibition, publicizing the terrors of the developing war. The painting now hangs in Madrid.

In 1955 a tapestry replica was woven by Jacqueline de la Baume Durrbach and hung in the entryway to the Security Council chambers of the United Nations in New York. In 2003, when US officials attended the United Nations to brief members on the war in Iraq, the tapestry was covered with a large blue sheet so that "the unappealing images" would not appear as a backdrop to official pictures and television appearances.

Visual art can be comforting, but can also be provocative. For example, both war and peace monuments have important functions to inspire serious thought about conflict, possibly to take action. The largest concentration of peace monuments is probably in the Japanese city of Hiroshima, the site of atomic bombing by the United States in 1945. The first monument was built in 1948 to commemorate the Hiroshima Girls High School casualties at ground zero of the bombing. The inscription on the monument reads "$E = MC^2$," reportedly because the occupying US authorities would not permit direct reference to the bombing. In another example, the sculpture of Yevgeny Vuchetich, "Let Us Beat Swords into Plowshares," was gifted to the United Nations by Russia, and was memorialized in a 1970 stamp (see Figure 12.4).

Art is also used therapeutically to transform traumatic feelings and memories related to violence and war, helping victims and even perpetrators of violence to heal, and inspiring broad social change (Levine, 2011). When conflict has ended, those affected are encouraged to use visual art forms such as drawing, quilting, and sculpture to remember and work through the wounds left by serious violence. The very act of expressing feelings visually becomes a medium for simultaneously memorializing, validating, and transforming brokenness, becoming a vehicle for healing and reintegration.

Figure 12.4 "Let Us Beat Swords into Plowshares"
Stamp based on the sculpture by Yevgeny Vuchetich.

Music Is a Transformative Medium

Music is a cultural universal: every culture, every family, every ethnic group loves and shares distinctive forms of music. Many have observed that communal singing is elemental communal breathing. Music affects individual emotion, mood, and perception, and can inspire hope; it can become a uniting interpersonal bond; it can change societies' understandings and practices.

According to Daniel Levitin (2008), music is transformative for three reasons: a) music inspires perspective-taking—the viewpoint of the composer is performed personally, literally exploring the other's ideas; b) music depicts realities from alternative times and places; and c) music combines and recombines elements of reality, belief, relationship, problems, and solutions, thus creatively inspiring the potential for transformation.

Though ancient, music is ubiquitous; though universal, it is particular. Levitin's analysis suggests that every song is a variant of six human themes:

- friendship and hatred—Music unites human experience, but also expresses and catalyzes discord and enmity.
- joy—Joy songs, often associated with dance or ceremony, express a broad and deep range of positive emotion.

- comfort—Music soothes distress and comforts sorrow, and becomes a preview of eventual healing.
- knowledge—Music can provide a "playground" to explore success and failure, and right and wrong ways of doing things.
- ceremony—Music celebrates notable events, organizing and communicating values and augmenting individual and collective memory.
- love—Songs explore the many shades of loving and of caring more for others than about ourselves.

Music documents and shapes history by becoming a signature of a cultural era or specific movement. The civil rights movement of the 1960s developed unique protest music. Hip hop music was generated by youth in the 1980s from ancient African American traditions to express nonconformity and to protest mainstream social values. Artists like the Beatles, Jimi Hendrix, and Bob Marley, U2 and Bono, and Eminem have had enormous influence on social discourse.

In conflict, music can express the related turmoil, helping to clarify problems, and thus modify reactions. Music can help rethink a harmful response, to discover more adaptive options. For example, in Great Britain, a campaign called "Love Music Hate Racism" spreads antiracism through music. Created by the Anti-Nazi League and Unite Against Fascism, their music encourages antiracist and antifascist activity, as well as discouraging Britains from supporting fascist election candidates.

Music therapy is an advanced type of therapy used to foster wellbeing and to assist troubled individuals' mental health. Working in a therapeutic relationship, patients compose or select music, then use it to explore problems and deepen awareness and personal growth. A variety of music is used to improve physical, emotional, and spiritual perspectives. Because it is nonverbal and creative, music therapy can be used with all ages and abilities.

Storytelling Is a Transformative Medium

Families and cultures use story to teach history and primary values, and to reinforce identities (Curthoys, 2012). Stories use structure and play, and elements of poetic recitation or comedy or suspense to combined art forms like drama and dance to encourage a listener's imagination. Story expresses the heart of meaningful experience (Behrman, 2016).

The National Storytelling Network notes that storytelling happens as an interaction between a storyteller and at least one listener. The responses of the listener influence the telling, so the teller must be attentive to the listener even as the story unfolds. Storytelling can be transformative for the teller when it is used to recount and clarify past events and to transmit deep feelings about them. Hearing can be transformative for the listener, too, as the story shapes feelings and imagination, even memory and identities.

Conflict stories are associated with strong emotion that can narrow perception to the most basic, sinister detail (Picard, 2015; Shapiro, 2017), altering the disputants' view of and commitment to a relationship, so the conflict can impact every subsequent interaction. The stories you tell about yourself and your conflicts construct coherent images and interpretations of the relationship and reactions to later conflicts (Baker, 2018; McAdams, 2013). For example, Donald Trump's narrative of his conflicts with the press and his political challengers is summarized in his phrase "witch-hunt," and this shapes his every interaction. When stories are transmitted within a culture, they can shape the core identity of a whole people and its opponents.

Storytelling is also activated to facilitate individual and social transformation (Senehi, 2020). For example, the Akron (OH) Story Circle Project facilitates rethinking race and hidden prejudice. Using Narrative Mediation or Narrative Facilitation (Winslade, 2000), a mediator provides a safe space to guide the retelling of an event from the contrasting perspectives of the disputants. In the process, parties break down the conflict into its elementary chapters and artic-ulate the assumptions that ignited it. This leads to a reinterpretation of the story (Shapiro, 2017). The goal is to rebuild a story with curi-osity, respect, and trust. The result can be a reconciled relationship (Beer, 2012).

> *My friends, love is better than anger; hope is better than fear; optimism is better than despair. So let us be loving, hopeful, and optimistic. Then we'll change the world.*
> —Jack Layton, 2011

Nonviolent Communication Facilitates Transformation

Nonviolent Communication (NVC) was developed by Marshall Rosenberg (2015), and is also called Compassionate Communication and Collaborative Communication. It is based on the assumption that behavior and communica-tion are linked with basic and valued human needs. Basic needs do not conflict because the universe holds plenty for everyone; conflict results when your ways of expressing and meeting needs clash with others' ways of doing so. When people become violent it is because your needs are frustrated and you lack other, more effective, ways of expressing them. As you develop deep interper-sonal connections, empathy grows and you can bridge the core needs between yourself and others. Core skills are centered in statements that express accurate self-awareness, empathic and accurate interpretation of others, and authentic understandings.

Rosenberg taught four NVC components that use personal awareness to facilitate caring connection with others:

1. Nonjudgmental observation of simple factual information;
2. Sensations and emotions associated with the observed facts;
3. Identify the related basic human needs, satisfied or frustrated; and
4. Clearly request, but do not demand, action to collaborate on meeting ev-eryone's needs.

NVC is a method of communication but, more, it is a worldview of shared needs and conflict prevention and a nonviolent lifestyle. Inner compassion in relationships with others means that your communication will lose the violent tendencies and take on nonviolent, collaborative patterns. NVC is applied in many intrapersonal ways, interpersonal conciliation, and within groups and social systems.

Think About and Discuss with Your Colleagues

Collect some of the phrases used by Donald Trump to describe his (perceived) political and journalistic opponents.

- What do these phrases suggest about his perception of and reaction to conflicts?
- Could you create for him alternative phrases that might be more objective and collaborative, and might alter his perceptions and reactions?

Transformative Mediation Facilitates Interpersonal Transformation (Bush and Folger)
Vigorous efforts have been made to develop professional ways to facilitate conflict transformation. Probably the most practical work is that of Baruch Bush and Joseph Folger (2005). They criticize traditional mediation for a simplistic problem focus that results at best in no change to the personal interpretations of a conflict, at worst in escalating injustice and a conflict spiral. Unsolved suspicion and anger are fundamentally alienating, and that interferes with ordinary skills and relationship functioning, and interactions degenerate. The negativity associated with conflict generates a sort of tunnel vision:

a. Vulnerability—Conflict destabilizes disputants' security and personal power, creating anxiety about weakness and defenselessness. Disputants therefore move to flee or to take control with unkindness, and the conflict stalls or becomes a power struggle.
b. Self-absorption—Negative conflict generates a perception of being unrecognized, insignificant, overlooked. Disputants react with defensive self-absorption, effectively shutting out the other party's concerns.

However disruptive, Bush and Folger believe that conflict can be the "motor of transformative change." To create sustainable peace, interpersonal mediation should interrupt the destructive cycle and improve conflict processing by helping the parties experience insight and regain positive connections. Transformation happens by reversing the central conflict dynamics, as illustrated in Figure 12.5.

a. An **empowerment shift** restores a sense of personal strength and mutual confidence, and reactivates skills. Transformative Mediation guides conflict parties to correctly identify deep needs, values, and priorities and to reinforce complementary strengths and capacities.
b. A **recognition shift** creates more realistic perception of the Self and the Other, and authentic interaction is regained. Transformative Mediation helps the parties to honestly and fully evaluate their own behavior and that of the Other, and to describe interactions that are satisfying and not.

The outcomes are healthier interactions, stronger ties, and more productive conflict patterns. When conflict interactions are altered with strength and

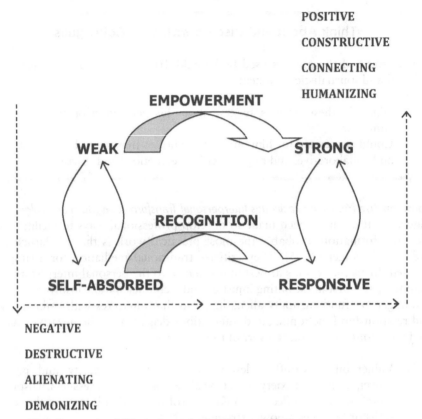

Figure 12.5 Dynamic shifts in transformative mediation
Reproduced with the permission of Robert A. Bush.

authentic interaction, transformation happens. Erica Fox (2010) called it **state-shifting**: "Confrontation gives way to connection, resistance to willingness, protectiveness to vulnerability ... a state-shift from alienation to alliance ... fragmentation to wholeness." Bush and Folger claim more straightforward decision making about relationships and other matters in conflict, and that even when the decision is to end a relationship, the end is accompanied by more compassionate understanding.

SOCIAL TRANSFORMATION WITH PEACEMAKING AND JUSTICE MAKING

People Must Be Enlisted to Join Social Transformation

George Lakey (2016) wrote that "strategy = power." If social change is to be successful, it must be guided by well thought strategy, and enlist many people on many levels of society. Lakey's five-staged framework illustrates a model for enlisting support.

1. *Cultural preparation* begins with public information, including exposure of the problem, dissemination of hope, and information about the goals aimed for. Gradual persuasion takes place. People must be convinced that

change is possible. A key motivating factor is the belief that the problem is important enough that you can do something to correct injustice. Virtually no one will invest significant effort into a trivial or hopeless cause.

2. Concerned people must be *organized* to generate enough influence to make a difference. Lakey encouraged this to happen through supportive interest groups and networks. Individuals, including politicians, make discrete decisions about their participation in a change that is underway. Anna Ortega-Williams (2017) added that organizing is formative: it shapes collective identity, helps heal collective trauma, and opens the way for new ways.

3. As the movement gains momentum, *direct action events expand and unify* the movement. Spreading awareness is crucial at this stage, so media relationships are cultivated. Information publicizes and promotes the cause, further expanding public support.

4. Noncooperative *mass action* is a natural development of the third phase. Grievances are expressed directly, and answers are proposed and negotiated. Movements are usually joined by many poorly informed individuals with highly mixed motives. In Black Lives Matter (see Case 12.2), for example, some people participate out of personal concern, some speak for affected populations, some have encompassing social concern, some hope to gain political points, and so on. This can result either in the expansion of issues included in the discontent or in the dilution of the momentum of the movement, and may also compromise its perceived legitimacy.

5. Extension to *parallel institutions* determines the durability of any social change. Pressure tactics diversify, and new power and decision making processes develop that include reformed structures and social process.

Weakness or incompletion at any stage of this framework usually results in a movement dwindling to nothing. The more organized and public the movement, the more likely it will generate opposition and a countercampaign.

In community **bottom-up peacebuilding**, locally designed processes such as relationship building and individual trauma healing work are used to address local grievances and losses. Formal, national changes through **top-down peace-building** are directed by national leaders, truth commissions, official apologies and other public events, legal reform, and national reparation. Both grassroots activists and powerful decision makers are important to successful strategies (Mac Ginty, 2012).

Not all social changes are uniformly adopted, and some simply decline and fade away. Everett Rogers (2003) noted that four forces influence the rate of change and whether a change will spread and endure: the new ideas and their applicability to everyday life, channels used to communicate both the problem and the possible solutions, the era and time frame, and the characteristics or resistance of the surrounding social system.

Social Problems and Injustice Necessitate Social Change
Virtually any problem that affects members of a society can become a social problem. *Personal problems*, such as underemployment, are challenges that people usually cope with privately or within a small circle of family and friends.

Social or *public problems*, such as high unemployment rates or poverty in a region, affect large numbers of people. Because personal and social concerns reinforce each other, the distinction between them is fluid. Public problems are beyond individual control, so one element of effective change is empowerment: persuading people that a broad solution is needed, is possible, and that they can be part of the change.

A *valence issue* is a problem about which reasonable consensus already exists in one direction. For example, virtually no one would condone valence problems of child abuse or political corruption (although the definitions of those conditions may vary). A *wedge issue* is a potentially divisive concern that is exploited to deliberately drive a wedge of fear and conflict. For example, calling the reform of marriage laws "world-shattering" or criticizing an education policy by stating that "society will never recover" could convert those into wedge issues. A *position issue* is a social problem connected to cultural principles that polarize popular opinion, about which strong consensus and agreement are *un*likely. For example, consensus or agreement is highly unlikely regarding Israeli settlements in Palestinian territories: few Palestinians would grant the legitimacy of the settlements while most Israelis continue to believe that they are necessary.

One of the primary motivators behind widespread change is collective frustration with an unworkable or unjust situation (Coser, 1956) like those taken on by Alvarado and Black Lives Matter: a political equilibrium, labor conditions, concern for the environment, or conflict and war (Giddens, 1982). The key is discontent, which then motivates collective justice making. Martin Luther King noted that when one person gets fed up enough to do something, that feeling spreads as if it were contagious. It was discontent with the "color coded framing" of society (Elias, 2020; Feagin, 2013) that inspired Black Lives Matter. As discontent with a current equilibrium spreads, related practices, norms for relationships, and cultural beliefs are debated and accompanied by some upheaval.

Social transformation occurs as an interaction between individuals and the collective. When a degree of consensus exists that a social change is needed, an inexact and unpredictable process starts. William Fielding Ogburn (1922) introduced the concept of **cultural lag** to describe that when social adjustment begins with progressive segments, culture and legislation "lag behind." The adjustment includes a time of social turmoil that ultimately results in a new equilibrium. Ogburn's conclusions outlined how society responds to social turmoil, and his stages of change can be adapted to broader social transformation processes (Del Sesto, 1983). A contemporary example of this process was illustrated in China, with the rethinking of the One Child Policy.

Systemic racism is a type of structural injustice (see Chapter 9) where racism is embedded within social power and cultural systems so invisibly and inescapably that it seems "normal." In Honduras, generations of rural poor farmers passively accepted the obvious injustice as "just the way life is." It took extraordinary thinking to begin shifting those conclusions to recognize that their situation was manipulated, and to mobilize groups for change. Systemic injustice is expressed in interlocking observable behavior, social structures, and policies that overlook the rights, needs, and dignity of marginalized groups, and attitudes that devalue certain characteristics while privileging others. Macpherson (1999) enumerated some of the causes: "It can be detected in processes, attitudes, and behavior that amount to discrimination through prejudice, ignorance, thoughtlessness, and racist stereotyping which disadvantage minority ethnic people."

A primary function of social conflict is systemic correction of underlying injustice. Discontent and unrest are signs that change or progress is about to happen. If society and its leaders attend to this emerging unrest, core systemic changes can transform exclusion and inequity into a better, beneficial society. Just as structural violence is expressed on three levels, so transformative solutions must occur on three levels: decisions and actions must reflect equity, organizations must provide equitable access to resources, and attitudes must move toward tolerance and appreciation of diversity. Such transformation necessitates critical assessment by individuals, organizations, and cultures that usually cannot happen in complete isolation but, rather, results from collective action.

Collective Transformation Is a Justice-Making Process

There is ongoing scholarly and philosophical debate and controversy defining justice and fairness, social inequity and injustice, and corrective social change. These concepts are hard to define by consensus. *Justice* means "right and fair"; *injustice* means "not right, unfair." However, perceptions of justice and injustice are contextually linked to views of human rights and varying tolerance for inequality, so actual thresholds for *in*justice vary from culture to culture.

Aside from abstract debates, there exist innumerable ordinary, universally human experiences of injustices, unfair and undeserved disadvantages that result from irresponsible neglect, misuse, or malevolence. Systemically, injustice is probably both negative and positive: events or a social status quo that deny or violate rights, *and* policies and actions that adversely affect the preconditions for wellbeing (Levy, 2006).

Social transformation must, therefore, be *both* negative and positive. The dual focus of transformative change is "what do we need to stop?" and "what do we hope to build?" Negative peace is the absence of conflict and positive peace is the presence of peaceable conditions. So, too, you can think of **negative justice** as the absence or failure of justice and **positive justice** as norms and proactive policies that provide fairly for the wellbeing of most people (Heinze, 2012; Shklar, 1990). To restore a community destroyed by conflict, multidimensional justices include all forms of retributive, distributive, restorative, procedural, and social justice.

Social justice exists when basic human needs are met and community members live peaceably with freedom to grow. Collective **social change** involves any significant alteration of existing order and accepted ways of living together. While such changes inescapably disturb an existing equilibrium, they lead to sometimes dramatic progress. If enduring solutions are to be found to troublesome issues that cause division and conflict, then solutions must be worked through on many synchronized fronts. It is unlikely that social change will occur quickly but, rather, it will be coordinated over significant periods and in many domains. It would help if you review the concept of nested conflict (drawn in our Introduction), which summarizes levels on which social conflict and change happen.

According to classical change theory (Udod, 2018), broad social change results from the dialectic equilibrium of complementary forces toward progress and resistance to change. A fluid equilibrium of progress and countermovement typically prevails across a social spectrum. A cultural practice persists and resists change, even if it is dysfunctional, until a better paradigm is accepted. When social life is broadly supported by a belief, resistance to change is strong; when discontent with the status quo develops, the dialectic moves toward progress. Social changes adopted by a substantial segment of society result in persistent change and progress. For example, ongoing resistance to changes in gender role balances and the place of women in global society can be attributed in part to the all-embracing foundations of womens' roles in every society.

Although the forces of resistance may be extensive, the need for progress is also strong (Waddell, 1998), so change becomes inevitable. Kurt Lewin (Cummings, 2015) recommended dealing with the progress-resistance dialectic in three parts: address and reduce resistance ("unfreeze" the existing order), compose a change, then promote movement in the desired direction ("refreeze" a new order).

The onset of a change that risks social instability may cause a significant backlash of distrust that animates a resistant countermovement working against the change. For example, racial segregation in some United States was, for many generations, the traditional, accepted social order (Benne, 1976). When the civil rights movement came to public attention, significant conflict and social division were caused, which continues today to some degree. The hope behind the turmoil is that a new perspective is formed that is both inclusive and realistically workable, thereby guiding new adaptive action. Rebecca Solnit (2016) defined hope as openings that arise from complexity and uncertainty to invite or demand action.

Transformation begins with individuals, and spreads to groups and society. Such structural changes can address the social inequities (such as slavery) that once were the foundation for long-term unrest and conflict. Systemic transformation rarely unfolds in orderly sequence, and the results are by no means certain or predictable. Two complementary processes can be observed:

1. *Incremental Progress*—Everyday experiences prompt incremental reformation of worldviews. Indisputable new data destabilizes existing ways of life almost invisibly over years and diverse cultures. Contrasting opinions and new ideas, especially expressed by respected peers, stimulate rethinking and change. New affiliations encourage reexamination of old ideas. New patterns of behavior, imposed and supported by collective social organizations can alter individual and family equilibrium. These gradual reformations coalesce over time into dramatic transformation.
2. *Paradigm Shift*—More dramatically but less commonly, worldview change occurs like a sudden leap. A **paradigm shift** is an alteration of the basic values and assumptions of a society, sometimes for the improvement of society, but sometimes not. A familiar traumatic paradigm shift was caused by the September 2001 9/11 terrorist attacks. Two deliberate plane crashes and two World Trade tower attacks in New York killed nearly 3,000 people and injured about 25,000 people. This event altered the assumptions of invulnerability and security of most people in the United States (Kakihara, 2003) and fundamentally changed government policies (Savitch, 2003).

An example of combined incremental and paradigm shifts occurred during the emancipation of women in the 19th and 20th centuries. Before that movement, women were not legal "persons." Awareness of the issue spread quietly and incrementally until moments when public campaigns advanced to dramatically challenge the existing paradigm.

Gradual Changes Adapt to Global Factors Naturally and Nonviolently

Many cultural advances occur gradually as new trends emerge (Dunfey, 2019). For example, as the world began to confront the recent coronavirus pandemic, striking changes occurred (and are ongoing) regarding health practices, relationship foundations, and social values. Other notable global trends currently underway correspond to potential social conflict:

- demographic shifts result in a drift from rural to urban ways of life and family style, increasing elderly and decreasing youth populations (with the exception of a developing "youth bulge" in parts of Africa), and increasing prosperity gaps between the people in developed and developing regions;
- gender role norms are rapidly shifting, affecting both home and work domains;
- rank and status criteria are being redefined, causing alterations of traditional prestige hierarchies; and
- power structures in government and in business are becoming more participatory, thus altering authority structures and decision making. This results in the inclusion of viewpoints from traditionally marginalized groups such as women and the poor.

It is not unusual for emergent changes to be cyclic, with recurring phases of growth and decline. A change in one aspect of social functioning disturbs an existing equilibrium and requires adjustment throughout the system. Though usually gradual, emergent transformation can lead to drastic change.

Revolutionary Change

Occasionally, revolution and terrorism arise from perceived social problems such as incompetent or unjust government. **Revolution** is a sudden, major, often violent, challenge of existing powers and social conditions. The origin of the concept is Old French <revolucion>, which means turning or even whirling around. Revolution results in a whirling and profound alteration of a society, but is not always progressive. Fidel Castro, for example, helped lead a sometimes violent revolutionary change in Cuba that created the first Communist state in the Western Hemisphere. Even Nelson Mandela at one time advocated violent sabotage in South Africa (then later relinquished that stance).

Early historical analysis by Crane Brinton (1938) distinguished some "uniformities" of revolutionary change:

- Context—Revolution begins in a group with ineffective, fractured, or corrupt leadership that causes general deprivation and growing resentment of injustice.
- Coercive revolution is initiated by people who have become disillusioned with legal, peaceful reformation. Subgroups direct the action process.

- Different motives rouse the people:
  a. Diversified *moderate reform groups* voice the discontent and negotiate revision within an existing structure.
  b. *Radical groups* split away from a moderate group to force immediate change through rebellious and adversarial opposition to authorities and moderate thinkers.
  c. Out of *extremist groups* a strong leader emerges who unites passionate protest and advocates forceful change.
- Conventional leaders have the options of attending to the discontent by addressing the revisions demanded, or of ignoring and degrading those who demand reform.

George Lawson's later scholarship (2019) added these insights:

- A *confluence* of events and specific social conditions, people, and leaders forms the foundation from which revolution emerges;
- Revolutionary action is *malleable*, shape-shifting to adapt its tactics to the historical and geographic context; and
- Revolution tends to be *intersocial*, crossing national and cultural boundaries.

A belief system called the **myth of redemptive violence** seems to motivate violent social change. There are some common elements: an entirely villainous enemy has disempowered legitimate authorities, but is opposed by an entirely good hero who triumphs over evil by using violence to force a sort of justice. *Redemptive violence* is the concept that short-lived violence can save people from perpetual violence. This dynamic is illustrated by the plots of many superhero stories. The myth is that necessary, justifiable force redeems peace from violence (Wink, 2014), so violence is regrettable but necessary to bring order into chaos. "Thou shalt sometimes kill." This myth has deep implications for strategies for social change. Peter Ackerman and Christopher Kruegler (1994) noted that when violence is widely accepted to oppose injury or tyranny, there is little or no incentive to consider less damaging alternatives.

Forceful or violent methods do shape social change. Revolutions are often followed by at least a brief period of peace and optimism (Brinton, 1938). For example, in the 1990s, the Taliban, a Sunni Islamic fundamentalist sect, initiated drastic changes in Afghani society by enforcing strict Sharia (Islamic) Law. At first these changes were welcomed as an orderly antidote to long-term corruption, civil turmoil, and war. However, harsh and sometimes arbitrary enforcement practices eventually eroded support among the Afghani people. Although the Taliban lost their widespread control in the early 2000s, they are still part of the ongoing violence in that region.

Hoped-for redemption is merely temporary, as Hannah Arendt (1972) said. "Violence is able, for a time, to instill fear, invite submission, and destroy lives and property, but not able to endow its users with legitimate consent they would require to keep their authority or power." As Martin Luther King said during his 1964 Nobel lecture, "Violence never brings permanent peace. It solves no social problem: it merely creates new and more complicated ones."

Violent action does cause social change, but the ever-present risk is that violence will force opponents or authorities to maintain their power with counter-violence. Coerced changes are usually grudging at best and scorned at worst, so they tend not to last.

Potential Methods for Social Transformation

Organized Social Movements Encourage Nonviolent Transformation
Groups of people who become impatient with the pace of evolving society organize to challenge specific social conditions. Their tactics are called *strategic disruption* because they tend to disrupt a status quo. Their actions are sometimes viewed as *peace movements* when their underlying purpose is to promote a better society. Diffused, multilevel, transnational activists use a repertoire of action for altering the conditions of diverse peoples (Porta, 2005; Tarrow, 2005). Movements and protests typically develop in cycles of contention (Tarrow, 2011, 2013) in four phases: from emergence to growth and coalescence, mainstream adoption, and decline (McAdam, 1996).

Social movement groups are not uniform or static. There is constant internal debate, and the groups stimulate broader public discussion of issues like what to campaign for (individual or social change, subtle or radical change, independent or with governmental support, one solution or many) and how to campaign (practical or idealistic, with or without force), and so on. Dispersed movements have different focus (for example, agriculture, climate, national armaments, or health), but their actions challenge those with decision and public policy-making power to address unjust disparities.

Historic Peacebuilder Guidance (Gandhi and King)
Many strategic decisions are made along the way to forming a change strategy. Martin Luther King advocated beginning with gathering evidence before taking orderly action, and Mohandas Gandhi's experiences expanded the repertoire.

1. Gather information to identify the problem—King believed that objective findings establish the legitimacy of a social movement. He promoted careful investigation of the facts to objectively establish that social injustice and inequity do exist, over and above any personal frustration or discontent.
2. Create a vision for change, and inform and educate the uninformed.
3. Commitment yourself to act congruently— Gandhi used community retreat and King advocated a "pause" from activity for a period of contemplation. Your own motives must be clear, and personal complacency and bitterness resolved. A peaceful attitude of a protest is very important because resentment, bitterness, and hatred compromise a movement and quickly escalate the conflict.
4. Negotiate—Map the allies, opponents, and decision makers. Begin negotiation to address the injustice officially with authorities who have the power to modify the discriminatory conditions.
5. Direct nonviolent action—Only when negotiations are unsuccessful, brainstorm tactics to responsibly take nonviolent direct action. You should do this openly, communicating both the discontent and the proposed or demanded solution. Nonviolent protesters, regardless of the tactics chosen, must be willing to accept any penalties that result from your actions. Both Gandhi and King endured numerous arrests for civil disobedience.

Gandhi's recommendations were designed to prevent uncontrolled conflict escalation (Wehr, 2019). Activists need training so that their first reactions are nonviolent, and not humiliating or destructive of an "enemy." Focus an immediate campaign on a well-defined issue that is a component of a larger, more basic problem. Intensify pressure in a planned, stepwise manner to prevent escalation into hostility.

6. Reconcile with opponents and begin the healing process—Understanding and friendship between opponents is the goal, and injustice, not people, are the target of protest.

CONFLICT CASE 12.2 ▪ BLACK LIVES MATTER, 2020

Systemic activism is an old phenomenon. For centuries, groups and movements across the globe have advocated for justice for marginalized groups such as women and racial minorities. In the past 70 years, justice making for people of color has been an important theme driven by several notable events.

In 1955, in Mississippi, a black 14-year-old named Emmett Till was beaten and lynched by Roy Bryant and J. W. Milam after teasing Bryant's white wife. Subsequent outrage resulted in the formation of the Emmett Till Memorial Commission with a mandate to foster racial harmony and reconciliation. The killing added impetus to the US civil rights movement.

In 1993, in London, England, black teenager Stephen Lawrence was stabbed in a racially motivated attack by Gary Dobson, David Norris, and other boys. A judicial inquiry led by William Macpherson (1999) resulted in some startling new insights into systemic racism, and 70 recommendations. This caused much social discussion and eventual reform.

In 2012, Florida police officer George Zimmerman shot black teenager Trayvon Martin. His acquittal in 2013 moved Alicia Garza, Patrisse Cullors, and Opal Tometi to found the Black Lives Matter movement.

The movement gained strength after 2014, mostly spurred by police violence. American police officers shot more than 1,000 people in 2019. The incident rate for white suspects was 13 fatalities per million, for black suspects it was 31 fatalities per million (Statista, 2020). The police murder of George Floyd in Minneapolis, MN, then sparked global participation in the summer of 2020.

Black Lives Matter unites a wide variety of people who are concerned about social injustice. It is many things at once: it is a phrase loaded with meaning, a slogan; it is a social dialogue and conversation about unjust conditions that underlie violence; it is a loosely structured international network of activist groups; and it is a decentralized political-social movement advocating nonviolent protest of social injustice. Though it is a "fuzzy" movement, Black Lives Matter is connected behind 13 guiding principles and goals that promote justice through direct action and policy change (BLM, 2015). Ninety-three percent of Black Lives Matter protests have been nonviolent (ACLED, 2020).

As is common with social movements, Black Lives Matter is accompanied by controversy. Support is generally positive (Thomas, 2020), but the movement has inspired some violent tactics from citizens, counterprotest groups, and government militarized violence toward protesters and journalists. Because it is not a centrally organized movement, different perceptions of the movement exist, even among supporters. There is disagreement about the actual degree of racial bias in society, due to different types of reporting that do not always include racial data.

Think About and Discuss with Your Colleagues

- What was, or is, your own experience with the Black Lives Matter movement?
- What is your view on the grievances that motivated the movement?
- Is the movement complete and finished? How would you judge its success or failure?
- What possibilities would there have been to address the grievances in ways other than a Black Lives Matter protest movement?

A Comprehensive Strategy for Social Transformation

You might discern from this discussion that real social change is not likely unless scattered strategies become integrated within a comprehensive approach (Zelizer, 2018). In the context of deep injustice and historical animosity, justice and peace are not separate or isolated. David Bloomfield (2006) described the complementary tasks of broad and deep justice making, peacebuilding, and reconciliation. Successful changes happen when systems connect a problem with the people, the process(es) of change, and strategies for decision making. Transformative ways to address a problem are integrated and synchronized across personal, interpersonal, structural, and cultural systems.

John Paul Lederach is an advocate and practitioner of a thorough, integrated approach to peacebuilding, summarized in Table 12.3. His conclusions are much like those of Alvarado. The peacebuilder must take into account:

- the peacebuilder must be patient with many abrupt *deviations* along the way because a peacebuilding process never unfolds in orderly sequence; at each point relapse into violence is possible;
- for success, *momentum* must be maintained; possibly as a continuously evolving process rather than a goal;
- *immediate* crisis intervention quiets crisis-driven factors that jeopardize peace (a time frame of days and months);
- the *intermediate* task is to equip people to take better action (1 to 2 years);
- a practical *plan* of peacebuilding discovers ways to solve the underlying problems (5 to 10 years); and
- a hoped for vision is of a *long-term* changed society based on peaceable conditions (more than 20 years); peacebuilding is, in fact, endlessly long term; and
- find ways to engage the *pyramid of actors* that represent all levels of society (Lederach, 1998).

Table 12.3 Long-Term Strategy for Peacebuilding Activity

Emphasis	Time Frame	Focus of Attention	Question to Be Considered
Conflict issue, crisis intervention	Immediate (2–6 months)	Action, peace enforcement	1. How do we manage the immediate crisis?
Relational systems, preparation, training	Medium term (5–10 years)	Social revision, peacekeeping	2. How do we prevent this crisis from recurring?
Social subsystems	Medium term (5–10 years)	Design, peacemaking	3. How do we move from crisis to desired change?
Past social systems	Long-term past	Design for peacebuilding	4. What are the root causes of the crisis?
Future social systems	Long-term future (20+ years)	Stable peace	5. What are the social structures and relationships we desire?

Source: Based on Lederach, 1997

This type of peacebuilding is currently being attempted in postgenocide Rwanda and several other regions.

Collective Peacemaking Is Justice Making

Bloomfield (2006) agreed with Lederach. He examined the process of a whole society moving from widespread distrust and suspicion, fear, and division to a genuinely shared future. He noted that social healing is unlike individual or interpersonal experiences. His research focus was on South Africa, Yugoslavia, and Rwanda after violence. In neighborhoods and regions like these, where incalculable trauma and harm have occurred, peacebuilding activities evolve from the urgent management of ongoing conflict to a long, deep, and demanding community-wide shift to peaceful methods.

Nancy Fraser (1999) suggested social justice making activities should include *redistribution*, *recognition*, and *representative participation*. In Honduras, for example, Elvia Alvarado uses land reform (redistribution), education and empowerment (recognition), and community action (participation) to promote social justice and progress.

Amela Puljek-Shank (2007) implied that attitude change is the ground of collective change that makes way for structural change. Four tightly linked instruments help to (re)build trust and humanize the enemy. Core *justice* addresses past violence, *truth* acknowledges experiences and uncovers previously secret events, *healing* helps victims to come to terms with suffering, and *reparation* provides real and/or symbolic compensation for losses. Collective reconciliation then leads to *redesign* of a society characterized by positive peace conditions.

Puljek-Shank mapped four unfolding waves of tasks for seemingly overwhelming transformation (not necessarily occurring in orderly sequence). As you read the following descriptions, watch for both negative and positive correctives.

Wave One: Acknowledgment concentrates on *psychological transformation* through individual mourning and grief, storytelling, uncovering perpetrator motivation, dismantling myth, and symbolic rituals and ceremonies facilitate psychological transformation. Personal and group therapy and counseling are common. Public admission of past injustices is also instrumental. Public holidays of remembrance, museums, monuments, living memorials, documentation and research on violence and aggression facilitate this aspect of transformation.

A significant innovation in social conflict resolution is the development of Truth and Reconciliation Commissions (TRC) that try to resolve historic injustices perpetrated by governments. To date, more than 50 countries have established resolution commissions. Some commissions are still operating and more are in the design stages. Beginning as early as 1982 in Bolivia, justice seeking commissions made attempts to negotiate reconciliation between historically antagonistic groups. Perhaps the most publicly known TRC was South Africa's Truth and Reconciliation Commission, 1995–1998, which in some ways formed a template. Most TRCs are viewed as at least partially successful in altering the psychology of injustice, but they often fall short of their lofty goals (Petoukhov, 2011).

Although the commissions are known by different names and their methods vary, their common goal is to help a society transcend injustice to build a new future. The operations of the TRCs typically include:

- discover the factual truth of what happened by publicly ending secrecy;
- promote large group healing;
- promote reconciliation between socially divided groups; and
- rewrite the future of a society or nation.

Wave Two: Restoration mends the broken spirits of victims through *spiritual transformation*. Systemic wrongdoing of the past implicitly declared the victims to be of no value, unworthy of dignity. Spiritual restoration begins to explore varieties of contrition, confession, and granting and receiving forgiveness. Collective transformation occurs through media reports such as forgiveness stories, religious rallies, and offender mediation.

In the reconstruction process, a public apology made by a legitimate official, speaking for the guilty institution and addressed to all victims of the wrong, begins to restore lost dignity and worth in several ways:

1. It can reverse or "unsay" the insulting indignity and worthlessness of victims.
2. It publicly acknowledges the injuries of the primary and secondary victims, and the legitimacy of their resentment.
3. It offers practical amends or official memorials for losses. And
4. It is a commitment to reform society to prevent reoffense (Govier, 2002).

It is essential that the apology be thorough. Most official apologies admit the least liability initially, but as the enormity of the systemic injustice is collectively understood, the apology can unfold in six degrees of contrition and negotiation (Mayer, 2004):

- passively acknowledge that mistakes were made,
- disown the blame with finger-pointing,
- allow the truth to be known with full information gathering,
- offer compensation starting with a minimum possible, salving the official conscience,

- seek someone to scapegoat and demand their removal, then
- the "bareheaded bow" shows true contrition, but is a rare gesture of official humility and repentance.

Wave Three: Revision of history begins a broader *cultural transformation* by rewriting distorted history, including recovery of lost Indigenous peace and reconciliation customs. Collective peacebuilding usually starts with community education in peace, human rights, dignity, tolerance of diversity, and nonviolence. These measures promote peoples' reconnection and cooperation among previously disempowered local communities, and a new culture based on recognition of equal rights and responsibilities.

Search for Common Ground is an international organization with a mandate to transform adversarial conflict to create sustainable peace. It has field offices in 36 countries, with headquarters in Belgium and the United States. Their emphasis is on culture change through public events involving mobile cinema, radio, and television programming, diplomacy, and traditional peacebuilding. More than 600 employees work in areas of high conflict, mediating between enemy groups to foster dialogue and peaceful cooperation.

Wave Four: Restructuring unjust public institutions reshapes *structural factors*, replacing political and economic hierarchies with democratic participation, equal rule of law, political accountability, and economic redistribution, development, and cooperation. Broad reforms include democratic elections with checks and balances, establishing rights and freedoms, effective law and policing mechanisms, reform of legal systems to use restorative practices and correction systems to emphasize rehabilitation and alternative dispute resolution.

Many formerly violent societies illustrate gradual reformation and reconciliation through a slow, deep, costly process of resettlement (Abu-Nimer, 2001; Bar-Siman-Tov, 2004). When violence has ended, there is a sort of collective *shock*. Practical *coexistence* means that enemies agree not to engage in open conflict and destruction. The risk of relapsing conflict is high, but this period of negative peace opens a breathing space to begin *restructuring*.

SUMMARY OF CONFLICT TRANSFORMATION THEORY

This chapter is presented from the conflict transformation point of view, which is starkly different from the efforts of conflict resolution and conflict management. The principles point to deep changes to society, based on assumptions that conflict can be constructive (Dayton, 2009; Indartono, 2014).

- Conflict transformation is a way of thinking about and understanding conflict.
- Conflict should not be treated as an isolated event but, rather, as an integral part of social development and progress.
- Transformation of violence to peace is always based in relationships. The actions of each participant affect the perception and actions of the others. Therefore, transformation is shaped by changes that occur within and between the participants.
- Conflict transformation occurs on all levels: intrapersonal, interpersonal, group, and international, sometimes all at once, sometimes naturally, sometimes suddenly.

- When harnessed constructively, social conflict can be a productive part of social change that potentially challenges harmful and unjust norms, power structures, and values.
- Conflict transformation is designed to address formerly intractable conflicts in which deeply rooted issues fueled violence. It pursues transformation of the root causes of social conflict.
- Conflict transformation is a gradual, complex process that requires sustained engagement and long term interaction.

SOCIAL TRANSFORMER AND NONVIOLENT PEACEBUILDER: DR. MARTIN LUTHER KING JR. (1929-1968)

Martin Luther King was a peacemaker in the southern United States whose influence extended internationally. His vision was to dissolve systemic racism and establish racial equality. Like Elvia Alvarado, his work advocated responses to injustice that are nonviolent but not passive, particularly civil defiance, massive protest marches, political lobbying, and public information and education.

Cultural Background

Jim Crow was a folk character fictionalized in a racist comedy originally written to portray blacks as dimwitted, inept, and ridiculous. Over time, "Jim Crow" became a pejorative reference to all people of African ancestry. The Jim Crow Laws were enacted after the American Civil War (1861–1865) that outlawed human trafficking. That web of laws justified white supremacy and segregation of so-called people of color (blacks and Aboriginals) in states that had formerly trafficked in slaves. The laws were enforceable until 1965 under a 1896 Supreme Court ruling that established the controversial "separate but equal races" fiction. For nearly a century, the laws more and more harshly enforced the racist tradition. The reality was that the practices resulted in degrading suffering for people of color.

Civil Rights Movement

In the early 1950s, some American southerners began to protest the unjust laws with acts of civil disobedience. A famous incident occurred in Montgomery, Alabama, when a tired black woman, Rosa Parks, refused to stand on a public bus to give up her seat to a white man. Parks was arrested and jailed, fired from her job, and received death threats for decades. A sympathetic protest boycott of the Montgomery bus transportation system virtually crippled the city after 382 days. Segregation of public transportation ended. Parks recalled later, "The only tired I was, was tired of giving in." She collaborated with other civil rights activists, becoming known as "the first lady of civil rights" when she was awarded a congressional gold medal for her contributions to the nation.

Thus began the social campaign known as the civil rights movement. After 1955, innumerable events of protest and successful acts of legal challenge resulted in a gradual erosion of the Jim Crow laws until segregation and discrimination of public services and employment were outlawed by the Civil Rights Act of 1964. The campaign also resulted in widespread social turmoil and conflict.

At about the same time, Martin Luther King became the pastor of the Dexter Avenue Baptist Church in Montgomery. Like Alvarado, he was a "second-class" citizen, despite his admirable education, superior thinking, and eloquent speech. His symbolic and real leadership was vital to the spread and success of the civil rights movement. After Rosa Parks's arrest, the Montgomery Improvement Association was formed, Dr. King was chosen to lead it, and they organized the Montgomery bus boycott. Thereafter, King used his influence to preach justice for all races, and condemned the segregation in which he had been raised. He is best known for his poetic "I Have a Dream" speech, delivered during a mass protest march in 1963 in Washington, D.C. (see his photo in Figure 12.6). In this speech, King communicated a sense of urgency and of hope as he insisted that society "make real the promises of democracy."

King continued to be a prominent activist in the movement. He was awarded the Nobel Peace Prize in 1964, which he acknowledged as the "profound recognition that nonviolence is the answer to the crucial political and moral question of our time—the need for us to overcome oppression and violence without resorting to violence and oppression. Civilization and violence are antithetical concepts." King was assassinated in 1968, in Memphis, Tennessee.

The civil rights movement has had no termination point. Many of the original actors in the movement, such as Stokely Carmichael, Diane Nash, James Lawson, and John Lewis, are well known today for their lifetime activism to confirm full civil rights.

Figure 12.6 Martin Luther King in Washington, D.C., 1963

CHAPTER SUMMARY AND STUDY GUIDE

This discussion is presented in minichapters that look at transformation on three levels: intrapersonal, interpersonal, and social.

- People affected by harm, injustice, and conflict choose to settle their turmoil with passive, violent, or nonviolent methods. The focus of intrapersonal transformation is on settling inner trouble and conflict, to create peaceable character.
- Interpersonal transformation is usually accomplished with reparative processes of apology, forgiveness, and reconciliation when a relationship is safe.
- Intrapersonal and interpersonal transformation are intricately entwined, each having implications for the other and facilitating peace on each level.
- Social and collective transformation involves long-term social processes that can affect large groups of conflicted people, address deeply rooted problems of injustice and inequity, and establish constructive interaction patterns that sustain a peaceable society.

TERMS IN FOCUS

agency   372
bottom-up peacebuilding   391
change agent   372
compassionate nonviolence   376
conflict transformation   371
cultural lag   392
empowerment shift   389
empty universal   379
forgive   379
moral amend   378
moral blindness   375
moral imagination   375
negative justice   393
nonviolence   376
paradigm shift   394

positive justice   393
practical amend   378
principled nonviolence   376
pseudoforgiveness   381
recognition shift   389
reconciliation   383
revolution   395
social change   393
state-shifting   390
strategic nonviolence   376
systemic racism   392
top-down peacebuilding   391
transformative justice   393
worldview skills   374

Conclusion

Professional Practice and Careers in Peace and Conflict Resolution

■ ■ ■

"Be the Change"

In Focus in This Chapter:

- ■ The discipline of conflict resolution is an interdisciplinary social science that takes knowledge from several human services disciplines.
- ■ Careers have a double nucleus of practice and theory, and triple career options;
- ■ Pathways to a meaningful career can be mapped through nondegree practical skills courses and/or college and university programs, and continuing education. Conflict Resolution Studies (CRS) education incorporates both theoretical and practical knowledge.
- ■ Professional activities and settings are highly varied, but most use reflective practice as they focus on process design, third-party intervention, teaching, and research;
- ■ Respectful ethical practice and specialized organizations are very important professional connections when working with vulnerable people.
- ■ The future of the discipline of CRS is in view.

CONFLICT CASE C.1 ■ PEACE AND CONFLICT PRACTITIONER LOIS EDMUND

I, the author, did not start my career as a conflict specialist; in fact, at the beginning I did not know that such a career even existed. I completed a bachelor of science in psychology, a master's degree in counseling, and a doctorate in psychology. After interning in several hospital settings, I was certified as a clinical psychologist. I began my career as a college professor of psychology, and provided mental health and illness treatment.

About 10 years later, "Fred," a former student who had become a conflict mediator, asked me to assist with the mediation of a young couple's conflict. Fred was concerned about mental illness and violence on the part of the young man. Although that mediation was quite a wild ride, Fred and I were successful in helping the couple to come to a peaceable place in their relationship.

Fred's gift to me was to introduce me to conflict resolution and mediation practices that built on my skills and experience as a psychologist. My career was never the same! I became involved with families and groups in serious conflict, some having experienced abuse or trouble with the law. In addition to my professional psychology networks, I began to interact with other mediators, lawyers, and professors of CRS. I was excited when I was asked to teach a core university course on conflict in groups. This, then, lead to a full-time teaching position in a conflict resolution program, mostly with undergraduate students but with some involvement with graduate students and research.

You might notice several things about my career story:

- My conflict-related work has been with individuals, pairs of affiliated people, families, and groups; I have not done any international work.
- My mediation practice, while extensive and very rewarding, has not been the sole focus of my work.
- For more than 30 years I have engaged in providing intervention, teaching, and research activities, all related to conflict.
- I entered the field through the discipline of psychology, a very helpful base from which to work. However, there has been a steep and never-ending conflict learning curve ever since.

This chapter (and, in fact, the whole textbook) is motivated by my excitement about CRS and the myriad marvelous career options. My hope is to inspire you to pursue the study and, when feasible, seek employment in this richly diverse field.

PEACE AND CONFLICT STUDIES IS A DISCIPLINE WITH A DOUBLE NUCLEUS AND TRIPLE CAREERS

CRS, interchangeably called Peace and Conflict Transformation Studies, is a relatively young social science. A periodic upsurge of interest in conflict prevention and peace can always be observed following major wars like the Napoleonic Wars, the American Civil War, the two world wars, recent revolutionary upheavals across Europe and Africa, and so on (Harris, 2008). CRS began differentiation as a field of study separate from its parent origins only in the middle 20th century, and this development is ongoing (Mayer, 2012). By the beginning of the 21st century, more than 400 academic programs were offered in 40 countries (Harris, 2008).

CRS is now at an exciting stage of development (Mayer, 2004). The goals of the discipline are to discover the origins of conflict, to improve the strategies chosen to process conflict, to minimize the harm that often accompanies escalated conflict, and to establish more peaceable relationships. This field incorporates contributions from many parent areas of scholarship such as history, political science, psychology, economics, and international relations. The body of CRS knowledge is sometimes criticized as an eclectic or hybrid discipline (Alberstein, 2013), but other scholars believe the breadth of knowledge is its core value.

This fast-rising body of knowledge has already become a foundation for many different, worthwhile careers. In fact, in almost any field of work, the principles and skills related to conflict resolution and transformation are useful, and many students of CRS go on to related employment fields. CRS could be called a **master discipline** because the knowledge and skills augment almost any other discipline or profession. A study of Coyahuga Community College students concluded overwhelmingly that students who participate in and successfully complete CRS courses learn important skills and knowledge that has lasting value in their personal and professional lives.

> *How wonderful it is that nobody need wait a single moment before starting to improve the world.*
> —*Anne Frank*

CRS is a useful, intriguing specialty with ever-expanding study and professional opportunities. While this is an obvious piece of good fortune, planning a path through can be confusing (Haas, 2018; Zelizer, 2006). There are many different routes to a rewarding career. As you study this chapter, notice the dual focus on theory and practice, and notice the triple career options of design and intervention, teaching, and research. There are many roads to resolution and peace (Schellenberg, 1996).

Professional conflict resolution practice applies theory in an ever-expanding variety of settings. Triple professional career opportunities are available:

- *process design and intervention* involves working with people in conflict;
- *teaching* and training focuses on developing practitioner knowledge and skills; and
- *research* into peace and conflict to determine effective conflict resolution methods.

Donald Schon integrated these activities, writing "Research is an activity of practitioners. It is triggered by the nature of the practice situation, undertaken on the spot, and immediately linked to action…. The exchange between research, theory, and practice is immediate, and reflection-in-action is its own implementation" (Schon, 1983). Practice, theory, and research operate in concert, complementing and enlarging each other. Theoretical concepts and hypotheses are reviewed and tested in light of research findings and practical experience, and results further refine theory.

Fieldwork occurs in several domains: intrapersonal (counseling and coaching), interpersonal (mediation), intergroup (facilitation), and international (mediation, facilitation, diplomacy). Professionals are typically involved in one or two activities; only a few professionals work simultaneously in all three domains. Recall the embedded nature and scope of conflict in the Introduction. This concept can be correlated with professional practice areas.

INCREASE YOUR KNOWLEDGE OF PEACE AND CONFLICT RESOLUTION

Preparation of your knowledge base incorporates many opportunities to study both theoretical knowledge and practical skillsets.

> *In theory, theory and practice are the same; in practice, they are not.*
> —*Albert Einstein*

Theoretical Education

A **theory** is proposed to explain observed facts and known principles. Theories are not "correct": all represent potential explanations. Theories cannot be proven; they can only suggest direction as you try to sort out a set of facts. Theories necessitate using inference to form a conclusion that unifies existing information. Therefore, theories vary in plausibility and usefulness because the ideas are closely linked to the information and facts selected. A "good" theory is one that provides insight, fits with most actual experiences, and is practically useful.

At times, theories might seem somewhat distant from real situations, but the explanations contained in theory provide scholars with the "big picture" of conflict. Conflict theory can be used to discover what in the past lead parties to this point, explain what is observed in the present, and suggest possible directions for a future relationship and peace and conflict strategies. Theory helps organize what is already known, and points to new insights, suggests directions for further inquiry that might extend existing knowledge, and also supports practical strategies which can lead to effective new actions.

Theories produce four types of information:

1. Description—We observe behavior and peaceful and conflict patterns, describing and sequencing them in ways that suggest causal relationships. Using this type of data, we can identify factors that contribute to constructive and destructive conflict. For example, we can observe men and women in conflict, quantifying and comparing the behaviors and strategies typically used, to describe an exemplary "feminine approach" or "masculine approach" to conflict. No one individual will fit these descriptions fully, but the types described can extend our understanding gender-based conflicts (see Chapter 5).

2. Analysis and Explanation—Using theory, we attempt to explain the "why" of conflict, looking at causes and contributions from the past. For example, it is useful to formulate and explain the process by which conflict escalates, unfolds, and deescalates (see Chapter 4).

3. Prediction—As theory becomes more advanced, it can be used to predict the probabilities that certain conflict behavior and dynamics will occur under particular circumstances. For example, although violence cannot be reliably predicted, we can use theory to anticipate the risk that violent conflict will erupt in a specific situation (see Chapters 8 and 9).

4. Change and Control—Theoretical data can be used to modify the ways people behave in conflict, to encourage them toward more peaceful and productive strategies while minimizing destructive patterns. This might take the form of education, alteration of potential triggers for conflict, adjustment of peoples' reactions and behavior, and so forth. For example, we use theoretical ideas to extend justice (see Chapter 10), deepen peace (see Chapter 11), and initiate changes to social discrimination (see Chapter 12).

There are many conflict theories that currently influence our understandings of conflict and approaches to practical resolution. Each theory selects a specific dimension of conflict as a focal interest, usually while deemphasizing others. Theories are under constant revision as research findings confirm hypotheses or point in new directions for investigation. There are so many theories that an exhaustive catalogue is impractical, and there is at present no overarching theory (Schellenberg, 1996). Here are a few of the categories of theory in CRS at present:

- **Individual Characteristics Theories** deal with distinct individual tactics and interactions. They are related to the human sciences such as psychology and sociology. The Psychoanalytic Theory and the Sociological Theory of Conflict fall into this group.
- **Social Process Theories** are based on analysis of conflict development and peacebuilding. Game Theory and Postmodern Theory focus on conflict process.
- **Social Bias Theories** investigate the realities of discrimination experienced by specific groups of people while envisioning a more constructive way. Critical Theory, Feminist Theory, Postcolonial Studies, Queer Theory, Social Identity Theory, and the Race Conflict Approach all focus on specific experiences of unjust exclusion and inequality.
- **Social Analysis Theories** use extensive and intensive examination of social systems, issues, and trends. Structuralism and World Systems Theory are examples.

Think About and Discuss with Your Colleagues

- Discuss the four goals of theory (description, explanation, prediction, and change or control). Which of these involves the least or greatest intrusion into the lives of other people, cultures, and situations?
- How do you think theory can apply in real-life situations?

Practical Training

Alongside theoretical knowledge, practical skill is another central focus of CRS. This is, in fact, the reason most people enter the profession: they want to make a difference in their world and need strong skills to do so. In this area, known principles are applied to real-life conflicts. This realm of knowledge focuses on ongoing skill development that is learned, practiced, and continually refined, then used to improve practical effectiveness. Of course, the use of skills and techniques must be safe when used with parties already experiencing harmful conflict. Most conflict practitioners are trained and certified in a specific professional discipline such as education or family or psychology, and have additional training in the dynamics and ethics of conflict and conflict intervention. There are multiple pathways of practical training.

Basic Skills Training

First, many organizations sponsor short seminars that focus on skill development, testing, and practice. Most workshops are styled to match the situation and needs of the audience, and they develop specific conflict intervention skillsets such as reflective practice, communication skills for difficult situations or relationships, and mediation skills. Typically, these seminars are 1 to 5 days in length in a face-to-face setting. A few are available for online learning, such as the Massive Open Online Seminar (MOOS) series at Beyond Intractability.

> *I have been impressed with the urgency of doing. Knowing is not enough; we must apply. Being willing is not enough; we must do.*
> —Leonardo da Vinci

Certification

After completing a prescribed series of seminars, trainees have the opportunity to become certified in a specialized type of conflict intervention such as family, environmental, or international mediation. Certification typically requires at least 40 hours' training, passing an assessment and skills testing process, and membership in a professionally accountable organization. Certification is one tool used to protect vulnerable consumers by ensuring appropriate qualifications, skill competency, and safe and ethical practice.

Advanced Training

A formally accredited route toward a conflict resolution and transformation career involves college or university training. Again, multiple pathways are offered in academic departments such as law, political science, psychology, and sociology. Increasingly, universities are forming distinct CRS and Peace Studies departments that offer interdisciplinary courses leading toward a bachelor's degree (3 or 4 years), or a masters' degree (often 2 or more years' training beyond the bachelor's). Even doctoral-level training, which tends to be theoretical (often 3 to 5 years), is available. Opportunities are expanding with the creation of new programs every year (Hansvick, 2007; Harris, 2008). Focused university programs are now available in most large city centers in North America and in Europe. Currently, nearly 500 worldwide programs are devoted to peace and conflict studies, and about 100 of these include graduate programs. Most programs include a practicum or cooperative learning component, so that students are assigned to agencies working in the field for credit based on supervised practical experience. These courses qualify graduates to do specialized interpersonal, group, or regional-national intervention work. After completion, many graduates participate in certification examinations (Zelizer, 2006, 2018). Figure C.1 illustrates a few of the common training pathways toward professional conflict qualification.

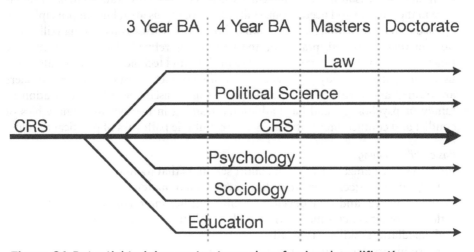

Figure C.1 Potential training routes toward professional qualification

Continuing Education

For a responsible professional, training is never truly completed, and continuing education is part of an ethical career path. Most professionals read journals and periodicals that update the most recent ideas. At present, nearly 100 journals are published regularly, each with a unique interest within scholarship. Journals are accessed by subscription or directly through libraries, particularly of those institutions associated with formal conflict training. Annual conferences are held by organizations such as the Association for Conflict Resolution, the Peace and Justice Studies Association, and the World Mediation Summit.

Think About and Discuss with Your Colleagues

- If you were to extend your study of CRS and begin to establish a career, where would you begin?
- Do you know of someone who could advise you? Check with your professor to begin this search.

Conflict professionals work with a wide range of activities, in a gratifying variety of professional settings that will be explored in the next section.

PRAXIS: PROFESSIONAL ACTIVITIES AND SETTINGS

Most CRS careers focus on one or more practice activities, called praxis: intervention with parties in conflict, conflict process design, teaching, or research. A single expert might typically engage in one or two activities, but relatively few have the skills or desire do all of them. The range of professional roles depends on interests, training and skills, work setting, and goals.

CRS practitioners are hired in many conflict fields (illustrated in Figure C.2), such as independent practice, business, family counseling, mediation of legal matters, or in corrections systems. Some practitioners work in government settings, with military forces, or with nongovernmental organizations (NGO) involved in areas where conflict affects the functioning of a society.

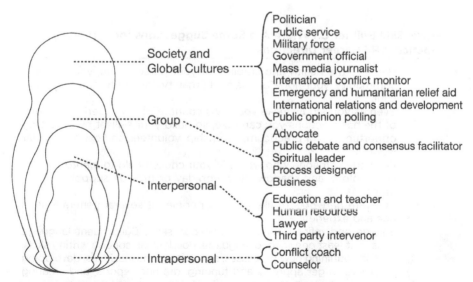

Figure C.2 Embedded conflict scope and professional practice diagram

It can be challenging to find a job providing conflict resolution services, but the skills learned in the field are applicable in many settings (Haas, 2018). A minimum of a bachelor's degree is necessary to do professional work, but an advanced degree is highly recommended. More than 60% of successful working professionals report that they have a master's degree or a degree in law (Smith, 2018), and this proportion is increasing.

There are many benefits from a CRS career:

- Financial Rewards—CRS practitioners are well paid as professional experts. Although many practitioners begin their careers as unpaid volunteers, the annual salary for an experienced professional typically begins at US$60,000 (Rhudy, 2014).
- Intriguing Opportunities—Skilled CRS practitioners have many worldwide prospects, and are usually in demand. In 2012, the US Bureau of Labor Statistics (2015) projected a 14% growth rate in the next decade in conflict resolution opportunities (Rhudy, 2014). In 2019, the website for the Bureau of Labor Statistics listed more than 200 possible jobs with a conflict focus.
- Worthwhile Work—People working in the CRS field report good satisfaction and reward, for many reasons. Many report that they believe they are helping to improve the current lives and relationships of clients. Most centrally, conflict workers have immediate opportunities to change their world.

Forrest Mosten's book (2001), though somewhat dated, provided detailed guidance to CRS students who want to explore career options. See Praxis Skill Builder C.1 for suggestions for exploring CRS careers.

Third-Party Conflict Intervention and ADR

CRS practitioners deal with specific parties in conflict, attempting to facilitate a constructive resolution of their conflict. Generalists provide services to clients with a range of problems, while specialists provide expert services to limited types

---

Praxis Skill Builder C.1 ■ Here Are Some Suggestions for Exploring Practical CRS Career Directions

- *Preserve the health* and stability of your personal life, your roots in community, your hopefulness for humanity, the contentment of your soul.
- Even as you study, *make your jobs count.* Earning experience is one of the basic actions you can take, so build your skillset by accessing opportunities for practicum, internship, volunteer, and extracurricular work.
- Persuade someone who works in your chosen field to *mentor* you as you explore, and shadow their workday or provide support in their office.
- Cultivate *networks* of like-minded people, of several generations in age and experience.
- Enlarge and refine your *communication* skills. Build fluent language skills in at least one second language. Polish clear, concise writing skills. Practice outlining new processes, advocating unusual ideas, developing proposals to get approval and funding, drafting reports, and creating summaries. Learn tools for using visuals in writing and presentation.

- *Maintain at least one area of backup skill and activity beside CRS.* It takes time to build experience and a reputation in conflict resolution. In the meantime you'll probably need something else to live on.
- *View a career as a long-term objective,* building on coursework, learning on the job, and testing your strengths and improving on your weaknesses in the field. Do not think your first choice will be your last; rather, many CRS professionals work in several settings before discovering a comfortable niche.
- *Expand your vocational goal to peacebuilder.* Mediation is a valuable but narrow technique. Peacebuilding is a way of being and contributing to constructive resolution of conflict that can find expression in any number of roles and functions. There will never be enough dedicated peacebuilders.
- *Get experience in community* work. This will expose you to people willing to help you, important issues in peoples' lives, and teach you useful problem solving skills.

Adapted with thanks from Bob Rhudy (2014), Ron Kraybill (2016), Chip Haas (2018).

of clients. **Third-party intervention** is provided by a trained professional who is not involved in the dynamics of the conflict and does not become involved. The third-party intervenor maintains an objective supportive role through the process while the disputants collaborate to deal with the heart of their conflict. Such experts usually work with highly sensitive people and issues, and sometimes with long-standing conflicts. This can be the unpredictable, edge-of-your-seat kind of work that is quite stressful but also extremely rewarding.

Intervention goes by different names in what is sometimes called an *intervention landscape*. Professionals might provide intervention like mediation, clinical counseling, third-party facilitation, or adjudication, usually in an agency or private office setting. Collectively, these processes are called **alternative dispute resolution** (ADR) approaches. Although specific roles are different, they use common procedures and skills to gently enter a conflict system and help maintain an orderly discussion process. Over time, the solutions reached are tested and possibly modified to be most effective.

Conflict Advocacy

—A third party, usually with discernible power or influence, speaks on behalf of someone else to promote justice and reduce conflict. Advocates support processes that identify the roots of conflict, establish facts and accurate information, find appropriate opinion leaders and decision makers, help form recommendations for programs of change, and, occasionally, become the spokespeople on behalf of the cause. Most lawyers and ombudspeople are advocates, but many causes such as voter rights, racial inequity, and international peacekeeping also utilize this type of intervention.

Conflict Facilitation

—A third party becomes involved in a group such as a workplace or committee that is in conflict. "Facilitate" literally means to "make easier," and the facilitator's role is to help calm existing conflicts so that they can be processed in constructive ways, challenge inaccurate assumptions that are impediments to peaceful relationship, prevent escalation and potential violence, and help conflicting parties to reach their actual goals.

Mediation
—Mediators help organize a conflict discussion, in a role somewhat like a sports referee, by structuring the flow of communication and negotiation (Moore, 2014). The goal of mediation is for the parties to find their own way to settle the conflict.

Conflict Coaching
—Conflict coaches support individuals whose own role is to deal directly with conflict. The clients are often managers, human resources personnel, or complainants, who lack the understandings, skills, and strategies to be effective. The coach uses conversation and readings to help the client reach insight into conflict dynamics, escalation and deescalation patterns, develop skills for conflict management, and set realistic goals and expectations for constructive resolution.

Conflict Process Design
Practitioners are hired with a mandate to design, operate, and monitor conflict resolution procedures. These experts work with systems of people such as schools and workplaces. A **process design** describes the steps that should be followed when a conflict cannot be solved simply. To be successful, design practitioners must have strong experience with a repertoire of intervention procedures and knowledge of their advantages and disadvantages, as well as be able to negotiate skillfully with group leaders to institute productive methods. Sometimes process design is conducted by human resources personnel, or these functions might be designated to committees or other contractors (Amsler, 2015).

Typically, a process is designed when there is no crisis, and system members have opportunities to contribute their ideas and give their consent. The design usually includes an outline of the problems to be addressed, goals for the process, a proposal of how change might occur, a facilitation plan, and anticipated outcomes (Shapiro, 2005).

Teaching Peace Education and Skills
Conflict and peace education takes place informally in the arena of everyday life and functioning, and also formally in community agencies or accredited educational institutions like schools, colleges, or universities. Most instructors are aware of the influence of their own behavioral modeling as they deal with conflict, and they add their own experiences to the teaching content. Formal trainers have a variety of backgrounds, but will often be working at a postdoctoral rank.

Teaching activities tend to focus on four linked spheres of knowledge:

a. *Personal qualities and practices* like self-reflection, perspective taking and empathy, personal resiliency, courage, and ethical decision making;
b. *Skills* for collaboration, communication, problem solving, prosocial leadership, and a repertoire of conflict responses operating at multiple system levels;

c. *Conflict resolution procedures*, including negotiation, consensus formation, cooperative decision making, and mediation; and

d. *Social concepts and visioning* that makes use of a peace and conflict continuum, the roots of violence, power, a peaceable environment, collective rights and responsibilities, and systemic bias.

Teaching methods have undergone several important trends in recent decades. First, lessons learned through personal encounter rely on **experiential learning**. It is based on five interwoven phases: experiencing an event, observation and self-reflection on the experience, gathering additional information and data, formation of an explanation and new insight, and testing new ideas in a new, similar encounter. Even formal training increasingly makes use of experiential learning, so that most courses now include active practice components like roleplay, application to hypothetical situations, and live observation of experienced facilitators.

Second, education is shifting away from the prescriptive approach toward an elicitive approach. **Prescriptive teaching** methods employ instruction that directs specific behaviors, problems and deficits with expert advice that students then absorb and memorize. An **elicitive approach** emphasizes students' existing knowledge, discovery learning, and shared peer teaching in the context of participants' own challenges.

Research

Advancement of the conflict discipline is dependent on continuing research that improves and refines both theoretical and practical knowledge (Pruitt, 2014; Wallensteen, 2011). Much of the data contained in this textbook draws from the product of half a century of researchers. Their activities fall within the broad directions taken by the social sciences that investigate human relationship dynamics.

> *Social research involves interaction between ideas and evidence. Ideas help researchers make sense of evidence, and researchers use evidence to extend, revise and test ideas.*
> —Charles Ragin

Practitioners investigate, use, and explain principles that clarify conflict dynamics and promote effective resolution, continually adding to our understanding of the complex nature of conflict. Useful paradigms of research are generated from genuine curiosity and promote the interaction of theoretical concepts with real-life situations. Examples of a few typical research themes include:

- describing historical trends and movements in conflict and peace;
- addressing practice issues of training and core skills competency;
- identifying the sources, igniters, and accelerators of conflict at any and all levels and in all settings, ideally to form the basis for successful intervention;
- addressing diversity issues (culture, gender, life development, etc.);
- analyzing the interactions within and between systems;
- appropriate use of conflict suppression, management, resolution, and transformation;
- designing intervention strategies and measuring their effectiveness; and
- preventing violent conflict.

Researchers work with different types of analysis using Urie Bronfenbrenner's (1994) insights about the embedded systems of the human network. Primary interests are to explore the functions of conflict in relationships: the mechanisms of igniting and escalating or deescalating conflict, pathways toward peaceable fulfillment of its purposes, and its growth and constructive value (Pruitt, 2014). A majority of research is related to and grows out of actual struggles in the field. Observed data, evidence, and known facts from those real situations are used to extrapolate general principles or procedures using **inductive inquiry**. Another method is **deductive inquiry**, which proposes abstract hypotheses or "guesses" derived from theory and then tests them to real-world situations.

Research usually happens within academic institutions such as universities and teaching institutes that are part of a cooperating research network (Cheldelin, 2008). Proposals are evaluated according to mandated criteria that include procedures that maintain safe and ethical interactions, methodology, and public reporting of results and conclusions. Some projects are publicly funded through government-related agencies; a few projects are privately funded by foundations and groups interested in promoting effective conflict process.

All responsible conflict professionals, regardless of their specific activities, work hard to provide ethical, safe, and respectful services. Ways of doing this will be discussed next.

ETHICS AND PROFESSIONAL ORGANIZATIONS

Practical intervention is work with vulnerable people immersed in distressing conflict. Decisions are often made under conditions of crisis and intense pressure. Practitioners therefore work carefully to protect the rights of especially vulnerable people. They use codes of professional conduct that assist them to make decisions and take actions that are ethical, safe, and respectful, while also promoting improvements to the parties' situations and relationships.

Experiential Reflective Practice

This self-correcting learning method is based on experiential learning and **reflective practice** (illustrated in Figure C.3). It uses a cycle of thinking that begins with experiences that are compared with existing evidence and knowledge. Insights from this technique are used to guide further exploration. It is part of the ongoing improvement of all CRS professionals (Mayer, 2012). Michael Lang's recent publication (2019) provides a context for exploring reflective learning and practice, case studies, and self-guided exercises.

Professional Ethics

An ethical dilemma was experienced by family mediator, "Laura." She was working with a separating couple, "Pete" and "Donna," to minimize any difficulties their children would experience during the family separation. The sessions seemed to be going well, with a fairly amicable tone, good planning for the kids, and the couple even spoke occasionally about reconciliation in the future.

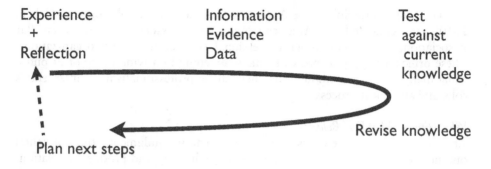

Figure C.3 Experiential learning and reflective practice technique

During one session that Donna was unable to attend, Pete disclosed to Laura that he had begun a secret affair with a new girlfriend. He was afraid that if Donna knew about this she would stop sleeping with him and the mediation might sour, so he insisted that Laura must maintain his confidentiality. Laura had a dilemma: if she kept Pete's secret, she would be seen to condone this unhealthy imbalance and the mediation would proceed under false assumptions; if she informed Donna, she would have to disrespect his demand for privacy and Pete might end the sessions. After consulting with her colleagues, Laura decided that the secret must be disclosed, and that Pete must be encouraged to do so.

Professional ethics are principles that define professional responsibilities and guide right and wrong actions. Codes of ethics are documents designed "to guide the conduct of mediators, inform the mediating parties, and promote public confidence in mediation as a process for resolving disputes" (Cohen, 2010). Most codes of ethics are available as public information.

Some principles of ethical practice sound deceptively simple. In actual practice, many things can go wrong, and many complications can arise because of factors like heated emotion and deeply rooted animosity. Many, if not most, parties in serious conflict present ethical dilemma that must be carefully thought through. The most common ethical problems involve working with unwilling parties, maintaining confidentiality, power imbalances, unregulated or incompetent practice (Noll, 2003), preserving participant autonomy while offering support, and providing procedural fairness while accepting a good-enough (not perfect) outcome (Waldman, 2011).

Rule Based Ethics: What Should or Shouldn't I Do?

Ethics of rules focus on the rules and regulations that define proper actions. The central questions addressed are "What should or shouldn't I do?" *Prescriptive ethics* describe and encourage appropriate behavior that should happen (for example, all disputing parties should be treated with equal respect); *prohibitive ethics* address exploitive actions that should never happen (for example, a professional should never have sex with a client). Rules-based ethics are often fairly simple (if not easy) to follow because they are framed as "do's and don'ts," such as "do keep information confidential" and "don't exploit a client financially."

The Ethical Principles (The Association for Conflict Resolution, and Cohen, 2010), are endorsed by American Arbitration Association, American Bar Association, and several other professional conflict resolution organizations. These principles apply to professionals intervening in a wide range of disputes, using many different methods. They help shape professionalism, an intervenor's role, and an ethical process.

Values Ethics: What Do I Believe?

At a deeper level that requires more discernment and judgment, **ethics of values** outline the ideals that are believed to promote healthy and productive relationships, especially in professional contexts. Values must be repeatedly examined, pursued, and refined. The core question addressed is "What do I believe?" This type of ethics describes fundamental beliefs held by ethical conflict practitioners. The precise list of "core values" is under development, with much scholarly debate and little consensus at present (Neufeldt, 2016).

Ethics of Character: What Kind of Person Should I Be?

Ethics of character (sometimes called **virtue ethics**) reach even deeper to the ongoing moral commitments of a practitioner that transcend a workplace and professional relationships. These ethics address the question, "What sort of person do I choose to be"? They focus on ideals toward which a practitioner aspires, such as generosity, humility, integrity, and respect (Handelsman, 2011).

Ethics of character are not quickly developed but, rather, represent the ongoing, struggling commitment of the professional to be careful in every action, mindful of the consequences of every decision made. Two moral intelligence skills are essential: a clear sense of right and wrong, *and* the ability to translate that understanding into good and correct behavior. As a skill, moral intelligence matures with practice. Michele Borba (2001) identified seven component virtues: empathy, conscience, self-control, respect, kindness, tolerance, and fairness. Readers of this textbook will find these ethical concepts referenced throughout. Doug Lennick and Fred Kiel's later research (2007) identified four component abilities that make up strong moral intelligence: integrity, responsibility, forgiveness, and compassion.

Students of all levels of experience are encouraged to learn and practice peacebuilding as a lifestyle that might or might not develop into a career (Mayer, 2012). Although the International Peace Practitioners' Network has now ceased functioning, their "Principles for Peace Practitioners" summarize well the concept of ethical character and lifestyle (see Table C.1). They are housed in several places including the American Psychological Association (Connors, 2003).

Think About and Discuss with Your Colleagues

Considering the "Principles for Peace Practitioners",

- Which of these principles already guide your lifestyle, and why?
- To which of these principles do you aspire?
- With which of these principles do you disagree, and why?

Table C.1   Peace Practitioner Agreement

International Peace Practitioners' Network

PEACE PRACTITIONER AGREEMENT

As an agent of peace on individual, group, social, and political levels, I agree to uphold the following ethical responsibilities:

1. to be respectful of the human rights of all persons and groups with whom I work;
2. to refrain from exploitation, abuse, and derogatory language about anyone;
3. to speak out against unethical behavior, exploitation, and abuse committed by others;
4. to work to support and educate my own employees, and to support and consult with colleagues in the peace advocacy community as needed;
5. to use my role and power to empower others, instead of doing for them what they can do for themselves;
6. to work to empower local authorities, mechanisms, and peace workers;
7. to ensure that my participation is invited and welcome by local peoples if at all possible;
8. to focus on restoring the healthy functioning of communities as I work with them;
9. to be honest and give full information about the agendas, dynamics, and limitations I am aware of for those parties involved in negotiations;
10. to strive to make clear financial arrangements that respect the best interests of my clients;
11. to practice respectful journalism and research that guards against violating the confidentiality of people discussed or otherwise harming clients, especially those who are victims of trauma;
12. to encourage conservation of the natural environment;
13. to seek continuing education, consultation, or supervision to gain a broader perspective on my work;
14. to withdraw or seek help if I suffer impairment of my judgment or burnout;
15. to work to see the peace process through to its end and to avoid abandoning the situation if possible.

Source: Connors, 2003. Reprinted with permission from Joanie V. Connors.

John Paul Lederach (2005) emphasized both the burdensome responsibility and the immense creativity of a **moral imagination,** which he defined as the capacity to recognize moments of possibility and turning points in conflict that can dramatically alter previous habits and create a new peace that does not yet exist. In practice, the moral imagination is the capacity to imagine and generate constructive processes that are rooted in, but transcend, familiar day-to-day destructive and violent patterns. Using the moral imagination in conflict situations will inevitably lead to diminished violence and constructive social interactions.

Lederach recommended four demanding ways to foster this imaginative, creative problem solving:

- imagine yourself in a web of relationships that includes your enemies;
- sustain curiosity that comprehends complexity and avoids dichotomous, simplistic contrasts;
- believe in and pursue creative action;
- accept the inherent risk of working with the unknown, and never resort to a familiar habit of violence.

Ethical decisions are almost always tricky and require careful deliberation and consultation with colleagues. Ellen Waldman (2011) advocated taking each dilemmas seriously and not accepting any easy answers. While codes of conduct are very important protections for vulnerable parties, they are not enough. Codes are guiding principles that do not provide direction in any specific situation.

In a real situation, there may be no single right course of action; often, there is a range of acceptable action (Waldman, 2011). When an ethical puzzle exists, consultation with colleagues is usually critical to finding the best course of action. A stepwise process for deliberating ethical dilemma, such as the one followed above by Laura, is outlined in Figure C.4.

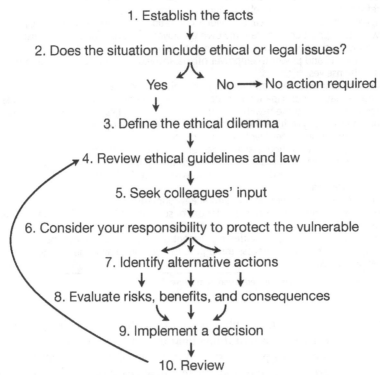

Figure C.4 Steps to guide ethical deliberation

Professional Practice Organizations

In addition to training and intervention skill, many practitioners are members of professional practice organizations where they network with supportive specialists, keep up to date with the most recent research and skills available, and are exposed to procedures designed to improve the effectiveness of intervention. The assortment of organizations is fast evolving as the CRS discipline differentiates and gains recognition. Many professional disciplinary organizations, for example in psychology, law, and education, sponsor subgroups of people who are interested in peace and justice. The many organizations promote relevant research, teach skills, and guide practice, and some regularly publish journals and periodicals that present cutting-edge information. There are approximately 150 organizations in North America, many of which are affiliated with local groups and with related European organizations.

As mentioned earlier, CRS is at an exciting stage of development, and we all can have a part in creating its future.

THE PAST AND FUTURE OF THE PEACE
AND CONFLICT DISCIPLINE

The discipline of CRS is now about 50 years old and is vigorously expanding and refining. The body of knowledge is extensive. As we move forward, our focus can be on what we confidently do know rather than what we do not know.

As the discipline continues to develop, ten principles will guide scholars and practitioners alike:

1. Our work must not accept simplistic or dichotomous solutions, in case we lose sight of the complex nature of relationship systems and conflict process;
2. We must continue to negotiate the complexity of diversity issues with an unwavering commitment to antibias education, equity, equality, and inclusion;
3. Our attention must remain on the tensions among the human systems;
   In intervention work,
4. Conflict and violence prevention need to be emphasized;
5. The field must continue to strive for ethical excellence;
   As we teach and train,
6. Ongoing learning must continue to incorporate disciplinary, interdisciplinary, and transdisciplinary data;
7. We must continue to focus on personal social-emotional development and management skills;
   In our research
8. Research and conflict intervention must continue to systematically explore methodologies demonstrated to be effective, and find robust ways of assessing outcomes;
9. We should extend our curiosity to include longitudinal analysis; and
10. Our focus should be on synergetic knowledge more than on segmented data.

CHAPTER SUMMARY AND STUDY GUIDE

- The discipline of peace and conflict resolution has a double nucleus of practice and theory, and leads to triple career options of process design and direct conflict intervention, skills and concept teaching, and research.
- CRS training includes both theoretical and practical knowledge; nondegree practical skills courses and/or college and university programs are part of a web of multiple education pathways.
- Professional activities and settings are nearly unlimited at our time in history.
- Ethical principles are central to guide the provision of safe, respectful services. Most practitioners must navigate ethical dilemma that require significant deliberation, so ethical practitioners use experiential learning and reflective practices. Responsible practitioners belong to at least one professional organization for ongoing networking, discussion, and training.
- The future of CRS is mixed and complex. Scholars and practitioners will need to be cautious in the directions the work takes in the future. Ten principles for future work are suggested.

TERMS IN FOCUS

Glossary

■ ■ ■

4-P analysis A method for analyzing the complexity of conflict, using people, problem, process, and potential solutions

A

Acculturation The painful relinquishment of the familiar culture

Active attention The deliberate concentration on a specific stimulus

Actual self The self that represents the truth in all of its complexities

Adjudication A form of adversarial conflict resolution in which a dispute is submitted for judgment to a fair, authoritative third party who has the power to issue a binding decision

Adversarial conflict resolution Using opposition, resistance, and argumentation to determine the "winning" version of justice

Affective conflict Occurs when people have significant feelings about the disagreement and use emotional heat, animosity, or antagonistic remarks; also called the emotional conflict

Agency The freedom and power to accomplish things

Aggression Violent behavior with the intent to dominate or master another party

Alternative dispute resolution (ADR) A variety of techniques to divert conflict from formal legal settings, and used to assist disputants to settle their problems and improve their relationship

Androgyny Neither feminine nor masculine but, rather, a mix of typically gender role features

Apartheid South African segregation of the races

Apathy Absence of feelings, concern, or interest

Approach-approach conflict One person has two mutually exclusive needs or goals, both of which are desirable

Approach-avoid conflict A single goal has both positive and negative consequences and the person wants both to approach and to avoid it

Approach motive Yearns for a desired goal

Antisocial actions Cause or aggravate conflict and hasten the deterioration of a relationship with passive, aggressive, or passive-aggressive tactics

Arbitration Conflict and resolution are controlled and decided by an expert third party called an *arbiter* or *arbitrator*

Argument culture Shared communication values of agonistic debate, dichotomous viewpoints, and winning an argument

Arms control Restricts national arms production, inventory, and use

Arms race Escalating rivalry to accumulate the strongest defensive capacity and stay ahead of the adversary

Articulated conflict Tangible but low-intensity conflict (also called manifest conflict)

Assertive communication Respectful communication that directly and reasonably states needs, thoughts, and opinions in nonthreatening, nondefensive ways

Assimilation The process of adopting the ways and values of the new culture

Associative culture Form of culture that emphasizes, at its core, interdependent associations, relationships, and family (also called collectivist culture)

Asylum seeker A refugee who has been granted that legal status by the United Nations or a cooperating state

Asymmetrical power relationship One side has more power and higher international legitimacy and status

Attachment A safe-haven relationship, a base from which the core of the individual self operates

Attachment Theory A broad body of work that focuses on the lifelong benefits of attachment and the potentially harmful consequences of unhealthy attachment relationships (Bowlby, 1969)

Atrocious violence Conflict is taken to almost inconceivable extremes of violence

Avoid-avoid conflict A person is forced to choose between two unpleasant options,

Avoid motive Aims to prevent something or avoid doing something unpleasant

B

Baasskap South African belief in white supremacy and domination

Belief Ideas and assumptions about actions that are true, right, and moral

Behavioral violence Intermitten, intentionally violent actions with identifiable victim(s), and identifiable perpetrator(s), not usually intended to express a defined cause or support a group

Bid for connection Any action that communicates, "I want to feel connected"

Binary Having one of two distinct and opposite forms

Biracial identity Results from the mix of two heritages

Blame Find fault, criticize, or condemn a person for their actions or for the assumed intentions; the contrast is to take responsibility

Blended family Creates a household comprised of members from at least two families

Blunted emotion Deny an emotional reaction even exists and, therefore, excessively control and fail to communicate their feelings

Bottom-up peacebuilding Locally designed processes such as relationship-building and individual trauma-healing work are used to address local grievances and losses

C

Change agent A leader from any social system who accepts responsibility for driving social change; may be a positive peacemaker or a negative troublemaker

Chosen glory Repetition of stories of heroism and triumph

Chosen trauma Repetition of stories of violence, victimization, and humiliation

CIMIC Civilian-Military Cooperation

Civil society An idea and an ideal that describes a peaceful society, engaged citizens, ethical government with a balance of powers, and connected governmental and global networks

Class conflict Occurs when social tension and conflict result from competing interests and intergroup interference, also called class struggle

Class Studies A specialty within Diversity Studies that explores social strata and class, working-class culture, class-based inequity, and social policy (also called Working Class Studies)

Classism Any practices that assign differential value to people based on social status

Climate (Relationship climate) Generalized energy and attitudes that characterize a relationship or social group

Closed system Norms for desirable behavior are rigid, so that individuals making changes often encounter disapproval

Code of conduct Describes behaviors expected of individual employees

Code of ethics Principles and values of the company

Code of practice Professional standards for using specialized knowledge and information

Coercive power Authorities exercise through monitoring, threats, and consequences to force someone else to follow expectations

Cognitive distortions Changes to beliefs, attitudes or behavior

Cold peace Hostility continues in a frozen sort of way, with no aggressive action, but also no efforts to build trust or collaboration

Cold war Characterized by mutual hostility but no direct engagement; the war consists of indirect tactics

Collective violence Violent behavior is used by groups of people to cause injury to others

Collectivist culture Form of culture that emphasizes interdependent associations, relationships, and family (also called associative culture)

Communication Reciprocating process of conversation using symbols to express and comprehend ideas, thoughts, feelings, and inquiries

Communication content Obvious topics of communication

Communicative competence A cluster of skills that support positive relationship and productive conflict process

Community resilience The ability of a social system to protect against, prepare for, and respond to a variety of emergencies that affect many people at once

Compassionate nonviolence Belief in the responsibility to promote deeply respectful interactions in every human connection, also called principled nonviolence

Competitive communication An adversarial interaction with the goal of being right or winning a perceived contest

Competitive conflict Tend to expand and escalate because they are approached disagreeably, from a negative, suspicious perspective; parties use obstructed, inconsistent communication; efforts are divided, duplicated, and often aim to overpower the opponent because of a willingness to impose a resolution. The result is almost always unsuccessful to resolve the problem and destructive of the relationship

Competitive power Used "against" other people, for personal gain at someone else's expense

Complementary conflict Parties use contrasting, sometimes opposite behavior

Complementary power Each member has a domain of power, with little sharing or overlap of control

Compromise problem solving Parties settle their differences by giving up on some goals and yielding to the needs of others

Conciliation Conflict resolution directed by disputants with professional guidance of practical inquiry into the reasons for a conflict results in a thorough understanding of conflict themes while avoiding confrontation, also called problem-solving mediation

Conflict Tension or an interactive struggle between two or more seemingly incompatible participants

Conflict advocacy A third party, usually with power or influence, speaks on behalf of someone else to promote justice and reduce conflict

Conflict analysis Attempts to gain understanding by clearly defining the problem, describing the dynamics of the conflict, and exploring possible routes to resolution

Conflict assessment Attempts to gain understanding by clearly defining the problem, describing the dynamics of the conflict, and exploring possible routes to resolution

Conflict coaching A third party supports other people whose role is to deal directly with conflict

Conflict crisis People become frustrated with efforts to solve a problem privately or collaboratively, and tensions reach a desperation point

Conflict curve Conceptual tool that presents a simplified view of how conflicts progress over time

Conflict facilitation A third party becomes involved in a group such as a workplace or committee that is in conflict

Conflict of interests Specific type of role conflict that arises from potentially incompatible interests

Conflict management Control of the processing of a problem to express the conflict within acceptable or safe limits, and to minimize losses for all parties

Conflict paradigm A mental model of conflict that affects both perception and response

Conflict resolution Addresses the causes of a conflict in a way that solves the problem, and preserves or even improves the relationship

Conflict transformation A thorough process by which disputants interests and problems, interactions, and conflict strategies are addressed in integrated ways, reforming destructive, intractable conflict into peaceful relationships

Construction of the Other The process of defining and reducing another person's identity to labels

Contact hypothesis States that stereotypes are best dissolved in real relationships

Content conflict Expressed in differences of opinion or priorities or viewpoints; also called the substantive issue

Context Any influence that contributes both to individual behavior and to collective practices, particularly in close relationships, social status, and personal and collective history

Continuity Provides security through consistency, reliability, and predictability

Contrient interdependence The belief that one group member's success is contrary to that of another member, leading to negative, group-hindering tactics and sabotage

Control Talk Directive communication, positive when done with consent and respect, negative when done without consent, or critically

Conventional warfare Two equipped and trained states are engaged in military combat. The goal is to fulfill national priorities. The "enemy" is clearly defined and the rules of engagement are roughly honored.

Convergent process Problem-solving process that narrow choices to make decisions

Cooperative communication Concentrates on reinforcing or strengthening relationship, mutual interests, and closer bonds

Cooperative conflict The parties have similar and compatible goals for problem resolution; dialogue includes a friendly attitude of respect, curiosity, and humility, with a feeling of agreement; divergence of interests is treated as a joint problem; parties communicate clearly and openly; they work together to enhance the chances of resolution. The result is almost always a constructive resolution.

Core identity Unique personal qualities, independent of others

Covert intent Hidden, unexpressed intention

Corporal punishment Spanking causes pain with slapping or hitting

Corrosive adversarial relationship Predictive of relationship unhappiness, conflict, and dissolution

Criminal justice system Network of laws and enforcement through many branches of police work, as well as accusation in response to infractions and imposition of penalties on the guilty

Critical Race Theory A field of inquiry that examines social functioning at the intersection of race, national origin, power, and law

CRS Conflict Resolution Studies, also called Peace Studies and Conflict Transformation Studies, uses multidisciplinary data to explore the origins, dynamic processes, and outcomes of conflict in the personal, interpersonal, group, and international spheres

Cultural diffusion The spread of one society's cultural distinctives to another

Cultural genocide Extreme form of cultural imperialism that attempts to obliterate the cultural heritage and

identity of a group completely, also called ethnocide

Cultural imperialism Cultural conquest waged to establish dominance and control, when members of one culture or religion aggressively impose their own worldview on others, supposedly to reform or civilize the Other; also called holy war

Cultural lag Cultural and legislative changes lag behind social progress

Cultural Studies An interdisciplinary area of scholarship that analyzes contemporary culture, concentrating on its history, defining traits, influences on everyday living, political dynamics between cultural groups, conflict, and peace making

Cultural values Shared with groups of people

Cultural violence Unintentional and invisible violence that rises when behavioral or structural violence is legitimized and justified by the attitudes, beliefs, and values of a society

Culture Complex patterns of behavior, values, and belief systems learned from and shared by members of a group

Culture of conflict Culturally specific practices, institutions, and norms associated with conflict

Culture of peace and nonviolence A system of attitudes that are likely to promote peaceful coexistence and the nonviolent resolution of conflicts

Culture of war and violence A system of values, beliefs, and attitudes essentially rooted in fear, insecurity, and distrust and, therefore, supportive of defensive violence

D

Deductive inquiry Research methods that extrapolate general principles or procedures from observed data and known facts

Demobilization Disbanding an armed group

Deportation Expulsion of a person or group by a government, usually as a punishment, also called extradition

Dialectic tensions Seemingly contradictory forces that are realities of all connected relationships

Diplomacy Formal activities that manage international relationships and conflicts between states through designated diplomats who represent the interests and policies of their sending nation

Disarmament Surrender, removal, or destruction of combat arms

Discipline Instruction and practice in a physical or mental skill

Discontinuity Occurs when consistency and predictability break down, resulting in uncertainty and insecurity

Distributive justice paradigm Correcting inequity by redistributing the resource or, even better, dismantling unjust ways of accessing resources

Distributive negotiation Competitive negotiation in which parties assume that their interests are in direct competition: what one party wins, the other party loses, also called positional bargaining and hard bargaining

Deception Intentionally, knowingly, or purposely misleading another person

Deescalation Occurs when calming words and actions are used to decrease the severity of a conflict through limiting the factors in dispute

Defensiveness Communication with the intent of protecting one's own interests and opinions

Deficiency need A basic need that, when threatened, will motivate urgent action

Descriptive norm Social ideas about what people do, plus the expectation that you will follow the pattern

Dialectic tension Seemingly contradictory elements that challenge the core of every relationship; cannot be solved with an either-or dichotomy (Baxter, 2008)

Discrimination Actions that treat someone unfavorably because of a perceived (but incorrect) correlation between ability and a personal characteristic such as age, religion, gender, or gender identity; results in unjust exclusion and exploitation

Disenfranchisement Identifiable groups are deprived of rights, privileges, or opportunities

Disrespect Expressed in behavior that you reasonably expect would cause harm or humiliation

Diversity The quality of being different

(Workplace) Diversity Refers to the extent of heterogeneous mixing versus homogeneous similarities among workers

Diversity Studies Explores social diversity and inequality and its influence on relationships and culture

Debilitative emotion Exaggerates the intensity of the moment, interferes with clear thinking or problem solving, and hinders effective relationship functioning

Differentiation phase Initial phase of conflict that intensifies differences

Differentiation process The phase of problem solving that focuses on differences among disputants, also called problem expansion

Directive listening Listening with the intention of correcting the ideas with argument, advice, or imposing the listener's viewpoint

Disclosure Occurs when normally private personal information is expressed out loud

Disinformation Intentionally spreads information that is known to be false, with the purpose of misleading opinion leaders

Dissonance Contradiction between two ideas, especially between self-concept and the views of others

Distributive negotiation Positional bargaining, hard bargaining, competitive negotiation with the intent to gain as much as possible

Divergent process Problem-solving process that creates new choices

Divided attention Occurs when we simultaneously receive several relevant sensations, and they compete for our attention and interfere with each other

Durable peace Orderly, demonstrates cooperative negotiation between opponents, and is dominated by JustPeace, also called sustainable peace

Dysfunctional conflict Harmful, poorly processed conflict

Dysfunctional family An unsafe or neglectful family that does not adequately fulfill the members' needs for any number of reasons

E

Effective outcome Solves a problem, improves parties' interactions, and uses a fair process (Laue, 1990)

Egocentric perspective Self-centered

Elicitive teaching Emphasizes students' existing knowledge, discovery learning, shared peer teaching in the context of participants' own challenges

Emotion Conscious feelings experienced in response to circumstances or experiences

Emotional contagion Emotion is communicated and transmitted interpersonally, so that a person feels emotion that is not genuinely their own

Emotional conflict Occurs when people have significant feelings about the disagreement, use emotional heat, animosity, or antagonistic remarks

Emotional flooding Overwhelming intensity of emotion

Emotional hijacking Intense emotion interferes with rational, logical thinking, activates an intense fight or flight impulse

Emotional Intelligence (EI or EQ) The capacity to identify, make sense of, and control emotions within ourselves, in others, and in groups

Empathic listening Listening with the intention of understanding, both intellectually and emotionally, deeper thoughts from another person's point of view

Empathy The ability to sense and react with understanding to others' emotions and viewpoint

Empowerment shift In Transformative Mediation, restores a sense of personal strength and mutual confidence, and reactivates skills

Empty universal A universal experience that is objectively blank because each person completes its meaning with their own subjective meanings

Enculturation The process by which you absorb the rules of a group's culture

Enhanced self Describes an ideal person or the way a person hopes to be; also called ideal self

Entitlement The attitude that "I am, or we are, better than other people, and therefore deserve special treatment"

Equity-restoring justice Methods focus on an aspect of the imbalance caused between the disputing parties

Escalation Increase in the severity of a conflict

Escalation threshold The point at which conflict becomes war

Ethical principles Useful guidelines when planning correct actions, and preventing wrong ones

Ethics of character Ongoing moral commitments of a practitioner that transcend professional relationships

Ethnic group A group whose members share the same culture, history, and language

Ethnic Studies An interdisciplinary study of ancestral origins, racial differences, diverse forms of ethnicity and national identity

Ethnocentrism Judges the Other against the standards and customs of your own group

Ethnopolitical conflict Large-scale conflict in which ethnic or religious differences and political disputes compound one another

Equifinality Refers to the existence of many pathways to a desired end

Experiential learning Learning through experience

Explicit conflict system What the organization says it does with conflict

Explicit rules Relationship rules that are definite, specific, and agreed by the parties

Exploitive power Taking power "from" others to fuel one's own private ends, without concern for other peoples' needs; least healthy, most destructive, and abusive power

Extradition Expulsion of a person or group by a government, usually as a punishment, also called deportation

Extrastate conflict Involves one state and an armed group from outside its borders

Extremism Fanaticism, holding extreme beliefs, with the rare outcome of discrimination

F

Face Measure of respectability or honor gained through correct behavior, social status, and conformity to expectations and duties

Facilitative emotion Helps clarify the meanings of events, providing insight into the dynamics of a relationship, and leading to constructive behavior

Faith A personal system of belief and practice (also called spirituality)

Fake news Distributes misleading content, sometimes based on so-called alternative facts

Family A group of people bonded in time and space by a variety of factors

Family competence The ability of the whole family to organize and manage itself as a cohesive unit, to productively accomplish its tasks

Family culture Family-owned objects, habits, beliefs, and ideals that form the shared identity of family members

Family developmental theory The theory that a family has phases of individual development that may contradict each other, causing conflict

Family resilience The ability of the whole family system to withstand and moderate changes within the family and in the environment, and recover equilibrium

Fear monger Motivated by a specific interest, cause, or benefit to stir up troublesome fear

Fight Talk Harsh, negative, and judgmental communication that vents anger or animosity and often ignites conflict

Flooding Experiencing overwhelming intensity of emotion

Forced migration Unplanned movement of a person or family away from their original homeland, also called involuntary displacement

Forcible population transfer An entire group is forced to migrate because a weak minority is considered undesirable by the powerful

Foreignness Subjective sense of resemblance versus strange or alien

Forgive To offer pardon for an offense—a noun and a verb

Friendly intent Designed to solve a problem, and/or improve an interaction or a relationship

Functional conflict Beneficial, meaningful conflict

Functional family Diverse forms of family who operate to protect members from trouble, and also proactively prepare them to confront and manage adversity

Functional immunity Protects the actions or functions carried out by professionals on behalf of a state

G

Game changer A tactic or event that completely upsets the familiar system of relationship rules or assumptions about them

Gender Cultural expectations for gender-based behavior

Gender analysis Study of and comparison of gendered experiences, and the examination of society from the differing standpoints of gendered individuals

Gender-based violence (GBV) Violence directed toward one gender, most often females, that violates sexual identity or sex organs

Gender expression How a person chooses to communicate gender identity

Gender identity Psychological identification with a particular gender

Gender literacy Awareness of gender diversity, associated expectations, and the consequences of those expectations

Gender role Patterns of behavior that are considered appropriate feminine or masculine behavior, also called sex role

Gender Studies A scholarly discipline devoted to the exploration of gender effects on relationships, social organization and functioning, and values and attitudes

Gender wage gap The difference of earnings between male and female workers

Generational strata Identifiable groups loosely defined by demographics and key life events

Genotype Biological genetic inheritance

Gini Coefficient One comparative measure of global economic justice

Global citizen Someone who is attentive to needs beyond the local community to include concerns beyond the narrow "I" or "us"

Globalization Cross-pollination of resources, ideas, and viewpoints, brings faster-paced cultural change

Good governance Ensures responsible, productive decision making. Just decisions are made that benefit everyone.

Governance The system by which political authority is exercised: how decisions are discussed and made, plans are formed and implemented, and public resources are managed

Ground rules Guidelines for behavior that participants agree to, to set the tone for intervention

Group climate Prevailing interactions, energy, and attitudes within a group environment

Group-level conflict Occurs among multiple parties who are associated in some significant way

Growth need A human need, not essential for survival but crucial for thriving and being

H

Habits Routine actions, interactions, or tendencies that are acquired through regular repetition

Harassment Hostile, destructive use of power in a workplace

Hard influence tactic Use of power that does harm to a relationship

Hard power Use of politically coercive economic and military methods

Hate speech Degrades or attacks, or incites prejudice or violence, ostensibly because of personal characteristics

Hatred Psychological and relational antipathy that develops in response to perceived offenses. It aims to shame, humiliate, and disempower the Other.

Hegemony A nation's dominance of global politics

Heterosexism Prejudicial attitude or active discrimination against alternative sexualities, based on belief in the superior or sole legitimacy of heterosexuality

Hidden agenda An individual has concealed goals that indirectly and subtly disrupt working behavior and communication

High-context culture The pattern that communicates meaning indirectly through mostly unspoken context; also called associative or collectivist culture

High-context group Clear communication requires sensitivity to the context of the relationship and setting in which it occurs

Holy war Wars waged to establish dominance and control through religion or culture, also called cultural imperialism

Hostile aggression Impulsive dominance or revenge, often unplanned and linked to a very hot emotion, also called retaliatory aggression

Hostile intent Driven not to solve a problem but deliberately to defeat or harm another person

Hot peace Active bridge building and cooperation between enemies

Hot war Hostility is acted out with the intention of harming or defeating an enemy

Household A group of people occupying a home

Human Development Index (HDI) Compiled from statistically compared education levels, per capita income, and life expectancy, used by the UN Development Program to rank national wellbeing

Human security Focus on qualities of life that sustain citizen wellbeing: freedom from want, freedom from fear

I

Ideal self Describes an ideal person or the way a person hopes to be; also called enhanced self

Identity The core factors that shape personal individuality, also called the self-concept

Identity-based conflict Develops when a person or group believes that their identity is threatened or denied legitimacy or respect

Identity conflict Based on core factors that shape personal identity and self-concept, those factors that provide personal uniqueness and consistency

Identity needs Affiliated, competent, consistent, and independent. These are foundations of self-respect, personal freedom, gender and cultural integrity, and respectful interaction

Immunity The principle that actions taken in an official capacity cannot be prosecuted. Functional immunity, personal immunity, and state immunity are different forms.

Implicit conflict system What members of a system do in conflict

Implicit rules Relationship rules that are unspoken and therefore subconscious, but agreement by the parties is assumed

Impunity Not having to face negative consequences or punishment after aggression

Incarceration Restriction of an individual's human rights in balance with the harm or injustice the crime caused to society

Individual characteristics theory Deals with patterns of distinct conflict tactics and interactions

Individualistic role Behavior is shaped by self-interested needs or goals more than contributions to the collective good

Inductive inquiry Research method that extrapolates general principles or procedures from observed data and known facts

Ineffective outcome Leaves a problem unsolved, or the problem is solved at the cost of a damaged or broken relationship

Inequality-Adjusted Human Development Index (IHDI) Measures national achievements against potential social contributions lost to inequalities in health, education, and life expectancy

Influence tactic Expresses power in actual behavior

Injustice Unfair—may refer to particular abusive or malicious actions, to a broader situation of imbalance or inequity, or to the failure of social systems to maintain justice

Instrumental violence Used in a strategy to accomplish a goal in the relationship or resolve a contentious issue, also called intentional violence

Intangible power Fluid dynamic of relative power among nations, has its origins in factors that affect the effectiveness of diplomatic and international negotiation

Integration phase Deescalating, stabilizing phase, during which emotions cool, issues are prioritized, and peripheral issues are set aside

Integration process The phase of problem solving that focuses on agreed methods, also called problem reduction

Integrative negotiation Cooperative negotiation with the intent of satisfying the needs of all parties, also called collaborative negotiation and soft bargaining

Integrative power Healthy power used "with" others, to unite, collaborate, advocate, and promote cooperation

Intent, intention Motive behind actions, the purpose or aim toward which actions are directed

Intention statement Openly states what is or is not intended

Interdependence Mutual dependency

Interest Underlying goal a person wants to fulfill, their needs and hopes

Interests-based conflict resolution Conflict parties identify their own interests, acknowledge common interests, and then negotiate satisfactory solutions

International conflict Occurs between governments, large groups of people in different geographical regions. Sometimes involves one government and another group desiring change through revolution or rebellion.

Interpersonal conflict Occurs between at least two parties who are affected by the problem in dispute

Interpersonal power The ability to influence other people's activities or environment, often a direct product of a relationship

Interpersonal violence Intentionally antisocial actions, relationship patterns, or attitudes that result from multiple source problems, develop and escalate over time, harm countless people, and suggest many potential solutions

Intersectionality A mosaic of personal and social identities that affect one's point of view or perspective

Intersex individuals Individuals born with ambiguous chromosomes, genitalia, and/ or hormonal functioning

Interstate conflict Involves two or more sovereign parties

Intervention Work done during and shortly after a violent crisis to improve the immediate situation or lower the harm caused by it

Intractable conflict Complex, long-lasting problems and conflicts that seem to resist solution, also called wicked conflict

Intrapersonal conflict Occurs within an individual, the "conflicted self"

Intrastate conflict Between a state government and a group within distinct boundaries, also called civil war

Involuntary displacement Unplanned movement of a person or family away from their original homeland, also called forced migration

Irreconcilable problem The problems between parties cannot be solved or resolved, so parties generally look for an exit strategy

J

Johari window Explanatory concept of interpersonal disclosure

Journalism Gathering information and distributing it to a consumer audience; tends to focus on violence and war

Judgmental listening Listening with a motive criticize or blame

Justice Experienced when conditions are right, fair, reasonable

Justice making Both the process and outcome of restoring justice and fairness to all parties to a conflict

JustPeace The foundation of peace is justice

Just war The belief that force may legitimately be used to correct a wrong, for a just purpose

K

Kinship A group of people who develop attachment and mutual loyalty through historical origins

L

Latent conflict Tangible, but subtle, conflict that results from hidden and unspoken differences, with the potential to erupt

Large-scale violence Hostile actions, relationships, and attitudes intersecting to increase risks and experiences of danger for an identifiable group of people in a community, nation, or international setting

Left-wing politics Summarizes progressive principles that emphasize egalitarian sharing of power and resources, with particular attention to reformation of conditions that cause social inequality.

Legal, procedural justice Settling family disputes through family court systems that address the legal and contractual dimensions of marriage, child custody, adoption, and inheritance.

Legitimate fear Adaptive fear associated with a primal threat to survival

Legitimate power Authority and power derived from a position within the hierarchy

Linear flow A communication process is organized, sequential, and shared by all parties

Linear thinking Logical examination of the causes and complications of disagreement. It is a method that sequentially examines the constituent parts of a complicated concept to reach understanding.

Low-conflict society Harmonious relationships are valued, and individual and community interests are linked together.

Low-context culture The pattern that communicates meaning literally, directly with words, and little contribution from implied context; also called individualistic culture

Lose-lose problem solving A conflict devolves into a focus on mutual defeat rather than on solving the initial problem

M

Maintenance role Activities that support the interpersonal functioning of the system by regulating and strengthening the group's cohesion

Malevolent intent Attempting to harm or defeat an opponent through hostility, spite, or malice

Manifest conflict Tangible, open conflict of varied intensity, also called articulated conflict

Manipulative power Used "over" others, to control through persuasion and management, can be healthy or destructive

Marginality Unchosen and probably undeserved situation of an individual or group on the margins of mainstream systems and institutions

Master discipline Knowledge and skills are applicable to and augment other disciplines

Media literacy The ability to identify types of media, and to understand, interpret, and use the information conveyed

Mediation Nonadversarial negotiation through a third party who helps disputants to organize the flow of discussion to focus on communicating needs, rights, and interests, and a satisfactory solution

Metacommunication Objectively noticing a communication process and commenting on it

Metamessage Information implicit, but not verbal, about parties' relationship

Metaproblem Disagreement about whether a problem exists or not, or whether it is important or not

Microaggression An insensitive act that causes interpersonal indignity or insult, usually subtle and unintended

Mindfulness A popular silent meditation used to maximize attention

Misandry Perception that men are treacherous, with accompanying distrust or hatred of males, or overlooking men's' needs and full contributions

Misinformation Inadvertent spread of incorrect, mistaken information based on data available at the time

Misogyny Perception that women are dangerous, resulting in distrust or even hatred of females, or neglecting women's' needs and positive contributions

Mixed-culture family A family that includes individuals with diverse origins in race, culture, country of origin or birth, or religion

Mixed-race identity Racial identity made up of scattered sources of genetic inheritance

Moral amend An apology that addresses a victim with dignity

Moral blindness Insensitivity to or denial of the deep individual and collective implications of injustice and violence, and to possible alternatives

Moral conflict Reflect deepest convictions and personal measures of what is good and meaningful; also called values conflict

Moral imagination Uses empathy to recognize possibilities and turning points in conflict that can alter previous habits and create a new peace that does not yet exist

Moral intelligence The ability to clearly distinguish right from wrong, and the ability to behave in right ways

Morphological level of culture First level of culture, the most visible and expressive distinctive customs, manners, and etiquette, as well as material artifacts (Das, 2007)

Multiculturalism The respectful coexistence of diverse forms of culture, each retaining some of the original distinctives but sharing core values

Multidimensional Poverty Index (MPI) Records acute gaps in standards of family living

Multiracial identity Racial identity made up of scattered sources of genetic inheritance

Multitrack diplomacy Simultaneous and interconnected methods conducted through different representative groups using similar methods

Muted voice Assumptions of the powerful result in voicelessness for the powerless (Ardener, 2005)

N

Narrative frame Inner story told to explain problems, events, and conflict

Nationalism The belief that societies or nations should be "pure"

Nationality Names the political state in which a person is a citizen

National security Focus on the security and safety of the state as a guarantor of personal security

Nature-nurture debate Classic debate about the sources of individual aggression

Negative frame Perception and negative interpretation steadily add to the dispute

Negative justice The absence or failure of justice

Negative paradigm Beliefs about conflict that divide the parties because they are connected to fear and can lead to silence or inauthentic communication

Negative peace The absence of tension, threat, open conflict, or violence

Negative peacebuilding Activity that ends conflict and violence, emphasizing crisis management, and violence containment or reduction

Negative sentiment override A negative perspective that is based on core habits that turn disputants away from each other and toward opposition—harsh behaviors and comments outweigh shared positive history.

Negotiable values Open to priority setting

Negotiation Voluntary decision making that results from complex give-and-take dialogue and exchange of information, ideas, and promises, usually between two parties

Nonadversarial conflict resolution Differences and disputes are resolved, and justice is created through cooperative discussion

Nonlinear flow A communication process is not rigidly organized, includes emotional content and tends to be authentic; also called chaotic communication

Nonlinear thinking Uses experience and knowledge to provide many starting points to explore conflict, with the expansion of the ideas in many directions at once

Nonlinguistic communication Communication through vocal quality and body language

Nonnegotiable values Closed to priority setting

Nonproliferation Restricts national arms production, inventory, and use

Nonviolence Far-reaching concept that goes beyond both passive acceptance and violent aggression to solve problems.

Norm Behavior patterns, "scripts" used as you function in relationships, sometimes the basis for judgments of "normal"

Normativity Assumes specific qualities are a valid standard for judging everyone

Nuclear family A traditional definition of a family as containing one man, one woman, and at least one child.

Nurturant power Healthy, prosocial power is used "for" others, to provide caring strength to support others

O

Ombudsperson An official appointed to communicate between disputing parties, clarify the limits of reasonable conflict, interpret positions, and suggest potential resolution

Open system Norms are flexible, so that individuals can make changes easily

Orchestrated violence Specific conditions and group dynamics are instrumental in generating risk of violent outbreaks

Order-restoring justice Methods to correct the disorderly nature of injustice, replacing it with orderliness

Othering The process of defining and reducing another person's identity to labels

Ought self What you believe you should be to measure up

Overt conflict Open conflict that can vary in intensity from mild and transitory to unrestrained and violent.

Overt intent Spoken, expressed intention

P

Paradigm Mental model based on assumptions that frame conflict, affect both perception and response, and determine a course of resolution

Paradigm shift A social change process that alters the basic values and assumptions of a society

Parenting style Pattern of parent behaviors toward children, is formed by the cluster of strategies a parent uses

Party Someone who has an interest in or cares about a conflict or its outcome

Patriarchy A society or culture organized with exclusively male leadership and power

Peacebuilding A comprehensive concept that refers to all efforts to decrease violence, increase security, and create more peaceable relationships

Peace enforcement Interposition of third-party military forces or trained civilians (usually unarmed) between violent adversaries

Peace journalism Selection and distribution of nonviolent stories with the goals of sensitizing the consumer public to the true costs of violence and the real effectiveness of peaceful and constructive conflict solutions

Peacekeeping Used to avert a developing confrontative crisis, designed to moderate intense hostility that is on the verge of becoming violent, also called preventive peacebuilding

Peacemaking Activities that bring hostile parties to resolve their grievances, with the objective of winning an enduring peace accord

Peace spoiler Individuals or group that adopts violent strategies to undermine peace processes and agreements

Perception The process by which a person makes sense of experienced information

Perceptual defense A subconscious censor that may prevent attention to or perception of obnoxious stimuli

Perceptual set The predisposition to perceive things in a specific, expected way

Perceptual suggestion Modification of perception that comes from similar experiences

Perpetrator A person who carries out an illegal, immoral, or intentionally harmful act

Perpetration Induced Trauma Stress (PITS) Results from a perpetrator's active participation in violent actions, especially prolonged or repeated

Perpetual problem A conflict rising out of nonnegotiable differences of personality or lifestyle, no amount of processing is likely to resolve

Personal competence The ability to successfully apply knowledge and skill to master life's real challenges

Personal ethics Guide individual actions in interpersonal relationships

Personal identity Unique, independent aspects of ourselves

Personal immunity Immunity from prosecution based on official position, applied to state officers acting within the mandate of their office

Personality The complex pattern of factors and traits that describe and distinguish one individual from others, unique but relatively consistent in the variety of settings

Personal power A fundamental human need that gives people the ability to control themselves and their immediate environment

Personal values Held by individuals

Persuasive listening Listening with the intention of persuading someone that your position is best

Phenotype Visible racial differences

Political power The ability to ensure that a party's own interests prevail

Political violence Hostile aggression led by a government or groups of people, with the goal of achieving a political aim

Poor governance Looks out for the wellbeing of a selected few, but not most people

Position Particular opinion about the problem and/or the solution

Positional argument Competitively arguing a rigidly held opinion without disclosing the underlying interest

Positional role Behavior expected of family member because of their position in the configuration

Positive frame Respectful, assertive perception that helps parties to perceive and interpret both the opponent and the conflict in friendly terms

Positive justice Norms and proactive practices that ensure the wellbeing of most people

Positive paradigm Beliefs about conflict that tend to draw parties together in a joint effort to restore harmony

Positive peace Multidimensional peace that actively prevents conflict and limits violence by addressing the roots of the conflict

Positive peacebuilding Difficult and long-term peacebuilding, intended to resolve the deep causes of conflict and violence by generating equitable conditions

Post-Traumatic Stress Disorder (PTSD) A psychological condition caused by experiencing or witnessing a seriously stressful or traumatic event

Postvention Work dealing with the aftermath of violence

Power The freedom to make choices and the capacity to direct other peoples' actions through authority or control, to accomplish a particular outcome

Power/authority-based conflict resolution A third party imposes a solution on conflict parties

Practical amend Restore to the victim any material losses caused by a wrongdoing

Precipitating event The event that sparks or triggers a conflict

Preemptive peacebuilding Focuses on actions that deescalate a pending crisis, by encouraging calm, calling for help from peaceable people, and peace dialogue

Prejudice Prejudge the Other unfavorably based on unfounded beliefs and expectations about a group rather than on personal experience

Prescriptive ethics Ethical principles that describe what should happen

Prescriptive norm Social expectations of what people must do if you want to remain a member of a group

Prescriptive teaching Employs instruction that targets specific behaviors, problems, and deficits with expert solutions that students then memorize

Preventive peacebuilding Explicitly cultivates goodwill and fosters positive interpretations of the Other through collaborative activity projects and informed debate

Prevention Activity that inhibits disputes from arising between parties, prevents existing disputes from escalating into violence, and limits the spread of violent conflicts when they do occur

Primary party Central people involved in a conflict

Primary or primal emotions Basic and rudimentary emotions, linked to tangible needs and survival

Primary territory Space under individual or small group control

Principal values The foundations on which a personal value system is built

Principled negotiation Starting point for negotiation is agreement to cooperatively follow four process principles, also called problem-solving negotiation

Principled nonviolence Belief in the responsibility to promote deeply respectful interactions in every human connection also called compassionate nonviolence

Privilege An unearned right, honor, or advantage that is granted to a particular person or group

Problem The stimulus for conflict that can arise from incompatible needs, goals, principles, or values; must be resolved if a relationship is to continue functioning

Problem expansion In problem solving, broadens the matters for consideration, also called differentiation

Problem reduction In problem solving, narrows the scope of a complex problem and reduces the matters for consideration, also called integration

Problem-solving mediation Conflict resolution directed by disputants with professional guidance of practical inquiry into the reasons for a conflict results in a thorough understanding of conflict themes while avoiding confrontation, also called conciliation

Problem-solving strategy Separation of positions from interests (Fisher, Ury, & Patton, 2011)

Procedural conflict People disagree about how to solve substantive problems, or how to fulfil the central purposes of the relationship

Procedural justice paradigm Fair process that addresses disputes or injustice

(Communication) process The relationship of one topic or focus to another, how a conversation is organized, and the meaning of the unfolding flow

Process Used to describe how a conflict unfolds

Process design Explores how conflict is processed within an organization and recommends process steps that should be followed when a conflict cannot be resolved simply

Process role Contribute to smooth relationships among family members

Professional ethics Guide professionals' duties and responsibilities toward clients, patients, or students, guide right and wrong actions

Professional misconduct Use of power violates established policies or becomes intense enough to be abusive and unacceptable

Prohibitive ethics Ethical principles that describe what should never happen

Promotive interdependence The belief that any one person's success promotes the entire group

Promotive peacebuilding Promotes relationship building across intersectional divides indirectly through activities like sports and international conferences

Proscriptive norm Social expectations about what people must not do to be "normal"

Prosocial actions Support relationship and peaceful interactions and conflict processing with assertive tactics

Prospective goal The goal or aim that begins a conflict

Protective factors Act as buffers, either decreasing the likelihood of experiencing violence or moderating the harm

Proximate cause Factors that contribute to a readiness for conflict or for its escalation

Pseudoforgiveness Pretended or careless forgiveness

Pseudolistening Going through the motions of listening while thinking of something else

Pseudopeace A state of pretending that peace exists, but with the tension of peace-at-all-costs

Psychological resilience An individual's ability to remain calm and successfully cope with crisis without enduring negative consequences

Public territory Space available to anyone who needs it

Punishment Imposes an unpleasant penalty with the goal of reducing improper behavior

Q

Qualitative research Focus research on detailed interpretation of limited case material and complex process

Quantitative research Uses measurement, mathematics, and statistics to examine the behavior of large groups of people

R

Rapport speech Person-focused communication intended to reinforce connection and cooperation

Race A concept that refers to classification of human groups based on inherited physical characteristics like skin color, hair color and texture, and eye color

Racial profiling Discrimination that relies on visible race, religion, or national origin when suspecting or investigating possible criminal behavior

Racism Any belief or attitude, action or practice that is founded on a racialized worldview

Radicalization Factors that converge to produce extreme activism

Reactivity Hasty and intense reaction to emotional stimuli

Recidivism Fall back into criminal behavior and the criminal justice system despite undergoing its negative consequences

Recognition shift In Transformative Mediation, creates more realistic perception of the self and the Other, and authentic interaction is regained

Reconciliation Creation of a new, peaceable relationship and interaction

Recreational diversity Sampling the morphological aspects of alternative cultures

Reflection-in-action Careful thought during a conflict

Reflection-on-action Retrospective analysis and thought after a conflict has ended

Reflective practice Self-reflection and insight, used to self-correct conflict resolution skills

Reframe Explore the perspectives of each party will often create new points of view, broaden understandings and insight

Refugee Someone who has fled their homeland because of war-related violence

Religion A sacred belief in the transcendent or supernatural dimension of life, shared with other devotees

Religious extremism Fuses a political interpretation of religious doctrine or a scriptural justification for political aims

Reparative peacebuilding Applies after violence and damage has happened, to repair relationships and improve root conditions

Report speech Task-focused communication intended to accomplish a task through information-sharing, expressing opinion, and exploring problems and solutions

Resilience The ability to adapt to sudden misfortune or to ongoing difficulty and stress

Responsibility Acknowledging that someone suffered as a result of specific actions, regardless of intention; the contrast is blame

Restorative justice paradigm Works out ways of restoring relationships, repairing the harms, and reintegrating the community

Restorative practices Practical methods used to restore justice

Retribution Punishment

Retributive justice paradigm Correcting injustice through equivalent payment or compensation for hurt and loss

Retrospective goal Conflict goals that becomes evident only in hindsight

Revolution Sudden, major, often violent, challenge of existing powers and social conditions

Rights-based conflict resolution The focus of conflict resolution is on individual rights, exploring the reasons for competing or incompatible rights, and then asserting appropriate rights in ways that do not undermine each other

Right-wing politics Conservative principle that supports decision making by leaders, and policies that conserve existing family and political order, existing laws, established institutions and borders, and a singular culture

Risk factor Life events, conditions, and experiences linked with problems, antisocial behavior, and violence

Role Recurring behavior patterns members are expected to fulfill as part of the whole system

Rule Regulations that dictate conduct in a specific situation

Rules-based ethics Ethical principles that focus on the rules of proper action

S

Savoir etre Knowing how to be

Savoir faire Knowing how to do things

Savoir vivre Knowing how to live well with Others

Search Talk Careful inquiry into uncertain or ambiguous personal opinions and feelings, with the purpose of understanding

Secondary emotion Elaborations of primary emotions that garner their significance from past experiences becoming emotionally associated with current events

Secondary party People involved indirectly in conflict, who are affected by the conflict or its resolution

Secondary territory Space used regularly by many people, but only if they comply with agreed-upon norms

Secure attachment Relationship security with little or no anxiety about separation or abandonment

Security dilemma Uncertainty or mistrust that grows in concert with another state's power or perceived threat, and leads to increasing state defensiveness

Settlement mediation Conflict resolution procedure directed by the disputing parties, but the dialogue is guided by a professional third party

Schema Templates for comparing data as similar to or contrasting something experienced earlier

Selective listening Hearing only what is familiar or acceptable while ignoring undesirable information

Sex Biological, genetic nature at birth

Sex role Patterns of behavior that are considered appropriate feminine or masculine behavior (also called gender role)

Sexism Prejudice or discrimination based on sex, gender, or gender roles

Sexual orientation Expresses sexual attraction toward other individuals

Shame-based culture Shame and embarrassment are used to penalize nonconformity to expectations; honors are used to reward those who live up to social ideals

Shop Talk Impersonal communication that focuses on task

Skill-based conflict resolution Uses education and training to improve the parties' Emotional Intelligence

Small Talk Impersonal communication that initiates rapport and trust

Social analysis theory Use extensive and intensive examination of social systems, issues, and trends

Social bias theory Address the realities of exclusion experienced by specific groups of people while envisioning a more constructive way

Social capital Three primary components of status: education, income, and occupational prestige

Social change Any significant alteration of existing order and accepted ways of living together—can happen violently or nonviolently

Social identity Identity characteristics expressed in relationship to other people, and can denote group affiliation, also called relational identity

Socialization Lifelong training of behaviors, relationships, and attitudes necessary to act appropriately in relationships and society, also called social learning

Social media All forms of electronic communication that distribute information, ideas, and commentary

Social norm An expected behavior pattern that defines and controls actions considered to be "normal," "scripts" used as you function in relationships

Social process theory Based in detailed techniques for analysis and peacebuilding

Socioeconomic status (SES) Stratified social rank, shared by a group of people with similar levels of wealth and power, also called socioeconomic class (SEC)

Soft influence tactic Use of power that does not harm a relationship

Soft power Use of direct appeals and demonstrations of superior national wealth and resources to persuade other nations to cooperate

Solvable problem From here-and-now, situational, and time-limited problems

Sovereign immunity A head of state or a government cannot commit an illegal act and is, therefore, immune from prosecution for official actions

Sovereignty Authority of a government over land, sea, airspace, a body of people, and independence from outside interference

Spanking Corporal punishment causes pain with slapping or hitting

Spirituality A personal system of belief and practice (also called faith)

Spite Talk Attack the opponent, leading to all-out emotional war

Spoiler Civilian and/or military groups opposed to peacemaking efforts, may sabotage or undermine peace negotiations and attempt to reignite the war

Stable peace The risk of conflict developing is insignificant

Stakeholder Someone who has a stake or interest, or something to lose or gain in the outcome of a conflict

Standpoint A particular position for viewing the world and gathering knowledge

State immunity A head of state or a government cannot commit an illegal act and is, therefore, immune from prosecution for official actions

State-shifting Conflict interactions are altered with strength and authentic interaction, and interpersonal transformation happens

Stereotype A simplistic perception of the Other that obscures personality and dignity, and labels someone merely as a member of a class

Stonewall Refuse to answer questions or cooperate, resulting in a stalled dialogue

Straight Talk Mutually disclosing communication of personal opinions and feelings, with the purpose of deep understanding

Strategic nonviolence Uses nonviolence because it works

Stratification Different groups are placed on different levels (strata) of society, which can strongly influence the opportunities of individuals within those strata

Strategic misrepresentation Misstating or distorting information in public media in a way that influences decision makers

Strategy Deliberated, planned response to conflict

Structural cause Pervasive tensions that are built into habits or policies, party relationship issues, or the fabric of relating that create the preconditions for conflict

Structural level of culture Second level of cultural identity, which is less tangible and must be inferred from observing how relationships are organized and interactions are enacted (Das, 2007)

Structural violence Unintentional violence that occurs when a society is organized or stratified in such a way that significant groups of people are disadvantaged by unequal access to collective resources, operates to preserve social order and existing power hierarchies

Style Patterns or clusters of behavior that are used repeatedly in a variety of conflict situations

Substantive conflict Expressed in differences of opinion or priorities or viewpoints

Suspicion Fear that is disproportionate to threat and does not reflect actual risk

Sustainable conflict resolution Has three qualities:A) the problem has been addressed in a satisfactory way;B) the relationship is preserved and, in fact, becomes stronger with improved communication and trust; andC) the parties remain engaged with each other, with no one having withdrawn.

Sustainable peace Orderly, demonstrates cooperative negotiation between opponents, and is dominated by JustPeace, also called durable peace

Symmetrical conflict Parties match or exaggerate each other's actions

Symmetrical power Influence is collaboratively shared and exchanged, fluctuating evenly according to individual strengths

Symmetrical power relationship Sides are somewhat balanced and are of equal standing in the global political scene and have independent military, political, and diplomatic resources

Synchronicity Conflict partners come to a decision simultaneously

System A multilevel network of interacting elements (parties, relationships, roles, events, process sequences, even ideas) that relate to each other

Systemic racism A type of structural injustice where racism is embedded within social power and cultural systems so invisibly and inescapably that it seems "normal"

Systemic violence Operates throughout a group of people, often so subtly that it is invisible even to those affected by it

Systems analysis Acknowledges the role of individual behavior and decisions in the development of conflict, but also maps the sequences of events as one action results in reactions from others with impact on the relationship network or system of conflict

T

Tactics Specific behaviors and methods that emerge as opponents pursue the goal of the conflict

Tangible power A nation's power potential beyond its declared borders, backed by resources such as population, economic strength, technology, the administration of laws, and military capacity

Task role Contribute to efficient family and home operations

Theory Organized statement of ideas that unifies principles, explanations, and interpretations of observed facts.

Theory of Intersectionality Explores individual and social identities, and social and political systems as they relate to social domination and subordination, and discrimination (Crenshaw, 1994)

The Other A term that refers to another person who is obviously different from yourself

Therapeutic mediation Conflict resolution directed by a professional like a psychologist or a family therapist with the goal of insight into the underlying causes of a conflict

Third party Helper-facilitator from outside a conflicted relationship system who becomes involved

Third-party facilitation Someone who is not involved in a conflict works with the parties to assist them to stop the conflict and to solve the source problems

Third-party intervention Conflict processing assistance is provided by a trained, objective professional who is not involved, and does not become involved, in the conflict

Top-down peacebuilding Formal peacebuilding lead by national and international leaders

Toxic workplace An organization with a negative, mistrusting, or threatening climate

Track I diplomacy Interstate negotiation conducted through designated professional representatives like appointed ambassadors

Tragic Drama Theory The theory that conflict is embedded in family patterns of persecutor, victim, rescuer, and scapegoat (Karpman, 2007)

Transactive goal Emerge during the course of the conflict

Transformative justice Unjust situations occur in the context of self-centered value systems. Justice making has a focus on making things right with ambitious aims: all parties are potentially "healed," and just outcomes are quite expansive

Transformative learning Relinquishing an old interpretation to construct a new viewpoint. This is usually unsettling but can lead to perspective change.

Transitional justice (TJ) Governs legal and political decisions in a newly stabilizing region by addressing existing balances of power and providing reparation for victims of large-scale violence

Trauma An intense threat to wellbeing and the damage that results from a disturbing or distressing event

Trauma-Informed Practice Deals with conflict issues with sensitivity to past trauma, consequences, and coping mechanisms

Trauma storytelling Tells of past conflict and trauma, from one generation to the next

Trauma studies A social science that investigates healthy and maladaptive responses to traumatic events like conflict

Triangular Theory of Love The theory that committed love has three essential, balanced components: erotic connection, friendship, and commitment (Sternberg, 1986)

Trigger Key actions or events (sometimes only anticipated and not yet happened) that will set off or escalate conflict

Trust Experienced as confidence (but not certainty) of a partner's goodwill, demonstrated in positive actions, reliability when it counts, and predictable concern and responsiveness

Type I trauma A one-time traumatic event

Type II trauma A traumatic event, repeated

Type III trauma Traumatic events so numerous and pervasive that the events mingle together

U

Uncivil behavior Low-intensity behavior that violates common social norms, without a clear intent to harm, often veiled and mostly unintentional

Unconventional warfare Between asymmetric opponents with the aim to exploit enemy vulnerabilities and persuade them

Unrightable wrong Unjust inequity becomes brutal atrocity, to quell conflict or eliminate a people

Unstable peace Intermittent periods of order and conflict, but with crisis looming, also called cold war

V

Values Relatively permanent principles and standards of behavior that are considered important and worthwhile

Values conflict Reflect deepest convictions and personal measures of what is good and meaningful

Values ethics Ethical principles that outline the ideals that are believed to promote healthy and productive relationships, especially in professional contexts

Victim Is a controversial term. Generally, a person who has experienced or witnessed the harm of a significantly violent event

Victim identity Ongoing coping patterns that compromise a victim's ability to cope

Violence An act of aggression that has the intent to harm another party

Violence (World Health Organization) The intentional use of physical force or power, threatened or actual, against oneself, another person, or a group or community, that either results in or has a high likelihood of resulting in injury, death, psychological harm, maldevelopment, or deprivation

Violent communication Any words or actions that degrade other people and undermine the dignity of its target

Violence engineer Motivated to create violence to make a dramatic point or to further a cause

W

War Chaotic turmoil among multiple organized parties

War crime Serious violation of conventional agreements and international rules of war

Wicked conflict Complex, long-lasting problems and conflicts that seem to resist solution, also called intractable conflict

Win-lose problem solving Based on the perception of a competitive either-or solution

Win-win problem solving An effective, enduring resolution by solving the problem, addressing the needs of each individual, preserving the relationship, and using a fair process

Working Class Studies A specialty within Diversity Studies that explores social strata and class, working-class culture, class-based inequity, and social policy (also called Class Studies)

Worldview A working model of the world from a specific standpoint

Worldview level of culture Third, deepest and most hidden level of cultural identity presents values and meaning, going beyond outward symbols to encompass your reason for being in the world. Values are subconscious and must be inferred (Das, 2007).

Worldview skills Challenge existing assumptions and worldviews, inspiring rethinking

X

Xenophobia Fear or distrust of a stranger

References

■ ■ ■

INTRODUCTION

Baxter, Leslie A., and Dawn O. Braithwaite. 2008. "Relational Dialectics Theory." In *Engaging Theories in Interpersonal Communication: Multiple Perspectives*, by Dawn O. Braithwaite and Leslie A. Baxter (Eds.), 349–61. Sage.

Boulding, Elise, and Kenneth Boulding. 1995. *The Future: Images and Processes.* Sage.

Braithwaite, Alex, and Douglas Lemke. 2011. "Unpacking Escalation." *Conflict Management and Peace Science* 28, 2, 111–23.

"Chief Black Kettle." 2020. *Washita Battlefield.* July 30. Accessed September 29, 2020. https://www.nps.gov/waba/learn/historyculture/black-kettle.htm.

Coleman, Peter T. 2004. "Paradigmatic Framing of Protracted, Intractable Conflict: Toward the Development of a Metaframework II." *Peace and Conflict: Journal of Peace Psychology* 10, 3, 197–235.

DFID. 2017. *Joint Analysis of Conflict and Stability: Guidance Note.* Analysis, DFID: Department for International Development.

Dugan, Maire A. 1996. "A Nested Theory of Conflict." *A Leadership Journal: Women in Leadership* 1, 1, 9–20.

Fisher, Ronald J., and Loraleigh Keashly. 1991. "The Potential Complementarity of Mediation and Consultation within a Contingency Model of Third Party Intervention." *Journal of Peace Research* 28, 1, 29–42.

Gottman, John Mordechai, and Julie Schwartz Gottman. 2008. "Gottman Method Couple Therapy." In *Clinical Handbook of Couple Therapy,* by Alan S. Gurman (Ed.), 4rth ed., 138–65. Guilford.

Harjo, Susan Shown. 2014. *Nation to Nation: Treaties between the United States and American Indian Nations.* Smithsonian.

Hauss, Charles. 2019. *From Conflict Resolution to Peacebuilding.* Rowman and Littlefield.

Hoig, Stan. 1990. *The Peace Chiefs of the Cheyennes.* University of Oklahoma.

Laue, James H. 1987. "Resolution: Transforming Conflict and Violence." *Inaugural Lecture of the Vernon M. and Minnie I. Lynch Chair in Conflict Resolution.* George Mason University, November 17.

Lawrence-Lightfoot, Sara. 2012. "Respect: On Witness and Justice." *American Journal of Orthopsychiatry* 82, 3, 447–54.

Mayer, Bernard S. 2009. *Staying with Conflict: A Strategic Approach to Ongoing Disputes.* Jossey-Bass.

———. 2012. *The Dynamics of Conflict: A Guide to Engagement and Intervention.* 2nd ed. Jossey-Bass.

443

———. 2015. *The Conflict Paradox: Seven Dilemmas at the Core of Disputes*. Jossey-Bass.

Meadows, Donella H. 2008. *Thinking in Systems: A Primer*. Chelsea Green.

Moore, John H. 2011. "Cheyennes." In *Encyclopedia of the Great Plains*, by David J. Wishart (Ed.). University of Nebraska, Lincoln.

Noll, Douglas. 2003. *Peacemaking: Practicing at the Intersection of Law and Human Conflict*. Cascadia.

Portwood, Sharon G., Richard G. Lambert, Lyndon P. Abrams, and Ellissa Brooks Nelson. 2011. "Evaluation of the Adults and Children Together against Violence: Parents Raising Safe Kids Program." *Journal of Primary Prevention* 32, 147.

Pranis, Kay. 2014. *Circle Keeper's Handbook*. Edutopia.

Rummel, R. J. 1991. *The Conflict Helix: Principles and Practices of Interpersonal, Social, and International Conflict and Cooperation*. Routledge.

Smith-Christopher, Daniel L. (Ed.). 2007. *Subverting Hatred: The Challenge of Nonviolence in Religious Traditions*. Orbis.

USAID. 2012. *Conflict Assessment Framework, 2.0*. Analysis, USAID: United States Agency for International Development.

CHAPTER 1

Agbalajobi, Damilola Taiye. 2010. "The Role of Women in Conflict Resolution and Peacebuilding." *Institute for Security Studies Monograph #173*, 233–253.

Antonioni, David. 1998. "Relationship between the Big Five Personality Factors and Conflict Styes." *International Journal of Conflict Management* 9, 4, 336–355.

Aristotle. n.d. "Nicomachean Ethics by Aristotle." *classics.mit.edu*. Accessed June 21, 2018. classics.mit.edu/Aristotle/nicomachaen.2.ii.html.

———. n.d. "Rhetoric, Book 1, 1109a.27." *Perseus Digital Library*. Accessed 2018. http://www.perseus.tufts.edu/hopper/nebrowser?mode=search&id=meteorol%2 Caristotle.

Baron-Cohen, Simon. 1997. *The Maladapted Mind: Classic Readings in Evolutionary Psychopathology*. Psychology Press/Taylor Francis.

Bar-Tal, Daniel, and Nehemia Geva. 1986. "A Cognitive Basis of International Conflict." *Psychology of Intergroup Relations* 118–133.

Bartlett, Robert C., and Susan D. Collins. 2011. *Artistotle's Nichomachean Ethics*. University of Chicago.

Bowen, Murray. 1978. *Family Therapy in Clinical Practice*. Jason Aronson.

Bronfenbrenner, Urie. 1979. *The Ecology of Human Development: Experiments by Nature and Design*. Harvard University.

Burton, John W. 1990. *Conflict: Human Needs Theory*. Macmillan.

———. 1998. "Conflict Resolution: The Human Dimension." *International Journal of Peace Studies* 3, 1.

Bushman, B. J. 2002. "Does Venting Anger Feed or Extinguish the Flame? Catharsis, Rumination, Distraction, Anger, and Aggressive Responding." *Personal and Social Psychology Bulletin* (American Psychological Association) 28, 724–731.

Canary, Daniel J., Ellen M. Cunningham, and Michael J. Cody. 1988. "Goal Types, Gender, and Locus of Control in Managing Interpersonal Conflict." *Communication Research*, August 1, 15, 4, 426–446.

Christakis, Nicholas A., and James H. Fowler. 2010. *Connected: The Surprising Power of Our Social Networks*. Little Brown.

Claes, Marie-Therese. 1999. "Women, Men, and Management Styles." *International Labour Review* 138, 4.

Coltri, Laurie S. 2020. *Alternative Dispute Resolution: A Conflict Diagnosis Approach*. 2nd ed.. Pearson.

De France, Kalee, and Gary W. Evans. 2020. "Expanding Context in the Role of Emotional Regulation in Mental Health." *Emotion*. Online publication.

DeSteno, David, James J. Gross, and Laura Kubzansky. 2013. "Affective Science and Health: The Importance of Emotion and Emotional Regulation." *Health Psychology* 32, 5, 474–486.

Digman, J. M. 1990. "Personality Structure: Emergence of the Five Factor Model." *Annual Review of Psychology* 41, 417–440.

Domenici, Kathy, and Stephen W. Littlejohn. 2006. *Facework: Bridging Theory and Pactice*. Sage.

Dreher, Diane E. 2000. *The Tao of Inner Peace: A Guide to Inner and Outer Peace*. Penguin.

Eddy, William A. 2005. "High Conflict Personality in Family Mediation." *ACResolution*, Summer, 14–17.

Erikson, Erik H. 1980. *Identity and the Life Cycle*. Norton.

Festinger, Leon. 1957. *A Theory of Cognitive Dissonance*. Stanford University.

Fisher, Ronald J., and Herbert C. Kelman. 2011. "Perceptions in Conflict." In *Frontiers of Social Psychology. Intergroup Conflicts and Their Resolution: A Social Psychological Perspective*, by D. Bar-Tal (Ed.), 61–81. Psychology Press.

Frankl, Viktor E. 2006. *Man's Search for Meaning (Revised and Updated)*. Beacon.

Galtung, Johan. 1969. "Violence, Peace, and Peace Research." *Journal of Peace Research* 6, 3, 167–191.

Gehricke, Jean-Guido, and Alan J. Fridlund. 2002. "Smiling, Frowning, and Autonomic Activity in Mildly Depressed and Nondepressed Men." *Perception and Motivation Skills* 94, 1, 141–151.

Gibbs, Graham. n.d. *Learning by Doing: A Guide to Teaching and Learning Methods*. Further Education Unit.

Goffman, Erving. 1982. Interaction Ritual: Essays on face to face behavior. Pantheon.

Goleman, Daniel. 1998. *Working with Emotional Intelligence*. Bantam.

———. 2012. *Emotional Intelligence: Why It Can Matter More Than IQ*. Bantam.

Greenspan, Miriam. 2003. *Healing through the Dark Emotions: The Wisdom of Grief, Fear, and Despair*. Shambhala.

Gross, James J., and Robert W. Levenson. 1997. "Hiding Feelings: Acute Effects of Inhibiting Negative and Positive Emotion." *Journal of Abnormal Psychology* 106, 1, 95–103.

Guo, Zheng-rong. 2011. "Comparison and Analysis about Face in Chinese and Western Cultures." *Journal of Xinzhou Teachers University*.

Halperin, Eran. 2016. *Emotions and Conflict: Inhibitors and Facilitators of Peace Making*. Routledge.

Hammer, Mitchell R. 2009. "Solving Problems and Resolving Conflict Using the Intercultural Conflict Style Model and Inventory." In *Contemporary Leadership and Intercultural Competence*, by Michael A. Moodian (Ed.), 219–232. Sage.

Hanh, Thich Nhat. 1999. *The Miracle of Mindfulness: An Introduction to the Practice of Meditation*. Beacon.

———. 2010. *Peace Is Every Step: The Path of Mindfulness in Everyday Life*. Random.

Hatfield, Elaine, Megan Carpenter, and Richard L. Rapson. 2014. "Emotional Contagion as a Precursor to Collective Emotions." In *Collective Emotions: Perspectives from Psychology, Philosophy, and Sociology*, by Christian von Scheve, Mikko Salmela (Eds.), 108–123. Oxford.

Hatfield, Elaine, Richard L. Rapson, and Yen-Chi L. Le. 2009. "Emotion Contagion and Empathy." In *The Social Neuroscience of Empathy*, by Jean Decety, Wilham Ickes (Eds.), 19–30. MIT.

Heitler, Susan. 1997. *The Power of Two: Secrets to a Strong and Loving Marriage*. New Harbinger.

Hermans, Hubert J. M. 2014. *Handbook of Dialogical Self Theory*, by Thorsten Geiser and Hubert J. M. Hermans (Eds.). Cambridge University.

Hermans, Hubert. 2006. "Moving through Three Persons, Yet Remaining the Same Thinker." *Cognitive Psychology Quarterly* 19, 5–25.

Hill, Christina L. M., and John A. Updegraff. 2012. "Mindfulness and Its Relationshp to Emotional Regulation." *Emotion* 12, 1, 81–90.

Ho, D. Y. 1972. "Face, Social Expectations, and Conflict Avoidance." Edited by Walter Lonner John Dawson. *International Association for Cross-Cultural Psychology*. Hong Kong University. 240–251.

Izard, Carroll E. 2010. "The Many Meanings/Aspects of Emotion: Definitions, Functions, Activation, and Regulation." *Emotion Review* 2, 4.

Johns, Gary, and Alan M. Saks. 2020. *Organizational Behaviour: Understanding and Managing Life at Work*. 11th ed. Pearson.

Kammhuber, Stefan. 2010. "Intercultural Conflict Management and Mediation." In *Handbook of Intercultural Communication and Cooperation*, by Alexander Thomas, Eva-Ulricke Kinast, Sylvia Schroll-Machl (Eds.), 2nd ed., 265–271. Vandenhoeck & Ruprecht.

Keashly, Loraleigh, and William Warters. 1996. "Conflict and Conflict Management." In *Applied Social Psychology*, by Stanley W. Sadava and Donald R. McCreary (Eds.), 248–273. Prentice-Hall.

Larsen, Jeff T. Nicholas A. Coles, and Deanna K. Jordan. 2017. "Varieties of Mixed Emotional Experience." *Current Opinion in Behavioral Sciences* 15, 72–76.

Le Bon, Gustav. 1895. *The Crowd: The Study of the Popular Mind*. Macmillan.

Lerner, Harriet. 2014. *Dance of Anger*. Harper Collins.

Lewin, Kurt. 1935. *A Dynamic Theory of Personality*. McGraw-Hill.

Lindner, Evelin G. 2014. "Emotions and Conflict: Why It Is Important to Understand How Emotions Affect Conflict and How Conflict Affects Emotion." In *Handbook of Conflict Resolution: Theory and Practice*, by Peter T. Coleman, Morton Deutsch, and Eric C. Marcus (Eds.), 2nd ed., 283–309. Jossey-Bass.

Maslow, Abraham H. 1943. "A Theory of Human Motivation." *Psychological Review* 50, 4, 370–396.

Mayer, Bernard. 2012. *The Dynamics of Conflict: A Guide to Engagement and Intervention*. 2nd ed. Jossey-Bass.

Mayer, John D., and Peter Salovey. n.d. "What Is Emotional Intelligence?" In *Emotional Development and Emotional Intelligence*, by Peter Salovey and D. Sluyter (Eds.), 3–31. Basic.

McCrae, Robert, and Paul T. Costa. 2008. "Five Factor Theory of Personality." In *Handbook of Personality: Theory and Research*, by Richard W. Robins, Lawrence A. Pervin and Oliver P. John (Eds.), 159–80. Guilford.

Merchant, Karima. 2012. *How Men and Women Differ: Gender Differences in Communication Styles, Influence Tactics, and Leadership Styles*. CMC Senior Thesis, Claremont McKenna College.

Miller, Sherod, Daniel Wackman, Elam Nunnally, and Phyllis Miller. 1988. *Connecting with Self and Others*. Interpersonal Communication.

Millon, Theodore, Seth Grossman, Carrie Millon, Sarah Meagher, and Rowena Ramnath. 2014. *Personality Disorders in Modern Life*. 2nd ed. John Wiley.

Morrison, Andrew P. 1998. *The Culture of Shame*. Jason Aronson.

Ogunsanya, Kemi. 2007. "Women Transforming Conflicts in Africa: Descriptive Studies." *ACCORD Occasional Papers* 2, 3, 1–52.

Ortony, A., and T. J. Turner. 1990. "What's Basic About Basic Emotion?" *Psychological Review*, 315–31.

Potter-Efron, Ronald. 2007. *Rage*. New Harbinger. Novalis.

Riskin, Leonard L. 2007. "Awareness in Lawyering: A Primer on Paying Attention." In *The Affective Assistance of Counsel: Practicing Law as a Healing Profession*, by Marjorie Silver (Ed.), 454–460. Carolina Academic.

Riskin, Leonard L., and Rachel Wohl. 2015. "Mindfulness in the Heat of Conflict: Taking STOCK." *Harvard Negotiation Law Review* 20, 121–154.

Sansone, Randy A., and Lori A. Sansone. 2010. "Road Rage: What's Driving It?" *Psychiatry* 7, 7, 14–18.

Scheff, Thomas J. 2000. *Bloody Revenge: Emotions, Nationalism, and War*. iUnives.

Schon, Donald. 1983. *The Reflective Practitioner: How Professionals Think in Action*. Basic.

Schwartz, Richard C. 2013. "Moving from Acceptance toward Transformation with Internal Family Systems Therapy." *Journal of Clinical Psychology* 69, 8, 805–816.

Schwartz, Richard, and Martha Sweezy. 2020. *Internal Family Systems Therapy*. 2nd ed. Guilford.

Segal, Jeanne. 2015. *Raising Your Emotional Intelligence: A Practical Guide*. 2nd ed. Henry Holt.

Segal, Jeanne, Melinda Smith, Lawrence Robinson, and Jennifer Shubin. 2019. "Improving Emotional Intelligence." *HelpGuide*. October. Accessed May 7, 2020. https://www.helpguide.org/articles/mental-health/emotional-intelligence-eq.htm.

Shapiro, Daniel L. 2017. *Negotiating the Nonnegotiable*. 2nd ed. Penguin.

Shaver, Phillip, Judith Schwartz, Donald Kirson, and Gary O'Connor. 1987. "Emotion Knowledge: Further Exploration of a Prototype Approach." *Journal of Personality and Social Psychology* 52, 6, 1061–1086.

Smith-Christopher, Daniel L. (Ed.). 2007. *Subverting Hatred: The Challenge of Nonviolence in Religious Traditions*. Orbis.

Stone, Douglas, Bruce Patton, and Sheila Heen. 2010. *Difficult Conversations*. 2nd ed. Penguin.

Stuster, Jack. 2004. "Aggressive Driving Enforcement: Evaluations of Two Demonstration Programs." *one.nhtsa.gov*. March. Accessed May 4, 2020. https://one.nhtsa.gov/people/injury/research/aggdrivingenf/pages/ExecSumm.html.

Ting-Toomey, Stella, and Tenzin Dorjee. 2019. *Communicating Across Cultures*. 2nd ed. Guilford.

Tupes, Ernest C., and Raymond C. Cristal. 1961. *Recurrent Personality Factors on Trait Ratings*. Technical Report #61–97. US Air Force.

Vignoles, Vivian L. Camillo Regalia, and Claudia Manzi, et al. 2006. "Beyond Self-Esteem: Influence of Multiple Motives on Identity Construction." *Journal of Personality and Social Psychology* 90, 2, 308–333.

Wade, Barry. 1989. *Conkers: Poems*. Oxford University.

Welbourne, Theresa. 2005. *Women "Take Care," Men "Take Charge": Stereotyping of US Business Leaders Exposed*. Research. Catalyst.

Wong, Ying, and Jeanne Tsai. 2007. "Cultural Models of Shame and Guilt." In *The Self-Conscious Emotions: Theory and Research*, by Jessica L. Tracy, Richard W. Robins, June Price Tangney (Eds.). Guilford.

CHAPTER 2

Adler, Ronald, Lawrence Rosenfeld, and Russel Proctor. 2016. *Interplay: The Process of Interpersonal Communication*. 4th ed. Oxford University.

Alson, Sheila, and Gayle B. Burnett. 2003. *Peace in Everyday Relationships*. Hunter.

Antonini, David. 1998. "Relationship between the Big Five Personality Factors and Conflict Styes." *International Journal of Conflict Management* 9, 4, 336–355.

Baker, Sherry, and David L. Martinson. 2001. "The TARES Test: Five Principles for Ethical Persuasion." *Journal of Mass Media Ethics* 16, 2–3, 148–175.

Bartos, Otomar J., and Paul Wehr. 2002. *Process and Outcome of Negotiations.* Columbia University.

Bateson, Gregory. 1972. *Steps to an Ecology of Mind: Collected Essays in Anthropology, Psychiatry, Evolution, and Epistemology.* University of Chicago.

Bock, Joseph G. 2012. *The Technology of Nonviolence: Social Media and Violence Prevention.* MIT.

Bolton, Robert. 1979. *People Skills: How to Assert Yourself, Listen to Others, and Resolve Conflicts.* Simon & Schuster.

Braithwaite Dawn O., and Paul Schrodt (Eds.). 2015. *Engaging Theories in Interpersonal Communication: Multiple Perspectives.* 2nd ed. Sage.

Buller, David B., Judee K. Burgoon. 1996. "Interpersonal Deception Theory." *Communication Theory* 6, 3, 203–242.

Cai, Deborah A., and William A. Donahue. 1997. "Determinants of Facework in Intercultural Negotiation." *Asian Journal of Communication* 7, 1, 85–110.

Cai, Deborah, and Edward Fink. 2002. "Conflict Style Differences between Individualists and Collectivists." *Communication Monographs*, 69, 1.

Canary, Daniel J., and Sandra G. Lakey. 2006. "Managing Conflict in a Competent Manner." In *Sage Handbook of Conflict Communication: Theory, Research, and Practice*, by John C. Oetzel and Stella Ting-Toomey (Eds.), 185–210. Sage.

Cupach, William R. 2015. "Communication Competence in the Management of Conflict." In *Communication Competence*, by Annagret F. Hannawa and Briah H. Spitzberg (Eds.) 341–365. Walter de Gruyter.

Deutsch, Morton. 2014. "Cooperation and Competition." In *The Handbook of Conflict Resolution: Theory and Practice*, by Peter T. Coleman, Morton Deutsch and Eric C. Marcus (Eds.), Chapter 1. Jossey-Bass.

Donahue, William A., and Deborah A. Cai. 2014. "Interpersonal Conflict: An Overview." In *Managine Interpersonal Conflict: Advances through Meta-analysis*, by Nancy, Mike Allen, et al (Eds.) Burrell, 22–41. Routledge.

Donnerstein, Edward. 2008. "Mass Media: A General View." In *Encyclopedia of Violence, Peace, and Conflict*, by Lester Kurtz and Jennifer Turpin (Eds.), 1184–1192. Academic.

Eddy, William A. 2005. "High Conflict Personality in Family Mediation." *ACResolution*, Summer, 14–17.

Eidelson, Roy J., and Judy I. Eidelson. 2003. "Dangerous Ideas: Five Beliefs That Propel Groups toward Conflict." *American Psychologist* 58, 3, 182–192.

Ellison, Nicole, Rebecca Heino, and Jennifer Gibbs. 2006. "Managing Impressions Online: Self-Presentation Processes in the Online Dating Environment." *Journal of Computer-Mediated Communication* 11, 2, 415–441.

Erickson, Bonnie, Allan Lind, Bruce C. Johnson, and William O. Barr. 1978. "Speech Style and Impression Formation in a Court Setting." *Journal of Experimental Social Psychology* 14, 226–279.

Fisher, Roger, William Ury, and Bruce Patton. 2011. *Getting to Yes: Negotiating Agreement without Giving In.* 3rd ed. Penguin.

Fixmer-Oraiz, Natalie, and Julia T. Wood. 2019. *Gendered Lives: Communication, Gender, and Culture.* 13th ed. Cengage.

Follett, Mary Parker. 2012. "Constructive Conflict." In *Sociology of Organizations: Structures and Relationships*, by Mary Godwyn and Jody Hoffer Gittell (Eds.). Sage.

Gallois, C., and Howard Giles. 2015. "Communication Accommodation Theory." *The International Encyclopedia of Language.*

Galtung J., Fischer D. 2013 High Road, Low Road: Charting the Course for Peace Journalism. In: Johan Galtung. SpringerBriefs on Pioneers in Science and Practice, vol 5. Springer, Berlin, Heidelberg. https://doi.org/10.1007/978-3-642-32481-9_8

Gibb, Jack R. September 1961. "Defensive Communication." *Journal of Communication* 11, 3, 141–148.

———. 1978. *Trust: A New View of Personal and Organizational Development.*

Giles, Howard. 2016. *Communication Accommodation Theory: Negotiating Personal Relationships and Social Identities across Contexts.* Cambridge University.

Gottman, John, and Nan Silver. 2015. *The Seven Principles for Making Marriage Work: A Practical Guide.* Harmony.

Greenman, John. 2008. "On Communication." *Michigan Law Review* 1337.

Hall, Edward T. 1976. *Beyond Culture.* Random.

Hannawa, Annegret F., and Brian H. Spitzberg (Eds.). 2015. *Communication Competence.* Walter de Gruyter.

Hawkins, Virgil. 2011. "Peace Process or Just Peace Deal? The Media's Failure to Cover Peace." In *Expanding Peace Journalism: Comparative and Critical Approaches,* by Ibrahim Seaga Shaw, Jake Lynch, Robert A. Hackett (Eds.), 261. Sydney University.

Ivy, Diana K. 2016. *Genderspeak: Communicating in A Gendered World.* Kendall Hunt.

Kadam, Rashmi Ashish. 2017. "Informed Consent Process: A Step Further towards Making it Meaningful." *Perspectives in Clinical Research* 8, 3, 107–112.

Kegan, Robert, and Lisa Laskow Lahey. 2007. *Seven Languages of Transformation.* Jossey-Bass.

Kehoe, Dalton. 2013. *Communication in Everyday Life.* 5th ed. Pearson.

Kempf, Wilhelm. 2007. "Peace Journalism: A Tightrope Walk between Advocacy Journalism and Constructive Conflict Coverage." *Conflict & Communication Online.*

Kim, Min-Sun. 2002. *Non-Western Perspectives on Human Communication: Implications for Theory and Practice.* Sage.

Levine, Timothy R. 2014. "Truth-Default Theory (TDT): A Theory of Human Deception and Deception Detection." *Journal of Language and Social Psychology* 33, 4, 387–392.

Lewicki, Roy J. 2006. "Trust, Trust Development, and Trust Repair." In *The Handbook of Conflict Resolution: Theory and Practice,* by Morton Deutsch, Peter T. Coleman, Eric C. Marcus (Eds.) 2nd ed., 92–120. Jossey-Bass.

Lewis, Michael, and Carolyn Saarni, ed. 1993. *Lying and Deception in Everyday Life.* Guilford.

Littlejohn, Stephen W., and Kathy Domenici. 2007. *Communication, Conflict, and the Management of Difference.* Waveland.

Luft, Joseph, and Harrington Ingham. 1955. "The Johari Window: A Graphic Model of Interpersonal Awareness." *Western Training Laboratory in Group Development.* University of California.

Lynch, Jake. 2008. *Debates in Peace Journalism.* Sydney University.

Lynch, Jake, and Annabel McGoldrick. 2005. *Peace Journalism.* Hawthorn.

Maiese, Michelle. 2003. "The Need for Dialogue." *Beyond Intractability.* September. Accessed August 30, 2018. beyondintractability.org.

Malek, Cate, and Susana Hayek. 2018. "Peacebuilding Simulation." *Beyond Intractability.* Accessed November 8, 2018. beyondintractability.org.

Maltz, Daniel, and Ruth Borker. 1982. "A Cultural Approach to Male-Female Miscommunication." In *Language and Social Identity,* by John J. Gumperz, Chapter 11. Cambridge University.

Mehrabian, Albert. 1972, 2007. *Nonverbal Communication.* Routledge.

Merchant, Katrina. 2012. "How Men and Women Differ: Gender Differences in Communication Styles, Influence Tactics, and Leadership Styles." *MCM Senior Theses.* Claremont McKenna College.

Miller, Sherod, Daniel Wackman, Elam Nunnally, and Phyllis Miller. 1988. *Connecting with Self and Others.* Interpersonal Communications Programs.

Mindell, Arnold. 2014. *Sitting in the Fire: Large Group Transformation Using Conflict and Diversity.* Deep Democracy Exchange.

Nelde, Peter H. 1987. "Language Contact Means Language Conflict." *Journal of Multilinguage and Multicultural Development* 8, 1–2, 33–42.

Northrup, Terrell A. 1989. "The Dynamic of Identity in Personal and Social Conflict." In *Intractible Conflct and Their Transformation*, by Louis Kriesberg, Terrell A. Northrup and Stuart J. Thorson (Eds.), 55–82. Syracuse University.

Omer, Haim. 2004. *Non-Violent Resistance: A New Approach to Violent and Self-Destructive Children*. Cambridge University.

Ong, Jonathan Corpus, and Jason Vincent A. Cabanes. 2018. *Architects of Networked Disinformation*. Accessed March 10, 2020. https://newtontechfordev. com/wp-content/uploads/2018/02/ARCHITECTS-OF-NETWORKED-DISINFORMATION-FULL-REPORT.pdf.

Pearce, W. Barnett. 2007. *Making Social Worlds: A Communication Perspective*. Blackwell.

Robin, Arthur L. 2007. "Problem-Solving Communication Training: A Behavioral Approach to Treatment of Parent-Adolescent Conflict." *American Journal of Family Therapy* 7, 2, 69–82.

Rosenberg, Marshall. 2001. *Nonviolent Communication: A Language of Compassion*. Puddledancer.

Sclafani, Jennifer. 2017. *Talking Donald Trump: A Sociolinguistic Study of Style, Metadiscourse, and Political Identity*. Routledge.

Siann, Gerda. 1985. *Accounting for Aggression: Perspectives on Aggression and Violence*. Unwin Hyman.

Sillars, Alan L., and Daniel J. Canary. 2013. "Communication, Conflict, and the Quality of Family Relationships." In *Handbook of Family Communication*, by Anita L. Vangelisti (Ed.), 2nd ed., 338–357. Routledge.

Smetana, Judith G. 1988. "Concepts of Self and Social Convention: Adolescents' and Parents Reasoning." In *Development during the Transition to Adolescence*, by Megan R. Gunnar and W. Andrew Collins (Eds.), 79–122. Lawrence Erlbaum.

Spitzberg, Brian H. 2015. "Composition of Communication Competence." In *Communication Competence*, by Annegret F. Hannawa, Brian H. Spitzberg (Eds.), 237–270. Walter de Gruyer.

Spring, Janis. 2004. *How Can I Forgive You?* HarperCollins.

Stone, Douglas, Bruce Patton, and Sheila Heen. 2010. *Difficult Conversations: How to Discuss What Matters Most*, 2nd ed. Viking Penguin.

Tannen, Deborah. 1984. "The Pragmatics of Cross-Cultural Communication." *Applied Linguistics* 5, 3, 189–195.

———. 1994. *Gender and Discourse*. Oxford University.

———. 1999. *Argument Culture: Stopping America's War on Words*. Ballantyne.

———. 2006. *You're Wearing That? Understanding Mothers and Daughters in Conversation*. Ballantine.

———. 2007. *Talking Voices: Repetition, Dialogue, and Imagery in Conversational Discourse*. Cambridge University.

Tavris, Carol. 1989. *Anger: The Misunderstood Emotion*. 2nd ed. Touchstone.

Ting-Toomey, Stella, and Ge Gao, et al. 1991. "Culture, Face Maintenance, and Styles of Handling Interpersonal Conflict: A Study in Five Cultures." *International Journal of Conflict Management* 2, 4, 275–296.

Truss, Lynne. 2005. *Talk to the Hand: Rudeness in the World Today*. Penguin Random.

Ury, William L. 1991. *Getting Past No: Negotiating with Difficult People*. Bantam.

Ury, William, Jeanne M. Brett, and Stephen B. Goldberg. 1988. *Getting Disputes Resolved: Designing Systems to Cut the Costs of Conflict*. Jossey-Bass.

Waldron, Jeremy. 2012. *The Harm in Hate Speech*. Harvard University.

Walker, Gregg. 2018. *Communicating Well in Conflict: Competence Skills and Collaboration*. Accessed March 10, 2020. oregonstate.edu/instruct/comm440-540/comptent.htm.

Wang, Qi, Edward L. Fink, and Deborah A. Cai. 2012. "The Effect of Conflict Goals on Avoidance Strategies: What Does Not Communicating Communicate?" *Human Communication Research* 38, 2, 222–252.

Wells, H. G. 1898 (2014). *The War of the Worlds*. Millenium.

Wertheim, Emmy. 1996. "Negotiations and Resolving Conflicts: An Overview." *europarc.org*. 11 21. Accessed May 17, 2018. https://www.europarc.org/communication-skills/pdf/Negotiation%20Skills.pdf.

Wiseman, Theresa. 1996. "A Concept Analysis of Empathy." *Journal of Advanced Nursing* 23, 6, 1162–1167.

Yang, Aimei, Maureen Taylor, and Adam J. Saffer. 2016. "Ethical Convergence, Divergence, or Communitas? An Examination of Public Relations and Journalism Codes of Ethics." *Public Relations Review* 42, 1, 146–160.

Yang, Wengi, and Shenghua Jin, et al. 2015. "The Impact of Power on Humanity: Self-Dehumanization in Powerlessness." *PLOS One* https://doi.org/10.1371/journal.pone.0125721.

Young, Nigel J., ed. 2010. *Oxford International Encyclopedia of Peace*. Oxford University.

Zimbardo, Philip, R. L. Johnson, and V. McCann. 2009. *Psychology: Core Concepts*. Pearson.

CHAPTER 3

Bransford, John D., and Barry S. Stein. 1993. *The Ideal Problem Solver*. Macmillan.

Brewer, Neil, Patricia Mitchell, and Nathan Weber. 2002. "Gender Role, Organizational Status, and Conflict Management Styles." *International Journal of Conflict Management* 13, 1, 78–94.

Cobb, Sara. 2013. *Speaking of Violence: The Politics and Poetics of Narrative in Conflict Resolution*. Oxford.

Coleman, Peter T. 2014. "Intractible Conflicts." In *The Handbook of Conflict Resolution: Theory and Practice*, by Morton Deutsch, Peter T. Coleman, Eric C. Marcus (Eds.), 708–744. John Wiley.

Conklin, Jeffrey. 2006. *Dialogue Mapping: Building Shared Understanding of Wicked Problems*. Wiley.

Deutsch, Morton. 1969. "Conflicts: Productive or Destructive?" *Journal of Social Issues* 7–41.

Donahue, William A., Randall G. Rogan, and Sanda Kaufman (Eds.). 2011. *Framing Matters: Perspectives on Negotiation Research and Practice in Communication*. Peter Lang.

Druckman, Daniel, and James Druckman. 2011. "The Many Faces of Framing in Negotiation." In *Framing Matters: Perspectives on Negotiation Research and Practice in Communication*, by William A. Donahue, Randall G. Rogan, and Sandra Kaufman (Eds.). Peter Lang.

Fisher, Roger, and Loraleigh Keashley. 1991. "The Potential Complementarity of Mediation and Consultation within a Contingency Model of Third Party Intervention." *Journal of Peace Research* 29–42.

Fisher, Roger, William T. Ury, and Bruce Patton. 2011. *Getting to Yes: Negotiating Agreement without Giving In*. 3rd ed. Penguin.

Folger, Joseph P., Marshall Scott Poole, and Randall K. Stutman. 2018. *Working through Conflict: Strategies for Relationships, Groups, and Organizations*. 8th ed. Routledge.

Garz, Detlef. 2009. *Lawrence Kohlberg: An Introduction*. Barbara Budrich.

Gottman, John. 2012. *The Gottman Institute*. February. Accessed August 5, 2020. www.gottman.com/blog/managing-conflict-solvable-vs-perpetual-problems/.

Gottman, John M., and Nan Silver. 2015. *The Seven Principles for Making Marriage Work*. Harmony.

Herman, Luc, and Bart Vervaeck. 2019. *Handbook of Narrative Analysis*. 2nd ed. University of Nebraska.

Hocker, Joyce L., and William W. Wilmot. 2018. *Interpersonal Conflict*. 10th ed. McGraw-Hill.

Holt, Jennifer L. and Cynthis James DeVore. 2005. "Culture, Gender, Organizational Role, and Styles of Conflict Resolution: A Meta-analysis." *International Journal of Intercultural Relations* 29, 2, 165–196.

Ivy, Diana K. 2016. *Genderspeak: Communicating in A Gendered World*. Kendall Hunt.

Knutson, Thomas J., and John C. Hwang,. 2000. "Perception and Management of Conflict: A Comparison of Taiwanese and US Business Employees." *Intercultural Communication Studies* IX–2.

Kohlberg, Lawrence. 1969. "Stage and Sequence: The Cognitive-Developmental Approach to Socialization." In *Handbook of Socialization Theory and Research*, by David A. Goslin (Ed.), 347–480. Rand McNally.

Kolb, Deborah M., and Judith Williams. 2000. *Shadow Negotiation: How Women Can Master the Hidden Agenda*. Simon & Schuster.

Kriesberg, Louis. 2020. *Constructive Conflicts: From Escalation to Resolution*. 5th ed. Rowman and Littlefield.

Lulofs, Roxane S., and Dudley D. Cahn. 2000. *Conflict: From Theory to Action*. 2nd ed. Allyn and Bacon.

McGoldrick, Monica, and Deidre Ashton. 2012. "Culture: A Challenge to Concepts of Normality." In *Normal Family Processes: Growing Diversity and Complexity*, by Froma Walsh (Ed.), 4th ed., 249–272. Guilford.

Meadows, Donella. 1999. *Leverage Points: Places to Intervene in a System*. Sustainability Institute.

Rittel, Horst W. J., and Melvin M. Webber. 1973. "Dilemmas in a General Theory of Planning." *Policy Sciences* 4, 2, 155–169.

Thomas, Kenneth W., Gail Fann Thomas, and Nancy Schaubhut. 2008. "Conflict Styles of Men and Women at Six Organizational Levels." *International Journal of Conflict Management* 19, 2, 148–166.

Ting-Toomey, Stella. 2010. "Intercultural Conflict Competence." In *Competence in Interpersonal Conflict*, by William R. Cupach, Daniel J. Canary and Brian H. Spitzberg (Eds.), 2nd ed., 139–162. Waveland.

Volkema, Roger J. 1997. "Managing the Problem Formulation Process: Guidelines for Team Leaders and Facilitators." *Human Systems Management* 16, 1, 27–34.

Walton, Richard E. 1987. *Managing Conflict: Interpersonal Dialogue and Third-Party Roles*. 2nd ed. Addison Wesley.

Wolfe, Michelle Anne. 2016. *Problem Expansion and Solution Containment: News Coverage and the Climate Debate*. (Unpublished doctoral dissertation, Austin, TX: University of Texas).

Wright, Diana, and Donella Meadows. 2013. *Thinking in Systems: A Primer*. Taylor and Francis.

Zartman, William I. 2008. "'Ripeness': The Importance of Timing in Negotiation and Conflict Resolution." *e-International Relations*.

CHAPTER 4

Afifi, Tamara D., and Kellie Steuber. 2010. "The Cycle of Concealment Model." *Journal of Social and Personal Relationships* 27, 8, 1019–1034.

Anedo, O. 2013. "Cultural Analysis of Harmony and Conflict: Towards an Integrated Model of Conflict Styles." *UJAH: Unizik Journal of Arts and Humanities* 13, 2.

Avruch, Kevin. 1998. *Culture and Conflict Resolution*. US Institute of Peace.

Axelrod, Robert. 2006. *The Evolution of Cooperation*. 2nd ed. Basic.

Blake, Robert R., and Jane S. Mouton. 1970. "'The Fifth Achievement." *Journal of Applied Behavioral Science*.

Brett, Jeanne, Kristin Behfar, and Jeffrey Sanchez-Burks. 2014. "Managing Cross-Culture Conflicts: A Close Look at the Implication of Direct Versus Indirect Confrontation." In *Handbook of Conflict Management Research*, by Oluremi B. Ayoko, Neal Ashkanasy, Karn A. Jehn (Eds.), 136–154. Edward Elgar.

Brew, Frances P., and David R. Cairns. 2004. "Do Culture or Situational Constraints Determine Choice of Direct or Indirect Styles in Intercultural Workplace Conflicts?" *International Journal of Intercultural Relations* 28, 5, 331–352.

———. 1973. *The Resolution of Conflict: Constructive and Destructive Processes*. Yale University.

Deutsch, Morton. 1994. "Constructive Conflict Resolution: Principles, Training, and Research." *Journal of Social Issues* 50, 1, 13–32.

———. 2014. "Cooperation and Competition." In *Handbook of Conflict Resolution: Theory and Practice*. 3rd ed., by Peter T. Coleman, Morton Deutsch, and Eric C. Marcus (Eds.), Chapter 1. Jossey-Bass.

Folger, Joseph P., Marshall Scott Poole, and Randall K. Stutman. 2017. *Working through Conflict: Strategies for Relationships, Groups, and Organizations*. 7th ed. Routledge.

Gabrielldis, Cristina, and Walter G. Stephan, et al. 1997. "Preferred Styles of Conflict Resolution: Mexico and the United States." *Journal of Cross-Cultural Psychology* 28, 6, 661–677.

Gallo, Giorgio. 2012. "Conflict Theory, Complexity and Systems Approach." *Systems Research and Behavioral Science*. Wiley.

Gottman, John M. 1993. "Roles of Conflict Engagement, Escalation, and Avoidance in Marital Interaction: Longitudinal View of Five Types of Couples." *Journal of Consulting and Clinical Psychology* 61, 1, 6–15.

Gottman, John M. 2013. *Marital Interaction: Experimental Investigations*. Academic Press.

Haines, Fiona, and David Gurney. 2003. "The Shadows of the Law: Contemporary Approaches to Regulation and the Problem of Regulatory Conflict." *Law and Policy* 25, 4, 353–380.

Heaphy, Brian, Catherine Donovan, and Jeffrey Weeks. 1999. "Sex, Money, and the Kitchen Sink: Power in Same-Sex Couple Relationships." In *Relating Intimacies: Explorations in Sociology*, by J. P. Bagguley Seymour (Ed.), 222–245. Palgrave Macmillan.

Holt, Jennifer L., and Cynthia James DeVore. 2005. "Culture, Gender, Organizational Role, and Styles of Conflict Resolution: A Meta-analysis." *International Journal of Intercultural Relations* 29, 2, 165–196.

James, P. D. 2003. *A Certain Justice*. Ballantine.

Keashly, Lorialeigh, and William C. Warters. 1996. "Working It Out: Conflict in Interpersonal Contexts." In *Patterns of Conflict, Paths to Peace*, by Larry J. Fisk and John L. Schellenberg (Eds.). University of Toronto.

Klein, Renate C. A., and Helmut Lamm. 1996. "Legitimate Interest in Couple Conflict." *Journal of Personal and Social Relationships* 13, 4, 619–626.

Kozan, Michel Kamil. 1997. "Culture and Conflict Management: A Theoretical Framework." *International Journal of Conflict Management* 8, 4, 338–360.

Kriesberg, Louis. 2020. *Constructive Conflicts: From Escalation to Resolution (5th)*. 2nd. Rowman and Littlefield.

Lederach, John Paul. 1992. "Understanding Conflict: Experience, Structure, and Dynamics." In *Mediation and Facilitation Training Manual*, by Carolyn Schrock-Shenk (Ed.), 70–72. Mennonite Conciliation Service.

Leung, Kwok. 2009, June 15. "Harmony and Conflict: Towards an Integrated Model of Conflict Styles." *22nd Annual IACM Conference Paper*. http://dx.doi.org/10.2139/ssrn.1484932.

Leung, Kwok, Frances P. Brew, and Zhi-Xue Zhang, et al. 2010. "Harmony and Conflict: A Cross-Cultural Investigation in China and Australia." *Journal of Cross-Cultural Psychology* 42, 5, 795–816.

Lewin, Kurt. 1951. *Field Theory in Social Science*. Harper.

Maiese, Michelle. 2003. "Destructive Escalation." In *Beyond Intractability*, by Heidi Burgess and Guy Burgess (Eds.). Conflict Information Consortium. 9. Accessed February 27, 2018. https://www.beyondintractability.org/essay/escalation.

Miller, Sherod, Daniel Wackman, Elam Nunnally, and Phyllis Miller. 1992. *Connecting with Self and Others*. 2nd ed. Interpersonal Communications.

Park, Heejoon, and David Antonioni. 2007. "Personality, Reciprocity, and Strength of Conflict Resolution Strategy." *Journal of Research in Personality* 41, 1, 110–125.

Peterson, Andrew. n.d. "Systems Modeling." *Beyond Intractability*, by Gus Burgess and Heidi Burgess (Eds.). Conflict Information Consortium. Accessed February 27, 2018. https://www.beyondintractability.org/essay/systems-modeling.

Price, Owen, and John Baker. 2012. "Key Components of De-Escalation Techniques: A Thematic Synthesis." *International Journal of Mental Health Nursing* 21, 4, 310–319.

Rahim, M. A. 1983. "A Measure of Styles of Handling Interpersonal Conflict." *Academy of Management Review* 26, 369–376.

Redekop, Vern Neufeld, and Jean-Francois Rioux. 2012. *Introduction to Conflict Studies: Empirical, Theoretical, and Ethical Dimensions*. Oxford University.

Reiger, Kerreen. 1987. "All but the Kitchen Sink: On the Significance of Domestic Science and the Silence of Social Theory." *Theory and Society* 16, 497–526.

Rodrigues, David L., and Aleksandra Huic, et al. 2019. "Regulatory Focus in Relationships and Conflict Resolution Strategies." *Personality and Individual Differences* 142.

Rosenberg, Marshall B. 2015. *Nonviolent Communication: A Language of Life*. 3rd ed. PuddleDancer.

Ruble, T. L., and K. W. Thomas. 1976. "Support for a Two-Dimensional Model of Conflict Behavior." *Organizational Behavior and Human Performance*, 143–155.

Rummel, Rudolph J. 1991. *The Conflict Helix: Principles and Practices of Interpersonal, Social and International Conflict and Cooperation*. Routledge.

Steele, Katie, and H. Orri Stefansson. 2016. "Decision Theory." In *The Stanford Encyclopedia of Philosophy*, by Edward N. Zalta (Ed.). Stanford University.

Stuart, Richard B. 2004. *Helping Couples Change: A Social Learning Approach to Marital Therapy*. Rev. ed. Guilford.

Susskind, Lawrence and Jennifer Thomas Larmer. 1999. "Conducting a Conflict Assessment." In *The Consensus Building Handbook: A Comprehensive Guide to Reaching Agreement*, by Sarah McKearnan, Jennifer Thomas Larmer, and Lawrence Susskind (Eds.). Sage.

Thomas, Kenneth. 1976. "Conflict and Conflict Management." In *The Handbook of Industrial and Organizational Psychology*, by Marvin Dunnette (Ed.). Rand McNally.

Ting-Toomey, Stella. 1985. "Toward a Theory of Conflict and Culture." In *Communication, Culture, and Organizational Processes*, by Lea P. Stewart, William B. Gudykunst, and Stella Ting-Toomey (Eds.). 71. Sage.

Ting-Toomey, Stella, Ge Gao, and Paula Trubisky, et al. 1991. "Culture, Face Maintenance, and Styles of Handling Interpersonal Conflict: A Study in Five Cultures." *International Journal of Conflict Management* 2, 4, 275–296.

Tyler, Tom R., E. Allan Lind, and Yuen J. Huo. 2000. "Cultural Values and Authority Relations: The Psychology of Conflict Resolution across Cultures." *Psychology, Public Policy, and Law* 6, 4, 1138–1163.

Ury, William L., Jeanne M. Brett, and Stephen B. Goldberg. 1993. *Getting Disputes Resolved: Designing Systems to Cut the Costs of Conflict*. Harvard.

Waller, Altina L. 1988. *Hatfields, McCoys, and Social Change in Appalachia, 1860–1900*. University of North Carolina.

Walton, Richard E. 1969. *Interpersonal Peacemaking: Confrontation and Third Party Consultation*. Addison-Wesley.

Wang, Qi, Edward L. Fink, and Deborah A. Cai. 2012. "The Effect of Conflict Goals on Avoidance Strategies: What Does Not Communicating Communicate?" *Human Communication Research* 38, 2, 222–252.

Wehr, Paul E. 2019. *Conflict Regulation*. 2nd ed. Routledge.

CHAPTER 5

Adams, Maurianne, Warren J. Blumenfeld, and D. Chase J. Catalano, et al. (Eds.). 2018. *Readings for Diversity and Social Justice*. 4th ed. Routledge.

Aerts, Diederick, Leo Apolstel, and Bart de Moor, et al. 1994. *World Views: From Fragmentation to Integration*. VUB Press.

Allport, Gordon W. 1979. *The Nature of Prejudice*. 3rd ed. Perseus.

Anandakugan, Nithyani. 2020. "The Sri Lankan Civil War and Its History." *Harvard International Review*.

Ardener, Shirley, and Edwin Ardener. 2005. "'Muted Groups': The Genesis of an Idea and Its Praxis." *Women and Language* 28, 2, 50–54, 72.

Armstrong, Karen. 2010. *Twelve Steps to a Compassionate Life*. Alfred A. Knopf.

Avrach, Kevin. 1998. *Culture and Conflict Resolution*. US Institute of Peace.

———. 2008. "Culture." In *Conflict: From Analysis to Intervention*, by Sandra Cheldelin, Daniel Druckman, Larissa Fast (Eds.), 2nd ed., 167–180. Continuum.

———. 2009. "Cross-Cultural Conflict." In *Conflict Resolution*, by Keith William Hipel (Ed.), 1:45–57. Encyclopedia of Life Support Systems.

———. 2015. *Context and Pretext in Conflict Resolution: Culture, Identity, Power, and Practice*. Routledge.

Bauman, Zygmunt. 1996. "From Pilgrim to Tourist—or a Short History of Identity." In *Questions of Cultural Identity*, by Stuart Hall, Paul du Gay (Eds.), 18–36. Sage.

Berger, John M. 2018. *Extremism*. MIT.

Black, Peter W. 2008. "Identities." In *Conflict: From Analysis to Intervention*, by Sandra Cheldelin, Daniel Druckman, Larissa Fast (Eds.), 2nd ed., 147–166. Continuum.

Bock, Joseph G. 2001. *Sharpening Conflict Management*. Praeger.

Boyden, Jo, Alula Pankhurst, and Yisak Tafere. 2012. *Harmful Traditional Practices and Child Protection: Contested Understandings*. Working Paper, University of Oxford.

Cavanaugh, William T. 2009. *The Myth of Religious Violence: Secular Ideology and the Roots of Modern Conflict*. Oxford.

Chang, Robert S., and Jerome M. Culp. 2002–2003. "After Intersectionality." *UMKC Law Review* 71, 2, 485–491.

Cho, Sumi, Kimberle Williams Crenshaw, and Leslie McCall. 2013. "Toward a Field of Intersectionality Studies: Theory, Applications, and Praxis." *Signs: Journal of Women in Culture and Society* 38, 4, 785–810.

Claes, Marie-Therese. 1999. "Women, Men, and Management Styles." *International Labour Review* 138, 4.

Cloke, Kenneth. 2001 (2007). *Mediating Dangerously: The Frontiers of Conflict Resolution*. Jossey-Bass.

Collins, Patricia Hill, and Sirma Bilge. 2016. *Intersectionality (Key Concepts)*. Polity.

Coltri, Laurie S. 2009. *Alternative Dispute Resolution: A Conflict Diagnosis Approach*, 2nd ed. Pearson.

Council on Foreign Relations. 2021. "Rohingya Crisis in Myanmar." Global Conflict Tracker. Accessed February 3, 2021. https://www.cfr.org/global-conflict-tracker/conflict/rohingya-crisis-myanmar.

Crenshaw, Kimberle Williams. 1994. "Mapping the Margins: Intersectionality, Identity Politics, and Violence against Women of Color." In *The Public Nature of Private Violence*, by Martha Albertson Fineman and Rixanna Mykitiuk (Eds.), 93–118. Routledge. https://www.racialequitytools.org/resourcefiles/mapping-margins.pdf.

Crenshaw, Kimberle, Neil Gotanda, Gary Peller, and Kendall Thomas (Eds.). 1995. *Critical Race Theory: The Key Writings That Formed the Movement*. New Press.

Das, Kalpana. 2007. "Culture, Identity, and Governance." *Summer Institute*, Intercultural Institute of Montreal.

Delgado, Richard, and Jean Stefancic (Eds.). 2017. *Critical Race Theory: An Introduction*. 3rd ed. New York University.

Dervin, Fred. 2012. "Cultural Identity, Representation, and Othering." In *The Routledge Handbook of Language and Intercultural Communication*, by Jane Jackson (Ed.). Routledge.

Docherty, Jayne. 2004. "Culture and Negotiation: Symmetrical Anthropology for Negotiators." *Marquette Law Review* 87, 711–722.

Dolinski, Dariusz, and Tomasz Grzyb, et al. 2017. "Would You Deliver an Electric Shock in 2015?" *Social Psychological and Personality Science* 8, 8, 927–933.

Doosje, Bertjan, and Fathali M. Moghaddam et al. 2016. "Terrorism, Radicalization, and De-Radicalization." *Intergroup Relations* 11, 79–84.

Farmer, Paul. 2003. *Pathologies of Power*. University of California Press.

Feagin, Joe R. 2006. *Systemic Racism: A Theory of Oppression*. Routledge.

Ferber, Abby L., and Christina M. Jimenez et al. (Eds.). 2008. *The Matrix Reader: Examining The Dynamics of Oppression and Privilege*. McGraw-Hill.

Fitzpatrick, Brian. 2014. *National Cultural Values Survey*. Special Report, Culture and Media Institute.

Fixmer-Oraiz, Natalie, and Julia T. Wood. 2019. *Gendered Lives: Communication, Gender, and Culture*. 13th ed. Cengage.

Galtung, Johan. 1969. "Violence, Peace, and Peace Research." *Journal of Peace Research* 6, 3, 167–191.

Gentry, Caron E. 2016. "Religion: Peace through Nonviolence in Four Religious Traditions." In *Palgrave Handbook of Disciplinary and Regional Approaches to Peace*, by Oliver P. Richmond, Sandra Pagodda, and Jasmin Ramovic (Eds.), 168–180. Palgrave.

George, John, and Laird Wilcox. 1992. *Nazis, Communists, Klansmen, and Others on the Fringe: Political Extremism in America*. Prometheus.

Goetz, Anne Marie, and Anne-Kristin Treiber. 2006. *Policy Briefing Paper: Gender and Conflict Analysis*. Briefing Paper, UN Development Fund for Women.

Goldberg, Rachel, and Brian Blancke. 2011. "God in the Process: Is There a Place for Religion in Conflict Resolution?" *Conflict Resolution Quarterly* 28, 4, 377–298.

Griffin, John Howard, and Robert Bonazzi. 1961 (2010). *Black Like Me*. Penguin.

Hackett, Conrad, and David McClendon. 2017. *The Changing Global Religious Landscape*. Survey, Pew Research Center.

Hall, Edward T. 1977, 1989. *Beyond Culture*. Random.

Hardy, Kenneth V. 2001. "Soul Work." *Psychotherapy Networker* September–October: 36–53.

Harro, Bobbie. 2018. "The Cycle of Socialization." In *Readings for Diversity and Social Justice*, by Maurianne Adams et al. (Eds.), 4th ed., 27–33. Routledge.

Higley, John, and Gyorgy Lengyel. 2000. "Elite Configurations after State Socialism." In *Elites after State Socialism: Theories and Analysis*, by John Higley and Gyorgy Lengyel (Eds.), 1–22. Rowman & Littlefield.

Holck, Lotte, Sara Louise Muhr, and Florence Villeseche. 2014. "Identity, Diversity, and Diversity Management: On Theoretical Connections, Assumptions, and Implications for Practice." *Equality, Diversity and Inclusion: An International Journal* 35, 1, 48–64.

Horowitz, Donald J. 2001. *The Deadly Ethnic Riot.* University of California Press.

———. 2009. *Human Development Reports.* National Statistics, UNDP.

Iannaccone Laurence R., and Eli Berman. 2006. "Religious Extremism: The Good, the Bad, and the Deadly." *Public Choice* 128, 1/2, 109–129.

IHRA. 2013. "Intersex Population Figures." *Intersex Human Rights Australia.* September 28. Accessed January 6, 2020. https://ihra.org.au/16601/intersex-numbers/.

Jenkins, Richard. 2014. *Social Identities.* Routledge.

Jorde, Lynn B., and Stephen P. Wooding. 2004. "Genetic Variation, Classification, and 'Race.'" *Nature Genetics Supplement* S28–S33.

Keashley, Loraleigh, and William C. Warters. 2000. "Working It Out: Conflict in Interpersonal Contexts." *University of Toronto Quarterly* 70, 1, 289–290.

Kroeber, Alfred L., and Clyde Kluckhohn. 1952. "Culture: A Critical Review of Concepts and Definitions." *Peabody Museum of Archaeology and Ethnology Papers* 47, 1, 223.

LeBaron, Michelle. 2003a. "Cultural and Worldview Frames." *Beyond Intractability.* August. Accessed May 24, 2019. https://www.beyondintractability.org/essay/cultural_frames.

———. 2003b. "Culture-Based Negotiation Styles." *Beyond Intractability.* July. Accessed May 24, 2020. http://www.beyondintractability.org/essay/culture_negotiation/.

Leopold, Till Alexander, Vesseline Ratcheva, and Saadia Zahidi. 2017. *Global Gender Gap, 2017.* Data, World Economic Forum.

Martin, Mercedes, and Billy Vaughn. 2014. "Cultural Competence: The Nuts and Bolts of Inclusion." *Diversity Officer Magazine.* Accessed June 4, 2020. https://diversityofficermagazine.com/cultural-competence/cultural-competence-the-nuts-bolts-of-diversity-inclusion–2/.

Mason, Stan (S.J.). 2018. "reddit." *Detailed Ethno-Racial Map of the World 2018.* May. Accessed May 31, 2019. https://www.reddit.com/r/Masastan/comments/7wruln/detailed_ethnoracial_map_of_the_world_2018/.

McCall, Leslie. 2005. "The Complexity of Intersectionality." *Signs* 30, 3, 1771–1800.

McClymond, Michael J., and David N. Freedman. 2006. "Religious Traditions, Violence and Nonviolence." In *Stress of War, Conflict, and Disaster,* by George Fink (Ed.), 397–407. Elsevier.

Mead, Margaret. 1935 (1963). *Sex and Temperament in Three Primitive Societies.* Perennial.

Merchant, Karima. 2012. *How Men and Women Differ: Gender Differences in Communication Styles, Influence Tactics, and Leadership Styles.* CMC Senior Thesis #513, Claremont McKenna College.

Meyer, Erin. 2014. *The Culture Map: Breaking through the Invisible Boundaries of Global Business.* PublicAffairs.

Midlarsky, Manus I. 2011. *Origins of Political Extremism.* Cambridge University.

Milanovic, Branko. 2016. *Global Inequality: A New Approach for the Age of Globalization.* Harvard University.

Morton, Samuel George. 1849. *Catalogue of Skulls of Man and the Inferior Animals.* Merrihew and Thompson.

Nash, Jennifer. 2008. "Rethinking Intersectionality." *Feminist Review* 89, 1, 1–15.

Nisbett, Richard E., Kaiping Peng, and Incheol Choi Ara Norenzayan. 2001. "Culture and Systems of Thought: Holistic versus Analytic Cognition." *Psychological Review* 108, 2, 291–310.

Noll, Douglas. 2003. *Peacemaking: Practicing at the Intersection of Law and Human Conflict.* Cascadia.

Paczynska, Agnieszka. 2008. "Globalization." In *Conflict: From Analysis to Intervention*, by Sandra Cheldelin, Daniel Druckman, and Larissa Fast (Eds.), 2nd ed., 217–220. Continuum.

Pieterse, Jan Nederveen. 2020. *Globalization and Culture: Global Melange*. 4th ed. Rowman and Littlefield.

Poushter, Jacob. 2017. *Majorities in Europe, North America Worried about Islamic Extremism*. Global Attitudes Survey, Pew Research Center.

Ritzer, George. 2009. *The McDonaldization of Society*. Pine Forge.

Rosenberg, Noah A., Jonathan K. Pritchard, and James L. Weber et al. 2002. "Genetic Structure of Human Populations." *Science* 2381–2385.

Rubenstein, Richard E. 1993. "Analyzing and Resolving Class Conflict." In *Conflict Resolution Theory and Practice*, by Dennis J. D. Sandole and Hugo van de Merwe (Eds.), 146–157. Manchester University.

Savage, Mike, Fiona Devine, and Niall Cunningham et al. 2013. "A New Model of Social Class? Findings from the BBC's Great British Class Survey Experiment." *Sociology* 47, 2, 219–250.

Shields, Stephanie A. 2008–2009. "Gender: An Intersectionality Perspective." *Sex Roles* 59, 5–6, 301–311.

Smith-Christopher, Daniel L. (Ed.). 2007. *Subverting Hatred: The Challenge of Nonviolence in Religious Traditions*. Maryknoll.

Stausberg, Michael (Ed.). 2009. *Contemporary Theories of Religion: A Critical Companion*. Routledge.

Stenou, Katerina. 2002. "Universal Declaration on Cultural Diversity." *UNESDOC*. Accessed May 28, 2019. https://unesdoc.unesco.org/search/4a2c4454-54cf-47be-80d8-6bb3093574fa.

Sternberg, Robert J. 2003. "A Duplex Theory of Hate: Development and Application to Terrorism, Massacres, and Genocide." *Review of General Psychology* 7, 3, 299–328.

Stueland, Eirik. 2013. *Religion Is a Motivator, Not a Motive for Conflict*. Technical Report, Defense Technical Information Center.

Tajfel, Henri. 1981. "Social Stereotypes and Social Groups." In *Intergroup Behaviour*, by John C. Turner, Howard Giles (Eds.), 144–167. Blackwell.

Thomas, Alexander. 2010. "Theoretical Basis: Intercultural Communication and Cooperation." In *Handbook of Intercultural Communication and Cooperation*, by Alexander Thomas, Eva-Ulrike Kinast, and Sylvia Schroll-Machl (Eds.), 2nd ed., 17–27. Vandenhoeck & Ruprecht.

Thomas, William Isaac, and Dorothy Swaine Thomas. 1928. *The Child in America: Behavior Problems and Programs*. Knopf.

Thomson, Robert, Masaki Yuki, et al. 2018. "Relational Mobility Predicts Social Behaviors in 39 Countries...." *Proceedings of the National Academy of Sciences of the USA*.

Ting-Toomey, Stella. 1982. "Toward a Theory of Conflict and Culture." Speech Communication Association.

Ting-Toomey, Stella, and Leeva C. Chung. 2011. *Understanding Intercultural Communication*. 2nd ed. Oxford University.

Ting-Toomey, Stella, and Tenzin Dorjee. 2019. *Communicating Across Cultures*. 2nd ed. Guilford.

Ting-Toomey, Stella, and John G. Oetzel. 2001. *Managing Intercultural Conflict Effectively*. Sage.

Ting-Toomey, Stella, Ge Gao, Paula Trubisky et al. 1991. "Culture, Face Maintenance, and Styles of Handling Interpersonal Conflict: A Study in Five Cultures." *International Journal of Conflict Management*, 2, 4, 275–296.

Triandis, Harry C. 1994. *Culture and Social Behavior*. McGraw-Hill.

Trujillo, Mary Adams, and S. Y. Bowland et al. (Eds.). 2008. *Re-Centering: Culture and Knowledge in Conflict Resolution Practice*. Syracuse University.

Ury, William L. 2000. *The Third Side: Why We Fight and How We Can Stop.* Penguin.

Venter, J. Craig, et al. 2001. "The Sequence of the Human Genome." *Science* 291, 1304–1351.

Wadesango, Newman, Symphorosa Rembe, and Owence Chabaya. 2011. "Violation of Women's Rights by Harmful Traditional Practices." *The Anthropologist* 13, 2, 121–129.

Watson, Jennifer. 2020. *Culture, Tradition, Power, and Sexuality: The Difficulties in Understanding and Ending Female Circumcision.* Master's thesis, Aalborg University.

Williams, David R. 1997. "Race and Health: Basic Questions, Emerging Directions." *Annals of Epidemiology* 7, 5, 322–333.

Wimmer, Andreas. 2013. *Ethnic Boundary Making: Institutions, Power, Networks.* Oxford.

Winthrop, John. 1838. "A Modell of Christian Charity." Vol. Series 7. New York Historical Society, 31–48.

WVS. 2019. *World Values Survey.* Accessed May 26, 2020. http://www.worldvaluessurvey.org/WVSContents.jsp.

Yang, Wengi, and Shenghua Jin et al. 2015. "The Impact of Power on Humanity: Self-Dehumanizaton in Powerlessness." *PLoS ONE* 10, 5.

Young, Evelyn Y. 2011. "The Four Personae of Racism: Educators' (Mis)understanding of Individual vs. Systemic Racism." *Urban Education* 46, 6, 1433–1460.

Young, Iris Marion. 2012. "The Five Faces of Oppression." In *The Community Development Reader*, by James DeFilippis, Susan Saegert (Eds.), 2nd ed., 328–337. Routledge.

Young, Michael. 2008. *The Rise of the Meritocracy.* 11th ed. Transaction.

Zenn, Jacob, and Elizabeth Pearson. 2014. "Women, Gender, and the Evolving Tactics of Boko Haram." *Contemporary Voices: St. Andrews Journal of International Relations* 5, 1.

CHAPTER 6

Adoption Network Law Center. 2018. *Adoption Statistics.* Accessed January 30, 2019. https://adoptionnetwork.com/adoption-statistics.

Afifi, Tracie O., Natalie P. Mota, and Patricia Dasiewicz et al. 2012. "Physical Punishment and Mental Disorders: Results from a Nationally Represented US Sample." *Pediatrics* 130, 2, 1–9.

Ainsworth, Mary D. S., Mary C. Blehar, Everett Waters, and Sally N. Wall. 2015. *Patterns of Attachment: A Psychological Study of the Strange Situation.* Psychology Press.

Amato, Paul R. 2014. "The Consequences of Divorce for Adults and Children: An Update." *Društvena istraživanja: časopis za opća društvena.*

Baker, Amy J. L., and Naomi Ben-Ami. 2011. "To Turn a Child against a Parent Is to Turn a Child against Himself." *Journal of Divorce and Remarriage* 52, 7, 472–489.

Baumrind, Diana. 1967. "Child Care Practices Anteceding Three Patterns of Preschool Behavior." *Genetic Psychology Monographs* 75, 1, 43–88.

———. 2012. "Differentiating between Confrontive and Coercive Kinds of Parental Power-Assertive Disciplinary Practices." *Human Development* 55, 35–51.

Baxter, Leslie A. 1990. "Dialectical Contradictions in Relationship Development." *Journal of Social and Personal Relationships* 7, 69–88.

Blackstone, Amy, and Mahala Dyer Stewart. 2012. "Choosing to Be Childfree: Research on the Decision Not to Parent." *Sociology Compass* 6, 9, 718–27.

Bodin, Arthur M. 1996. "Relationship Conflict." In *Handbook of Relational Diagnosis and Dysfunctional Family Patterns*, by Florence W. Kaslow (Ed.), 371–93. Wiley.

Boulding, Elise. 1978. "Families and the Creation of Futures." In *Cultures of the Future*, by Magoroh Maruyama, et al (Eds.), 7–31. Mouton.

———. 1988. *Building a Global Civic Culture: Education for An Interdependent World.* Syracuse University.

Bowlby, John. 1969. *Attachment and Loss, Volume 1.* Hogarth.

———. 1988. *A Secure Base: Parent-Child Attachment and Healthy Human Development.* Routledge.

Braithwaite, Dawn O., and Paul Schrodt. 2013. "Stepfamily Communication." In *The Routledge Handbook of Family Communication*, by Anita L. Vangelisti (Ed.), 161–175. Routledge.

Burgess, Ernest W. 1931. "Family Tradition and Personality." In *Social Attitudes*, by K. Young (Ed.), 188–207. Henry Holt.

Bush, Robert Baruch, and Joseph P. Folger. 2002. "Changing the Quality of Conflict Interaction: The Principles and Practice of Transformative Mediation." *Pepperdine Dispute Resolution Law Journal* 3, 1, 39–65.

Byron, Kristin. 2005. "A Meta-analytic Review of Work-Family Conflict and Its Antecedents." *Journal of Vocational Behavior* 67, 2, 169–198.

Canada, Statistics. 2017. "Portrait of Childrens' Family Life in Canada in 2016." *Statistics Canada.* August 2. Accessed February 1, 2019. https://www12.statcan.gc.ca/census-recensement/2016/as-sa/98-200-x/2016006/98-200-x2016006-eng.cfm.

2017. "Family Rules Setting." In *SAGE Encyclopedia of Marriage, Family, and Couples Counseling*, by John Carlson and Shannon B. Dermer (Eds.). Sage.

Carter, Betty E., and Monica McGoldrick. 1989. *The Changing Family Life Cycle: A Framework for Family Therapy.* Prentice Hall College.

Chandra, Anita, Joie Acosta, and Stefanie Howard et al. 1, 1, 2011. *Building Community Resilience to Disasters.* Rand Health Quarterly. National Institutes of Health.

Crane, Jeffrey Paul. 2013. *Family Implicit Rules, Shame, and Adolescent Prosocial and Antisocial Behaviors.* M.Sc. Dissertation, Brigham Young University.

Darling, Nancy. 1999. *Parenting Style and Its Correlates.* ERIC Digest. ERIC Institute of Education Sciences.

Eddy, William A. 2005. "High Conflict Personalities in Family Mediation." *ACResolution* Summer, 14–17.

Eidelson, Roy J., and Judy I. Eidelson. 2003. "Dangerous Ideas: Five Beliefs That Propel Groups toward Conflict." *American Psychologist* 58, 3, 182–192.

Emerald, David, and Robert Lanphear. 2015. *The Power of TED.* Polaris.

Enright, Robert D., and Richard P. Fitzgibbons. 2014. *Helping Clients Forgive: An Empirical Guide.* American Psychological Association.

Enright, Robert D., Elizabeth A. Gassin, and Ching-Ru Wu. 1992. "Forgiveness: A Developmental View." *Journal of Moral Education* 21, 2, 99–114.

Epstein, Robert. 2010. "What Makes a Good Parent?" *Scientific American Mind*, 46–51.

Falicov, Celia Jaes. 1988. *Family Transitions: Continuity and Change over the Life Cycle.* Guilford.

Ford, Frederick R. 1983. "Rules: The Invisible Family." *Family Process* 22, 2, 135–145.

Ford, Frederick R., and Joan Herrick. 1974. "Family Rules: Family Lifestyles." *American Journal of Orthopsychiatry* 44, 1, 61069.

Gardner, Richard A. 1985. "Recent Trends in Divorce and Custody Litigation." *Academy Forum* 29, 2, 3–7.

Gelles, Richard J., and Murray A. Straus. 1988. *Intimate Violence.* Simon & Schuster.

Gershoff, Elizabeth. 2010. "More Harm Than Good: A Summary of Scientific Research on the Intended and Unintended Effects of Corporal Punishment on Children." *Law and Contemporary Problems* 31.

Goldman-Wetzler, Jennifer. 2020. *Optimal Outcomes.* Harper Business.

Gottman, John, and Julie Gottman. 2017. "The Natural Principles of Love." *Journal of Family Theory and Review* 9, 1, 7–26.

Gottman, John M., and Julie Schwartz Gottman. 2015. "Gottman Couple Therapy." In *Clinical Handbook of Couple Therapy*, by Alan S. Gurman, Jay L. Lebow, and Douglas K. Snyder (Eds.), 129–157. Guilford.

Gottman, John M., and Robert W. Levenson. 1999. "Rebound from Marital Conflict and Divorce Prediction." *Family Process* 38, 3, 287–292.

Gottman, John M., and Nan Silver. 2015. *The Seven Principles for Making Marriage Work* (2nd ed.). Harmony.

Gottman, John M., Janice Driver, and Amber Tabares. 2002. "Building the Sound Marital House: An Empirically Derived Couple Therapy." In *Clinical Handbook of Couple Therapy*, by Alan S. Gurman (Ed.), 373–399. Guilford.

Grogan-Kaylor, Andrew, Julie Ma, and Sandra A. Graham-Bermann. 2018. "The Case against Physical Punishment." *Current Opinion in Psychology* 19, 22–27.

Gurman, Alan S., Jay L. Lebow, and Douglas K. Snyder. 2015. *Clinical Handbook of Couple Therapy* (5th ed.). Guilford.

Haley, Jay, and Madeleine Richeport-Haley. 2007. *Directive Family Therapy*. Haworth.

Hawkins, Melissa W., Sybil Carrere, and John M. Gottman. 2002. "Marital Sentiment Override: Does It Influence Couples' Perception?" *Journal of Marriage and Family* 64, 1, 193–201.

Karpman, Stephen B. 1968. "Fairy Tales and Script Drama Analysis." *Transactional Analysis Bulletin* 7, 26, 39–43.

———. 2007. "The New Drama Triangles." *United States of America Transactional Analysis Association*. USATAA/ITAA.

Kaslow, Florence W. (Ed.). 1996. *Handbook of Relational Diagnosis and Dysfunctional Family Patterns*. John Wiley.

Kazdin, Alan E. (Ed.). 2002. *Encyclopedia of Psychology*. American Psychological Association.

Kelly, Joan B. 2012. "Risk and Protective Factors Associated with Child and Adolescent Adjustment Following Separation and Divorce." In *Parenting Plan Evaluations: Applied Research for the Family Court*, by Kathryn Kuehnle and Leslie Drozd (Eds.) 49–84. Oxford University.

Kressel, Kenneth, and Morton Deutsch. 1977. "Divorce Therapy: An In-depth Survey of Therapists' Views." *Family Process* 16, 4, 413–443.

Larzelere, R. E., and B. R. Kuhn. 2005. "Comparing Child Outcomes of Physical Punishment and Alternative Disciplinary Tactics: A Meta-analysis." *Clinical Child and Family Psychology Review* 8, 1, 1–37.

Maccoby, Eleanor E., and Robert H. Mnookin. 1992. *Dividing the Child: Social and Legal Dilemmas of Custody*. Harvard.

2018. *Marriage and Divorce Rates*. Chart SF 3.1.C Crude Divorce Rate, 2017. Organization for Economic Cooperation and Development.

Martin, Judith N., and Thomas K. Nakayama. 1999. "Thinking Dialectically about Culture and Communication." *Communication Theory* 9, 1–25.

McCoy, Monica L., and Stefanie M. Keen. 2014. *Child Abuse and Neglect*. Psychology Press.

McGoldrick, Monica, and Tazuko Shibusawa. 2012. "The Family Life Cycle." In *Normal Family Processes: Growing Diversity and Complexity*, by Froma Walsh (Ed.), 375–398. Guilford.

McKee, Laura, Erin Roland, and Nicole Coffelt et al. 2007. "Harsh Discipline and Child Problem Behavior." *Journal of Family Violence* 22, 187–96.

Meadows, Donella H., and Diana Wright. 2008. *Thinking in Systems: A Primer*. Chelsea Green.

Miller, Sherod, Daniel Wackman, Elam Nunnally, and Phyllis Miller. 1992. *Connection with Self and Others*. Interpersonal Communication Programs.

Morrison, Mary Lee. 2015. *Elise Boulding: A Life in the Cause of Peace*. McFarland.

Mosten, Forrest, and Elizabeth Potter Scully. 2015. *The Complete Guide to Mediation: How to Effectively Represent Your Clients and Expand Your Family Law Practice* (2nd ed.). American Bar Association.

Murphy, Jane C., and Robert Rubinson. 2012. *Family Mediation: Theory and Practice* (2nd ed.). LexisNexis.

Murphy, Patrick E., and William A. Staples. 1979. "A Modernized Family Life Cycle." *Journal of Consumer Research* 6, 1, 12–22.

Ortega, Josue, and Philipp Hergovich. 2018. *The Strength of Absent Ties: Social Integration via Online Dating*. September 14. Accessed April 30, 2019. https://arxiv.org/abs/1709.10478.

Papernow, Patricia. 2015. "Therapy with Couples in Stepfamilies." In *Clinical Handbook of Couple Therapy* (5th ed.), by Alan S. Gurman, Jay L. Lebow, and Douglas K. Snyder (Eds.) 467–487. Guilford.

Parker, David. 2004. "Mixed Race." In *Social Identities: Multidisciplinary Approaches*, by Gary Taylor, Steve Spencer (Ed.) 107–128. Routledge.

Parker, David, and Min Song (Eds.). 2001. *Rethinking "Mixed Race."* Pluto.

Pediatrics, American Academy of. 1998. "Guidance for Effective Discipline." *Pediatrics* April: 101, 4.

Peterson, Gary W., and Kevin R. Bush I (Eds.). 2013. *Handbook of Marriage and the Family*. Springer.

Red Horse, John G. 1980. "Family Structure and Value Orientation in American Indians." *Social Casework* 61, 8, 462–7.

Regina, Wayne F. 2011. *Applying Family Systems Theory to Mediation: A Practitioner's Guide*. University Press of America.

Rodgers, Roy H., and James M. White. 2009. "Family Development Theory." In *Sourcebook of Family Theories and Methods: A Contextual Approach*, by William J. Doherty, Pauline C. Boss et al. (Eds.) 225–257. Springer US.

Rolland, John S. 2004. "Anticipatory Loss Framework." In *Living beyond Loss: Death in the Family* (2nd ed.), by Froma Walsh, Monica McGoldrick (Eds.) W. W. Norton.

Rummel, R. J. 1991. *The Conflict Helix: Principles and Practices of Interpersonal, Social, and International Conflict and Cooperation*. Routledge.

Santisteban, Daniel A., Lourdes Suarez-Morales, and Michael S. Robbins et al. June 2006. "Brief Strategic Family Therapy: Lessons Learned ..." *Family Process* 45, 2, 259–271.

Schneewind, Klaus A., and Anna-Katharina Gerhard. 2002. "Relationship Personality, Conflict Resolution, and Marital Satisfaction in the First Five Years of Marriage." *Family Relations* 51, 1.

Selman, Robert L., and Amy P. Demorest. 1984. "Observing Troubled Children's Interpersonal Negotiation Strategies: Implications of and for a Developmental Model." *Child Development* 5, 288–304.

Shannon, Samuel, and Jana Sutton et al. 2018. "Family Rules." In *Encyclopeda of Couple and Family Therapy*, by Jay Lebow, Anthony Chambers, and Douglas C. Breunlin (Eds.) 1111–18. Springer.

Sternberg, Robert J. 1986. "A Triangular Theory of Love." *Psychological Review* 93, 2, 119–135.

Sternberg, Robert J. (Ed.). 2005. *The Psychology of Hate*. American Psychological Association.

Steuber, K. R. 2005. "Adult Attachment, Conflict Style, and Relationship Satisfaction: A Comprehensive Model." Master of Arts Thesis, University of Delaware.

Stewart, Ron. 2001. *Early Identification and Streaming of Cases of High-Conflict Separation and Divorce: A Review*. Review. Department of Justice Canada.

Straus, Murray A., Richard J. Gelles, and Suzanne K. Steinmetz. 1980 (2006, 2017). *Behind Closed Doors: Violence in the American Family*. Routledge.

Tannen, Deborah. 2012. *I Only Say This Because I Love You*. Penguin Random.

Turner, Lynn H., and Richard West. 2015. "The Challenge of Defining Family." In *The SAGE Handbook of Family Communication*, by Lynn H. Turner, Richard West (Eds.) 10–25. Sage.

UNDESA. 2009. *Child Adoption: Trends and Policies*. Research. United Nations Department of Economic and Social Affairs.

VanBreda, Adrian DuPlessis. 2001. *Resilience Theory: A Literature Review*. Literature Review. South African Military Health Service, Military Psychological Institute.

Vidyarthi, Lalita Prasad, and Binay Kumar Rai. 1976. *The Tribal Culture of India*. Concept.

Walsh, Froma. 1994. "Healthy Family Functioning: Conceptual and Research Developments." *Family Business Review* 7, 2, 175–198.

———. 2012. *Normal Family Processes: Growing Diversity and Complexity* (4th ed.). Guilford.

Walsh, Michael R., and J. Michael Bone. 1997. "Parent Alienation Syndrome: An Age-old Custody Problem." *The Florida Bar Journal* 93–97.

Wang, Wendy. 2018. *Institute for Family Studies*. January 10. Accessed May 2, 2019. https://ifstudies.org/blog/who-cheats-more-the-demographics-of-cheating-in-america.

Winnicott, D.W. 1973. *The Child, the Family, and the Outside World*. Penguin Random.

Young, Michael, and Peter Willmott. 1973. *The Symmetrical Family*. Pantheon.

Zeanah, Charles H., and Mary Margaret Gleason. 2010. *Reactive Attachment Disorder: A Review for DSM-V*. Research Review. American Psychiatric Association.

CHAPTER 7

Adler, Ronald B., Lawrence B. Rosenfeld, Russell F. Proctor, and Constance Winder. 2012. *Interplay: The Process of Interpersonal Communication*. Oxford.

Altman, Irwin, and Martin M. Chemers. 1984. *Culture and Environment*. Cambridge.

Apfelbaum, Evan, Michael I. Norton, and Samuel R. Sommers. 2012. "Racial Color Blindness: Emergence, Practice, and Implications." *Current Directions in Psychological Science* 21, 3, 205–209.

Axelrod, Larry, and Rowland Johnson. 2006. *Turning Conflict into Profit*. University of Alberta.

Barnlund, Dean C., and Franklyn Saul Haiman. 2012. *The Dynamics of Discussion*. Houghton Mifflin, Literary Licensing.

Bartlett, Katharine T. 2009. "Making Good on Good Intentions: The Critical Role of Motivation ...." *Virginia Law Review* 95, 8, 1893–1972.

Bendersky, Corinne. 1998. "Culture: The Missing Link in Dispute Systems Design." *Negotiation Journal* 14, 4, 307–311.

Benne, Kenneth, and Paul Sheats. 1948. "Functional Roles of Group Members." *Journal of Social Issues* 4, 4–49.

Bennett, James, Michael Pitt, and Samantha Price. 2012. "Understanding the Impact of Generational Issues in the Workplace." *Facilities* 30, 7/8, 278–288.

Bersin, Josh. 2015. "Becoming Irresistible." *Deloitte Review* 16.

Brown, Graham, Thomas B. Lawrence, and Sandra L. Robinson. 2005. "Territoriality in Organizations." *Academy of Management Review* 30, 3, July 1, 577–594.

Chen, Ming-Huei. 2006. "Understanding the Benefits and Detriments of Conflict on Team Creativity Process." *Creativity, Innovation, and Management* 15, 1, 105–116.

Commission, Public Service. 2020. "The Cost of Conflict." *Government of Newfoundland and Labrador*. 3 12. Accessed August 14, 2020. https://www.psc.gov.nl.ca/psc/rwp/costofconflict.html.

Cortina, Lilia M. 2008. "Unseen Injustice: Incivility as Modern Discrimination in Organizations." *Academy of Management Review* 33, 1, 55–75.

Coy, Brent, and William H. O'Brien et al. 2011. "Associations between Evaluation Anxiety, Cognitive Interference, and Performance on Working Memory Tests." *Journal of Analytical Psychology* 25, 5, 823–832.

Deutsch, Morton. 1973. *The Resolution of Conflict: Constructive and Destructive Processes*. Yale University.

Dougherty, Debbie S. 2006. "Gendered Constructions of Power during Discourse about Sexual Harassment: Negotiating Competing Meanings." *Sex Roles* 54, 7–8, 495–507.

Einarsen, Stale, and Helge Hoel et al. 2003. "The Concept of Bullying at Work: The European Tradition." In *Bullying and Emotional Abuse in the Workplace: International Perspectives in Research and Practice*, by Stale Einarsen and Helge Hoel et al. (Eds.), 3–30. Taylor & Francis.

Ellison, Sara Fisher, and Wallace P. Mullin. 2014. "Diversity, Social Goods Provision, and Performance in the Firm." *Journal of Economics and Management Strategy* 23, 24, 465–481.

Feldblum, Chai R., and Victoria A. Lipnic. June, 2016. *Select Task Force on the Study of Harassment in the Workplace*. Task Force Study Report. US Equal Employment Opportunity Commission.

Fisher, Roger, William T. Ury, and Bruce Patton. 2011. *Getting to Yes*. Penguin.

Folger, Joseph P., Marshall Scott Poole, and Randall L. Stutman. 2018. *Working through Conflict: Strategies for Relationships, Groups, and Organization* (8th ed.). Routledge.

Ford, Robert C., and Myron D. Fottler. 1995. "Empowerment: A Matter of Degree." *Academy of Management Perspectives* 9, 3.

Frey, Carl Benedikt, and Michael Osborne. 2013. *The Future of Employment: How Susceptible Are Jobs to Computerization?* Research. Oxford Martin School, University of Oxford.

Fu, Ping Ping, and T. Taber. 1998. "National Cultural Similarities and Differences: A Comparison between US and Chinese Managers." *Journal of Management*. Southern Management Association.

Fu, Ping Ping, and Gary Yukl. 2000. "Perceived Effectiveness of Influence Tactics in the United States and China." *Leadership Quarterly* 11, 2, 251–266.

Gersick, Connie J. G. 2017. "Time and Transition in Work Teams: Toward a New Model of Group Development." *Academy of Management* 31, 1.

Giles, Howard 2016. "Communication Accommodation Theory." In Erik Barnouw, *International Encyclopedia of Communication Theory and Philosophy*. Wiley-Blackwell.

Glassdoor for Employers. 2014, November 17. Accessed August 15, 2020. https://www. glassdoor.com/employers/blog/diversity/.

Global Human Capital Report. 2008, July. Research Report. CPP, Inc.

Hall, Edward T. 1976. *Beyond Culture*. Anchor/Doubleday.

Hickson, Gerald B., James Pichert, Lynn Webb, and Steven Gabbe. 2007. "A Complementary Approach to Promoting Professionalism: Identifying, Measuring, Addressing. ..." *Academic Medicine* 82, 11, 1040–1048.

Hinds, Pamela J., and Mark Mortensen. 2005. "Understanding Conflict in Geographically Distributed Teams: The Moderating Effects of Shared Identity, Shared Context, and Spontaneous Communication." *Organizational Science* 16, 3, 203–325.

Hofmann, Eva, and Barbara Hartl et al. 2017. "Authorities' Coercive and Legitimate Power: The Impact on Cognitions Underlying Cooperation." *Frontiers in Psychology*.

Huxham, Chris, and Siv Vangen. 2005. *Managing to Collaborate: The Theory and Practice of the Collaborative Advantage*. Routledge.

Ilgaz, Zeynep. 2014. "Conflict Resolution: When Should Leaders Step In?" *Forbes. com*. May 15. Accessed December 5, 2018. https://www.forbes.com/sites/85broads/2014/05/15/conflict-resolution-when-should-leaders-step-in/#7f1ed5613357.

Ilgen, Daniel R., and John R. Hollenbeck et al. 2005. "Teams in Organizations: From Input-Process-Output Models to IMOI Models." *Annual Review in Psychology* 56, 517–543.

Kabanoff, Boris, Robert Waldersee, and Marcus Cohen. 2017. "Espoused Values and Organizational Change Themes." *Academy of Management Journal* 38, 4.

Kearl, Holly. 2014. *Unsafe and Harassed in Public Spaces: A National Street Harassment Report.* National Survey Report. Stop Street Harassment.

Keashly, Loraleigh. 2012. "Hostile Work Relationships." In *Problematic Relationships in the Workplace,* by Janie M. Harden Fritz and Becky L. Omdahl (Eds.), Vol. II. Peter Lang.

Kehoe, Dalton. 2013. *Communication in Everyday Life* (5th ed.). Pearson.

Kolb, Judith A. 2013. "Conflict Management Principles for Groups and Teams." *Industrial and Commercial Training* 45, 2, 79–86.

Leape, Lucian L., and Miles F. Shore et al. 2012a. "A Culture of Respect, Part 1: The Nature and Causes of Disrespectful Behavior by Physicians." *Academic Medicine* 87, 7, 1–8.

———. 2012b. "A Culture of Respect, Part 2: Creating a Culture of Respect." *Academic Medicine* 87, 7, 853–858.

Lerner, Harriet G. 1997. *Dance of Anger.* HarperCollins.

Lewin, Kurt. 1943. "Defining the "Field" at a Given Time." *Psychological Review* 50, 292–310.

Lorenzo, Rocio, Martin Reeves. 2018. "How and Where Diversity Drives Financial Performance." *Harvard Business Review.*

Lytle, Anne L., Jeanne M. Brett, and Debra L. Shapiro. 2007. "The Strategic Use of Interests, Rights, and Power to Resolve Disputes." *Negotiation Journal* 15, 1, 31–51.

Mackenzie, Hugh. January 4, 2016. *Staying Power: CEO Pay in Canada.* News Release. Canadian Centre for Policy Alternatives.

Mathews, Andrew. 1990. "Why Worry? The Cognitive Function of Anxiety." *Behavior Research and Theory* 28, 6, 455–468.

Michel, Kathleen. 1994. "Conversation On-Line: Girls' Rapport Talk and Boys' Report Talk." *Women and Language* 17, 1.

Moberg, Paul J. 2001. "Linking Conflict Strategy to the Five Factor Model: Theoretical and Empirical Foundations." *International Journal of Conflict Management* 12, 1, 47–68.

Moule, Richard K., and Danielle M. Wallace. 2017. "An Experimental Investigation into Perceptions of Disrespect during Interpersonal Conflict." *Social Science Research* 62, 134–149.

Namie, Gary. 2003. *Workplace Bullying: Escalated Incivility.* Research. Ivey Business Journal, University of Western Ontario.

———. June, 2017. *2017 WBI US Workplace Bullying Survey.* Survey Report. Workplace Bullying Institute.

NDVH. 2020. "Relationship Spectrum." *National Domestic Violence Hotline.* Accessed August 14, 2020. https://www.thehotline.org/healthy-relationships/relationship-spectrum/.

Nielsen, Morten Birkeland, Lars Glaso, and Stale Einarsen. 2017. "Exposure to Workplace Harassment and the Five Factor Model of Personality: A Meta-analysis." *Personality and Individual Differences* 104, 195–206.

Northrup, Terrell A. 1989. "The Dynamic of Identity in Personal and Social Conflict." In *Intractable Conflicts and Their Transformation,* 61-. Syracuse University.

Oetzel, John G., and Stella Ting-Toomey. 2003. "Face Concerns in Interpersonal Conflict: A Cross-cultural Empirical Test of the Face Negotiation Theory." *Communication Research* 30, 6, 599–624.

Raven, Bertram H., and John R. P. French. 1958. "Legitimate Power, Coercive Power, and Observability in Social Influence." *Sociometry* 21, 2, 83–97.

Rayner, Charlotte, and Loraleigh Keashly. 2005. "Bullying at Work: A Perspective from Britain and North America." In *Counterproductive Work Behavior: Investigations of Actors and Targets*, by Suzy Fox and Paul E. Spector (Eds.), 271–296. American Psychological Association.

Robbins, Stephen, and Timothy A. Judge. 2018. *Organizational Behavior*.

Rospenda, Kathleen M., and Judith A. Richman. 2004. "The Factor Structure of Generalized Workplace Harassment." *Violence and Victims* 19, 2.

Salin, Denise. 2009. "Organisational Reponses to Workplace Harassment: An Exploratory Study." *Personnel Review* 38, 1, 26–44.

Schein, Larry E, and Virginia E. Greiner. 1988. *Power and Organizational Development: Mobilizing Power to Implement Change*. Addison-Wesley.

Shewchuk, Richard M., and Windsor Westbrook Sherrill. 2009. "Managing a Diverse Health Services Workforce." In *Strategic Management of Human Resources in Health Services Organizations* (3rd ed.), by S. Robert Hernandez, Stephen J. O'Connor (Eds.), 117–132. Delmar.

Stainback, Kevin, and Donald Tomaskovic. 2012. *Documenting Desegregation: Racial and Gender Segregation in Private Sector Employment since the Civil Rights Act*. Russell Sage Foundation.

Statistics, US Bureau of Labor. 2015. *Workplace Homicide*. Annual Injuries, Illnesses, and Fatalities. United States Department of Labor.

———. 2017. "Survey of Occupational Injuries and Illnesses." Annual.

Stewart, L. 2008. "Pride Comes before a Claim: The Psychology of Dispute Resolution." *Field, Fisher, Waterhouse Secretary Review*. Accessed December 5, 2018. http://www. ffw.com/publications/all/articles/psychology-dispute-resolution.aspx.

Tannen, Deborah. 2007. *You Just Don't Understand: Women and Men in Conversation*. HarperCollins.

Ting-Toomey, and Stella, John G. Oetzel. 2001. *Managing Intercultural Conflict Effectively*. Sage.

Tolbize, Anick. 2008. *Generational Differences in the Workplace*. Literature Review. University of Minnesota.

Triandis, Harry C. 2018. *Individualism and Collectivism* (2nd ed.). Routledge.

Triandis, Harry C., Lois L. Kurowski, and Michele J. Gelfand. 1994. "Workplace Diversity." In *Handbook of Industrial and Organizational Psychology*, by Harry C. Triandis, M. D. Dunnet, and L. M. Hough (Eds.), 769–827. Consulting Psychologists.

Tuckman, Bruce W. 1965. "Developmental Sequence in Small Groups." *Psychological Bulletin*, 63, 6, 384–399.

Tuckman, Bruce W., and Mary Ann C. Jensen. 1977. "Stages of Small Group Development Revisited." *Group and Organization Studies* 2, 4, 419–427.

Urick, Michael J., and Elaine C. Hollensbe et al. 2017. "Understanding and Managing Intergenerational Conflict: An Examination of Influences and Strategies." *Work, Aging, and Retirement* 3, 2.

Ury, William, Jeanne M. Brett, and Stephen B. Goldberg. 1993. *Getting Disputes Resolved: Designing Systems to Cut the Costs of Conflict*. Harvard.

Watson, Warren E., Kamalesh Kumar, and Larry K. Michaelssen. 2017. "Cultural Diversity's Impact on Interaction Process and Performance: Comparing Homogeneous and Diverse Task Groups." *Academy of Management* 36, 3.

Wood, Julia T., and Natalie Fixmer-Oraiz. 2018. *Gendered Lives: Communication, Gender, and Culture*. Wadsworth.

Yukl, Gary. 2012. "Effective Leadership Behavior: What We Know and What Questions Need More Attention." *Academy of Management Perspectives* 26, 4.

Yukl, Gary A., and Cecilia M. Falbe. 1990. "Influence Tactics and Objectives in Upward, Downward, and Lateral Influence Attempts." *Journal of Applied Psychology* 75, 132–140.

Yukl, Gary, and J. B. Tracey. 1992. "Consequences of Influence Tactics When Used with Subordinates, Peers, and the Boss." *Journal of Applied Psychology* 77, 525–535.

CHAPTER 8

Arendt, Hannah. 1963. *Eichmann in Jerusalem: A Report on the Banality of Evil.* Viking.

Bandura, Albert. 1973. *Aggression: A Social Learning Analysis.* Prentice Hall.

Berkowitz, Leonard. 1993. *Aggression: Its Causes, Consequences, and Control.* McGraw-Hill.

Black, Michele C., and Kathleen C. Basile, et al. 2010. *The National Intimate Partner and Sexual Violence Survey.* National Center for Injury Prevention and Control.

Byrne, Sean, and Jessica Senehi. 2012. *Violence: Analysis, Intervention, and Prevention.* Ohio University.

Cashman, Greg. 2013. *What Causes War? Introduction to Theories of International Conflict.* Rowman and Littlefield.

Center for Strategic and International Studies. 2019. *2019 Global Peace Index: A Snapshot of the Global State of Peace.* June. Accessed June 28, 2019. https://www.csis.org/events/global-peace-index-2019-launch.

Centers for Disease Control. 2020. "National Center for Injury Prevention and Control, Division of Violence Prevention." *Centers for Disease Control and Prevention.* March 2. Accessed August 26, 2020. https://www.cdc.gov/violenceprevention/youthviolence/riskprotectivefactors.html.

Christie, Daniel J., Richard V. Wagner, and Deborah DuNamm Winter (Eds.). 2001. *Peace, Conflict, and Violence: Peace Psychology for the 21st Century.* Prentice Hall.

Conflict and Political Violence Index. 2014. "Conflict and Political Violence Index 2014." *Relief Web.* May 7. Accessed June 7, 2019. https://reliefweb.int/sites/reliefweb.int/files/resources/Conflict_and_Political_Violence_Index_2014_Map.pdf.

Crowe, Timothy. 2000. *Crime Prevention through Environmental Design: Applications of Architectural Design and Space Management Concepts* (2nd ed.). Butterworth-Heinemann.

Department for Child Protection. 2013. *Perpetrator Accountability in Child Protection Practice.* Resource. Government of Western Australia.

Fineman, Martha Albertson. 2008. "The Vulnerable Subject: Anchoring Equality in the Human Condition." *Yale Journal of Law and Feminism* 20, 1.

———. 2017. "Vulnerability and Inevitable Inequality." *Oslo Law Review* 4, 3, 133–149.

Galtung, Johan, and Tord Hoivik. 1971. "Structural and Direct Violence: Operationalization." *Journal of Peace Research* 8, 1, 73–76.

Garcia-Moreno, Claudia, Alessandra Guedes, and Wendy Knerr. 2012. *Understanding and Responding to Violence against Women.* Violence and Health. World Health Organization.

Garcia-Moreno, Claudia, and Henrica A. G. F. Jansen et al. 2006. "Prevalence of Intimate Partner Violence: Findings from the WHO Multicountry Study on Women's Health and Domestic Violence." *Lancet* 368, 9543, 1260–1269.

Group, Strategic Foresight. 2019. *Peace, Conflict, Terrorism.* June. Accessed June 12, 2019. https://strategicforesight.com/focus.php?id=1.

Hansen, Paul A. 1991. *Survivors and Partners: Healing the Relationships of Sexual Abuse Survivors.* Heron Hill.

Hawkins, J. David, and Brian H. Smith et al. 2007. "Promoting Social Development and Preventing Health and Behavior Problems during Elementary Grades: Results." *Victims and Offenders* 2, 2, 161–181.

Herman, Judith L. 1997 (2015). *Trauma and Recovery: The Aftermath of Violence—from Domestic Abuse to Political Terror*. Basic.

Howell, James C. 2010. *Gang Prevention: An Overview of Research and Programs*. Research. US Department of Justice, Office of Juvenile Justice and Delinquency Prevention.

Howell, James C., and Elizabeth A. Griffiths. 2019. *Gangs in America's Communities* (3rd ed.). Sage.

Institute for Economics and Peace. 2019. "Positive Peace Report 2019: Analysing the Factors That Sustain Peace." *Institute for Economics and Peace*. October. Accessed January 14, 2020. http://visionofhumanity.org/reports.

IRIN. 2017. *The World's Conflict*. Map. The New Humanitarian.

Khan, Roxanne. 2018. "Attitudes towards 'Honor' Violence and Killings in Collectivist Cultures." In *The Routledge International Handbook of Human Aggression: Current Issues and Perspectives*, by Jane L. Ireland, Philip Birch, and Carol A. Ireland (Eds.). Routledge.

Kraybill, Ron. 1992. "Powerlessness in Systems." In *Mediation and Facilitation Training Manual*, by Carolyn Schrock-Shenk (Ed.), 243–244. Mennonite Conciliation Service.

Krug, E. G., et al. (Eds.). 2002. *World Report on Violence and Health*. Public Health. World Health Organization.

Kuypers, Joseph A. 1992. *Man's Will to Hurt: Investigating the Causes, Supports, and Varieties of His Violence*. Fernwood.

Lamb, Sharon. 1996. *The Trouble with Blame: Victims, Perpetrators, and Responsibility*. Harvard.

———. 1999. "Constructing the Victim: Popular Images and Lasting Labels." In *New Visions of Victims: Feminists Struggle with the Concept*, by Sharon Lamb (Ed.), 108–138. New York University.

Langhinrichsen-Rohling, Jennifer. 2005. "Top Ten Greatest 'Hits': Important Findings." *Journal of Interpersonal Violence* 20, 1, 108–118.

Larieu, Julie, and Paul Mussen. 2010. "Some Personality and Motivational Correlates of Childrens' Prosocial Behavior." *Journal of Genetic Psychology* 147, 4, 529–542.

MacNair, Rachel M. 2012. *The Psychology of Peace: An Introduction* (2nd ed.). Praeger.

Matsakis, Aphrodite T. 1996. *I Can't Get Over It: A Handbook for Trauma Survivors* (2nd ed.). New Harbinger.

May, Rollo. 1998. *Power and Innocence: A Search for the Sources of Violence*. W. W. Norton.

McCann, I. Lisa, and Laurie Anne Pearlman. 2015. *Psychological Trauma and Adult Survivor: Theory, Therapy and Transformation*. Routledge.

Mc Evoy, Claire, and Gergely Hideg. 2017. *Global Violent Death, 2017*. Small Arms Survey. Graduate Institute of International and Development Studies.

Milgram, Stanley. 1963. "Obedience to Authority: The Experiment That Challenged Human Nature." *Journal of Abnormal and Social Psychology* (Harper Perennial) 67, 4, 371–378.

Monahan, John, and Jennifer L. Skeem. 2016. "The Evolution of Violence Risk Assessment." In *Violence in Psychiatry*, by Katherine D. Warburton and Stephen M. Stahl (Eds.), 17–23. Cambridge University.

Morris, Stephen C. 2007. *The Causes of Violence and the Effects of Violence on Community and Individual Health*. Education Summary. Global Health Education Consortium.

Museilak, Natalia. 2018. *Exploring Dimensions*. PhD dissertation, University of Western Ontario, Graduate and Postdoctoral Studies.

Nation, Maury, and Cindy Crusto, et al. 2003. "What Works in Prevention: Principles of Effective Prevention Programs." *American Psychologist* 58, 6/7, 449–456.

National Institutes of Health. 2014. *Treatment for PTSD in Military and Veteran Populations*. Committee Report. National Institutes of Health.

Noor, Masi, and Marina Cantacuzino (2018). *Forgiveness Is Really Strange*. Singing Dragon.

Pepler, Debra J. 2018. "The Development of Aggression in Childhood and Adolescence: A Focus on Relationships." In *The Routledge Handbook of Human Aggression: Current Issues and Perspectives*, by Jane L. Ireland, Philip Birch, and Carol A. Ireland (Eds.). Routledge.

Portwood, Sharon G., and Richard G. Lambert et al. 2011. "An Evaluation of Adults and Children Together (ACT) Against Violence: Parents Raising Safe Kids Program." *Journal of Primary Prevention* 32, 3–4, 147–160.

Quinn, Katherine A., Jennifer L. Walsh, and Julia Dickson-Gomez. 2019. "Multiple Marginality and the Variation in Delinquency and Substance Abuse among Adolescent Gang Members." *Substance Use and Misuse* (Published online November 5, 2018). doi: 10.1080/10826084.2018.1528465) 54, 4, 612–627.

Roccas, Sonia, Lilach Sagiv, and Shalm H. Schwartz et al. 2002. "The Big Five Personality Factors and Personal Values." *Personality and Social Psychology Bulletin* 28, 6, 789–801.

Rosenberg, Marshall B. 1983. *A Model for Nonviolent Communication*. New Society.

———. 2015. *Nonviolent Communication: A Language of Life*. PuddleDancer.

Rushton, J. Philippe. 2004. "Genetic and Environmental Contributions to Prosocial Attitudes: A Twin Study of Social Responsibility." *Proceedings of the Royal Society B: Biological Sciences* 271, 1557.

Saxe, Glenn N., B. Heidi Ellis, and Julie B. Kaplow. 2009. *Collaborative Treatment of Traumatized Children and Teens: The Trauma Systems Therapy Approach*. Guilford.

Sheng, Yap Kioe. 2009. "What Is Good Governance?" *United Nations Economic and Social Commission for Asia and the Pacific*. July 10. Accessed February 8, 2019. https://www.unescap.org/sites/default/files/good-governance.pdf.

Siann, Gerda. 1994. *Gender, Sex, and Sexuality: Contemporary Psychological Perspectives*. Taylor Francis.

Singer, Margaret Thaler, and Janja Lalich. 1995. *Cults in Our Midst*. Jossey-Bass.

Straus, Murray A., and Ethel L. Mickey. 2012. "Reliability, Validity, and Prevalence of Partner Violence Measured by the Conflict Tactics Scales in Male-Dominant Nations." *Aggression and Violent Behavior* 17, 5, 463–474.

Vigil, James Diego. 2016. "Multiple Marginality: A Comparative Framework for Understanding Gangs." In *Methods That Matter: Integrating Mixed Methods for More Effective Social Science Research*, by M. Cameron Hay (Ed.), 284–305. University of Chicago.

Volkan, Vamik. 2004. *Blind Trust: Large Groups and Their Leaders in Times of Crisis and Terror*. Pitchstone.

Walker, Lenore E. A. 2017. *The Battered Woman Syndrome* (4th ed.). Springer.

World Bank. 2018. *The Economic Cost of Conflict*. March 1. Accessed June 12, 2019. https://www.worldbank.org/en/news/infographic/2018/03/01/the-economic-cost-of-conflict.

World Health Organization. 2016. *World Health Statistics 2016*. Annual Progress. World Health Organization.

Xu, Xiaohe, Kent R. Kerley, and Bangon Sirisunyaluck. 2011. "Understanding Gender and Domestic Violence from a Sample of Married Women in Urban Thailand." *Journal of Family Issues* 32, 6, 791–819.

Zimbardo, Philip. 2007. *The Lucifer Effect: Understanding How Good People Turn Evil*. Random House.

CHAPTER 9

Arendt, Hannah. 1970. *On Violence*. Houghton Mifflin Harcourt.

Bandura, Albert. 1973. *Aggression: A Social Learning Analysis*. Prentice Hall.

Barash, David P., and Charles P. Webel. 2018. *Peace and Conflict Studies* (4th ed.). Sage.

Bar-Siman-Tov, Yaacov (Ed.). 2004. *From Conflict to Resolution*. Oxford.

Berkowitz, Leonard. 1993. *Aggression: Its Causes, Consequences, and Control.* McGraw-Hill.

Boulding, Kenneth E. 1990. "The Nature of Power." In *Three Faces of Power*, by Kenneth E. Boulding (Ed.), 15–34. Sage.

Boutros-Ghali, Boutros. 1992. "An Agenda for Peace: Preventive Diplomacy, Peacemaking, and Peacekeeping." *International Relations* 11, 3, 201–218.

Brecher, Michael. 2016. *The World of Protracted Conflicts.* Rowman and Littlefield.

Burke-White, William W. 2004. "Human Rights and National Security: The Strategic Correlation." *Harvard Human Rights Journal* 17, 249.

Byrne, Sean, and Jessica Senehi. 2012. *Violence: Analysis, Intervention, and Prevention.* Ohio University.

Cashman, Greg. 2013. *What Causes War? Introduction to Theories of International Conflict.* Rowman and Littlefield.

Center for Strategic and International Studies. 2019. *2019 Global Peace Index: A Snapshot of the Global State of Peace.* June. Accessed June 28, 2019. https://www.csis.org/events/global-peace-index-2019-launch.

Cordeiro-Rodrigues, Luis, and Danny Singh (Eds.). 2020. *Comparative Just War Theory: An Introduction to International Perspectives.* Rowman and Littlefield.

Christie, Daniel J., Richard V. Wagner, and Deborah DuNamm Winter (Eds.). 2001. *Peace, Conflict, and Violence: Peace Psychology for the 21st Century.* Prentice Hall.

CPVI. 2014. "Conflict and Political Violence Index 2014." *Relief Web.* May 7. Accessed June 7, 2019. https://reliefweb.int/sites/reliefweb.int/files/resources/Conflict_and_Political_Violence_Index_2014_Map.pdf.

Diehl, Paul F. 2016. "Exploring Peace: Looking beyond War and Negative Peace." *International Studies Quarterly* 60, 1, 1–10.

Dudouet, Veronique. 2006. *Transitions from Violence to Peace: Revisiting Analysis and Intervention in Conflict Transformation.* Analysis. Berghof Research Center for Constructive Conflict Management.

Dukes, E. Franklin. 2008. "Unrightable Wrongs." *ACResolution* Summer, 15–18.

Dupuy, Kendra, and Siri Aas Rustad. 2017. *Trends in Armed Conflict, 1946–2017.* Peace Research Institute of Oslo.

Du Toit, P. 1989. "Bargaining about Bargaining: Inducing the Self-Negating Prediction in Deeply Divided Societies—The Case of South Africa." *Journal of Conflict Resolution* 32, 2, 210–230.

Farmer, Paul. 2003. *Pathologies of Power: Health, Human Rights, and the New War on the Poor.* University of California Press.

Fisas, Vicenc. 2008. *Peace Process Yearbook.* Icaria Editorial.

Fisher, Roger J., and Loraleigh Keashly. 1991. "The Potential Complementarity of Mediation and Consultation within a Contingency Model of Third Party Intervention." *Journal of Peace Research* 28, 1, 29–42.

Galtung, Johan, and Tord Hoivik. 1971. "Structural and Direct Violence: Operationalization." *Journal of Peace Research* 8, 1, 73–76.

Glassner, Barry. 2009. *The Culture of Fear.* Basic.

Group, Strategic Foresight. 2019. *Peace, Conflict, Terrorism.* June. Accessed June 12, 2019. https://strategicforesight.com/focus.php?id=1.

Guelke, Adrian. 2012. *Politics in Deeply Divided Societies.* Polity.

Haidt, Jonathan. 2013. *The Righteous Mind: Good People Are Divided by Politics and Religion.* Random.

Haywood, Andrew. 2017. *Political Ideologies: An Introduction* (6th ed.). Macmillan International.

HIIK. 2019. *Conflict Barometer.* Annual Political Conflict Report. Heidelberg Institute for International Conflict Research.

Hinton, Alexander L., Andrew Woolford, and Jeff Benvenuto (Eds.). 2014. *Colonial Genocide in Indigenous North America.* Duke University.

Holmes, John W. 2020. "Middle Power." *Historica Canada.* May 27. Accessed September 4, 2020. https://www.thecanadianencyclopedia.ca/en/article/middle-power.

Horowitz, Donald L. 1993. "The Challenge of Ethnic Conflict: Democracy in Divided Societies." *Journal of Democracy* 4, 4, 18–38.

———. 2001. *The Deadly Ethnic Riot.* University of California Press.

IRIN. 2017. *The World's Conflict.* Map. The New Humanitarian.

Jolly, Richard, and Deepayan Basu Ray. 2007. "Human Security—National Perspectives and Global Agendas: Insights from National Human Development Reports." *Journal of International Development* 19, 4, 457–472.

Kaufmann, Daniel, Aart Kraay, and Massimo Mastruzzi. 2011. "Worldwide Governance Indicators: Methodology and Analytical Issues." *Hague Journal on the Rule of Law* 3, 2, 220–246.

Kraybill, Ron. 1992. "Powerlessness in Systems." In *Mediation and Facilitation Training Manual,* by Carolyn Schrock-Shenk (Ed.), 243–244. Mennonite Conciliation Service.

Kriesberg, Louis. 2005. "Nature, Dynamics, and Phases of Intractability." In *Grasping the Nettle: Analyzing Cases of Intractable Conflict,* by Fen Osler Hampson, Pamela R. Aall, and Chester A. Crocker (Eds.), 65–98. US Institute of Peace.

Krug, E. G., et al. (Eds.). 2002. *World Report on Violence and Health.* Public Health. World Health Organization.

Lama, Mahendra P. 2018. *Human vs. National Security.* Analysis. 21st Century Global Dynamics Initiative, 11, 22.

Levy, Jack S., and William R. Thompson. 2010. *Causes of War.* Wiley-Blackwell.

Lindner, Evelin. 2006. *Making Enemies: Humiliation and International Conflict.* Praeger, ABC-CLIO.

Lund, Michael. 2001. "A Toolbox for Responding to Conflict and Building Peace." In *Peacebuilding: A Field Guide,* by Luc Reychler and Thania Paffenholz (Eds.), 16–20. Lynne Rienner.

Lynch, Derek F. 2008. "Balance of Power Relationships." In *Encyclopedia of Violence, Peace, and Conflict,* by Lester Kurtz and Jennifer Turpin (Eds.), 175–186. Academic Press.

March, Luke. 2012. *Radical Left Parties in Europe.* Routledge.

Margolis, J. Eli. 2010. "Understanding Political Stability and Instability." *Journal of Civil Wars* 12, 3.

Mc Evoy, Claire, and Gergely Hideg. 2017. *Global Violent Death, 2017.* Small Arms Survey. Graduate Institute of International and Development Studies.

McAdams, Dan P., and Kate C. McLean. 2013. "Narrative Identity." *Current Directions in Psychological Studies,* 22, 3.

McLean, Kyle, and Scott E. Wolfe et al. 2019. "Police Officers as Warriors or Guardians: Empirical Reality or Intriguing Rhetoric?" *Justice Quarterly.*

Mearsheimer, John J. 1990. "Instability in Europe after the Cold War." *International Security* 15, 1, 5–56.

Miall, Hugh. 2013. "Conflict Transformation: A Multidimensional Task." In *Transforming Ethnopolitical Conflict: The Berghof Handbook,* by Alex Austin, Martina Fischer, and Norbert Ropers (Eds.), 67–90. Springer.

Midgley, Tim. 2015. "An Alternative Approach to Conflict Analysis." *Saferworld.* June 11. Accessed September 4, 2020. https://www.saferworld.org.uk/resources/news-and-analysis/post/161-an-alternative-approach-to-conflict-analysis-.

Mudde, Cas. 2019. *The Far-Right Today.* Polity.

National Conference of Catholic Bishops. 1983. *The Challenge of Peace: God's Promise and Our Response.* Pastoral Letter. National Conference of Catholic Bishops.

National Institutes of Health. 2014. *Treatment for PTSD in Military and Veteran Populations.* Committee Report. National Institutes of Health.

Newman, Edward, and Oliver Richmond. 2006. "Peace Building and Spoilers." *Conflict, Security, and Development* 6, 1, 101–10.

NVDRS. 2018. *National Violent Death Reporting System*. Accessed June 12, 2019. https://www.cdc.gov/violenceprevention/datasources/nvdrs/index.html.

Nye, Joseph S. 1990. "The Changing Nature of World Power." *Political Science Quarterly*, 105, 2, 177–192.

Office for Coordination of Humanitarian Affairs. 2017. *World Humanitarian Data and Trends*. Annual Report. UN Office for Coordination of Humanitarian Affairs.

Pettersson, Therese, and Magnus Oberg. 2020. "Organized Violence, 1989–2019." *Journal of Peace Research* 57, 4.

Project, The Kurdish. 2015. *Kurds and the Refugee Crisis*. Accessed January 10, 2019. https://thekurdishproject.org/infographics/kurds-and-the-refugee-crisis.

Rahr, Sue, and Stephen K. Rice. 2015. *From Warriors to Guardians: Recommitting American Police Culture to Democratic Ideals*. Bulletin. US Department of Justice, National Institute of Justice.

Ramsbotham, Oliver, Tom Woodhouse, and Hugh Miall. 2011. *Contemporary Conflict Resolution: Prevention, Management, and Transformation of Deadly Conflicts* (3rd ed.). Polity.

Ross, Marc H. 1993. *The Culture of Conflict: Interpretations and Interests in Comparative Perspective*. Yale University.

Rothman, Jay. 1997. *Resolving Identity-Based Conflict in Nations, Organizations, and Communities*. Jossey-Bass.

Rothman, Jay, and Michal Alberstein. 2013. "Individuals, Groups, and Intergroups: Theorizing about the Role of Identity in Conflict and Its Creative Engagement." *Ohio State Journal on Dispute Resolution* 631.

Rummel, Rudolph J. 1981. "The Just Peace." In *Understanding Conflict and War*, by Rudolph Rummel (Ed.), Vol. 5. Sage.

Rupasinghe, Kumar, and Sanam Naraghi Anderlini. 1998. *Civil Wars, Civil Peace: An Introduction to Conflict Resolution*. Pluto.

Ryan, Stephen. 2007. *The Transformation of Violent Intercommunal Conflict*. Ashgate.

Schellenberg, James. 1996. *Conflict Resolution: Theory, Research, and Practice*. SUNY.

Sheafer, Tamir, and Shira Dvir-Gvirsman. 2010. "The Spoiler Effect: Framing Attitudes and Expectations toward Peace." *Journal of Peace Research* 47, 2, 205–15.

Sheng, Yap Kioe. 2009. "What Is Good Governance?" *United Nations Economic and Social Commission for Asia and the Pacific*. July 10. Accessed February 8, 2020. https://www.unescap.org/sites/default/files/good-governance.pdf.

Smith-Christopher, Daniel L. (Ed.). 2007. *Subverting Hatred: The Challenge of Nonviolence in Religious Traditions*. Orbis.

Stedman, Stephen John. 1997. "Spoiler Problems in Peace Processes." *International Security* 22, 2, 5–53.

Subedi, D. B. 2013. "'Pro-Peace Entrepreneur' or 'Conflict Profiteer'? Critical Perspective on the Private Sector and Peace Building in Nepal." *Peace and Change* 38, 2.

Taras, Raymond C., and Rajat Ganguly. 2016. *Understanding Ethnic Conflicts* (4th ed.). Routledge.

Thorhallsson, Baldure, and Sverrir Steinsson. 2017. "Small State Foreign Policy." *Oxford Research Encyclopedia of Politics*, May 24.

TNH. 2017. *The New Humanitarian (formerly IRIN News)*. April 4. Accessed January 13, 2020. https://www.thenewhumanitarian.org/maps-and-graphics/2017/04/04/updated-mapped-world-war.

UCDP. 2019. *Uppsala Conflict Data Program*. Annual Armed Conflict. Uppsala Universitet.

United Nations. 1997. "Programme of Action on a Culture of Peace." *UN General Assembly*. New York.

UN Development Programme. 1994. *Human Development Report*. Analysis. United Nations Development Programme.

UNHCR. 2018. Statistical Yearbook. United Nations Refugee Agency.

US Institute of Peace. 2020. "Cessation of Large Scale Violence." *United States Institute of Peace*. Accessed September 1, 2020. https://www.usip.org/guiding-principles-stabilization-and-reconstruction-the-web-version/safe-and-secure-environment/nece.

Volkan, Vamik. 2004. *Blind Trust: Large Groups and Their Leaders in Times of Crisis and Terror*. Pitchstone.

Wilson, Maureen E. 2019. *Post-Conflict Justice and Legal Traditions: A New Conceptual Framework*. Dissertation, Kennesaw State University.

World Bank. 2018. *The Economic Cost of Conflict*. March 1. Accessed June 12, 2019. https://www.worldbank.org/en/news/infographic/2018/03/01/the-economic-cost-of-conflict.

World Health Organization. 2016. *World Health Statistics 2016*. Annual Progress. World Health Organization.

Zahar, Marie-Joelle. 2008. "Reframing the Spoiler Debate in Peace Processes." In *Contemporary Peacemaking* (2nd ed.), by John, Roger Mac Ginty (Eds.) Darby, 159. Palgrave Macmillan.

Zartman, I. William. 2015. *Preventing Deadly Conflict*. Polity.

Zartman, I. William, and Lewis Rasmusen (Eds.). 1997. *Peacemaking in International Conflict: Methods and Techniques*. US Institute of Peace.

Zartman, I. William, and Maureen Berman. 1983. *The Practical Negotiator*. Yale University.

CHAPTER 10

Ajayi, Adeyinka Theresa, and Lateef Oluwafemi Buhari. 2014. "Methods of Conflict Resolution in African Traditional Society." *African Research Review* 8, 2, Serial 33, 138–157.

Beer, Jennifer E., and Caroline C. Packard. 2012. *Mediator's Handbook* (4th ed.). New Society.

Blader, Steven, and Tom R. Tyler. 2003. "A Four-Component Model of Procedural Justice: Defining the Meaning of a 'Fair' Process." *Personality and Social Psychology Bulletin* 29, 6, 747–758.

Brett, Jeanne M. 2010. "Culture and Negotiation." *International Journal of Psychology* 97–104.

Civil Service Commission, UK Government. 2019. *British Diplomatic Service Manual*. Available at https://civilservicecommission.independent.gov.uk/wp-content/uploads/2019/03/03a_diplomatic.pdf.

Butler, Paul. 2016. "The System Is Working the Way It Is Supposed To: The Limits of Criminal Justice Reform." *Georgetown University Law Journal* 1419–1433.

Carens, Joseph H. 2000. *Culture, Citizenship, and Community: A Contextual Exploration of Justice as Evenhandedness*. Oxford University.

Central Intelligence Agency. 2019. *The World Factbook*. Accessed April 11, 2019. https://www.cia.gov/library/publications/the-world-factbook/rankorder/2172rank.html.

Correctional Service of Canada. 2018. *Offender Statistics*. March 26. Accessed April 10, 2019. https://www.csc-scc.gc.ca/index-en.shtml.

Decker, Scott, Cassia Spohn, Natalie Ortiz, and Eric Hedberg. 2014. "Criminal Stigma, Race, Gender, and Employment: An Expanded Assessment." *National Institute of Justice*, January.

Fisher, Roger, William Ury, and Bruce Patton. 2011. *Getting to Yes: Negotiating Agreement without Giving In* (3rd ed.). Penguin.

Follett, Mary Parker. 2013. *Dynamic Administration: The Collected Papers of Mary Parke Follett*. Martino.

Fortune, Marie M. 2001. *No Justice without Healing*. FaithTrust Institute.

Foucault, Michel. 1977. *Discipline and Punish: The Birth of the Prison*. Vintage.

Hyle, Ken. 2018. "Annual Determination of Average Cost of Incarceration." *US Federal Register, Prisons Bureau*, April 30.

Konow, J. 2001. "Fair and Square: The Four Sides of Distributive Justice." *Journal of Economic Behavior and Organization* 46, 137–164.

Kuhn, Andre. 2001. "Incarceration Rates across the World." In *Penal Reform in Overcrowded Times*, by Michael Tonry (Ed.), 101–114. Oxford.

Laue, James. 1990. "The Emergence and Institutionalization of Third-Party Roles in Conflict." In *Conflict: Readings in Management and Resolution*, by John Burton and Frank Dukes (Eds.), 256–272. Macmillan.

Longres, John F., and Edward Scanion. 2001. "Social Justice and the Research Curriculum." *Journal of Social Work Education* 37, 3, 447–463.

Maise, Michelle. 2013. "Procedural Justice." *Beyond Intractability*. June. Accessed April 16, 2019. https://www.beyondintractability.org/essay/procedural_justice.

Mauer, Marc. 2017. "Incarceration Rates in International Perspective." *Oxford Encyclopedia of Criminology and Criminal Justice*. June 28. Accessed June 8, 2020. https://oxfordre.com/criminology/view/10.1093/acrefore/9780190264079.001.0001/acrefore-9780190264079-e-233.

Newmark, Lisa C. 2006. *Crime Victims' Needs and VOCA-Funded Services: Findings and Recommendations from Two National Studies*. Research. National Institute of Justice.

Novak, Michael. 2000. "Defining Social Justice." *First Things First*, December: 108, 11–13.

Pely, Doran. 2011. "Where East Not Always Meets West: Comparing the Sulha Process to Western-Style Mediation and Arbitration." *Conflict Resolution Quarterly* 28, 4, 427–440.

Public Safety Canada. 2003. *Restorative Justice and Recidivism*. Research Summary. Government of Canada.

Redekop, Paul. 2008. *Changing Paradigms: Punishment and Restorative Discipline*. Herald.

Sen, Amartya. 2009. *The Idea of Justice*. Harvard University.

Sherman, Lawrence W., and Heather Strang et al. 2007. *Restorative Justice: The Evidence*. The Smith Institute, Teeside University.

Sitka, Linda. 2009. "Exploring the 'Lost and Found' of Justice Theory and Research." *Social Justice Research* 22, 98–116.

Trujillo, Mary A. 2008. *Recentering: Culture and Knowledge in Conflict Resolution Practice*. Syracuse University.

Tutu, Desmond. 2012. "The Spirit of Ubuntu." Clinton Foundation. Available at https://stories.clintonfoundation.org/the-spirit-of-ubuntu-6f3814ab8596.

Van Ness, Daniel W., and Karen H. Strong. 2010. *Restoring Justice: An Introduction to Restorative Justice*. Bender.

van Tuijl, Peter. 1999. "NGOs and Human Rights: Sources of Justice and Democracy." *Journal of International Affairs* 52, 2, 493–512.

Walker, Polly O. 2004. "Decolonizing Conflict Resolution: Addressing the Ontological Violence of Westernization." *American Indian Quarterly* 28, 3/4, 527–549.

Walmsley, R. 2003. "Global Incarceration and Prison Trends." *United Nations: Forum on Crime and Society* 3, 1 & 2, 65–78.

Walmsley, Roy. 2018. *World Prison Population List* (12th ed.). September. Accessed March 4, 2020. https://www.prisonstudies.org/sites/default/files/resources/downloads/wppl_12.pdf.

Wertheim, Emmy. 1996. "Negotiations and Resolving Conflicts: An Overview." *europarc.org*. 11 21. Accessed May 17, 2018. https://www.europarc.org/communication-skills/pdf/Negotiation%20Skills.pdf.

Western, Bruce, and Becky Pettit. 2010. "Incarceration and Social Inequality." *Daedalus* 139, 3, 8–19.

Zehr, Howard. 1990. *Changing Lenses: A New Focus for Crime and Justice*. Herald.

———. 1995. "Justice Paradigm Shift? Values and Visions in the Reform Process." *Mediation Quarterly* 12, 3.

———. 2014. *Little Book of Restorative Justice* (2nd ed.). Good.

Zutter, Deborah Lynn. 2007. *Preparing for Mediation: A Dispute Resolution Guide* (2nd ed.). Abundance Solutions.

CHAPTER 11

Armstrong, Karen. 2006. *The Great Transformation: The Beginning of Our Religious Traditions*. Knopf.

———. 2010. *Twelve Steps to a Compassionate Life*. Knopf.

Asfaruddin, Asma. 2013. *Striving in a Path of God: Jihad and Martyrdom in Islamic Thoughts*. Oxford University.

Avruch, Kevin. 1998. *Culture and Conflict Resolution*. US Institute of Peace.

Bainton, Roland H. 1960. *Christian Attitudes toward War and Peace: A Historical Survey and Critical Re-evaluation*. Wipf and Stock.

Barash, David P., and Charles P. Webel. 2018. *Peace and Conflict Studies* (4th ed.). Sage.

Bock, Joseph G. 2001. *Sharpening Conflict Management: Religious Leadership and the Double-Edged Sword*. Praeger.

Boulding, Elise. 1988. *Building a Civic Culture: Education for an Interdependent World*. Syracuse University.

Boulding, J. Russell (Ed.). 2017. *Elise Boulding: A Pioneer in Peace Research, Peacemaking, Feminism, Future Studies, and the Family*. Springer.

Bouta, Tsjeard, S. Ayse Kadayifci-Orellana, and Mohammed Abu-Nimer. 2005. *Faith-Based Peacebuilding: Mapping and Analysis of Christian, Muslim, and Multi-faith Actors*. Analysis. Netherlands Institute of International Relations "Cingendael."

Boutros-Ghali, Boutros. 1992. "An Agenda for Peace: Preventive Diplomacy, Peacemaking, and Peacekeeping." *International Relations* 11, 3, 201–218.

Brantmeier, Edward J. n.d. "Connecting Inner and Outer Peace: Buddhist Mediation Integrated with Peace Education." *Journal of Peace Education and Social Justice* 1, 2, 120–157.

Brennan, Donald G. 1960. "Arms Control, Disarmament, and National Security." *Daedalus* 89, 4, 681–707.

Britannica, Encyclopaedia. 2019. "Indian Mutiny." *Encyclopaedia Britannica*. May 8. Accessed June 25, 2019. https://www.britannica.com/event/Indian-Mutiny.

Bruneau, Thomas C., and Florina Christiana Matei (Eds.). 2013. *The Routledge Handbook of Civil-Military Relations*. Routledge.

Burgess, Heidi. 2018. "Limiting Violence and Intimidation—for Researchers." *Beyond Intractability*. Accessed June 20, 2019. https://www.beyondintractability.org/userguide/limitviolence-researchers.

Burton, John. 1990. *Human Needs Theory*. Macmillan.

Cader, Aram Abdul. 2017. "Islamic Principles of Conflict Management: A Model for Human Resource Management." *International Journal of Cross Cultural Management* 17, 3, 345–363.

Christie, Daniel J., and Barbara Tint et al. 2008. "Peace Psychology for a Peaceful World." *American Psychologist* 63, 6, 540–552.

Cottey, Andrew. 2013. *Reshaping Defence Diplomacy: New Roles for Military Cooperation and Assistance* (2nd ed.). Routledge.

Diamond, Louise, and John W. McDonald. 1996. *Multitrack Diplomacy: A Systems Approach to Peace*. Kumarian.

Dietrich, Wolfgang. 2012. *Interpretations of Peace in History and Culture*. Palgrave Macmillan.

Dyck, Harvey L. (Ed.). 1996. *The Pacifist Impulse in Historical Perspective*. University of Toronto.

Edwards, A. J. C. 1986. *Nuclear Weapons, the Balance of Terror, the Quest for Peace*. Palgrave Macmillan.

Epstein, Ron. 1988. "Buddhist Ideas for Attaining World Peace." San Francisco State University, November 7, 9.

Firchow, Pamina. 2018. *Reclaiming Everyday Peace: Local Voices in Measurement and Evaluation after War*. Cambridge University.

Fisher, Roger, William L. Ury, and Bruce Patton. 2011. *Getting to Yes: Negotiating Agreement without Giving In*. Penguin.

Franke, Volker. 2006. "The Peacebuilding Dilemma: Civil-Military Cooperation in Stability Operations." *International Journal of Peace Studies* 11, 2, 5–25.

Freedman, Alan. 2016. "Peace: Shalom Is More Than the Absence of War." *Global Virtue Ethics Review* 7, 3, 53–60.

Galtung, Johan. 1971. "A Structural Theory of Imperialism." *Journal of Peace Research* 13, 2.

———. 1976. "Three Approaches to Peace." In *Peace, War, and Defense: Essays in Peace Research*, by Johan Galtung (Ed.), 282–462. Christian Ejlers.

Galtung, Johan, and Carl G. Jacobsen. 2000. *Searching for Peace: The Road to TRANSCEND*. Pluto.

Global Peace Index. 2019. *Global Peace Index*. Annual Ranking. Institute for Economics and Peace.

Green, Clifford J. 2005. "Pacifism and Tyrannicide: Bonhoeffer's Christian Ethic." *Studies in Christian Ethics* 18, 3, 31–47.

Grieves, Vicki. 2009. *Aboriginal Spirituality: Aboriginal Philosophy, the Base of Aboriginal Social and Emotional Wellbeing*. Discussion Paper #9. Cooperative Research Centre for Aboriginal Health.

Groff, Linda, and Paul Smoker. 1996. "Spirituality, Religion, Culture, and Peace: Exploring the Foundations for Inner-outer Peace in the 21st Century." *International Journal of Peace Studies* 1, 1, 57–113.

Gutierrez, Juan. 2009. "Factors Helping to Overcome the Use of Violence for Political Purposes in the Basque Country." In *Conflict Transformation and Peace Building: Moving from Violence to Sustainable Peace*, by Bruce W. Dayton and Louis Kriesberg (Eds.), 220–234. Routledge.

Hahn, Thich Nhat. 2008. *The World We Have: A Buddhist Approach to Peace and Ecology*. Parallax.

Havel, Vaclav. 1997. *The Art of the Impossible: Politics as Morality in Practice*. Knopf.

Herz, John H. 1951. *Political Realism and Political Idealism*. University of Chicago.

———. 2003. "The Security Dilemma in International Relations: Background and Present Problems." *International Relations* 17, 4, 411–416.

Hoffman, Ross. 2013. "Respecting Aboriginal Knowing in the Academy." *AlterNative: An International Journal of Indigenous Peoples* 9, 3, 189–203.

ICC. 2020. *The Court Today*. March. Accessed June 4, 2020. https://www.icc-cpi.int/iccdocs/pids/publications/thecourttodayeng.pdf.

International Court of Justice. 2018. *Handbook of the International Court of Justice*. December. Accessed September 16, 2020. https://www.icj-cij.org/files/publications/handbook-of-the-court-en.pdf.

Institute for Economics and Peace. 2020. *Structures of Peace: Identifying What Leads to Peaceful Societies*. Annual Global Peace Index. Institute for Economics and Peace.

Johnson, James Turner. 1987. *The Quest for Peace: Three Moral Traditions in Western Cultural History*. Princeton University.

———. 2002. *The Holy War Idea in Western and Islamic Traditions*. Pennsylvania State University.

Kaldor, Mary. 2003. "Civil Society and Accountability." *Journal of Human Development* 4, 1, 5–27.

Kaufmann, Daniel, and Aart Kraay. 2018. "Worldwide Governance Indicators." *World Bank*. Accessed June 27, 2019. https://info.worldbank.org/governance/wgi/#home.

Kaufmann, Daniel, Aart Kraay, and M. Mastruzzi. 2011. "The Worldwide Governance Indicators: Methodology and Analytical Issues." *Hague Journal on the Rule of Law* 3, 2, 220–246.

King, Martin Luther. 1992–1993. "Letter from a Birmingham Jail." *Martin Luther King Papers*. University of California Davis.

Koontz, Theodore J., and Andy Alexis-Baker (Eds.). 2009. *Christian Attitudes to War, Peace, and Revolution: John Howard Yoder*. Brazos.

Kraft, Kenneth (Ed.). 1992. *Inner Peace, World Peace: Essays on Buddhism and Nonviolence*. State University of New York.

Lederach, John Paul. 1998a. *Building Peace: Sustainable Reconciliation in Divided Societies*. US Institute of Peace.

———. 1998b. "Remember and Change." In *Transforming Violence: Linking Local and Global Peacemaking*, by Judy Zimmerman Herr and Robert Herr (Eds.). Herald.

Lederach, John Paul, and R. Scott Appleby. 2010. "Strategic Peacebuilding: An Overview." In *Strategies of Peace: Transforming Conflict in a Violent World*, by Daniel Philpott and Gerard F. Powers (Eds.), 19–44. Oxford.

Lopez, Donald S. 2004. *Buddhist Scriptures*. Penguin.

Mac Ginty, Roger. 2008. "Indigenous Peacemaking versus Liberal Peace." *Cooperation and Conflict* 43, 2, 139–163.

Mac Ginty, Roger, and Pamina Firchow. 2016. "Top-Down and Bottom-Up Narratives of Peace and Conflict." *Politics* 36, 3, 308–323.

McDonald, John W. 2003. "Multi-track Diplomacy." *Beyond Intractability*. September. Accessed June 25, 2019. https://www.beyondintractability.org/essay/multi-track_diplomacy.

Myers, David. 2015. *Exploring Social Psychology* (7th ed.). McGraw-Hill.

Nasir, Mohammed Abdun. 2020. "Conflict, Peace, and Religious Festivals: Muslim-Hindu-Christian Relations on the Eastern Indonesian Island of Lambok." *Interreligious Studies and Intercultural Theology* 4, 1, 102–123.

Neidjie, Bill. 2002. *Gagudju Man*. JB Books.

Newman, Edward, and Oliver Richmond. 2006. *The Impact of Spoilers on Peace Processes and Peacebuilding*. United Nations University Press.

Nilsson, Desiree, and Mimmi Soderberg Kovacs. 2011. "Revisiting an Elusive Concept: A Review of the Debate on Spoilers in Peace Processes." *International Studies Review* 13, 4, 606–626.

Pandia, P. K. 2017. "Hindu Tourists as Pilgrims in Quest of Spiritual Peace." *International Journal of Current Research in Education, Culture, and Society* 1, 1.

Peace Building Initiatives. 2013. "Introduction to Peacebuilding." *Peacebuilding Initiatives (PBI)*. April 25. Accessed September 16, 2020. http://www.peacebuildinginitiative.org/index8be4.html?fuseaction=cmc_printall.print&pageId=1681&printview=true&printchild=1.

Peterson, Timothy J., and Jon Van Til. 2004. "Defining Characteristics of Civil Society." *The International Journal of Non-for-Profit Law*, February.

Ross, Marc Howard. 1993. *The Management of Conflict: Interpretations and Interests in Comparative Perspective.* Yale University.

——. 2009. "Culture in Comparative Political Analysis." In *Rationality, Culture, and Structure* (2nd ed.), by Mark Irving Lichbach and Alan S. Zuckerman (Eds.), 134–160. Cambridge University.

Rouner, Leroy S. (Ed.). 1990. *Celebrating Peace.* University of Notre Dame.

Royce, Anderson. 2004. "A Definition of Peace." *Journal of Peace Psychology* 10, 2, 101–116.

Sandy, Leo, and Ray Perkins. 2002. "The Nature of Peace and Its Implications for Peace Education." *Online Journal of Peace and Conflict Resolution* 4, 2, 108.

Schattle, Hans. 2008. *The Practices of Global Citizenship.* Rowman and Littlefield.

Schlichtmann, Klaus. 2016. *A Peace History of India: From Ashoka Maurya to Mahatma Gandhi.* Vij.

Sheng, Yap Kioe. 2009. "UNESCO United Nations Economic and Social Commission for Asia and the Pacific." *What Is Good Governance?* July 10. Accessed February 8, 2020. https://www.unescap.org/sites/default/files/good-governance.pdf.

Sinha, Jai B. 1982. "The Hindu (Indian) Identity." *Dynamische Psychatrie* 15, 34, 148–160.

Smith, Linda Tuhiwai. 1999. *Decolonising Methodologies: Research and Indigenous Peoples.* University of Otago.

Smith, Michael J. 1998. "Humanitarian Intervention: An Overview of the Ethical Issues." *Ethics and International Affairs* 12, 63–79.

Soeung, Bunly, and SunYong Lee. 2017. "The Revitalisation of Buddhist Peace Activism in Post-War Cambodia." *Conflict, Security, and Development* 17, 2, 141–161.

Soni, Varun. 2010. "Religion, World Order, and Peace: A Hindu Approach." *CrossCurrents* 60, 3, 310–313.

Tanabe, Juichiro. 2016. "Exploring Buddhist Peace Theory." *Cultural and Religious Studies* 4, 10, 633–644.

——. 2019. "Buddhism and Post-Liberal Peacebuilding: Building a Holistic Peace Model Interconnecting Liberal Peace and Buddhist Peace." *Eubio Journal of Asian and International Bioethics* 29, 2, 46–52.

Tavares, Rodrigo. 2008. "Understanding Region Peace and Security: A Framework for Analysis." *Journal of Contemporary Politics* 14, 2, 107–127.

Turner, Dale. 2006. *This Is Not a Peace Pipe.* University of Toronto.

Wilson, T. 2004. "Racism, Moral Community, and Australian Aboriginal Autobiography Testimony." *Biography* 27, 1, 78–103.

Winston, Robert P. 2005. *Buddhist Scriptures.* Penguin Global.

Yeh, Theresa De-Ian. 2006. "The Way to Peace: A Buddhist Perspective." *International Journal of Peace Studies* 11, 1, 91–112.

Yoder, Perry B. 2017. *Shalom: The Bible's Word for Salvation, Justice, and Peace* (2nd ed.). Wipf and Stock.

Zelizer, Craig (Ed.). 2013. Integrated Peacebuilding: Innovative Approaches to Transforming Conflict. Westview.

CHAPTER 12

Abu-Nimer, Mohammed (Ed.). 2001. *Reconciliation, Justice, and Co-Existence: Theory and Practice.* Rowman and Littlefield.

Ackerman, Peter, and Jack DuVall. 2000. *A Force More Powerful: A Century of Nonviolent Conflict.* St. Martin's Press.

Ackerman, Peter, and Christopher Kruegler. 1994. *Strategic Nonviolent Conflict: The Dynamics of People Power in the Twentieth Century.* Praeger.

ACLED. 2020. "Demonstrations and Political Violence in America: New Data for Summer 2020." *Armed Conflict Location and Events Data.* August. Accessed September 21, 2020. https://acleddata.com/2020/09/03/demonstrations-political-violence-in-america-new-data-for-summer–2020/.

Altmaier, Elizabeth M. 2019. "Forgiveness." In *Promoting Positive Processes after Trauma*, by Elizabeth Altmaier (Ed.), 65–75. Elsevier.

Alvarado, Elvia, and Medea Benjamin. 1987. *Don't Be Afraid, Gringo: A Honduran Woman Speaks from the Heart—The Story of Elvia Alvarado*. Harper and Row.

Arendt, Hannah. 1972. *Crisis of the Republic*. Harcourt Brace.

Baker, Mona. 2018. *Translation and Conflict: A Narrative Account*. Routledge.

Bar-Siman-Tov, Yaacov (Ed.). 2004. *From Conflict Resolution to Reconciliation*. Oxford University.

Bar-Tal, Daniel, and Gemma H. Bennink. 2004. "The Nature of Reconciliation as an Outcome and as a Process." In *From Conflict Resolution to Reconciliation*, by Yaacov Bar-Siman-Tov (Ed.), 11–38. Oxford University.

Bartunek, Jean M. 2013. *Organizational or Educational Change: The Life and Role of a Change Agent Group*. Psychology Press.

Bauman, Zygmunt, and Leonidas Donskis. 2013. *Moral Blindness: The Loss of Sensitivity in Liquid Modernity*. Polity.

Beer, Jennifer E., and Caroline C. Packard. 2012. *Mediator's Handbook* (4th ed.). New Society.

Behrman, Carolyn, and Bill Lyons et al. 2016. *The Akron Story Circle Project: Rethinking Race in Classroom and Community*. University of Akron.

Benne, Kenneth D. 1976. "The Processes of Re-Education: An Assessment of Kurt Lewin's Views." *Group and Organizational Studies* 1, 1, 26–42.

Black Lives Matter. 2015. "Black Lives Matter: Guiding Principles." *Black Lives Matter*. October 4. Accessed September 21, 2020.

Bloomfield, David. 2006. *On Good Terms: Clarifying Reconciliation*. Research Report #14. Berghof Research Center for Constructive Conflict Management.

Brinton, Crane. 1965. *The Anatomy of Revolution* (3rd ed.). Random.

Bush, Robert A. Baruch, and Joseph P. Folger. 2005. *The Promise of Mediation: The Transformative Approach to Conflict* (2nd ed.). Jossey-Bass.

Butcher, Charity, and Maia Hallward. 2018. "Religious vs. Secular Human Rights Organizations: Discourse, Framing, and Action." *Journal of Human Rights* 17, 4, 502–523.

Byrd, W. Carson. 2011. "Conflating Apples and Oranges: Understanding Modern Forms of Racism." *Wiley Peer Review* 5, 11, 1005–1017.

Chenoweth, Erica, and Maria Stephan. 2011. *Why Civil Resistance Works: The Strategic Logic of Nonviolent Conflict*. Columbia University.

Coser, Lewis A. 1956. *The Functions of Social Conflict*. Routledge.

Cummings, Stephen, Todd Bridgman, and Kenneth G. Brown. 2015. "Unfreezing Change as Three Steps: Rethinking Kurt Lewin's Legacy for Change Management." *Human Relations* 69, 1, 33–60.

Curthoys, Lesley, Brent Cuthbertson, and Julie Clark. 2012. "Community Story Circles: An Opportunity to Rethink the Epistemological Approach to Heritage Interpretive Planning." *Canadian Journal of Environmental Education* 17, 173–187.

Dayton, Bruce W., and Louis Kriesberg. 2009. "Introduction." In *Conflict Transformation and Peacebuilding: Moving from Violence to Sustainable Peace*, by Bruce W. Dayton and Louis Kriesberg (Eds.), Chapter 1. Routledge.

Del Sesto, Steven L. 1983. "Technology and Social Change: William Fielding Ogburn Revisited." *Technology Forecasting and Social Change* 24, 3, 183–196.

Donais, Timothy. 2009. "Empowerment or Imposition? Dilemmas of Local Ownership in Post-conflict Peacebuilding Processes." *Peace and Change* 34, 1, 3–26.

Drumwright, Minette E., and Patrick E. Murphy. 2004. "How Advertising Practitioners View Ethics: Moral Muteness, Moral Myopia, and Moral Imagination." *Journal of Advertising* 33, 2, 7–24.

Dunfey, Theo Spanos. 2019. *What Is Social Change and Why Should We Care?* May 29. Accessed September 26, 2020. https://www.snhu.edu/about-us/newsroom/2017/11/what-is-social-change.

Elias, Sean, and Joe R. Feagin. 2020. "Systemic Racism and the White Racial Frame." In *Routledge International Handbook of Contemporary Racisms*, by John Solomos (Ed.). Routledge.

Enright, Robert D. 2001. *Forgiveness Is a Choice: A Step-by-Step Process*. American Psychological Association.

Enright, Robert D., and Richard P. Fitzgibbons. 2015. *Forgiveness Therapy: An Empirical Guide for Resolving Anger and Restoring Hope*. American Psychological Association.

Enright, Robert D., and Joanna North (Eds.). 1998. *Exploring Forgiveness*. University of Wisconsin.

Exline, Julie Juola, Everett L. Worthington, and Peter Hill, et al. 2003. "Forgiveness and Justice: A Research Agenda for Social and Personality Psychology." *Personality and Social Psychology Review* 7, 4, 337–348.

Feagin, Joe R. 2013. *White Racial Framing: Centuries of Racial Framing and Counterframing* (2nd ed.). Routledge.

Fischer, Louis. 2004. *Life of Mahatma Gandhi*. HarperCollins.

Fisher, Stephen. 2018. "Valence Issue." In *A Concise Oxford Dictionary of Politics and International Relations* (4th ed.), by Iain McLean (Ed.). Oxford University.

Flanigan, Beverly. 1992. *Forgiving the Unforgivable: Overcoming the Bitter Legacy of Intimate Wounds*. Wiley.

Fox, Erica Ariel. 2010. "State-Shifting: Advancing the Art of Conflict Intervention." *ACResolution*, Spring: 7–11.

Fraser, Nancy. 1999. "Social Justice in the Age of Identity Politics: Redistribution, Recognition, and Participation." In *Culture and Economy after the Cultural Turn*, by Larry Ray and Andrew Sayer (Eds.), 25–52. Sage.

Galtung, Johan. 1965. "On the Meaning of Nonviolence." *Journal of Peace Research* 2, 3, 228–256.

Giddens, Anthony, and David Held (Eds.). 1982. *Classes, Power, and Conflict: Classical and Contemporary Debates*. University of California.

Goldberg, Rachel, and Brian Blancke. 2011. "God in the Process: Is There a Place for Religion in Conflict Resolution?" *Conflict Resolution Quarterly* 28, 4, 377–298.

Govier, Trudy, and Wilhelm Verwoerd. 2002. "The Promise and Pitfalls of Apology." *Journal of Social Philosophy* 33, 1, 67–82.

Guerra, Nestor B. 2017. *The Life of Elvia Alvarado as the Voice of the Voiceless Women in Honduran Culture*. Thesis, University of North Carolina at Pembroke.

Hauss, Charles (Chip). 2003. "Apology and Forgiveness." In *Beyond Intractability*, by Guy Burgess and Heidi Burgess (Eds.). September. Accessed October 16, 2019. https://www.beyondintractability.org/essay/apology_forgiveness.

———. 2015. *Security 2.0: Dealing with Global Wicked Problems*. Rowman and Littlefield.

Heinze, Eric. 2012. *The Concept of Injustice*. Routledge.

Indartono, Setyabudi. 2014. *Conflict Management*. Aksara Media Pratama, Yogyakarta State University.

Jenkins, Alan. 2009. *Becoming Ethical: A Parallel, Political Journey with Men Who Have Abused*. Russell House.

Kakihara, Kuniharu. 2003. *The Post-9/11 Paradigm Shift and Its Effects on East Asia*. Policy Paper. Institute for International Policy Studies.

Kan, Melanie M., and Ken W. Parry. 2004. "Identifying Paradox: A Grounded Theory of Leadership in Overcoming Resistance to Change." *Leadership Quarterly* 15, 4, 467–491.

King, Martin Luther, and Clayborne Carson (The Legacy Series). 1958, 1986. *Stride toward Freedom: The Montgomery Story*. Beacon.

King, Martin Luther, Jr., Clayborne Carson, and Tenisha Hart Armstrong. 2014. *The Papers of Martin Luther King, Jr.* University of California.

Kohn, Sally. 2016. *The Opposite of Hate: A Field Guide to Repairing our Humanity*. Algonquin.

Kraybill, Donald W., Steven M. Nolt, and David L. Weaver-Zercher. 2007. *Amish Grace: How Forgiveness Transcended Tragedy*. Jossey-Bass.

Kraybill, Ronald S. 2000. "From Head to Heart: The Cycle of Reconciliation." In *Mediation and Facilitation Training Manual* (4th ed.), by Carolyn Schrock-Shenk (Ed.), 31–33. Mennonite Conciliation Service.

Lakey, George. 1987. *Powerful Peacemaking: A Strategy for a Living Revolution*. New Society.

———. 2016. *Toward a Living Revolution: A Five-Stage Framework for Creating Radical Social Change*. Wipf and Stock.

———. 2018. *How We Win: A Guide to Nonviolent Direct Action Campaigning*. Melville House.

Lawson, George. 2019. *Anatomies of Revolution*. Cambridge.

Lederach, John Paul. 1997. *Building Peace: Sustainable Reconciliation in Divided Societies*. US Institute of Peace.

———. 2003. "Conflict Transformation." *Beyond Intractability*. October. Accessed February 20, 2020. https://www.beyondintractability.org/essay/transformation.

——— 2014. *Little Book of Conflict Transformation*. Good Books.

———. 1999. *The Journey Toward Reconciliation*. Herald.

———. 2005a. "On Pied Pipers: Imagination and Reactivity." In *The Moral Imagination: The Art and Soul of Building Peace*, by John Paul Lederach (Ed.). Oxford University.

———. 2005b. *The Moral Imagination: The Art and Soul of Building Peace*. Oxford.

Lederach, John Paul, Reina Neufeldt, and Hal Culbertson. 2007. *Reflective Peacebuilding: A Planning, Monitoring, and Learning Toolkit*. Joan B. Kroc Institute for International Peace Studies.

Levine, Ellen G., and Stephen K. Levine (Eds.). 2011. *Art in Action: Expressive Arts in Therapy and Social Change*. Jessica Kingsley.

Levitin, Daniel J. 2008. *The World in Six Songs*. Penguin.

Levy, Barry S., and Victor W. Sidel (Eds.). 2006. *Social Injustice and Public Health*. Oxford.

Lewicki, Roy J., Beth Polin, and Robert B. Lount. 2016. "An Exploration of the Structure of Effective Apologies." *Negotiation and Conflict Management Research* 9, 2, 177–196.

Lollins, E. 2010. "Focus on Education: Monuments to Peace." *Peace Chronicle*, 16.

Lunenburg, Fred C. 2010. "Managing Change: The Role of the Change Agent." *International Journal of Management, Business, and Administration* 13, 1, 1–6.

Mac Ginty, Roger, and Gurchathen Sanghera. 2012. "Hybridity in Peacebuilding and Development: An Introduction." *Journal of Peacebuilding and Development* 7, 2, 3–8.

Macpherson, William. 1999. *The Stephen Lawrence Inquiry: Report of an Inquiry by Sir William Macpherson of Cluny*. Judicial Inquiry. Home Office, Government of the United Kingdom.

McAdam, Doug, John D. McCarthy, and Mayer N. Zald (Eds.). 1996. *Comparative Perspectives on Social Movements: Political Opportunities, Mobilizing Structures, and Cultural Framings*. Cambridge University.

McAdam, Doug, Sidney Tarrow, and Charles Tilly. 2001. *Dynamics of Contention*. Cambridge University.

McAdams, Dan P., and Kate C. McLean. 2013. "Narrative Identity." *Current Directions in Psychological Studies*, 22, 3.

McCandless, Erin. 2020. "Peacebuilding." In *Understanding International Conflict Management*, by Charity Butcher and Maia Hallward (Eds.). Routledge.

McCullough, Michael E., and Lindsey M. Root et al. 2009. "The Psychology of Forgiveness." In *Oxford Handbook of Positive Psychology* (2nd ed.), by C. R. Snyder and Shane J. Lopez (Eds.), 427–436. Oxford.

McCullough, Michael E., Kenneth I. Pargament, and Carl E. Thoresen (Eds.). 2000. *Forgiveness: Theory, Research, and Practice*. Guilford.

Meyer, Karl E. 2004. "Six Degrees of Contrition." *World Policy Journal* 21, 2, 108–110.

Mindell, Arnold. 2014. *Sitting in the Fire: Large Group Transformation Using Conflict and Diversity*. Deep Democracy Exchange.

Moyer, Bill, J. A. MacAllister, and M. L. F. S. Soifer. 2002. *Doing Democracy: The MAP Model for Organizing Social Movements*. New Society.

Noll, Douglas E. 2003. *Peace Making: Practicing at the Intersection of Law and Human Conflict*. Cascadia.

Ogburn, William Fielding. 1922. *Social Change with Respect to Culture and Original Nature*. B. W. Huebsch.

Ortega-Williams, Anna. 2017. *Is Organizing a Pathway for Wellbeing and Post-Traumatic Growth*. Doctoral Dissertation, Fordham University.

Partridge, Erin. 2021. *Getting On in the Creative Therapies: A Hands-On Guide to Personal and Professional Development*. Jessica Kingsley.

Petoukhov, Konstantin. 2011. *An Evaluation of Canada's Truth and Reconciliation Commission (TRC) through the Lens of Restorative Justice and the Theory of Recognition*. Graduate Study Thesis, University of Manitoba.

Picard, Cheryl. 2015. "Practicing Insight Mediation." May.

Porta, Donatella della, and Sidney Tarrow. 2005. "Transnational Processes and Social Activism: An Introduction." In *Transnational Protest and Global Activism*, by Donatella della Porta and Sidney Tarrow (Eds.), 1–19. Rowman and Littlefield.

Puljek-Shank, Amela. 2007. "Trauma and Reconciliation." In *20 Pieces of Encouragement for Awakening and Change: Peacebuilding in … Yugoslavia*, by Helena Rill, Tamara Smidling and Ana Bitoljanu (Eds.), 181–204. Centre for Nonviolent Action.

Rogers, Everett M. 2003. *Diffusion of Innovations (5th ed.)*. The Free Press.

Rosenberg, Marshall B. 2015. *Nonviolent Communication: Language of Life* (3rd ed.). PuddleDancer.

Savitch, H. V. 2003. "Does 9/11 Portend a New Paradigm for Cities?" *Urban Affairs Review* 39, 1, 103–127.

Senehi, Jessica. 2008. "Building Peace: Storytelling to Transform Conflicts Constructively" In *Handbook of Conflict Analysis, Intervention, and Resolution*, by Dennis Sandole, Sean Byrne, et al. (Eds.). Taylor and Francis.

———. 2020. "Theory-Building in Peace and Conflict Studies: The Storytelling Methodology." In *Routledge Companion to Peace and Conflict Studies*, by Sean Byrne, Thomas Matyok, et al. (Eds.), Chapter 4. Routledge.

Senge, Peter. 2006. "System Citizenship: The Leadership Mandate for this Millenium." In *The Leader of the Future 2*, by Frances Hesselbein and Marshall Goldsmith (Eds.), 31–46. Jossey-Bass.

Senge, Peter, Hal Hamilton, and John Kania. 2015. *The Dawn of System Leadership*. Position Statement. Stanford Social Innovation Review.

Shapiro, Daniel L. 2017. *Negotiating the Nonnegotiable* (2nd ed.). Penguin.

Sharp, Gene. 1973a. *The Politics of Nonviolent Action, Volume 1: Power and Struggle*. Porter Sargent.

———. 1973b. *The Politics of Nonviolent Action, Volume 2: Methods*. Porter Sargent.

———. 1985. *The Politics of Nonviolent Action, Volume 3: Dynamics*. Porter Sargent.

Shklar, Judith N. 1990. *The Faces of Injustice*. Yale.

Shriver, Donald W. 1995. *An Ethic for Enemies: Forgiveness in Politics*. Oxford.

———. 1998. "Is There Forgiveness in Politics? Germany, Vietnam, and America." In *Exploring Forgiveness*, by Robert D. Enright and Joanna North (Eds.). University of Wisconsin.

Smith-Christopher, Daniel L. (Ed.). 2007. *Subverting Hatred: The Challenge of Nonviolence in Religious Traditions*. Orbis Books.

Solnit, Rebecca. 2016. *Hope in the Dark: Untold Histories, Wild Possibilities* (2nd ed.). Haymarket.

Statista, Research. 2020. "Number of People Shot to Death by Police in the US 2017–2020." *Statista*. August 31. Accessed September 21 21, 2020. https://www.statista.com/statistics/585152/people-shot-to-death-by-us-police-by-race/.

Sutherland, Jessie. 2005. *Worldview Skills: Transforming Conflict from the Inside Out.* Worldview Strategies.

Tarrow, Sidney. 2013. "Contentious Politics." In *The Wiley-Blackwell Encyclopedia of Social and Political Movements*, by Donatella della Porta and Bert Kandermans et al. (Eds.). Blackwell.

Tarrow, Sidney G. 2011. *Power in Movement: Social Movements and Contentious Politics* (3rd ed.). Cambridge University.

Thomas, Deja, and Juliana Menasce Horowitz. 2020. "Support for Black Lives Matter Has Decreased since June." *Pew Research Center, Fact Tank*. September 16. Accessed September 21, 2020. https://www.pewresearch.org/fact-tank/2020/09/16/support-for-black-lives-matter-has-decreased-since-june-but-remains-strong-among-black-americans/.

Tutu, Desmond, and Mpho Tutu. 2014. *The Book of Forgiving: Four-fold Path for Healing Ourselves and Our World.* HarperCollins.

Tzu, Sun. 2019. *The Art of War.* Ixia Press.

Udod, Sonia, and Joan Wagner. 2018. "Common Change Theories and Application to Different Nursing Situations." In *Leadership and Influencing Change in Nursing*, by Joan Wagner (Ed.), Chapter 9. University of Regina.

Waddell, Dianne, and Amrik S. Sohal. 1998. "Resistance: A Constructive Tool for Change." *Management Decision* 36, 8, 543–548.

Wade, Nathaniel G., and Everett L. Worthington. 2005. "In Search of a Common Core: A Content Analysis of Interventions to Promote Forgiveness." *Psychotherapy: Theory, Research, Practice, Training* 42, 2, 160–177.

Wehr, Paul. 2019. *Conflict Regulation* (2nd ed.). Routledge.

Wenzel, Michael, Lydia Woodyatt, and Kyli Hendrick. 2012. "No Genuine Self-Forgiveness without Accepting Responsibility: Value Reaffirmation as a Key to Maintaining Positive Self-Regard." *European Journal of Social Psychology* 42, 5, 617–627.

Wink, Walter. 2014. "Facing the Myth of Redemptive Violence." *Ekklesia*, November 15.

Winslade, John, and Gerald Monk. 2000. *Narrative Mediation: A New Approach to Conflict Resolution.* Jossey-Bass.

Woehrle, Lynne, and Susan French. 1992. "Unlocking the Paradox of Nonviolence and Self-Defense: A Feminist Analysis." Annual Consortium on Peace Research and Education.

Worthington, Everett L. 2009. *A Just Forgiveness: Responsible Healing without Excusing Injustice.* IVP Books.

Worthington, Everett L. (Ed.). 2005. *Handbook of Forgiveness.* Routledge.

Zelizer, Craig (Ed.). 2018. *Integrated Peacebuilding: Innovative Approaches to Transforming Conflict.* Routledge.

CONCLUSION

Alberstein, Michal, and Jay Rothman. 2013. "Taking Stock of the Field: Past, Present, and Future." *International Journal of Conflict Engagement and Resolution* 1, 1, 3–7.

Amsler, Lisa Blomgren, Janet K. Martinez, and Stephanie E. Smith. 2015. "The State of System Design." *Conflict Resolution Quarterly* 33, S1, S7–S26.

Borba, Michele. 2001. *Building Moral Intelligence: The Seven Essential Virtues That Teach Kids to Do the Right Thing.* Jossey-Bass.

Cheldelin, Sandra, Daniel Drickman, and Larissa Fast (Eds.). 2008. *Conflict: From Analysis to Intervention* (2nd ed.). Continuum.

Cohen, Jeffrey. 2010. "Ethical Principles: Final Report of the Ethics Committee, Association for Conflict Resolution." *Association for Conflict Resolution*. May. Accessed March 21, 2019. https://acrnet.org/page/EthicalPrinciples.

Connors, Joanie V. 2003. "Principles for Peace Practitioners." *American Psychological Association*. June. Accessed March 21, 2019. https://www.apa.org/monitor/jun03/principles.

Haas, Chip. 2018. "Making Other Plans." *ACResolution*, December: 6–8.

Handelsman, Mitchell M., Samuel Knapp, and Michael Gottliebe. 2011. "Positive Ethics." In *Handbook of Positive Psychology* (2nd ed.), by C. R. Snyder and Shane J. Lopez (Eds.), 105–113. Oxford.

Hansvick, Christine L., and Ian M. Harris. 2007. "Peace and Conflict Programs within Higher Education: Changes Observed since the Year 2000." *Proceedings of the International Education for Peace Conference*. International Education for Peace Institute. 276–288.

Harris, Ian M., and Mary Lee Morrison. 2013. *Peace Education* (3rd ed.). McFarland.

Harris, Ian M., and Amy L. Shuster. 2008. *Global Directory of Peace Studies and Conflict Resolution Programs* (7th ed.). Periodic Review. Peace and Justice Association and International Peace Research Association Foundation.

Kraybill, Ron. 2016. "Tips for a Conflict Resolution Career." *River House Press*. April 26. Accessed March 13, 2019. https://www.riverhouseepress.com/blog/career-in-conflict-resolution/.

Lang, Michael D. 2019. *The Guide to Reflective Practice in Conflict Resolution*. Rowman and Littlefield.

LeBaron, Michelle, and V. C. Robinson. 1994. *Conflict Resolution and Analysis as Education*. University of Victoria.

Lederach, John Paul. 2005. *The Moral Imagination: The Art and Soul of Building Peace*. Oxford University.

Lennick, Doug, and Fred Kiel. 2007. *Moral Intelligence*. Pearson.

Mayer, Bernard S. 2004. *Beyond Neutrality: Confronting the Crisis in Conflict Resolution*. Jossey-Bass.

———. 2012. *The Dynamics of Conflict: A Guide to Engagement and Intervention* (2nd ed.). Jossey-Bass.

Moore, Christopher W. 2014. *The Mediation Process: Practical Strategies for Resolving Conflict* (4th ed.). Jossey-Bass.

Mosten, Forrest S. 2001. *Mediation Career Guide: A Strategic Approach to Building a Successful Practice*. Jossey-Bass.

Neufeldt, Reina. 2016. *Ethics for Peacebuilders: A Practical Guide*. Rowman and Littlefield.

Noll, Douglas. 2003. *Peacemaking: Practicing at the Intersection of Law and Human Conflict*. Cascadia.

Pruitt, Dean G., and Katherine G. Kugler. 2014. "Some Research Frontiers in the Study of Conflict and Its Resolution." In *The Handbook of Conflict Resolution: Theory and Practice*, by Peter T. Coleman, Morton Deutsch, and E. C. Marcus (Eds.), 1087–1109. Jossey-Bass/Wiley.

Ragin, Charles C., and Lisa M. Amoroso. 2018. *Constructing Social Research: The Unity and Diversity of Method*. Sage.

Rhudy, Robert J. 2014. *Engaging Conflict for Fun and Profit: Current and Emerging Career Trends in Conflict Resolution*. MACRO—Maryland Mediation and Conflict Resolution Office.

Schellenberg, James A. 1996. *Conflict Resolution: Theory, Research, and Practice*. State University of New York.

Schon, Donald A. 1983. *The Reflective Practitioner: How Professionals Think in Action.* Basic.

Shapiro, Ilana. 2005. "Theories of Change." *Beyond Intractability.* January. Accessed March 15, 2019. https://www.beyondintractability.org/essay/theories_of_change.

Smith, David J. 2016. *Peace Jobs: A Student's Guide to Starting a Career Working for Peace.* Information Age.

——. 2018. "Career Changers and Job Seekers: Who Are They? What Do They Need?" *ACResolution*, December: 20–22.

Waldman, Ellen (Ed.). 2011. *Mediation Ethics: Cases and Commentaries.* Jossey-Bass.

Wallensteen, Peter. 2011. *Peace Research: Theory and Practice.* Routledge.

——. 2019. *Understanding Conflict Resolution.* Sage.

Zelizer, Craig (Ed.). 2018. *Integrated Peacebuilding.* Routledge.

Zelizer, Craig, and Linda Johnson. 2006. *Career Advice for the Field of International Peace and Conflict Resolution.* Survey. Alliance for Conflict Transformation.

Index

∎ ∎ ∎

Page numbers in italics refer to figures and tables.

About the Author

■ ■ ■

Dr. Lois Edmund is a trained clinical psychologist (BSc, Wayne State University; MA, PhD, Rosemead Graduate School). Her professional practice is in psychology, mental health, and conflict mediation, and she has membership in several related professional organizations. For 40 years, she taught many university courses in psychology, medicine, theology, and peace and conflict resolution, and her research interests focused on healthy relationships, abuse, trauma recovery, and interpersonal forgiveness. She holds the position of Professor Emeritus at Menno Simons College, Canadian Mennonite University. She served as Secretary to the Board of Directors of the Association for Conflict Resolution, and is a member of the Peace and Justice Studies Association.

Association for Conflict Resolution®

VOICES, CHOICES, SOLUTIONS

About the ACR

The Association for Conflict Resolution (ACR) is a professional organization enhancing the practice and public understanding of conflict resolution. An international professional association for mediators, arbitrators, educators, and other conflict resolution practitioners, ACR works in a wide range of settings throughout the United States and around the world. Our multicultural and multidisciplinary organization offers a broad umbrella under which all forms of dispute resolution practice find a home. Website: www.acrnet.org; Twitter: @ACRgroup.